Mars Hill Graduate S

mhgs.edu/l

DATE DUE

DATE DUE

Jesus Christ in Modern Thought

John Macquarrie

JESUS CHRIST
IN
MODERN
THOUGHT

SCM PRESS
London

TRINITY PRESS INTERNATIONAL
Philadelphia

First published 1990

SCM Press Ltd
26–30 Tottenham Road
London N1 4BZ

Trinity Press International
3725 Chestnut Street
Philadelphia, Pa. 19104

British Library Cataloguing in Publication Data

Macquarrie, John, *1919–*
    Jesus Christ in modern thought.
    1. Christology
    I. Title
    232

    ISBN 0–334–02457–9
    ISBN 0–334–02446–3 pbk

Library of Congress Cataloging-in-Publication Data

Macquarrie, John.
    Jesus Christ in modern thought / John Macquarrie.
        p.   cm.
    Includes bibliographical reference.
    ISBN 0–334–02457–9 : $29.95 (U.S.).
    ISBN 0–334– 2446–3 (pbk.)
    1. Jesus Christ —History of doctrines.   2. Jesus
Christ—Person and offices.   I Title.
BT198.M295 1990
232'.09—dc20   90–31831

Typeset at The Spartan Press Ltd, Lymington, Hants
Printed in Great Britain by
Dotesios Printers Ltd, Trowbridge, Wiltshire

In Memory of
Harry Sutton
1925–1987

Contents

Preface

This book was originally planned as the third part of a trilogy which began with *In Search of Humanity* (1982) and continued with *In Search of Deity* (1984). If I had adhered to that plan, the present work would have consisted mainly of Part 3, together with some introductory material. That is to say, drawing on the findings of the two earlier books on humanity and deity, it would have attempted to make sense in modern terms of the conception of the God-man, as applied to Jesus Christ. In the meantime, I had been invited by the editors of the German *Theologische Realenzyklopädie* to write a two-part article (virtually a small book) on Jesus Christ, the first part to consist of a historical survey of the major christologies from the Enlightenment to the present day, the second to offer a systematic or dogmatic statement for our own time. This second part obviously corresponded to the task which I already had in mind, but it now became apparent to me that one could hardly go about the systematic task without first of all giving some account of the vast amount of thinking that has been devoted to christology over the past two hundred years and more. But this great quantity of post-Enlightenment writing on christology was in constant dialogue with the christology of earlier times. In particular, much of it was critical of classical christology produced by the theologians and councils of the early centuries, a christology which is enshrined in the widely accepted formulation of the council of Chalcedon (451). Furthermore, the christologies developed after the Enlightenment have been largely philosophical in character, concerned with the abstract *possibility* of a God-man. Quite a large number of theologians working on christological problems during this period were anxious to get rid in one way or another of the troublesome historical problems (and they have become increasingly troublesome) that arise when one introduces the concrete historical figure of Jesus of Nazareth and considers the claim that he is the God-man. This made it clear to me that one cannot begin the story at the Enlightenment but must go back to the sources, to the earliest witness to Jesus Christ in the New Testament, and to trace how, out of these early testimonies, the classical theology developed.

So I found myself engaged in the task of writing a book which itself falls into three parts. The first part, entitled 'The Sources and the Rise of Classical Christology' takes us back to the earliest testimonies to the Christ-event, the development from these of the classical christology and then, in highly compressed form, the continuing dominance with minor variations of the classical christology for something like thirteen centuries, right down to the beginning of the modern period. The second part is called 'The Critique of the Classical Christology and Attempts at Reconstruction' and considers in some detail the more or less radical criticisms directed against the classical christology and the search for constructive alternatives. The third part bears as its title the question which Bonhoeffer found himself asking in prison and which remains a question for us: 'Who Really Is Jesus Christ for Us Today?'

Quotations from the Bible are mostly from the Revised Standard Version. My debt to many writers past and present is evident from the notes. I especially want to express thanks to two of my former colleagues at Christ Church, the Rev. Professor Maurice F. Wiles and the Rev. Canon John C. Fenton. They gave generously of their time to read much of the material in Part One. They both made many valuable suggestions for improvements, and I have greatly benefited from their help. Where errors and misunderstandings remain, I am entirely to blame. I wish to thank also the SCM Press for their help and encouragement. It is thirty-five years since I submitted my first book to the Press, and during that long time I have received from the Press unfailing courtesy and co-operation.

John Macquarrie

PART ONE

The Sources and the Rise of the Classical Christology

Problems of Christology

Christology is the study which has for its subject-matter Jesus Christ, his person and his work, or, to put it in a slightly different way, who he was (or is), and what he did (or does). Christianity, as the name implies, has Jesus Christ at its very centre, so that if christology is concentrated on a study of Jesus Christ, it is not so much a branch of Christian theology as its central theme; or, at least, it shares the centre with the equally fundamental doctrine of God.

Possibly the beginnings of christology belong to the time of Jesus himself. According to Mark's Gospel, he put to his disciples the question, 'Who do men say that I am?' (Mark 8.27). This suggests that there was already speculation among the populace about who this teacher from Nazareth might be – John the Baptist, or Elijah, or some other prophet come back from the past? At once, however, Jesus follows up with a second question, addressed directly to the disciples: 'But who do you say that I am?' They were not just members of the public who might have some vague opinion on the matter, but persons who had made at least some measure of commitment to Jesus and were recognized to be disciples. Peter answered, 'You are the Christ' (Mark 8.29). Whether Mark is correct in placing this incident within the period of Jesus' teaching ministry or whether this incident (or something like it) happened only after the disciples had come to believe in the resurrection, is not of great importance. There must have been a time when the first somewhat vague attachment of the disciples to their teacher began to take the form of a more definite faith that he was a theologically significant figure. It might be claimed that it is only at this point that one can properly speak of the beginning of christology, or even of the beginning of Christianity. Thus Tillich writes: 'Christianity was born, not with the birth of the man who is called "Jesus," but in the moment in which one of his followers was driven to say to him, "You are the Christ."'[1] Of course, the term 'Christ' was only one of the interpretative titles given to Jesus in the earliest days of Christianity, and then as now it had more than one meaning. Tillich himself gives a very broad interpretation of the term, and it is doubtful that any early Christian would have understood it in his way, for he talks of 'the Christ, namely, he who brings the new state of things, the New Being.'[2] All I want to say is that at this point an explicitly theological content appeared in what the disciples had to say about Jesus. It was at least a minimal confession of faith. But while there is a distinction between the disciples' confession of faith and what I have called the 'vague opinions' of the uncommitted populace, one should not make this distinction absolute. For these vague opinions, as reported by Mark, seemed to be of an honorific nature and were tending toward some kind of recognition or even commitment. The people were thinking of him as a prophet, and what title could have been more honourable in the eyes of many Israelites? Among recent writers on christology, Schillebeeckx has claimed that 'the choice of the very first followers of Jesus (later to become Christians) fell upon the Jewish model of the eschatological prophet, with which they were familiar.'[3] Though I think that Schillebeeckx exaggerates his case, his view is at least a possible one, and illustrates my contention that no absolute distinction can be made between those anonymous Jews who thought of Jesus as one of the prophets and the disciples who more boldly called him the Christ. It may well be the case, as Schillebeeckx suggests, that some of those who began by surmising that Jesus was a prophet went on from that beginning to become committed Christians.

I have said that christology is concerned to ask who Jesus Christ was (or is) and what he did (or does), and perhaps I should now explain more fully this somewhat odd choice of words. Let us begin with 'Who was he?' This is a historical question, or group of questions. When did Jesus live? What can we discover about the background against which he lived – his family and the kind of society of which it was a part? And since Jesus Christ became the centre of a worldwide faith, we have to ask in particular about his relation to the Jewish faith in which he grew up, how he might have understood himself or been understood by his followers in the context of that Jewish faith. It has been recognized for a long time that our historical information about Jesus is scanty, and that we do not have the material that a modern biographer would consider necessary if he were invited to write the life-story of some well-known person. Still, we do have some historical data concerning Jesus, and the question, 'Who was he?' is perhaps the first question that will naturally arise in our minds.

However, I have suggested that the question needs to be expanded to 'Who was he (or is he)?' This may seem an odd question to ask about someone who died nearly two thousand years ago. But if one is engaging in christology, it is a question that cannot fail to be asked. For christology is not simply an investigation into the history of Jesus. It is true that in spite of the paucity of information about him, one can write historical studies of Jesus, and people are still doing this.[4] Whatever else or whatever more he may have been, Jesus was certainly a human being who can be assigned a time and a place in history, and though christology is more than the history of this human being, his history enters into it as part of the total fabric of christology. How important or how unimportant the historical element may be within the totality of a christological study is a question that must be deferred for the present. At present I am simply making the point that christology is more than a historical study of the man Jesus of Nazareth. It is also (and even primarily, a theological study), putting Jesus in the context of Christian faith, asking about his relation to God on the one hand and to the human race on the other, and asking how we must think of a person who can sustain these relations. It is this further theological question (or group of questions) that seems to demand the formulation, 'Who *is* he?' rather than 'Who *was* he?' For we are concerned here with a present or continuing reality, a reality which did not come to an end with the death of Jesus. Indeed, it only began to shape people's lives in a radical way *after* his death. Those whose lives had been deeply influenced by Jesus spoke of a 'resurrection.' Later we shall have to examine critically what could be meant by the assertion that Jesus had risen from the dead and was still known as a living presence. But certainly this is how generations of Christians have experienced Jesus, from the earliest days to our own time. One eminent theologian of the present, E. L. Mascall, has linked the historical Jesus and the present Christ in the following words: 'That the Christ whom we know today is the historic Christ is basic to our faith, but we do not depend for our acquaintance with him on the research of historians and archaeologists. He is also the heavenly Christ, and as such is the object of our present experience, mediated through the sacramental life of the Church.'[5]

Having briefly explained in what sense christology deals with the question of who Jesus was (and is), I turn now to the other question, the question of what he did (and does). Traditionally, theologians have distinguished between the doctrine of the person of Christ and the doctrine of the work of Christ, and in textbooks of theology, these are usually treated in separate chapters. But such separation is artificial, and is made only because for the sake of clearer discussion we must limit our problems. Who one is and what one does belong together.

Our reason for speaking both of what Jesus did and of what he does is the same as for speaking both of what he was and what he is. What he did, his actual career, his deeds and words, comprise a moment in universal history so impressive that after two thousand years it is still 'revelation' – and here I am using the word 'revelation' not in some subtle theological sense, but for a phenomenon which, though rare, belongs to general human experience. Let the atheistic Nietzsche say it better than I could: 'The concept of revelation – in the sense that suddenly, with indescribable certainty and subtlety, something becomes visible, audible, something that shakes one to the last depths and throws one down – that merely describes the facts.'[6] It would not be inappropriate to apply these words to the career of Jesus Christ and to its impact on the human race. One might perhaps question Nietzsche's stress on the sudden and dramatic nature of revelation, for a revelatory happening – and I think this is clearly the case with the event of Jesus Christ – may demand a long time for its preparation and an equally long time for its recognition and reception. But there are many Christians who at the mention of Jesus Christ think in the first instance of what he did at a particular time in the past, of his work as a great moment in the spiritual history of humanity, and they emphasize the uniqueness of this datable moment by describing it in a New Testament phrase as 'once for all' (*ephapax*) (Rom. 6.10, etc.) Others, however, especially in the modern period (examples are Schleiermacher, Ritschl, Bultmann, Schillebeeckx) seem to attach less importance to the past event transmitted to us in the tradition than to the present experience of wholeness or salvation known to the believer or to the believing community through faith in Christ. For them, what Christ does has a certainty greater than what he did or is reported to have done. Yet even those who would lay most of the stress on present experience would rarely go so far as to say that the tradition of a past revelatory event is dispensable. It would seem that Christianity has to point us to something more than its present-day effects which, one must frankly say, are often unimpressive. It has still to appeal to some great moment of revelation at its beginning, even if this means getting involved in the uncertainties that arise as soon as we begin to investigate any event of the past, and especially an event so distant and so obscure as the career of Jesus Christ. We can see many modern theologians desperately struggling to free themselves from any dependence on historical research. Later we shall critically consider some concrete examples. But we shall see that they never quite succeed, and that the 'he was' and the 'he is', the 'he did' and the 'he does' remain tied together. Though we might gladly be rid of it, the historical problem is part of the christological complex and will not go away. But what is arguable is the extent to which historical questions are determinative for christology, and whether in some way yet to be clarified we have to acknowledge two sources for the knowledge of Jesus Christ – the testimony of the past and the experience of the present.

The discussion which has engaged us in the last few paragraphs leads to another problem – the problem of being and doing. We have seen that there are two sets of questions that may be asked about Jesus Christ – the question of his being or person (who he was, or is), and the question of his doing or work (what he did, or does). I ventured to say that these two lines of questioning are inseparable. But not everyone would agree. There is at the present time a powerful tendency to concentrate on what Jesus did (or does) and to leave aside the question of his being or person. This is called 'functional' christology, and it is part of a wider tendency to understand Christianity in primarily practical terms and to avoid the more strictly intellectual and theological issues. To some extent this is understandable. For a long time, the intellectual climate in the West has not been hospitable to theological and metaphysical questions. Even those who have some interest in such questions often feel impatience on reading some of the christological debates of the past, whether from the patristic or the mediaeval or the Reformation periods. Arguments about the two natures, the hypostatic union, whether Jesus had a human nature but not a human personality – these seem unreal to the modern reader. Just as some theologians would like to get rid of the historical problems and the shifting sands of historical research, so others would gladly escape from the subtle intricacies of traditional christological speculation. But can we really get away from it? The question is really whether a human being can be reduced to a collection of roles or functions, or whether there is not also a person who is the centre and subject of these roles or functions. 'Functional man', as he is sometimes called, and *a fortiori* a 'functional Christ', is an artificial abstraction, not a concrete living person. Later in the book, I shall return to the criticism of any supposedly merely 'functional' christology, and seek to show that we cannot avoid the problems of an 'ontological' christology, that is to say, a christology that asks about who Jesus is as well as about what he does. Meanwhile, however, I may refer to the discussion by Donald MacKinnon of the use of the concept of 'substance' (*ousia*, also translated 'being') in christology. Although the New Testament itself is almost devoid of philosophical terms, we cannot reflect theologically on its claims for Jesus Christ without getting involved in ontology. As MacKinnon puts it,

> The simplest affirmation, for instance, concerning Christ's relation to the Father, must include the use of the sort of notions of which ontology seeks to give an account. If we think or speak of Christ as subordinate to the Father, or argue whether as a person – understood in Boethius' terms as *individua substantia rationabilis naturae* – he is distinguished from his Father, we are immediately involved willy-nilly in the use of and reconstruction of ontological notions . . . One can only dodge the use of these notions if one supposes that the doctrine of Christ's person is something that excuses rather than compels full intellectual effort in the attempt to grasp its implications.[7]

The implied warning against anti-intellectualism in the last quoted sentence is not to be ignored. It would be dangerously irresponsible to commend faith in Jesus Christ without having thought as deeply as possible on the grounds for such faith. We note, however, that MacKinnon asks not just for the use of ontological notions but also for their 'reconstruction'. When the church took over from Greek philosophy such a notion as 'substance', that notion was enlarged and modified in the theological context. So this is not a plea for the incorporation of philosophical terms in their pre-theological usage. Indeed, it is not even a plea that the same words should be used. The word 'substance' (or 'being'), though it has been in continuous use in the church for centuries and is enshrined in that most ecumenical of all confessions of faith, the Nicene creed, may not be a necessity, *if one can find other and more up-to-date expressions in which one can express the problems formerly discussed in the language of 'substance' and the like*. Maurice Wiles, for instance, admits that the traditional terminology may have been appropriate in the early Christian centuries but believes that it is so no longer. But he does not think that this implies that we have to throw away all the insights that the earlier language tried to express. He himself offers an affirmative statement which, he believes, captures much of the traditional teaching. About Jesus he is prepared to say:

> He was not just one who had taught about God; he was not just one who had lived a life of perfect human response to God. He had lived a life that embodied and expressed God's character and action in the world. As prophets in the past had expressed the word of God that had come to them not only in speech but in symbolic action, so in a far more comprehensive way did Jesus. The impact not merely of his teaching but of his whole person communicated the presence and the power of God with an unprecedented sense of directness and finality.[8]

These are obviously very large claims to make for Jesus Christ, and I think they may fairly be called ontological claims. They do not, of course, make use of the traditional ontological terms, but are these claims asserting any less than the older language asserted? To answer this question, one would have to weigh very carefully such expressions as 'a life that embodied and expressed God's character and action in the world' and 'communicated the presence and the power of God with an unprecedented sense of directness and finality'. My own impression is that Wiles, in his own language, is reproducing the essentials of the traditional christological teaching. It is true that he himself thinks that the difference between his formulation and the traditional one is wider than I may seem to have suggested, for he thinks that in the history of Christian thought the traditional metaphysical language was understood in a more direct and even literal way than he would allow. He is probably correct – there has been too much literalism, and too much elaboration and drawing of fine distinctions on the basis of that literalism. Yet there have always been some perceptive theologians who have recognized the gulf between the finite and the infinite, the human and the divine, and that whether we are talking about human language or a human life, these cannot exhibit the divine in direct literal fashion, but only analogically, as scaled down to the finite.

Maurice Wiles' language about Christ would also lie well within the limits of tolerance sketched out by James Dunn on the basis of the New Testament. He acknowledges that there is considerable diversity among the New Testament writers in what they have to say about the person of Christ, and there is no single view that could be described as the 'orthodox' New Testament position. But he does claim to find an element of unity among the diversity, namely, 'the conviction that the historical figure, Jesus the Jew, is now an exalted being – that this Jesus is and continues to be the agent of God, supreme over all other claimants to the titles, Lord and Son of God.'[9] Here is a different language again, and the expressions with ontological implications are 'exalted being', 'the agent of God', 'Lord', 'Son of God'. To acknowledge these points about Jesus is, in Dunn's view, 'the irreducible minimum, without which Christianity loses any distinctive definition'.[10] But he goes on at once to deny that anyone should require some particular elaboration of the basic confession or some particular form of words.

It may be useful to pause for a moment at this point and to sum up our findings so far, because we are already becoming aware of the enormous complexity of the study called christology. It involves us in historical questions, questions concerning the career of Jesus Christ, the origins of Christianity and the subsequent development, including the development of christology itself. But this is all further complicated by the fact that for Christian faith Jesus is not just a figure of the past but a reality of present experience – 'the heavenly Christ' (Mascall) or 'an exalted being' (Dunn). What can such expressions mean? They direct us to the question of Christ's relation to God the Father. Although the New Testament writers succeeded in making these basic points with only the minimal involvement in philosophical language, this situation soon began to change in the decades which followed and in which the church's beliefs about Jesus Christ were receiving the formulation which they retained for many centuries. Now the ontological implications already hidden in some of the New Testament pronouncements about Christ were being made explicit in a language derived from philosophy, and we find him described, for instance, as *homoousios* ('one in substance or being') with the Father. Admittedly, christology took a decidedly metaphysical turn around this time. But if we accept with MacKinnon that Christian faith, among other things, demands and deserves our 'full intellectual effort,' it is hard to see how Christian theology could have developed in any other adequate way.

The complexity of christological language therefore arises from its harnessing together of history on the one hand with theology on the other, and this theology (which can never divest itself of some indirect or analogical element) expresses itself sometimes in forms which are more obviously symbolic or even mythological, sometimes in forms which are more conceptual and ontological. Does this strange complex of discourse remind us of anything? Yes, it does. It reminds us of what the New Testament writers call the 'gospel' (*euangelion*). In the New Testament itself, the word 'gospel' is used in a broad sense for the good news of Jesus Christ, and only later, about the middle of the second century, did the word begin to be used in a more restricted way for the four writings which today we call the 'gospels'. It is in the broad sense that I want the word to be understood when I compare the language of christology to the language of gospel. In this broad sense, we can say there is a gospel according to Paul as well as a gospel according to Mark or John – in fact, Paul uses the word 'gospel' more frequently than any other New Testament writer. Clearly, there is a considerable difference between, say, Paul's letter to the Romans and Mark's Gospel. The obvious difference is that the latter is largely narrative, the former is largely theological reflection. Yet is it not rather the case (and I shall try to show this in more detail later) that each of these two writers has varied the mix, so to speak? In Paul, the narrative is assumed, for the most part, tacitly; in Mark, the narrative provides the framework for his book, but the story is the vehicle for theological teaching.

But although the language of christology reminds us of the language of gospel, christology and gospel are not the same. Gospel is preaching or proclamation, it is a first-order language which is unselfconscious, a language in which faith speaks in order to awaken faith through the transmission of the good news on which faith has been founded. Christology, on the other hand, has taken a step back, so to speak, and has become self-conscious and self-critical. We could say (and this might be an alternative definition of christology) that it is *gospel that has been reflected upon and criticized*. It is a second-order language which nevertheless continues to reflect the characteristics of the first-order language on which it is directed. However, if the reflective and critical tendencies in this language reach a certain pitch, it may acquire an ontological character which was only latent in the language of the gospel.

But does this comparison of the language of christology with that of gospel take us anywhere? It has sometimes been claimed that the four books called 'gospels' constitute a distinct literary *genre*, and I suppose one could include in this the 'gospel' in the wider sense in which I have been using the term. But the concept of gospel remains elusive. It may be, as I have said, that it includes history, theology and (when one begins to think it out) ontology. But these are not, so to speak, lying side by side, so that one can isolate them from one another. They interpenetrate one another. What looks like a simple historical assertion, as that Jesus was born in Bethlehem, has its theological meaning, for Bethlehem is the city of David, and David was king of Israel, and God made promises to David and his descendants, and so on . . . Again, a theological assertion, as that Jesus Christ came into the world to save sinners, is not a piece of timeless mythology. It is something which is referred to an actual human being who lived in a particular area at a particular time of world-history. This point was discussed in some detail a generation ago in connection with Bultmann's theory of demythologizing. The question was raised whether the term 'myth' can rightly be applied to the stories about Jesus Christ, for stories which are typically regarded as myths are indefinite as to time and place. They are often stories about what happened 'in the beginning' or, in the case of eschatological myths, about what will happen 'in the end'. The stories about Jesus are, by contrast, at least in principle datable. Luke may have got things wrong when he attempted near the beginning of his gospel (Luke 2.1–2 and 3.1–2) to date the career of Jesus Christ by citing some contemporary moments in secular history, but the very fact that he makes the attempt shows that he believed himself to be writing about the realm of history, not mythology. There is in fact very little pure mythology in the New Testament, though there are many passages where mythological and historical motifs are combined, in order to express some theological truth not as a timeless free-floating assertion, but as embodied in those events which, it was believed, constituted the climax of a particular line of history, what Paul called 'the fulness of the time' (Gal. 4.4).

Even a quick glance at all this composite and diverse material that is lumped together under the word 'gospel' may make us doubt the very possibility of christology, if the task of christology is to clarify, reflect on, criticize and generally try to make sense of it all. And even if one were apparently succeeding with this task, what would this mean? If one were able to arrive at a more or less coherent christology, the complaint might then be made that this is possible only by a *tour de force* which combines in an artificial unity items which do not and cannot belong together. For instance, James Dunn, in the book from which I have already quoted, writes that 'what many Christians both past and present have regarded as orthodox christology may be regarded (not altogether unfairly) as a curious amalgam of different elements taken from different parts of first-century Christianity – personal pre-existence from John, virgin birth from

Matthew, the miracle worker from the so-called "divine man" christology prevalent among some Hellenistic Christians, his death as atonement from Paul, the character of his resurrection from Luke, his present role from Hebrews and the hope of his parousia from the earlier decades.'[11] Admittedly, this does look rather like a rag bag. The human mind does have a tendency to harmonize and systematize the sundry items of information which it collects from diverse sources, and no doubt there is a temptation to impose an artificial or at least premature unity on these items. But while that is indeed a danger, it can equally well be argued that understanding progresses and deepens as we see connections between items which at first seemed quite unrelated. The significance of Jesus Christ was not seen all at once. Furthermore, it was not grasped by one particular individual. The construction of a christology generally accepted in the Christian community inevitably took place by stages, and combined the different insights of different writers. An illustration of this is afforded in another of Professor Dunn's books, in which he argues that a belief in Jesus' personal pre-existence emerges clearly only with the Fourth Gospel, near the end of the New Testament period, but that this can be seen as a development from the wisdom christology of earlier Christian thought.

The point I am making is that to bring together material from different sources, especially when this material can be exhibited as constituting a process of development, is not necessarily a bad thing and may in fact bring about important new insights. We happen to live at a time when there is great stress on the importance of analysis, but we must not forget that knowledge demands synthesis as well as analysis, though certainly an honest and thorough analysis can save us from making superficial syntheses. It is not so long ago that in the period of 'biblical theology' we were being pressured by biblical scholars into recognizing the unity of the Bible, but their arguments were often so flimsy that it is not surprising that the present generation of scholars are insisting on the diversity of the biblical writings. This has been a needed corrective, but it is important that it should not be pushed to the point where analysis becomes dissolution. As we have noted, Dunn himself recognizes a unifying idea amid the diversity of the New Testament, an idea which he expresses as the conviction that the historical figure, Jesus the Jew, becomes an 'exalted being'.[12]

The points we have just been considering certainly highlight the difficulties in the way of a christological inquiry, but they do not suggest that it is a hopeless task. Nevertheless, they should temper our expectations about what is possible, and what it is reasonable to expect. We must expect that there will continue to be a variety of christologies, though one would also expect that there would be some unifying thread among them. This would seem to imply in turn that we should not seek a description of Christ's person or work that is too closely detailed. I have already mentioned that traditional discussions about the two natures, the hypostatic union, the view that Christ had a human nature but not a human personhood, and similar questions, seem unreal to the modern reader. This is not just because of the quaintness of the language and concepts, but perhaps even more arises from the sense that at such points we are being tempted into an overdetermination of the person of Christ. We are, so to speak, getting out of our depth. We are trying to describe Jesus Christ with a precision and detail without having adequate grounds for the assertions we are making. It is at this point that we might usefully recall the so-called 'principle of reserve' employed by J. H. Newman and other theologians of the Oxford Movement. It is a recognition of the limits of theological understanding, an acknowledgment that there is always an indirect or analogical element in theological language so that minute description must always be suspect. Although I defended the need for ontological language in christology, the sad truth is that in the early centuries the distinctions became more and more minute and the debates more and more abstract until finally it is doubtful if anything of genuine significance was being discussed at all – for instance, did Jesus Christ have one will or two wills? A good theologian will have to judge the point at which a legitimate and even necessary analysis of the several elements that enter into the constitution of Christ's person, passes over into baseless speculation. It seems to me that even very great theologians have sometimes transgressed the limits. For instance, Barth offers an extended and profound discussion of christology, stretching through several part-volumes and many hundreds of pages of his *Church Dogmatics*. But sometimes the discussion, especially when it touches on differences of opinion between Lutheran and Reformed theologians of an earlier time, seems to move into a realm of unreal distinctions. As we have already seen, some Christian theologians, such as Professor Wiles, would be content to say of Jesus Christ that he 'embodied and expressed God's character and action in the world'.[13] This is a pretty far-reaching assertion, and certainly says what was most important in the Christian acknowledgment of Jesus as the Christ. Some theologians may want to go further, and try to clarify some of the ontological relations which the assertion seems to imply, relations between the human Jesus and God the Father, or relations within the person of Jesus Christ himself. But there is a limit to how far one can or should go along such lines. Coming back to Karl Barth, I think he is pressing the limits, if not overstepping them, when, discussing the traditional view that in Jesus Christ there concur two 'natures' (Barth prefers to speak of two 'essences', but in each case it is the Greek word *physis* that is intended), he holds that these natures 'participate' in each other, and that this participation is asymmetrical, for, as 'his divine essence is that which is originally proper to him, and his human is only adopted by him and assumed to it . . . the determination of his divine essence is *to* his human, and the determination of his human essence *from* his divine.'[14] I find myself asking, 'How does Barth, or any theologian of finite intelligence, know this?' And even if he could know it, does not this teaching undermine the full humanity of Christ and push us in a monophysite direction? And I may add that whatever we say about Jesus Christ or whatever claim we make, we must never cast doubt on his full humanity.

Perhaps we have to remind ourselves again that the language of christology, especially when it is attempting to speak of the theological significance of Jesus Christ, is inevitably a language having a measure of indirect and analogical character. Though we have seen that christology cannot ignore ontological questions, we have also seen that its roots lie in what we have labelled as 'gospel' in the broadest sense, the kind of language employed in the original Christian proclamation (*euangelion* or *kerygma*). Though christology adopts a reflective and even critical stance towards the gospel, it cannot disavow its origin or depart altogether from the kind of language, both concrete and symbolic, out of which it arose. Sometimes, indeed, christology has attempted to become a purely conceptual, even 'scientific' language. I would say that the Chalcedonian definition is an example of such an attempt, though the four great negative adverbs in that definition also illustrate the principle of reserve. They acknowledge an element of mystery and hold open the door for further exploration. Nevertheless, the language of Chalcedon has moved far from that composite of history, legend, mythology and so on that we designate by the term 'gospel'. And here we see both the usefulness and the limits of such a formula. It is useful because it brings a second kind of language alongside the first kind, and these languages mutually illumine one another. The ontology of Chalcedon throws light on the meaning of the gospel, but equally the gospel brings to life the abstractness of Chalcedon. There is a parallel case nearer our own time. Bultmann's demythologizing used the conceptuality of existentialism to elucidate the meaning of the gospel for persons to whom mythological discourse was no longer meaningful. But Bultmann's existential version of Christianity would not perhaps make much appeal if it were not illustrated and embodied in the concrete narratives of the Bible. Further, as we have seen in the case of Barth, an excessive preoccupation with the *minutiae* of speculative theology can lead into the discussion of questions which are at best adiaphora and at worst meaningless.

These remarks suggest that christology (and theology in general) is as much an art as a science – a suggestion which is strengthened when we remember that most christological heresies have arisen from a lack of proportion. The language of christology, in so far as it reflects the language of gospel, is perhaps better understood when we compare it to art than when we compare it to science. I am not saying that theology is art, or that its truth is the same as, say, the truth of a poem, for these things can all be distinguished, but I believe that distinctively christo-logical discourse can be illuminated by a comparison with art. If we think of some typically theological assertions about Jesus Christ, as that he came into the world to save sinners, that he is the incarnate Word, that God raised him from the dead, and so on, we are at once aware of an elusiveness in such statements. It is not just, as we have already noted, that they are not straightforward historical assertions. They are not *simpliciter* descriptive language at all. But can we say more clearly what they are?

A philosopher who has, I believe, helped to throw light on the problem is Hans-Georg Gadamer. He has investigated the question of what kind of knowledge and what kind of truth come to expression in art. Do we acknowledge that the artist, of whatever kind, is seeking to convey knowledge and to open up truth? Gadamer has no doubt that this is the case. 'Art is knowledge, and the experience of the work of art is a sharing in this knowledge . . . Does not the experience of art contain a claim to truth which is certainly different from that of science, but equally certainly is not inferior to it?'[15] Again, he claims (and this claim is more obscure): 'The esthetic experience is not just one kind of experience among others, but represents the essence of experience itself . . . An esthetic experience always contains the experience of an infinite whole.'[16] Going further, he holds that the artistic representation (for he seems to be talking about representative art) reveals truth more than the original which it represents, the work of art more than the material out of which it has been constructed. To quote his own illustration, 'With regard to the recognition of the true, the being of representation is superior to the being of the material represented, the Achilles of Homer more than the original Achilles.'[17] Such representation is not, of course, a mere copying of the original. In Gadamer's language, 'it is not merely a second version, a copy, but a recognition of the essence.'[18]

Gadamer does seem to be saying something important here. Suppose we had an eye-witness account of the siege of Troy, or even suppose we were somehow able to see for ourselves the events that then took place, it would not be particularly edifying, only a brutal episode in the continu-ous cycle of violence that went on in the eastern Mediterranean at that time. The poet (or poets) whom we call Homer has by consummate art transfigured these sordid scenes into a panorama of human nature. The poet has, in Gadamer's expression, 'recognized the essence' and enabled the reader to see it also. And then for hundreds of years literary critics and commentators have gone to the poem and unpacked its seemingly inexhaustible treasures.

Let us now see whether this situation can illuminate our problems with christology. Here too there are, so to speak, three layers. There is the original, the so-called 'historical' Jesus. What would we have made of him, if we had seen him, or if someone had left a factual, realistic account of his career? If we were like most of the people living at that time, we would not have made very much of him. Most likely we would have seen just the busy rabbi, expounding the scriptures and arguing with other teachers, the one of whom Karl Barth wrote, 'Jesus Christ is also the rabbi of Nazareth, one whose activity is so easily a little commonplace alongside more than one founder of a religion.'[19] Even if we had seen him dying on the cross and knew something of the reasons for his execution, at most we might have felt only a mingling of pity and respect for a teacher who had suffered for his devotion to what he believed to be truth. The whole career and person of Jesus is transfigured by the New Testament writers who present it as 'gospel'. Are we to say that they have 'recognized the essence', that they have brought to light the 'truth' of Jesus Christ and have enabled their readers to share their vision of the truth? I suppose this is what Martin Kähler had in mind when he wrote that 'the real Christ is the preached Christ', the Christ presented in the gospel or kerygma, not the figure revealed by historical research.[20] He goes so far as to say that 'the Jesus of the "life of Jesus" movement is merely a modern example of human creativity, and not an iota better than the notorious dogmatic Christ of Byzantine christology'.[21] This last comparison is surely not justified, since the dogmatic Christ of Chalcedon is ultimately derived from the kerygmatic Christ, not from whatever abstraction historical research may claim to have found underlying the gospel.

Let us remind ourselves of my provisional definition of christology as 'gospel that has been subjected to reflection and criticism'. Gospel is, in relation to the original, the second layer, corresponding to an art-work. A gospel does resemble a work of art in the sense that it does not merely copy the original or offer a second version of it, but, dare we venture to say, exposes the essence of the original, so that there takes place the event of the recognition of truth, the setting forth in unconcealedness (aletheia) of the fundamental meaning and reality of the original? A detailed history of Jesus, if we had been left one, would have been a copy or second version of the original – though it would necessarily have been an imperfect copy, since a personal life can never be fully transcribed in words. But a gospel is concerned (to use Gadamer's phrase) with the recognition of the essence. It achieves its aim by weaving together

historical incidents, teachings and sayings, mythological ideas, legendary accretions, theological reflections into a unique kind of discourse.

The writers of the gospels are not usually supposed to have been very
erudite, but their products are surely analogous to works of art, and from
time to time rise to the level of works of genius. We know virtually
nothing about the author of John's gospel, though, as I shall show later,
he had an extraordinary gift of language. But I can give one example now
of his literary power. The example is his account of the trial of Jesus. If
there had been a clerk of court and he had left us a transcript of the trial, it
might have made us see it very differently from the account in the Fourth
Gospel. But the evangelist whom we call John, by what Bultmann calls 'a
remarkable interweaving of tradition and specifically Johannine narration',[22] has dramatically presented the essential meaning as he perceived
it and as we are enabled to perceive it – a reversal of the roles of Jesus and
his judges, so that Jesus emerges as the judge while the ecclesiastical and
political establishments are put on trial and found wanting. It is a
remarkable transfiguration of the facts, not a distortion but rather an
exposure of the reality. This is not just analogous to a work of art – it is
itself an art-work of genius.

All art-works are executed in a style that belongs to a particular time
and culture. This is as true of the New Testament writings as of any other
literature. The ideas and devices used to set forth the significance of Jesus,
to bring about the recognition of the essence, belong to the first-century
near-eastern cultural milieu, and many of them do not readily achieve
their purpose today. For instance, the attribution of miracles to Jesus may
have impressed the first readers of the gospels and led them to see Jesus
in a new depth, but for the modern reader, such stories are likely to be a
barrier, hence Bultmann's project of demythologizing. Even so, it is
remarkable that so much in the New Testament still communicates
directly with us, and of course it is the mark of a great work of art that it
can communicate across cultural boundaries. But one must not minimize
the gaps that separate us from the kerygma of the New Testament
writers. And this is where we see the necessity of christology, which has
the task, through reflection and criticism, of renewing and interpreting
the insights of gospel. From this point of view, christology is like a third
layer, as we move from the original happenings first to gospel as their
setting forth by the New Testament writers and then to christology as the
continuing task of interpretation and renewal.

In talking of the progression and transformation that takes place as we
move from the original events in space and time to their expression in the
form of gospel to their critical reinterpretation in christology, we are
brought once again to a problem at which we have glanced more than
once without giving it more than passing attention – the problem,

namely, of the place of the historical in the study of christology. We have accepted that neither gospel nor christology is simply the history of Jesus of Nazareth, though they both contain historical assertions. We have seen too that the theological assertions of gospel and christological discourse are not timeless, like the utterances of mythology, but are referred to a particular stretch of history. Also, we have seen reason to believe that we must hold fast to the complete humanity of Jesus Christ, and this would not be possible if we regarded him as either a fictitious or a supernatural character. So we suppose that there is an original series of events in the actual world underlying both christology and the gospel which christology seeks to re-express in more critical and sophisticated ways.

But what can we know about this supposed original series of events? Or how do we think of it? Sometimes people speak as if this original were just some bare happening, a brute fact to be perceived in its sheer givenness. But not only are we no longer in a position to perceive these happenings of long ago. Even if by some miracle we could perceive them taking place – let us say, by a journey back through time such as writers of science fiction imagine – we would not see bare unvarnished facts. Our minds would be interpreting those facts even as we saw them happen. If we took our twentieth-century mentality with us on this supposed journey, we might interpret some of these facts differently from the evangelists, for instance, what they recount as a miracle might not seem so to us. But there would never be facts without interpretation, for history itself is a human phenomenon, and therefore even as it happens it is being interpreted one way or another. There are no uninterpreted brute facts which can serve as a norm by which to judge subsequent interpretations. That is why, near the beginning of this book, it was said that christology, even Christianity itself, did not begin with the birth or conception of Jesus of Nazareth, but in the moment when Peter (or some other disciple) said to him, 'You are the Christ!' The event includes its perception and reception in a human community if it is to count as history, as distinct from mere natural happening. We do not first of all have a bare happening, and then someone comes along and attaches a meaning or interpretation to it. From the beginning, meanings and interpretations form part of the event, though this does not exclude the possibility that these meanings and interpretations may later be challenged or deepened or regarded as mistaken.

Among contemporary theologians, no one has been more insistent in criticizing the separation of history into facts and interpretation than Wolfhart Pannenberg. He writes:

Such a splitting up of historical consciousness into a detection of facts and an evaluation of them (or into history as known and history as experienced) is intolerable to Christian faith, not only because the message of the resurrection of Jesus and of God's revelation in him necessarily becomes merely subjective interpretation, but also because it is the reflection of an outmoded and questionable historical method. It is based on the futile aim of the positivist historians to ascertain bare facts without meaning in history. Against this we must reinstate today the original unity of facts and their meaning.[23]

Pannenberg, of course, is writing as a Christian theologian, but the criticisms he offers of the positivist view of history had already been forcibly stated a generation earlier by the philosopher R. G. Collingwood.[24]

It will help us to hold together history and theology, event and interpretation, if we consider at this point an expression which has gained a lot of currency in recent years among biblical and theological writers – I mean, the expression 'Christ-event', I am not sure who first used this phrase, though it may very likely have been Bultmann, for it occurs rather frequently in his writings, and in the writings of scholars who have been strongly influenced by Bultmann, notably John Knox.

In Bultmann's own use of the expression 'Christ-event', it seems to me that he is wanting to stress a dynamic idea of christology, that is to say, the Christ as a happening in history, rather than as a person considered as an ontological reality. This latter way of looking at Christ is understood by Bultmann to lead to an 'objectification' – a supposedly static or abstract understanding of Christ as person or nature or substance or timeless ideal. Whether Bultmann is successful in evading the ontological question, and whether his existentialist christology stands up to criticism, are questions to which we shall return in a later chapter. But for the moment, we note that Bultmann repeatedly declares that Jesus Christ is the *event* of God's acting in the world, the bearer of the word which God speaks; and since it is the word rather than the bearer which matters, the Christ-event is not confined to the career of Jesus Christ but is prolonged in all subsequent proclaiming of the word by the church, down to this present time. 'Jesus Christ', writes Bultmann, 'is the eschatological event, as the man Jesus of Nazareth, and as the word which resounds in the mouths of those who preach him.'[25] He can also speak of 'the proclamation of the word as a continuation of the Christ-event'. So for Bultmann the Christ-event extends a long way, perhaps indefinitely, beyond the temporal life-span of Jesus, certainly later than Jesus in the proclamation of the church, and perhaps also prior to Jesus in the formation of messianic expectations in Israel.

In the usage of John Knox, the conception of a Christ-event is extended not only in time but in a social sense. Knox takes seriously the point made above that a historical event includes its perception and interpretation. We have also expressed this by saying that christology and Christianity begin not with the isolated figure of Jesus of Nazareth but with his recognition as the Christ. One can speak of a revelation in Christ only when that has become a revelation for someone. The Christ-event includes the response of faith. Knox does in fact tell us that the 'event of Christ' includes 'the personality, life and teaching of Jesus, the response of loyalty he awakened, his death, his resurrection, the receiving of the Spirit, the faith with which the Spirit was received, the coming into being of the Church.'[26] So the Christ-event is for him a very complex reality, though he does not explicitly extend it so far in time as Bultmann appears to do. Clearly, for Knox, the church has a very important place in all this. He does say that the only difference in the world before and after the coming of Christ was that the church had now appeared. 'The only adequate way to define the [Christ-] event is to identify it with the Church's beginning,' so that one can also say that 'the event is the moment of the Church's beginning.' Knox acknowledges of course that the beginning certainly included the more limited event of the career of Jesus of Nazareth, and he even accords to this career a normative value by which the subsequent life of the church may be judged. But 'the event has no historical reality except within the history of the church.'[27]

Knox's understanding of the Christ-event is certainly broader than Bultmann's in the sense that it understands the event as a social happening, but the two views are not seriously conflicting. Rather, Knox has filled out the concept by taking more seriously that social aspect of human existence, not adequately recognized by Bultmann. But both scholars are agreed in seeing the Christ-event as something larger than the career of Jesus of Nazareth. In that larger reality there were joined inseparably the career of Jesus and its impact on the believing community, the history of Israel and the history of the church, the tradition of the past and the experience of the participants in the event. They are inseparably joined because each lends meaning to the other. This is in no sense to downgrade Jesus Christ. Like any other human being, he did not exist apart from his relations to other human beings, and could not be isolated from them without mutilation. And, as has been stated, it is not denied that he was the inspiring centre of the complex which we call the 'Christ-event' – even, as Knox claims, a kind of norm by which to judge the legitimacy of subsequent developments. But Knox seems to be introducing a new problem by this claim, for if Jesus himself is to be a norm, must we not find ourselves again with the obligation of sorting out precisely what comes from him and what derives from other elements in the complex? Perhaps we should be satisfied with the more modest claim of Maurice Wiles, who says: 'That [Jesus] was the prime creative force in that historic movement of change seems to me beyond question. But the exact nature of that prime creative force, of his specific contribution, is something of which we can be much less confident. A considerable degree of doubt on that score is simply a fact of life with which we have to learn to live.'[28]

When at an earlier stage we were discussing the theological implications of the gospel and the need to engage in a measure of ontological explication, we decided that there are limits to such explication. We were suspicious of over-ambitious attempts to dissect and analyse the person of Christ, his relation to God the Father and the conjunction in him of the divine and the human. The limiting factor here is our own lack of mental capacity for understanding the mysteries of divine and human life, and we invoked the principle of reserve. It now seems that we come to a corresponding limit when we inquire into the historical data that lie behind the discourse that we call 'gospel'. This time it is not the weakness of our understanding that is the trouble, but the paucity and uncertainty of our information concerning Jesus of Nazareth. So we see that there are both ontological and historical limits to the christological enterprise. Perhaps from a religious point of view, these limitations do not matter – it is possible to have an existential or 'saving' faith in Jesus Christ without assenting to or even understanding something like *anhypostasia*, or without having an opinion as to whether he actually stilled a storm on the Sea of Galilee. We shall have to decide as we go along just where the limits lie, and to resist the temptation to make claims or assertions beyond our resources. ——

Coming back to the conception of a Christ-event, which we have just been discussing, I think we can say that the use of this conception does to some extent relieve the problems that arise from our lack of information about the historical Jesus. The coming into being of the church or the Christian movement is, shall we say, more visible and clearly attested in history than the personal career of the rabbi of Nazareth. And if we think of Jesus and the community as together embraced in the Christ-event, this is not only being true to the inescapably social character of all human existence, it also dissolves some questions that used to be debated with some heat among churchmen, who disagreed about what comes from Jesus and what comes from the community. Whether, for instance, the so-called 'dominical' sacraments were instituted by Jesus or by his followers or perhaps partly by both is a question of little consequence once it is acknowledged that there is no sharp dividing line between Jesus and the community. Even more importance was attached in some of the older books on christology to the question of how Jesus understood himself. Did he think of himself as Messiah, or did he call himself Son of Man in some special eschatological sense of that term? Did he first apply to himself the imagery of the suffering servant of deutero-Isaiah? Did he think of himself as standing in a unique relationship to the Father? Or did some or all of these ways of thinking originate among his disciples? There can, I think, be no certain answers to these questions. But I also think that the importance of such questions has been exaggerated. We do not need to know the inner thoughts of Jesus, and in any case we cannot. When one places him in his context and acknowledges that he cannot be abstracted from his community and the response of that community, to be gathered from the appellations it applied to him, then many of our questions, although they continue to have a certain historical interest, are of no great moment for christology.

Another problem which appears in a different light when we focus attention on the Christ-event rather than on the individual person of Jesus Christ is the idea of incarnation itself. This too has often been considered in isolation and in ways which give it a strongly mythological colouring. We meet such speculative ideas as the 'implanting' of the divine Logos in Jesus, and this is conceived as a unique intervention by God in human history. But if we think of Jesus in all the relationships that went to constitute him as a person, in his continuity with Israel on the one hand and with the new Christian community on the other, then it is within this complex human reality that God has come to expression in that new and fuller way that we call 'incarnation'. This was not just the work of a moment; it did not happen in a flash on the day of the annunciation; it was a lengthy process which had been long preparing in the history of Israel and then continued in the life of the church – the coming into being of a new humanity. It was not just the formation of an individual (though, as we have seen, there is no reason to doubt that Jesus was at the centre of it) but it was the creation of a new humanity, so that the wider community in which Jesus has his setting can be called his body, and even by some persons an extension of the incarnation.

But while I believe that to refuse to separate the individual Jesus of Nazareth from the wider reality which we call the Christ-event does ease some of the questions that have vexed theologians in their study of christology, it would be idle to pretend that serious questions do not remain. Sometimes, where there are conflicting traditions, it may still be necessary or desirable to ascertain what came from Jesus and what from his followers. For instance, is divorce totally prohibited for the Christian (Mark 10.2–9), or is it permissible in certain circumstances (Matt. 5.31–2)? In some cases we may be able to reach a probable answer to a question like this, but in other cases not. But a more general and more troublesome question lies behind the particular cases. What is the ground of our confidence for believing that there is such close continuity between Jesus and his community? Have we good reason to assume that Jesus and the community do constitute a unity so close that the mind and words of

Jesus are the mind and words of the community, and *vice versa*? Some scholars, after all, have held that there was a radical break between Jesus and the church, and certainly there were some differences. For instance, Jesus proclaimed the imminence of the kingdom of God, while the church proclaimed the Lordship of Jesus. We can hardly go along with Newman's close identification of the church's word with Christ's, when in his hymn he takes 'her teaching as his own'. The systematic theologian will never be in a position where he can ignore the uncertainties arising out of historical research, and when some reputable historian has cast doubt on some particular tradition, the theologian will avoid placing weight on that tradition.

There is still another criticism of the conception of a 'Christ-event', and we must take note of it. It can be objected that the expression is too vague to be of much use. Of course, that objection could be made to any use of the word 'event'. One cannot set fixed boundaries to an event, for one event merges into another in a continuous stream of happening, and to try to specify an event too closely would seem to be an arbitrary act. But the notion of a 'Christ-event' is particularly vulnerable. As we have seen, some writers extend the event indefinitely – it reaches to the present time, and also extends back into the history of Israel. But it then becomes so nebulous that it loses all definition and ceases to be useful in christological discussion. John Knox, as we have noted, thinks of the Christ-event in a more limited way; it originates in the personal career of Jesus Christ and extends to the coming into being of the church, as the response to Christ. This may be arbitrary, but at least it makes the idea manageable and is a useful convention. It also corresponds roughly with the period covered by the New Testament.

The title of this book is 'Jesus Christ in Modern Thought', and we seem to have said virtually nothing about the second half of that title. By 'modern thought' I mean the thinking, both theological and philosophical, that took shape in that vast transforming movement of the human spirit which took place in the seventeenth and eighteenth centuries, and which won for itself the title of the Enlightenment. It touched virtually every aspect of European thinking, and was deeply influential in science, history, politics, philosophy, theology, economics, as well as giving birth to new sciences which applied the principles of the Enlightenment to further areas of nature and human society.

Not least did it shake to its very base our own theme of christology. For very many centuries, there had been little change in the estimate of Jesus Christ. The New Testament was taken to be a faithful and, indeed, divinely inspired account of his life and teaching. He himself was believed to be the God-man in the sense that had been formulated in four hundred years of controversy in the early church, culminating in the

Chalcedonian definition of 451, according to which Jesus Christ is a divine person in whom are perfectly conjoined, without either mixture or separation, a complete divine nature and a complete human nature, so that he is both truly God and truly man. That understanding of Jesus Christ, based on the New Testament and on the subsequent dogmatic development, continued essentially intact through the stormy upheavals of the Reformation and the religious wars, so that, as has often been noted, the Enlightenment brought more radical changes to Christian theology than did the Reformation. But from the Enlightenment onward the situation has changed, and challenges have continually been offered both to the historical trustworthiness of the New Testament and to the theological claim that God was uniquely present and revealed in the person of Jesus Christ.

The new religious beliefs that appeared in the Enlightenment period are known generally as 'deism'. But the advocates of deism would not have regarded these beliefs as 'new', for they thought of themselves as returning to 'natural' or 'rational' religion, to fundamental beliefs about God and man that are innate to the human mind and discoverable by reason without the aid of any alleged revelation. Deism originated in England in the thought of Edward Herbert (1582–1648), better known as Lord Herbert of Cherbury, older brother of the Anglican priest-poet George Herbert. Lord Herbert's book *De Veritate*[29] (1624) listed five basic beliefs as the rational foundation of religion – belief in a Supreme Being (the usual Enlightenment title for God), the duty to worship him, the equation of such worship with a virtuous life, the need for repentance, and a future life bringing rewards and punishments. The deists accepted that God had created the world in the beginning, and many of them accepted the argument from design as the strongest evidence for God's existence. But as the science of the time, especially Newton's account of the solar system, was exhibiting the universe as a self-regulating mechanism, the deists virtually excluded the possibility of divine intervention in the world, by way of miraculous action or revelation. Creation itself had been the only miracle, for it seemed to be needed to account for the existence of an ordered world. But after the beginning, God let the world go its own way in accordance with the laws he had laid down at the beginning. Deism was therefore a kind of dualism. However, God was needed for another purpose besides accounting for creation – he was the author of the moral law, as well as the laws of physics. This twofold doctrine of God, as lawgiver for both the natural and the moral order, found classic expression in the famous words of Kant: 'Two things fill the mind with ever new and increasing admiration and awe, the oftener and the more steadily we reflect on them: *the starry heavens above and the moral law within*'.[30]

As time went on, deism became more diversified. It spread from England to France, Germany and other European countries, and was influential among the founding fathers of the United States. Though most deists thought of God as transcendent, some moved toward pantheism. Again, though many deists believed that Christianity embodies the truths of natural religion, they also believed that revelation is superfluous, and the implication is that Jesus Christ is superfluous. Some deists became increasingly hostile to Christianity. One of the first to offer a radical reinterpretation of the New Testament, Herbert Samuel Reimarus (1694–1768), claimed that the 'real' Jesus had been a political revolutionary who led a revolt against the Romans but was frustrated. Traces of this, he believed, are still visible in the gospels – the triumphal entry into Jerusalem, the violence in the Temple, the disillusioned cry from the cross. But the disciples covered up the truth and gave us the gospels as we have them. By means of two falsehoods – the story that Christ had risen from the dead and the promise that he would come again – they won over many of the people and succeeded in launching the Christian church. These startling views were published only after the death of Reimarus, through the agency of another Enlightenment scholar, Lessing.[31] Reimarus was only one of the anti-Christian deists. Voltaire (1694–1778) while he was a deist and held that belief in God is a necessity – 'If God did not exist, it would be necessary to invent him'[32] – was at the same time one of Christianity's bitterest enemies. But as the combination of the scientific spirit, rationalism, empiricism and scepticism increased in strength, deism found itself threatened just as much as Christianity. A new wave of atheistic materialism was breaking on the Western world. God himself was disappearing, and traditional affirmations about Jesus Christ were further than ever removed from the beliefs of most men and women in the modern world. As God seemed to become increasingly redundant, man had to fall back on himself, on his rationality and responsibility. In 1784, Kant published a famous essay with the title, 'An Answer to the Question, "What is Enlightenment?"' He described it as man's coming of age. Up till that time, the human race had depended on powers beyond itself. But human beings have reason, and they must have the courage to think and choose for themselves. 'Dare to know!' wrote Kant. 'Have the courage to make use of your own understanding – this is the motto of the Enlightenment.'[33]

It is true that many things in the Enlightenment have been left behind. We no longer share its naive, even pathetic, belief in human perfectibility (though neither did Kant). The crude materialism of some of the French *philosophers* has long since been discredited by the advances of science itself. We recognize the poverty and shallowness of a merely secular life style, though we have not found how to deal with this problem. Yet in other important respects we remain inevitably children of the Enlightenment. Some of its lessons can never be unlearned. We cannot go back to the mythology of a former age, or to its supernaturalism, or to the spiritual authoritarianism of an infallible church or an infallible Bible. So if we want to ask the question about Jesus Christ and think it worth asking, we have to confront not only all the difficulties and complexities mentioned in the earlier parts of this chapter, but the equally difficult problems of making sense of it all within the constraining framework of modern thought.

] 2 [

The Prehistory of Christology

No matter how novel any event or any idea may be, it is almost certain that it has not just come 'out of the blue', as we say. When we begin to consider it, we learn that it has antecedents and has been in preparation for perhaps a very long time. This is as true of the event of Jesus Christ as of any other event. In saying this, one is not denying the possibility of novelty in human history, and certainly not trying to minimize the novel impact of Jesus Christ. I have already used the word 'revelation' for that impact, and quoted the dramatic definition which Nietzsche gave to that word. When the event takes place – whether it is the Christ-event or a scientific discovery or an explorer stumbling on a new continent – we are at first overwhelmed with the novelty. But very soon our minds are busy trying to relate the new phenomenon to the context of what we already know. This is a necessity of our thought. If we were confronted with something really out of the blue, something quite unrelated to anything else that we had ever seen or had ever crossed our minds, we would be speechless. We could have no understanding of this strange new apparition.

If we are to understand, we have to begin looking for a context. We begin asking 'Who?', 'What?', 'Whence?' . . . The first Christian disciples, after they had been 'thrown to the ground', to use Nietzsche's expression, picked themselves up and began wondering what had happened or was still happening. Near the beginning of the book, I alluded to what has traditionally been believed to be the first approximation to an answer to their wondering – Peter's confession, 'You are the Christ!' Whether Peter actually said this or whether Jesus accepted the description or whether it was an appropriate description are all debatable matters, but what is important is that from the very beginning the disciples placed Jesus in the context of Hebrew and Jewish religion, and tried to understand him in terms of the images and conceptions arising out of that religion. There is nothing surprising about that. Although Christians seem often unaware of the fact, Jesus was a Jew, not a Christian. His own teaching, even when he is engaging in polemics against Jewish traditionalists, belongs within the tradition which he is criticizing. Likewise his first disciples were Jews. They continued to frequent the Temple and the synagogues, and to begin with appeared to be a movement within Judaism. Before long it became clear that the new movement could not be contained within Judaism, but even as the Christian church emerged as a distinct entity, it held fast to its Jewish heritage, and even today claims the Hebrew scriptures as its Old Testament. Though many philosophers and theologians from Kant onward have tried to minimize the relation of Christianity to Judaism or to deny it altogether (as did also the Nazis in a more sinister manner), the fact remains, and no one can advance very far in the understanding of Christianity, and perhaps especially christology, without looking back to the Jewish tradition. It was the expectations arising out of Judaism and the Hebrew scriptures that shaped the earliest thinking about the person of Jesus Christ and that were used to answer the question, 'Who was he (or is he)?' That is the reason that demands a backward look at the heritage of Judaism before we directly consider Christian thought about Jesus Christ. It is this heritage that I mean when I speak of the 'prehistory' of christology.

To guard against possible misunderstanding, I should say at this point that I am not being so arrogant as to suggest that Judaism is *merely* a prelude to Christianity, or that the Old Testament is *merely* a prolegomenon to the New. Both the Hebrew scriptures and the Judaism that eventually developed from them have their own independent worth and dignity. In view of the tragic history of Jewish–Christian relations, it is important to say this. So in speaking of the 'prehistory' of christology I am simply acknowledging the debt which Christianity owes to the older tradition. No doubt the separation of the two faiths was inevitable, but even in the earliest days of rivalry, Paul warned the Christians against any illusions of superiority. They are, he wrote, like new branches that have been grafted into an ancient olive-tree; 'remember it is not you that support the root, but the root that supports you' (Rom. 11.18).

There is quite a different misunderstanding against which we must also guard, namely, the possible confusion of what I am calling a 'prehistory' of christology, and the practice of looking for predictions of Jesus in the Old Testament. Many apologists of earlier times, including important patristic writers, made much of what they took to be prophecies concerning Jesus in the religion of Israel. There is evidence that even in the very earliest days of the Christian movement, there was a diligent searching of the ancient writings for predictions of Jesus. An example occurs in the much loved story of the two disciples returning to Emmaus after the crucifixion of Jesus, and sadly discussing the turn which events had taken. They had expected Jesus to restore the fortunes of Israel, but now he was dead. But the risen Christ appears to them, 'and beginning with Moses and all the prophets, he interpreted to them in all the scriptures the things concerning himself' (Luke 24.27). David Friedrich Strauss believed that this searching of the scriptures was an activity that went on for a generation as the disciples tried to reconcile their faith in a crucified Lord with the prophetic expectations of a messiah.[1] No doubt in the process they pressed into service many passages that were never intended to be messianic predictions. Yet they found plenty of material which, to an uncritical person, might seem quite remarkable and explicitly applicable to Jesus. A good example is Psalm 22, which describes a sufferer whose misfortunes bear a close resemblance even in detail to the sufferings of Jesus on the cross, as narrated in the gospels. But such resemblances can be explained in more ways than one. Strauss pointed out that one has to reckon with the possibility that the gospel narrative has been constructed with the alleged prediction in mind, and made to fit it. The old-fashioned appeals to prophecy have been largely discredited, and one does not meet them today among reputable scholars.

But if the prehistory of christology is not to be found in specific promises or predictions in the ancient texts, in what sense are we claiming that there is a prehistory? In any case, Jesus simply did not fulfil many of the messianic expectations of former times but rather contradicted them, so that he was as much an unexpected as an expected messiah. We have to look for the connection in a broader correspondence between the themes of the Old Testament and those of the New. The Old Testament created a framework of beliefs and expectations in which Christianity, and, in particular, the christological beliefs about Jesus could emerge. We have to remember also, of course, that it was only a small group of Jews who saw in Jesus the culmination of Israel's history.

We may begin by asking, who was this people, Israel, who produced the scriptures which we still read and whose faith formed the matrix from which Christianity was born? Although there is uncertainty, it would seem that the people called Hebrews are related to the Habiru, who are already mentioned early in the second millennium BC. These Habiru do not seem to have been a definite nation or ethnic group. They were vagrants or people of indefinite affinity, something like gypsies, perhaps, who went from one country to another, taking what employment they could get. A consciousness of this lowly origin seems to have lingered in the Hebrew memory, for we are told that in the cult the Israelite confessed his identity thus: 'A wandering Aramean was my father, and he went down into Egypt and sojourned there . . .' (Deut. 26.5). According to their own understanding of their history (and we have to remember that every nation's history, especially its early history, is heavily laden with mythology and ideology – this is as true of England and the United States as it is of Israel) – the Hebrews or at least a considerable number of them were enslaved in Egypt but eventually were marvellously delivered, owing, as they believed, to the intervention on their behalf of their God. This obscure people who had not even been a people had been called to become the people of God. They would never be a 'great' people, in any usual sense in which we might use that expression, but this small and despised section of humanity would nevertheless attain to a spiritual leadership through the purity and nobility of its religious faith. There is a parallel here to what is unveiled in the New Testament. The obscure Jesus of Nazareth – we have already noted how difficult it is to get any reliable historical information about him – is none the less the chosen (elect) one of God, just as Israel had been his chosen (elect) people. And those who joined themselves to Jesus and became the nucleus of the church were, like the Habiru, people of no worldly consequence. Jewish Christians who knew the history of their own people would understand Paul very well when he wrote to one of the churches: 'Consider your call, brethren; not many of you were wise according to worldly standards, not many were powerful, not many were of noble birth; but God chose what is foolish in the world to shame the wise, God chose what is weak in the world to shame the strong, God chose what is low and despised in the world, even things that are not, to bring to nothing things that are, so that no human being might boast in the presence of God' (I Cor. 1.26–9). So a major theme of the New Testament, the condescension of God, was already being expressed in the Old.

But perhaps it will be asked whether the God of Israel is not represented in the Old Testament as a transcendent, monarchical God. Certainly there are elements of such imagery attaching to God. He is transcendent of his creation, and this is brought out especially in the prohibition of idols. The religion of Israel is differentiated from that of other near-eastern peoples of the ancient world because it has no images to represent or symbolize the presence of God. How could a strictly monotheistic imageless religion, which posed the rhetorical question, 'To whom will you liken God?' (Isa. 40.18), foreshadow Christianity with its central assertion that God became incarnate or that a man was the embodiment of God's presence and action in the world? We have to remember that the ban on images is counterbalanced in the Old Testament by the teaching that the first human couple were made in the divine image. 'God said, "Let us make man in our image, after our likeness . . . So God created man in his own image, in the image of God he created him; male and female he created them' (Gen. 1.26–7).

Thus, although the human being is a creature, such a being is nevertheless made in the image of God and therefore must have some possibility of manifesting God in the world. So some idea of incarnation is not ruled out altogether by the Hebrew insistence on the transcendence of God. Again, when we examine the idea of God in the Old Testament, we learn that his transcendence is not to be interpreted as sheer otherness, as distance or inaccessibility. On the contrary, he is near to his creation and cares for it. The dialectical relation of God to the world has been expounded in detail by the Jewish scholar Abraham Heschel, through his concept of the *pathos* of God. In the biblical tradition, he tells us, God is not isolated in a transcendent realm, but is present and manifests himself in the world. He is not understood as detached and unaffected by what goes on in the world. 'God does not simply command, and expect obedience. He is also moved and affected by what happens in the world . . . God does not stand outside the range of human suffering and sorrow. He is personally involved in, even stirred by, the conduct and fate of man.'[2] This pathos or deep feeling on the part of God is linked by Heschel to the phenomenon of prophecy that was so characteristic of Israel's religion. 'The prophet is stirred by an infinite concern for the divine concern. Sympathy is the essential mode in which he responds to the divine situation.'[3] The prophet is not just a mouthpiece for God, not an instrument, but – and I use Heschel's words – a 'partner' and 'associate'.[4] But it is insisted that even this degree of intimacy does not infringe the difference between God and the creature. It is a union in will and feeling, but there is no 'fusion of being'. Therefore, although I said that Heschel's teaching does not seem to rule out as impossible 'some idea of incarnation', I have been very guarded in my language, because it is clear that he would find inacceptable the Nicene language of *homoousios* ('of the same being' or 'of one substance') and it is important not to misrepresent him by exaggerating what he says about the intimacy between the prophet and God.

The objection may be made that this pathos of which Heschel writes is a primitive anthropomorphism which continued to cling to Israel's idea of God even in the age of the great prophets. But such a view depends on a very low estimate of the feelings or emotions in the life of a human being. While some of them are manifestations of states of the body, there are also feelings that have a definitely spiritual quality. If man is indeed made in the image of God, it is not just in his rationality or capacity for thought that he reflects God, but in the entire range of spirit, and we cannot exclude the feelings. If there really is a mysterious affinity between the divine and the human, then in some way the emotional life in the creature must point to an analogue in God.

The pathos of God is not the only way in which the writers of the Hebrew scriptures seek to express God's interest in and concern for his creation. Although it is only in Christian theology that the Holy Spirit emerges as a distinct hypostasis or person within the divine being, there is already much teaching about the Spirit of God in the religion of Israel. The Spirit is like a wind or breath proceeding from God into the world. The Spirit moves across the face of the waters in creation (Gen. 1.2), renews the face of the earth (Ps. 104.30), declares justice through the mouths of the prophets (Micah 3.8), bestows special talents on individuals (Ex. 35.31). So the Spirit, who descends on Jesus at his baptism (Mark 1.10) and on the nascent church at Pentecost (Acts 2.1–4), was already there in the Hebrew heritage and known as the immanent activity of God in the world. But it was not the Spirit who, in the thought of Christian theology, became incarnate in Jesus Christ, but the Word. In the Old Testament, the Word is closely allied to the Spirit. The Word too goes forth from God into the world, and comes to the prophets who proclaim it. Neither the Word nor the Spirit were hypostatized in the way that happened in Christian theology, but the possibility for such hypostatization was there. And if, as we have seen, a specially intimate link was formed between God and the prophets through whom his Word was heard, may not this have suggested a still more intimate union in which the Word would actually be embodied in a human life?

Thus, although the God of Israel was certainly transcendent and not to be confused with the creation, he was also present in the creation by his Spirit and his Word, and was even mirrored in the creation because humanity bore his image and likeness. The deep connection between God and the creatures, especially his elect people, Israel, found more formal expression in an idea which was very characteristic of Hebrew religion – the idea of a covenant.[5] A covenant is a solemn agreement in which those who enter into it accept certain obligations toward each other. It would hardly be going too far to say that the history of ancient Israel is a history of covenants with her God. No doubt later historians sometimes imposed the covenant pattern on earlier history, but even before the making of formal covenants there was the sense that God had committed himself to his people and demanded their commitment to him in return. This conception of a covenant-relationship eventually passes over into Christianity. Jesus is called 'the mediator of a new covenant' (Heb. 12.24) and in the accounts of the Last Supper he is quoted as saying, 'This cup is the new covenant in my blood' (I Cor. 11.25). It is obvious that the idea of covenant as solemn promise has a strong future reference. So if we say that the history contained in the Old Testament is largely a history of covenants, we are also saying that Old Testament history is strongly oriented to the future. Certainly, it tells of origins and events of the past, but it is peculiar in constantly directing attention to what is to come. In the words of Gerhard von Rad, 'The Old Testament can be read only as a book of ever increasing anticipation.'[6] Each covenant points us to a future, yet before that future has been realized or we can perceive its full significance, events take a different turn and a new covenant is struck, but this is equally provisional and may well be superseded. Christians have believed that their own history as a community of faith can be inserted into this open-ended process as a 'new' covenant and a possible *dénouement*, though in my earlier acknowledgment of the independent worth and dignity of the Jewish tradition, I was careful to make it clear that I am not saying that Christianity is the *only* possible fulfilment.

When we place the religion of ancient Israel within the framework of comparative religion, its future-oriented or eschatological outlook is one of its principal distinguishing features. Most archaic religions looked back to a 'Golden Age' in the beginning, and found in it archetypes for their imitation.[7] There were, of course, traces of this in the religion of Israel, but at some point in the history of that religion attention shifted to the end-time. History was then understood not as the gradual falling away of the human race and the cosmos from an initial Golden Age, but as the theatre in which the God of Israel was fulfilling his purposes – righteous purposes that would bring justice, mercy and peace. This was what was to become known as the 'kingdom of God' or the 'reign of God,' and which was to constitute the main theme of the preaching of Jesus. To begin with, the kingdom of God was still identified with the kingdom of Israel, and was visualized as a renewed and purified revival of the kingdom of David to which the scattered sons and daughters of Israel would return with joy. That dream continued to be cherished by some, but it was so improbable and met with so many disappointments that the eschatological hope took a new form. This was apocalyptic. Perhaps it was simply the product of disillusionment. The apocalyptists looked not for a political renewal but for a cosmic cataclysm, the end of the old age with all its evils and the beginning of a new age or even a new world. This would be brought about by the supernatural action of God.

These ideas were very much in the air in the time of Jesus, and they lie behind his proclamation, recorded by the evangelist: 'The time is fulfilled, and the kingdom of God is at hand; repent, and believe in the gospel' (Mark 1.15). 'With such a message,' writes Bultmann, 'Jesus stands in the historical context of Jewish expectations about the end of the world and God's new future.'[8] Bultmann also points out that Jesus' teaching about the kingdom is consistently of the apocalyptic sort, and there is no mention in that teaching of such political expectations as that of the messianic king who would rid the people of their enemies, or that of the lordship of Israel over the earth, or that of the gathering together of the twelve tribes. Though such political ideas had been present in the expectations of Israel, they do not have a place in the kind of kingdom which Jesus was proclaiming. The signs that this kingdom or reign of God was imminent, indeed, was already dawning, were not to be seen in political events of the time. Rather, these signs were visible in the healings which, according to the gospels, Jesus himself effected: 'The blind receive their sight and the lame walk, lepers are cleansed and the deaf hear, and the dead are raised up, and the poor have the good news preached to them' (Matt. 11.5). We shall, of course, have to ask just what credence can be placed on these reports of miracles of healing attributed to Jesus. For the present, we can only note that there are many such reports and that they can hardly be dismissed out of hand as mere legends, for Jesus' initial popularity with the people in Galilee seems to have rested largely on his reputation as a healer, and it would be difficult to account for it if there was no truth in that reputation. So the kingdom that was breaking in was not a new political set up, but an overcoming of the evil, supposedly demonic, powers which brought so much affliction into human life. The reign of God would be a new, fuller, better life for ordinary people. No doubt this might include changes of a political kind (and this might seem more obvious to us than to people of that time, since we are more conscious of the extent to which the lives of individuals are shaped by the sociopolitical structures in which they exist) but such political changes were not of importance in Jesus' interpretation of the reign of God. His parables expound in detail the nature of God's reign but they call not for political activity but simply for a readiness to let God be God, to let his Spirit have free course in the world so that the creation might become what God intended for it. If we ask what that may be, we can only go to the parables for hints and pictures and indications. John's gospel sums it up in the word 'life' – not just biological life, but the flourishing in every way of the whole creation, and especially of those creatures who are said to be made in the image and likeness of God and whose flourishing extends furthest. It is this gospel which sums up the purpose of Jesus himself by attributing to him the words, 'I have come that they may have life, and have it abundantly' (John 10.10).

These words also relate the coming of the kingdom and the mission of Jesus. This brings us to one of the most difficult problems of early Christianity. Jesus appears announcing the imminent coming of the reign of God, and we have seen that this is how he is presented in the synoptic gospels. But it would seem that only a generation later the focus had shifted, and the disciples of Jesus were proclaiming not the kingdom of God but the person of Christ. Was this a mistake? Jesus, it seems clear, had expected that the supernatural inauguration of the kingdom would take place very soon. We may even speculate (and the point will be discussed later) that when he went up to Jerusalem before the crucifixion, he expected that the end would come during his sojourn in the city. But the end did not happen. If Jesus did indeed expect the end at that time, he was mistaken – and since we have already determined[9] to take the humanity of Jesus with full seriousness, there is nothing surprising in the fact that he might be mistaken about the time of the coming of the kingdom, for only a supernatural being and therefore a docetic and non-human Christ could have a knowledge of future events. In fact, according to Mark and Matthew, while Jesus speaks of the speedy coming of the kingdom, he also admits that he does not know the day or the hour: 'Truly, I say to you, this generation will not pass away before all these things take place. Heaven and earth will pass away, but my words will not pass away. But of that day or that hour, no one knows, not even the angels in heaven, nor the Son, but only the Father. Take heed, watch; for you do not know when the time will come' (Mark 13.30–33). Presumably, as the prospect of an early end of the age faded, the disciples attached themselves more and more to Jesus and to what they remembered of his promises.

I have been trying to show that there is a prehistory of christology in the religion of Israel, a foreshadowing of the New Testament in the Old. Yet one can speak of this prehistory only in a general way. It was not nearly anything so simple as a prediction of the Christ by far-sighted prophets of a past age, nor is there any straightforward continuity of the old into the new. While Jesus fulfilled some of the expectations of Israel, he contradicted others. Still, the point made at the beginning of this chapter remains undeniable, namely, that when we are confronted with something novel, our first move is to relate it to what we know already. Thus, we recall that when Jesus asked his followers, 'Who do you say that I am?' Peter replied, 'You are the Christ', and this word 'Christ' is simply the Greek equivalent of the Hebrew term 'messiah' which was a title given to a figure associated with certain of the eschatological expectations of Israel. So Jesus was, so to speak, assigned a place in the field of the religious understanding. Yet what do we mean when we say, 'assigned a place'? It will soon become clear to us that we do not mean that he was put into a premanufactured slot. Although the title 'Christ' has stuck so that today we may hardly think of it as a title but just part of a name, Jesus Christ, yet if we are forced to think of it as a title, as when Tillich speaks, as he regularly does, of Jesus *the* Christ, it is unlikely that we shall be understanding that title in the same way as people did in New Testament times. As soon as the title was applied to Jesus, a shift was taking place in its meaning or meanings. The same holds of other titles that were applied to Jesus in the early Christian community and that were derived from the religion of Israel. None of them were simply taken over as moulds into which the person of Jesus was then made to fit. Rather, they all underwent changes so that they could accommodate the new content. There are more than half a dozen titles that were commonly used of Jesus, titles derived from the Jewish tradition. Although these titles were not used in their unchanged pre-Christian sense, they nevertheless establish contact at various points with the 'prehistory' of christology, and show how in the early decades of Christianity, people were searching for expressions that would more or less adequately say what they wanted to say about Jesus Christ in his relation to God on the one side and to his fellow human beings on the other. Following the changing patterns of both Old Testament and New Testament scholarship as they seek to identify the meanings of the various titles assigned to Jesus is not easy. The number of opinions seems almost equal to the number of scholars engaged in the investigations. One expects that when studies are pursued on supposedly scientific principles, there will be a large measure of unanimity about the results obtained. But this does not appear to have been the case in biblical studies. The systematic theologian almost despairs of finding assured conclusions, and one can understand the impatience of Tillich and others who try as far as possible to make their theological constructions independent of the shifts in biblical studies. I do not myself believe that one can dispense with history in theology or escape the uncertainties which inevitably attend any historical assertions, but there is a principle which I try to follow, and which ought to be stated at this point. It is as follows. Where there are two rival historical views on a matter, and one does not seem to have a clear weight of evidence over the other, then the systematic theologian should follow the more sceptical point of view. He may not in fact be persuaded of the sceptical view, but if he acknowledges that at least it puts a question mark against what has been traditionally believed on the matter, then he will try to construct his theological argument without relying on the matter which has been put in question. There will be examples of this in the discussions immediately following, on the titles of Jesus drawn from the Jewish and Old Testament heritage, and it is to these that we now turn.

Christ

We consider first the title 'Christ'. As I remarked a few sentences back, this is the title that has stuck, so to speak. It became so closely attached to Jesus of Nazareth that before long its original connotations were forgotten and it was virtually part of his name. But these 'original connotations', so far as we can discover what they were, were not particularly apposite to Jesus. As Oscar Cullmann has said, 'One might consider it really ironical that the title "messiah" ("Christ" in Greek) should have been deliberately, permanently connected with the name Jesus.'[10] What then did this word 'Christ' or 'messiah' mean?

Literally, both words, the one derived from Greek and the other from Hebrew, mean 'one who has been anointed'. Various people might be anointed in ancient Israel – the king, likewise the priests, some of the prophets. But the idea of a coming messiah, as part of the eschatological expectation of Israel, was associated chiefly with kingship. It was believed that God had promised to David that his descendants would continue to occupy the throne of Israel, and even when prophets had lost respect for contemporary rulers of the house of David, they looked for a future ruler who would restore the Davidic kingdom. Isaiah, for instance, visualizes a ruler on whom the Spirit of God would bestow his gifts, who would establish justice among the people and destroy the oppressors, and whose reign would be a period of peace, indeed, a paradise on earth (Isa. 11.1–8). The question of these messianic expectations is enormously complicated, and we cannot become entangled in it here. Von Rad believes that as time went on, the link with the house of David was weakened and that the messiah might make an entirely new beginning.[11] Eichrodt, on the other hand, suggests that in spite of the nationalistic language, what was to be restored was God's own kingship over Israel.[12] There is no denying, however, the strongly nationalist and political associations of the messianic hope. Admittedly, of course, the political and the religious strands were closely related to each other. As the image of the messiah became increasingly varied and also became conflated with other related images, the priestly aspects of the office might be stressed more than the royal aspects. According to some scholars, there were even Jewish groups which hedged their bets, so to speak, and hoped for two messiahs, one political and one ecclesiastical![13] One is tempted to say that they must have been the Anglicans of the ancient world.

It seems clear from the points we have already considered that the messianic idea could not easily be applied to Christ, though it is also seen to be a possibility that it could be so modified or so combined with other ideas that it could be made to fit. But what then are we to make of the confession of Peter? It has sometimes been said that this marks the turning-point in Jesus' ministry. I have said myself at the beginning of this book that it was in the moment that one of the disciples (very likely, Peter) confessed Jesus as the Christ that Christianity came into being. I was, however, careful to add that the incident may have occurred not in the midst of Jesus' ministry but after his resurrection.[14] Bultmann's comment on the story of Peter's confession is brusque. 'This passage is to be characterized as legend.'[15] It is not historically the turning-point of Jesus' ministry, though it is the turning-point of Mark's gospel, where it serves as a literary device. Bultmann gives several reasons for his judgment. One is that the story breaks off after Peter's confession. We are not told, for instance, how Jesus replied. Bultmann thinks the original conclusion of the story is the one given by Matthew, where Jesus blesses Peter and names him as the rock on which he will build his church (Matt. 16.13ff.). The reply to Peter, with its reference to the church, certainly has the appearance of being a post-resurrection tradition.[16] On Bultmann's view, then, the belief that Jesus is the messiah arises with the resurrection, and since it was traditionally Peter who rallied the disciples after the crucifixion, it is natural to see him as the first to confess Jesus as the Christ. However, the fact that in Mark's gospel Jesus does not answer Peter's confession may be more significant than Bultmann allows. He neither accepts nor denies the description of himself as the Christ. When he is asked directly by the high priest, 'Are you the Christ?' then according to Mark he replies 'I am' (Mark 14. 62), but Matthew and Luke have altered this reply to the ambiguous, 'You say so.'[17] So Jesus shows a certain reluctance to accept the title of Christ. This was often explained by saying that he did not want people to misunderstand him as a political leader. But perhaps Bultmann (and before him, Wrede) were right in their view that Jesus did not think of himself as messiah at all. Of course, before many years had passed, the disciples were indeed calling Jesus the Christ, but the word was already changed in meaning, and it has continued to change down to such sophisticated definitions as Tillich's 'bearer of the new being', a phrase that would never have entered the head of any early Christian.

Another major difficulty which we have not yet considered is the fact that the messiah was visualized as a victor, not a sufferer. So when the disciples did come to the point where they recognized Jesus as the Christ, they had to find justification in the tradition for a suffering messiah. They did this by pushing the political connotations of messiah-hood into the background and introducing into the content of the idea characteristics originally associated with other images, such as the 'suffering servant' of deutero-Isaiah. But, as Cullmann points out, this was going against the 'mainstream of contemporary messianism' in which 'one can at best find faint traces of a suffering messiah'.[18]

It is time for us to sum up this discussion of the application of the messianic title to Jesus. It seems most probable that Jesus did not think of himself as messiah or accept the title in his lifetime, but that it came to be used by his followers after the resurrection, and then took on new meanings and discarded some of the old meanings. Yet in saying this, one must not exaggerate. Would the disciples have used messianic language after the resurrection if they had not some suspicions during the ministry that Jesus might be messiah? I find the following remarks of Günther Bornkamm very persuasive:

With all due attention to the critical examination of tradition, we have seen no reason to contest that Jesus actually awakened messianic expectations by his coming and by his ministry, and that he encountered the faith which believed him to be the promised saviour. The faith which is expressed by the two disciples at Emmaus, 'But we hoped that he was the one to redeem Israel' (Lk. 24, 21) seems to express quite accurately the conviction of the followers of Jesus before his death. This, too, is the only explanation of the attitude of the Jewish authorities and of Pilate's verdict . . . We should therefore not speak about Jesus' non-messianic history before his death, but rather of a movement of broken messianic hopes, and of one who was hoped to be the messiah, but who, not only at the moment of failure, but in his entire message and ministry, disappointed the hopes that were placed in him.[19]

Even after the resurrection, these hopes could only be revived if they were thoroughly rethought. So the traditional concept of messiah does not take us very far in our search for an answer to the question, 'Who was (or is) Jesus of Nazareth, called the Christ?' It need hardly be added that although the messiah, as God's anointed, would certainly be a highly exalted being, he was also understood as fully human, and the original use of the title did not imply the kind of relation of Jesus to the Father which developed in later belief.

Son of Man

If we have encountered problems in discussing the title 'Christ', we can look for even more severe problems when we turn to 'Son of Man'. Was this a title at all? Did Jesus use it of himself? Was the Son of Man supposed to be someone other than Jesus, and did Jesus expect this other to come and inaugurate the new age? These are difficult if not impossible questions, and again the systematic theologian finds that clear answers are not to be had. We can only follow what seem to be the more probable opinions among the biblical scholars.

There is however a starting-point on which most writers on the topic agree, and it is quite important. The expression 'Son of Man' (in Hebrew, *ben adam*; in Aramaic, *bar nasha*) was commonly used in these languages as a periphrasis for 'man', just as in English we occasionally use such an expression as 'every man jack'. So when the psalmist asks, 'What is man that thou art mindful of him, or the son of man that thou dost care for him?' (Ps. 8.4), the expressions 'man' and 'son of man' are used synonymously in a parallelism, and each of them means simply 'human being'. This is the common informal sense of 'son of man'.

Much attention has been paid to a particular passage in the Old

Testament where the expression 'Son of Man' is used. This is the vision of
Daniel in which, we read, 'there came one like a son of man, and he came
to the ancient of days and was presented before him; and to him was
given dominion and glory and kingdom, that all peoples, nations and
languages should serve him; his dominion is an everlasting dominion,
which shall not pass away, and his kingdom one that shall not be
destroyed' (Dan. 7.13–14). It has sometimes been claimed that here the
Son of Man is an apocalyptic figure who will bring in the new age and will
himself be exalted in that age. Some have gone so far as to see in these
verses a prophecy of the coming exaltation of Jesus Christ. But that would
be a most improbable explanation. It is true that the appearance of the
'Son of Man' in Daniel does suggest the possibility of a link with
apocalypticism, but the most likely interpretation is that in Daniel's vision
of the end, a human figure or son of man symbolizes Israel as 'the true
descendant of Adam' in Morna Hooker's phrase,[20] in contrast to the
animals mentioned earlier in the vision, apparently symbolizing pagan
empires. In the non-canonical literature, especially the Book of Enoch, the
Son of Man makes his appearance again, and there has been hot debate
among scholars about his significance and whether he is of importance for
interpreting the New Testament. But there seem to be no strong reasons
that would make us read any more into this literature than into Daniel.
Again, Morna Hooker's view seems the most likely, namely, that Adam,
Son of Man and Israel are closely connected with each other.

When we turn to the New Testament, we find the expression 'Son of
Man' being used frequently in its informal sense as 'human being'. When,
for instance, Jesus says, 'The Son of Man is lord even of the sabbath'
(Mark 2.28), it is fairly obvious that he is speaking not of himself but of
human beings generally, for he has just said, 'The sabbath was made for
man, not man for the sabbath' (Mark 2.27). Sometimes, of course, Jesus
does use the expression 'Son of Man' in reference to himself, but then it
would seem to be simply a substitute for the first personal pronoun, for
example, 'Foxes have holes, and birds of the air have nests; but the Son of
Man has nowhere to lay his head' (Matt. 8.20). But even when we have
disposed in these ways of some of the 'Son of Man' passages, there are
others where the expression, used in the mouth of Jesus himself, seems
unmistakably to have a future reference to the definitive end of the age
and the coming of the reign of God. When he is asked by the high priest
whether he is the Christ, Jesus, as we have seen, gives an answer which is
not completely unambiguous; but then he goes on surprisingly to talk not
about the Christ but about the Son of Man: 'And you will see the Son of
Man seated at the right hand of Power and coming with the clouds of
heaven' (Mark 14.62). Does this mean that Jesus, while remaining non-
committal about being called the Christ (perhaps because the title was too

political) refers to himself by the apocalyptic title 'Son of Man' and expects
to have a role in the final *dénouement*? Or how do we understand the
words of Jesus in his apocalyptic vision when he says, 'And then they will
see the Son of Man coming in clouds with great power and glory' (Mark
13.26)? We read these passages as if Jesus were referring to himself when
he talks of the coming of the Son of Man, but I think that Bultmann is
correct when he claims that in these third-person mentions of the Son of
Man, Jesus 'points ahead to the Son of Man as another than himself'.[21]
One might think that this view receives considerable support from the
fact that according to Mark Jesus warned that 'whoever is ashamed of me
and of my words in this adulterous and sinful generation, of him will the
Son of Man also be ashamed when he comes in the glory of the Father
with the holy angels' (Mark 8.38). This seems to refer pretty clearly to a
Son of Man other than Jesus. But according to Matthew, Jesus said,
'whoever denies me before men, I also will deny before my Father who is
in heaven' (Matt. 10.33). One must suppose that Matthew has changed
the saying to conform to the belief, by this time prevalent, that Jesus and
the Son of Man are identical. Perhaps we can go even further than
Bultmann, and speculate whether the Son of Man is not to be considered
as an *individual* other than Jesus but symbolizes (as we may suppose the
expression originally did in Daniel) the new community, the true Israel,
the genuine descendants of Adam, who would be established on the
great day of the coming of the kingdom. This is a humanistic interpretation of the imagery, one which dispenses with all thought of a terrifying
apocalyptic supernatural being (whether a returning Jesus or someone
other than Jesus), but rather sees Jesus both as fulfilling the goal of a true
humanity and as himself inaugurating the new age in which the
community of a new humanity or people of God (symbolized by the Son
of Man) will be the primary reality. Of course, one must frankly say that
this interpretation is given from the point of view of modern post-
mythical thought and does not pretend to reconstruct (if that is possible)
what Jesus and his contemporaries intended by their 'Son of Man'
language. I would, however, point out that what I am here calling a
humanistic interpretation of the Son of Man symbol coheres very well
with my earlier insistence on relating the history of the individual Jesus to
the wider reality of the Christ-event.

Ethelbert Stauffer has claimed that 'the idea of the "Son of Man" lives
on in the Pauline epistles under a new christological word that gives
linguistic expression to the same thing'.[22] He is referring, of course, to
Paul's language about the first and last Adams, and we shall take up this
point when we come to our specific discussion of Paul's thinking on
christology. But we have already seen enough to persuade us that the
'Son of Man' language about Jesus does not demand of us that we move

into apocalyptic ideas or into mythology about a primal Man, but can be understood as a way of talking about Jesus in his humanity, a way capable of producing far-reaching developments, and that has in fact produced such developments in the subsequent history of Christian thought, and still offers resources for theological reflection on Jesus in our own post-Enlightenment age.

Son of God

'I believe that Jesus Christ is the Son of God' was, according to some versions, the confession made by the Ethiopian eunuch on the occasion of his baptism. Even today, it is commonly held that to be a Christian is to acknowledge Jesus Christ as the Son of God. But then we have to ask just what is meant by this expression, 'Son of God'?

There is inevitably a mythological ring about the phrase, 'Son of God'. It perhaps reminds us of the stories of the lascivious deities of Olympus who by devious stratagems had intercourse with mortal women. There are no associations of this kind in the Christian use of the idea. When Justin the martyr in the course of his argument with Trypho the Jew made an unguarded comparison between Jesus and Perseus, said to have been begotten by Zeus of a mortal, Trypho very properly rebukes him: 'Christians should be ashamed of making comparisons with such as Perseus.'[23] There is of course a fragment of similar mythology early in Genesis when the 'Sons of God' take wives from among the daughters of men (Gen. 6.2), but this has nothing to do with the application of the expression to Jesus. There is a literalness in the old mythological usage which, even for those Christians who believed in the virginal birth or, rather, conception of Jesus, was not possible.

To speak of Jesus as 'Son of God' is to use a metaphor. It is certainly an important metaphor and affirms a close relation to God, but it does not imply deification. Martin Hengel holds that in the Old Testament, the expression 'Son of God' has the fairly broad, general sense of 'belonging to God'. Its application was also broad – to the people of Israel (Ex. 4.22), to the Davidic king and his successors, including, presumably, any messianic ruler of the future (II Sam. 7.14).[24] We need not be surprised that Jesus was called 'Son of God' but we need not suppose that this title originally had the decisive meaning that it acquired later. It arises within a long traditional usage, in which a person close to or considered to be an agent of God might be called his son. Jesus does not appear to have called himself 'Son of God' any more than he called himself 'messiah', but the tradition does indicate that he had a special sense of the fatherhood of God, and expressed this in a word of peculiar intimacy, *abba*. Thus Reginald Fuller writes that 'although there is no indubitably authentic logion in which Jesus calls himself the "Son", he certainly called God his

Father in a unique sense.'[25] But we might ask, 'How unique?' After all, he did teach his disciples to pray, 'Our Father . . ' And there are passages in the New Testament that call Christians generally the sons or children of God (John 1.12, etc.) Admittedly, Christians would acknowledge that their filial relation to God has been bestowed through Jesus Christ, but once bestowed, is it a different relation? It is sometimes said to be different in kind and not merely in degree. But surely those who speak in this way are taking the expression 'Son of God' with a literalness and conceptual precision which it does not have and was not intended to have. Referring back for a moment to our discussion of 'Son of Man', I would argue that the potentiality for becoming a Son of God belongs to humanity as such, and that it is because Jesus Christ is Son of Man, in the sense of the Man, the true Man, that he is also Son of God. To the extent that Christians share in his new humanity, they too are sons and daughters of God – not slaves or second-class citizens, but full members of the household. Surely God's salvation would not be less than this.

But although I am stressing the metaphorical character of the expression 'Son of God', I do not think this detracts in any way from its theological significance. A Father and a Son are distinct persons, so the Son is not simply being identified with the Father. Yet the Father–Son relationship is such that such language as 'one in being' or 'of the same substance' is justified. Or again, as Anthony Harvey has indicated, the agency of the Son on behalf of the Father, would have been, in Hebrew eyes, a natural consequence of the filial relationship.[26] The theological implications of all this are developed with great subtlety of language in John's gospel, as we shall see in due course.[27]

Word

Jesus is also designated the Word or Logos. The use of the Greek expression 'Logos' has perhaps encouraged the belief that this term came in from Greek philosophy. Certainly the patristic writers availed themselves of philosophical notions concerning the Logos, but biblical scholars have increasingly tended to the view that as far as the New Testament is concerned, the use of the 'Logos' or 'Word' concept can be quite adequately explained in terms of the Jewish heritage. This is not to deny that some Hellenistic influence may have been felt, for already in New Testament times Philo of Alexandria had been combining Hebrew and Greek ideas, and his work may have been known to the author of the Fourth Gospel, the New Testament writing which makes the most significant use of the Logos concept. Even so, the idea that the Word or Logos is a kind of hypostasis or distinct entity within the being of the Godhead might indicate a development beyond the Hebrew understanding of the Word of God. Although in the Old Testament God 'sends' his

Word and the Word 'comes' to the prophets, the Word is hardly a distinct entity.

But precisely here lies the beauty and aptness of this particular expression. It hovers, shall we say, between metaphor and metaphysics. If we think of the Word as personified in Jesus Christ, then it acquires distinctness from God; yet as God's Word, it is like any word, an utterance of the speaker, something that proceeds from the being of the speaker and reveals that being, something which, we may say, is an extension of the speaker. This is the complex relationship that finds remarkable expression in the opening verse of the prologue to John's gospel: 'In the beginning was the Word, and the Word was with God, and the Word was God' (John 1.1). 'The Word was with (*pros*) God' recognizes distinctness; 'the Word was God' recognizes identity. The Word cannot be identical with God for it has gone forth or been uttered as a distinct entity, yet because it proceeds from God and reveals God, it is still 'one in being' with God, an extension of God, if one may use such language. The Word hovers between distinctness and identity, and this is brought out in John's remarkable language. Furthermore, the Word was 'in the beginning', so God has never been without his Word. These remarks also show us the resemblances between the metaphor of the Word and the metaphor of the Son of God, and in fact as soon as we get beyond the prologue, we find that John ceases to talk about the Word, and now talks about the Son. Yet the transition is so smooth that we are scarcely aware of it, and this shows how close in meaning the two expressions are. One could say that the expression 'Son' has the advantage of being personal; on the other hand, 'Word' is more universal and breaks out of the specifically Jewish associations of 'Son of God', which might also acquire the unwanted pagan associations that were common in the Hellenistic world.

So we may say that when Christians began to speak of Jesus as the Word, they were not only renewing the Old Testament's understanding of a God who comes out from himself and communicates himself, they were also employing a term that had great possibilities for communication beyond the Jewish community, and that is still useful in our own day in relating Christian faith to other faiths.

Lord

The title 'Lord' is somewhat different from those already considered, for 'Lord' is not so much a descriptive term as one that expresses rank or worth. To acknowledge Jesus Christ as Lord (Rom. 10.9) appears to have been one of the earliest Christian confessions of faith. To say, 'Jesus is Lord', is certainly to say something about him, but equally it is to express one's own devotion and allegiance. It is to recognize Christ as an exalted being. But just how far exalted is he? When people addressed Jesus as 'Lord' in the course of his ministry, this was probably just a respectful title used in speaking to a teacher. When the evangelists refer to him as 'the Lord', no doubt there is much more implied in the title, but then we have to remember that the evangelists are calling him 'the Lord' a full generation after he had been going around in Palestine, and by now there had arisen the belief that he was the Christ. Paul's frequent use of such expressions as 'our Lord Jesus Christ' and 'the Lord Jesus Christ' are considerably nearer the lifetime of Jesus, but are again post-resurrection. They are honorific ways of speaking of Jesus, already recognized as the Christ.

The words of Thomas, 'My Lord and my God!' (John 20.28) carry the exaltation to the furthest lengths, and appear to equate Lordship and Godhood. Presumably this reflects the whole Johannine christology. It seems likely that something less is implied in the early preaching of Peter, as reported in Acts: 'This Jesus, whom you crucified, God has made both Lord and Christ' (Acts 2.36). Yet a high christology must have emerged at quite an early stage. Paul (quoting, as is often believed, a still earlier pre-Pauline hymn), writes: 'Therefore God has highly exalted him and bestowed on him the name which is above every name, that at the name of Jesus every knee should bow, on heaven and on earth and under the earth, and every tongue confess that Jesus Christ is Lord, to the glory of God the Father' (Phil. 2.9–11). What is this name that is above every name? Clearly, it is the name 'Lord', and 'Lord' as a devout Jew would understand it, that is to say, as standing for the name Yahweh, God's own name, considered too holy to be pronounced. Paul's letter to the Philippians probably dates from about the middle fifties, and the hymn, as mentioned above, is commonly supposed to be even earlier. So very early in Christian history the title 'Lord' must have been used of Jesus in a way which put him into a relation of near-identity with the one true God of Israel. Here we are reading the word 'lord' (*Kyrios*) in terms of its Jewish background. An alternative view, favoured at least in part by Bultmann, traces the *Kyrios* title to Hellenistic sources, in which it was used for the deities of the mystery cults. If this were true, it would mean that the designation 'Lord' makes Jesus one deity among others and does not associate him with the one God. But what then do we make of Paul's words: 'For although there may be many so-called "gods" in heaven or on earth – as indeed there are many "gods" and many "lords" – yet for us there is one God, the Father . . . and one Lord, Jesus Christ' (I Cor. 8.5–6)? The question of origins may not be very important in any case, for Bultmann concedes 'that the figure of Jesus as *Kyrios* increased in content and weight'.[28]

Because the *Kyrios* title is, as I have said, a term denoting rank or worth and therefore involves the attitude of the believer, it tends toward an existential type of christology. As Graham Stanton has expressed it, 'The *Kyrios* christology expresses the authority of the Lord over the individual and the Christian community, and is often related to ethical statements.'[29] Bultmann's own christology, as we shall see later,[30] could be described in very similar terms. But assuming that the decision to accept Jesus as Lord is not just an arbitrary one, but is made deliberately and intelligently, one may then ask about the grounds on which it has been taken. This is the point at which we have to ask just how much weight has been assigned to the term 'Lord', or how closely it approximates to 'God'.

God

It required a surprisingly short period of christological development before the point was reached at which Christians designated Jesus as God. And they did not mean simply 'a god', another deity to swell the number of the many gods and lords whose cults proliferated in the Mediterranean world of those days. We have seen from our study of the word 'Lord' that as early as the time of Paul, Jesus was receiving the 'name that is above every name'. I say it was surprising that this happened so quickly. It was so, because the strict monotheism of the religion of Israel might have been expected to militate against the emergence of this Christian belief that a man who had lived not very long ago was now, in the traditional pictorial language, 'at the right hand of God' (Rom. 8.34, etc.), sharing in the divine being and glory. We have, of course, been trying to show in this chapter how the basic beliefs of Christianity relate to the heritage of Israel, but it must also have been the case that some of these new beliefs would only be accepted by the early Jewish Christians after a long struggle. By the time we come to the second century, we find Jesus is often called 'God', for instance, by Ignatius in the early years of the century. But in the New Testament, Jesus is scarcely ever called 'God' in a direct straightforward way, though there are cases where he may be said to be called 'God' indirectly, as seemed to us to be the case in the hymn of Philippians, where the word 'Lord' is virtually equivalent to 'God'.

Bultmann may be cited as a New Testament scholar who thinks that it is very hard to show that in New Testament times Jesus was actually called 'God'. 'Neither in the synoptic gospels,' he wrote, 'nor in the Pauline epistles, is Jesus called God; nor do we find him so called in the Acts of the Apostles or in the Apocalypse.'[31] There are a few ambiguous passages in the deutero-Pauline literature, but Bultmann's conclusion is that 'the only passage in which Jesus is undoubtedly designated or, more exactly, addressed as God, is John 20.28, that is, at the end of the story of Thomas, where Thomas makes the confession, "My Lord and my God!"' Bultmann does acknowledge that some of the other expressions applied to Jesus in the New Testament (and, as we have seen, he tends to think of a Hellenistic rather than an Old Testament provenance for these terms) elevate Jesus into the divine sphere, perhaps as a cultic deity or world ruler, but not so as to put him on a level with the one God.

Of course, not all New Testament scholars take such a negative view of the matter as Bultmann. Raymond Brown, for instance, claims that 'in three clear instances and in five instances that have a certain probability, Jesus is called God in the New Testament.'[32] The three allegedly clear instances are; the confession of Thomas, also cited by Bultmann; the opening verse of John's gospel, 'the Word was God'; and a verse in the epistle to the Hebrews where a psalm is addressed to Jesus as God, 'Thy throne, O God, is for ever . . .' (Heb. 1.8). The second and third instances, of course, are indirect, especially the third. The five probable cases are admittedly marginal or ambiguous, but Brown thinks that Bultmann's neglect of such cases leads him to unnecessarily sceptical conclusions. One must also mention the case made by John Fenton for accepting Matthew's use of the word *Emmanuel*, ('God with us') as an instance of Jesus' being called God in the synoptics (Matt. 1.23).[33] Though Bultmann may be unduly negative, it cannot be denied that he shows the reluctance of New Testament writers to call Jesus God, compared with Christians of later times. Yet over against this one has to set the less direct evidence, some of which we have examined in connection with other titles and which has pointed in the direction of increasingly exalted conceptions of Jesus as one moves through the New Testament.

In this chapter we have been concerned to explore some of the expectations, images and ideas that were already current when Christianity came into being, and which helped to shape the first disciples' understanding of the Christ-event, though, as we have seen, this pre-Christian material was itself subjected to change as it was applied to a new content. We now turn to a more systematic study of the New Testament itself, as the primary source of our knowledge of Jesus Christ.

The Witness of Paul

When we go to the New Testament to inquire about the Christ-event, where do we begin? It might seem that we should begin with the gospels which offer us an ordered chronological account of the career of Jesus. Yet the gospels come from a period which is, we may suppose, a full generation after the time of the events which they narrate. Can we get closer than that? Unquestionably there were traditions about Jesus circulating among the disciples in those decades between the crucifixion and the writing of Mark's gospel, commonly believed to be the oldest of the four. Form critics have analysed these units of tradition, and shown how they were linked together by the evangelists. To some extent it is possible to discern layers of tradition, so one might try to isolate the oldest traditions of all. But obviously this would be a risky procedure. Schillebeeckx has attempted it in his christology,[1] but many critics are dissatisfied with the result. Karl Barth warns us, 'It is only with the help of very doubtful procedures that we can separate out from the gospels a genuinely pre-Easter tradition.'[2]

So rather than get involved in these 'doubtful procedures' where even New Testament specialists are in disagreement with each other, it seems to me to be preferable to begin with the writings of Paul. As I pointed out earlier, these too belong within the category of 'gospel' just as much as the four gospels called explicitly by that name. Paul's writings show the same combination of different kinds of language – history, theology, mythology and so on – but the mix is different from that of the evangelists. Paul has reduced the historical element to a bare minimum (though there is more than is often supposed) while extended theological reflection gets most of the space. So Paul's letters constitute the earliest written evidence for the 'gospel' or 'kerygma', which in turn constitutes the raw (or not so raw) material for christology. These letters bring us up to twenty years nearer to Jesus than do the gospels. Of course, there is debate also about the dating of Paul's life and of his letters. On the whole, I follow the careful scholarship of John Knox.[3] John Robinson advocated a somewhat later dating,[4] but in any case we are dealing with documents that belong to the first generation after Jesus, while the four gospels belong to the generation after that. I have omitted from consideration Ephesians and the Pastoral Epistles, since they are not nowadays generally believed to be the work of Paul himself, though they may reflect his teaching as it was understood by his followers. For the convenience of the reader, I list here the letters of Paul, with the dates suggested by Knox and Robinson.

	Knox	Robinson
I Thessalonians	Early 40s	50
II Thessalonians	ditto	50
I Corinthians	51/53	55
II Corinthians	ditto	56
Galatians	51	56
Romans	53/54	57
Philippians	47/50	58
Philemon	ditto	58
Colossians	ditto	–

Both Knox and Robinson would allow that their chronological schemes are full of uncertainties, and a reading of their arguments confirms this. Also, there are many other scholars who have produced still different schemes. Even so, the differences relate mainly to the dating of individual letters, and there remains broad agreement that the Pauline corpus as a whole is a product of the period extending from the middle forties to the late fifties, say AD 45–60. This raises a difficult question. Is it conceivable that the very high christology which we find in Paul could have developed so quickly? If, for instance, we accept Knox's surprisingly early dating for Philippians, and if we also accept the 'high' interpretation of the Christ-hymn in that epistle, as we saw reason to do in the preceding chapter,[5] then we seem driven to say that less than twenty years after the crucifixion, Jesus was already exalted as the Lord, already, it seems, recognized as (to use the much later language of Nicaea) 'God from God, true God from true God'. Now, one might say that the whole of later classical christology was already encapsulated or concentrated in the initial years (months? days?) of the Christ-event, just as, according to some cosmologists, the whole future pattern of the development of the universe was already manifesting itself in the first three minutes. In the words of an American cosmologist, 'After the first three minutes, the universe will go on expanding and cooling, but not much of interest will occur for seven hundred thousand years'.[6] One can hardly help being struck by the similarity of this remark to a sentence that we read in Martin Hengel: 'More happened (in christology) in this period of less than two decades than in the whole of the next seven centuries . . . Indeed, one might even ask whether the formation of doctrine in the early church was essentially more than a considered development and completion of what had already been unfolded in the primal event of the first two decades.'[7] Some writers have been critical of what might be called the 'big bang' theory of Christian origins,[8] and the emergence of the new faith may well have been more hesitant, piecemeal and multiform than we usually imagine. Yet even allowing for this, it is still necessary to posit a focal creative event, the so-called 'Christ-event', from which these diverse movements sprang, and it still remains a problem to explain how the doctrinal explications of the event took shape so quickly.

Perhaps the first scholar to be aware of this problem was David Friedrich Strauss in the first half of the nineteenth century. He stated the problem in these words: 'The space of about thirty years, from the death of Jesus to the destruction of Jerusalem, during which the greater part of the narratives must have been formed; or even the interval extending to the beginning of the second century, the most distant period which can be allowed for the origin of even the latest of these gospel narratives and for the written composition of our gospels; is much too short to admit of the rise of so rich a collection of mythi.'[9] His solution of this problem did in fact account for the shortness of the time, though whether it is acceptable may be questioned on other grounds. The solution was:

> The greater part of these mythi did not arise during that period, for their first foundation was laid in the legends of the Old Testament, before and after the Babylonish exile; and the transference of these legends with suitable modifications to the expected messiah was made in the course of the centuries which elapsed between that exile and the time of Jesus. So that for the period between the formation of the first Christian community and the writing of the gospels, there remains to be effected only the transference of messianic legends, almost all ready formed, to Jesus, with some alterations to adapt them to Christian opinions and to the individual character and circumstances of Jesus: only a very small proportion of mythi having to be formed entirely new.[10]

Obviously, this corresponds to what I have called the 'prehistory' of christology, treated in Chapter 2. However, there is the difficulty that, as we have seen, Christianity did not (as Strauss himself was aware)[11] take over passively the traditional messianic expectations, and, in particular, had to argue the case for a suffering messiah. But it may have been the case that once the identification of Jesus with the messianic images of Judaism had begun, it went ahead with great speed, even admitting quite major 'modifications' and 'alterations', as visualized by Strauss. Seventy years after Strauss, Wrede was claiming that Paul had constructed a mythological archetype of the Christ out of the Jewish traditional material, then at the time of his conversion, when he had a vision of the glory of Jesus, he transferred his theological construct of the Christ to Jesus. According to Wrede, Paul believed 'in a celestial being, a divine Christ, before he believed in Jesus'.[12] At least, one can say that Paul was steeped in Jewish theology, and also that he appears to show little interest in the historical Jesus, so the theory is not to be summarily dismissed. Wrede, however, goes to extremes in his theory of what we might call a 'prefabricated' Christ in the theology of Paul. Probably closer to the facts of the matter is the more moderate view that there was a good deal of ready-made imagery in the Jewish tradition that could be applied with suitable adaptations to Jesus, and it is quite possible that this process could have been well advanced two or three decades after the crucifixion. If Wrede had been correct, one might have expected Paul's christology to have been decidedly docetic, and indeed the whole history of Christian theology would probably have been different. But such is simply not the case. Paul certainly believed that Jesus Christ was a definite historical and human personage.

It has to be admitted that there is not much in the way of historical assertion in the Pauline epistles, though once we begin to look for it, we may be surprised to find how much there actually is. Of course, we have not yet discussed the question of how much history is needed in christology, and we may remember that many Christians who have had deep insights into the person of Christ have set a low value on historical information about him – Kierkegaard is an obvious example. Much of what Paul teaches about the historical Jesus is implicit, not explicit. He obviously had some traditions about Jesus in mind, and in some cases at least these traditions appear to have been familiar to those whom he addresses, so that he needs only to allude to events about which they already know. Thus, although Paul has no passion narrative, the crucifixion of Jesus is assumed to be a fact, and clearly a fact well known to those whom he is addressing. On a few occasions he is more explicit. He says that he has 'received' the tradition which he is now 'delivering' or 'handing on' to those to whom he is writing. So one can extract from Paul's letters at least a bare outline of the life of Jesus.

The bare outline would include at least the following points, and perhaps it could be supplemented, though not to any great extent:

1. As distinct from the views expressed in any docetic christology or in any Christ-myth theory, Paul teaches that *Jesus existed as a human being*, born of a woman (no mention of a virgin birth), born under law (Gal. 4.4), more specifically, a member of the race of Israel (Rom. 9.4) and a descendant of David (Rom. 1.3).[13]

2. *Jesus had brothers* (I Cor. 9.5), of whom one was called James (Gal. 1.19) and was considered to be a 'pillar' of the church at Jerusalem (Gal. 2.9).

3. *Jesus had followers*, and Paul is in agreement with other New Testament writers in making special mention of the Twelve among these followers (I Cor. 15.3).

4. *Jesus' ministry had been directed to the Jews*, in accordance with the promises given to the patriarchs (Rom. 15.8).

5. *Jesus instituted the eucharist on the night when he was betrayed* (I Cor. 11.23–26). This is the longest connected historical narrative about Jesus that we find in Paul. Is this surprising? In some ways, perhaps it is. But if the liturgy was at the heart of the Christian community, it need not be surprising. Again, at an earlier point we just touched on the question whether, in some sense, Christians might have or claim to have some encounter with the living Christ as a way of knowing him, alongside what they may know through the tradition. Certainly Paul claimed some direct knowledge of Christ, not mediated through other disciples. These questions are tied up with the enigma of the resurrection and cannot be answered until we have come to that topic.[14]

6. *Jesus was crucified* (II Cor. 13.4, and many allusions elsewhere).

7. *His death was brought about by the Jews* (I Thess. 2.15).

[8. *He was raised on the third day* (I Cor. 15.4).]

I have bracketed point No. 8, because it is arguable whether the resurrection of Jesus, even if one believes in it, can properly be regarded as an event in the historical order. To fill out this list, one might add two sayings of Jesus which Paul has preserved and which have parallels in the synoptic gospels. One relates to the prohibition of divorce (I Cor. 7.10, similar to Mark 10.9), and it is interesting that Paul explicitly says that this is Jesus' teaching, not his own, in contrast to what follows, which is the teaching of Paul, not of Jesus. The other saying (I Cor. 9.14) claims the right of an apostle to be supported by those among whom he works, and could be compared to the words ascribed to Jesus in Luke 10.7.

But returning to the list of seven or eight historical facts asserted by Paul, we might find it interesting to compare them with a list of basic facts which a modern historian is willing to consider virtually certain. E. P. Sanders has attributed this virtual certainty to eight facts in the career of Jesus. Sanders has confined his attention to events, excluding sayings from consideration. The eight events which qualify are these:

1. Jesus was baptized by John the Baptist.
2. Jesus was a Galilean who preached and healed.
3. Jesus called disciples and spoke of there being Twelve.
4. Jesus confined his activity to Israel.

5. Jesus was engaged in a controversy about the Temple.

6. Jesus was crucified outside Jerusalem by the Roman authorities.

7. After his death Jesus' followers continued as an identifiable movement.

8. At least some Jews persecuted at least parts of the new movement.[15]

One cannot help noticing the close correspondence between this list by a modern historian of the more or less indisputable facts about Jesus with the list given above of those basic facts that can be extracted from Paul's letters. Points 3, 4 and 6 are virtually identical. Point 1 on the Pauline list, asserting Jesus' existence as a human being, does not appear on Sanders', perhaps because nowadays no reputable historian appears to hold a Christ-myth theory, and no reputable theologian is consciously docetic. But there is a rough correspondence with Point 2 in Sanders. Paul makes Jesus an Israelite, Sanders more specifically a Galilean; Sanders also omits the Davidic descent, probably correctly, though Paul's mention of it in Romans shows that very early the recognition of Jesus as the Christ (not, as we have seen, a clearly defined term) had led some to attribute to him Davidic descent. Although Sanders alone has mentioned the baptism of Jesus by John – and this is undoubtedly a very well attested fact – one does not find any mention of it in Paul. But Paul does in fact have quite a lot to say about baptism in the Christian church and it might be possible to argue that a knowledge about Jesus' own baptism is implicit in what he says about baptism in the church. But the question does not seem important. Again, Sanders mentions controversy between Jesus and some of the Jews over the Temple, and this may have been a major factor leading to Jesus' trial and execution. Paul says nothing about this, but he does mention something not included by Sanders – the institution of the eucharist, which would seem of major importance to someone belonging to the worshipping Christian community. Another very obvious difference is that Paul includes the resurrection of Jesus among his historical facts, while Sanders does not. But, as mentioned already, the precise historical status of the resurrection is arguable. What undoubtedly is a strongly attested historical event and one that will call for explanation is the rise of a belief in the resurrection, and Sanders has included this by implication in his assertion that Jesus' followers continued as an identifiable movement after the crucifixion.

There is one further difference to be noted. Paul attributes the killing of Jesus to the Jews (Point 7). Sanders mentions the Romans as his executioners (Point 6), but also asserts that 'at least some Jews' persecuted at least some members of the new Christian movement (Point 8). Delicate issues arise here. For many centuries, Christians have blamed the Jews for the death of Jesus and this has been used to stir up anti-Semitic passions. But certainly Paul was no anti-Semite, but proud of his Jewishness and a lover of his race: 'I could wish that I myself were accursed and cut off from Christ for the sake of my brethren, my kinsmen by race' (Rom. 9.3). Sanders for his part has been active in promoting better Jewish–Christian relations, and by his scholarly work has dispelled many of the old misrepresentations of Judaism as a hard legalistic system. But as an honest historian, he has also pointed to the tension between Jesus and the Sadducees of the Jewish establishment (Point 7). Both Jews and Romans found it expedient to get rid of Jesus, and though one might debate the degree of responsibility attaching to each, neither group can be excluded from some share.

It may be asked why, in our consideration of Paul as the author of the first written witness to the Christ-event, we have gone into this question of how much history there is in Paul, and how it compares with the views of a contemporary historian. More than one answer can be given to the question. The first answer is that it has been necessary to show that Paul's understanding of Jesus Christ is rooted in history. He was not a heavenly being, in the sense of an alien form of existence, but a human being, a fellow-Israelite who had moreover been humiliated and subjected to a degrading execution as a criminal. Paul does not make many historical assertions, but he certainly does not cut the link with history. Though he says that he no longer knows Christ 'after the flesh' (*kata sarka*) as he once did, this does not mean that he has forsaken the historical reality of Jesus in favour of some spiritualized docetic Christ, but that his understanding of Christ is no longer based on worldly standards of what is worthy and what unworthy. So this passage about knowing Christ according to the flesh simply means that while Paul had once accepted the common judgment on Christ as a malefactor, he does so no longer (II Cor. 5, 16; see the modern translations in RSV and NEB). A second answer to our question is that it seemed useful to show that the historical material about Jesus in Paul, scanty though it seems, is very similar to what a modern critical historian will take to be the basic reliable historical facts about Jesus. A third answer is that at some point in this book, we shall have to ask just how much history is needed for an adequate christology. Many people might think that Paul's christology is adequate, or even extravagant. It is therefore instructive to note that he neither posits an elaborate historical basis for it, nor does he dismiss history as of no importance.

However, as has been insisted before, we are never confronted with bare facts of history, but with facts that have been interpreted and given a place in a structure of thought. The attempt to isolate the historical statements about Jesus Christ in Paul's writings is bound to appear a somewhat artificial proceeding, because they are all incorporated into the texture of his general teaching, which I have called 'gospel' in the basic sense of that term. But I thought it desirable first of all to make it clear that for Paul Jesus is beyond any question a human being who lived and taught and suffered on this planet. This had to be done because (and Paul cannot be exonerated from all guilt on the matter) he has appeared to many able scholars, such as Wrede, to have conceived Christ primarily as a heavenly being and his humanity as, at best, accidental. This impression may well have been reinforced by the only item in the Pauline christology to which we have so far paid any attention, the attribution to Jesus of the 'name that is above every name', the name of the holy God himself.

Much will turn here on the answer that we give to a difficult question. Did Paul think of Jesus Christ as a pre-existent being? Did he already accept a full doctrine of incarnation in which this heavenly pre-existent being 'came to earth', to speak mythologically, as a man? Many people, including learned scholars, might think that this is obvious. Let me quote a scholar from the early part of the century, the American, William Porcher DuBose, whose book, *The Gospel according to St Paul*, must still be judged a brilliant work by any standard and was one of the major influences that determined me to begin this examination of the New Testament witness to Jesus with Paul's letters rather than with the synoptic gospels, as writers on christology have more commonly done. The words I wish to quote from DuBose are these: 'That St Paul realizes profoundly the truth of the pre-existence and the deity of our Lord, there can be no question.'[16] This statement, and there are many others like it in DuBose's writings, would nowadays bring shrill howls of protest not only from radical theologians like those who contributed to the symposium, *The Myth of God Incarnate*,[17] but would also call forth a demur from many moderate biblical scholars who might perhaps themselves be firm believers in a doctrine of the incarnation, but whose scholarly integrity would compel them to deny that 'the pre-existence and the deity' of Jesus Christ are as clearly taught by Paul as DuBose supposed. Even a moderately conservative scholar, James Dunn, who acknowledges that 'historically speaking, Christian faith has been faith in the incarnation', warns strongly against reading the later doctrines of the church into the New Testament. 'What would it have meant,' he asks, 'to their hearers when the first Christians called Jesus "Son of God"? We must endeavour to attune our listening to hear with the ears of the first Christians' contemporaries. We must attempt the exceedingly difficult task of shutting out the voices of church fathers, councils and dogmaticians down the centuries, in case they drown the earlier voices, in case the earlier voices were saying something different, in case they intended their words to speak with different force to their hearers.'[18]

Of course, no reasonable person will deny that there takes place development of doctrine, and that the faith-utterances of the earliest

Christians needed several centuries of reflection before their full theological content could be unfolded. But no reasonable person will deny either,
that in the long history of theological controversies, development has
sometimes gone astray, and that one has got to go back to the origins to
check whether a particular development has any rootage in the early
witness. Even so central and venerable a dogma as the incarnation is not
exempt from this kind of test. We must not force the biblical text to
conform to later developments which are alien to it.

So how does it stand with this idea of pre-existence which DuBose and
a host of other scholars have confidently ascribed to Paul's understanding
of Jesus Christ? Admittedly, they seem to have much evidence to support
their point of view. We can think at once of passages which seem to admit
of no other interpretation than that Christ pre-existed his being sent into
the world. 'When the fulness of the time was come, God sent forth his
Son' (Gal. 4.4). 'God, sending his own Son in the likeness of sinful flesh,
condemned sin in the flesh' (Rom. 8.3). 'For you know the grace of our
Lord Jesus Christ, that though he was rich, yet for your sakes, he became
poor' (II Cor. 8.9). Above all, one thinks of the Christ-hymn in Philippians: '[Christ Jesus,] though he was in the form of God, did not count
equality with God a thing to be grasped, but emptied himself, taking the
form of a servant, being born in the likeness of men' (Phil. 2.6–7).

DuBose, as we have noted, considers that such passages put Paul's
belief in the pre-existence of Jesus Christ beyond question. This conclusion might seem to be demanded by logic rather than exegesis – if God
sent forth his son, must not that son have already been in existence? But
we are dealing with language that is metaphorical or even mythological,
and the language and logic of common sense may not be directly
applicable. God's metaphorical 'sending' of his metaphorical 'son' can be
understood in ways that do not imply pre-existence, once we accept that
the language is metaphorical and not literal. Here I come back to the views
of James Dunn, who does in fact argue that passages in Paul which, at first
sight, seem to entail a doctrine of the pre-existence of Jesus Christ, do not
do so. The discussion of the question of Christ's pre-existence extends
through much of Professor Dunn's important work, *Christology in the
Making*, and it would be foolish to try to summarize his arguments. What I
shall do is to attempt to convey Dunn's interpretation of the Philippians
passage, as possibly the most important place in the Pauline epistles
where pre-existence is an issue.

Professor Dunn acknowledges that the Philippians passage 'seems on
the face of it to be a straightforward statement contrasting Christ's pre-
existent glory and post-crucifixion exaltation with his earthly humiliation'.[19] In other words, Jesus came from heaven to earth and then went
back to heaven. But Dunn believes that we interpret the words in this way

because we bring to them the background of long cherished popular Christian beliefs. If we try to understand the words against the background in which we may judge that Paul understood them, we interpret them in a very different sense. The original background of the passage was probably the stories of the creation and fall in the early chapters of Genesis. Paul's christological teaching here turns on a contrast between Adam and Christ, or between the sinful humanity of the fallen human race and the new humanity that came into being in Christ. Adam was made in the image or form of God (Dunn says that the words *eikon* and *morphe* are virtually synonymous) but grasped at something more – to take God's place, we may suppose; through this grasping, he lost the likeness that was already within his reach. Jesus Christ, by contrast, 'faced the same archetypal choice that confronted Adam, but chose *not* as Adam had chosen (to grasp equality with God). Instead, he chose to empty himself of Adam's glory and to embrace Adam's lot.'[20] As Professor Dunn can also express it, 'the programme is run through again, and the divine intention for man is now fulfilled in the one who became Lord'.[21] These words are to be carefully noted, for they are a clear indication that the interpretation of the Christ-hymn offered by Professor Dunn is not reductionist. It still brings us to the point where Christ receives the 'name that is above every name'. But it is equally clear that the order of the reasoning has been reversed. The conventional way of taking the Philippians hymn, as the story of a heavenly being who lays aside his pre-existent glory to become man, is, in the terminology fashionable at the present time, a 'christology from above', or, in more technical language, a 'catabatic' christology. The alternative interpretation represents the hymn as the story of a man who lays aside any desire to displace God, and who offers everything, even life itself, to God for the furtherance of God's purpose. This is what is popularly called 'christology from below' or 'anabatic' christology. This second type of interpretation not only fits well with the modern insistence on the full humanity of Christ (a view with which I have already expressed wholehearted agreement[22]), but also dispenses with the mythological idea of a personal pre-existence of Jesus Christ. This does not mean that it dispenses with all thought of pre-existence. It is perfectly compatible with (and probably demands) the idea that Jesus Christ pre-existed in the mind and purpose of God, and I doubt if one should look for any other kind of pre-existence. As Karl Barth has said about Jesus' pre-existence, 'he has a basic reality in the counsel of God, which is the basis of all reality'.[23] If one wants to go beyond this and claim that Jesus Christ had prior to his birth a conscious, personal pre-existence in 'heaven', this is not only mythological but is, I believe, destructive of his true humanity.

Professor Dunn has directed us away from following that road, and I think we should be grateful. But many people have followed that road, and Professor Dunn may be mistaken. The advocates of a kenotic christology, which was very popular in England in the later part of the nineteenth and the early part of the twentieth century, made the notion of pre-existence central to their christology and relied heavily on the Christ-hymn of Philippians. We shall be examining their christology later,[24] but here we note that they offer a different view from that of Professor Dunn. Still another view is found in Rudolf Bultmann and adherents of the 'history of religions' school. According to Bultmann, the background of the Christ-hymn is a Gnostic myth of the Primal Man who came from heaven to awaken all human beings to an awareness of their heavenly origin and to conduct them to the realms of light.[25] Bultmann supposed there had been a pre-Christian Gnosticism in which these ideas circulated, but he admitted that we have 'little information' about it, and more recent research suggests that the Gnostics borrowed from Christianity rather than the other way round. But obviously when one is inquiring about the background of Paul's teachings and what these teachings meant to Paul himself, one is surrounded by uncertainties. Dunn's interpretation of the Christ-hymn is not only possible but even plausible, yet the alternative views have also some strength. But I think there are two points still to be considered which, in my judgment, tip the scales in Dunn's favour.

The first point is this. The Christ-hymn of Philippians was only one of several passages quoted above[26] which all seemed to indicate that Paul believed in a (personally) pre-existent Christ. Even if Professor Dunn's interpretation works rather nicely for the Philippians passage, how does it fare in the other cases? One must say that Dunn puts up a good case. Let me take just one instance, the passage from II Corinthians, 'For you know the grace of our Lord Jesus Christ, that though he was rich, yet for your sakes he became poor, so that by his poverty you might become rich' (II Cor. 8.9). This passage is often associated with the Philippians passage in advocacy of a kenotic christology. But Dunn reads it differently. 'Adam's enjoyment of God's fellowship could readily be characterized as a "being rich", just as his fall resulted in his "becoming poor" . . . Though he could have enjoyed the riches of an uninterrupted communion with God, Jesus freely chose to embrace the poverty of Adam's distance from God, in his ministry as a whole, but particularly in his death, in order that we might enter into the full inheritance intended for Adam in the first place.'[27]

Even if we think that the exegetical arguments remain indecisive, there is a second important point. Perhaps it carries more weight with a systematic theologian than it would with a New Testament scholar. It is simply that Dunn's interpretation allows us to see Paul's general christology as much more coherent than it would otherwise appear. For the effect of Dunn's exegetical work is to annex the passages about 'self-emptying' and 'becoming poor' to what may be called the 'Adam' christology, which, one may claim, is the mainstream of Paul's christological reflection and which seems to have been current even before Paul so that it must be considered the most ancient christology of all. It is not only the most ancient, it is also the most intelligible, and one that is relatively free from speculation and mythology, so that right at the beginning of Christian theology, in the earliest written witness to Jesus Christ, we find a theology of his person which can serve as a model even for our post-Enlightenment mentality two thousand years later. For, put at its simplest, the career of Jesus Christ is seen as a rerun of the programme which came to grief in Adam but has now achieved its purpose in Christ and in those who are joined with him in the Christ-event. The talk of 'rerunning a programme' (which I borrow from Professor Dunn)[28] may seem like an attempt to be up-to-date, but I do not think it expresses anything different from what Cardinal Newman expressed in his hymn:

> O loving wisdom of our God!
> When all was sin and shame,
> A second Adam to the fight
> And to the rescue came.
>
> O wisest love! that flesh and blood,
> Which did in Adam fail,
> Should strive afresh against the foe,
> Should strive and should prevail.

Let me say at once that this is *not* a complete christology, and obviously not a complete account of Paul's christology. But it is, I think, the beginning of christology, a frankly human beginning in which two human beings are contrasted, and therefore a beginning from 'below', if anyone likes that kind of language. It is obviously too quite different from the Gnostic myth. In that myth, the Primal Man or perfect humanity stands at the beginning and from then on, human history is increasingly engulfed in darkness. But in Paul's story, it is the flawed man or fallen man who stands at the beginning, while it is the second or last Adam who brings humanity to its completion. The working out of the details of the story would take us far beyond Paul, to Irenaeus and finally to the christologies of the present day.

Our next step must be to look more carefully at the use of the Adam imagery in Paul's teaching. We shall concentrate attention on two passages, one in Romans and one in I Corinthians, where Paul explicitly juxtaposes the figures of Christ and Adam, though there are other passages which seem to have Adam in view.

In the Romans passage (5.12–19), the argument and imagery are dense, complicated and – in spite of what I said a few sentences back about coherence in Paul – not entirely self-consistent. Two human beings (*anthropoi*) are contrasted. Through one of them (Adam) sin has entered into the world, and through sin, death, which has spread to all members of the human race, because all have sinned. Through the other (Jesus Christ) has come the opposite of sin, namely, righteousness, and this too has spread out from the one man to many through justifying grace. And just as sin brought death, so righteousness brings life. Let us try to sort out these ideas somewhat. Both Adam and Jesus are human beings (*anthropoi*). Probably Paul thought of both of them as historical figures, though nowadays we would regard Adam as a mythological personage. But this does not make any great difference to Paul's argument. The important point is that both Adam and Jesus are set forth by Paul as *representative* figures, but they perform their representative roles in different ways. Adam, as Kierkegaard saw, is 'Everyman' or the 'average man', in the sense that every human being repeats Adam's experience of temptation and fall into sin. We could say then that Adam is a mythical construct representing a universal human experience. Adam is a hypothetical figure postulated to account for the universality of sin in the human race. The further deduction is drawn that the universality of death is a consequence of the universality of sin, for the creation narrative contained the threat that the sin of disobedience would be punished by death (Gen. 3.3). The background of the idea is mythological, but one might say that sin is itself a form of death, a loss of being or a diminution of human life. Jesus Christ, on the other hand, is a historical figure, and we have seen how Paul fully acknowledges this. If we think of him too as a representative figure, we have to proceed in the opposite direction from the one we followed in the case of Adam. Jesus Christ is not 'Everyman', not the average man who is also the fallen man, but rather the exceptional man who is also the true man, the fulfilment of the humanity which God intended in his work of creation. Jesus represents humanity by having fulfilled the form of the human, a form in which the form or image of God in which human beings have been created shines clearly forth and the humanity is transfigured. This is all clearly expressed by Paul in other passages. He calls Christ 'the image (*eikon*) of the invisible God, the first-born (*prototokos*) of all creation' (Col. 1.15). He may have known the story of the transfiguration of Christ and have had it in mind when he compares Christ to Moses whose face is said to have shone after he came down from the mountain at the giving of the law. Whatever splendour may have belonged to that occasion is exceeded, thinks Paul, in the new revelation in Christ, for now we are given 'the light of the knowledge of the glory of God in the face of Christ' (II Cor. 4.6).

But how can a man, or two men, Adam and Christ, have the representative status assigned to them by Paul, and have such an enormous significance for great masses of other people? In the case of the mythological Adam, it is not hard to answer the question, for he himself is a construct from universal human experience. He is the hypothetical archetypal sinner, and whether we suppose there was one Adam or many Adams (to say nothing of many Eves), there is plain evidence that human history has gone dreadfully wrong, and that, as Paul puts it, 'there is no distinction: all have sinned and fall short of the glory of God' (Rom. 3.23). And to believe this does not imply that one has also to subscribe to some theory of the hereditary propagation of sin. In the case of Christ, as we have briefly noted, the problem of representation is different. He is not a hypothesis constructed out of universal experience, but a concrete historical figure who in many respects contradicts the universal experi- ence, and likewise, as we have seen in Chapter 2, contradicts our finest spiritual expectations. The assertion here that he is a concrete historical figure in contrast to a myth will be discussed in more detail later in the appropriate place, but we can accept it for the present on the historical testimony of Paul and other early witnesses, and leave till later the theological assessment of the need for a historical reality for Christ.[29] But how then can Christ represent all or some human beings if he is not merely a member of the human race, but, as Christians themselves claim, an objective reality that stands over against the human race, exposing both human sinfulness and the true destiny of the human being to bring to fulfilment the image of God and grow into likeness to God? It seems to me quite impossible to maintain, as Karl Barth appears to do, that the entire human race, whether people like it or not, whether they under- stand it or not, are somehow included in Christ as the one true human being and destined to salvation in him. I do not object to Barth's universalism, but to the fact that he really destroys the humanity of those whom he is so anxious to save, because he makes salvation a purely objective and external matter, quite independent of their will or choice. God's purpose would be defeated, not attained, if this interpretation were true, for the peculiar characteristics of the human being, freedom and responsibility, would be abolished. Paul, I think, takes a different and much more convincing view of the matter. Those whom Christ represents are those who, in the frequently occurring and much debated phrase, are 'in Christ' (Rom. 8.1, etc.). Some interpreters have taken this phrase primarily in a mystical or sacramental sense; the believer is united with Christ by some deep inner bond, so that he shares in the risen nature of Christ as once he had shared in the fallen nature of Adam. Thus

Deissman speaks of Paul's 'Christ-mysticism', explained as follows: 'Paul was not deified nor was he transformed into spirit nor did he become Christ . . . but he was transformed by God, he became spiritual, and he was one whom Christ possessed and a Christ-bearer.'[30] This may be too individualistic, and John Knox gives the words 'in Christ' a social interpretation. After saying that this phrase expresses most fully Paul's understanding of the relation of the believer to Christ, Knox claims that 'he is saying in effect that the Church is Christ's body; membership in the Church is membership "in Christ"'.[31] Of course, these two interpretations do not exclude one another. Especially when we remember the importance that the sacraments of baptism and the eucharist had for Paul, we can readily believe that to be 'in Christ' was both an inward personal relation to Christ and an outward objective relation to the church.

Let us now turn our attention to the second of the two passages of Adam christology which I mentioned, the one in I Corinthians. It is even more complicated and difficult than the passage in Romans. 'Thus it is written,' says Paul, '"The first man Adam became a living being"; the last Adam became a life-giving spirit. But it is not the spiritual which is first but the physical, and then the spiritual. The first man was from the earth, a man of dust; the second man is from heaven. As was the man of dust, so are those who are of the dust; and as is the man of heaven, so are those who are of heaven. Just as we have borne the image of the man of dust, we shall also bear the image of the man of heaven' (I Cor. 15.45–49). The contrast here is between Adam, the man who sank into sin and death, and Jesus, the 'man from heaven' who has risen above death (for the comparison takes place in the context of Paul's discussion of resurrection). But there is a complication in the I Corinthians passage which is not present in Romans. In his earlier letters (including I Corinthians), Paul was much preoccupied with the Christ of the future who would come as the 'man from heaven' at the end of the age. Does this language about the 'man from heaven' indicate a docetic tendency, as if Jesus were a supernatural being, in contrast to the all-too-human Adam? If that were so, then this teaching in I Corinthians would give a very different interpretation of Paul's christology from what we believed we saw in Romans. Perhaps one could explain the change by saying that by the time he wrote Romans, Paul had moved away from his earlier expectations of a dramatic return of Christ. Even so, however, I do not think that the two passages conflict with one another. The man from heaven is continuous with the Jesus who lived a human life, was crucified, then raised from the dead and exalted to God's presence. He is not a member of an alien race but a human being who has attained the true humanity – indeed, one way of defining resurrection would be to say that it is the lifting of human life on to a new level. If Paul's language about the 'man from heaven' contains some allusion to near-eastern mythology, perhaps the myth of a 'primal man', then the story has been turned around completely. In Paul, the man from heaven is not there at the beginning of the story, he is not the primal man, but comes at the end. He emerges at the resurrection, he exists now 'in heaven' as the 'life-giving Spirit' leading and vivifying the church, and (in the belief of the primitive Christians) he will come again at the end of the age. He is 'from heaven' not in the sense of being non-human or superhuman, but because he is sent or destined or called by God to bring to light the true nature of man – a nature which was concealed as a potentiality even in the first Adam, the man of dust, and is now revealed in the risen and glorified Christ. So Paul says – and a modern evolutionist could not have said it better – 'It is not the spiritual which is first but the physical, and then the spiritual.' The teaching here is not different from what we have already met in Paul, namely, that the first Adam remains on the level of the earthly, the second or last Adam is transfigured into the true humanity which reflects the glory of God.

But although the teaching in I Corinthians is on essentially the same lines as we have seen in Philippians and Romans, the early 'man from heaven' language should not be forgotten. In the earlier exposition of the Christ-hymn[32] in Philippians, I said that Paul's imagery leads to a christology that is 'from below', but I was careful to add quite explicitly that this 'is not a complete christology and obviously not a complete account of Paul's christology'.[33] While I believe (in common with most Christian theologians who are writing about christology at the present time) that one has to begin at the human end, so to speak, I do not think one has to remain there. In I Corinthians, Paul puts Adam at the beginning, and acknowledges him as a 'living being', though a 'man of dust'. Only after the physical do we come to the spiritual, to the 'last Adam', the transfigured man whom he describes as a 'life-giving Spirit'. The christology 'from below' is incomplete because it considers only the unfolding of the human, the exfoliation of the immense potentialities of the creature made in the image and likeness of God. The story needs to be completed by speaking of God's own action in all this. In the words of Hans Urs von Balthasar, 'The raising of a man to the unique, the only-begotten, calls for the yet deeper descent of God himself, his humbling, kenosis.'[34] The full significance of these words will become apparent only at a much later stage in our inquiry. We could express the same point by saying that any merely adoptionist christology must be completed by an incarnational christology. The rising of a man is made possible only by the condescension of God.

This is surely the case with Paul, who frequently emphasizes the weakness and helplessness of the merely human, and the need for divine grace. He has, I think, got the order right. He begins with the human, with that which is closest to us, and only after he has laid the anthropological foundations does he show the implications for the divine action and presence. Thus, as we have seen, his basic christology contrasts the first Adam, the man who failed, with the last Adam, the man Christ Jesus who fulfilled God's intention for humanity. He begins Romans by speaking of Jesus' human descent from David, and then goes on to say that by his resurrection, understood as some basic transformation of his being, he is 'designated' Son of God in power (Rom. 1.1–4). He begins I Corinthians by reminding us that God carries out his work by choosing the weak and despised things of the world, specifically the crucified Christ, whom he then proceeds to call the power of God and the wisdom of God (I Cor. 1.14). In the Christ-hymn of Philippians, if the interpretation we have adopted is correct, he begins not with the glory of the pre-existent Christ but with the man who refuses to grasp at equality with God but who nevertheless ends up with the name of God himself (Phil. 2.11). The teaching that it is God himself who is present and at work in Jesus Christ is summed up in another epistle, where, after speaking of the creation of a new humanity in Christ, Paul says, 'All this is from God, who through Christ reconciled us to himself . . . that is, in Christ God was reconciling the world to himself' (II Cor. 5.17–19). Paul's christology, I am claiming, though it bears the mark of his own powerful and individual mind, is not revolutionary, but restates the christology already current among the earliest Christians. Many scholars believe that the opening chapters of Acts give us a trustworthy account of the earliest Christian preaching and teaching. According to that source, Peter declared in his Pentecost sermon: 'Let all the house of Israel know assuredly that God has made him both Lord and Christ, this Jesus whom you crucified' (Acts 2.36). Critics reading this in the light of later controversies are inclined to dismiss Peter's christology as primitive and adoptionist. But was Paul saying anything different? Have we not seen the same determination to make the crucified man, Jesus of Nazareth, the foundation of the Christian story, rather than a 'man of heaven' or a pre-existent divine being? Within the New Testament itself, one can trace the development from a christology like that of Peter at Pentecost (we may call it in a very general way, 'adoptionist', if that is not too much an anachronism), to the 'incarnational' christology of John (and here too we must add to 'incarnational' the qualification, 'in a general way'). But I insisted that these two are not sheer opposites. The adoptionist view, in recognizing that 'all this is from God', has an inner tendency toward a more incarnational account; while if an incarnational christology skips over the 'primitive' christology that began from the crucified Jesus, it runs a grave danger of becoming docetic.

Paul, as it seems to me, shared the 'primitive' christology which Acts attributes to Peter, though of course it is all worked out in greater detail by Paul. But his statement that 'all this is from God' can be paralleled by Peter's words that Jesus was 'delivered up according to the definite plan and foreknowledge of God' (Acts 2.23). Paul probably does not intend any more than this when he talks of Christ as the 'wisdom' of God (I Cor. 1.24), for his use of this wisdom language does not seem to be sufficiently formal or definite to allow one to argue for a wisdom christology, with wisdom as a divine hypostasis incarnate in Jesus.

If indeed, as seems highly probable, Paul teaches a christology 'from below', this has considerable significance. Among other things, it means that in a secular age like ours when teaching that begins from 'God' or 'heaven' or the 'logos' falls on deaf ears, Paul's christology, and in particular his use of the imagery of the two Adams, acquires a new relevance.

It has to be remembered too that Paul, more than any other New Testament writer, had a very comprehensive anthropology or doctrine of what constitutes a human being. It is, perhaps, not very coherent and is drawn from various sources, but it does provide a terminology for describing the basic experiences that characterize the Christian life, temptation, sin, conscience (Paul seems to have been the first to introduce the Greek word *syneidesis*, 'conscience', into Christian discourse), faith, understanding and many other ideas. One of Bultmann's major achievements was to expound and analyse this Pauline anthropology.[35] The importance of such an anthropology for christology hardly needs to be argued. If we are determined to maintain the full humanity of Jesus Christ and to resist every current of docetism, then we need to have as clear an idea as we can achieve of what constitutes humanity, and if we also believe that Jesus Christ has significance for other human beings, then we have to understand their humanity also and how it might possibly be related to his.

Although, as we have noted, Paul tends to stress the weakness of the human being and the universality of sin among the members of the human race, his anthropology is, on the whole, a hopeful one. It is so because he does not envisage a static human nature, fixed for all time. Humanity is, for Paul, a dynamic mode of being, capable of undergoing profound transformations. No doubt this was not a theoretical conviction only, but had its roots in his own dramatic conversion experience. Humanity for him is something always moving out into new possibilities, capable of 'transcendence', to use the term favoured by many philosophical anthropologists of the present time. This idea helps on the one hand to elucidate the status of Jesus Christ, who has 'transcended' the ordinary reaches of humanity so that he is not simply a 'living creature' as was the first Adam, but a 'life-giving spirit', himself a creative source. Obviously this ties in very closely with Paul's idea of resurrection. Whether 'resurrection' could be called an anthropological concept is clearly a controversial matter. Paul himself seems to prefer to say that Jesus 'was raised' from the dead, rather than that he 'rose' from the dead, thus making the resurrection God's act rather than a consequence of Jesus' fulfilment of the form of the human. But here again, I would hesitate to think that we are dealing with opposites which exclude each other. Resurrection, like life itself, can be seen from one point of view as an anthropological phenomenon – the final step in human transcendence; it can equally well be seen as the gift of God, made possible by the divine grace and goodness. In a well-known passage, Paul mentions Christ's resurrection, using the passive voice ('was raised') and thus stressing the divine agency in the event, yet he includes it as one in a series of natural or everyday events, such as dying and being buried. He says: 'For I delivered to you as of first importance what I also received, that Christ died for our sin in accordance with the scriptures, that he was buried and that he was raised on the third day in accordance with the scriptures' (I Cor. 15.3–4). Paul makes a valiant effort to clarify the idea of resurrection, and clearly it has a key position in his christology. We have already noted that according to Paul it was 'by his resurrection' that Christ was 'designated' Son of God in power, and though there is some doubt about what this word 'designated' (*horisthentos*) means, it does seem to indicate that recognition of Jesus as Son of God depends on the resurrection. Paul can also say, 'If Christ has not been raised, your faith is futile and you are still in your sins' (I Cor. 15.17). At this point of our inquiry, we simply note that Paul did not equate the resurrection of Jesus with anything so naive as the belief that the dead body had come alive again. He introduces the idea of a 'spiritual body', but this is so obscure that we shall leave it aside until we come to a general discussion of resurrection.[36] For the time being, let us be content with the broad definition of resurrection I have given above – the attainment of the goal of human transcendence.

For Paul, the resurrection of Jesus Christ is not an isolated or individual occurrence only, it is the 'firstfruits' of a general resurrection. Resurrection is the destiny of all believers, perhaps even of all human beings. It is one element in that potentiality for being that was given to the human race as created in the image and likeness of God. All human beings are summoned to transcendence and therefore to resurrection, and Paul believes that it is through a union in faith to Christ that this path can be followed and the goal eventually attained. Paul gives a vivid picture of the process of human transcendence 'in Christ'. 'We all,' he says, 'beholding (or, reflecting) the glory of the Lord are being changed into his likeness from one degree of glory to another; for this comes from the Lord, who is the [life-giving] Spirit' (II Cor. 3.18). The use of the word 'glory' in this sentence suggests again the idea of transfiguration, and the understanding of the human being as faced with an openness in which he can transcend one horizon after another helps to explain Bultmann's success in applying the categories of existentialism to the interpretation of the Pauline anthropology.

But how are we to suppose that Christians can become so united with Jesus Christ that they are able to 'reflect' in their own transcendence and eventual resurrection the glory that appeared in Jesus Christ? We have already touched on this question when I drew attention to the expression frequently used by Paul, 'in Christ'. We have seen that this has been interpreted in two ways, one more mystical and individualistic, the other more social and objective, taking 'in Christ' to mean 'in the church' or 'in the body of Christ'. Paul himself seems to bring these two possible meanings together in the stress which he lays upon the Christian sacraments as establishing and developing the bond between Christ and the members of his body.

Concerning baptism, by which the bond is established, Paul writes: 'Do you not know that all of us who have been baptized into Christ Jesus were baptized into his death? We were buried therefore with him by baptism into death, so that as Christ was raised from the dead by the glory of the Father, we too might walk in newness of life' (Rom. 6.3–4). In this view of baptism, the life of the Christian becomes a participation in the life of Christ, though 'life' and 'death' are understood here metaphorically. The 'death' of baptism means that 'our old self was crucified with him so that the sinful body might be destroyed and we might no longer be enslaved to sin' (6.6). The 'newness of life' is not a life beyond physical death, but a risen life now, sustained by the union with Christ.

Then there is the eucharist. The new life established in baptism is developed and nourished in the sacrament of the altar. We have noted that the Last Supper is one of the relatively few events in the life of Jesus which Paul records, and he does so in unusual detail. His account of the event is substantially similar to what we find in the three synoptic gospels, but it is Paul alone who, after the giving of both the bread and the cup, quotes Jesus as having said, 'Do this in remembrance of me' (*eis ten emen anamnesin*) (I Cor. 11.24–25). Whether Jesus himself commanded the repetition of the eucharistic acts or whether his disciples simply felt the need to relive the occasion is debatable, and in our earlier consideration of the Christ-event, as including both the words and works of Jesus *and* the response of the disciples, we decided that it is not of vital importance to know exactly who contributed what. That is the view also of Joachim Jeremias, author of a classic study of eucharistic origins. He thinks that the background of the eucharist is to be found in the memorial meals of

Palestinian Judaism rather than supposed pagan parallels adduced by the 'history of religions' school. He makes the interesting point (also made nowadays by many liturgical scholars)[37] that if we ask *who* is to be reminded of Jesus, it is less likely to be the disciples, and more probably God himself. The sacrifice of Jesus is being pleaded before God in the hope that it might hasten the consummation of the kingdom which Jesus had inaugurated.[38] A further point made by Jeremias and again commonly accepted by liturgical scholars is that *anamnesis* does not mean just a remembering of the past, 'God's remembrance is never a simple remembering of something, but always an effecting and creating event.'[39]

Much earlier in this book, I raised the question whether people may still have something like a personal encounter with Christ, and whether we could know him in this way as well as through historical testimony. Paul obviously believed that such an encounter is possible. He may have had intense personal experiences of this kind, such as his conversion and possibly visions, and these would be private to him and quite extraordinary, but must we not suppose that some such encounter is also found in the eucharist, not only by visionaries and mystics, but by many Christians? Whether we are willing to entertain this possibility or whether we rule it out at once will depend on what meaning we attach to the belief in Christ's resurrection. Paul may well have been correct when he said that if Christ is not risen, then Christian faith is vain. Is it possible to give an adequate and convincing account of Jesus' resurrection? This question lies ahead of us. It is still quite far down the road, but in the end we shall not be able to evade it.

Meanwhile, however, we shall continue to explore the New Testament witness to Jesus Christ.

] 4 [

The Witness of the Synoptists

In the last chapter, I expounded the christology of Paul as I understand it, and deliberately chose this as our starting-point for investigating the New Testament witness, because Paul's letters are our oldest written evidence for Jesus Christ and for the Christ-event. Certainly there were traditions about Jesus and words ascribed to Jesus circulating in the churches before Paul wrote his first epistle. There may even have been some written material relating to Jesus – collections of his sayings, accounts of his passion, stories of his deeds. As we have seen, Paul himself was acquainted with such traditions, and assumed that those whom he was addressing were also conversant with some basic facts about Jesus. But the attempts of scholars to isolate the earliest layers of tradition or to reconstruct such supposed documents as Q (containing material that is common to Matthew and Luke) or *Urmarkus* (a hypothetical source of Mark's gospel) have not produced enough in the way of assured results to serve as a safe guide for the student of christology. The putative documents behind the New Testament have not survived in their original form, and many scholars question whether some or all of them ever existed; the oral material has been modified and edited so that only here and there do we have glimpses of what the original traditions were. We can only go to the New Testament as it has come down to us, and especially to the four gospels, and then, with the aid of biblical scholars, learn as much as we can about Jesus and about the faith which he inspired. This means that we are reading these first-century writings through the eyes of modern critical scholarship. We cannot understand them in the relatively direct way of the first readers, because we do not bring to them the same presuppositions. But we do have to try to enter into their ways of thinking, as well as asking what it all might mean for us today.

So although we began with the 'gospel according to Paul' and were able to derive from his writings both a basic history of Jesus and a theological account of his person that still makes a good deal of sense, we have now to turn to those books called 'gospels' in the narrower and more usual sense of the word, the four books of the New Testament which purport to give us in mainly narrative form an account of the career and teaching of Jesus Christ. Of the four gospels, Matthew, Mark, Luke and John, the last named has been recognized since ancient times to stand somewhat apart from the others. But Matthew, Mark and Luke are strikingly similar among themselves, both in their contents and in the order in which these contents are presented. Because of their resemblances, which are often verbal, they can be set out side by side in parallel columns. For this reason they are called the 'synoptic' gospels, and it is with these three synoptic gospels that we shall be concerned in this chapter.

In some ways, they constitute the heart of the witness to Jesus Christ. This explains why they have been subjected to more intense critical examination than any other body of writings. It is the case that both in the past and even today there are people who have such a reverential attitude towards these books that any critical examination of them or any doubting of their credibility seems wrong. But in modern times the necessity for criticism has become almost universally accepted. These books about Jesus and the claims that they make must be subjected to the same type of questioning that we would apply to other books coming down from the past. We have to ask, for instance, about dating – how close are the documents to the events they profess to describe, and, in particular, are they close enough to be reliable? We ask questions about authorship – were any of the authors eyewitnesses, or did they have access to eyewitnesses? We ask about the influence upon these writers of contemporary ideas which might not be acceptable today – for instance, ideas about miracles or demon-possession or some of the ways of thinking that arose out of the Old Testament and Jewish background which we considered in Chapter 2. We ask about the relations between one author and another, because although these synoptic gospels are very similar to one another, there are many differences of detail and some of them are quite significant.

We have noted that some people are determined to exclude the findings of critical research from their attitude to the gospels, but surely such people can do this only by being willing to live with a split mind. When occasion demands, they are members of the modern world and make use of all the facilities of modern medicine, fast travel, instant communication and so on. But as both Strauss in the nineteenth century and Bultmann in the twentieth stated, one cannot logically accept the modern world-picture in which events are meshed together in an immanent system of interaction and at the same time give credence to the world of the gospels with its supernatural happenings, such as miracles, demonic agencies, angelic visitations, voices from heaven and so on. Perhaps the literalists and fundamentalists think that once a person has begun to doubt, there can be only a downward slide into utter scepticism. But we are not in a take-it-or-leave-it situation. One can surely be more selective than that. We may put question marks against many things in the gospels, and yet find that there is much else of great value. Let us try first of all to set out in somewhat more detail some of the major changes which two hundred years of criticism demand in our attitudes to the synoptic gospels. Apart from general considerations, like those just mentioned concerning the virtual disappearance of belief in supernatural agencies, there are more specific forms of criticism.

Source criticism is the attempt to show how documents, as we have them today, have been put together from earlier documents, because no matter how skilfully this has been done, some tell-tale traces usually remain. This kind of criticism has a special importance when we are considering the synoptic gospels. We have noted that these three gospels have a great deal in common. By far the greater part of Mark appears also in Matthew, and about half of Mark appears in Luke. How do we explain this, and what significance does it have? For many centuries, people believed that Matthew's gospel is the oldest. Even last century, such eminent scholars as Schleiermacher and Strauss (at the time when he wrote *The Life of Jesus*) believed that Matthew was the first to write a gospel. Those who thought that Matthew was the first evangelist had to suppose that Mark had composed his gospel by summarizing Matthew. But already in the eighteenth century some scholars were beginning to have doubts about this theory, and the opinion was expressed that Mark might be the earliest of the gospels.

It was not until 1835 that a German scholar, Karl Lachmann, published an article in which he adduced a well reasoned case for the priority of Mark.[1] Although some scholars have even now remained unconvinced – and it has been argued that there is a fallacy in Lachmann's reasoning[2] – the great majority of students of the New Testament have come to believe that Mark is the earliest of our gospels, and that it was used by both Matthew and Luke in the composition of their gospels. Obviously, a number of consequences flow from this change in opinion about the order in which the gospels were written, and who was dependent on whom. As long as Matthew had been regarded as the first of the evangelists in time, that lent considerable authority to the gospel which bears his name, for Matthew was one of the Twelve and an eyewitness, and therefore his record could be presumed trustworthy. Mark, by comparison, was a lesser figure, and not one of the Twelve. He belonged to a younger generation than the original disciples, and would not have firsthand knowledge of Jesus. But this consideration was in part offset by the tradition, ascribed to Papias and reported by Eusebius,[3] that Mark had been the companion of Peter and had learned from him of the sayings and doings of Jesus, though Papias adds that he did not set them down in order. The fact that Mark was not a person of great importance in the New Testament makes it quite likely that the tradition is correct in naming him as author of the gospel ascribed to him. Mark's gospel is usually dated about the year 67, roughly a decade later than the last of Paul's letters, and soon after the deaths of Peter and Paul at Rome in the persecution of Nero. If this is correct, then Mark's gospel, even though it is not by an original disciple, does take us well back into the first century. Matthew and Luke would be fifteen to twenty years later. Matthew would not be the work of one of the Twelve, for then he would not have needed to rely on Mark for his information, while as far as Luke is concerned, it has never been supposed that he was an eyewitness, though he does claim to have used traditions that had come from eyewitnesses. So the synoptic gospels are not so close to the events they record as was once supposed.

A further problem is raised by form criticism. When we read the synoptic gospels, we can hardly fail to notice that they divide up into fairly short paragraphs, many of which are complete in themselves and joined only loosely to the preceding or following material. These paragraphs can be classified according to their form. Some tell of incidents which have become the settings for sayings of Jesus. Others are miracle stories which again may be conjoined with sayings. Still others are stories of conflict. The theory is that these units circulated in the early Christian congregations, where they were used for teaching purposes. Some of these sayings or incidents may indeed go back to Jesus, but inevitably secondary material would be introduced, or incidents would be expanded by legendary accretions. After a time, it would become difficult or even impossible to know what came from Jesus and what from the church.[4] Of course, I have pointed out earlier that if we see the origin of Christianity in the Christ-event rather than in the individual man, Jesus of Nazareth, the question of precisely what is dominical and what is not, appears less important than it may have done at one time.

Form criticism has another consequence. Papias, it will be remembered, said that Mark had got his information from Peter, but did not present it in order. One would naturally assume that Papias has in mind chronological order. The separate units that had come down in the tradition have been, in a commonly used simile, strung together like beads, but without much regard for the order in which they happened. Inevitably there are some constraints of chronology. There is a teaching and healing ministry in Galilee, followed by the journey to Jerusalem which leads in turn to the final conflict with the enemies of Jesus, the arrest, trial, crucifixion and resurrection. This pattern imprinted itself on subsequent attempts to write the life of Jesus, but it seems to be derived as much from common sense as from historical evidences as such. Thus form criticism seems to have removed us still another step away from the actual Jesus. But again it must not be supposed that we are being driven into utter scepticism. Rudolf Bultmann, a leading advocate of form criticism, declared: 'Form critics do not dispute the view that the Church had its origin in the works of Jesus, and has preserved many of his sayings in its literary creations.'[5] I suppose, however, that when we instance any particular saying or any particular incident, there must be some doubt. So we seem to be in the paradoxical situation of saying that the church has preserved some authentic material about Jesus' deeds or sayings, but we cannot be sure which! But this may not be so bizarre as it seems at first sight. Any university – and this is certainly true of Oxford – preserves the memory of outstanding teachers who lived a generation or so before the present body of teachers and students. Various stories are told about them, and various sayings are attributed to them. Many of these may have a basis in fact, some may even have come down unaltered. One suspects that most of them have been embellished. Nevertheless, a picture of the person concerned may still come through with a fair measure of truth.

I mention also redaction criticism. In the gospels, we have not only the material that the various evangelists have gathered out of the tradition, we have also their own contributions as they have edited this material and formed it into a more or less continuous narrative. In Mark himself, the repeated commands of Jesus to the disciples to remain silent about what he has said or done would appear to originate with Mark, and, as we shall see shortly, introduce some confusion into his narrative. Editorial work is even more evident in Matthew and Luke, where they have taken over material from Mark. We met an interesting illustration of this in our discussion of the expression 'Son of Man' which Mark uses apparently in reference to a person other than Jesus and which Matthew has re-expressed so that it does refer to Jesus.[6] The freedom of these editorial modifications of the traditional material is another consideration that weighs against any fundamentalist or literalist belief in a verbally inspired text. On the other hand, this same freedom to alter existing material or to insert new editorial material introduces one more hazard between the reader and the historical realities to which the synoptists witness.

The discovery of the antiquity of Mark's gospel and of its key position among the synoptics made this thitherto somewhat neglected gospel the prime favourite with those nineteenth-century scholars who were engaged in the quest for the historical Jesus, that is to say, who were seeking a straightforward historical account of the man, Jesus of

Nazareth, before he was swallowed up in the theological and mythological imagery which the church soon put upon him. These investigators
were seeking a human and humanistic picture, from which had been
stripped away all the supernatural connotations that had gathered
around Jesus. But it was already too late, for even our most ancient
witnesses know nothing of an untheological Jesus and already speak
from the attitude of faith. If this is true of any of the New Testament
writers, it is especially true of Mark. In Bultmann's words, 'Mark is
thoroughly mythological, and shows Jesus as the very Son of God,
walking the earth.'[7] So anyone looking back from the position which New
Testament studies have reached today must find it astonishing that
scholars ever expected to find in Mark the material for a simple
unvarnished account of the man Jesus. As we shall shortly see, there are
additional features of Mark's gospel that are very puzzling. Even the
abrupt ending of the book – 'and they said nothing to anyone, for they
were afraid' (Mark 16.8) – is so strange that many readers have felt that
something has got lost here, and even in ancient times well-intentioned
editors were supplying smoother endings of their own. But the abrupt
ending in silence and fear may well be authentic, and is even characteristic of a gospel whose author makes much of secrecy and mystery.

Why did Mark decide to write a gospel at all? This is a question that
cannot be answered with any confidence. It has been suggested that the
first generation of disciples was dying out – this would fit in well with the
dating of the gospel to a year shortly after the death of Peter at Rome – and
it was therefore necessary to write down what was still remembered of
Jesus before the demise of those who had preserved these memories. It
has been objected to this answer that Christians at that time were still
expecting that the end of the age would come very soon, and so they
would not be concerned to leave records for the future. But it may have
been the case that when Mark decided to write his book, the expectation
of a speedy end to the world was beginning to diminish. After all, by the
time Matthew's gospel appeared, say fifteen years or so later, the
institutional church was taking shape and a world mission was being
contemplated, both signs that apocalyptic expectations had been dimmed
down. Another possibility is that, if we may assume that epistolary
material such as the letters of Paul were circulating round the churches,
Mark (and presumably others) thought that something less rabbinical and
more concrete was needed to communicate the gospel of Jesus Christ,
and so began to collect into a book the units of tradition that existed in the
churches, and some knowledge of which seems to be assumed in Paul's
letters.[8] We can only speculate about possible motives. But whatever the
motive may have been, Mark produced his gospel and thereby launched a
new type of Christian literature.

If then we are talking of 'gospel' in the broad sense as a type of discourse having the characteristics described in Chapter 1,[9] then Paul comes first in the production of written gospel. But if we are following the commoner usage in which the word 'gospel' is applied to the same type of discourse, but with a different 'mix' in which the narrative element predominates and provides the framework, then Mark has a good claim to the honour of having written the earliest gospel. If we date it a couple of years or so before 70, then we do have to admit that a full generation had passed since the events of which the gospel tells, and it would have been good to have had something earlier, an actual eyewitness testimony from one or more of the companions of Jesus, as people at one time believed that they did have in Matthew's gospel. Even so, we might still hope that Mark could give us a reliable picture of earliest Christianity, of Jesus and the impact which he made upon his first followers. But unfortunately we find that Mark's gospel presents us with quite a host of problems.

In 1901 William Wrede produced a book entitled *The Messianic Secret*. Wrede accepted the priority of Mark and the dependence upon him of Matthew and Luke, but he regarded this as something of a disaster. 'It would indeed,' he wrote, 'be most highly desirable that such a gospel [as Mark's] should not be the oldest.'[10] Why did Wrede pass such a harsh verdict on Mark? There were several reasons, and these will emerge in our discussion. But let us begin from the point that appears in the title of Wrede's book – the so-called 'messianic secret'. Wrede believed that Jesus, like many other teachers in the ancient world, gave both teaching that was public (exoteric) and teaching that was reserved for an inner circle of initiates (esoteric). Mark, he thought, makes a clear distinction between these two types of teaching. Thus, after Jesus has told the parable of the sower and the seed, when the crowd has departed and he is left alone with his intimate disciples, he says to them: 'To you has been given the secret of the kingdom of God, but for those outside, everything is in parables; so that they may indeed see but not perceive, and may indeed hear but not understand; lest they should turn again and be forgiven' (Mark 4.11–12). He then goes on to explain to the Twelve and 'those who were about him' the meaning of the parable. Even within the Twelve, there seems to have been an inner circle, consisting of Peter and James and John, who, for example, were the only companions of Jesus with him at the raising of Jairus' daughter (Mark 5.37) and on the mount of transfiguration (Mark 9.2). But the great secret, the one which is mentioned in the title of Wrede's book, is the fact that Jesus is the messiah. So when Peter makes his confession, 'You are the messiah (or Christ)', Jesus' reply is not quoted in Mark, who simply says, 'and he charged them to tell no one about him' (8.30).

Why does Mark represent Jesus as having an esoteric body of teaching, including his own messiahship? A traditional answer that might have been given to this question was to say that Jesus was concerned that if he publicly announced himself as messiah, this would be misunderstood because of the political and nationalist associations of the term. But when we considered at an earlier stage[11] the application of the title Christ or messiah to Jesus, we saw good reasons for accepting Bultmann's view of Peter's confession in Mark's gospel, namely, the view that it was only after the resurrection that Peter and the others came to believe that Jesus was the Christ, and that Mark has brought forward the confession into the middle of Jesus' ministry, where in fact it serves as a literary device, dividing the earlier, hopeful ministry of Jesus in Galilee from the sombre period that begins with his journey up to Jerusalem. If this is the case, then Jesus' charge to the disciples to keep silent about his messiahship was not due to any anxiety that the title might be misunderstood, but to the fact that during his lifetime no one called him messiah and he did not think of himself as messiah. But Mark, as we shall see shortly, ascribed to Jesus supernatural powers of knowledge, so Jesus must have known that he was the messiah. So the silence about this during his ministry has to be accounted for by the fiction that he imposed a ban on his disciples' making any public mention of his messiahship. To quote Wrede's words, 'If our view could arise only where nothing is known of an open messianic claim on Jesus' part, then we would seem to have in it a positive historical testimony for the idea that Jesus did not actually give himself out as messiah.'[12]

Those parts of Wrede's teaching just considered simply confirm and help to explain the view which we had already reached in our consideration of the use of the title Christ or messiah in relation to Jesus. But we are as yet only at the beginning of Wrede's critique of Mark. He goes on to point out that Mark is not at all consistent in the matter of the messianic secret. He holds that long before Peter's confession in Mark's account, Jesus was already well-known as messiah. In the very first chapter of Mark's gospel, Jesus heals 'a man with an unclean spirit'. Such a healing was, in Mark's eyes, a messianic sign. But on this occasion Jesus did not tell the man to be silent about an act which proclaimed his messiahship. Clearly, the man was not silent, for 'at once [Jesus'] fame spread everywhere throughout all the surrounding region of Galilee' (1.28). In the case of the Gerasene demoniac, whose 'unclean spirit' had recognized Jesus as 'Son of the most high God', Jesus actually tells him to go and spread the news of the miraculous healing: '"Go home to your friends, and tell them how much the Lord has done for you, and how he has had mercy on you." And he went away and began to proclaim in the Decapolis how much Jesus had done for him; and all men marvelled'

(5.19–20). I think, however, that Wrede overreaches himself when he cites in support of his view two 'Son of Man' passages from the early part of Mark, and identifies the Son of Man with Jesus on the one side and with the messiah on the other. He says, 'If "Son of Man" means the messiah, then, according to Mark, Jesus designates himself as such long before Peter's confession, and in the full glare of publicity at that.'[13] The passages which he cites (2.10 and 28) do not, in my view, demand an apocalyptic or messianic interpretation, or even require us to refer the expression 'Son of Man' to Jesus in particular. I think that in both cases 'Son of Man' means no more than a human being.

We can freely grant, however, that Wrede shows that Mark is inconsistent in his use of the idea of a messianic secret. Sometimes, indeed, Mark himself reduces the idea to absurdity. If Jesus 'came into Galilee, preaching the gospel of God', presumably he wanted to be understood. He used parables in his teaching, and parables are admittedly an indirect form of language, but it is absurd to suggest that they were used to prevent people from understanding the message. Parables are an educational device for illuminating mysteries that cannot be directly described. And if, as Mark suggests, the parables were meant to confuse the public while Jesus enlightened the disciples with his esoteric explanations, we would have to conclude that he had been singularly unsuccessful with these explanations, for there are several complaints about the disciples' *lack* of understanding (7.18; 8.17; 9.32).

Can we discern a christology in Mark's gospel? I think we can, but it is not well developed or coherent, and it has neither the simplicity nor the profundity of what we found in Paul. Nevertheless, the narrative form gives to Mark's presentation of Jesus a liveliness which can still be impressive. It is no accident that even in the late twentieth century, a famous British actor[14] can hold an audience for an hour and a half by reading straight through Mark's gospel. Perhaps this says something too about the necessity for some definitely historical assertions in an adequate christology. Mark has been praised for the vividness of his narrative, and there are many passages where we have glimpses of the human Jesus, in what we might call his 'naturalness'. As we shall see, this humanity is overshadowed in the total Marcan picture by a heavy stress on the supernatural qualities ascribed to Jesus, but a man existing amidst the chances and changes of human life is certainly there. Jesus was 'tempted by Satan' (1.12) at the outset, the middle and the end of his ministry, as Mark depicts it; he prayed to God the Father, 'in the morning, a great while before day, he rose and went out to a lonely place, and there he prayed' (1.35) – and there is no suggestion that he prayed from any other motive than the need of God's help; he accepted John's baptism of repentance (1.9) and Mark, unlike Matthew, offers no apology for this;

when someone calls him 'Good teacher', he replies, 'Why do you call me good? No one is good but God alone' (10.18). He was subject to the common human emotions: he could be angry and upset, as when 'he looked around him with anger, grieved at their hardness of heart' (3.5); equally, he might have an impulse of affection, as when 'Jesus, looking upon him, loved him' (10.21); he was afflicted with distress at the approach of death, for he 'began to be greatly distressed and troubled, and he said to them, "My soul is very sorrowful, even to death"' (14.34); on another occasion, emotions were running so high that his family tried to restrain him, because people were saying that he was out of his mind (*exeste*) (3.21) – an incident which Mark alone records, and is suppressed by the other synoptists. This is only a selection of passages, but they make it quite clear that Mark understood Jesus as a human person, subject to the limitations that belong to any human being.

But so far we have looked at only half the picture, or not even half. Jesus, as Mark regards him, is certainly a man, but just as certainly no ordinary man, but a superman or even a divine man, filled with supernatural power. We have already noted Wrede's view that Jesus' miracles were the evidences of his messiahship – 'nothing is more obvious than that Mark understood the miracles as manifestations of the messiah.'[15] This frank appeal to the supernatural obviously raises serious questions for the modern reader. It is not simply that our understanding of nature has changed from the understanding that prevailed in New Testament times. There is the further difficulty that, if Jesus is the Son of God, to use the expression common in Mark, he would choose to manifest the fact through miraculous actions. Jesus himself indicates that he did not think highly of those whose faith needed to be created or supported by a 'sign from heaven'. When some Pharisees asked for such a sign, he replied: 'Why does this generation seek a sign? Truly, I say to you, no sign shall be given to this generation' (8.12). And here Mark adds one of his vivid touches, for he tells that when Jesus said these words, 'he sighed deeply in his spirit', as if in exasperation and despair at those who thought that his authority could be settled by some sensational wonder. Yet, if Mark is to be trusted, he did in fact give the people plenty of signs – miracles of healing the sick and raising the dead, of feeding multitudes with some scraps of food, of stilling a storm and walking on the lake, to say nothing of voices from heaven at his baptism and transfiguration. If these things did happen, then they did not impress Jesus' enemies, and he was proved to be right when he challenged their demand to be given a sign. Mark, however, believed that they did happen, and that they were evidences that Jesus was the Christ or the Son of God. How can we resolve this problem?

I think we may begin by making a distinction that has often been made in the past, between miracles of healing and nature miracles. Even today, we still hear reports of remarkable healings. Whether they should properly be called 'miracles' is another question, for it is more likely that we simply do not understand how such events happen or what are the intricate linkages between mental and bodily states. Whatever energies are involved, it would be very rash to deny that such healings take place. Very often, it seems they are only temporary, but sometimes they are long lasting. Again, it seems that some people (not always religious believers) have a gift for bringing about such healings. The tradition that Jesus was gifted with healing power is so strong that it can hardly be set aside, and the fact that there are people today with such powers is a further argument in favour of the tradition. Of course, in New Testament times it was commonly believed that these extraordinary acts of healing were exorcisms, the expulsion from the sick persons of demons or evil spirits, and Jesus himself understood the matter in this way. Here Mark is unconsciously testifying to the genuine humanity of Jesus, whose understanding of the world and of nature was that of his contemporaries.

We begin now to see the point in distinguishing between miracles of healing and nature miracles. The former still occur within our experience, and so reports of such happenings from the past have to be treated with respect, especially in the case of Jesus where the tradition is so strong, and where it would be difficult to account for his early popularity among the uneducated masses if he had not done something extraordinary for them. Further, Mark in his frank way reports that sometimes Jesus *failed* to perform works of healing (6.5) and this report of failure renders more credible the reports that on other occasions he succeeded.

There is another important point to be noted about these stories of healing miracles. In early Christianity (though Mark does not directly mention it) there was the expectation that the messianic age would be signalized by miracles of healing, as promised by ancient prophets: 'Then the eyes of the blind shall be opened, and the ears of the deaf unstopped; then shall the lame man leap like a hart, and the tongue of the dumb sing for joy' (Isa. 35.5–6). These were envisaged not primarily as impressive manifestations of power but as acts of deliverance from the ills of human life, as the raising up of life on to a new level. If we remember this, then the healing miracles are signs or pointers to the central saving mission of the messiah (if we may use that particular designation). Such nature miracles as walking on the lake, by contrast, apart from their legendary character, do not have the significance of fuller life attaching to the healing miracles, but seem to act only as impressive evidences of supernatural power.

Mark, one must say, is not free from the idea that Jesus' authority and his status as Son of God are evidenced by his miracles of all kinds. When I said earlier that in Mark Jesus is no ordinary man but a 'divine man', this choice of words was quite deliberate. The 'divine man' (*theios aner*) was a recognized type in the Hellenistic world, a man whom the gods endowed with superhuman powers. It was in this sense that Mark seems to have understood the appellation 'Son of God' when applied to Jesus, rather than in the more sober senses discussed in Chapter 2.[16] Bultmann uses the expression *theios aner* ('divine man') to describe the Christ of Mark's gospel, and says, 'In Mark, and most of all in his miracle stories, Hellenism has made a vital contribution.'[17] Here Bultmann is again following the views of the 'history of religions' school, and hitherto we have declined to follow him in that direction. But he does seem to be correct in the case of Mark, as indeed we might almost expect, if Mark's gospel was written in Rome in the late sixties. In confirmation of this, we may note that Reginald Fuller, who consistently resists the attempts of Bousset and Bultmann to find Hellenistic origins for early christological teachings, is nevertheless of opinion that the *theios aner* type of christology has found its way into Mark's miracle stories.[18] He cites as a clear instance of this the story of how a quasi-physical healing power (*dunamis*) flows out from Jesus to the woman with a haemorrhage, without any conscious volition on Jesus' part (Mark 5.30).

One hardly needs to point out that the idea of a Christ who establishes his claims through wonders and miracles is in sharpest contrast to what we found in Paul's teaching. In Paul, as we have seen, Christ is reckoned in worldly terms among the things that are weak and foolish. He does not think equality with God is something to be grasped, but rather he empties himself and humbles himself. Fuller speculates that the preachers of 'another Jesus' (II Cor. 11.4) whom Paul opposed were representing Christ in terms of a *theios aner*, and this seems quite a plausible suggestion.

The supernatural element in Mark's presentation of Jesus is found not only in the miracle stories but also in the ascription to Jesus of supernatural knowledge. In particular, he is said to have knowledge of future events. Immediately after Peter's confession, Jesus began to teach the disciples 'that the Son of Man must suffer many things, and be rejected by the elders and the chief priests and the scribes, and be killed, and after three days rise again' (8.31). The prediction is repeated more than once (9.31–2 and 10.33–34). Even so, the disciples do not understand. One may suppose that, looking back on events from an interval of nearly forty years, Mark assumed that Jesus, the divine man, went up to Jerusalem knowing clearly what would happen there. We shall discuss this point later,[19] but it does look as if Mark was using hindsight to put these predictions into the mouth of Jesus, and that the disciples' lack of understanding is his way of accounting for the fact that the crucifixion apparently took them by surprise and quite overwhelmed them. But again, Mark has not made his story consistent, for although he ascribes to Jesus on the way to Jerusalem a clear knowledge of what is going to happen, he tells us that on the very brink of the passion, Jesus could still pray, 'Remove this cup from me', as if the future were still open. Supernatural knowledge on Jesus' part is, however, limited. He proclaims the coming end of the age, but he confesses that he does not know precisely when it will come. 'Of that day or that hour no one knows, not even the angels in heaven, nor the Son, but only the Father' (13.32). These words indicate that the Son does not have the omniscience of the Father, but his knowledge is compared to that of angels. The demons or evil spirits likewise have supernatural knowledge, so that the messianic secret is not a secret for them. 'I know who you are, the Holy One of God', cries a demon-possessed man to Jesus (1.24). Jesus too is filled with a spirit that gives him supernatural powers and supernatural perception. His enemies declared that he was possessed by Beelzebul, the prince of demons, and owed his powers of exorcism and healing to Beelzebul. But Jesus replies that it is not a demonic power that casts out demons, as if it had turned against itself. It is the Holy Spirit of God that is at work (3.22–30). This can hardly fail to remind us of the story of Jesus' baptism by John, recounted near the beginning of Mark. John's baptism is described without any blurring as a baptism of repentance (1.4), but in fact the idea of baptism is given a new meaning, for in the case of Jesus the Spirit descends upon him and a voice attests, 'Thou art my beloved Son, with thee I am well pleased' (1.10–11). This idea of baptism by or into the Holy Spirit becomes the type of Christian baptism, as we noted in our discussion of Paul, whose understanding of baptism seems to imply a knowledge that Jesus had been baptized by John and of the traditions associated with that event.

So it would seem not unfair to say that Mark's christology is a Spirit christology. The Spirit of God rests upon Jesus – there are obvious echoes of the Old Testament in this (Isa. 11.2 and 61.1) – and some modern writers have tried to revive a Spirit christology, believing that it is simpler and more intelligible than the classical christology. But a Spirit christology brings its own problems, for apparently simple language about the Spirit's descending on a human being or resting on a human being conceal their own ontological mysteries. I ventured to say that Mark's christology is not well developed or coherent. He very rightly clings to the humanity of Christ, but overlays it with a supernaturalism which is never properly integrated with the humanity. So I would think of Mark's christology as something of a regression from the first and last Adam christology of Paul.

But there are still large stretches of Mark's gospel which we have not considered. I mean the chapters which deal with the final events in the career of Jesus, his passion and resurrection. All the gospels devote what is proportionately a large amount of space to the passion of Christ, for the cross was believed to be at the very heart of the new faith. It is as if the life of Jesus was told backwards by these early Christian writers, or, better expressed, was thought backwards. By this I mean that, assuming again that it was after the resurrection that Jesus was confessed as Christ, Son of God, Lord or whatever other titles may have been pressed into service to express his unique significance for Christians, it was from this moment of confession, perhaps an extended moment, that the Christ-event was perceived as God's salvific act for his people. Could we say that now the messianic secret was revealed, the incognito of the man from Nazareth was penetrated? The whole story is told and understood in the light of its dénouement. This point emphasizes again the danger of trying to probe back into a pre-resurrection faith, as some writers on christology have attempted. Neither the New Testament writers nor ourselves today can exclude from our minds the end of the story even when we are thinking of its beginnings.

We have already seen how Mark's telling of the story was (in all probability) profoundly affected by the hindsight that arose from knowing the end. Those predictions of the passion and resurrection which, as Strauss maintained,[20] are too detailed to be explained merely as intelligent guesses, are inserted by Mark because he thinks it necessary to show that Jesus went knowingly to his passion. Peter's confession is brought forward into the middle of the ministry because, as Bornkamm has suggested, there were some stirrings of messianic hope.[21] To account for the earlier silence about Jesus' messiahship, Mark employs his device of the messianic secret, though it would seem that the injunctions to silence were largely disobeyed. Mark's reconstruction of the past extends back as far as the ministry of John the Baptist and Jesus' baptism at his hands. The later synoptists, Matthew and Luke, carry the story back to the birth of Jesus, but their accounts differ from one another and by now one has moved so far back into the past from the central events of crucifixion and resurrection that any historical reliability has faded.

Let us now look at what Mark tells us about the passion and resurrection of Jesus. We have already noted that he is insistent that Jesus went to Jerusalem knowing that he would die, and if the death of Jesus is to have any significance for human salvation, then there must be some way in which it can be understood as a voluntary act, though this does not entail that he would have to have had the detailed knowledge of future events which Mark attributes to him. But if for the moment we assume that Jesus' death had a voluntary character, in what sense could it be understood as salvific? There is a somewhat striking passage in Mark where, much more in the spirit of Paul's kenotic christology than in the spirit of the *theios aner* christology that we noted in some parts of Mark, Jesus is quoted as follows: 'You know that those who are supposed to rule over the Gentiles lord it over them, and their great men exercise authority over them. But it shall not be so among you; but whoever would be great among you must be your servant, and whoever would be first among you must be slave of all. For the Son of Man also came not to be served but to serve, and to give his life as a ransom for many' (10.42–45). The language here and the christology it expresses reminds us of the Christ-hymn in Philippians, also, of course, of the suffering servant image in the Old Testament (Isa. chapters 42, 49, 50, 52, 53). The main difficulty in understanding this passage is to know what meaning to give to the word 'ransom' (*lutron*).

Probably a majority of scholars today would think that the use of the word 'ransom' in this passage does not come from Jesus himself but from the community. Even if we agree (as we saw reason to do) that the predictions of his passion made by Jesus in Mark's gospel are *vaticinia ex eventu*, inserted by the evangelist as he looks back on the incidents some decades later, there must have come a moment when Jesus recognized that his death was inevitable, and he must have had some thoughts about it. We cannot know just how he understood his death, though, as we have seen, there would need to have been a measure of voluntariness in it if it was ever to have the place in Christian faith that it came to have. But interpretations of that death in such terms as 'ransom' and 'sacrifice' come almost certainly from the Christian community, rather than from Jesus in person. Whether they originated in the one or the other seems usually to be of little importance – they all come, as we have seen, out of the Christ-event, which is a social event. But it is reasonable to believe that these interpretations by the community were consonant with what they knew of Jesus, and certainly not in violent contradiction. When Vincent Taylor writes that 'it is reasonable to believe that Jesus interpreted his death, or, to speak more exactly, his surrendered life as a sacrificial offering',[22] I would have grave doubts about agreeing with him. But if he had written that 'it is reasonable to believe that the followers of Jesus interpreted his death as a sacrificial offering, and did so in the light of all they knew about him,' then that would seem to me very reasonable indeed. Some things we can learn about only through the *testimony* of others, and if we are not willing to admit some testimony into our study of the beginnings of christology, we may as well give up. So we come back to the question, 'What was meant by speaking of the death of Jesus as a "ransom"?'

I think we have first of all to put out of our minds many of the later theological doctrines of atonement which thought of the ransom as some kind of appeasement. Christ's surrendered life might be a ransom paid to the devil (Gregory of Nyssa) or a satisfaction offered to the Father for the outrage done to his honour (Anselm) or a propriatory sacrifice (Council of

Trent). All such views are open to serious objections – the first because it assumes that the devil has proprietary rights over the fallen human race, whereas, if there are any devils, they are not to be bought off, but annihilated; and the second and third because they picture an angry God and set the Son over against the Father. The underlying problem with such theological theories is that they fail to recognize the metaphorical character of the language and try to impose on it a more precise interpretation than it is intended to bear. If we put Mark's words about 'a ransom for many' back into context, they occur not in any grandiose theory of atonement, but in a commendation of the life of service as opposed to a life of rule and self-assertion. And it was in this servant-role that Jesus was remembered by the Christian community – not only in this passage of Mark's gospel but, as we noted above, in the very similar Christ-hymn in Paul's letter to the Philippians and, as we shall be seeing in due course, in John's account of the supper.

It might be better if we approached the interpretation of the 'ransom' language from the other end, as it were, that is to say, from what is implied in it for Christian discipleship. After Mark has told the story of Peter's confession that Jesus is the Christ, and we have then heard the first prediction of the passion and resurrection, Jesus goes on to teach what discipleship will mean: 'If any man would come after me, let him deny himself and take up his cross and follow me. For whoever would save his life will lose it; and whoever loses his life for my sake and the gospel's will save it. For what does it profit a man to gain the whole world and forfeit his life?' (8.34–36). The use of the word 'cross' here might seem to suggest that this saying was an invention of the community, after the crucifixion. But this may not be the case. Already before the crucifixion of Jesus, a cross (*stauros*) could symbolize suffering and sacrifice.[23] This teaching about taking up the cross, together with the passages on servanthood, seems to me to bring us close to the very heart of Christianity, to the centre of the Christ-event. For the Christ event, from one point of view, is the true transvaluation of all values, the exaltation of servanthood and even self-emptying above domination and acquisition. The 'cross' which the disciple must take up is his or her 'dying' to the standards and values of the 'world' and becoming united with Christ in the new life he offers. The 'ransom' paid by Jesus was his own sacrificial death on the cross which is seen as the price of human deliverance from enslavement to sin. But the further working out of these difficult questions must wait until we have heard some further witnesses from the New Testament, and until we are in a position to attempt a dogmatic or systematic study of the work of Christ.

Continuing with Mark's account of the last days of Jesus, we move on to the triumphal entry into Jerusalem. Such a way of speaking of the incident is probably far too grand. It is likely to have been no more than an obscure happening in which Jesus was enthusiastically greeted by a handful of followers. If it had been a big event with political implications, then, as E. P. Sanders points out, it is almost certain that the Roman authorities would have acted immediately against Jesus and his disciples. Nevertheless, the incident would be inflated as rumours of it spread, so that on the one hand it became for the disciples a messianic sign, while on the other hand it could be used by Jesus' opponents as evidence that he had the ambition to be king. Could Jesus himself have understood it in that way? We cannot answer this question with any certainty, but this story of the triumphal entry, assuming that it really happened, though on a smaller scale than Mark suggests, would give support to Bornkamm's view that even if Jesus was recognized as messiah only after the resurrection, he had awakened messianic hopes in the course of his ministry.[24] But I do not think that modern attempts to impose a political interpretation on Jesus get much support from Mark at this point. In the disputes which he had with religious teachers after his arrival in Jerusalem, Jesus is represented by Mark as explicitly denying that the messiah would be a Son of David. 'How can the scribes say that the Christ is the Son of David?' (12.35). Whether this denial goes back to Jesus or to the evangelist hardly matters. It evidences a desire to keep political and nationalist causes at a distance. If Jesus did in some sense think of himself as a king, then, as the words about rule, authority and servanthood, quoted above,[25] make clear, and as further evidence will tend to confirm,[26] it was a very special kind of kingship appropriate to the kingdom of God, not a kingship founded on force of arms.

We must bear this in mind when we consider the next major incident in the story, the so-called 'cleansing of the Temple', when he 'began to drive out those who sold and those who bought in the Temple' (12.15). This event too has tended to be exaggerated from the time of Reimarus onward into a major political demonstration, almost like the taking of the Bastille. But it was probably no more than a noisy protest, observed by only a few people but magnified in the telling about it, so that it became for Jesus' followers some sort of messianic sign, and for his enemies an overt act of rebellion. John Knox, I believe, puts things in their proper perspective when he writes about the triumphal entry and the cleansing of the Temple as follows:

It is altogether likely that actual incidents lay back of these two gospel pericopes and that these incidents were not unlike what Mark has described. But this only means that when Jesus entered Jerusalem, he was hailed by a group of Passover pilgrims, presumably Galileans, as 'the prophet Jesus from Nazareth of Galilee', or even as messiah; and that when, a few days later, he observed what seemed to him the desecration of the Temple, he made a vigorous and effective protest.[27]

Knox shows how Matthew in his gospel gives these incidents a messianic slant that they do not have in Mark. One may suppose also that Jesus' enemies would report the incidents with such embellishments and exaggerations as would help to convince the authorities that he was a dangerous man who had to be liquidated. Sanders, on the other hand, regards these incidents as more serious than Knox allows, and even believes that Jesus intentionally 'managed' them. Sanders does seem to have a point in drawing attention to the fact that it was only after the incident in the Temple that the authorities acted. That incident was, in Sanders' view, the trigger which set off the series of events which followed.[28]

But before we come to that sombre series of events – betrayal, arrest, trial, crucifixion, burial – there are two incidents in which Jesus is depicted still with his disciples; the supper on the eve of the crucifixion, and the 'agony' in the garden of Gethsemane.

The supper may surely be considered a well attested event. We have seen at an earlier point that Paul includes it among the very few historical events from the life of Jesus which he mentions. In addition, it finds a mention in all four gospels. But when we read these five accounts, we find that they differ considerably among themselves. Paul mentions the last supper because he believed that it was there that Jesus instituted the eucharist, and he quotes Jesus as having used both the word over the bread, 'This is my body', and the word over the wine, 'This cup is the new covenant in my blood', and also reports that after each of these words, Jesus commanded a repetition of the rite, 'Do this in remembrance of me.' Mark, by comparison, has not dissimilar words concerning the bread and the cup, but there is no command to continue doing this in remembrance, so that if we had only Mark's account, we would not know that a continuing rite had been instituted. Matthew is similar to Mark. Luke, who is closest to Paul, does have a command to repeat the rite after the bread word, but not after the cup word. John tells of the supper, but does not connect it with the eucharist.

Most of these variations can be fairly plausibly explained. John does not quote the eucharistic words because he wanted to protect the sacred formula, and in any case he gives eucharistic teaching elsewhere in the gospel – so Jeremias.[29] The same scholar explains Luke's omission of the command to repeat after the blessing of the cup by saying that in the poorer Christian congregations wine was not always available, and the celebration took place in one kind only; this would agree with Luke's use of the expression 'the breaking of bread' for the eucharist (Acts 2.46).[30]

The fact that Mark and Matthew do not explicitly include a command for repetition is of little moment since, for all these writers, the eucharist was regularly celebrated in their churches and had been for decades on the basis of a liturgical tradition, before there was any scriptural account of a dominical institution. Inevitably, when the New Testament writers mentioned the supper which Jesus and his disciples had shared on the eve of his passion, then, they read into it those characteristics which had come down to them in the liturgical tradition. It may be regarded as probable that Jesus did institute some continuing rite at that last meeting, but what may have come from Jesus and what was contributed by his followers cannot now be precisely determined, and perhaps especially in this case, we see that it does not really matter. It is no accident that the eucharist came to have a central place in the life of the church because in a unique way it links the church to the Jesus of history and at the same time unites it with the Christ of present and future. In fact, the eucharist brings together and throws light on several of the themes that have emerged in our discussion so far of Christ's last days in Jerusalem.

Even if the supper which Jesus held with his disciples in the upper room had had no eucharistic elements – if, for instance, John's account of the supper with no mention of the eucharist is due not to a desire to protect the sacred formulae but derives from a primitive tradition which knew only of a common meal – one could still find a great deal of significance in it, and this is the reason for its being remembered. For the kingdom which Jesus had preached had been compared to a banquet, and the meal of Jesus with his disciples has an eschatological significance. It is an anticipation of the heavenly banquet, and in Mark's account Jesus seems to have this in mind when he says, 'I shall not drink again of the fruit of the vine until that day when I drink it new in the kingdom of God' (14.25). When we perceive the eschatological character of the meal, the other descriptions fall into place. The language about Jesus's giving his life as a ransom for many, or about the disciple taking up his cross, or about the new covenant, are all brought into a unity of meaning in the eucharist. There is already in germ here a doctrine of eucharistic sacrifice. Whether or not the word *anamnesis* ('remembrance') is used in any particular gospel tradition, the idea is there of bringing the sacrifice of Christ before God, of reminding him of the cross, the ransom, the new covenant. In Jeremias's words, 'As often as the death of the Lord is proclaimed at the Lord's supper, and the *maranatha* rises upwards, God is reminded of the unfulfilled climax of the work of salvation.'[31] A modern liturgical scholar, Geoffrey Wainwright, claims: 'The eucharist is a dominically instituted memorial rite which, not only serving to remind men but being performed before God, is sacrificial at least in so far as it recalls before God with thanksgiving that one sacrifice, and prays for the

continuing benefits of that sacrifice to be granted now.'[32] At the same
time, the eucharist, like baptism, unites the believers with Christ in his
self-offering. They take up the cross or, in Bultmann's language, accept
Christ's cross as their own.[33] There is another important point that should
not be ignored, though it is historical rather than theological. It touches
on the question to which we shall turn in a moment – why was Jesus put
to death? Whatever may have been the specific accusation, the real issue
was that he threatened the security of the established powers and did so
not by force of arms but by a transvaluation of values, in which the values
of his non-worldly kingdom were supplanting the values of this world. So
Wainwright remarks: 'By keeping open the vision of a divine kingdom
that transcends anything yet achieved, the Christian liturgy is to that
extent subversive [of the existing order.].'[34] The point has been put more
generally by Richard Holloway: 'The man who worships God is a threat to
every other power which claims absolute authority.'[35]

Even at the supper which we have just been discussing the clash
between the two kinds of power was preparing to emerge into the open.
The traditions are agreed that it was one of the Twelve who betrayed Jesus
to his enemies, and his name has been remembered, Judas. No doubt he
had joined himself to Jesus in good faith in the first place, but his attitude
had changed. It is often supposed that he had expected Jesus to lead a
political rebellion, and was disillusioned when he discovered that this
was not on the agenda. Or it may be simply the case that the lure of a
reward tempted him away from his allegiance. It is not even clear what
was the substance of his betrayal. Did he betray that Jesus and the
disciples were discussing a kingdom and that Jesus had ambitions to be
king? Or did he simply betray to them the place called Gethsemane on the
Mount of Olives where Jesus and his friends were accustomed to meet
together? In any case, we need not pursue the matter further.

We pass on to Jesus' agony in the garden of Gethsemane, and this does
confront us with questions that cannot be avoided. On the one hand, this
scene in Gethsemane, apart from its dramatic importance, does seem to
me to make an important contribution to our understanding of Jesus. But,
on the other hand, it once more places Mark's credibility in question. We
have seen already that he is sometimes seriously inconsistent. The story
of Gethsemane is quite inconsistent with the preceding chapters which
tell of Jesus' predictions of the passion and give the impression that he has
gone up to Jerusalem knowing that he will die and prepared for his death.
Now he is overcome with natural human shrinking in the face of death.
Now he prays that if possible the hour might pass from him. 'Abba,
Father, all things are possible to thee; remove this cup from me; yet not
what I will, but what thou wilt' (14.36). If we have to choose between
Gethsemane and the predictions, then we must choose Gethsemane, for

it depicts Jesus in his full humanity, grieved, perhaps tempted to escape, throwing himself in prayer on the Father, while the predictions represent him as superhuman and supernatural. But is the choice really open to us? For who reported these agonized prayers of Jesus, assuming that he uttered them aloud? We are told that the disciples were asleep, overcome with weariness. And in the crowded hours that followed Gethsemane, it does not seem possible that Jesus would be able to communicate his thoughts and feelings to his intimates.

It is not surprising that many scholars dismiss the story as legend. Bultmann talks of its 'thorough-going legendary character'.[36] I doubt very much if this could be disputed, but if we cast our minds back to earlier discussions of the nature of the discourse that we call 'gospel', it may not sound too paradoxical to say, 'yes, this is legend, but it is true legend!' For there is indeed *true legend*, just as there is true myth. In this case we can say that Mark (or someone before Mark) has given an imaginative interpretation of what must have been going on in the mind of Jesus in those hours in the garden before his arrest. I say *must*, for the imaginative depiction of the scene rests on the belief that anyone whose powers bring him to a position of leadership is bound to be faced with decisions about how to use these powers or what kind of leadership to exercise. We have already taken note that Mark mentions temptations at three points in Jesus' career – at the beginning (1.12), in mid career (8.33), and now at the end. That may be Mark's way of saying that Jesus was tempted throughout his life. But to what was he tempted? Perhaps to the way of violence, or perhaps to rely on the sensational impressions created by the works of a *theios aner*. Unlike Matthew and Luke, Mark gives no detailed account of the nature of Jesus' temptations at the beginning of his ministry, though presumably the stories in Matthew and Luke are legendary. But all these stories, including the Gethsemane story, are what I would call 'true' legends, imaginative and sympathetic insights into the mind of Jesus as the evangelists were able to understand it. The case of Gethsemane is important because it shows us Jesus as truly human – even at the last moment uncertain about the precise course of the future, even at the last moment assailed by the temptation to evade suffering and death. One might also say that this is a decisive moment for Mark (or for some source that he may have used) for now the image of the 'divine man' prominent in earlier sections of the gospel is finally overcome by the image of the servant.

Judas leads the arresting officers to the garden, and Jesus is taken into custody. The story of the trial, like so much of this narrative, is complex and ambiguous, and it is impossible to be quite clear about what happened. New Testament scholars take different views. It is not clear just how the Jewish and Roman jurisdictions were related to one another.

It is not clear either what charge was brought against Jesus – was it blasphemy (as A. E. Harvey holds),[37] or was it the ambition to be king (as is claimed by E. P. Sanders)?[38] Again, it is hard to know whether the chief responsibility for the execution lay with the Jews or the Romans. The gospels come from a time when rivalry between church and synagogue was very acute, so they tend to lay the blame on the leaders of the Jews, and to exculpate the Romans. They even represent Pontius Pilate as troubled with scruples, though we know from ancient authorities such as Josephus and Philo that he was harsh, brutal and unjust.[39] On the other hand, some modern writers (Moltmann is an example),[40] partly out of guilt feelings about Christian persecutions of the Jews, partly out of ideological revulsion against Roman imperialism, have tried to shift the onus of responsibility to the Romans. I doubt very much if these questions can ever be decisively settled, or even that there was a 'due process' of law. Whatever the technicalities may have been, the death of Jesus, like the deaths of many prophets and dissidents before and since, would have been brought about for one reason or another in law, but the underlying truth is that he had become too much of a threat to both the Jewish and the Roman establishments. This would have been the case whether or not there was any possibility of revolutionary violence, for those who exercise power and embrace an ideology of power are well aware of the truth expressed by Richard Holloway and quoted a few pages back, that the man who worships God threatens every other power that lays claim to absoluteness.

The story in Mark goes on from the trial to the crucifixion, and all that it may be necessary to say here is that this is the final proof of the humanity of Jesus Christ. He dies, as all human beings die. The various gnostic and docetic heresies that soon arose in the church were at one in denying that Jesus had really died, and invented several ingenious explanations to show that he only seemed to die, but, of course, he could not die because he was a divine being. There is something of an irony in placing side by side Bultmann's words, 'In Mark [Jesus] is a *theios anthropos*, indeed more: he is the very Son of God walking the earth,'[41] with Mark's own words about the death of Jesus: 'And when the centurion who stood facing him saw that he thus breathed his last, he said, "Truly this man was a Son of God"' (15.39). Jesus is here being recognized as a Son of God in his mortal act of breathing his last, that is to say, in his human finitude. If the 'divine man' christology appears in the early chapters of Mark, it is not to be observed in the account of the passion.

This point is reinforced by the report that Mark gives of Jesus' last words from the cross: 'And at the ninth hour Jesus cried with a loud voice, "*Eloi, Eloi, lama sabachthani?*" which means "My God, my God, why hast thou forsaken me?"' (15.34). The fact that Mark quotes these words is another tribute to his frankness, for they might easily be interpreted (as Reimarus did indeed interpret them) as meaning that Jesus had finally become disillusioned. It is interesting too that he quotes the Aramaic, as if these words of Jesus had been often quoted and the saying was well-known. So one cannot dismiss the possibility that this is an authentic memory of what Jesus did actually say. At the same time, the words are clearly taken from the opening verse of Psalm 22. There are other reminders of that psalm in Mark's description of the crucifixion – the soldiers dividing Jesus' clothes, the passers-by mocking him. So it is quite possible that Mark or some pre-Marcan transmitter of the tradition has come to believe that Psalm 22 is a prediction of the passion, and has then told the story with details that fit the alleged prediction. But in either case, the cry of God-forsakenness can be understood only as another pointer to the humanity, even the human weakness, of Jesus. It contrasts with the cries of the mockers, 'Come down from the cross!' But Jesus was no superman, about to work a miracle or give a supernatural sign. Rather, this gospel of Mark shows him as truly man, or even as the true man, who simply by being man in the fullest sense is also Son of God.

The gospel goes on to tell of the burial of Jesus and then of his resurrection. Mark gives a much briefer account of the resurrection than any of the other evangelists. Possibly, as we have already noted, the original ending of his gospel has been lost, and it may have contained accounts of the appearances of the risen Christ. But if we accept that the text of Mark as we now have it ends at the words, 'for they were afraid' (16.8), then we have here an account of the resurrection that contrasts sharply with Paul's. The latter's belief in the resurrection of Jesus rested on a series of appearances or encounters, including one to himself. Mark rests his belief on the fact that a group of women, going to anoint the body of Jesus in the tomb, found the tomb open, and a young man (or angel?) there who told them that Jesus had risen and was going to Galilee, where they would see him. The other evangelists combine the two accounts and speak both of an empty tomb and of appearances.

We cannot say much about this until we are in a position to examine the meaning and possibility of resurrection much more thoroughly than we can at this stage. Many commentators take the view that the story of an empty tomb is a later tradition, and they rightly point out that little, if anything, could be deduced from the bare fact that the tomb was discovered empty. To the modern mind, at any rate, a resurrection would be just about the last explanation to be considered. However, some highly competent scholars have taken a different view. Geza Vermes writes: 'But in the end, when every argument has been considered and weighed, the only conclusion acceptable to the historian must be that the opinions of the orthodox, the liberal sympathizer and the critical agnostic alike – and even perhaps of the disciples themselves – are simply interpretations of the one disconcerting fact: namely, that the women who set out to pay their last respects to Jesus found, to their consternation, not a body, but an empty tomb.'[42] Wolfhart Pannenberg takes the view that the empty tomb story is not a secondary creation but an ancient tradition of the Jerusalem church, and that the rise of a belief in Jesus' resurrection 'is hardly understandable except under the assumption that Jesus' tomb was empty'.[43] Of course, even if one were to accept that the tomb was found empty, it would be a long way from there to belief in a resurrection. Also, one has to ask whether the two traditions, the appearances and the empty tomb, are compatible with each other. Paul, as we have seen, did not seem to envisage the rising of the physical body of Jesus, but this would seem to be part of the empty tomb tradition.

Let us now sum up the results of our examination of the witness of Mark, the first in time among the synoptists. We have seen that there are many problems and some inconsistencies in Mark. Yet the main outlines seems clear. Jesus is baptized by John, but this baptism is different from the others which John performed, for the Spirit of God descends upon Jesus and a heavenly voice declares, 'Thou art my beloved Son.' After John's arrest, Jesus begins preaching that the kingdom of God is at hand. To learn what this kingdom is, we have to look at his parables, simple comparisons with everyday realities. Mark is surely mistaken in thinking that Jesus used parables to conceal his message, for they are designed to make it clear even to ordinary people that this kingdom is not a political dominion founded on human power, but a kingdom that will be inaugurated by God and in which our customary human values will be reversed. In the early chapters of Mark, Jesus' authority to proclaim the kingdom is attested by his miracles, especially miracles of healing. He is a man on whom the divine Spirit has conferred superhuman powers, and therefore Son of God. Jesus is also supposed to have superhuman knowledge, especially of the future. But as the gospel progresses, the 'divine man' type of christology moves in the direction of a servant or kenotic christology, nearer to the teaching of Paul. If Wrede's theory of the messianic secret is correct, as we inclined to think, then although Mark places the confession of Jesus as the Christ in the middle of the ministry, one would infer that (again like Paul) he knew that it was only with the resurrection that Jesus was recognized as the Christ, though some messianic hopes may have been aroused before.

We have seen that most modern biblical scholars believe that the gospels of both Matthew and Luke are heavily dependent on Mark for their knowledge of Jesus. We cannot examine these gospels of Matthew and Luke in any detail, but we must briefly note where and how they change or develop or supplement the material borrowed from Mark. Both of these gospels are more than half as long again as Mark.

It was said above[44] that in composing their stories, the evangelists took the crucifixion-resurrection as their centre of reference, and thought back from there. Mark carried his story back as far as the baptism of Jesus by John. Matthew goes back to the birth of Jesus, and even gives an account generation by generation of his descent from David. This introduces a new dimension beyond what we have seen in either Paul or Mark. In some respects, both Paul and Mark think of Jesus as a supernatural or divine figure, but both Paul's 'last Adam' christology and Mark's 'Spirit christology' can, without violence, be given what would later have been called an 'adoptionist' interpretation, in the sense that they show us a human being whom God elects to be *the human being* in and through whom *he reveals himself*. So Matthew includes in his story of Jesus' birth the detail of a virginal conception, something unknown to Paul and Mark and also John. Jesus appeared to be the descendant of David, as the traditional messianic expectation required, but according to Matthew, he had no human father but had been conceived by the Holy Spirit. So from the moment of his birth, or, more precisely, his conception, Jesus was Son of God, though in a more literal and mythological way than that expression required. Thus reverence for Jesus is heightened in Matthew beyond what we have found in Mark. As we have noted already, Matthew calls Jesus 'God' in applying to him the title Emmanuel, 'God with us'.[45] Not all scholars agree with John Fenton, whose interpretation of the title we decided to follow, but he receives support from other passages of the gospel, such as Matthew's repeated use of the verb 'worship' (*proskunein*) to describe the disciples' attitude to Jesus, perhaps especially in the case of the risen Christ (28.17); C. F. D. Moule sees this as an implication that they accord Jesus the honour due to God.[46] Further indications are to be seen in some of the editorial changes that Matthew makes to Mark's narrative. He represents John as unwilling to baptize Jesus, because John thinks it would be more fitting for Jesus to baptize him (3.14); again, the story about Jesus declining the title 'good' when a young man calls him 'Good master', has been altered by Matthew so that Jesus asks the somewhat bland question, 'Why do you ask me about what is good?' However, the story of Jesus' ministry that we find in Matthew is not essentially different from Mark, and even the messianic secret, though of less importance than it was in Mark, is still visible.

The major difference between the two gospels is that Matthew has included a large quantity of Jesus' teaching, not present in Mark and usually supposed to be derived from the source known as Q. This teaching is mainly ethical in character and includes the so-called 'Sermon on the Mount'. It has therefore made a special appeal to many modern readers who may not be attracted by the more historical and theological teachings of the gospels, but who find the moral demands of Jesus just as valid for society today as they were in his own time. Whether, of course, they can be separated from their theological context is debatable. Matthew was writing after the institutional church was beginning to take shape, and so something like an 'ordered' life was required. The first flush of eschatological expectations had passed, and the church was having to adjust to the possibility of a long history. Furthermore, Matthew was a Jewish Christian, and had to present the Christian message in terms appropriate to a Jewish readership – that is why he so often claims that the actions of Jesus fulfilled Old Testament prophecies, and why he tries to relate Jesus' moral teaching to the Law of Moses. Jesus' teaching is novel and demands an inwardness which was not explicit in the traditional commandments. But Matthew shows that teaching as a fulfilling or surpassing of the law, rather than its abrogation. According to W. D. Davies, the relation of Jesus' teaching to the Law of Moses is better understood as completion than as antithesis.[47] But Davies gives only a modified assent to the view that Jesus is the new Moses, or that the Sermon on the Mount is the Christian version of the law that had been given on Mount Sinai. Clearly, however, there is some parallel between the two figures, Moses and Jesus, and to Jews who reverenced Moses as the deliverer of the people and the communicator of God's demands, there must have been considerable significance in the thought of Jesus as the new Moses. It was believed, after all, that Moses himself had said, 'The Lord your God will raise up for you a prophet like me from among you, from your brethren – him you shall heed' (Deut. 18.15).

A third point at which Matthew augments the Marcan account is in the matter of Jesus' resurrection. Mark, it will be remembered, contains a promise that the disciples will see their risen Master in Galilee, but the text of the gospel breaks off before any appearance is recorded. In Matthew, Jesus appears to the Eleven and speaks solemn words of command and promise, words that have reverberated in the mind of the church down to the present time: 'All authority in heaven and on earth has been given to me. Go therefore and make disciples of all nations, baptizing them in the name of the Father and of the Son and of the Holy Spirit, teaching them to observe all that I have commanded you; and lo, I am with you always, to the close of the age (28.19–20).

Although Luke's gospel contains much material that is also in Mark and Matthew, he had sources of his own and has welded his material into a coherent whole. Renan judged this gospel to be 'the most beautiful book in the world', and even the hyper-critical Bultmann is willing to say that 'the gospel of Luke is the climax of the history of the synoptic tradition in so far as the development which that tradition had undergone from the beginning has attained its greatest success in Luke: the editing and connecting of isolated sections into a coherent continuity.'[48]

Like Matthew, Luke takes the beginning of the story back to the birth of Jesus, and even beyond it, though he gives a quite different account of the birth. The two writers, however, are agreed in dating the birth in the reign of Herod the Great, who died in 4 BC, so that Jesus must have been born at least four years earlier than the traditional date. Luke also agrees in teaching a virginal conception of Jesus. No doubt the details of both Matthew's and Luke's birth narratives are legendary, though they also illustrate the power of a concrete story when one considers how these nativity scenarios have impressed themselves on Christian imagination. Luke in particular furnishes us with a striking example of what I earlier called 'true legend', in discussing Mark's account of the agony in the garden of Gethsemane. I have in mind the story of Christ's birth in a stable. Marxist philosopher Ernst Bloch wrote this about it:

> Prayers are said to a child born in a stable. No glance into the heights can be broken downwards in a closer, more humble, more homely way. At the same time, the stable is true, such a lowly origin for the founder is no invention. Legend does not paint misery, certainly not that which lasts a whole lifetime. The stable, the carpenter's son, the visionary among simple people, the gallows at the end, this is taken from historical stuff, not the golden stuff beloved of legend.[49]

The stable is true! Ernst Bloch knew well enough that any scientific historian is prepared to write off the stable as legend, but it is true theologically, in fact, very near to that transvaluation of all values which I said lies at the very core of Christianity. Luke's story of the temptations (which is not very different from Matthew's) at the beginning of Jesus' ministry is another example of 'true legend'. It can be interpreted as the rejection of any *theios aner* image of the Christ. Yet this does not mean that Luke broke free from those elements of the *theios aner* idea which he inherited from Mark – and this lends point to Wrede's complaint that it was a pity that Mark's gospel came first, and left its stamp on the two other synoptic gospels.

We have noted that Bultmann gives Luke credit for composing a more coherent gospel than did Matthew and Mark, and in fact he sets out to give something like a historical account. He relates the events of the gospel narrative to events in secular history. We have noted already his mention of Herod the Great. Next he places the date of Christ's birth at the census of Quirinius, governor of Syria. Then he gives no less than six contemporary references to fix the date of John the Baptist's preaching of repentance (3.1–2). This seems to promise firm ground for a chronology, but unfortunately when the various secular references are checked, they do not fix a date with any exactitude.[50] The belief, still quite common, that Luke was a careful historian, cannot be sustained.

One of the most valuable features of Luke's gospel is that it contains several parables attributed to Jesus which are among his best known but are not to be found in the other gospels. These include the story of the rich fool (12.13–21); the parable of the unjust steward (18.1–8); the story of the rich man and Lazarus (16.19–31); the contrast of the Pharisee and the publican (18.9–14); the parable of the lost coin (15.8–10); the story of the two sons (15.11–32); and the story of the good Samaritan (10.25–37). It has often been said that Luke imparts a universality to the Christian gospel, and has a particular regard for the socially excluded and for aliens, and these parables shows that this is indeed the case.

Like Matthew, Luke adds to the story of the empty tomb stories of the appearances of the risen Christ. He also mentions that at this time the scriptures were being searched for predictions or supposed predictions that would justify the church's faith in a suffering messiah (24.27 and 45–7). The appearances of the risen Jesus continued for forty days after the resurrection, and ended with his ascension, an event which is peculiar to Luke. This period between resurrection and ascension (to use the scheme of Luke) was seen by Barth as the time of revelation.[51] In a sense, we can accept this. It means that there was a time, whether forty days or four hundred scarcely matters, when the meaning of the Christ-event sank into the disciples' minds, so to speak. They came to terms with the crucifixion, and they came to believe in the resurrection. At one time, perhaps, they had hoped that Jesus would restore the fortunes of Israel (Luke 24.21). But now they had come to the point of believing that 'God has made him both Lord and Christ, this Jesus whom you crucified' (Acts 2.36). And with this we have made the transition from Luke's gospel to his second volume, The Acts of the Apostles, and to the primitive preaching of the church. But essentially it is the same christology that we have met in all the synoptists – a christology in which the man Jesus receives the Spirit of God and through his obedience even to death is raised to christhood and lordship.

5

The Witness of John

We have already become aware of the great difficulties and complexities which beset the study of christology. These increase enormously when we take account of the Johannine contribution to the subject – the gospel of John and the three letters traditionally attributed to the author of that gospel. At the beginning of the last chapter I spoke of John's gospel as standing 'somewhat apart' from the synoptics, and that was no doubt an understatement. The differences between John and the other gospels are major, and since our present task is to collect the early evidences for the Christ-event, it is not easy to see how the witness of John fits in with the witness of the synoptics, to say nothing of Paul or any other New Testament witness whom we may have to call. Yet since the current tendency in New Testament studies is perhaps to overstress the differences among the several writers, it may be best to begin by mentioning some of the more obvious agreements to be found between John and the synoptics, to make it clear that we are still concerned with the same Jesus of Nazareth, who he was and who he is. John too places the activities of Jesus in Palestine, though with less emphasis on Galilee, and John too records how these activities brought Jesus into conflict with the authorities and eventually led to his arrest, trial and execution under the Roman governor, Pontius Pilate. John occasionally narrates incidents in terms close to those used by the synoptists, such as the miraculous feeding of the five thousand and Jesus' walking on the water (both incidents in 6.1–21). Sometimes John does not narrate incidents recorded by the synoptists, but makes unmistakable allusions to them – for instance, he does not tell of Jesus' agony in the garden of Gethsemane, but *before* the supper he quotes Jesus as saying, 'Now is my soul troubled. And what shall I say? "Father, save me from this hour?" No, for this purpose I have come to this hour' (12.27). I accepted Bultmann's view that the Gethsemane story is legendary, for reasons stated earlier,[1] but the

Johannine passage would indicate that behind the legend there was an actual incident, Jesus' natural human emotions of shrinking in the face of an imminent and cruel death. Because of the occasional agreements or partial agreements between John and the synoptists, there has been much discussion of the question whether John knew the synoptic gospels, and whether his own gospel was intended to supplement or even to take the place of these other gospels. The arguments have been inconclusive, but in any case they would not be of importance for the theological questions which are the main concern of this book.

The differences between John and the synoptists are more striking than the similarities. Sometimes they are differences in matters of detail. Thus, while John agrees with the synoptists that Jesus 'cleansed' the Temple by driving out those who were engaging in a profitable trade with the pilgrims, he puts this incident near the beginning of Jesus' ministry, whereas Mark and the others position it a few days before the crucifixion. Only if we follow the synoptic gospels, therefore, can we see this event and the public disorder which presumably accompanied it, as the immediate occasion which roused the authorities to take action against Jesus. Again, despite broad similarities in the passion narrative, there is another difference about dates, John placing the Last Supper and the crucifixion a day earlier in relation to the Passover feast than do the synoptists. But the major differences in John's gospel are not points of detail or connected with specific incidents but have a general character affecting his teaching as a whole. Some of the main points of difference are as follows.

1. In the synoptic gospels, Jesus' teaching and preaching are centred in the kingdom of God; in John, Jesus' own person has become the focus of interest. While in the synoptics Jesus is apparently reluctant to accept the title of Christ or messiah, in John he himself claims a relation to the Father going far beyond anything that the title 'Christ' had originally signified. So John's gospel is a very christological account, and its author could even be called the Christ-intoxicated man. As Bultmann has put it,

> In John, Jesus appears neither as the rabbi arguing about questions of the law, nor as the prophet proclaiming the breaking in of the kingdom of God. Rather, he speaks only of his own person, as the Revealer whom God has sent. He does not argue about the sabbath or fasting or purity and divorce, but speaks of his coming and his going, of what he is and what he brings the world. He strives not against self-righteousness and untruthfulness but against disbelief toward himself.[2]

2. Not only is the content of Jesus teaching different in John, the form of the teaching is also markedly changed. In the synoptics, Jesus' teaching is given sometimes in the form of short sayings, which are given a setting

in some incident or argument or instruction – the kind of sayings which the form-critics loved to analyse and classify; sometimes it is given in the form of parables, a highly distinctive literary form in which a brief narrative is used to elucidate a moral or spiritual truth. In John, we find not just isolated sayings, but longer, connected discourses; and we do not find parables,[3] but extended metaphors, which are of quite a different literary type – I mean, of course, such passages as 'I am the living bread' (6.51ff.), 'I am the door of the sheep' (10.7), 'I am the good shepherd' (10.11), 'I am the true vine' (15.1).

3. In John's gospel, Jesus knows his special vocation and his unique relation to the Father from the very first. Likewise, from the beginning of his ministry he is at once recognized as the Christ or Son of God, both by John the Baptist and by those whom he calls to be his disciples (1.29–51). There is no history of a deepening knowledge and recognition such as one can discern in the synoptics, where Jesus himself is said to have 'increased in wisdom' (Luke 2.52) and the disciples on their side come to a moment of recognition when they acknowledge him as the Christ – though we have seen reasons for believing that this moment may not have come until the resurrection.[4]

4. Because Jesus is the Christ from the beginning, his story is, in John's gospel, actually reversed, in a theological sense. In the synoptic gospels, as also in the letters of Paul and in the primitive preaching of Acts, we begin with a human, earthly Jesus, who, in the course of his history and in particular of his resurrection is manifested as the Christ. It is an 'ascending' christology, popularly called a christology 'from below' or in the more technical language of Grillmeier an 'anabatic' christology. As we noted in an earlier context,[5] the synoptic writers and Paul constructed their story backwards, so to speak, that is to say, their fixed point of reference was the resurrection, and from there they looked backward over the life of Jesus. Mark looked as far as Jesus' baptism and the beginning of his ministry, Matthew and Luke traced the story further back to his birth, now embellished with legendary details in the light of subsequent events. But John was not content to stop at the birth, or even at the genealogies with which Matthew and Luke preceded it. He does not mention such matters, but goes back to the ultimate beginning, to the Word or Logos dwelling with the Father before the creation of the world. The story is reversed in a theological sense because here we do not have any longer an anabatic christology but what we must call a 'catabatic' one – the story of a heavenly being who comes down to earth; or, to speak more accurately, a christology which is both catabatic and anabatic, for the one who came down is also the one who returns to the place where he had been. 'No one has ascended into heaven but he who descended from heaven, the Son of Man' (3.13). In other words, we now have a more

complicated christological pattern, a pattern of descent followed by ascent. John's gospel itself falls into this pattern. The first part (1.1 to 12.19) tells of the origin of the Son and his sojourn on earth; the second part (12.20 to the end) tells of his departure. For better or worse, this was destined to become the pattern of the classic christology of the church, and remains so to this day in the Nicene creed. It could be argued, of course, that it is only a more emphatic and detailed version of the christology already taking shape in Paul, as when he calls Christ the 'wisdom of God' (I Cor. 1.24) or, more importantly, when he consciously reverses the theological order of the christological story and puts God at the beginning as its only sufficient ground: 'All this is from God, who through Christ reconciled us to himself and gave us the ministry of reconciliation; that is, in Christ God was reconciling the world to himself' (II Cor. 5.18–19).

5. While the synoptists and Paul are (at least, in the main) still in the grip of a future-oriented eschatology, John has (again, we must say, in the main) abandoned this for a view in which the events once expected in the future have been brought into the present: 'Now is the judgment of this world, now shall the ruler of this world be cast out' (12.31). John, of course, did not cause the decline of the eschatological expectations that had been so important for the earliest Christians, but he accepted the change and gave a consistent expression to it in his writings.

6. John was a master of symbolism, as of language generally, and this will be made apparent later when we consider in greater detail some of the expressions which he attributes to Jesus – 'I am the true vine, the living bread', and so on. But his preference seems to have been for verbal symbolism, and some scholars have concluded that he did not attach much value to the sacraments of the Christian community. He tells the story of the Last Supper of Jesus with his disciples, but makes no mention of the institution of the eucharist on that occasion, though, as we have noted,[6] all the synoptists and Paul claim that the eucharist was instituted at that time, so the event must be considered well attested. Again, John describes an early encounter between Jesus and John the Baptist, and even reports John as saying, 'I saw the Spirit descend as a dove from heaven, and it remained on him' (1.32); but although this mention of the Spirit seems definitely to allude to the tradition about the baptism of Jesus by John, the Fourth Gospel omits to say that Jesus was baptized by John. It may be granted that these silences of the evangelist can be explained in more ways than one. Over against the silences, one has to note that Jesus in John's gospel gives what has usually been regarded as eucharistic teaching (6.41ff.) but not in the context of the Last Supper; and he tells that the disciples of Jesus, perhaps even Jesus himself, baptized those who came to them (3.22 and 4.1–2). So it is by no means certain that John

had a negative attitude to the sacraments, though if his book is rightly described as a 'spiritual' gospel (the expression was already used by Clement of Alexandria[7] about the year 200) then John may have believed that the physical symbols used in the sacraments are inappropriate and that they ought to be spiritualized and internalized (as happened also among the Quakers many centuries later).

The long list of differences between John and the synoptists, just stated, points to the fact that when, in the course of our study of the early witnesses to Christ, we turn from the synoptists to John, we are confronted with a massive shift. It should not be exaggerated, for as I said at the beginning of the chapter, they are both talking about the same Jesus of Nazareth, and they tell the same basic story, with many points of agreement as well as of difference. Yet undoubtedly there is a massive shift. With the composition of the Fourth Gospel, christology entered new phase, and even today it is still argued whether the new development was a step forward or a step back.

I mentioned the expression used by Clement of Alexandria – a 'spiritual' gospel. I suppose all the Christian gospels are fundamentally spiritual writings, but Clement was contrasting John with the synoptics which, he claimed, had exhibited 'bodily' things. By that, I suppose he meant that they had set forth historical matters that could be observed by the senses. Thus, the synoptists begin their story with the appearance of Jesus in his public ministry (Mark) or with his birth (Matthew and Luke) while John bypasses these historical or empirical beginnings to go back to the ultimate beginning in the life of God. This, in turn, found expression in two different types of christology: the anabatic, which tells of a man (admittedly, one on whom the Spirit had descended) rising to Lordship and Christhood, while the catabatic tells of a heavenly being who comes from the spiritual realm to dwell among human beings, yet perhaps we wonder if he is ever quite one of them. As we look over the list of differences between the Johannine and the synoptic gospels, we can hardly fail to conclude that there has been a shift away from the humanity of Jesus in the direction of turning him into an otherworldly figure. Our uneasiness may increase when we remember that Clement, who thought so highly of this 'spiritual' gospel, also taught that although Jesus Christ went through the motions of eating and drinking, he had no need to take physical nourishment.[8] This would not seem to be compatible with a belief in the true humanity of Jesus.

Clement's understanding of John's gospel and of the Johannine Christ has come back in a different form to trouble us in the twentieth century. We live in a time when the majority of theologians (including the present writer) are determined to maintain the full humanity of Jesus Christ. But at the same time some eminent New Testament scholars have been finding in John evidences, as they believe, of a strong Gnostic influence, and the question has to be asked whether this brings John under suspicion, together with all the Christian theology that has drawn its inspiration from John.

The scholar who has made the major contribution to the question of Gnostic influences in John was Rudolf Bultmann, and he was writing on these questions long before he produced his magnificent commentary, *The Gospel of John*. Hitherto we have been unwilling to follow Bultmann very far when he invites us to walk along the path of the 'history of religions' school, but I think he has a stronger case in his view of John. What impressed Bultmann was the general similarity between the redemptive narratives circulating among the Gnostics and the story of Jesus as it is told by John. Generally speaking,[9] Gnostics believed in a dualistic universe, the scene of a conflict between light and darkness. Light stands for the forces of God, spirit, truth, knowledge while darkness represents demonic forces, matter, falsehood, ignorance. God, in this scheme of belief, is a distant God, virtually unknown. The world is in the power of demonic rulers, and in conflict with God. Human beings are trapped in the world and ignorant of the fact that, so far as they are spiritual, they have their origin in God. But God sends to them an emissary or Revealer who will impart to them the knowledge (*gnosis*) of the truth, and as they learn the truth, they are delivered from the bondage of the world and the way is opened for their return to the realm of light.

Almost all of these points can be paralleled in John. He too recognizes a dualistic background of light and darkness, already mentioned in the prologue (1.5). For John too God is hidden: 'No one has ever seen God' (1.18). But God has sent the Son to make the Father known (1.18b) – and these notions of 'sending' and 'making known' are pervasive of the gospel, so that Jesus may be rightly called an 'emissary' and 'revealer'. The world, in John, is hostile to God and rejects his emissary; but those who receive him are enabled to reclaim their true status as children of God (1.11–12). The extent of the resemblance is increased if we attend to John's use of such words as 'light', 'truth', 'knowledge' and so on, and, on the dark side, his mention of the (demonic) 'ruler of this world' (12.31).

The Gnostic/Johannine comparison just made seems at first sight very persuasive. It rests on the assumption, however, that there existed a pre-Christian or, at least, pre-Johannine Gnosticism on which the writer of the gospel drew. Bultmann even speculated that there was 'probably' a Gnostic or gnosticizing source for the discourses in John. Not only has this view that there was a Gnostic source found little favour, there has been the more sweeping objection that Gnosticism was a later phenomenon than Bultmann believed. This may be true of the developed Gnostic systems, but there can be little doubt that many of the leading ideas of

Gnosticism were already circulating when the Fourth Gospel was composed. I do not think there is any reason to question the quite modest claim of Walter Schmithals in his Introduction to the English translation of Bultmann's commentary: 'The influence of pre-Christian Gnosticism can be discerned in Philo of Alexandria, and particularly in speculations of late Judaism (such as the wisdom myth), as well as in the Qumran writings'. Detailed evidences supporting this view may be found in Bultmann's own book, *Primitive Christianity in its Contemporary Setting*.

Even those scholars who minimize the connection between John's gospel and early Gnosticism do not go so far as actually to deny it. Thus, in the introduction to his 'Anchor Bible' commentary on John, Raymond Brown says: 'one cannot claim that the dependence of John on a postulated early oriental Gnosticism has been disproved', though he holds that the 'hypothesis remains very tenuous'. It seems undeniable that Bultmann exaggerated the extent of the dependence, yet it is equally undeniable that the significant parallels described above do point to some relation. If we set alongside each other the early manifestations of Gnosticism or proto-Gnosticism and the *late* date which most scholars have assigned to John's gospel, then the hypothesis of some Gnostic influence on John will not seem improbable, as an explanation of the parallels. It is true, of course, that in recent years the question of the date of John's gospel has been reopened by the work of John Robinson. His careful researches and ingenious arguments have shown that there are in John some very early elements of tradition, and that we have been too ready to accept as established fact some of the text-book theories about the dating of the New Testament writings.[10] But even so, Robinson has hardly shaken the view that what we know as John's gospel probably comes from the closing years of the first century. For instance, one would have to set against Robinson's work the interesting researches of J. L. Martyn, who sees the sharp rivalry in John between Christian and Jew as reflecting the historical situation at the end of the first century. He argues in detail that the story of the healing of the man born blind and his expulsion from the synagogue (John 9) refers to an actual incident in the city where the Johannine church was located, though the incident has been projected back by the evangelist into the time of Jesus.[11]

On the whole, I think we must give a cautious assent to Bultmann's thesis about the Gnostic affinities of John. Perhaps we could even say that John's attitude to Gnosticism was something like Bultmann's own attitude to existentialism, because both Gnosticism and existentialism expressed the alienation of an age together with its longing for spiritual satisfaction, and so these movements offered a language and conceptuality through which the Christian message might make contact with the needs of the time. In fact, Hans Jonas, in his masterly study of

Gnosticism, does compare it to existentialism. Though the latter is a movement 'of our own day, conceptual, sophisticated, and eminently "modern" in more than the chronological sense; the former from a misty past, mythological, crude, and even something of a freak in its own day, and never admitted to the respectable company of our philosophic tradition', he finds they have a good deal in common.[12]

But does not its relation to Gnosticism disqualify John's gospel as a credible witness to Jesus Christ and the Christ-event? For surely a Christ presented in the context of Gnostic ideas must be a docetic Christ, a purely spiritual disembodied and otherworldly being free from contamination of anything physical or bodily – in short, not a human being. Some scholars have not hesitated to claim that this is indeed the case. Käsemann, for instance, once a pupil of Bultmann but in his later work striving hard to get out from under Bultmann's shadow, declares bluntly that the Johannine Christ is 'God striding over the earth'.[13] When the reader hears this phrase, it will almost inevitably act as a reminder of the very similar words which Bultmann used about the Jesus of Mark's gospel – 'the very Son of God walking the earth'.[14] The point is worth remembering, because it shows that the difference between the Christ of John's gospel and the Christ of Mark's gospel is not so great as is sometimes supposed. We have seen that Mark's Christ too could be presented as the 'divine man' and that his humanity was thereby obscured, but we did not conclude that Mark's picture is a purely docetic one, for we found many compensating passages which speak clearly of the humanity of Christ and even of his servant role. May not the same be true of John's gospel? Käsemann accepts that there are some passages in John which seem to ascribe humanity and even humility to Jesus, but that these are only features of the outward appearance of this heavenly being who visits the earth. What Käsemann does not recognize, but I think we must recognize, is that John has been critical and selective in his use of the Gnostic or proto-Gnostic ideas, just as Bultmann, many centuries later, was critical in his use of existentialist categories.

The crucial point, I think, is this. In the comparison made a few paragraphs above between the major ideas of Gnosticism and some corresponding elements in the gospel of John there was one obvious omission: I said nothing about the Gnostic belief that the material world is inherently evil and that it is the creation not of the one true God but of demonic powers of one sort or another. I omitted that central tenet of Gnosticism because there is nothing corresponding to it in John. This is a part of Gnosticism which John rejects, but it is precisely the part that would entail a docetic understanding of Jesus. John makes it clear in his prologue that everything derives its being from the Father, acting though the agency of the Logos: 'all things were made through him, and without him was not anything made that was made' (1.3). This carefully constructed sentence seems to be explicitly designed to affirm that everything that is in existence has been created by God through the Logos, and at the same time to deny that anything has been brought into existence through any other creative agency. Once this crucial point has been established, then the human, bodily, historical existence of Jesus is made secure. This is quite compatible with acknowledging that John, like Mark before him, may sometimes ascribe to Jesus' supernatural powers and that modern criticism will call into question the veracity of reports of such powers. John is not alone among New Testament writers in trying to express his sense of the uniqueness of Jesus by depicting him as 'passing through this world some inches off the earth' (the words are borrowed from John Robinson).[15] But while this feature of his gospel calls for critical treatment, it certainly does not amount to a full-blown docetism.

I mentioned above that John had used a 'carefully constructed sentence'. We do not know who 'John' was, or whether there was one John or more than one. But one thing that will become apparent to us as we go along is that 'John' was a master of language – I do not think the word 'genius' would be out of place if applied to him. Those first-century Christians had undergone a revelatory experience that had 'thrown them to the ground'[16] and in the years after it, they were searching for words to express it. Inevitably they made mistakes as they tried to give their witness, but one can only admire the extraordinary inventiveness they showed. John was the most inventive of all, perhaps especially by his use of paradox, a way of speaking which employed two contradictory statements, neither of which is cancelled out by the other but which together point to a state of affairs that cannot be itself directly expressed. We meet an example of this in the very first verse of John's gospel, the opening of the prologue, possibly the most celebrated passage in the whole of the New Testament.

Let me first of all simply quote the words, since they seem to be capable of lending themselves to inexhaustible meditation and interpretation:

1. In the beginning was the Word, and the Word was with God, and the Word was God.

2. He was in the beginning with God;

3. all things were made through him, and without him was not anything made that was made.

4. In him was life, and the life was the light of men.

5. The light shines in the darkness, and the darkness has not overcome it.

9. The true light that enlightens every man was coming into the world.

10. He was in the world, and the world was made through him, yet the world knew him not.

11. He came to his own home, but his own received him not.

12. But to those who received him, to those who believed in his name, he gave power to become children of God;

13. who were born, not of blood, nor of the will of the flesh nor of the will of man, but of God.

14. And the Word became flesh and dwelt among us, full of grace and truth; we have beheld his glory, glory as of the only Son from the Father.

16. And from his fulness have we all received, grace upon grace.

17. For the law was given through Moses; grace and truth came through Jesus Christ.

18. No one has ever seen God; the only Son, who is in the bosom of the Father, he has made him known. (John 1.1–18, omitting 6–8 and 15).

Some years ago, I attempted (as many others have done) to write my own translation (or, rather, paraphrase) of these verses, not because I was so foolish as to think it would be better than the traditional English versions, but to help both myself and others in the process of meditation and appropriation. Perhaps the major innovation in my paraphrase was the translation of Word or Logos by 'Meaning', which seemed to me the most comprehensive rendering for Logos and the one which would respond most directly to feelings of alienation and lostness, both as they are known in the contemporary world and as they were experienced at the time when Gnosticism made its appeal. Here then is the paraphrase.

Fundamental to everything is Meaning. It is closely connected with what we call 'God', and indeed Meaning and God are virtually identical. To say that God was in the beginning is to say that Meaning was in the beginning. All things were made meaningful, and there was nothing made that was meaningless. Life is the drive toward Meaning, and life has emerged into self-conscious humanity, as the (finite) bearer and recipient of Meaning. And Meaning shines out through the threat of absurdity, for absurdity has not overwhelmed it.

Every human being has a share in Meaning, whose true light was coming into the world. Meaning was there in the world and embodying itself in the world, yet the world has not recognized the Meaning, and even humanity, the bearer of Meaning, has rejected it. But those who have received it and believed in it have been enabled to become the children of God. And this has happened not in the natural course of evolution or through human striving, but through a gracious act of God. For the Meaning has been incarnated in a human existent, in whom was grace and truth; and we have seen in him the glory toward which everything moves – the glory of God. From him, whom we can acknowledge in personal terms as the Son of the Father, we have received abundance of grace. Through Moses came the command of the law, through Jesus Christ grace and truth. God is a mystery, but the Son who has shared the Father's life has revealed him. [17]

This paraphrase can, at the best, give a general idea of how the words of the prologue might be interpreted in our post-Enlightenment and evolutionary era, but it does not, of course, excuse us from a careful verse by verse study of John's actual words in an accurate and unvarnished translation.

1. In the beginning was the Word, and the Word was with God, and the Word was God.

There has been endless discussion about John's understanding of the Word or Logos. Had he read the works of Philo of Alexandria, who had tried to blend Greek and Jewish ideas and who visualized the Logos as a kind of intermediary between the transcendent God and the physical universe? Or, as recent scholarship has tended to believe, had John derived his understanding of the Logos in the main from Old Testament and Jewish sources – and we must remember that for a long time Greek ideas had already been influencing the Jewish tradition? After all, in the Hebrew scriptures, it is through his word that God creates the heavens and the earth, and through his word that he reveals his will to the prophets. It is true that in John the Word has been hypostatized and personalized, so as to become virtually a second entity alongside the Father. But this tendency toward hypostatization is to be found in the Old Testament, if not in relation to the Word, at least in relation to the Wisdom of God. One can discern parallels between what is said about wisdom in Proverbs and what is said about the Word in John.

'The Lord created me at the beginning of his work, the first of his acts of old. Ages ago I was set up, at the first, before the beginning of the earth. When there were no depths, I was brought forth, when there were not springs abounding with water. Before the mountains had been shaped, before the hills, I was brought forth; before he had made the earth with its fields, or the first of the dust of the world. When he established the heavens. I was there, when he drew a circle on the face of the deep, when he made firm the skies above, when he established the fountains of the deep, when he assigned to the sea its limit, so that the waters might not transgress his command, when he marked out the foundations of the earth, then I was beside him like a master workman; and I was daily his delight, rejoicing before him always, rejoicing in his inhabited world and delighting in the sons of men.' (Prov. 8.22–31)

But it is not necessary for us to get into a detailed discussion of what ideas and influences may lie behind John's use of the Logos concept. I remind the reader of the brief discussion of the 'Word' in an earlier part of the book where we considered some of the terms from the religious traditional vocabulary that came to be applied to Jesus as what we might call 'first approximations' to an interpretation.[18] I wrote at that point that there is a 'beauty and aptness' in this expression, Word or Logos, when applied to Jesus. It is through words that one expresses what is in one's mind. Otherwise one's thoughts would remain hidden. 'God speaks', writes Karl Barth, and he intends this to be an assertion of something that characterizes the very being of God.[19] Barth is talking about the God of the Bible who, unlike God in some other traditions, does not remain closed in upon himself in contemplation or self-sufficient bliss, but directs himself outward, or communicates himself. Through his word, 'Let there be light!' he inaugurates the creation of the universe. Through his word, he speaks to Israel. According to John, Jesus Christ is God's Word. Barth claims that when it is said that God speaks, the language is literal, not figurative. But he is surely mistaken about this. God does not speak words and sentences like those of a human language. If we think of Jesus Christ as supremely God's Word, then in him there is expressed far more than could be expressed in words, understood only in the verbal sense. Admittedly, part of the Word communicated in Christ is verbal, Christ's own teaching, and this is clearly affirmed in John: 'He who hears my word and believes him who sent me, has eternal life' (5.24). But it is the whole person and history of Jesus Christ that constitute the Word – the Word which makes known what is in the mind of the Father.

The second half of the first verse of the prologue is also of the highest importance. It is the first use by John of paradox, which I have already mentioned as characteristic of this evangelist. We have two statements, which on the surface appear contradictory: 'The Word was with (*pros*) God, and the Word was God.' When we say 'The Word was with God', that seems to imply that God and the Word are two distinct, though closely related, entities. When we say 'The Word was God', that seems to imply that God and the Word are one, or are identical. By this subtle use of language, John is in effect saying that the Word, as coming forth or proceeding from the Father, is distinct; yet, when he immediately adds, 'The Word was God', he seems to be virtually identifying God and Word. But is this not entirely true to the 'apt and beautiful' metaphor he is using? When I speak a word, that word acquires a kind of separateness or independence, it has been 'uttered' or externalized, it can be heard and appropriated by others, it can even be written down. It has 'proceeded' from the speaker, to use a traditional theological term. Yet in another way that word is still an extension or part of the speaker, it is my word in which I have expressed myself. In this sense a word is, to use another traditional term of theology, 'of the same being' (*homoousios*) as the one who speaks it. Even within the prologue, John soon ceases to talk about the Word, and talks instead of the Son. The language of the Son is more obviously personal than the language of the Word, but the fundamental metaphor remains very similar. A son is distinct from his father, yet a son too is, in a sense, a continuation of the father. In Jewish society, a son was considered the agent of his father, and this is another point of similarity, for the Word is depicted by John as God's agent in creation.[20] But John shows the same subtle use of paradox when he uses 'Son language' as when he uses 'Word language'. So, later in the gospel, we find Jesus saying, 'I and the Father are one' (10.30), but we must not leap to the conclusion that Jesus is here identified with God the Father. We have to take account of other subtle statements that qualify a near identity with a measure of separateness, such as 'I am in the Father and the Father in me' (14.10). John also appears in some verses to subordinate Jesus to the Father, 'The Father is greater than I' (14.28) for we are still far from the doctrine of the triune God, as it was eventually formulated.

Before we leave the first verse of the prologue, let us look at the difficult question whether, when it is said that 'the Word was God', Jesus is actually being called 'God', albeit indirectly. We have touched already on this question, and have seen that the experts disagree, Raymond Brown affirming and Bultmann denying that Jesus is here called God.[21] It must be said that, on the surface at least, Brown would seem to be correct. For (although the identification of Jesus with the Word will be made only later in the prologue) we are told here that 'the Word was God', so if Jesus was the Word, then it seems to follow that Jesus is God. But I have already suggested that John's use of the paradox, 'The Word was with God and the Word was God' hovers somewhere between identity and difference, and does not permit us to say that God and the Word are simply identical. Thus even if we are correct in speaking of the 'identification' of Jesus with the Word, we could not go on to infer an identification of Jesus with God. Here, I think, we have to take note of the many subtle variations of meaning in the little word 'is'. Sentences in which the word 'is' asserts identity are convertible, that is to say, they can be turned around. An illustration would be, 'George Bush is President of the United States', which entails the assertion, 'The President of the United States is George Bush.' But it is not at all clear that by conversion we can assert that 'God is the Word' or, still less, 'God is Jesus'. In fact, the logic of Christian theology positively forbids us to say any such things. We can say that 'The

Word is/was God' or that 'Jesus is/was God', but when we make God the subject of the sentence, we have to allow that God is 'more' than the 'Word' or Jesus, God is also the Father from whom the Word proceeds or the Son is begotten – indeed, if we were to move on from John to the developed Christian doctrine of the Trinity, we would have to say that God is Father, Son and Holy Spirit, and cannot be identified with any one of these in isolation, as would be implied in saying 'God is the Word' or 'God is Jesus'. (There have been a few theologians who have indeed identified God and Jesus, and later we shall consider and criticize what they have said).[22] But if we do not have an 'is' of identity in the assertion, 'The Word was God', what kind of 'is' is it?

I note first of all a point made by Anthony Harvey concerning John's language in this verse. Harvey claims that if the Word were being identified with God, the Greek text would not have the simple word *theos* (God) but would precede it with the definite article, *ho theos* (which might be rendered 'the one and only God'). Is the simple *theos* then to be treated as an adjective, perhaps with the meaning 'divine'? I do not think that is a satisfactory explanation either, for there is a perfectly acceptable Greek adjective with that meaning, namely *theios* (which we have already met in the expression *theios aner*). But to turn *theos* into an adjective is not only to usurp the usage of an already existing adjective, it is also to suggest that there is a class of divine beings to which the Word belongs, and such an idea would have been intolerable from the point of view of Jewish monotheism. There is another possibility, suggested to me by some remarks of Professor Bowman Clarke.[23] Admittedly, the usage about which he is talking is only analogous to what we have in John, for the Christian way of talking about God has its own specific logic, and this cannot be subsumed under anything else. Nevertheless, an analogy might throw some light on it. Clarke draws our attention to what he calls 'mass terms'. Examples are 'gold', 'water', 'matter'. If I say, for instance, 'This bracelet is gold', I am not identifying it with all the gold in the world, but I am saying that it is of 'the same substance' or that it is 'one in being' with gold. It is in some sense analogous to this that we must understand John's claim that 'The Word was God', and its implication that if Jesus was the word, then Jesus was, in the same sense, God.

2. He was in the beginning with God.

The second verse of the prologue does not seem to add anything that was not already contained in the first verse, but it does draw out an important implication. If indeed the Logos is of the same substance as God, then he must share the essential characteristics of God. Therefore, if God has been from the beginning, the Logos too has been from the beginning. To express this in another way, we could say that there never was a time when there was no Word, and there never was a time when God was wholly contained within himself. God has always been uttering his Word, that is to say, going forth in self-communication, positing another than himself, yet another who shares the same being as the Father. This may sound very Hegelian, for in Hegel the Absolute Spirit has from all eternity been going out into the realm of the finite. But this resemblance to Hegelianism need occasion no surprise, since Hegel's fundamental conceptions of the Spirit originated out of his reflections on the Christian doctrine of the Trinity.

3. All things were made through him, and without him was not anything made that was made.
This verse introduces the notion of the Logos as God's agent, specifically as the agent in creation. Although agency is a functional notion, it has already been given an ontological ground in the assertion in verse 1 of the intimate relation between God and the Word. The importance of verse 3 is that it makes clear that even if there is some Gnostic influence on John, he is not uncritical, and in fact rejects a basic Gnostic tenet. John is declaring that creation is the work of God, acting through his Logos, whereas the Gnostics believed the material creation to be utterly alien to God, and to be the work of demons or false gods. It may be asked, then, why does John have to introduce an agent between God the Father and the creation? Why did God not create the universe directly, so to speak? Perhaps the answer to this is that although John is setting his face against the Gnostic point of view, he was nevertheless sensitive to the Hellenistic influences that had been working on Judaism for a long time, and which tried to protect God's otherness from and transcendence of the world by introducing intermediate beings between God and the world. It may even have been Philo of Alexandria from whom John takes his teaching about the Logos as the agent of creation, as many scholars believed for a long time. But even if John did not get the teaching from Philo, he could have got it elsewhere, for it was part of the stock of ideas in the Hellenistic culture. It could be argued too that distinctions within God arise almost necessarily from reflection on what God, if there is a God, must be. As we have seen, Hebrew writers were tending to think of a hypostatized Wisdom of God long before John's time, while after his time there arose the full-blown Christian belief in a triune God. So the idea of the Logos as God's agent in creation is not un-Jewish or un-Christian, but as John interprets it, it is decidedly anti-Gnostic.

4. In him was life, and the life was the light of men.
With this verse, we begin to move in the ambience of the typical

Johannine language, for 'light' and 'life' are symbols that will come and go through the entire gospel. 'Life' here is, of course, far more than merely biological life. Perhaps we might be permitted to call it 'metaphysical life' and its highest form is what the evangelist calls 'eternal life'. The fulness of life is the life of God himself. Later on in the gospel, Jesus will tell us that the communication of this more-than- natural (or, if the word is permitted, supernatural) life was the basic purpose of his coming: 'I came that they may have life, and have it abundantly' (10.10).

Although, as I have pointed out, 'life' in John's prologue is not simply biological life, the teaching of the prologue lends itself very readily to a comparison with evolutionary theory. The second part of the verse we are presently considering says that 'the life was the light of men'. With the emergence of the human race, life has emerged into the light of reason and self-consciousness, and we begin to see the full dimensions of 'life' in the Johannine sense. These dimensions were well expressed many years ago by William Porcher DuBose, at a time when evolution was still regarded by many theologians as a threat to Christian faith. Commenting on John's words, DuBose spoke of 'the life that has at last culminated in rational, free and ultimately divine humanity'.[24]

5. The light shines in the darkness, and the darkness has not overcome it.

The dualistic contrast of light and darkness in this verse may well be of Gnostic origin, but it seems clear that for John the dualism is not ultimate, and that the light will not be extinguished by the darkness. Admittedly, the darkness is real and poses a threat to the light. Yet the very fact that life and light have appeared in the darkness seems to imply that the potentiality for life and light were hidden in the darkness, that God was hidden in the darkness until he spoke his word, 'Let there be light!' In his first epistle, John gives expression to the light symbol in a somewhat different way: 'This is the message we have heard from him and proclaim to you, that God is light and in him is no darkness at all' (I John 1.5).

John does not say what is the origin of the darkness. Although I have said that he does not teach an ultimate dualism, he may well have believed in demonic powers of some sort, as is suggested by his mention of the 'ruler of this world' (12.31). But although the world (kosmos) is fallen and lies under sin, so that John usually speaks of the world as hostile to God and to believers, it is still the creation of God through his Word, and God loves the world and has sent the Son as the Revealer who will bring salvation (3.16–17). So although the dualistic background of light and darkness is reminiscent of Gnosticism, John is far from embracing a Gnostic metaphysic of two equal and opposed Powers.

9. The true light that enlightens every man was coming into the world.

As is well known, this verse can be read in either of two ways, depending on how it is punctuated; either in the version given here (following RSV), or 'That was the true light, that enlightens every man who comes into the world' (essentially what we find in AV). Whichever way we read it, the verse strikes a note of universalism. It suggests that every human being is to some degree enlightened by the Logos, perhaps even (as some later writers would have said) has a share in the Logos, at least as a potency. It is important to bear this in mind when one finds later in the gospel such passages as 'No one comes to the Father but by me' (14.6). This later passage is often taken to be an exclusive claim for the revelation in Christ, but if we take it in conjunction with the teaching that Christ is the Logos, we see that it need not be taken in an exclusive sense. For if Christ is the Logos through whom all things (including all human beings) have been created, then wherever there remains a trace of the Logos, there is something of the true light and of a genuine knowledge of God. This verse of John in the prologue opens the door to the teaching of Justin only fifty years later, a teaching which quite probably alludes to the prologue: 'We are taught that Christ is the first begotten of God and that he is the Word of whom all mankind partakes. Those who lived by the Word are Christians, even though they have been considered atheists, such as, among the Greeks, Socrates, Heraclitus and others like them'.[25]

10. He was in the world, and the world was made through him, yet the world knew him not.

In this verse the shadow-side again obtrudes itself. The universe (*kosmos*) manifests order (the very name 'kosmos' implies this), and order, in turn, implies mind and form, and could never arise out of sheer chance or chaos. Yet the world as we see it also manifests disorder. It is certainly not obvious to immediate inspection that everything has been made what it is through divine wisdom. As in verse 5, John does not speculate on the reason for the disorder, though the general sense of the present verse would seem to point to human beings as the source of the disorder, rather than to the creative Logos or to demonic forces intent on frustrating his work. But the tragic fact remains. The world was made by God through his Logos, but even those finite spiritual beings within the world (the human race) who are enlightened by the Logos do not recognize their origin in God. Here we seem to see the Gnostic influence again, though in this case the teaching is compatible with Christianity – the teaching namely that human beings come from God but have 'forgotten' whence they come. They live in the ignorance of sin and unbelief, alienated from the life that is truly theirs.

11. He came to his own home, but his own received him not.

This verse continues the tragic theme of the preceding one. Christ comes to his own, and the language here is important – he comes not as a stranger of an alien race (that would be Gnosticism!) but truly as one of the human race – as the true man, shall we say, the man who has not forgotten his origin but stands in intimate relation to the Father? And in saying this, we see that in spite of all the differences, the 'massive shift', as I called it, the essential christology of Paul and the synoptists has not been abandoned by John. In John, Jesus remains, in the words of Charles H. Dodd, 'the *alethinos anthropos*, the real or archetypal Man',[26] and this expression is perfectly adequate to embrace both the solidarity of Jesus with the human race ('his own') and his distinctness from fallen or sinful humanity.

The question has been raised whether 'his own' in this verse means specifically the Jewish people. That would add a special poignancy to the verse, since the Jews had been elected by God and prepared as a people for the elect one, Jesus the Christ, yet they had rejected him. Such an interpretation would at the same time raise the question whether John is anti-Semitic. It can hardly be denied that the gospel abounds in hostile or derogatory mentions of 'the Jews'. But the term 'anti-Semitic' is not applicable here, and is in fact anachronistic and misleading if it suggests a comparison with the anti-Semitism of later times. The hostility to the Jews in this gospel is not based on race – indeed, it is unlikely that the concept of race played any part in John's thinking. Very likely, John himself was a Jew, even if we do not identify him with the apostle of that name. The gospel comes from a time when rivalry between Jew and Christian had reached a high level of intensity. There is much to be said for Lou Martyn's hypothesis, mentioned earlier,[27] that the Fourth Gospel may have come out of a Christian congregation located near a powerful synagogue and reflecting the hostility between the two groups in the closing years of the first century. But it would seem that for the most part, 'the Jews' of who John speaks disparagingly are not the Jews as such or the whole Jewish people but those leaders and officers who, either in Jesus' time or his own, were combatting the new Christian movement. Even so, although John neither shared nor could foresee the fanaticism of later anti-Semitic movements, his writings may have fuelled such movements.

My own view, however, would be that, in view of the context, Christ's 'own' who rejected him were, in this particular verse, the human race as a whole and not specifically the Jews.

12. But to all who received him, who believed in his name, he gave power to become children of God.

The universalistic interpretation given to 'his own' in the preceding verse gets support from verse 12. Christ has not been rejected by all of his own. Some have received him. But these some are no longer Jews or Samaritans or Greeks, or, rather, these worldly differences no longer matter, for they are all included in a new category, 'children of God'. At this point, John is in agreement with Paul and other early writers in seeing the Christian community as a new nation or a new humanity, defined not in worldly terms but in terms of the new relation to God brought about by the coming of Christ. The point is made again in Jesus' conversation with the Samaritan woman later in the gospel. 'The woman said to him, "Our fathers worshipped in this mountain; and you say that in Jerusalem is the place where men ought to worship". Jesus said to her, "Woman, believe me, the hour is coming when neither on this mountain nor in Jerusalem will you worship the Father . . . But the hour is coming, and now is, when the true worshippers will worship the Father in spirit and truth, for such the Father seeks to worship him"' (4.20–21 and 23). The first epistle also mentions the status of the believers as children of God, and the close relation to Christ which this new status brings to them. 'See what love the Father has given us, that we should be called children of God. The reason why the world does not know us is that it did not know him. Beloved, we are God's children now; it does not yet appear what we shall be, but we know that when he appears we shall be like him, for we shall see him as he is.' (I John 3.1–2). These words will remind us too of similar teaching which we met in Paul.[28]

13. Who were born, not of blood nor of the will of the flesh nor of the will of man, but of God.

Now we are given a closer definition of what is meant by 'children of God'. Though they are conceived and born like other human beings, their specific being as children *of God* is not bestowed through reproduction or race or special parentage or any other earthly distinction. They receive it from God by an act of grace. They were born 'not of bloods' (the Greek word is plural, suggesting particular strains of race or ethnic group or family) 'nor of the will of the flesh nor of the will of man, but of God'.

It was mentioned above that John says nothing about the birth or genealogy of Jesus Christ, and omits any mention of a virgin birth, such as we find in Matthew and Luke. Perhaps John had never heard the tradition of a virgin birth, but whether he had or not, the verse we are presently considering may be taken as the teaching in John which corresponds theologically to the virgin birth stories in Matthew and Luke. But here the 'virgin birth' has been universalized and allegorized. It is universalized because the significance of the story has been transferred from the individual Jesus to all Christian believers. They have experienced a birth which has come about not through any human will or agency, but a birth that has been brought about by God and is a birth into a new life or even a new humanity. It is allegorized, for the birth of which this verse speaks is not biological birth but a spiritual birth or rebirth, through which the believers have entered that 'life' which Jesus had come to bring and which may rightly be called a 'more-than-natural' life. That is why, in my paraphrase of the prologue, I said that becoming children of God 'has happened not in the natural course of evolution or through human striving, but through a gracious act of God'. Yet this gracious act need not be crudely conceived as intervention. If anyone believes that in some sense Jesus reveals God, or that God was in Christ, then he certainly seems to be claiming that Jesus Christ was not just a product of blind chance, but he may believe that in all the ages before Christ, a process was going on that had been initiated in the beginning by God and which culminated in the Christ-event.

This way of interpreting verse 13 is supported when we think of the encounter between Jesus and the religious leader Nicodemus, described two chapters further on in the gospel. Here indeed the idea of a new birth by the Spirit of God is universalized. 'Unless one is born anew', says Jesus, 'he cannot see the kingdom of God'. And again, 'Unless one is born of water and the Spirit, he cannot enter the kingdom of God' (3.3 and 5).

14. And the Word became flesh and dwelt among us, full of grace and truth; we have beheld his glory, glory as of the only Son from the Father.

Now we have come to the culmination, and this verse with its assertion that the Word became flesh must rank with verse 1 as the very essence of the prologue or even of the entire Johannine teaching. And, as between these two crucial verses, the weight seems to lie with verse 14. As Augustine said in his Confessions, the teaching that there is a Word and what has been said on this subject in the prologue so far is something he could have learned from Plato and his followers. But that the Word was made flesh is the distinctively new teaching that he has learned from Christianity.

The Word was made flesh. How can we understand this? If we try to understand it literally, it is nonsense. The Word is Meaning, and Meaning cannot be transformed into the biological tissue we call flesh. The word 'flesh' is being used in a figurative sense for the realm of the human, the empirical, the historical. It is true, of course, that John says quite simply, 'The Word became flesh' (*ho Logos sarx egeneto*), and that we have traditionally spoken of this event as the 'incarnation', derived from the Latin word *caro*, 'flesh', and signifying, 'becoming flesh'. Unfortunately this language does all too easily conduce to a literal and crudely mythological way of thinking, as if the Logos were animating, or enclosed

in, a framework of flesh and bones and blood. Some such view is alleged
to have been taught by Apollinarius, and was condemned at the Council
of Constantinople in 381. In opposition to that, the church taught that in
Jesus Christ the Logos assumed a complete humanity. It might have been
better therefore if the church had not used the word 'incarnation' but had
devised a term corresponding to the Greek *enanthropesis*, 'becoming
human'. But clearly whatever term may be used, one has to move away
from any supposedly literal meaning and to recognize the figurative
character of the language. If it is nonsense to say that Meaning can be
transformed into flesh in a literal way, there are still very formidable
difficulties in the way of understanding what could be meant by God
becoming man. For God is infinite, eternal, immortal and so on, while a
human being is finite, temporal, mortal, and has a good many more
characteristics that are apparently the opposites of those that belong to
God. If the divine is to be expressed in terms of the finite, then there must
take place a 'dimming down', so to speak. This is the kind of problem with
which the kenotic christologies of the nineteenth century tried to deal,
and a fuller discussion must be deferred until a later stage in our inquiry.
But these questions are already latent in the startling claim of John that in
Jesus Christ the Word that has been from the beginning has become man.
John does not appeal to the ancient doctrine of an image of God in man,
though it might have helped his case, as it does that of Paul. But perhaps
he already believed, as Justin did not many years after, that all human
beings participate in the divine Word and so have some potentiality for
manifesting that Word.

John's blunt assertion that the Word became flesh, with all the
materiality that 'flesh' conveys, may be taken as a further evidence that he
believed Jesus to be a man, and did not follow the Gnostics into docetism.
This evidence is strengthened when we read the opening words of the
first epistle of John, words which could hardly have been stronger in
affirming that Jesus was a real human being within this world: 'That
which was from the beginning, which we have heard, which we have
seen with our eyes, which we have looked upon and touched with our
hands, concerning the word of life – the life was made manifest and we
saw it, and testify to it, and proclaim to you the eternal life which was with
the Father and was made manifest to us – that which we have seen and
heard, we proclaim also to you' (I John 1.1–3). It is true that the same
epistle mentions a dissident group who had apparently adopted docetic
views of Jesus. But John himself has no sympathy with them and warns
against them in strong terms: 'Beloved, do not believe every spirit, but
test the spirits to see whether they are of God; for many false prophets
have gone out into the world. By this you know the Spirit of God: every
spirit which confesses that Jesus Christ has come in the flesh is of God,

and every spirit which does not confess Jesus is not of God. This is the spirit of antichrist, of which you heard that it was coming, and now it is in the world already' (I John 4.1–3).

We have seen that Käsemann argues that John himself is an uncritical docetist and that his Jesus is God striding over the world. Käsemann claims that commentators on verse 14 have laid all the stress on the words, 'The Word became flesh,' and have not paid attention to the second part of the verse, 'We have beheld his glory.' But surely the glory of Christ was not the glory of a being endowed with supernatural power. If we said this, we would miss the central paradox in John, that Christ's exaltation and humiliation are one and the same, that his lifting up on the cross is his lifting up in glory. This is surely a central belief of the Christian faith, that the true glory is not the glory of power but the glory of love.

16. And from his fulness have we all received, grace upon grace.

The word 'grace' (*charis*) is not common in John, as it is in Paul. On Bultmann's exegesis, 'grace' is here equivalent to 'life', which we have met already in the prologue and which in this gospel Jesus tells us is the principal gift which he brings (10.10). It is its gift-like character that is stressed by the word 'grace'.

17. For the law was given through Moses; grace and truth came through Jesus Christ.

The contrast between law and grace sounds more like Paul than John, and in any case may not be quite fair to Judaism. But the contrast between Moses and Jesus Christ is entirely typical of John, and is the first of several such contrasts between Jesus and heroes of the Jewish faith, always to the detriment of the latter. But, as already pointed out, this is not evidence of any anti-Semitism, but arises out of the immediate situation of Jewish – Christian rivalry around the year 100.

18. No one has ever seen God; the only Son, who is in the bosom of the Father, he has made him known.

Perhaps there is a final Gnostic touch in this concluding verse. The first part agrees with Gnosticism in saying that God is unseen and unknown. The second part acknowledges that God has sent a Revealer to make known the mystery of himself. The Revealer is now designated by the personal description, 'Son', first introduced in verse 14b, and this will continue through the rest of the gospel. But, as we have seen, 'Word' and 'Son' are metaphors with a good deal in common, and the transition from the one to the other is entirely smooth and scarcely noticeable.

The prologue, which we have examined in some detail, already foreshadows what is to follow in the body of the gospel. God has sent forth his Word or Son in the person of Jesus Christ. Through his words and deed, will be given a revelation of God superior both to that of Judaism and of any Gnostic sect which claims a revealer other than Jesus.

What then is this revelation that is brought by the Revealer, Jesus Christ? Here we must pay attention to an assertion made more than once by Bultmann and often quoted. One formulation of it runs thus: 'It turns out in the end that Jesus as the Revealer of God reveals nothing but that he is the Revealer.'[29] The same point is asserted in somewhat different words: 'John in his gospel presents only the fact (*das Dass*) of the revelation without describing its content (*ihr Was*).'[30] I must however declare frankly that I regard that statement that Jesus revealed nothing except that he was the Revealer as mere tautology. If anyone reveals anything, then *ipso facto* that person is a Revealer. We need say only, 'He revealed', and nothing is added to this by saying, 'He revealed that he is Revealer.' But when we strip down this pretentious form of words to 'He revealed', we see that something is still wrong. To 'reveal' is a transitive verb, and the sentence is incomplete until we supply an object for the verb. Unless *something* has been revealed, nobody has performed an act of revealing. In spite of what he says, Bultmann himself offers some content for the revelation.

But certainly John supplies a content, and we have already seen what it is. It is 'life,' in the sense of life in its fulness, the life of God mediated to human beings in Jesus Christ. We have noted already that in John's gospel Jesus is reported as saying that the purpose of his coming among men was 'that they might have life and have it abundantly' (10.10). The whole purpose of the gospel is summed up in what was originally its last verse, before the present chapter 21 was added: 'These [things] are written that you may believe that Jesus is the Christ, the son of God, and that believing you may have life in his name' (20.30). This theme of life, more-than-natural life, expressed in the words and deeds of Jesus, runs through all that range of metaphors which are applied to him. The water which the Samaritan woman drew from the well originally dug by Jacob becomes a symbol of the living water of Christ and he is likewise the living bread and the light of the world and the true vine (contrasted with the vine which symbolized Israel) and the good shepherd (contrasted with hirelings and false prophets). This is admirably summed up by Bultmann himself in his great commentary: 'Just as all the waters of the earth point to the one living water, and as all bread on the earth points to the one bread of life, and as all daylight points to the one light of the world, just as every earthly vine is contrasted with the "true" vine, so too every shepherd in the world is contrasted with the "good" shepherd.'[31] The revelation, we could say, is this: Jesus is the true Man who at every point draws the fulness of life from the Father, and who in turn mediates this fulness of life to those who believe in him. The revelation is not some esoteric *gnosis*, a secret formula which Jesus will reveal in words, but is just his own person.

But can we really say that the Christ of the Fourth Gospel is the 'true Man' or must we still be troubled by some lingering doubts of docetism? All that magnificent imagery of water, bread, light and so on is introduced by the formula, 'I am' (*ego eimi*), reminiscent of the name of God in the Old Testament: 'I am who I am' or simply 'I am' (Ex. 3.14). Would it not be megalomania for any truly human person to ascribe to himself all these descriptions which are appropriate to a divine being but scarcely to a human being? What man could say, 'I am the living bread', 'I am the light of the world', 'I am the true vine', and so on? Bultmann does make the point that the 'I am' formula had different usages, and that in the examples cited, we have a 'recognition formula' in which not the *ego* but the descriptive phrase is the subject, so that one could (or should) translate: 'The living bread – it is I', 'The light of the world – it is I,' 'The true vine – it is I'. These sentences do not answer the question, 'Who are you?' but the questions 'What is the living bread?' and so on. These phrases express deep human aspirations which find their focus in Jesus. I am not sure that this suggestion of Bultmann makes much difference to our understanding of the passage, but we may suppose that it was not Jesus himself but John or the Johannine community that applied these descriptions to him to express what he had meant for their faith.

But what are we to say of Christ's miracles in this gospel – changing water into wine, for instance, at the wedding party in Cana? Was not that 'God striding over the earth', a docetic figure and no real human being? But then we have to ask whether John intended such stories to be taken literally. He calls the miracles signs, and just like the metaphors already considered, they point beyond themselves to the only true miracle, the new life from God which Jesus is bringing. As John Fenton has expressed it, 'The glory of Jesus which is revealed in this story is not the power to change water into wine, but to give eternal life'.[32] The various signs in John, from the first one at Cana to the last one, the raising of Lazarus, are all pointers to the true life which Jesus has come to communicate.

There is one more question that has to be faced concerning the humanity of Jesus Christ in John's gospel, and that is the question of his pre-existence. If Jesus Christ were personally pre-existent, would not that undermine his true humanity? I think the stress lies on the word 'personally'. If we say with Paul, 'All this is from God' and 'God was in Christ', then we seem to be committed to believing that in some sense Jesus Christ was there from the beginning in the mind or purpose of God, and was coming to be in the long ages of history prior to the historical incarnation. But none of that takes away his true humanity. What would threaten the genuineness of his humanity would be the belief that Jesus consciously pre-existed in 'heaven', almost, if one may say so, like an actor in the wings waiting for the moment when he must go on to the stage of history. Some such idea does seem to be present in John, when Jesus prays to the Father: 'Glorify thou me in thy own presence with the glory which I had with thee before the world was made' (17.5). The language here is mythological, and if allowance is not made for this, then it does seem hard to reconcile with a true humanity in Jesus. But if we think that John's mythological language in this part of his gospel is intended to say neither more nor less than he has said more soberly in the prologue concerning the Word that has been from the beginning and that becomes flesh in Jesus Christ then the humanity of Christ is not impugned.

John's final distancing of his gospel from Gnosticism is to be found in his passion narrative, where he goes out of his way to insist that Jesus really died. Gnostic and docetic writers always, in one way or another, manipulated the passion story in such a way that Jesus, as an immortal divine or angelic being only seemed to die or changed places with someone who died in his place or flew off to the heavenly places or in some other way avoided death. John's passion story resembles in some respects the other gospels, but has one peculiar feature which seems to be there for the explicit purpose of saying that Jesus really died and was therefore really human. 'Since it was the day of preparation, in order to prevent the bodies from remaining on the cross on the sabbath (for that sabbath was a high day), the Jews asked Pilate that their legs might be broken, and that they might be taken away. So the soldiers came and broke the legs of the first, and of the other who had been crucified with him; but when they came to Jesus and saw that he was already dead, they did not break his legs. But one of the soldiers pierced his side with a spear, and at once there came out blood and water' (19.31–34). The piercing with the spear made sure that Jesus was dead. In this gospel of signs, the reference to blood and water is surely significant, but the symbolism is not clear. Some have seen in water and blood an allusion to baptism and the eucharist, still pointing therefore to the gift of the new life. On the other hand, the same symbolism in the first epistle seems to assert that Jesus came not just in the spirit but in the flesh: 'This is he who came by water and blood, Jesus Christ, not with the water only but with the water and the blood' (I John 5.6).

The gospel ends, as do Matthew and Luke, with stories of some resurrection appearances. We recognize again that because of the importance of the resurrection for an understanding of Jesus, the theme will have to be treated in detail at a later stage. But since the central theme of John's gospel has been life, sometimes called 'eternal life' because it is a life grounded in God and thus not destructible, this concept of eternal life has in this gospel already anticipated the resurrection hope, so that stories of the appearances of the risen Lord are of less importance here than in Matthew and Luke. Indeed, the entire ending of Jesus' story has been transformed in John. The series of events, from crucifixion to the giving of the Holy Spirit, is all compressed into a single event. The most violent of all the Johannine paradoxes is, 'I, when I am lifted up from the earth, will draw all men to myself' (John 12.32). Here crucifixion and exaltation are identified. The full meaning of eternal life is manifested in the death of Christ, and one has to ask whether any subsequent resurrection or ascension or second coming is needed. We shall come back to this question near the end of the book.[33]

6

Other New Testament Witnesses

In successive chapters we have examined the testimonies concerning the Christ-event offered by the letters of Paul, the synoptic gospels with Acts, and the Johannine literature. These together constitute the main sources for our knowledge of Jesus Christ and of the response which he evoked from his contemporaries. But they do not exhaust the New Testament witness, and we must take note also of some other New Testament writings, which either add to the testimonies already considered or present different views.

Hebrews

The most substantial of the writings still to be considered is the epistle to the Hebrews. It is an impressive composition with a sustained train of thought, and though it does not make any significant addition to our knowledge of the history of Jesus, it opens up a new theological interpretation of his person and work by applying to him the imagery of sacrifice and priesthood.

In view of the importance of Hebrews, it is surprising that virtually nothing is known about who wrote it, when it was written, or to whom it was addressed. These questions have all been hotly debated, and although many answers have been given, none of these has clearly established itself. From the epistle itself, we may infer that the author had a good knowledge of Jewish traditions and worship, and also that he was acquainted with Platonism, perhaps specifically with the thought of Philo of Alexandria. We may also infer that he was writing for Christians who, for some reason or other, were thinking of lapsing from their Christian faith into apostasy. The epistle therefore stresses that in Christ God has spoken in a new way and makes a unique and incomparable offer of salvation. These features of the epistle seem to point to a date fairly late in the first century. John Robinson argued for a much earlier date, for he believed that Hebrews describes the Temple worship as if it were still going on, and that if the epistle had been written after the destruction of Jerusalem in 70, it would almost certainly have mentioned that shattering event.[1] But fifty years before Robinson's view was expressed, A. H. McNeile had claimed that 'the references in the present tense to Old Testament worship afford no evidence that the Temple was still standing'.[2] In fact, the epistle is not referring to the Temple at all, but to the ritual appointed in Leviticus for the Day of Atonement. So there is no good reason for thinking that Hebrews was written earlier than 70. On the other hand, a considerably later date is suggested both by the fact that the threatened lapses into apostasy suggest that the initial attraction of Christianity was wearing off, and by the relatively sophisticated christology taught in this epistle. This last remark finds its endorsement in the opening verses of the epistle: 'In many and various ways God spoke of old to our fathers by the prophets; but in these last days he has spoken to us by a Son, whom he appointed heir of all things, through whom also he created the worlds' (1.12). This seems to announce right away a christology of the 'catabatic' kind, and indeed we cannot fail to notice the close resemblance between the teaching of these verses and that of John's prologue. In both cases, our introduction to Christ is not to a human being but to the divine 'Son' or 'Word' who comes from God and through whom the worlds were made. Hebrews continues to speak of Christ in the most exalted language. 'He reflects the glory of God and bears the very stamp of his nature, upholding the universe by his word of power' (1.3).

I do not believe that the charge of docetism has been brought against Hebrews so forcibly as it has against John, for the writer of Hebrews, as he develops his thought, makes more than one unequivocal assertion of Jesus' true humanity. (Of course, I did try to show that John also, if we do him justice, is no docetist). But both John and Hebrews have reversed the order that we found in Paul and Mark and the primitive preaching of Acts. John and Hebrews begin from the side of the divine, from the exalted Christ as the agent of God in creation, and only subsequently do they speak of his humanity. This procedure, as is well-known, established the pattern for the classic christological statements of the church, and the pattern was firmly in place before the end of the first century.

Yet even in the exalted opening verses of Hebrews, there are some things which do not quite fit the heavenly pattern and suggest process, history, growth, becoming. It is after he has done his work of taking away sin that the Son sits down at the right hand of the Father and is declared to be superior to the angels. He bears the stamp (*charakter*) of God's nature or being (*hypostasis*), and he seems to have done so from the beginning. Yet something has really happened in his earthly lifetime. Even if he has borne the impress of the divine nature from before the creation, there is real struggle and real overcoming of temptation before he sits down by the right hand of God, '*having become* as much superior to angels as the name he has obtained is more excellent than theirs' (1.4). Just what is being said here and whether it is quite self-consistent are points we can scarcely decide as yet. The difficulties may simply be variations on those that arise whenever we seek to relate the eternal and the temporal, heaven and earth, God and man. It may turn out to be the case that Hebrews is less uncompromisingly catabatic than it appeared to be at first sight, and that theologically it lies somewhere between the christologies of Paul and John. Hebrews does share with John the threefold christological pattern that we noted there – descent from heaven, sojourn on earth, return to heaven. But perhaps in Hebrews more happened in the middle stage (sojourn on earth) than is the case in John, so that in this respect Hebrews is closer to Paul.

The author of Hebrews seeks to reconcile the two sides of his account of Jesus through the concept of priesthood. Jesus is the great High Priest, and the work of a priest is to reconcile the human race to God. But in order to do that, he must somehow span the gap that separates God and man. On the one hand, the priest must be authorized by God. This is the point of the opening verses. There Jesus is called the Son, and we have noted more than once that in Jewish society, to be a son was at the same time to be the agent of the father. The prophets of old had also been agents of God, but Jesus, as the Son, is superior to the prophets. If we ask about the grounds for this superiority, the answer given is that he exhibits the impress or stamp of the divine nature, which is this writer's equivalent way of saying what Paul meant when he declared Jesus to be the 'image' of the invisible God. Jesus is Son because he is the archetypal man who exhibits, to the extent this is possible in a finite existent, the impress of the divine nature. Even if there is a sense in which the earthly Jesus in his historical existence brings to perfect expression the divine image, there is also a sense in which that image has been there from the beginning. To revert for a moment to the Pauline language, the last Adam is also the first Adam, or, better expressed, the ideal Adam, the idea which God had in mind when he said within himself, 'Let us make man in our own image and likeness'. So the Son is here described as the 'firstborn' or 'firstbegotten' (*prototokos*). We need not understand this in terms of personal pre-existence, and if it originally was understood in such a way, it would be necessary to demythologize it. What we have in the first two chapters of Hebrews is a valiant attempt by the author to present Jesus as (1) sent by God, originating in God and the agent of God, and as such already present in the mind or purpose of God before his appearing in world-history; and as (2) a wholly human being who is in solidarity with all men and women. The two points are made with equal firmness. One might say, of course, that the author's problem is the problem of all christology, and in the end it may prove insoluble. Almost inevitably, the balance is tipped one way or the other. Either we end up with a man, who may indeed tower in incomparable moral and spiritual superiority over his fellows, but only by a misplaced courtesy could such a man be called God; or else we have an alien being from heaven who, whatever human qualities he may manifest or simulate, is finally of a different origin and kind. As we shall see, it was a brilliant stroke on the part of the author of Hebrews to choose the concept of priesthood to illuminate the mystery of the person of Christ, for all the elements of a powerful analogy are present. But whether the author carries it through with clarity and consistency is at least questionable, and demands from us a close examination of his argument.

Let us then look once more over the beginnings of this text, and without ceasing to be critical, let us try to put upon it the most sympathetic interpretation it will bear. It opens with a contrast between Jesus and the prophets of Israel. For the author of Hebrews, as for John and indeed for the Bible in general, God is a God who speaks, a God who sends his word and communicates himself to his human creatures. So the story begins from God who is the source of the action, both in creation and in redemption. God has 'in these last days' done something new. He has often spoken through his prophets, but now he has spoken through a Son. The Son is obviously more than a prophet. He is of the same nature or is one in being with the Father. He is clearly meant to be understood as some kind of divine hypostasis, a distinct form of being within the Godhead. It is not clear what is meant by saying that God has 'appointed him the heir of all things'. The words seem to refer to an event which has taken place in time. But the other things said about Christ seem to be eternal truths about him. The Son has always existed, and through him God created the worlds, as he did through the Logos in John. Again, the Son is said to reflect the glory of God, to bear the very stamp of his nature and to uphold the universe by his word of power. All this, in contrast to the phrase about being appointed heir, puts the Son firmly on the divine or eternal side. But what may have been uppermost in the author's mind was the purpose of his whole epistle, to be a 'word of exhortation' (13.22) to those Christians who were thinking of apostatizing. The author is seeking to state as strongly as he can that the Son is superior to all who came before him. Though he has always been the Son and borne the very stamp of the divine nature, something new, real and of supreme importance has happened in the Son's sojourn in history, 'When he had made purification for sins, he sat down at the right hand of the Majesty on high, having become as much superior to angels as the name he has obtained is more excellent than theirs.' Surely he has always been entitled to sit at the right hand of the Majesty on high? And why say he 'has become' superior to angels, for the preceding verses give him a status that was always superior to angels, indeed, superior to every being except the Father? And what is meant by saying he 'has obtained' a name more excellent than theirs, for surely his name has always been more excellent?

The answer to these questions can surely be only that 'in these last days', when the firstborn Son has come into the world in the person of Jesus of Nazareth, he has in his historical existence achieved something new that puts him above angels and any other beings that could be imagined. The Son, up to this point, has existed only in God or in heaven, the archetypal man with every perfection, yet these perfections were ideal and not yet realized in a finite historical life or exposed to the hazards of such a life. In the earthly life of Jesus, the archetype and its ideal qualities are actualized in the context of finite and temporal existence, even when beset by temptations. So the Son can be said to 'have become' superior to angels and heavenly beings generally, and to 'have obtained' a more excellent name than theirs. He can even be said to have been 'made perfect' (*teleiotheis*): 'Although he was a Son, he learned obedience through what he suffered; and being made perfect, he became the source of eternal salvation to all who obey him, being designated by God a high priest after the order of Melchizedek' (5.9–10).

Perhaps there is something more to the discussion about angels and human beings in Hebrews. When God resolved to create a finite being in his own image and likeness, he did not create an angel. It was the human race that he created and elected for his purpose. The author of Hebrews cites no less than seven passages from the Old Testament in support of his contention that Jesus is superior to angels. Whether one can in every case accept his exegesis is debatable, but the summary of his discourse about angels is this: 'Are they not all ministering spirits sent forth to serve, for the sake of those who are to obtain salvation?' (1.14). Here he seems to be suggesting that human beings in general, not just the Son or Jesus, have a superior worth to angels, for God is concerned with the salvation of human beings and angels themselves exist to serve the cause of that salvation. God's purpose is not to put the world in subjection to angels (2.5) but to human beings. Admittedly, this has not yet happened, but a decisive breakthrough has been made by one human being, Jesus who is the Son. In his human historical life he has realized the ideal humanity that had been elected by God for the manifestation of the divine image and likeness. Jesus is thus the pioneer (*archegos*) of a new perfected humanity, no longer just an ideal in the realm of pre-existent possibility, but an actual man who has lived on earth. And Hebrews strongly emphasizes the close links between Jesus and the whole human race. He is said to taste death for everyone and to bring many sons and daughters to glory (2.9–10). And, 'he who sanctifies and those who are sanctified have all one origin. That is why he is not ashamed to call them brethren, saying, "I will proclaim thy name to my brethren, in the midst of the congregation I will praise thee"' (2.11–12). In bold language, the author goes on to say, 'Surely it is not with angels he is concerned, but with the descendants of Abraham. Therefore he had to be made like his brethren in every respect, so that he might become a merciful and faithful high priest in the service of God, to make expiation for the sins of the people. For because he himself has suffered and been tempted, he is able to help those who have been tempted' (2.16–18).

It has been suggested that in the two opening chapters of Hebrews the author is attacking an 'angel' christology, that is to say, an interpretation of the person of Christ as an angelic being. Whether in fact there was such a christology, or whether it is mentioned here, does not really matter. If there was, the author has given it the *coup de grace*, and the major blow is struck right at the end, when he points out that if Jesus Christ is to effect reconciliation as high priest, then he must have been fully and totally a human being, for only one who completely shared the human condition could be relevant to that condition and be a representative – a pioneering representative of his fellow human beings. I am not sure whether the argument of these opening chapters of Hebrews is entirely coherent, but I believe that the interpretation offered here makes a good deal of sense, and does so without making any concessions to a docetic reading. The initiative certainly lies with God – he is the sender of the Son and the ultimate author of salvation. Yet the Son is not a stranger from beyond, but one of us – 'he who sanctifies and those who are sanctified are all of one origin' (*ex henos pantes*). The earthly, human, historical experience is essential to the Son in his priestly work. The reasons have become clearer too for the belief that Hebrews teaches a christology that lies theologically (perhaps also chronologically) between Paul and John. We have seen parallels to both, and we have also seen the difficulties when one attempts to reconcile these two types of approach. But there is still much more material to consider before we can claim to have heard the witness of Hebrews.

We have to heed the author's own injunction: 'Consider Jesus, the apostle and high priest of our confession' (3.1). We have to consider in detail the meaning of priesthood, which is taken in Hebrews as the clue to the person of Christ. The author holds firmly to the two poles of priesthood, not always easily harmonized – the pole of authorization, of being sent from God (expressed in the verse just quoted by the word 'apostle'), and the equally important pole of being in solidarity with those to whom the apostle is sent. It may be best to begin with this second pole, as Hebrews lays great stress upon it and we must not underrate it, because it is a vital corrective to the exalted language at the beginning of the epistle. So we are told that 'we have not a high priest who is unable to sympathize with our weaknesses, but one who in every respect has been tempted as we are, yet without sin' (5.15). This seems to be a quite unequivocal assertion of the humanity of Jesus. He is tempted as all human beings are, as the synoptic gospels plainly state, and as even John seems to acknowledge in an apparent allusion to the Gethsemane scene. Hebrews, of course, makes an important qualification – he 'was tempted as we are, yet without sin'. How this 'yet without sin' is to be interpreted raises difficult questions and shows the acute difficulty in reconciling the two aspects of Christ's priestly being. If he is without sin, is he really participating in the human condition? But if we do not say this, then can he truly represent God or be an apostle from God to the human race? This question of what is called in a strangely negative way the 'sinlessness' of Jesus Christ will need to be faced at a later stage,[3] but as a provisional answer we may say that sin is not of the essence of humanity, it has no place in that 'archetypal' man conceived in the mind of God when he resolved to create a finite being in his image and likeness, so that even if sin is universally present in the human race as an empirical fact, there is not a contradiction in speaking, as Hebrews does, of a human being who is 'without sin'. Further on, Hebrews stresses Jesus' vulnerability to suffering. 'In the days of his flesh, Jesus offered up tears and supplications, with loud cries and tears, to him who was able to save him from death, and he was heard for his godly fear. Although he was a Son, he learned obedience through what he suffered; and being made perfect, he became the source of eternal salvation to all who obey him, being designated by God a high priest after the order of Melchizedek' (5.7–10). The first sentence in this quotation may refer to the Gethsemane scene, or possibly to the cry of dereliction from the cross, but in either case it indicates a degree of human suffering in Jesus that puts him on a level with those who have known pain and adversity at their most acute. The second sentence is even more striking in its assertion of the finitude of Jesus' being. His was no ready-made righteousness imported into earth from the heavenly realms. It was a righteousness forged in the struggles with affliction and temptation – indeed, could there be any other genuine kind of righteousness? Jesus must be counted among those of whom the hymn writer declared, 'Many a blow and biting sculpture polished well those stones elect'. So Hebrews says of this high priest, 'He can deal gently with the ignorant and wayward, since he himself is beset with weakness' (5.2). Perhaps we have to say the same about God himself, as was suggested to us by Abraham Heschel's claim that there is *pathos* in God.[4] But certainly one has to allow for *pathos* in the priest, and Hebrews does this.

Enough has been said then to show that Hebrews does not deny the humanity of Jesus Christ, even though it begins from the thought of the Son who was God's partner in creation and bore the imprint of the divine being. His relation to the Father was no static or eternal property laid up securely in the heavens, but had to be realized in history in the face of all the sufferings and temptations which afflict mortal men and women.

But a priest is not complete simply by sharing in the human lot. His office is to bring something from God into that human condition, to bring grace and hope and empowerment. We have seen that different New Testament witnesses have chosen different ways of expressing this 'extra' which Jesus brought with him and which differentiated him from the mass of fallen mankind. All are agreed with Paul's belief that God was in Christ, but they express it in diverse ways, theological, mythological, even philosophical. Mark tells of the descent of the Spirit on Jesus at his baptism; Matthew and Luke do the same but add the story of a virgin birth by the power of the Holy Spirit; John traces the origin of Jesus back to the Word that was with God in the beginning, and says that his birth was the result not just of human agency but of God. A quite different and novel direction is taken by Hebrews. As we have seen, the controlling image for Hebrews is that of the high priest. More specifically, it is the legendary figure of Melchizedek to whom the writer turns. According to Genesis, Abraham, on returning victoriously from a battle, was met by Melchizedek, described as king of Salem and priest of God most high (El Elyon). This Melchizedek brought to Abraham bread and wine, and also blessed him in the name of El Elyon. Abraham in return gave him 'a tenth of everything' (Gen. 14.17–20). Melchizedek is mentioned once again in the Old Testament, in Psalm 110, which has the appearance of being a coronation or enthronement psalm. It represents God as saying to the king, 'You are a priest for ever, after the order of Melchizedek' (Ps. 110.4). Unfortunately the text of the psalm is corrupt, and the meaning cannot be established with certainty. Nevertheless, the entire psalm was seized on very early by the nascent church as a messianic prediction, and applied to Jesus Christ. In the New Testament, it is quoted by Matthew, Acts, I Corinthians, Ephesians, as well as in Hebrews. But it is only in Hebrews that the verse concerning Melchizedek is cited. Hebrews makes the point that no one can arrogate priesthood to himself. A priest must be appointed and authorized, ultimately by God. 'For every high priest chosen from among men is appointed to act on behalf of men in relation to God. And one does not take the honour upon oneself, but he is called by God, just as Aaron was. So also Christ did not exalt himself to be made a high priest, but was appointed by him who said to him, "Thou art a priest for ever, after the order of Melchizedek"' (5.1, 4, 5 and 7). The writer of Hebrews elaborates on the figure of Melchizedek, partly by inference from the passage in Genesis, partly, it must be said, from pious imagination. King of Salem (a place-name, possibly Jerusalem) is allegorically interpreted 'king of peace (*shalom*),' while Melchizedek is rendered 'king of righteousness (*sedeq*)', and both titles are applied to Jesus. It is argued further that Melchizedek must have been superior to Abraham, for he blessed Abraham, and 'it is beyond dispute that the inferior is blessed by the superior' (7.7). Furthermore, Abraham paid him tithes. From the absence of any details about Melchizedek in the Genesis account, Hebrews claims that 'he is without father or mother or genealogy, and has neither beginning of days nor end of life, but resembling the Son of God, he continues a priest for ever' (7.3).

This characterization of Melchizedek is then used to establish the superiority of Christ's priesthood over the levitical priesthood of Israel. That levitical priesthood was tied to members of the tribe of Levi, that is to say, it was passed on through physical descent. Melchizedek does not have this physical link, he is without father or mother, and this is taken to mean that his priesthood derives directly from God. The fact that his priesthood was recognized and honoured by Abraham, proves its superiority over the levitical priesthood, for Abraham treated him as a superior, yet Abraham was the forefather of the Levites and, indeed, of all Israel. But the priesthood of Jesus was like that of Melchizedek, for did not God say to the messiah-to-be in Psalm 110, 'Thou art a priest for ever, after the order of Melchizedek'?

The argument used here by the author of Hebrews seems far-fetched to a modern reader, but it would not seem so at the time when it was written and it was believed that the Hebrew scriptures contained infallible predictions of events to come. Apart from the argument, however, we might be willing to believe that Christ's priestly office was indeed bestowed by God and had nothing to do with birth or ancestry, just as Matthew in his gospel indicates that descent from David is not important (22.41–46) – in spite of the genealogy at the beginning of the gospel!

Something like a modern parallel to the argument about the priesthood of Jesus in Hebrews is supplied by the famous *Tract One* of John Henry Newman. He is reminding the clergy of the Church of England that their priesthood does not depend on state recognition or university degrees, but is God's gift.

> There are some who rest their divine mission on their own unsupported assertion; others, who rest it on their popularity; others, on their success; and others, who rest it on their temporal distinctions. This last case has, perhaps, been too much our own; I fear we have neglected the real ground on which our authority is built – *our apostolical descent*. We have been born not of blood, nor of the will of the flesh, nor of the will of man, but of God.[5]

Hebrews now proceeds to speak in more detail of this unique priesthood of Jesus Christ, and to show how it differs, not only in origin but in its exercise, from the levitical priesthood, and in what respects it is superior. The function of a high priest is said to be to offer gifts and sacrifices to God on behalf of the people. The priests of the old dispensation offered their sacrifices day by day throughout their lifetime. The new high priest differs from them in two respects, which at first sight may seem to contradict one another. He offers not repeated sacrifices, but one sacrifice once offered; and it is said several times over that his priesthood is permanent, not just for a lifetime, after which another will succeed him, but for ever. But if he is high priest for ever, there must be a sense in which he offers 'gifts and sacrifices' for ever, that being the function which defines priesthood. Here we may notice a difference in interpretation which appears to depend less on exegesis than on the different approaches of Protestant and Catholic scholars. The former stress the 'once-for-allness' and unrepeatability of the sacrifice of Calvary and sometimes suggest that Jesus 'sitting' alongside God means that he was finished with sacrificing. Catholics teach rather that the Son continues 'a priest for ever' and that the sacrifice of Calvary, though unrepeatable, continues as an abiding reality not tied to a moment of time. So Myles Bourke comments, 'That Jesus is described as seated (8.1) does not mean that his sacrifice is "done and over" [as claimed by James Moffatt]. The author is using the imagery of Psalm 110 and is dealing with the double role, royal and priestly, that the exalted Jesus exercises. His being seated applies to his kingly status, and the metaphor should not be used as an argument against his present offering as ministering priest.'[6] More than that, there are suggestions in the epistle that the eternal self-giving of Jesus takes place beyond space and time altogether, in 'the inner shrine behind the curtain, where Jesus has gone as a forerunner on our behalf, having become a high priest for ever, after the order of Melchizedek' (6.19–20). The idea is echoed later: 'We have such a high priest, one who is seated at the right hand of the throne of the Majesty in heaven, a minister in the sanctuary of the true tent which is set up not by man but by the Lord' (8.1–2). The philosophy of Plato probably lies behind these ideas, as in the related claim that the tabernacle and the levitical sacrifices were only a shadow of the real thing. In modern times, the idea of an eternal sacrifice in the heart of God was taken up and given powerful expression by Hegel,[7] and his ideas have in turn reappeared in the theology of E. Jüngel.[8]

We may think, however, that the comparison in Hebrews between the old sacrifices and the new one is more successful on the negative side than on the affirmative. Few would disagree with the statement that 'it is impossible that the blood of bulls and goats should take away sins' (10.4), but they might still have difficulty in seeing how the new sacrifice of Christ avails while the old sacrifices failed. Is not this whole idea of sacrifice incredible? No doubt the application of the idea of sacrifice to the death of Christ is a controversial matter, and we have to be very careful about it if we are not to fall into primitive and even immoral ideas about God and about what reconciliation to God would mean. We have already briefly discussed the problem of the death of Jesus and distances ourselves from such interpretations as would see that death as a 'propitiatory sacrifice'. I believe that the teaching in Hebrews does take us a few steps nearer to a better understanding. First of all, it makes clear (as do other New Testament writers also) that Christ's death was voluntary. Just to what extent it was voluntary or why this voluntary character seems to be a theological requirement, are questions that will need to be investigated further.[9] But we may say provisionally that if the notion of sacrifice can be purged of morally dubious associations, so that it can find an acceptable place in Christian belief, then it can appear only as *self-sacrifice* or ultimate self-giving. There is, of course, nothing of this in the sacrifice of animals. The very idea of human sacrifice fills us with horror, unless it were shown as the willing or even heroic self-immolation of a person for his or her friends, fellow-citizens, or some great cause. Surely Hebrews is quite clear that these considerations are applicable to the death of Jesus. It is declared that 'he offered up himself' (7.27). This idea becomes associated in Hebrews with a verse from Psalm 40, a verse which later writers on the atonement have taken up: 'Sacrifices and offerings thou hast not desired, but a body thou hast prepared for me; in burnt offerings and sin offerings thou hast taken no pleasure. Then I said, "Lo, I have come to do thy will, O God", as it is written of me in the roll of the book' (Ps. 40.6–8 as quoted from Septuagint in Heb. 10.5–7). The teaching of Hebrews at this point is very much like that of Mark's narrative from the words about Jesus' giving his life a ransom for many on to the scene in Gethsemane where he submits to the will of the Father, or the Christ-hymn in Philippians leading up to obedience to the death of the cross.[10] If we use the word 'sacrifice', it means in all three cases the costly doing of God's will.

But Jesus, we have seen, is for Hebrews the pioneer (*archegos*) who has opened up a way for his brothers and sisters. 'Therefore, since we have confidence to enter the sanctuary by the blood of Jesus, by the new and living way which he opened for us through the curtain, that is, through his flesh, and since we have a great high priest over the house of God, let us draw near with a true heart in full assurance of faith' (10.19–22). Believers are invited to offer themselves with Christ, just as in Mark he tells the disciples that if they would come after him, they must take up the cross. It is not made quite clear in Hebrews just what is the relation of the Christian believers to Jesus or how they are joined with him in his sacrificial way. The use of the word 'pioneer' (which occurs twice in the epistle) in reference to Jesus' saving work might suggest that he is considered primarily as an exemplar. He blazes the trail so that others may follow after him. But that would hardly do justice to the images of 'priest' and 'mediator' which are also applied to him. He is the sacrificial victim as well as the priest who offers, and this points to a deeper relation than that of an example to be followed. Faith is important – both the faith of Jesus by which he pursued his obedient path and the faith which he himself awakens. But how is this faith mediated?

Again, commentators are divided. Catholics have seen eucharistic allusions in the later parts of Hebrews, Protestants have disputed this as it might seem to suggest a *repetition* of the sacrifice of Calvary, which Hebrews clearly rejects. But Catholic teaching does not say there is a repetition. The word used by the council of Trent was 're-presentation' (*repraesentatio*) which can be readily reconciled with what we claimed above about the eternal or perduring character of Christ's sacrifice, and with Paul's words that 'as often as you eat this bread and drink the cup, you proclaim (*katanggellete*) the Lord's death until he comes' (I Cor. 11.26).

One has to say that there is nothing in the actual words of Hebrews that refers unmistakably to the eucharist – indeed, it even omits to mention that Melchizedek brought forth bread and wine when he went to meet Abraham. Also, the author of Hebrews, like many other very early Christians, seems to have believed strongly that there is no forgiveness for sins committed after baptism, and although the inference is not quite clear, this might be held to conflict with belief in an eternal sacrifice. Of course, such a rigorist view seems to conflict with Christ's own teaching as reported by Matthew (18.22) that forgiveness should not be limited. Nevertheless, this was the general view of the matter, and only began to be relaxed a generation after Hebrews when The Shepherd of Hermas, recognizing the weakness of human nature, allowed the possibility of repentance for *one* sin after baptism.[11]

On the other side, it has to be said that the lack of an explicit reference to the eucharist may be deliberate. It could have been part of the policy of protecting the Christian mysteries from profane misunderstanding. We may remember that Jeremias accounted in this way for the fact that John's gospel, though it tells of the Last Supper, has no mention of the institution of the eucharist on that occasion.[12] So we find Schillebeeckx making a similar point about the reticence of Hebrews, when he asks: 'Is this an instance of the *disciplina arcani*, the injunction to silence?'[13] Certainly the eucharist could not have been unknown to either the writer or the readers of Hebrews, certainly too there are expressions which seem to allude to the eucharist, but nothing is said that puts the matter beyond all reasonable doubt. When we read, 'Let us continually offer up a *sacrifice of praise* to God' (13.15), the expression 'sacrifice of praise' is familiar to us from later liturgies – the *sacrificium laudis* of the Tridentine canon and the 'sacrifice of praise and thanksgiving' of the Anglican liturgy. One might also mention 'the blood of the eternal covenant' words which can hardly fail to recall the words of institution, 'This cup is the new covenant in my blood' (I Cor. 11.25). There is another verse which remains problematic: 'We have an altar from which those who serve the tent have no right to eat' (13.10). What is this altar? Perhaps the Christians had been taunted with the complaint that they had no altar or sacrifice. This is the answer that Hebrews gives. But what does the author have in mind? Is the altar Calvary itself? Or is it that invisible altar in the heavenly shrine? Or is it a reference to the eucharist? No dogmatic answer can be given, and as we are dealing here with imagery – and cryptic imagery at that – it is not unreasonable to suppose that all three possibilities are embraced in the allusion. In that case, the worship of the church on earth can be seen, in the words of Schillebeeckx, as 'a sharing of the heavenly liturgy of Jesus'.[14]

This last remark helps to ease another controverted point in relation to Hebrews. It has often been pointed out that in this epistle priestly language is used about Jesus Christ and about the discredited levitical priesthood, but never of Christian ministers, and this has sometimes been used as an argument to show that the use of priestly or sacerdotal language for Christian ministers is inappropriate. It is of course well-known that such language did not come into common use until two or three centuries after Hebrews was written. It could hardly have been otherwise, for the vocabulary of priesthood was associated with either Jewish or pagan worship and sacrifices. Christian ministry is modelled on the ministry of Christ, and to understand him as the high priest, as Hebrews does, is to open the door to the eventual application of priestly language to Christian ministry. In the words of the Anglican–Roman Catholic 'Agreed Statement' on ministry:

> The priestly sacrifice of Jesus was unique, as is also his continuing high priesthood. Despite the fact that in the New Testament ministers are never called 'priests' (*hiereis*), Christians came to see the priestly role of Christ reflected in these ministers and used priestly terms in describing them. Because the eucharist is the memorial of the sacrifice of Christ, the action of the presiding minister in reciting the words of Christ at the last supper and distributing to the assembly the holy gifts is seen to stand in a sacramental relation to what Christ himself did in offering his own sacrifice.[15]

This discussion of eucharist and priesthood, though it is helpful for understanding the main christological teaching of Hebrews, should not make us think that the epistle is narrowly ecclesiological. In the later parts of it, a universalistic note is struck. Again, one has to speak cautiously, for more than one interpretation is possible. The central purpose of the writer has been to set forth Jesus as the pioneer of salvation, the great high priest for all times. But in the great pageant of the men and women of faith whom Hebrews passes in review, the list does not begin, as we might have expected, with Abraham, but goes back to legendary or even mythological figures. 'By faith Abel offered to God a more acceptable sacrifice than Cain . . . By faith Enoch was taken up so that he should not see death . . . By faith Noah took heed and constructed an ark for the saving of his household' (11.4–7). The significance of this was picked up by John Baillie, who claimed that this passage shows us 'the earliest Christian way of recognizing and explaining the common elements that pervade all the religions and therefore all the moral traditions of mankind'.[16]

It is important not to miss this universalist moment in the epistle, for the author has spent so much of his time showing the superiority of Christianity over Judaism that we might get the impression that he is very narrowly sectarian. But the polemic is not directed against Jews as such – they figure very prominently among the exemplars of faith – but is incidental to the aim of confirming Christians in the new unique way of salvation provided by Christ.

I Peter

The New Testament writing known as the first epistle of Peter (though few scholars nowadays would uphold the tradition of Petrine authorship) may come from roughly the same time as Mark's gospel, and may be considered at this point because some of its teaching fits in rather well with the teaching of Hebrews. Thus, although I Peter does not use the term 'high priest' in relation to Jesus Christ, it does speak of him as the 'chief shepherd' (an expression also found in Hebrews 13.20) and as the shepherd and guardian or bishop (*episkopos*) of your souls (2.25). I Peter also delineates the other side of this relationship, not explicitly described in Hebrews, though, as we have seen, it may be considered implicit. I mean, the participation in Christ's priestly or pastoral office that belongs to Christian believers. Here in I Peter the church is called a 'holy priesthood, to offer spiritual sacrifices acceptable to God through Jesus Christ' (2.5). Again (in a rough translation of language applied to Israel in Exodus 19.6) the Church is called 'a chosen race, a royal priesthood, a holy nation, God's own people' (2.9). However, at the risk of mixing metaphors, I Peter has incorporated these ideas into a very different way of picturing the relation between Christ and his church: Christ is compared to the cornerstone of a building, and the members of the church are like 'living stones built into a spiritual house' (2.5).

Though the word 'sacrifice' appears in the quotations made above, I Peter does not present a theology of Christ's sacrifice as Hebrews does. But I Peter does devote much attention to the related topic of suffering. The letter appears to have come from a time when Christians were suffering in one of the outbreaks of persecution that were now befalling them in various parts of the Roman Empire. The writer encourages them in their trials by telling them that they are sharing in the sufferings of Christ, and that this is nothing strange but a part of true Christian discipleship. 'Rejoice in so far as you share Christ's sufferings, that you may also rejoice and be glad when his glory is revealed' (4.13). It would seem that when this document was composed, arguments about a suffering messiah[17] had long ago been settled and the picture of the suffering servant in deutero-Isaiah (to which there are clear allusions in 2.21–24) was generally accepted as a prediction of the fate of Christ. But I Peter makes a very important point about suffering, a point that was not always grasped by subsequent generations of Christians. The point is that there is nothing desirable or praiseworthy in suffering as such. There is no masochistic glorification of suffering for its own sake. Much of our suffering comes about as a result of our own misdeeds, so it is deserved suffering and really self-inflicted suffering. In the view of I Peter, such suffering does not call for any respect. But innocent suffering, where it is borne with patience and without anger, can and does work for the benefit both of the church and of those to whom its mission is directed. Christ suffered for the benefit of others, and such suffering is part of the vocation of the Christian, it is one way in which Christians are united with Christ. 'For to this you have been called, because Christ also suffered for you, leaving you an example, that you should follow in his steps. He committed no sin; no guile was found on his lips. When he was reviled, he did not revile in return; when he suffered, he did not threaten; but he trusted to him who judges justly. He himself bore our sins in his body on the tree, that we might die to sin and live to righteousness. By his wounds, you have been healed' (2.21–24).

There is another passage of christological import in I Peter, though it is so obscure and marginal that I might have been excused if I had passed it over, had the idea with which it seems to deal not managed to get included in the Apostles' Creed and so passed into theology. I mean, the purely mythological notion of Christ's descent into hell, in the interval between his death on the cross and his resurrection. This presupposes the ancient cosmology, according to which there was a vast cavern under the earth, forming the abode of the departed shades. The words which refer (or are supposed to refer) to the descent into hell are these: 'Christ also died for sins once for all, the righteous for the unrighteous, that he might bring us to God, being put to death in the flesh but made alive in the spirit; in which he went and preached to the spirits in prison, who formerly did not obey, when God's patience waited in the days of Noah, during the building of the ark, in which a few, that is, eight persons, were saved through water' (3.18–20). The allusion to being saved through water is linked by the writer to baptism, and later he comes back to the theme of these verses by saying, 'This is why the gospel was preached even to the dead, that though judged in the flesh according to men, they might live according to God in the spirit' (4.6).

All this is so obscure that there has been endless dispute among scholars about what it may mean. Among recent writers, Pannenberg and Schillebeeckx[18] have, in my opinion, had most success in making sense of the passage.

I would like to make the following points. (1) The beginning of the passage makes it clear that it is continuing the earlier theme, that the innocent sufferings of Christ bring benefit even to the undeserving. (2) Christ's purpose in this episode is therefore salvific. He was not going (as some commentators have suggested) to announce to the 'spirits in prison' that they had been finally frustrated (that would surely have been a somewhat malicious act) but to bring them the good news that salvation had been gained. Schillebeeckx points out that the verb used for Christ's communication to the spirits, 'preached' (ekeruxen), is 'a word which is always used in the New Testament in connection with the message of salvation.'[19] (3) On the question of who were these 'spirits in prison', I do not think they were 'fallen angels', as some have claimed, but sinful men who had died in their sins. Likewise Pannenberg thinks that the spirits were 'the shades of disobedient men who had died at the time [of the flood]'.[20] Whether or not the writer of the epistle was quite clear in his own mind, he is in fact coming very close to universalism. The people of Noah's time were supposed to have been particularly wicked, so if Jesus went and preached salvation to them, could anybody be finally left out? And even if one went back to the unlikely idea that the spirits in prison are the fallen angels, then an even more universalistic message seems to come through – even the demons will be saved!

As was said above, the passage in I Peter which we have been discussing is so obscure and also so fragmentary that very little can be made of it, and one is constantly in danger of reading into it later speculations. Nevertheless, there are some New Testament parallels which help toward understanding the issues. The letter to the Ephesians (to be considered in the next section) says parenthetically of Christ's ascension: 'In saying, "He ascended," what does it mean but that he had also descended into the lower parts of the earth? He who descended is he who also ascended far above all heavens, that he might fill all things' (4.9–10). We might also consider Paul's mention of an apparently common custom in the earliest days of Christianity, the custom of baptism by proxy for those who had died. 'What do people mean by being baptized on behalf of the dead? If the dead are not raised at all, why are people baptized on their behalf?' (I Cor. 15.29). This practice of being baptized on behalf of the dead does not, of course, relate directly to the belief that Jesus had preached to the spirits in prison, but it belongs to the same circle of ideas and shows clearly what lay behind them – the desire to extend the benefits of Christ to those who had lived and died before his time. In our study of Hebrews, we have already seen how Christ's self-sacrifice was understood as a once-for-all event, yet one having eternal significance that would stand for all future generations. But if it was to stand eternally in the future, what about the past? Could it not be visualized as also extending to all those generations of men and women who had lived in the time before Christ? This is one of the things that concerned the writer of I Peter, and though his ideas are, to our minds, wildly mythological, we can have some appreciation for the motives that lay behind this myth of Christ's descent into the underworld (if that is indeed the correct interpretation of the epistle's cryptic statements). When we come to the systematic part of this book, we shall take up the subject again.[21]

Ephesians

When in Chapter 3 we studied the christology of Paul, I deliberately omitted from consideration the epistle to the Ephesians, although for about eighteen centuries it had been included in the Pauline corpus. But the question of Pauline authorship has become a matter of dispute in modern times. I have to note that a majority of the New Testament scholars whom I have been citing and whose work seems to me especially helpful have come to the view that Paul was not the author of Ephesians, and I find their arguments persuasive. Of course, it is not denied that the epistle comes out of the Pauline churches, and much of it virtually recapitulates teaching from Colossians and other epistles of Paul. But there are significant differences from those epistles which are almost universally recognized to be Paul's own. Some of these differences are linguistic – differences in vocabulary and, perhaps even more obvious, in style, for Ephesians has many long involved sentences which make its arguments even harder to follow than most of Paul's.

In addition, there are changes in the subject-matter. The return of Christ, so prominent in the early epistles, is not mentioned. Instead, there is emphasis on the church as a continuing institution, suggesting that the epistle comes from a time after the strong eschatological expectations of the early Christians had subsided. The sufferings and death of Christ are de-emphasized, and instead there is stressed his exaltation and cosmic significance. Though there can be no certainty, the balance of evidence seems to come down against the traditional belief that the epistle is the work of Paul himself. But this in no way detracts from the value of the epistle, which offers a fascinating glimpse of the church as it existed in the second half of the first century, situated on the very margins of society and yet already bringing about a transformation of society as it gathered into its community those who had thitherto been divided by enmity. It would not be going too far to say that this epistle gives clear testimony to a new phase in the Christ-event, another step toward the universalizing of the new humanity that had been inaugurated in Christ and his immediate circle of disciples and was now spreading into the wider world.

According to this epistle, God's purpose for his creatures has been revealed in Christ. It is, to bring together in a unified community the many rival groups of human beings, whose differences are typified by the division between Jews and Gentiles. 'Before the foundation of the world' (1.4) God had already destined these warring groups to be brought into unity in Christ. As for Christ himself, he is a cosmic figure, and the church is a cosmic or universal community: God has 'raised [Christ] from the dead, and made him sit at his right hand in the heavenly places, far above all rule and authority and power and dominion, and above every name that is named, not only in this age but in that which is to come; and he has put all things under his feet and has made him the head over all things for the church, which is his body, the fulness of him who fills all in all' (1.20– 23). Though some of the language here is reminiscent of the Christ-hymn in Philippians, the teaching of Ephesians seems to go well beyond Philippians (at least, as we interpreted it) in making Christ a glorious cosmic figure. Also the church here seems to be invested with an aura of glory. It is the body, of which Christ is the head, and so its relation to Christ is very close. The metaphor of the body applied to the church is common in the epistles of Paul (Romans, I Corinthians, Colossians) but it is particularly so in Ephesians. In addition to the passage quoted above, there is mention of Christ's reconciling Jew and Gentile 'in one body through the cross, thereby bringing the hostility to an end' (2.16); Christ has given his gifts 'for building up the body of Christ, until we all attain to the unity of faith and of the knowledge (*epignosis*) of the Son of God, to mature (*teleios*) manhood, to the measure of the stature of the fulness (*pleroma*) of Christ' (4.12–13); the goal of the process is that 'we are to grow up in every way into him who is the head, into Christ, from whom the whole body, joined and knit together by every joint with which it is supplied, when each part is working properly, makes bodily growth and upbuilds itself in love' (4.15–16); finally, we are told that Christ loves the church 'because we are members of his body' (5.30). Two other related metaphors are used to express the closeness between Christ and the church. One we have already met in I Peter. It is the metaphor of Christians being built up into a holy temple, 'built upon the foundation of the apostles and prophets, Christ Jesus himself being the cornerstone' (2.20). The other is that of the church as the bride of Christ (5.12–27).

The idea of the church as the body of Christ, being steadily built up toward completion as new members are added, has been seen by Bultmann as yet another instance of Gnostic influence. Certainly, some of the Greek words used (and indicated in the quotations above) are common in the Gnostic vocabulary. More importantly, there was a Gnostic myth which depicted salvation as the gathering together of the souls of the elect so as to build the statue of the 'primal man'. A version of this myth is given by Hans Jonas as follows:

> At the end, when the cosmos is dissolved, this same Thought-of-Life (a title used for the primal man) shall gather himself in and shall form his self in the shape of the Last Statue. His net is his Living Spirit, for with his Spirit he shall catch the Light and the Life that is in all things, and build it on to his own body . . . Then, when this Last Statue is perfected in all its members, then it shall escape and be lifted up out of that great struggle through the Living Spirit, its Father, who comes and fetches the members out of the dissolution and end of all things.[22]

Undoubtedly there are some remarkable resemblances between this Gnostic excerpt and some of the passages in Ephesians. But as was the case with some of the other alleged Gnostic influences that have come to our notice, there is a serious problem about dating. The Gnostic quotation comes from the third century, though Jonas believes that it represents an archaic level of Gnostic thought.[15] Bultmann is one of the scholars who denies that Ephesians is the work of Paul himself, so he would push its date forward into the later decades of the first century. But even making it as late as possible – the limit would be around 90, since the epistle is quoted by Clement of Rome about the year 95 – it would still be much earlier than the Gnostic speculations about the Last Statue. At the very most, one might allow that some fragment of mythology concerning the primal man lay behind both Ephesians and the Gnostic teaching, but one would have to add immediately that the mythology was used very differently in each case. In Ephesians, the cruder elements have been eliminated, and the idea that the body is being built up *in love* has no parallel in the alleged Gnostic counterpart.

Another point in the christological teaching of Ephesians calls for comment. When we were discussing I Peter and its curious teaching about Christ's descent into hell and his preaching to the 'spirits in prison', I mentioned that there might be similar teaching in Ephesians. Speaking of the ascension of Christ, Ephesians adds: 'In saying, "He ascended," what does it mean but that he had also descended into the lower parts of the earth? He who descended is he who also ascended far above all the heavens, that he might fill all things' (4.9–10). Some of the language here – 'the lower parts of the earth' and 'far above all the heavens' seem to suggest an all-encompassing cosmic journey, from the highest heaven or beyond it to the depth of the underworld, and back again. Such an interpretation would consort well with Ephesians' vision of the cosmic Christ who fills all in all (2.22) – his dominion reaches even into hell. This is a permissible interpretation and may be correct, but many scholars take the view that there is no reference to the underworld here but simply to the descent to earth of the pre-existent Christ and his return to the heavenly places. That would mean that the writer, whoever he was, had a christology closer to John than to Paul, as we have interpreted them.

Summary and Assessment of Results

In this chapter and in the three that preceded it we have been passing in review the New Testament witness to Jesus Christ and the Christ-event, and it hardly needs to be said that the New Testament is the only substantial witness that we have concerning these matters. It is true that a handful of secular historians – Tacitus, Suetonius and possibly Josephus – makes brief mention of Jesus, but they add nothing of importance to our knowledge of him, though their mention of him could be reckoned a confirmation that he really existed at the time and place assigned to him by the New Testament. However, since no serious historian doubts this, virtually nothing is added to the New Testament witness.

But what are we to make of that witness itself, now it has been set before us? Probably the first thing that strikes us is the enormous diversity of the testimony given. The second Adam of Paul, the miracle-worker of Mark, the pre-existent Word of John, the priestly figure of Hebrews, together with many other characterizations, some more and some less important – how can these all elucidate this one man, Jesus of Nazareth, or even that group of men and women who were caught up in the Christ-event? Should we, in spite of the formidable difficulties, look for a thread of unity that would bring together all these diverse images of Jesus? Or would that be a falsification of the evidence, an artificial synthesis imposed on all this varied material? Or should we select one of the interpretations and try to show that it has a coherence and a claim to truth superior to what the others can show? But what would be our principle of selection? Would it be only a 'hunch', an intuition that in this or that formulation, we had caught a ring of truth? And could we then simply forget about the other ways of seeing Christ? To some extent, this is what actually happened in the centuries after the New Testament, when increasingly a metaphysical or ontological understanding of Christ came to dominate the theological scene, and displaced other possibilities. But these early attempts by the New Testament writers to express what they understood as the significance of Jesus Christ took the form of images, pictures, metaphors, such as messiah, Son, High Priest, Word and so on. These were not strictly defined concepts, but allusive ideas with somewhat blurred edges. When one is dealing with images of this sort, it is not desirable to set up one of them as normative, and to eliminate all the others. Even if it is not obvious how some of these images can be reconciled, we may still need a plurality of images to illuminate the subject-matter. Theology, and specifically christology, make use of concepts, but never altogether dispense with images. Images may be related paradoxically, and we did indeed take note of the use of paradox in the Johannine writings. In paradox, there is an element of contradiction, but the paradoxical ideas do not simply cancel one another out but correct and enhance one another and point beyond themselves to something which neither can express outside of the paradoxical relation.

We have also to remember that the New Testament did not come into being all at once. The writings included in it were produced over a period of, let us say, sixty years. Some of the differences as between authors or even within a single author are explicable in terms of the development of thought. We may regret that the New Testament does not give us what it was once supposed to give – eyewitness accounts of the life of Jesus. But is this really so regrettable? If an event or a person has any depth or significance that is more than transitory, it cannot be appreciated in an instant. Time and reflection are needed. A famous American journalist remarked that the difference between journalism and history is that history needs time. If Jesus Christ had even a fraction of the significance that has been claimed for him, then the sixty years of the New Testament and even the four hundred years from his lifetime until the Council of Chalcedon were not too long for pondering the questions, 'Who was he (or is he)?' and 'What had he done (or is he doing)?'

So the first step toward making sense out of the confused mass of material exposed by our exploration of the New Testament writings is to ask whether any pattern of development is to be seen in them. We did in fact study the material in a roughly chronological order, but the chronology was *only rough* – we began with Paul, then went on to Mark, Matthew and Luke–Acts, then to John, and finally moved back to Hebrews, I Peter, etc. Of course, even the greatest experts would have difficulty in putting all these documents in their *exact* order! And if this could be done, would it help very much? Sometimes a later writing may preserve fragments of earlier christology, for instance, Luke–Acts has relatively late material about the virginal conception, but, in the opinion of many scholars, gives us a reliable glimpse of the most primitive teaching of the church in the early chapters of Acts. Nevertheless, if we are careful, I think we can discern a pattern of christological development within the New Testament, and if we can discern even its broad outline, that is bound to help us in understanding later developments.

This outline can be traced through the diverse material set out in our last few chapters. As a kind of double-check, I shall compare it as we go along with the pattern of development which John Knox described in his book, *The Humanity and Divinity of Christ*, subtitled 'A Study of Pattern in Christology'. Knox, like myself, is convinced of the necessity of defending the genuine humanity of Jesus Christ against all pressures, though these pressures were already operating in New Testament times. So there is a fundamental agreement between us, though we diverge on certain points.

Knox claims that there are three stages in the development of christology up to the end of the first century, and he designates them by the names adoptionism (the belief that Jesus was a man who by his resurrection was made Lord and Christ by God); kenoticism (the belief that Jesus had pre-existed as a divine or heavenly being who by a voluntary emptying (*kenosis*) had become a man and lived on earth); docetism (a belief rejected by the church but held among dissident groups that Jesus was wholly an other-worldly figure who appeared on earth but only seemed to be a man).[23] Later, he slightly modifies this scheme to include between kenoticism and docetism what he calls 'incarnationism' (the belief that a pre-existent divine hypostasis took in Jesus a genuinely human life), but this fourth possibility is not so clearly defined as the others. It does not stress self-emptying, but at the same time it resists the fateful slip into docetism.[24] Knox, like myself, does not think that there is evidence enough to justify the attempts of some scholars (such as Robinson and Schillebeeckx) to reach back to a christology even more primitive than adoptionism.

At one point in the book, Knox seems to settle for adoptionism as a perfectly adequate christology. He says, 'I believe it can be said not only that the most primitive christology – what we have been calling "adoptionism" – is the minimally essential christology but that in its basic structure it was, and might conceivably have continued to be, an entirely adequate christology.'[25] I have a lot of sympathy with what Knox says here, but I did claim earlier that an 'anabatic' or 'adoptionist' christology is only half the story.[26] It does not acknowledge what Paul expressed in words I have quoted more than once, 'All this is from God.' Knox too feels that adoptionism is defective at this point. He believes that the idea of pre-existence was brought into christology to make it clear that God had not just found a man who happened to be suitable for elevation to christhood, but that this man had been sent from God. Here, regrettably, I have to take a different line from Dr Knox. As will be remembered, I found the arguments of Professor Dunn decisive in showing that the christological teaching of Paul can be understood without invoking the notion of pre-existence. On the other hand, Professor Knox, like Professor DuBose in an earlier time, thinks that Paul's belief in the pre-existence of Jesus is 'beyond doubt'.[27] If it were purely a question of exegesis, I would hesitate when two such eminent New Testament scholars differ. 'Who shall decide when doctors disagree?' But it seems to me that economy favours Dunn, and makes us shy away from such a dubious notion as pre-existence. If we can make sense of Paul without it, that is in itself supportive of Dunn. I remember another New Testament scholar, William Barclay, saying to me that he was an adoptionist in christology because it was the only christology he could understand! An excellent reason!

Actually, Professor Knox offers a very thorough critique of pre-existence. Once it had been introduced, he believes, it threatened belief in the true humanity of Christ. It reached its peak in John's gospel, which, he thinks, trembles on the very edge of docetism. He makes the interesting point that because a pre-existent Jesus is already immortal and beyond the reach of death, then 'the more fully the logic of pre-existence is allowed to work itself out in the story, the less important the resurrection is bound to become there'.[28] A docetic Lord might convey a revelation to the human race (as in Gnosticism) but could not *do* anything decisive for them unless he was himself fully human. More controversially, Knox also questions whether the teaching about Christ's sinlessness does not separate him from humanity. It is not enough, in his view, to say that Jesus was tempted. For, he asks, 'Am I really tempted, if I do not, however briefly or tentatively or slightly, consent?'[29]

These are very serious questions. As far as pre-existence is concerned, I have indicated in earlier passages of the book that I would reject any personal pre-existence as mythological and also as undermining a genuine recognition of the humanity of Jesus. I think this is Knox's ultimate position too. The question of sinlessness I shall leave till we come to the systematic or dogmatic part of the book.

Knox, surprisingly enough, ends up by expressing his preference for a form of kenoticism. It is, however, an 'interpreted' kenoticism, in which the more mythological and speculative elements have been removed.

While I have been very much in sympathy with Knox's insistence on the full humanity of Christ, I have some doubts about his way of understanding it. Like him, I have been willing to see the Christ-event, rather than the individual person of Jesus Christ, as the locus of incarnation or as the appearance of a new humanity, or however one may express it. Often he does use impressive language about Jesus as the creative centre of the Christ-event, but one cannot help wondering whether the church is displacing Jesus Christ at the centre, and whether the church, either now or at the beginning, is able to bear the weight being put upon it. Although I do not think John Knox actually quotes the words, there is a verse in John which seems to express his teaching: 'The glory which thou hast given me I have given to them' (John 17.22). But Christ is not only the creative centre and source of inspiration for the church, there is also a sense in which he stands over against the church, as its Redeemer and even as its Judge. Christ can have the significance claimed for him only if he is truly and fully a member of the human race. But equally he can have that significance only if we can make some affirmations about him that we cannot make about the church or about the human race in general. The New Testament writers, as we have seen, tried to make such affirmations as they witnessed to what they had learned of Christ, and they deployed a whole battery of terms in the attempt. Some were mythological, some may have undermined his true humanity. Some, we may hope, provide lasting insights. Nevertheless, here is the source material from which all serious reflection about Jesus Christ must begin, and the process of sifting, refining, revising, restating has gone on from then until now.

7

The Rise of Classical Christology

We have devoted several chapters to the christology of the New Testament, but in this chapter I propose that we should wing our way through about seventeen centuries to the dawn of the modern age. Have I lost all sense of proportion? No, I think I can justify the procedure. Let me remind the reader of some words of Martin Hengel, quoted earlier.[1] He said that in this subject of christology 'one is tempted to say that more happened in the period of two decades than in the whole of the next seven centuries, up to the time when the doctrine of the early church was completed.' The New Testament sets before us a dense mass of material, culled from a relatively short time, the initial Christ-event. Within the New Testament we can see development in the understanding and interpretation of the material, from the early adoptionism which told of a crucified man being made Lord and Christ by God, to the later incarnationism which told of the divine Word living as a human being in the midst of the human race. The process of reflection and development did not end with the last New Testament writing – in fact, no one was aware of being the 'last New Testament writer', for the collection of books which were given the special status of being included in the New Testament canon had still not been made and would not be made for a long time. But the process described in the last chapter as 'sifting, refining, revising, restating', already begun by the New Testament writers, continued without a break. We move into what is called the 'patristic' period, a very important period which was uniquely formative for the later history of the church, a period when a great deal happened, yet, as Hengel claimed, the great creative events had already been packed into a few short decades of the first century. It is no disparagement of the patristic writers and indeed of all theologians since them to say that they are all writing footnotes on the 'gospel' proclaimed by the first generation of Christians.

This does not prevent them from criticizing their sources, still less from criticizing one another, and it does not deny that they may bring much new knowledge and new experience to the elucidation of the material which has been passed on to them. Still, for several centuries,[2] the patristic writers were engaged in formulating into a coherent body of doctrine the material about Jesus they had derived from the New Testament. Most of this work, of course, was done in the face of opposition, sometimes fierce opposition, from other theologians who took a different view. Many of them were branded as heretics and their writings were condemned, because from time to time the church, in its official capacity, pronounced in favour of one of the competing views. That view then acquired the status of being the belief of the church, often called a 'dogma'. Sometimes worldwide councils of bishops were called to decide controversies over matters of belief. Some of these councils have been recognized as ecumenical. Such, for instance, were the great councils of Nicaea (325) and Chalcedon (451). The latter council, it was hoped, would put an end to controversies over the person of Christ, but it did not in fact do so. Nevertheless, the christological statements agreed at these early councils were to remain the norms of belief for more than a thousand years, all through the Middle Ages and even through the Reformation, until the Enlightenment.[3] We could agree with Martin Hengel that for many centuries no major changes took place in the church's beliefs about Jesus. In the earlier centuries, the official or classical christology was formulated; in the later centuries, it underwent only minor adjustments. The criticism and decline of the classical theology begins in earnest only in the eighteenth century. That explains why I am devoting only one chapter to the lengthy period between the end of the New Testament and the beginning of the Enlightenment. As Maurice Wiles has said about this part of the church's history, 'The great achievement of the Fathers was the establishment of a scheme of Christian theology which in its main features has remained normative for the church ever since. Today the value of that scheme – even indeed whether it has any meaning at all – is being called more and more into question.'[4]

We have seen that the christological teachings of the New Testament are very diverse. How then was it possible to build out of them anything like a unified christology, such as was eventually accepted by the majority of the Christian churches in east and west?

First of all, we have to note that a great change was coming over the membership of the church in those years. The first Christians were Jews, the writers of the New Testament were Jews, and the first attempts to interpret the person and work of Christ were formulated in categories drawn from the Jewish tradition. But already in the early years of the second century, the church had become more and more a church of the Gentiles. The Temple at Jerusalem had been destroyed in 70, and after the desperate revolt of Jewish nationalists in 132 to 135, Jerusalem was turned into a pagan city by the Romans. If Christianity was to be preached to the Gentiles and understood by them, it needed to be re-expressed in non-Jewish imagery. The expectations of the Jewish people had shaped the earliest formulations of the gospel, but these expectations were unknown and irrelevant to those whom the church was now addressing. So there was a pressure to move away from the Jewish circle of ideas to the more widely diffused medium of the prevailing Hellenistic culture.

A second point to be noted is that Christianity was beginning to make an appeal to educated people. Many of them had lost faith in the traditional polytheistic religion of the classical tradition and found spiritual nourishment in philosophical teachings, such as Platonism and Stoicism. Some of the early Christian apologists, of whom we shall say more shortly, presented Christianity as a new philosophy, and naturally they employed terms and ideas drawn from the Greek philosophical tradition in their dialogue with non-Christian philosophers.

A third thing happened, perhaps as a consequence of the two points already mentioned. Some things in the New Testament witness were more readily related to pagan ways of thinking than others. For instance, John's gospel begins by talking of the Logos or Word, and 'Logos' was a central conception in much Greek philosophy. It is unlikely that John himself had understood 'Logos' in a primarily philosophical sense but what he had written in his prologue certainly lent itself to philosophical interpretation, and the concept of Logos was a dominant influence in the theology of the early centuries. In a similar way, the idea of incarnation, which first received clear expression in John, was widely taken up by the theologians of the Gentile churches, for this idea was more congenial to their ways of thinking than it had been to the monotheistic Judaism from which the earliest generation of Christians had come.

Some Christian theologians of later times have expressed regret over what they call the 'Hellenization' of Christianity in sub-apostolic and patristic times. Among them was Adolf Harnack, one of the greatest Christian scholars of all time. Yet even he admitted that there was an inevitability about this development. If Christianity was to break out of its somewhat narrow origins and make an appeal to all peoples, then it had to come to terms with the wider culture of the ancient world. Furthermore, if it was to speak to the educated classes, it had to come to grips with the philosophical ideas of the time. Christianity has always been a whole way of life, and more than a philosophy or world-view. But it does have its intellectual aspects, and these need to be stated and defended. No doubt there have been theologians throughout history who have approached the Christian faith in too narrowly academic a spirit, and there were certainly times in the early centuries and later when abstruse metaphysical issues received far more attention than they deserved. But I wonder whether, on the whole, a graver threat to the church's integrity has come from anti-intellectualism than from any excessive preoccupation with intellectual issues.

The centuries between the last writings of the New Testament and the great councils of Nicaea and Chalcedon were a time of intellectual wrestling with the Christian faith. This was not a one-sided 'Hellenization' of Christianity, for just as Jewish ideas had already been modified as they were incorporated into Christian theology, now Greek ideas were also being modified as they were used to serve new purposes. In the words of Bernard Lonergan, who has written about this period, what we see is 'the drive toward drawing together the whole heritage of the Hebrews and the Greeks to form a new Christian mode of thought and style of life'.[5] He sums up the years to Nicaea in the following sentences:

> The Nicene dogma marks a transition from a multiplicity of symbols, titles and predicates, to the ultimate ground of these, namely, the Son's consubstantiality with the Father. Equally, it marks a transition from things as related to us, to things as they are in themselves, from the relational concepts of God as supreme agent, creator, omnipotent Lord of all, to an ontological conception of the divine substance itself. It makes, no less, a transition from the Word of God as accommodated to a particular people at a particular time under particular circumstances, to the Word of God as it is to be proclaimed to all people, of all times, under whatever circumstances – the transition from the prophetic oracle of Yahweh, the gospel as announced in Galilee, the apostolic preaching and the simple tradition of the Church, from all of these to catholic dogma.[6]

Obviously, some of Lonergan's assertions here are open to question, and some would strongly contest them. But I think we can accept his general justification of these early Christian thinkers. Just as the church sometimes thought of itself as a third people, a new nation, as it were, beyond the division between Jew and Gentile, so these early theologians could be said to be creating a third conceptuality, neither Hebrew nor Greek, though drawing resources from both. Today, when horizons have grown so much wider, Indian or Chinese Christians may complain that the language of 'catholic dogma' is less universal than Lonergan suggests, but it did achieve its purpose when it first arose, and continued to function throughout Christendom for many centuries.

One of the earliest Christian writers in the period following closely on the New Testament was Ignatius of Antioch. He had been bishop in Antioch, and was arrested by the Roman authorities and sent to Rome for trial. On his way to the imperial city, he wrote a number of letters, and though he was not himself a theologian or philosopher, these letters, dating from about 110, already show the direction in which christology was going to move. So while we found that the New Testament writers were very hesitant to call Jesus Christ 'God', and there are only two or three instances, Ignatius has no problem about using God-language of Christ: 'Permit me to be an imitator of the passion of Christ, my God.'[7] But although I said that the idea of incarnation was more congenial to Hellenistic thought than to Jewish monotheism, it would be wrong to think that it came easily. For how could God, conceived by Greek philosophers as remote, impassible, untouched by matter – how could such a God be incarnate in a human life? Ignatius was aware of the paradox contained in such a belief: 'There is one Physician who is possessed of both flesh and spirit; both made and not made; God existing in flesh; true life in death; both of Mary and of God; first passible, then impassible.'[8] As in John's gospel, one is aware of the pressure toward a docetic view of Christ, but like John, Ignatius repudiates docetism with vehemenence. His desire to suffer (and I use the word 'desire' deliberately, for Ignatius seems to have a different attitude to suffering from what we noted in I Peter) and his belief that this suffering belongs to his discipleship means that Christ's suffering too must have been real and no mere semblance. 'He suffered all these things for us; and he suffered them really, and not in appearance only, even as also he truly rose again. But not, as some of the unbelievers who are ashamed of the formation of man, and the cross, and death itself, affirm, that in appearance only and not in truth, he took a body of the Virgin, and suffered only in appearance, forgetting as they do him who said, "The Word was made flesh."'[9] Much more time and thought would be needed before more adequate theological statements would be found, but, like Kierkegaard many centuries later, Ignatius did not shrink from the paradoxes that inevitably arise from the Christian assertion that God has made himself known in a human life.

We move on to the middle of the second century, to Justin the Martyr. He had been a pagan philosopher, and even after his conversion to Christianity, he still regarded himself as a philosopher, and regarded Christianity as the true philosophy. Obviously this philosophical stance profoundly affected his way of understanding and presenting Christian faith. Inevitably he was attracted by the description of Jesus as the Word or Logos, and this was understood by him in the way in which the term was employed in Greek philosophy. The Logos has existed from eternity, and it mediates God's activity to the world. In an earlier discussion,[10] we saw that Logos or Word is a very apt metaphor to use of Jesus Christ, for a word is both distinct from the one who speaks it, yet in a sense is also an extension of the speaker. To believe in a Logos alongside God is not to abandon monotheism, though in fact Justin does speak of a 'second God'. For Justin, in accordance with the philosophy of the time, God was remote, nameless, unknowable. So he did not appear on earth or speak directly. 'The ineffable Father of all neither comes to any place nor walks nor sleeps nor arises, but always remains in his place, acutely seeing or hearing, not with eyes or ears, but with a power beyond description.'[11] When therefore the Old Testament speaks of God appearing on earth or speaking to patriarchs or prophets, this is the Logos. But how does this eternal Logos relate to the human Jesus? It is sometimes said that Justin is interested only in the eternal, pre-existent Logos, not in the earthly Christ. This is only partly true. While Justin identifies Christ with the Word of ancient times, he also holds that it is in Christ that the Word has come to full expression, having been only partially revealed in earlier manifestations. Like Ignatius, he is driven to acknowledge a paradox which he cannot explain: '[The pagans] proclaim our madness to consist in this, that we give to a crucified man a place second to the unchangeable and eternal God, the creator of all; for they do not discern the mystery that is herein, to which, as we make it plain to you, we pray you to give heed.'[12] So even for the philosophical Justin, the ultimate mystery is in the crucified man, and was not revealed to those 'Christians before Christ', such as Socrates and Heraclitus, even though he acknowledges that they had lived 'with the Word' (*meta logou*).[13]

We have seen that the two early writers just mentioned, Ignatius and Justin, both find themselves driven into paradoxes, though Justin's position is eased by making the Word subordinate ('in second place') to God. Some measure of paradox could hardly have been avoided if they were going to remain faithful to the New Testament witness, for according to that witness, Jesus Christ was, on the one hand, completely human, yet, on the other, sent by God and so close to God that Christians could no longer speak of God without also speaking of Christ, and could no longer speak of Christ without also speaking of God. In an early formulation of Paul, 'For us, there is one God, the Father, from whom are all things and for whom we exist, and one Lord, Jesus Christ, through whom are all things and through whom we exist' (I Cor. 8.6). It was not yet overtly the paradox of the God-man, yet that paradox was latent from the beginning.

Of course, also from the beginning, there were two obvious ways in which the paradox could be dissolved. One could deny that Jesus was really a man who had suffered and died, and claim that he was a

supernatural being who merely had the semblance of a man. We have
seen that already in the first century some members of the Johannine
community took this view and left the church. [14] Or one could dissolve the
paradox by saying that Jesus was merely a man, one more in the line of
Hebrew prophets, perhaps the greatest of them, but not in any sense
divine. Irenaeus, writing about the year 180, mentions a group of Jewish
Christians, called 'Ebionites', who held such beliefs and continued
various Jewish practices. [15] Both of the groups mentioned here, docetics
and Ebionites, were considered heretical, for if one subscribed to their
views, then Christianity *as a religion* became impossible. Jesus could only
be Son, Word, Mediator, High Priest and so on if somehow he bridged the
gap between God and the human race, and that seems to demand that
somehow he must belong to both sides. The mainline of Christian
theology was built up among the clash of rival beliefs, and it is important
to remember that Ignatius, Justin and their successors did not follow their
path out of a perverted love for paradox and dialectic, but because they
could not be contented with easy one-sided solutions which turned out
not to be solutions at all. But we owe something to the heretics also, for
they explored these other possibilities and found that they were blind
alleys. We should indeed be very careful in the use of the word 'heretic'
for it is not meant to rule out the necessity for experiment and innovation
in theology, but only when these are combined with a stubborn
individualism and contempt for the community. [16]

I have already mentioned the name of Irenaeus, and he is often
considered the first great Christian theologian after the New Testament.
He developed his teaching in controversy with heterodox points of view,
and his principal writing is therefore called *Against Heresies*. He spent
much of his energies battling against the Gnostics, but I think we have
sufficiently discussed Gnosticism in earlier chapters. Irenaeus is of special
interest for our own study because, unlike many of the theologians of his
time, he was unequivocal in his recognition and assertion of the humanity
of Christ. This found expression in his taking up again that christology
which we saw to be possibly the oldest and certainly the most persuasive
in the New Testament – the Adam christology of Paul, though very likely
it was already known in the church before Paul's time.

Underpinning Irenaeus' christology is an anthropology. According to
this anthropology, the human being is not conceived as confined within
rigid bounds, but is constituted rather by a possibility of becoming, by an
openness which allows for development and advance. So Irenaeus did
not take the story in Genesis that the human being was made in the image
and likeness of God to mean that Adam and Eve were perfect in the
beginning. Rather, they were like children who had to grow into
maturity. 'Created things must be inferior to him who created them . .

They come short of the perfect. Man could not receive this perfection, being yet an infant.'[17] The image of God, on this view, was given as a potentiality into which the human creatures might grow, though the possibility of growth and advance implies that equally there was the possibility that they might slip back through sin. Mistaking the Hebrew parallelism of image and likeness for two distinct concepts, Irenaeus supposed that man, as part of his existential constitution, had the potentiality for growing toward God (this was the 'image') and that the goal or realization of this potentiality would be the glory of closeness to God (this was the 'likeness'). So human life is (or is intended to be) the progression from the potency of the image to the realization of the likeness. In Irenaeus' words, 'Now, it was necessary that man should be in the first instance created; and having been created, should receive growth; and having received growth, should be strengthened; and having been strengthened, should abound; and having abounded, should recover from the disease of sin; and having recovered, should be glorified; and being glorified, should see his Lord.'[18] The close relation between God and the perfected human being is expressed in the words, 'The glory of God is a living man; and the life of man consists in beholding God.'[19] Like many other patristic writers, Irenaeus did not hesitate to call this perfected state of humanity 'deification'. Of course, he did not mean that man had become a god or a part of God, but that the divine image was now fully manifested in the creature, whose life was lived in God and out of God. A scriptural precedent for this way of talking is found in a late writing of the New Testament, II Peter, where Christians are promised that they will become 'partakers of the divine nature (*theias koinonoi phuseos*)' (1.4).

The christology of Irenaeus, making use of these anthropological ideas, is very close to Paul's. The first attempt to create human beings in the image and likeness of God failed through the sin of Adam and Eve. But 'in the last times, not by the will of the flesh, nor by the will of man, but by the good pleasure of the Father, his hands formed a living man, in order that Adam might be created [again] after the image and likeness of God.'[20] There is one difference (or perhaps I should say, addition) made by Irenaeus to the Pauline teaching. He speaks of Adam as having been animated by 'that breath of life which proceeded from God', whereas in the case of Christ he says that 'the Word . . . having become united with the ancient substance of Adam's formation, rendered man living and perfect, receptive of the perfect Father, in order that as in the natural [Adam] we were all dead, so in the spiritual we may all be made alive'.[21] But perhaps one should not make too much of the difference between the 'breath of life' given by God to Adam and the Word given to Christ, for surely the breath of life bestowed on Adam included some share or participation in the Logos. 'Breath of life' and 'Logos' are not added extras, but essential to the human constitution. Certainly, Irenaeus' desire to defend the genuine humanity of Christ would not seem to be compatible with making a fundamental difference between Christ and human beings generally.

Tertullian, a native of North Africa and about twenty years younger than Irenaeus, took a similar line. He too opposed Gnosticism and any other view that diminished Christ's true humanity, for he shared the belief of the author of Hebrews that Christ 'had to be made like his brethren in every respect'.

But we have noted that Irenaeus and those who thought like him were going against the tide in the second century, for the dominant tendency was to emphasize the divinity of Christ at the expense of his humanity. At an earlier point, we had occasion to notice Clement of Alexandria and his teaching that although Jesus ate and drank, he had no need to do so.[22] Clement had virtually conceded the Gnostic case, and the best we can say for him is that at least his own variety of Gnosticism was a highly Christianized one. But Clement had to a considerable extent set the tone for Alexandria which in those days was a great and influential centre of Christian theology. It used to be commonly believed that the theologians of Alexandria were preoccupied with the divinity of Christ while the rival school of Antioch were left to defend his humanity. R. D. Williams has warned us against pushing this contrast too far: 'The stark distinctions once drawn between Antiochene and Alexandrian exegesis or theology have come increasingly to look exaggerated.'[23] Nevertheless, some of the great Alexandrians – Cyril especially comes to mind – can hardly escape the charge of having been very one-sided.

But first we consider an Alexandrian theologian whose insight, learning and independence give him a good claim to be considered the greatest of all the Fathers, Origen (died about 254). Although a great biblical scholar, Origen was also steeped in the philosophy of Plato, as it had come to be understood in his time. From these two sources he developed a very complicated cosmology of spiritual beings and material beings, and it is in the context of this that we have to understand his christology. Origen's starting-point is the divine Wisdom, and this, he tells us, is not to be understood impersonally, but as a living hypostasis. This Wisdom is eternally begotten or generated by God. 'Who that is capable of entertaining reverential thoughts or feelings regarding God can suppose or believe that God the Father ever existed, even for a moment of time, without having generated this Wisdom?'[24] He goes on immediately to say that this Wisdom is also called the Word 'because she is, as it were, the interpreter of the secrets of the mind'.[25] So Christ is co-eternal with God the Father, who has generated Wisdom or the Word from the beginning. But there is a further complication. Because of his Platonism, Origen believes that all rational creatures have immortal souls, and their immortality means not only that they will live on for ever in the future but that they have also lived for ever in the past. Now, according to Origen, Jesus had a human soul: 'As he truly possessed flesh, so also he truly possessed a soul.'[26] The reader may remember that when we were discussing the prologue to John's gospel, I pointed out that the expression, 'the Word became flesh', could rather easily be misinterpreted to mean that the Word simply animated a human body, rather than becoming united with a complete human being. The first of these two possibilities was later to be deemed a heresy,[27] but Origen already avoids it by claiming that the soul of Christ (itself immortal) had always been united with the Logos. He illustrates the nature of the union by the famous simile of iron heated in a fire. 'If a mass of iron be kept constantly in the fire, receiving the heat through all its pores and veins, and the fire being continuous and the iron never removed from it, it becomes wholly converted into the latter . . . in this way then that soul which has been perpetually placed in the Word and perpetually in the Wisdom and perpetually in God, is God in all that it does, feels and understands.'[28] I suppose one must say that Origen's christology is catabatic, since it begins from the divine Wisdom or Word, who has been generated by the Father since eternity, but because it is a full humanity, both body and soul, which the Word takes in the incarnation, Origen cannot be accused of docetism. 'We see in him some things so human that they appear to differ in no respect from the common frailty of mortals, and some things so divine that they can appropriately belong to nothing else than the primal and ineffable nature of deity.'[29] On the other hand, like many other ante-Nicene writers, Origen strongly asserts the Word's subordination to the Father, even if they are co-eternal. We cannot see God directly in Christ, for the infinite has been scaled down to the finite. Christ is the 'image' or 'mirror' of the ineffable God.[30]

From the New Testament onward, we have sometimes come across universalist tendencies. In Origen, there are not just tendencies but explicit statements acknowledging that the truth and salvific action of God extend beyond the specifically Christian revelation, and that in the end God's salvation will embrace all those creatures who are capable of receiving it, even the demons. 'It was not true,' wrote Origen, 'that [God's] rays were enclosed in that man alone . . . or that the Light which is the divine Logos, which causes these rays, existed nowhere else . . . We are careful not to raise objections to any good teachings, even if their authors are outside the faith.'[31]

At the present day, many people would find it difficult to go along with Origen's Platonist belief in a substantial eternal soul, but the conception appears to be integral to his christology. Even so, his teaching made a powerful contribution to Christian thought and to the theological reputation of Alexandria.

Nevertheless, little more than half a century after Origen's death, Alexandria became the scene of possibly the fiercest theological dispute in the entire history of Christianity – the Arian controversy. Whatever one's view of Arius may be, he certainly said something important, for even in the present decade large and learned books have been rolling off the presses, arguing in the first place about what Arius really said, or intended to say, and in the second place, whether he had any justification for saying what he did.

'Abuse of one's opponents', writes Maurice Wiles, 'is frequently a sign of the weakness of the case that one is making out against them.'[32] This is the first sentence in a piece entitled 'In Defence of Arius'. Wiles' purpose was not to vindicate Arius' teaching, which he describes as 'certainly an inadequate account of the fulness of Christian truth'.[33] But he does seek to show – and, I think, with a considerable measure of success – that the difference between Arius and his opponents was not as clear-cut as is usually supposed and that to regard Arius as an arch-heretic is to go far beyond the evidence. The main thrust of the accusation against Arius was that he placed Christ with the creatures rather than with God. For him, only God the Father is unbegotten and self-subsistent. The Son is begotten, so there must have been when he was not (*en pote ouk en*). Wiles points out that Arius certainly did not invent this notorious expression, since Origen, who believed in the eternal generation of the Son or Word, had already repudiated it long before Arius was born.[34] Arius is also alleged to have said that the Son was a creature, but added 'but not as one of the creatures'. This is a good example of the kind of paradoxes I pointed out in discussing John's gospel, paradoxes which are inevitable when we just do not have words to say directly what we feel must be said. Origen too, we have seen, thought of the Son as subordinate to the Father, so if we were to take a charitable view of Arius, we could say that he was simply shifting the emphasis from identity to difference – and, however difficult it may be to find the words, the church has wanted to assert both identity and difference in the relation of the Father and the Son. So Arius may not have strayed too far from Origen or even from John. Of course, one would still have to ask whether he persisted too stubbornly in his views in opposition to the Christian community.

The bishop of Alexandria, Alexander, took action against Arius and suspended him from office.[35] But Arius stuck to his opinions and, as he had many friends and sympathizers, the dispute spread and became so bitter that Emperor Constantine was himself alarmed at the threat to the unity of the church and even of the Empire. It seems that at this time Constantine was advised on ecclesiastical matters by a Spanish bishop,

Hosius of Cordova, and as a consequence of this advice, he summoned the first great ecumenical council of bishops, to meet at Nicaea in 325. The council condemned Arianism, and drafted a creed to which all the bishops were required to give assent. This creed was not, of course, the one which we nowadays call the Nicene creed,[36] but it attempted the very difficult task of saying affirmatively what the essentials of Christian belief are, but saying this in such a way as to exclude any possible Arian interpretation. Whether in fact it is possible to devise a language so nuanced that it will exactly affirm the orthodox theological view and at the same time exclude what has been judged to be error is debatable. Perhaps it may not even be desirable, and the long story of controversies that unfolded even after Nicaea and Chalcedon shows how brittle were the achievements of those councils.

The most noteworthy feature of the creed of 325 was its assertion that Christ is 'of one substance as the Father' or 'of the same being as the Father'. The Greek word is *homoousios*, an unpopular word with many of the bishops because it was unscriptural and had already been used in controversies. The word *ousia* itself had several meanings,[37] and at a later stage I shall try to sort out some of the confused terminology.[38] But we may think it a good thing that there was some ambiguity in the terminology of the creed, for that meant that there remained some flexibility in interpretation, which in turn meant that some theological progress would still be possible, and dogma was not frozen at a particular moment in its history. But certainly some of the more extreme views on the person of Christ were excluded, and the negative aspect of the creed found expression in an appendix which stated that the Catholic Church anathematizes those who say, 'There was when he was not', or 'He was created out of nothing' or 'He was of a different subsistence (*hypostasis*) or being (*ousia*)' – this last point illustrates the slipperiness of the terminology and the confusion among such terms as *hypostasis*, *ousia* and *physis*.

So the hope that Nicaea would bring peace and harmony to the church was not realized, or, at least, not quickly realized. In 328 Athanasius had become bishop of Alexandria, and he assumed leadership of the Nicene or orthodox party in the church. He occupied the see for forty-five years, and the fact that he was driven out of it into exile no less than five times during his tenure shows how troubled these times were and how the ecclesiastical struggles swung now one way, now another. There is no need for us to go into the details of these seemingly never-ending disputes. But we should not fail to take note of a contribution which Athanasius made to christology before he became involved in the Arian controversy – his treatise entitled *De Incarnatione*, usually dated 318. The christology of Athanasius is a christology of the Word, which took a body of the virgin. But Athanasius supports this initially implausible idea of incarnation by a consideration which, I think, still has significance for a christology in the modern period. He draws an analogy between the human body and the whole cosmos. There is a sense in which the whole cosmos embodies the Word; why then should not the Word be embodied in a human being within the cosmos? 'The philosophers of the Greeks say the world is a great body; and rightly they say so, for we perceive it and its parts affecting our senses. If then the Word of God is in the world, which is a body, and he has passed into it all and into every part of it, what is wonderful or what is unfitting in our saying that he came in a man?'[39] Through sin, human beings created in the image of God had lost that image, or (as I believe Athanasius would have been willing to express the same thing) having been given a participation in the Logos had lost it, so the Logos returns in Jesus Christ and renews what had been lost. The event is compared to what might happen when a portrait made on a panel of wood has been effaced by stains, and the person whose likeness it was returns, so that the likeness may be restored. Thus Athanasius can say of Christ the Word that he became man that we might become God – again the idea of deification, in the sense explained in connection with Irenaeus.[40]

The views of Athanasius and his supporters finally triumphed only some years after his death, at an ecumenical council held at Constantinople in 381. It was this council which agreed to what we now call the Nicene creed, though it would be more accurately called the Niceno-Constantinopolitan creed. It enshrined the word *homoousios*, 'of the same being' or 'consubstantial', as the most accurate term the church could find to express the relation of Christ to the Father. Even to this day, the creed of 381 remains the most ecumenical of all dogmatic statements in the Christian churches. This does not make it immune from criticism or possible revision, but it does entitle it to a very high degree of respect.

The council of 381 had another important matter to consider as well as reaffirming the findings of Nicaea. I have mentioned that Origen insisted that Jesus had a human soul and, according to his teaching, this soul was united to the Logos. In many other writers, it was not clear whether in Jesus the Logos had taken a human soul or only a human body – an ambiguity already present in the wording, 'The Logos became flesh'. Grillmeier uses the terms 'Logos/man' christology and 'Logos/sarx' christology to distinguish the two positions.[41] The distinction appears to have attracted little attention for quite some time. Athanasius does not pronounce about it, and Arius was assailed for his denial of the full divinity of Christ, though it seems that he also denied that Christ had a human soul.[42]

But the question of whether Christ had a human soul and the importance of that question for christology was raised not by Arius but by someone who had been an opponent of Arianism and a friend of

Athanasius, Apollinarius, bishop of Laodicea. It seemed to Apollinarius that the Logos/man christology could not help introducing a tendency toward a dualism in our understanding of Christ, and that only the Logos/sarx christology could really safeguard the unity of his person. An element of uncertainty is introduced into the discussion of Apollinarius' view because he oscillates between the thought of man as compounded of body and soul, and the more complex theory of a threefold being of body, soul and spirit. I follow John Kelly's interpretation (which has the advantage of being simpler and more intelligible than the alternative).[43] According to Kelly, Apollinarius believed that 'the Word was both the directive, intelligent principle in Jesus Christ, and also the vivifying principle of his flesh' – that is to say, both mind (*nous*) and soul (*psyche*). This is confirmed by a fragment of Apollinarius which reads: 'The divine energy fulfills the role of the animating soul (*psyche*) and of the human mind (*nous*).'[44]

This teaching of Apollinarius was hotly debated in the years following 370. It had certain attractions, chiefly in avoiding any suggestion that Jesus had some kind of dual personality. But the great weight of opinion was against Apollinarius, and his christology was condemned by the council of Constantinople in 381. The main objection was that by denying to Jesus a human mind or soul, Apollinarius was denying an essential element in his humanity; or, to express the same thing in another way, the Logos/man theology was being preferred to the Logos/sarx theology, at least, if the term *sarx* was being understood as anything less than a complete human being historically existing. This objection to Apollinarianism was summed up in some often quoted words of Gregory of Nazianzus: 'That which he has not assumed, he has not healed; but that which is united to his Godhead is also saved. If only half Adam fell, then that which Christ assumes and saves must be half also; but if the whole of his nature fell, it must be united to the whole nature of him that was begotten, and so be saved as a whole. Let them not then begrudge us our complete salvation, or clothe the saviour only with bones and nerves and the portraiture of humanity.'[45] This is simply an adaptation to the case of Apollinarianism of an argument we have heard repeatedly from New Testament times onward, that unless Jesus Christ were truly and completely human, he could not have the soteriological significance that Christians have attributed to him.

This is an appropriate moment at which to take a sideways look at some other theological developments which strengthened the condemnation of Arianism and its teaching that the Son is subordinate to the Father. I mean, the development of the doctrine of the Trinity, due in large measure to those Cappadocian fathers, Basil of Caesarea, Gregory of Nyssa and Gregory of Nazianzus. In the West, a similar task was performed by Augustine, who completed his treatise *On the Trinity* in 419. It is outside our field to go into this trinitarian development, but it touches so closely on christology that we must briefly note it. Augustine claimed that 'in this Trinity, what is said of each is also said of all on account of the indivisible working of the one and same substance . . . The Father, the Son and the Holy Spirit are one and the same substance in an indivisible equality.'[46] Thus the rejection of subordinationism was now placed on a firmer basis by trinitarian theology. Though this might have been expected to heighten the emphasis on the divinity of Christ, Augustine preserved a lively sense of his humanity, and not least of Christ's solidarity with his human community. Thus, we find Augustine saying (and it is typical of him) 'The Head and body are one Christ', and even, 'We can rightly call all those "christs" who are anointed with his chrism, forasmuch as the whole body with its Head is one Christ.'[47] And we must not forget that although Augustine owed much to the 'books of the Platonists', he says himself: 'I read there that God the Word was born not of flesh nor of blood nor of the will of man nor of the will of the flesh, but of God. But that "the Word was made flesh and dwelt among us," I read not there.'[48]

However, we must return to our main theme, and it has to be said at once that neither the findings of the council of 381 nor developments in trinitarian theology were going to prevent the church from tearing itself apart with new controversies over the person of Jesus Christ. As I remarked a few pages back, the issues were frequently so obscure and such a fine balance had to be maintained between opposing interpretations that it was virtually impossible to find a language that would express what (in the view of the church) had to be said and would exclude what (again, in the view of the church) had to be denied. So in the fifth century it was not long before new controversies broke out, sparked once more by one-sided writings which came eventually to be judged heretical.

The most notorious of these new heresies was the one known as Nestorianism. Its originator was a certain Nestorius who became bishop of Constantinople in 428. Nestorius had come from Antioch, and we may see in this new dispute a continuation of the longstanding rivalry between the ancient sees of Antioch and Alexandria. The Antiochene scholars had traditionally been champions of the reality of Christ's humanity, and in fact Nestorius had been strongly opposed to Apollinarianism, as a diminution of that humanity. But his opposition extended to any views which seemed to him to obscure or minimize Christ's truly human nature, and he thought (perhaps not without reason) that there was a definite tendency toward such errors in the Alexandrian school. Unfortunately for Nestorius, as happened also in the case of many other heretics or alleged heretics, his views were for a long time known only as they had been quoted and criticized by persons who disagreed with him. It was only at the beginning of the present century that an important work by Nestorius was discovered, and this made it clear that he had been badly misrepresented. Nestorius, one has to say, was not a Nestorian, in the sense that he did not conform to the stereotype or rather caricature constructed by his enemies. He was opposed to what he considered the inappropriate use in his diocese of the title *Theotokos* ('God-bearer' or 'Mother of God') for the Blessed Virgin Mary, and from this the conclusion was drawn that he denied that Christ was God and regarded him merely as a man. But in his own writings,[49] Nestorius denies these allegations. He likewise denied another allegation, namely, that he separated the humanity and divinity of Christ so sharply that he ended up with two Sons or with a double personality in Christ. Now that scholars have access to what Nestorius actually taught, there is general agreement that although he may have expressed himself without sufficient care, he has been misrepresented by his opponents. The chief of these was Cyril (died 444), patriarch of Alexandria. Sydney Cave claimed that Nestorius's own writings make it clear 'that the traditional account of [his] teaching owes as much to Cyril's malice as to Nestorius' heresy, and that the condemnation of Nestorius was due less to his false teaching than to his own amazing tactlessness and the clever adroitness of Cyril'.[50] But whatever one may think of the methods used, Nestorius's views were condemned by an ecumenical council meeting at Ephesus in 431.

The christological teaching which Cyril opposed to that of Nestorius can be constructed from letters which he wrote to Nestorius during the months preceding the council of Ephesus.[51] At first glance, it might seem that Cyril's views were not much different from those of Apollinarius, condemned almost fifty years earlier. That is because Cyril from soteriological motives stressed the unity of Christ with the Word, as against what he believed (probably wrongly) was Nestorius' error of dividing Christ into two persons, one human and one divine. In this controversy, the waters were once again muddied by the ambiguities and fluctuations in such key-terms as *ousia*, *hypostasis* and *physis*. In the second of his letters to Nestorius, Cyril proposes to consider what is meant when it is said that the Word 'became incarnate and was made man'.

For we do not affirm that the nature (*physis*) of the Word underwent a change and became flesh, or that it was transformed into a whole or perfect man consisting of soul and body; but we may say that the Word, having in an ineffable and inconceivable manner personally (*kath' hypostasin*) united to himself flesh instinct with a living soul, became man and was called the Son of Man, yet not of mere will or favour, nor again by the simple taking to himself of a [human] person (*prosopon*), and that while the natures which were brought together into this true unity were diverse, there was of both one Christ and one Son: not as though the diverseness of the natures were done away by this union, but rather the Godhead and Manhood completed for us the one Lord and Christ and Son by their unutterable and unspeakable concurrence and unity.

Let me comment briefly on this statement from Cyril. First, there is a commendable modesty and agnosticism in some of the words he uses – 'ineffable', 'inconceivable', 'unutterable', 'unspeakable'. One can only wish that this modesty – what the Oxford Fathers called the 'principle of reserve' – had been more in evidence among those ancient Fathers who spent so much labour and ill-feeling over their meticulous efforts to anatomize (in a metaphysical way) the person of Christ. Second, in acknowledging that Christ had a soul, even a 'rational soul' (*psyche logike*) – an expression which gets rather lost in Dr Heurtley's translation – Cyril does seem to differentiate his view from that of Apollinarius, and he states explicitly toward the end of our quotation that the diversity of the natures is not done away by the union. Third, he achieves the desired unity in Christ by holding that this is the unity of his person (*hypostasis* or *prosopon*), though it appears that he has in mind not a human personhood but the person of the Word, who remains unchanged.

If the language of this quotation is still not unequivocal, we might refer to a passage in his third letter, written later in the same year of 430, in which Cyril speaks of 'the one incarnate hypostasis of the Word, for the Lord Jesus Christ is one according to the scriptures'. Although Cyril himself did not use the term, some of those who followed him used the word *anhypostasia* (literally, 'not having a hypostasis') for this view that in Christ there was no human personhood or hypostasis, and that his only hypostasis was that of the Word. At an earlier stage of the book, I mentioned this conception of *anhypostasia* as an example of theology's overreaching itself in speculation. I doubt very much whether it makes sense to say that Jesus or anyone else could have a human nature and yet lack human personhood. And if it does make sense, I would regretfully have to think of it as an error, because it would undermine the true humanity of Christ, and that is something which, in my view, is utterly inexpendable.

Of course, if Jesus Christ is, as the church has claimed, significant for the whole human race, then christology must offer some explanation of how it is possible for him to have this representative function. Near the beginning of our discussion, I did say that we should not look on Jesus as an isolated individual (which no human being actually is), but from the very beginning as the centre of a social happening, the so-called 'Christ-event'. The further explication of this broader, even universal, significance of Christ remains on our agenda, but I do not think that the idea of an anhypostatic humanity offers a successful way forward, even if in the context of modern thought we were still able to make sense of that idea.

Even after the condemnation of Nestorius, disputes still rumbled on. However, some points of agreement seemed to be emerging. Common sense alone would help to persuade people that Jesus Christ had been a unitary person, not a divided personality and, still less, 'two Sons', something that probably Nestorius himself had never believed. On the other hand, the paradox of the divine and human in Jesus Christ remained, and it could hardly have failed to become apparent that there is no way to escape that paradox short of a wholesale abandonment of the apostolic faith. So some compromise had to be reached, and to find that compromise was the task of yet another ecumenical council, summoned by the emperor to meet at Chalcedon in 451. The crisis which was the immediate occasion of this council had been precipitated by a certain Eutyches, who had the backing of Cyril's successor in the see of Alexandria. Eutyches gave a new twist to the Alexandrian insistence on the unity of Christ by teaching that in the incarnate Christ there are no longer two natures but one. This is the doctrine called 'monophysitism', the doctrine that in Christ there is only a divine, not a human, nature. This has some affinity with Cyril's teaching, but carries it to an extreme which Cyril himself did not sanction, and probably had not foreseen.

When the council met, it had before it certain 'resource documents', as we might nowadays call them: the creed agreed at Nicaea in 325 and the Niceno-Constantinopolitan creed produced by the council of 381; two letters of Cyril, including the second that he sent to Nestorius, described above;[52] and the Tome of Leo, who was bishop of Rome at that time. This Tome of Leo is actually a lengthy letter, sent by the Pope to the patriarch of Constantinople and supporting the latter's condemnation of the views of Eutyches. Leo strongly insists on the distinctness of the two natures in Christ, while at the same time asserting that 'one and the same person is truly the Son of God and truly the Son of Man'. But sometimes Leo writes as if there were a kind of alternation in Jesus Christ, who is now a divine being, now a human being, language again reminiscent of a dual personality. So we read: 'Each nature in union with the other performs the actions which are proper to it. The Word those which are proper to the Word, the flesh those which are proper to the flesh. The one is resplendent with miracles, the other succumbs to injuries.'[53] This language does seem to imperil the unity of Christ's person.

What then did the Chalcedonian fathers make of it all? I quote the central part of their definition of faith as it appears in the revised American Prayer Book of 1979.

Therefore, following the Holy Fathers, we all with one accord teach men to acknowledge one and the same Son, our Lord Jesus Christ, at once complete in Godhead and complete in manhood, truly God and truly man, consisting also of a reasonable soul and body; of one substance (*homoousios*) with the Father as regards his Godhead, and at the same time of one substance with us as regards his manhood; like us in all respects, apart from sin; as regards his Godhead, begotten of the Father before the ages, but yet as regards his manhood begotten, for us men and for our salvation, of Mary the Virgin, the God-bearer (*Theotokos*); one and the same Christ, Son, Lord, Only-begotten, recognized in two natures, without confusion, without change, without division, without separation; the distinction of natures being in no way annulled by the union, but rather the characteristics of each nature being preserved and coming together to form one person and subsistence, not as parted or separated into two persons, but one and the same Son and Only-begotten God the Word, Lord Jesus Christ; even as the prophets from earliest times spoke of him, and our Lord Jesus Christ himself taught us, and the creed of the Fathers has handed down to us.

Such then was the compromise which attempted to do justice to the opposing sides and to give fair expression to what Kierkegaard was to call many centuries later the 'absolute paradox'.[54] Perhaps there is no way in which that paradox can be fairly expressed. But for the time being the Fathers hoped they had succeeded. 'Peter has spoken through Leo. This is the teaching of Cyril. Anathema to him that believes otherwise.'

It hardly needs to be said that even Chalcedon did not bring the wrangling to an end. The Coptic Church of Egypt remains monophysite to this day, though in a newer language they are called 'non-Chalcedonian'. At the other extreme, Nestorianism flourished and established its own form of Christianity in Asian countries reaching as far as China, where there were already Nestorian Christian congregations in the seventh century. However, most of the Christian churches accepted the Chalcedonian settlement, and it has continued to be the norm for the church's belief concerning the person of Jesus Christ. As mentioned above, it is currently printed in the American Prayer Book, though how many American Christians read it and understand it is surely a question.

But the purpose of a dogmatic statement like the formula of Chalcedon is not – or, at any rate, ought not to be – to put an end to all further discussion of the matter. The church never reaches final truth. At the best – and we may hope this did in fact happen at Chalcedon – the church becomes aware that some avenues are dead ends, but is incited to pursue more promising ways in the hope of getting a fuller vision of truth. As

Karl Rahner has put it, 'The clearest formulations, the most sanctified formulas, the classic condensations of the centuries-long work of the Church in prayer, reflection and struggle concerning God's mysteries; all these derive their life from the fact that they are not the end but the beginning, not the goal but the means, truths which open the way to the ever greater truth.'[55] Chalcedon is an important milestone in the church's progress toward a deeper understanding of Jesus Christ, but it left plenty of scope for further reflection.

At the beginning of this chapter, I reminded the reader of Martin Hengel's claim that already in the New Testament period there was more development in the church's beliefs about Christ than took place in the next seven hundred years. I ventured to amend this to 'the next four hundred' years, because it seemed to me that the reflections and arguments which led up to Chalcedon were far more important and have been far more permanent in their influence than what happened in the centuries following Chalcedon. So I propose to pause for a little at this point, and ask just where we have reached in our inquiry. Certainly, the discussion, as compared with what we found in the New Testament, has taken an intellectual and philosophical turn. That in itself is not something to deplore. Christianity has to give a credible account of itself if it is to be taken seriously. But one has got to ask whether the tendency to concentrate on doctrinal formulas has not diminished the existential and soteriological understanding of faith in Jesus Christ, and indeed whether the whole discussion has not been in danger of slipping into artificial disputation over minutiae and fine distinctions. Alongside the intellectualizing tendency goes another. This is the tendency to assimilate Jesus Christ more and more to the being of God, and to obscure his humanity. It is of course true that Chalcedon seeks a balance, and asserts both that the Son is consubstantial with the Father and consubstantial with the human race. But the disputes that broke out after Chalcedon made it clear that the humanity of Christ had not been fully safeguarded.

The best known of this new crop of controversies was over the question whether Christ had one will or two wills, in consequence of the two natures. It was eventually decided that orthodoxy requires two wills (Third Council of Constantinople, 680, also known as the sixth ecumenical council). But this may be regarded as the *reductio ad absurdum* of the whole controversy. It proceeded on the false assumption that there is a faculty or organ of the mind called the 'will' which has the function of making decisions. This misleading idea may have arisen because many languages have a noun (will, *voluntas*, *thelema*, etc.) which might seem to indicate some distinct 'thing-like' part of our mental or spiritual equipment. But a little reflection on the use of the language shows that the 'will' is nothing but the activity of willing, and this is an activity of the whole person. The will is simply the self in action.[56] Two wills in one person would be a pathological condition, and this was surely not what the church wanted to say about Jesus Christ. Willing belongs to the self or personal centre, and although Chalcedon spoke of two natures, it acknowledged one person, and therefore a unitary willing. No doubt human nature has a plurality of desires, and these may conflict with one another, but this is something different from willing.

It is a decided relief to turn away from this dispute between monothelitism (the doctrine of one will in Christ) and dyothelitism (the doctrine of two wills) to something with more substance, and also more promise for the future. I mean the Byzantine christology which grew up in the Eastern churches after Chalcedon and continued right on into the Middle Ages. It brought to life again some of the insights of that christology which I described as the oldest of all and also judged to be possibly the most credible – I mean, the christology of first and second Adam, expounded by Paul but thereafter pushed into the background, except for a brief time when it was renewed by Irenaeus.

This type of christology now re-emerges in the writings of Maximus the Confessor (580–662). He is described by John Meyendorff as 'the real father of Byzantine theology'.[56] Maximus is difficult to understand, partly, I think, because he obscures his own thought with a mass of cosmological and anthropological speculation. I must admit too that he adhered to the doctrine of two wills in Christ and, in opposition to my own view expressed above, held that these wills belonged to the two natures rather than that willing is an activity of the one personal centre. But he has two great virtues – he firmly links christology to anthropology, and whether he is speaking of the divine or the human, he uses categories that are dynamic rather than static.

Every created thing, according to Maximus, has its *logos*, the idea which God had in mind in creating it; and this *logos* is also the end toward which the created thing in question tends. So throughout the universe there is a tendency or striving toward fulfilment. The nearest parallel to this in contemporary philosophy would, I think, be Bloch's *Principle of Hope*. Both see the world not as brute fact but as possibility. The human being too has his *logos*, and its fulfilment points him to God and a life in God, which Maximus, following the custom of Eastern theologians, calls 'deification'. The human being is also considered to be a microcosmos, summing up the several levels of creation. The first man, Adam, was created so that he might unite in himself the whole creation and, fulfilling the goal set by his *logos*, lead the whole creation to God in a kind of cosmic deification. This purpose was frustrated by the fall, and now we see the role of Christ in this scheme. In Christ is the divine Logos which integrates all the *logoi* of the created realm. In this connection, Maximus uses the verb *anakephalaioumai*,[57] the word used by Ephesians and Irenaeus to signify a 'gathering up' or 'recapitulation' of all things in Christ – again, perhaps, the idea of some kind of cosmic deification. Some of Maximus' language must raise the question whether he succeeds in maintaining the full humanity of Christ. I have already expressed unease about the 'two wills' doctrine. Maximus did not accept Cyril's idea of an anhypostatic humanity in Jesus, but he did accept that Jesus' humanity was 'enhypostatic'. This term had been used in the sixth century by Leontius of Byzantium, who did not take the view that Christ had no human hypostasis, but held that this had been taken into the hypostasis of the Logos. Perhaps this is just a clumsy way of saying what Origen more elegantly expressed in his metaphor of the iron being transformed by the fire,[58] but although *'enhypostasia'* has been welcomed by at least one modern writer on christology,[59] I doubt if it is any more intelligible or any less damaging to the full humanity of Christ than the defective notion of *anhypostasia* on which it was intended to be an improvement.

The best known of these Byzantine theologians was John of Damascus, living in an area which had already become part of the domains of Islam. His main endeavours were directed to synthesizing the teaching of the Greek Fathers, but in doing so, he introduced some insights that have a bearing on christology. Thus, for instance, he saw the role of the Holy Spirit in the incarnation as the personal sanctification of Mary, rather than in any magical terms.[60] He got into the usual tangles over two wills and two natures, but his defence of the use of icons, which was under attack at that time, shows how seriously he took the fleshly existence of Jesus to be, and how he linked the incarnation with a theology of matter. Commenting on John's part in the iconoclastic controversy, Bishop Kallistos Ware makes three important points.[61] (1) The veneration of icons is not in any sense idolatry, for the icon is a symbol of the personal or spiritual reality it represents. (2) Icons have an important educational function, and this was especially true in an age when many people could not read. The bishop quotes John of Damascus as follows: 'If a pagan asks you to show him your faith, take him into church and place him before the icons.'[62] (3) Icons have a doctrinal significance – they 'safeguard a full and proper doctrine of the incarnation'. The Old Testament forbade the making of images of God, but also claimed that the human being is made in the divine image. For Christians, as we have repeatedly seen, this image which was impaired at the fall has been restored in Christ. So John can say:

> Of old, God, the incorporeal and uncircumscribed was not depicted at all. But now that God has appeared in the flesh and lived among men, I make an image of the God who can be seen. I do not worship matter,

but I worship the creator of matter, who for my sake became material and deigned to dwell in matter, who through matter effected my salvation. I will not cease from worshipping the matter through which my salvation has been effected.[63]

The classical Chalcedonian christology continued virtually unchanged through the Middle Ages, though individual scholars sometimes contributed interesting new insights. First, we consider Anselm (1033–1109), Archbishop of Canterbury and author of the treatise *Cur Deus homo?*,[64] which may be translated 'Why the God-man?' Anselm's great merit is that he insists on relating the question about Christ's person to the question of his work. But against this merit has to be set a somewhat cold rationalism and a view of God which sets him over against Jesus Christ and represents him as more concerned with obtaining satisfaction for the infringement of his rights than with reconciling the world in love. As far as rationalism is concerned, Anselm sets out to show the necessity for incarnation on logical grounds, leaving out of account the Christian revelation and Christ himself. Stripped down to its barest essentials, his argument is this. God has created human beings for a good purpose, but because of their sin and disobedience (which he compares to incurring a debt) they have not achieved the goal that was set for them, and deserve punishment instead. But they have no resources either to repay the debt or offer the satisfaction or compensation which is additionally required for the affront offered to God. So man has the *obligation* to offer to God that which he does not have the *power* to bring. God has the *power* to settle the affair, but not the *obligation*. Hence the necessity for a God-man, Jesus Christ. As sharing the nature of God, he defeated sin; as sharing the nature of man, he fulfilled the human debt to God and paid the satisfaction due. As a piece of logical argument, *Cur Deus homo?* has some merit – perhaps it indicates that if there is a creator God who is concerned for his erring creatures, then some form of incarnation would be the way to help them. But as a piece of theology, *Cur Deus homo?* has repelled many readers because its legalistic God has seemed to them sub-Christian. That is no doubt why in modern times many theologians have been more attracted to the views of Anselm's younger contemporary. Abelard (1079–1144) who in a commentary on Romans argued that Christ did not die to appease the anger of God but to inspire human beings through an example of faithful love.

Thomas Aquinas (1225–74), the greatest of the Western mediaeval theologians, gave a full statement of the classical christology.[65] It occupies no less than eight volumes of the bilingual Blackfriars edition of the *Summa Theologiae* and there will be no attempt here to summarize his detailed treatment first of the problems raised by incarnation and the assumption by the Word of humanity, and then in chronological order of the events and mysteries of the career of Jesus. But a few points in his treatment may be picked out for mention. Like Anselm, he sees the incarnation as God's response to man's fall into sin, and though one cannot know what God might have done otherwise, the view seems to be that the incarnation of the Word would probably not have taken place. Also Thomas has interesting things to say about Christ's knowledge. From the New Testament onward, there has been a tendency to ascribe to Jesus a supernatural or even divine knowledge that would place his humanity in doubt. Unlike some mediaeval theologians, Thomas did not agree that Christ had divine knowledge of everything. Like other human beings, he had to acquire knowledge of empirical facts through experience and education. But Thomas did believe that Jesus enjoyed the full beatific vision of God and had an infused or revealed knowledge, including knowledge of his Christhood. A further point worth mentioning is that Thomas raised some highly speculative questions, for instance, whether the Father or the Holy Spirit might have become incarnate, rather than the Son. Some critics have blamed him for raising such questions. But while I admit they are unanswerable, I would say that they are not entirely useless, for they suggest interesting possibilities. I have never myself understood why theologians have maintained that there could be only one incarnation and it had to happen exactly as it did. Now that we are much more conscious than was Thomas both of the variety of revelations or so-called revelations that have come through saviour-figures on this planet, and of the possibility that there are in the universe other personal races of beings who stand in need of a knowledge of God, the notion of a plurality of incarnations or perhaps of degrees of incarnation cannot be dismissed without consideration. It will have to be discussed in the systematic part of this book, but for the moment we note that even so eminent a theologian as the angelic doctor seems to have been open to the possibility: 'It seems that after the incarnation the Son has the power to take up another human nature distinct from the one that he actually did.'[66]

We have seen that Thomas (in common with the Dominicans generally) believed that the incarnation took place to repair the damage of the fall. Duns Scotus (1265–1308) took the view favoured by his fellow Franciscans that the Word would have become incarnate in the creation in any case, and this view seems to commend itself to modern theologians more than that of Thomas.

In the churches of the East, the leading mediaeval theologian was Gregory Palamas (1296–1359), archbishop of Salonika. We have already learned of the high theology of matter which underlay the Orthodox veneration of icons. In Gregory we see this from another angle. He favoured the mystical practices of the Hesychasts, who attuned their prayers to the bodily rhythms of breathing and heartbeat. Gregory held that the entire human being, body and soul, is a unity. The whole human being is made in the image of God and this is implied also by the incarnation. The divine energies flow into the creation, and just as the body of Christ shone at the transfiguration, the Christian in his whole being is transfigured and deified by grace. This mysticism seems poles apart from the rationalism of Anselm in the West, but it may have something to tell us about the mystery of resurrection.[67]

We end this chapter at the Reformation. At first, it seemed that the Reformers might bring major changes in christology. Martin Luther (1483–1546) attacked the speculations of the scholastics and stressed 'saving' as distinct from 'sophistical' knowledge, that is to say, christology based on soteriology rather than on metaphysics. This new attitude was given classic expression by Philip Melanchthon (1497–1560). 'The mysteries of the Godhead are not so much to be investigated as adored. It is useless to labour long on the high doctrines of God, his unity and trinity, the mystery of creation, the mode of incarnation . . . To know Christ is to know his benefits, not to contemplate his natures and the modes of his incarnation.'[68] This is true if one is preaching, but it is hardly a recipe for theology, and both Luther and Melanchthon soon went back to the scholasticism which they professed to despise. However, something must have rubbed off on Lutheranism, for the momentarily more radical views mentioned above have reappeared in Ritschl, Herrmann, Bultmann and others.

John Calvin (1509–64) is by common consent the best of the Reformation theologians. It is true that he taught a doctrine of Christ's work even grimmer than that of Anselm and involving the substitutionary punishment of Christ in the place of the human race. But on the whole he remained firmly committed to Chalcedonian christology. Two points in his teaching are interesting. He noted that in the Old Testament three types of persons had been anointed – kings, priests and prophets. So in his *Institutes of the Christian Religion* (final edition) he made the threefold office (*munus triplex*) of prophet, priest and king, a basic ingredient of his christology, and has been widely followed in this by Reformed theologians. The other point is his difference from the Lutherans. Whereas they held that the incarnate Logos was wholly in Christ, Calvin denied this and taught that the Logos 'continuously filled the world even as he had done from the beginning'.[69] This teaching has been called *illud extra calvinisticum*. It is a point with some importance, and reappears in Barth.[70]

Thus, in the sixteenth century, the classic christology still stood more or less intact. It was not the Reformation but the Enlightenment that was to challenge its centuries-long dominance. The fact that it did stand for so long is an evidence of its strength and a warning that it may not lightly be set aside. But in the new age the ancient structure was shaken to the very foundations. To this new age we must now turn.

PART TWO

The Critique of the Classical Christology and Attempts at Reconstruction

8

Rationalist Christology

In the first chapter of this book, I referred to the famous 1784 essay of Immanuel Kant (1724–1804) entitled 'An Answer to the Question, "What Is Enlightenment?"'[1] I quoted only from the first paragraph of that essay, where Kant describes the enlightened person as one who uses his own understanding and does not rely on the guidance of others. In the remainder of the essay, Kant has much to say about religious belief, because that is an area in which many people have declined to think for themselves and have relied on the views taught by the church and sometimes even prescribed by the state. Kant, as one might expect, was eager to promote independent thought in this area as in others and to defend the rights of reason to question and criticize in the face of authority and tradition. It was with this purpose in view that he published his important work *Religion within the Limits of Reason Alone* (1793). Near the beginning of his book, he writes provocatively: 'Were biblical theology to determine, wherever possible, to have nothing to do with reason in things religious, we can easily see on which side would be the loss; for a religion which rashly declares war on reason will not be able to hold out against it in the long run.'[2]

The sentiment expressed here is very typical of the Enlightenment, and we shall indeed take Kant and his book on religion as our example of a 'rationalist' christology, that is to say, a statement about the significance of Jesus Christ by one who bases himself on the data and methods permissible 'within the limits of reason alone'. But perhaps it should be added at once – and it will become clear in what follows – that at certain points Kant is not at all typical of Enlightenment thought on these matters. Though one cannot assign precise dates, the Enlightenment had been going on for a long time before Kant. The early Enlightenment thinkers had glorified reason, and had found religion a fairly easy target for their criticisms in the name of reason. Kant took a different target, and his criticisms of religion have to be traced back to a more fundamental criticism. Kant had taken upon him to criticize reason itself. This is what the critical philosophy was about. When the first edition of *The Critique of Pure Reason* was published in 1781, the very title made it clear that what was being put on trial was reason itself. Kant claimed that his work in philosophy amounted to a Copernican revolution, and so it was, for reason was being turned inward to examine itself. Certainly, one had to have a profound faith in reason to do this. Yet, the result was also to show the limitations of reason. In Kant's view, reason has what might be called an 'imperialistic' tendency, that is to say, it tends to pronounce about matters beyond its competence. 'Human reason has this peculiar fate, that in one species of its knowledge it is burdened by questions which, as prescribed by the very nature of reason itself, it is not able to ignore, but which, as transcending all its powers, it is not able to answer.'[3] So there is a paradox here, and how serious it may turn out to be, we cannot yet say. Reason takes upon itself the awesome task of investigating its own foundations, but in the course of this inquiry, it discovers its own limitations.

This explains my remark that the criticisms of religion in the first *Critique* are incidental to the more fundamental criticism of reason. What Kant actually criticizes is the traditional natural theology with its alleged 'proofs' of the existence of God. But the fault in this is that reason has overshot itself; in particular, it has taken categories which are only applicable within space and time and has sought to apply them to supersensible realities. But then one must look more closely at what we can expect to know about religious realities 'within the limits of reason alone'. The word 'limits' has to be taken very seriously. If natural theology is 'transcendental illusion', how can religious ideas derived from reason be used to criticize (or support) the beliefs of a supposedly 'revealed' theology, as Kant seems to require? Perhaps he would reply that this objection would hold against 'pure' or 'theoretical' reason, but not against 'practical' reason, on the basis of which he tries to re-found faith. But this dualistic division of reason into theoretical and practical is something which he never clearly explains or justifies.

How did Kant see the relation of his rational theology to theology as it is understood in the churches, that is to say, theology founded on the Bible and tradition? This relation is stated quite clearly in the preface to the second edition of Kant's book. He compares the two types of theology to two concentric circles. The larger circle is 'revealed' or 'biblical' theology, containing all the historical and symbolic material on the basis of which Christian theology has been built up. The rational theologian or philosopher of religion must prescind from all this historical material, he must, in Kant's words, 'waive consideration of all experiences'. The ideal, apparently, would be for the philosopher to extract from traditional theology its timeless essence, and by this Kant understood its moral significance. This is *a priori*, capable of being derived from rational principles alone, apart from any historical experience. Kant modestly tells us that it is not necessary for us even to have an understanding of his own system of critical philosophy in order to understand his book on the religion of reason: 'To understand this book in its essential content, only common morality is needed, without meddling with *The Critique of Practical Reason*, still less with the theoretical *Critique*.' Reading Kant's words almost two hundred years after they were written, we cannot help being struck with the formidable gulf which now separates us even from the best thought of the Enlightenment. Could one possibly arrive at the 'essence' of Christianity or of any concrete form of religion by abstracting it from its history and its symbols, as if these were somehow extraneous additions? Or is there a reason (whether theoretical or practical) so pure that it can operate unaffected by the historical circumstances of the reasoner? The awakening of the human race (or, at least, the Western part of it) to a sense of human rationality and human responsibility, that awakening which we call the Enlightenment, certainly demanded that in every field, perhaps especially in religion and theology, authority and tradition must be called into question, yet even as sober a man as Kant was swept to the extravagant view that reason can operate in a vacuum, without regard to history and circumstance.

Of course, in this matter Kant is simply following a path that had already been marked out by some of his predecessors in the Age of Reason. The attempt to isolate a timeless essence of Christianity and to identify it with natural or rational religion had been made long before by Lord Herbert and the deists.[4] In Germany, Gotthold Ephraim Lessing, who died in the same year that Kant's first *Critique* was published, had exposed the difficulty of seeking to base universal moral or religious truths on events of history. In the first place, reports of such events are liable to be mistaken, especially if they took place a long time ago.

> If I had lived at the time of Christ, then of course the prophecies fulfilled in his person would have made me pay great attention to him; if I had actually seen him do miracles, I would have gained so much confidence that I would willingly have submitted my intellect to his. But I live in the eighteenth century in which miracles no longer occur. The problem is that *reports* of fulfilled prophecies are not fulfilled prophecies; that *reports* of miracles are not miracles. These reports have to work through a medium that takes away all their force.[5]

From this he draws the inescapable conclusion that 'if no historical truth can be demonstrated, then nothing can be demonstrated by means of historical truths. That is, accidental truths of history can never become the proof of necessary truths of reason.'[6] This last sentence, often quoted, brings a new consideration into the argument. The fact that alleged historical truths are never entirely certain is not the only reason for saying that one cannot demonstrate from them necessary truths of reason. An even more important reason is that even if one knew with certainty some historical truth, that truth would still be contingent or accidental, and would not have the universality that the true rationalist seeks. Lessing spoke of the 'ugly ditch' which separates accidental truths from necessary truths, and he said that though he had often and earnestly tried to leap across, he had never succeeded. In the next century, Kierkegaard thought that he had successfully made the leap, but we shall not prejudge his performance. What can be said at the moment is that Lessing did indeed expose an epistemological gap in Christian theology. But Lessing, as a good rationalist, believed that what reason in its critical capacity had taken away, it could restore from its own *a priori* treasures. The history of Jesus Christ and all the supporting apparatus of revelation is not strictly necessary, though it may be useful. 'Revelation gives nothing to the human race which human reason could not arrive at on its own; only, it has given, and still gives to it, the more important of these things sooner.'[7]

Kant's view on the questions mentioned in the preceding paragraph did not differ essentially from Lessing's. But there was one point at which Kant sharply separated himself not only from Lessing but from the majority of his predecessors in the Enlightenment. Lessing was an optimist, not to say a perfectionist and utopian. As man's rationality frees itself from ignorance and the dominance of the past, a new world, rational, moral, even religious in the somewhat attenuated sense in which Lessing understood that term, will open out. 'It will assuredly come! the time of a new eternal gospel . . . perhaps even some enthusiasts of the thirteenth and fourteenth centuries had caught a glimpse of this new eternal gospel.'[8] Did he have in mind various disciples of Joachim of Fiore, who in the centuries mentioned were looking for an 'age of the Spirit' in which the church would shed its dogmas, ceremonies and institutional trappings, and all society would be transformed into a society practising something like Lessing's rational religion of humanity? Kant had little patience with such utopianism, for he believed that it ignored a basic fact of human nature. On the very first page of his book on religion, he pours cold water on Enlightenment optimism by drawing attention to what theologians called 'original sin' and Kant calls the 'radical evil' in human nature.

That 'the world lieth in evil' is a plaint as old as history, old even as the older art, poetry; indeed, as old as that oldest of all fictions, the religion of priest-craft . . . More modern, though far less prevalent, is the contrasted optimistic belief, which indeed has gained a following solely among philosophers and, of late, especially among those interested in education – the belief that the world steadily (though almost imperceptibly) forges in the other direction, to wit, from bad to better; at least that the predisposition to such a movement is discoverable in human nature. If this belief, however, is meant to apply to *moral* goodness and badness (not simply to the process of civilization), it has certainly not been deduced from experience; the history of all times cries too loudly against it.[9]

So Kant feels bound to admit what he calls a radical innate principle of evil in the human species. I compared this to the 'original sin' of Christian theology, and the comparison is not without foundation, for Kant had a Calvinist background. (His grandfather, who spelt his name Cant, had come to East Prussia from Scotland, where the surname Cant is still common on the east coast.) Kant indeed rejected the idea that sin is propagated hereditarily in the human race, but he was much more sensitive to the threat of moral evil in human life than most of his philosophical contemporaries. He rejected too the Calvinist doctrine of a 'total depravity' of human nature, for if evil is a fact of experience, so is human seeking after good. But Kant was aware also of what may be called the sheer gratuitousness of evil in human affairs, both among primitive peoples and those who are judged to be civilized. Evil is done not only when it is expected to bring some advantage to the evil-doer, but sometimes evil is done apparently for its own sake. There is, so to speak, a mean streak in human beings, an aggressive desire to hurt the other, even if the other is in no way threatening.

The New Testament parable of the labourers in the vineyard is instructive in this respect. The owner of the vineyard pays a full day's wages to all who have worked for him, even those whom he hired late in the day. Those whom he had hired early in the morning complain. But why should they? They get the wage they have been promised. That the owner is being generous by paying the same wage to the others is not doing them any harm. The owner's question to them gets the point: 'Do you begrudge my generosity?' (Matt. 20.15). Kant distinguishes three degrees of immoral action. The action may spring from weakness – one wants to do the right thing, but is not strong enough to resist the inclination to do something else. Or the action may spring from the impurity of our motives, that is to say, we may do the right thing, but we do it from an unworthy motive, such as fear. But there is also a third case – the immoral action is done out of wickedness. The gospel parable quoted above gives an illustration readily recognized of how human beings will inflict harm on another or seek to deprive that other of a benefit just for the sake of putting that other person down. Decidedly sad though this may be, it is a far more realistic view of the human condition than the optimistic belief that people will normally do the right thing.

The fact that Kant puts the radical principle of evil in human nature at the beginning of his philosophical theology ensures therefore that we shall not be offered any utopian point of view, though equally he avoids the opposite extreme of representing human beings as so utterly disabled by sin that they can bring forth nothing that is good. But we have to ask the question whether Kant sees the moral deficiency of the human race as the sole justification for religion. There is no doubt that Kant laid the highest possible value upon morality, and that the tendency throughout his writings is to assign to religion only the derivative value that it strengthens the moral character and supplies the moral deficiency that is so widespread among human beings. But actually he is far from being consistent on these matters. He wants to conceive the human person as a rational and therefore moral being who lives quite autonomously in accordance with his reason. 'So far as morality is based on the conception of man as a free agent who, just because he is free, binds himself through his reason to unconditioned laws, it stands in need neither of the idea of another Being over him, for him to apprehend his duty, nor of an incentive other than the law itself, for him to do his duty.'[10] This insistence on the autonomy of the moral life is of the highest importance for Kant. As a rational being, man must give himself the law, he must derive it from his own rationality. If it is a law given to him by some authority outside himself or above himself, by God, in other words, then that is heteronomy and unworthy of a rational being. It is an offence against the first principle of enlightenment – have the courage to use your own understanding, rather than relying on the guidance of another! We may ask, of course, is God simply another, or might he not somehow be at the very heart of human life and human rationality itself? Kant throughout most of his career thought of God as the deists had done, as a distant Being external to the creation. Perhaps at the end of his career he had formed a better idea of divine immanence, and we shall have to consider that at a later stage. But here we are taking note of Kant's constant insistence on the autonomy of man himself as the source of the moral law. Then, beyond that, a pure morality must have as its motivation simply the performance of duty as required by rationality; if God is brought into consideration as holding out either rewards for the performance of duty or punishments for the failure to perform, that destroys the purity of the motive and the truly moral character of the action. So on Kant's own view of morality, it would be hard to argue that religion must be brought in as a supplement to make good our moral deficiency, for such a supplement would be itself a perversion of the true nature of morality. We shall see this plainly when we come to the point where we consider Kant's extraordinary struggle to come to terms with the theological idea of grace.

On the other hand, it must increase our admiration for Kant that he did have the courage and realism to insist on a radical and innate principle of evil in human nature, for by his honesty in insisting on this, he threw a spanner into the works of his own philosophy. His cherished Enlightenment conception of man as a rational being living in the autonomy of reason is not tenable if that same man is somehow a flawed being, unable to measure up to the demands of his own rational nature. And the inconsistency into which Kant is forced is increased on the other side by his unwillingness to allow any intrinsic worth to religion and to see it only as a prop for morality. If communion with God is a good in itself, even, as some would claim, the highest good, then one would not need to justify religion on the ground that it is good for morals – especially if, on one's own theory, it is destructive of the autonomy of morals.

These arguments about the relation of morality and religious faith may remind us of rather similar arguments among theologians about the motivation behind the incarnation. Did God send Christ to the human race because that race had fallen into sin, and only through the coming of the Word in Christ and his obedience even to death on the cross could the race be restored to a right relation to God? This, I think, is how Anselm and Athanasius and Paul and many others would have thought. Or was the incarnation something that would have taken place irrespective of the fall, a fuller identification of God with his creation so as to bring it nearer to the fulfilment he intended for it? This, perhaps, would have been the view of Abelard and Origen and John. Such questions, of course, are speculative and unanswerable, but they do have some value in stimulating theological reflection.

Let us now then ask what place Kant finds for Jesus Christ in his philosophical religion. Strictly speaking, perhaps, the answer would be that there is no place for Jesus Christ or for any historical figure in such a religion. Yet Kant is also trying to show that his religion within the limits of reason is, shall we say, the essence or inner meaning of Christianity, and presumably of other faiths as well. I use the word 'faiths' here because in Kant's usage, there is only one *religion* ('natural religion' or 'rational religion') but many faiths, the concrete historical forms of Christianity, Islam and the rest, which, to greater or less extent, may embody the one religion. Christian faith has at its centre Jesus Christ. The corresponding place in the one religion is occupied by what Kant calls the 'archetype' of a life 'well pleasing to God'. He tells us plainly that 'we need no empirical example to make the idea of a person morally well pleasing to God our archetype; this idea as an archetype is already present in our reason'.[11] Yet when he describes the content of this archetype, we can hardly fail to recognize in it something very like the content of the historical personhood of Christ: 'This ideal of a humanity pleasing to God (hence of such moral perfection as is possible to an earthly being who is subject to wants and inclinations) we can represent to ourselves only as the idea of a person who would be willing not merely to discharge all human duties and to spread about him goodness as widely as possible by precept and example, but even, though tempted by the greatest allurements, to take upon himself every affliction, up to the most ignominious death, for the good of the world and even for his enemies.'[12] The historical figure of Jesus Christ, his teaching and his passion, can be discerned as the content of this archetype, and may also begin to make us wonder whether the Enlightenment belief that accidental truths of history cannot serve as a foundation for universal truths is as persuasive as the eighteenth-century rationalists believed. A bare archetype of the life well pleasing to God, understood as the abstract conception of such a life as might be constructed from reason alone, a conception in which we 'waive consideration of all experience' (in Kant's phrase), would be empty, and so dull that it could hardly be expected to excite enthusiasm in anyone. It needs the concrete instantiation which exerts an appeal to the imagination. Furthermore, the concrete historical example has about it a kind of inexhaustibility. For instance, the witness of the gospels to Jesus Christ has been studied in the minutest detail for centuries, yet there seems to be always more to discover. In a well-known passage in which he is discussing our ordinary empirical knowledge of the world, Kant remarks: 'Thoughts without content are empty, intuitions without concepts are blind.'[13] This surely holds good also in religion and theology. Partly it arises within ourselves, out of the very constitution of our nature; partly it arises from the encounters of experience – encounters with other persons, with nature, with God.

It is not just the case (or so I would hold) that it would take much longer for reason to arrive at the conception of a life well pleasing to God without the stimulus of a concrete example (call it revelation if you wish) as Lessing believed, and Kant probably agreed. And it is not just the case that because human nature, for whatever reason, is flawed and perverted by sin that it needs something like a conversion experience (Kant calls it a 'change of heart') before it comes to perceive where its true good lies and still more to achieve it. It is that the input of experience and our appropriation of that experience are both needed, and it is not possible to say that one of these is more fundamental than the other or that one of them is sufficient without the other. A concrete saviour-figure (whether Jesus Christ or some other figure from salvation-history) is not an optional extra or a mere facilitation of the spiritual life, but indeed a revelation, an overwhelming opening up of the possibilities hidden in human life. On the other hand, there could be an endless succession of saviour-figures and we could remain blind to their significance were there not something within us (conscience? practical reason? mystical awareness? religious consciousness? or however one may describe it) which enables us to recognize in the saviour-figure our own highest good. In the case of Jesus, there were many who saw nothing special in him, but there were also witnesses who confessed 'Thou art the Christ' or used some other form of words. In Matthew's gospel, when Peter makes this confession, Jesus replies. 'Flesh and blood has not revealed this to you, but my Father who is in heaven' (Matt. 16.17). In modern language, we might say to Peter, 'It was not empirical observation that prompted your confession, but a recognition deep within you that this is the humanity to which you and all human beings are called, and this recognition come from God.'

Let me explain this point further, and with a more direct reference to Kant. For I think Kant has an important point here, and it must not be ignored or allowed to disappear because we are making some other justifiable criticisms of what he says. The point is this, that in religion there is a synergism or working together of revelation and our natural powers of knowing. This has to be maintained against theologians who make exaggerated claims for revelation and who deny that there is any genuine knowledge of God other than that which comes through the specific revelation in Christ. For how do they answer the question of recognizing a revelation as revelation? Kant, I believe, gives the correct answer to the question. We recognize the historical Christ as revelation because we already have in our constitution as human beings an ideal or archetype which, we believe, we see fulfilled in him. The reader may recall that in Chapter 2, which was entitled 'The Prehistory of Christology', we saw how over a long period certain expectations and aspirations had been formed, and that Jesus was interpreted in terms of these. We saw, of course, that this was a very complex process, nothing so simple as the straightforward fulfilment of prophecies, as some Christian apologists of the past had been accustomed to claim. Jesus, we acknowledged, was as much a contradiction as a fulfilment of expectations, certainly in the sense that he went beyond them. But is the case any different with that archetype or ideal of humanity which lies deep in every human person – the image of God in which he or she was created, to use the traditional theological language? For that archetype both draws us and beckons us through our conscience and moral awareness, and yet at the same time condemns us for falling so far short.

Now, I said that this is a natural knowledge within us, an understanding, however imperfect or impaired, of what authentic humanity is, and that means what I *ought* to be. When I see this ideal realized beyond my expectations in another, namely Jesus, I recognize him as revelation, as God's Word to us, as God's Son in the image of the Father, as the Christ or however I express it. This is what I mean by a synergism or co-working between revelation and natural knowledge. But it is important not to make that gap between revelation and natural knowledge too wide. I have written elsewhere that 'there is a sense in which all natural theology is revealed theology, for if God is the source of everything, he must also be the source of the knowledge of himself, and there is no "unaided" knowledge of God, any more than there is unaided knowledge of my neighbour. But there is also a sense in which all revealed theology is natural theology, since it comes through persons, things and events in this world and is appropriated by our universal human faculties.'[14] Although I have been calling this inner ideal of a humanity well pleasing to God 'natural' knowledge, which it is indeed as part of our human 'nature', we have to remember that we did not invent this nature for ourselves. Our constitution as rational, moral, personal beings is *given* to us, it is the donation of Being. In theological language, we are created by God in his image. Creation is itself a gift, the most fundamental act of giving. Therefore we cannot make an absolute distinction between nature and grace. Because nature is itself given, it is from the beginning infused with grace. Likewise, because the power of knowing is itself a gift, all our knowing is in some measure revelation. This point was clearly understood by Kant. The archetype of a life well pleasing to God or the ideal of a perfected humanity is not something we invent, but something that we discover as part of our original endowment as we learn who and what we are. So, claims Kant, 'just because we are not the authors of this idea, and because it has established itself in man without our comprehending how human nature could have been capable of receiving it, it is more appropriate to say that this archetype has *come down* to us from heaven and has assumed our humanity.'[15] This is a most important statement on Kant's part, an acknowledgment of 'revelation' and even something like 'incarnation', like the *descendit* of the Nicene creed.

But it is equally important to notice the difference here between what Kant is saying and what traditional Christian theology has said. For Kant, it is the archetype that has 'come down': that moral and spiritual ideal that lodges in every human being has its origin in the creative reality we call God. It is something like the early Christian idea of the Word in which all human beings to some extent participate. But what is being said specifically of Jesus Christ? The New Testament message is that the Word, which has indeed been in the world since the beginning and has manifested itself in various ways, has been fully embodied in Jesus Christ. I think that Kant, on the basis of the gospel records, believed that the earthly life of Jesus was indeed the fulfilment of the archetype, but this historical exemplar did not interest him as much as did the archetype itself. This is understandable from the point of view of any philosophy in which ideas and logic are more important than concrete living realities. What Augustine said about Plato could be repeated with slight modification about Kant. Here we learn that there is an archetype and that it has its origin in God, but we do not learn that the archetype has become flesh or has inserted itself into time and history. But if our understanding of the Christ is rationalized to this extent, has not something of vital importance been lost – the claim namely that the life well pleasing to God is not just a distant ideal or dream, but has been actualized in history, in the face of finitude, temptation, suffering and so on? And it could hardly be claimed that it is in fact realized in the whole human race, in every member of which the archetype or some trace of the archetype is present. Kant at least could not make that claim, even if some optimistic rationalists might have been bold enough to make it. For Kant, we remember, held that not only is the archetype present in human nature universally, but so is also a radical innate principle of evil. The author of John's gospel knew this too, for though he speaks of the Logos as the light which lightens every human being, he also declares that when the Word came to his own, they did not receive him.

What I have called the 'rationalist' christology of Kant (and it is probably the best statement of a rationalist christology that came out of the Enlightenment) seems to be fundamentally docetic. Kant seems to have done what Wrede wrongly accused Paul of doing – placing his faith in an eternal otherworldly Christ, and then only connecting this supernatural figure accidentally with the human Jesus of Nazareth. For Kant's archetype is, from another point of view, the eternal Christ, as distinct from the historical Jesus. This is the Christ who is the same yesterday, today and for ever, an unchanging timeless pattern who has pre-existed in the minds of rational beings, still lives (as the 'risen' Christ) in their minds, and will continue his 'post-existence' to all eternity, or at least so long as there are still rational beings. Indeed, as we shall see in due course, there may come a time when only the pure archetype will remain as the focus of a wholly rational religion, and the last links with the historical Jesus and with historical Christianity will have been snapped. However, we have not yet reached that point, either in our critical exposition of Kant or in the actual historical development of Christianity.

In fact, Kant does work out, often with great ingenuity, an interpretation of Christianity which shows it to be a narrative or pictorial representation of rational religion. We have seen that Jesus Christ, in Kant's view, does provide a concrete example of the life well pleasing to God, though since we have the archetype within ourselves we do not need Christ to teach us what the content of such a life is. Nevertheless, the fact of Christ brings home to us with a new vividness the claim of the archetype upon us. Especially when we remember that humanity carries in itself not just the archetype but also a principle of evil, it may well require the concrete example to bring about that 'change of heart' of which Kant speaks. 'Such a godly-minded teacher,' writes Kant, 'even though he was completely human, might nevertheless truthfully speak of himself as though the ideal of goodness were displayed incarnate in him.'[16] It might even be said of such a teacher that he has come from heaven, so that in a carefully interpreted sense, Kant can sanction the use of incarnational language. But he is quite definite in his teaching that Jesus was a human, not a supernatural person. Though I did say earlier that Kant is docetic because he lays all the stress on the archetype rather than on the historic person of Jesus as the exemplar of the archetype or even its living presence, he is not docetic in the sense of denying a true humanity to Jesus. And he does this for the right reason, namely, that Jesus is not to be separated from the rest of the human race, if indeed he is a significant figure for humanity. But here the position is complicated by Kant's insistence on the complete autonomy of every human being in the moral life. Each one of us has a duty to conform his or her life to the archetype set before us by our reason. In this connection, Kant invokes his famous principle usually expressed in the abridged form, 'Ought implies can'. In his own words, 'We *ought* to conform to it (the archetype); consequently, we must be able to do so.'[17] Jesus' realization of the life well pleasing to God would be significant for us only if he had realized it in the face of temptation, suffering and so on, that is to say, in a genuinely human situation. As we shall see in a moment, Kant had the greatest difficulty in coming to terms with the idea that human weakness might be supplemented by a divine grace, for how could that happen without infringing the principle of moral autonomy?

But for the moment, let us explore further how Kant explains Christian doctrine in terms of rational religion. Living in Protestant Prussia, he had to make something of the doctrine of justification by faith, since Luther had made it central to his Reformation. All of us are under obligation to conform to the demands of the archetype. Yet the distance separating us from the goal of perfect conformity is, according to Kant, 'infinite', so that at any given time we are falling short. His solution to the problem – and it seems somewhat strained – is this. The change of heart brought about in us by Christ has given us a *disposition* toward the good. God, 'who knows the heart through a purely intellectual intuition' accepts the disposition for the deed. Although Kant does not quote the Lutheran phrase *simul iustus et peccator* ('at one and the same time, both a righteous person and a sinner'), it would seem that he had something like this in mind.

Let us turn now to the difficult question of how the Christian experience of grace or of the divine assistance could find a place in Kant's theology, or in any rationalist theology of the Kantian type. On the one hand, any such experience as grace seems to be excluded. Morality requires that we ought to realize the good, and if the moral sense has the importance that Kant claims for it and is not an illusion, then we must have the ability to do what is required of us. Morality would be self-contradictory if it demanded what we cannot fulfil – unless, of course, morality completes itself in religion. But since Kant regards religion as merely ancillary to morality, he cannot allow that the moral life points onward to religion. On the other hand, Kant, with his undeniable perceptiveness and honesty, acknowledges that the practical reason does not have things its own way in human life, but is opposed and frustrated by a radical principle of evil. So although ought implies can, the sad truth is that we cannot, that weakness and even wickedness constantly deflect us from the pursuit of the good, so that even the most conscientious have to confess themselves unprofitable servants. So if we take this side of Kant's teaching seriously, we are led to the conclusion that something akin to grace is desperately needed. Once more then we have run into an inconsistency in this religion within the limits of reason. We are not able to measure up to the demands of morality; but if we are somehow lifted up to fulfil them, is that not an end of freedom, and therefore an end of morality, which entails freedom?

Kant himself states the dilemma, of which he was very well aware, in the following terms.

> The concept of a supernatural accession to our moral, though deficient, capacity and even to our not wholly purified and certainly weak disposition to perform our entire duty, is a transcendent concept, and is a bare idea, of whose reality no experience can assure us. Even when accepted as an idea in nothing but a practical context it is very hazardous, and hard to reconcile with reason, since that which is to be accredited to us as morally good conduct must take place not through foreign influence but solely through the best possible use of our own powers. And yet the impossibility thereof (i.e., of both these things occurring side by side) cannot really be proved, because freedom itself, though containing nothing supernatural in its conception, remains, as regards its possibility, just as incomprehensible to us as is the supernatural factor which we would like to regard as a supplement to the spontaneous but deficient determination of freedom.[18]

Kant's *aporia* arises from his relentless critical rationalism on the one side and his honest acknowledgment of certain aspects of human experience, especially our moral fallibility, on the other. But why then can he not acknowledge the human experience of grace? Why does he feel constrained to say that divine grace is 'a bare idea of whose reality no experience could assure us'? I would certainly have thought that for many religious believers, it is precisely an experience of grace that has led them to their faith, rather than some subtle argument to prove the existence of God. One has only to think of the testimonies of such great Christians as Augustine. Further, one would have thought that the *experience* of grace is itself indubitable, though questions arise as soon as an interpretation is offered – as, for instance, that the experience comes from God and is not wholly explicable in psychological terms. These reflections suggest that the difficulties may arise from Kant's conception of God. During most of his career, Kant, I think it would be fair to say, understood the word 'God' in the sense which it bore among the deistic thinkers of the seventeenth and eighteenth centuries. God, in this way of understanding, was somewhat abstractly conceived. Stripped of anthropomorphic characteristics, he was a transcendent being who had in the beginning created the world and laid down the laws of nature. Likewise he was the author of the moral law. This God is purely worshipped simply in one's obedience to the moral law.[19] We can recognize in this something very close to Kant's idea of religion within the limits of reason alone. If one asks whether, on such a view, there remains any distinction between religion and morality, the answer would seem to be that the religious believer not only seeks to obey the moral law but accepts it as God's command. Kant does speak in these terms, both in the book on religion and in *The Critique of Judgement*, where it is said that 'religion is morality in relation to God as lawgiver'.[20] But if Kant is prepared to acknowledge God as lawgiver, why not also as giver of grace? We have seen indeed that he is prepared to say that God justifies the sinner in the sense of accepting a *disposition* toward the good as counting for achievement.

One may also ask whether this talk of God as moral lawgiver is not in conflict with Kant's rejection of heteronomy. Must not the moral law be something that man, as a rational being, gives to himself? But possibly Kant does avoid inconsistency here, for he makes it clear that in his view we do not obey the moral law because it is God's command, but we recognize it as God's command because we have already accepted its moral authority on the basis of the practical reason.

If Kant had been able to allow for some experience of God, would this have resulted in a richer philosophy of religion than he is able to offer us? Perhaps it would, though it would place in doubt whether we are still talking about religion within the limits of reason *alone*, or whether we have moved at least a step toward Schleiermacher who found the roots of religion not in reason but in the depths of what he called 'feeling', an intuition which, to begin with, is inarticulate. Kant rejects the idea that we can have any experience of God and he is negative in his attitude to mysticism, but there are a few moments when he unbends slightly from his rather cold rationalism. He does believe that in moral experience and particularly in the exercise of freedom, the human being has an immediate experience of what he calls the 'supersensible'. 'In the whole faculty of reason it is the *practical reason only* that can help us to pass beyond the world of sense, and give us knowledge of a supersensible order and connection, which, however, for this very reason cannot be extended further than is necessary for pure practical purposes.'[21] In his shorter treatment of ethics in the writing called *Groundwork of the Metaphysic of Morals*, Kant introduces the feeling of *Achtung*, variously translated as 'reverence' or 'respect', and this he considers to be a feeling with a rational basis and appropriate to our acknowledgment of the moral law. But if in moral experience we have somehow come into relation with the supersensible, is not this emotion of respect something like a religious emotion, an experience of the holy? Only at the very end of his career do we find Kant in the fragments collected into the *Opus posthumum* moving away from the deistic notion of a purely transcendent and remote God to the thought that God is immanent in the world and in the very being of man. At this point it would not be too much to say that the moral experience, embracing both freedom and obligation, is an experience of God. For Kant, morality is the locus of the holy. We ourselves as rational beings give ourselves the moral law; but rationality is not just my rationality or yours, it is a universal principle in which we each participate. The idea of man's relation to God here is not altogether different from what Kant has said about the believer and Christ – the idea of the Christ is already within, and yet transcends the individual being; nor is it altogether different from the early Christian belief that there is a universal logos in which each rational (*logikos*) creature participates. So we find in the *Opus posthumum* sentences such as the following: 'God must only be sought *within* us . . . God is not a Being outside of me. The proposition "There is a God" means no more than, "There is in human reason, determining itself according to morality, a supreme Principle". There is a Being in me, distinguished from myself as the cause of an effect wrought upon me, which freely – that is, without being dependent on laws of nature in space and time – judges me within, justifying or condemning me; and I as man am myself this Being, and it is no substance external to me, and, what is most surprising of all, its causality is no natural necessity but a determination of me to a free act.'[22] Now we have moved so far from the notion of a distant God that he has been brought so close and made so immanent that one wonders if God-language is appropriate. Moreover, this Being or Principle seems scarcely personal, and for many people, one would not speak of God apart from some form of personality.[23] Nevertheless, I think one could say that these last reflections of Kant on the question of God are consistent with what he has said in the main period of his philosophical activity. They represent an austere kind of religion in which what we may call the 'ethical reality' is regarded with a reverence which is truly religious. It is not so much that religion has been reduced to morality as that morality has been elevated to become the centre of religious feeling. Some things about this religion within the limits of reason are quite admirable – it does stress the ethical aspect of religion and tries to exclude whatever is sentimental and self-indulgent, and in these respects it is very much in the tradition of Christianity, especially Protestant Christianity. It is not for nothing that Kant has been called the 'philosopher of Protestantism'. On the other hand, those aspects of religion which appeal to the imagination and which inspire emotions of loyalty and devotion are disregarded, and many Christians would undoubtedly think that their spiritual heritage has been seriously impoverished in the form it has been given by Kant.

And it can hardly be doubted that this process of impoverishment – or, as some might prefer to say, this process of slimming Christianity down to its simple essentials – is only the beginning of a much more drastic reduction. The religious observances of Christianity are to be valued only for their moral worth. Prayer has its value only in reminding us of our moral obligations and holding them before us. Church-going is justified only as it impresses in a public manner the sense of a moral community. The sacraments are not means of grace but solemn ceremonies with ethical rather than religious significance. It is true that Kant can find a place in his rational religion for virtually all the doctrines of Christian theology, once they have been reinterpreted as symbols having a purely ethical significance. But what is the end of this process?

It is that historical or ecclesiastical faith, appealing to supposed revelations and particular historical traditions, will gradually give way to a purely rational faith, in which the dogmas and traditions will have been completely transformed into philosophical concepts. This will be the realization of a pure rationalistic and universal religion, free from all particularities of history or geography. For Christianity, this would mean even the elimination of Jesus Christ as an historical figure. The pure archetype of a human life well pleasing to God would, of course, still be central, but there would be no need or advantage in associating it with a particular manifestation. In Kant's own words, 'The gradual transition of ecclesiastical faith to the exclusive sovereignty of pure religious faith is the coming of the kingdom of God.'[24]

It follows from this that the Christian church and the Christian faith are transitional phenomena, destined to be superseded by the one universal rational religion. In some ways, it might seem that Kant's views would have fitted Judaism rather than Christianity. In fact, roughly a century after Kant, the Jewish philosopher Hermann Cohen[25] brought together Kantianism and the prophetic religion of the Hebrews into an austere philosophical faith, stripped of all that he regarded as mythology. This religious philosophy of Cohen could be reckoned a lineal descendant of Kant's rational religion of 1793. But it was Christianity that Kant believed to be the historical embodiment of the pure religion of reason. Like many other German philosophers and theologians, Kant betrayed an anti-Jewish bias. 'The Jewish faith,' he tells us, 'was, in its original form, a collection of mere statutory laws upon which was established a political organization; for whatever moral additions were then or later appended to it in no way whatever belong to Judaism as such.'[26] Christianity, although it came immediately after Judaism in time, had, in Kant's view, no essential connection with it. (Many readers will see in this evidence of Kant's almost total lack of understanding of history.) 'Christianity, completely forsaking the Judaism from which it sprang, and grounded on a wholly new principle, effected a thoroughgoing revolution in doctrines of faith.' It is 'that Church which contained within itself, from its first beginning, the seed and the principles of the objective unity of the true and universal religious faith.'[27] I suspect that neither Jews nor Christians would be satisfied with what Kant says here. The 'wholly new principle' was surely the incarnation of the Word, with its prehistory in Judaism, but for Kant, that is all unimportant. His rationalist christology, in spite of his genius, simply fails to do justice to the substance of the Christian tradition.

9

Humanistic Christology

I have entitled this chapter 'Humanistic Christology', and this calls for a few words of explanation. I do not intend the expression to be taken in a reductionist sense. I am going to discuss the christology of Friedrich Schleiermacher, and although he explicitly rejected as illogical and incoherent the traditional two-nature christology, I think that he tried conscientiously to say *in his own terms* all that the classical christology had said. But his christology is humanistic in the sense that it presupposes a fairly definite anthropology or doctrine of man, and that the understanding of what a human being is or can become is the clue to that peculiar status which Christians ascribe to Jesus as the Christ or the Redeemer or the Mediator or whatever expression may be used. But that is still only a partial reason for using the expression, 'humanistic christology'. One could have said the same about Kant's christology, as we find it in *Religion within the Limits of Reason Alone*. I am using the word 'humanistic' for Schleiermacher's teaching rather than for Kant's because Schleiermacher had a more adequate view of what constitutes a human being. Kant thought not only of religion but of the human being 'within the limits of reason alone'. For Kant, the human being is first and foremost a rational being. But however important reason is in human life, it is wrong to isolate it as the characteristic that marks off men and women from other terrestrial creatures. It is too narrow a criterion for the human reality. We are more than rational intellects, and to lay all the stress on rationality is to move toward a one-sided and eventually impoverished understanding of what a human being is. That, I think, became clear to us in our examination of Kant's rationalistic christology. It certainly had its virtues, but it left out many important things which do not happen to fit Kant's narrow concept of the rational. At an early age, Schleiermacher became well acquainted with Kant's philosophy but soon came to believe that it did much less than justice to the human reality, and especially to that dimension of human life that we call 'religion'.

In 1799, only six years after Kant's book on religion, Schleiermacher expressed quite a different approach in a book of his own: *Reden über die Religion an die Gebildeten unter ihren Verächtern*, or, as it is entitled in English, *On Religion: Speeches to its Cultured Despisers*.[1] This book was revolutionary. It repudiated the scholastic orthodoxy of both Catholic and Protestant theology, and at the same time the dry conceptualism (a better term for it than 'intellectualism') of the rationalists of the Enlightenment. Schleiermacher was determined to come to grips with the living reality in all its complexity both of human nature and of religion in particular. It has often been said that his work was like a breath of fresh air blowing into the dust-filled studies of theologians and philosophers alike. He took his readers behind the creeds of the theologians and the abstract analyses of the philosophers to the experiences out of which these things had come. The use of the word 'experiences' here suggests that I might have just as well called this chapter 'Experiential Christology' as 'Humanistic Theology'. The word 'experiential' is very apposite, because for Schleiermacher present experience becomes a more important source for theology than the witness of scripture and tradition, or the *magisterium* of the church. Schleiermacher, while rejecting narrow rationalism, still stands with the Enlightenment in appealing to present experience and insight, rather than relying on the wisdom of the past. So he is also generally regarded as the father of modern liberal theology – one would have said until recently, modern liberal Protestant theology, but now his influence is evident in some Catholic theologians as well. Though perhaps there have been few theologians who could be called disciples of Schleiermacher, and very few today who would accept that title, it is impossible to be insulated from his thought. One of his most severe critics, Karl Barth, has written: 'The first place in a history of the theology of the most recent times belongs and will always belong to Schleiermacher, and he has no rival.'[2]

Schleiermacher was a many-sided thinker and it is important not to be misled by some of the oversimplified characterizations that have been attributed to him. He has been seen, for instance, as a 'romantic' in reaction against the rationalism of the Enlightenment. It is true that he had friends in the Romantic movement, and that he considered that a narrow rationalism, such as we find in Kant's view of religion, missed out much that is essential to humanity. But at the same time he had been deeply influenced from his youth by the Kantian philosophy and by the spirit of the Enlightenment generally, and was just as suspicious as Kant of appeals to authority, miracles, prophecies and so forth. As we shall see when we consider his criticism of the Chalcedonian christology, he was not inferior to other philosophers of his time in the capacity for critical analysis. Others have described Schleiermacher as a 'subjectivist'. It may be admitted that he did direct attention to inward religious experience and away from arguments which tried to establish either theism or atheism on the grounds of objective evidences in the world. This led Feuerbach to the (deliberate) mistake of claiming that Schleiermacher's theology supported his own view that God is nothing more than an idea in the human mind. But this was certainly not Schleiermacher's intention, and I do not believe that any fair-minded reader would think that it was. It cannot be denied that Schleiermacher's conception of God never achieves a high degree of clarity and, especially in his earlier writings, seems close to a vague pantheism, but it is never reduced to a mere idea in the human mind, but, on the contrary, exercises a powerful, perhaps even decisive, influence on what human beings are and become, the influence of a reality other and greater than themselves. If nowadays there are students of religion who hold that God-language refers to nothing outside of human life or transcending human life, but functions only subjectively in articulating the spiritual lives of those who use it, then such persons are not disciples of Schleiermacher, any more than was Feuerbach. It should be noticed too that although Schleiermacher had turned attention to the inner experience of religious persons, he was no individualist. His appeal was to the corporate experience of the believing community.

In rejecting subjectivism as an adequate description of Schleiermacher, we must be equally careful not to exaggerate the influence of pietism upon him. Pietism, encouraging as it did feelings of warmth and devotion, was a natural reaction against the cold rationalism and moralism that was characteristic of deism. Schleiermacher's family had been attracted to pietism and he was himself educated in a pietist academy. This experience certainly taught him that religion is much more than a collection of dogmas, whether orthodox or rationalist, and more likewise than moral duties, even when these are regarded as divine commands. But Schleiermacher's mind had been exposed to philosophy, both ancient and modern, and he was not in danger of being swept away by irrational emotions. He did indeed have a broader understanding of the human reality than the typical Enlightenment philosopher could offer, and in particular he recognized that feeling (*Gefühl*) is an essential constituent of a fully human person. What he understood by 'feeling' we shall consider shortly, but it was much more than mere subjective emotion. So if we wish really to come to grips with what is important in religion, going beyond its outward garb of dogma and ceremonial, we have to penetrate into its roots in the inward spiritual life of man.

Let us then turn to Schleiermacher's writings, and see how he goes about his task. I have already mentioned the early work, *On Religion: Speeches to its Cultured Despisers*. Already in this book Schleiermacher gives a central role to feeling, and he continues to do so throughout his career, though there are some significant differences in his ways of describing religious feeling. The neglect or even contempt which so many of the educated classes evince toward religion is, according to Schleier-macher, due to the fact that they consider it only from the outside. One must plunge more deeply into the life of the soul if one is to get a true picture. 'You must transport yourself into the interior of a pious soul and seek to understand its inspiration.'[3] It is such a sentence as this that arouses the suspicion that Schleiermacher is a thoroughgoing subjectivist, that for him religion is a narcissistic exercise in which the pious soul con-templates itself. I do not deny that such an interpretation is possible, though I certainly would deny that it is what Schleiermacher intended and that it pays proper attention to what he says.

A theology or a philosophy of religion which rests its case mainly on religious experience always encounters this kind of difficulty. Is its primary datum an experience *of God* (objective genitive) or merely an *experience* which the person having the experience describes by the expression 'of God?' In any case, it is this 'deep-down' experience, if we may call it such, that Schleiermacher sees as the root of religion. It is a feeling, in his language, but, as already indicated, for him 'feeling' is not just emotion. Feeling, in Schleiermacher's sense of the term, is an awareness of a reality which has called forth the feeling. Feelings do not arise in our minds at random, out of our own subjectivity. They are aroused in us by the impinging upon us of particular events and situations. Sometimes Schleiermacher speaks of feeling as 'intuition' (*Anschauung*). That word was used by Kant for the deliverances of the senses, and he believed that our intuitions are confined to the objects of sense. Schleiermacher, on the other hand, believes that our intuitions may reach beyond the things of sense to spiritual realities, not least to God. God is not someone or something whom we reach at the end of a line of argument to prove his existence or to posit him as a necessary cause or condition of some state of affairs. God is intuited in religious feeling as the holy, the infinite, mediated through the world. That intuition is grasped in an experience which is, to begin with, wordless. Only as we reflect on it do we put it into words. So dogmas and propositions are a kind of second-order formation in religion. In Schleiermacher's words, 'Dogmas are a knowledge about feeling, and in no way an immediate knowledge about the operations of the Universe that gave rise to the feelings.'[4]

The sentence just quoted calls for a brief comment. To say 'dogmas are a knowledge about feeling' certainly suggests that they are a transcript of the religious experience, but not, I think, that they are simply a *description* of the experience. If the dogma were no more than a description of how the religious person feels, then Schleiermacher would be merely a psychologist, not a philosopher of religion or a theologian. Dogmas are not a description of religious experience, but an attempt to articulate in words and propositions the content of that experience. Most theologians nowadays accept that if there is such a thing as revelation, the revelation does not come ready-made in propositional form. Before it can be presented in the form of scripture or creed or confession, it has to undergo a transmutation in the mind of the recipient of the revelation, or the recipients, if the revelation came to a community rather than an individual. But the 'raw material' of the revelation may have been a personal encounter or an impressive event of some kind. Then those who experienced that event as revelation put it into words in order to communicate it as best they could. It is in some such sense that we may understand Schleiermacher's claim that 'dogmas are a knowledge about feeling, and in no way an immediate knowledge about the operations of the Universe that gave rise to the feelings'. This same sentence makes it clear that for Schleiermacher these feelings refer to a reality beyond the being in whom they are aroused. They are induced by 'operations of the Universe', not by the subjective operations of one's own psyche.

But now it is the expression 'operations of the Universe' that calls for some explication. Operations of the Universe are, presumably, the everyday events which we can all see, but the religious person sees them, or sees at least some of them, as not just isolated events but as events that somehow light up the whole, events that speak of Unity which moves in and through all events. The religious vision sees everything in God. To talk of seeing things in God has been not uncommon among religious thinkers. In discussing Schleiermacher, however, we might take the liberty of altering the expression slightly, and talk of seeing things in their eternal aspect. This was the form of words used by the great Jewish philosopher of the seventeenth century, Spinoza, who declared that 'It is the nature of reason to see things under a certain aspect of eternity' (*res sub quadam aeternitatis specie contemplari*). At the time when he wrote the *Speeches*, Schleiermacher was an enthusiastic admirer of Spinoza. In the second speech, Schleiermacher bursts out emotionally:

> Offer with me a tribute to the manes of the holy, rejected Spinoza. The high World-spirit pervaded him; the Infinite was his beginning and his end; the Universe was his only and his everlasting love. In holy innocence and in deep humility he beheld himself mirrored in the eternal world, and perceived how he also was its most worthy mirror. He was full of religion, full of the Holy Spirit. Wherefore he stands there alone and unequalled; master in his art, yet without disciples, without citizenship, sublime above the profane tribe.[5]

After this eulogy of the God-intoxicated Spinoza, one wonders what Schleiermacher will find to say about Jesus Christ.

Spinoza was virtually a pantheist, and at this stage of his career, Schleiermacher too was close to that position. That is why he can speak more or less indiscriminately of God, the Universe, the All, the Whole, the Infinite and so on. Perhaps 'the Infinite' is the phrase that best catches his thought in the *Speeches*. If we look for a closer definition of the feeling which is peculiar to religion, we find it in this sentence: 'True religion is sense and taste for the Infinite.' It seems to me that this early definition of religion in Schleiermacher is preferable to his later and better known equation of religion with the 'feeling of absolute dependence'.[6] Possibly these two ways of speaking are quite compatible, and are like the obverse and reverse of a single coin. But there seems no doubt that 'the sense and taste for the Infinite' is the more affirmative notion. It draws our attention to the mystery that is at the heart of the human being, the mystery that issues not only in religion but in the whole range of spiritual character-istics that belong to humanity. A human being is finite, severely limited in power, intelligence, moral capacity, and finally given over to death. Yet this finitude is contradicted by that same being's reaching out beyond himself, and though finite, setting his sights, so to speak, on the infinite – looking beyond death to 'eternal life' (variously interpreted), or seeking fulfilment in God (even speaking of 'deification'). In modern language we talk of human 'transcendence' to designate this capacity of the human being to reach out, and although what can be achieved must be limited by human finitude, perhaps there is no limit to what can be imagined, so that to talk of a sense and taste for the infinite in this finite human creature is not nonsensical. It should be noted, however, that there is a potentially tragic element in transcendence. The very same capacity that makes possible the highest human aspirations also makes possible the quest for power and domination. Often it is in the religious institution itself that the ambiguity comes into view, and we find side by side the pursuit of piety and the pursuit of power. Using somewhat different language, we could say that the spiritual constitution of the human being is that which makes possible the capacity to go out into the apparently infinite room of what lies open to the human spirit. Yet we have also to remain aware that there are sins of the spirit more destructive than sins of the flesh. Kant was right in qualifying the rationalism of the human being with the radical principle of evil.

I mentioned the mystery of the human being, and this mystery is nowhere more evident than in the conjunction in our humanity of our actual finitude with the sense and taste of the infinite. For this 'sense and taste', to stick to Schleiermacher's terminology, seems to open before us a realm that stretches out indefinitely and the end of which we cannot see. We may be reminded of John's words: 'Beloved, we are God's children now; it does not yet appear what we shall be' (I John 3.2). Is this some kind of mysticism then? Was Schleiermacher commending mysticism when he declared that true religion is sense and taste of the Infinite? It would not help us to understand Schleiermacher just to apply to him the label of 'mystic'. As we shall see later, there was certainly an element of mysticism in Schleiermacher, but to some extent he shared that suspicion of mysticism which has been characteristic of most German Protestant theologians.

Schleiermacher himself prefers the broad term 'religion' for that activity of the human spirit which he is concerned to describe, and it would be wrong on our part to narrow 'religion' to 'mysticism', without a good deal more evidence. But even the broad and seemingly neutral term 'religion' has attracted criticism. I have mentioned Karl Barth as one of Schleiermacher's strongest critics, though Barth has also been generous in his appreciation of some of Schleiermacher's work. Nevertheless, for Barth, 'religion' is not a good word, though I am not sure that he would have wished to be considered one of its 'cultured despisers'. Religion, in Barth's view, is the opposite of revelation. In the latter, God comes to man and makes himself known. In religion, man grasps at God but never finds him.

> From the standpoint of revelation, religion is clearly seen to be an attempt to anticipate what God in his revelation wills to do and does do. It is the attempted replacement of the divine work by a human manufacture. The divine reality offered and manifested to us is replaced by a concept of God arbitrarily and wilfully evolved by man . . . In religion, man ventures to grasp at God. Because it is a grasping, religion is the contradiction of revelation, the concentrated expression of human unbelief. Revelation does not link up with a human religion which is already present and practised. It contradicts it.[7]

This criticism has to be taken very seriously, especially as we are engaged in a christological study. If the object of our study is the concrete person, Jesus Christ, and if, as Christians believe, he is, in a sense which we are trying to discover, the revelation of God, then is there not something wrong with an approach that begins from general considerations about the human 'sense and taste of the Infinite' and tries to fit Jesus Christ into this scheme? Are we not back to much the same place as we found in considering Kant's rationalistic christology? For there we were directed to an *a priori* idea of a life well-pleasing to God which is already part of the endowment of the human mind and which renders the historical Jesus strictly unnecessary; are we not now being directed by Schleiermacher to a somewhat vague capacity for the Infinite which will surprisingly turn out to be a Jesus-shaped blank into which the revelation (if indeed it can still be called a 'revelation') will fit?

It is important not to make too stark a contrast at this point. We do not have to choose between the alternatives of a revelation coming wholly from without or an innate knowledge that arises out of the mind's own resources. We said in the case of Kant's decision to give priority to the inward archetype over the empirical example that at least he was correct in claiming some reciprocity here, for we could never recognize Jesus as a person well pleasing to God unless we already had some idea of what is meant by a person well pleasing to God, and we do have that idea because of our own constitution as human persons. A very similar argument can be made in the case of Schleiermacher. It is not a fair reading of Schleiermacher to say that the divine is being forced to fit the contours of a God-shaped blank in the human mind; he is simply affirming that if we did not have some innate capacity for responding to God (some sense and taste of the infinite), then we would never have any experience of God. In spite of what Barth says, religion and revelation are not in conflict with one another. Religion is not merely a grasping for God, as if we could take him into our control. But it is an openness to God. I find myself in complete agreement with Maurice Wiles' criticism of Barth: 'The claim that Christianity is not a religion but a revelation is an illegitimate attempt to solve a complex problem in one's own favour by the simple process of an arbitrary definition.'[8] To do justice to the complexity of the problem, it seems necessary to me to acknowledge – as Schleiermacher does – man's quest for God as well as God's quest for man, and this does not mean that one is denying that God's quest comes before the human one and inspires it.

Schleiermacher explicitly makes room for revelation in his conception of religion and indeed puts it at the very source. 'What is revelation?' he asks. He answers, 'Every original and new communication of the Universe to man is a revelation, as, for example, every such moment of conscious insight as I have just referred to. Every intuition and every original feeling proceeds from revelation.'[9] Of course, whether this way of speaking of revelation would be acceptable to Barth and to some other theologians is open to question. Like Kant, Schleiermacher uses the word 'revelation', but he is enough of an Enlightenment man to play down any suggestion of a 'supernatural' element. Revelation, as in the definition of it which I quoted many pages back from Nietzsche,[10] is for Schleiermacher simply a startlingly new insight into a problem. It would be wrong to say that Schleiermacher subjectifies revelation. It has its ultimate origin in God or the Universe, but Schleiermacher is content to leave the matter somewhat vague. 'As revelation lies beyond consciousness, demonstration is not possible, yet we are not merely to assume it generally, but each one knows best himself what is repeated and learned elsewhere, and what is original and new.'[11] The attempt here to rehabilitate revelation by playing down its allegedly supernatural character and by assimilating it to 'natural' experience is paralleled in Schleiermacher's treatment of some other traditional religious ideas. Miracles, for instance, are a serious obstacle to belief in the mind of modern persons. Schleiermacher does not simply throw out the miraculous, but moves attention away from the conception of a miracle as an event which infringes the laws of nature to the conception of miracle as a sign – a conception which, as we have seen, was already beginning to appear in John's gospel. So, when we call some event a 'miracle', then, according to Schleiermacher, this description 'refers purely to the mental condition of the observer'.[12] When he says that 'miracle is simply the religious name for event', we might think he is going too far and abolishing any distinction between miracles and everyday 'natural' happenings. But this is not really so. Any event is potentially a miracle, for any event can be seen primarily from a religious point of view, that is to say, as a 'sign of the infinite'. No doubt some events are more suited than others to function as such signs, but to a religious mind which has become trained to see everything in God – *sub quadam aeternitatis specie* – even the meanest event has the potentiality of becoming a miracle. So Schleiermacher can declare: 'To me all is miracle. In your sense the inexplicable and strange alone is miracle, in mine it is no miracle. The more religious you are, the more miracle you would see everywhere.'[13]

In the *Speeches*, as I have said, Schleiermacher begins from a general defence of religion and, so far as christology is brought into this early work at all, Jesus Christ is interpreted within the general religious context that has already been established. The term which Schleiermacher uses for Christ is 'Mediator' and this of course links up with the ideas of revelation and miracle already discussed. In particular, Schleiermacher finds the Johannine presentation of Christ impressive, for here we have the paradox of the human longing for the infinite brought together with the common and the finite in the person of Christ.[14]

With his deep sense of the importance of signs and symbols, and of the role of feeling in religion, Schleiermacher does not, like Kant, exalt the claims of an abstract 'natural' religion above those of 'positive' or historical Christianity. But he does think that Christ 'never maintained he was the only Mediator'.[15] His followers should also be mediators, and he also visualizes the Deity as overcoming the alienation of the creatures by 'scattering points here and there over the whole that are at once finite and infinite, human and divine'.[16] But while he is open to recognize value in different forms of religion, he follows Kant in minimizing the debt of Christianity to Judaism. 'I hate that kind of historical reference', he exclaims. 'Each religion has in itself its own historic necessity, and its beginning is original.'[17]

We must now leave these early reflections of Schleiermacher to consider his closer engagement with Christianity and in particular with the person and work of Christ as we find it expressed in the works of his maturity. But we shall see that he continued to follow the general direction that had been marked out in the *Speeches*.

Fully twenty years elapsed between the appearance of the *Speeches*, and the publication of Schleiermacher's major theological work, *The Christian Faith*. The first edition of the latter work was issued in 1821, and an extensively revised second edition in 1830.[18] This book of Schleiermacher ranks with Calvin's *Institutes* and Barth's *Dogmatics* as one of the two or three most important systematic theologies of Protestantism. Of course, Schleiermacher had not been idle during the twenty years or so between his early and his later work. He took up problems in many areas, including hermeneutics and ethics, but during these years he was concentrating attention more and more on Christianity and the person of Christ. We have seen that the *Speeches* dealt with religion in general, though Schleiermacher was already distancing himself from the abstract 'natural religion' that had appealed to the deists and recognized that in actual communities of faith there is always a positive historical basis. As early as 1805, the preoccupation with Christianity manifested itself in the writing called *Weihnachtsfeier*, translated into English as *Christmas Eve*. This is a dialogue on the Platonic model among the members of a family who have gathered together to celebrate Christmas. The dialogue is a complex affair, with many points of view finding expression, from historical scepticism to confident faith. But two points come across and may be regarded as developments beyond the *Speeches* and pointers to what was to come in *The Christian Faith*. These two points are the centrality of Jesus Christ and the priority of the testimony of present experience over historical report.

The Christian Faith itself begins with various definitions. Dogmatics (or, as we might prefer to say, systematic theology) is said to be an activity of the church. It is therefore not a general theory of religion or an apologetic for religion in the face of rational criticism (as the *Speeches* were) but the setting forth in words of the faith of a believing community. So Schleiermacher is quite clear that there is no one Christian theology expressing immutable objective truth. Any systematic theology is the product of a particular church at a particular time in its history. A church is 'a communion or association relating to religion or piety', and piety, the defining characteristic of a church, is said to be (just as in the *Speeches*) neither a knowing nor a doing but a feeling.[19] Feeling, in turn, is equated with 'immediate self-consciousness'. So feeling is given a certain cognitive character. An immediate self-consciousness is an intuition of how it is with oneself, an intuition which has not yet been put into words, but which is capable of being put into words. Hence 'Christian doctrines are accounts of the Christian religious affections set forth in speech.'[20]

So far, apart from the concentration on specifically Christian experience, the teaching is much the same as in the *Speeches*. But if we inquire more exactly about the feeling which constitutes piety, there emerges a difference, which I mentioned briefly above.[21] The specific religious feeling is said to be the 'feeling of absolute dependence' (*schlechthinniges Abhängigkeitsgefühl*).[22] Schleiermacher has claimed that human experience falls into two parts – the area which we control, and the area in which we are passive. It is in this second area that we are aware of our dependence, and a moment's reflection shows us how universal and multiform this dependence is. But when we think of *absolute* dependence, this is not just a uniquely high degree of dependence, but something quite specific – the distinctively religious feeling.

I ventured to suggest earlier that Schleiermacher might have done better to stay with his early view that true religion is 'sense and taste for the infinite', rather than replacing it with the new conception of 'absolute dependence'. (The formula, incidentally, first appears in the edition of 1830.) My reason for taking that view was that 'sense and taste for the infinite' has a somewhat more active flavour and suggests man's *quest* for God. Absolute dependence seems to suggest complete passivity. It was Hegel who sarcastically remarked that if piety consists in absolute dependence, then the dog must be the most pious of creatures. I think, however, that Schleiermacher would have replied that to have an awareness of absolute dependence is correlative with and inseparable from a sense of the One on whom we are absolutely dependent. It must be said, however, that this is not obvious. To have a sense of finitude may possibly entail having some inkling of the infinite. In spite of the Enlightenment, the correlation of finite and infinite may still have seemed convincing in Schleiermacher's time. But I do not think that would still hold today. Even in the past two hundred years, man has vastly expanded that area of life over which he has control, and has correspondingly diminished the area where he can be only passive. So when Schleiermacher asserts that the consciousness of being absolutely dependent is 'the same thing' as being in relation with God,[23] and still more when he asserts that the feeling of absolute dependence is universal and does away with the need for the traditional proofs of God's existence, I do not think we can go along with him.[24] There are many people in the world today who do think of themselves as playthings of forces over which they have no control, but interpret this as meaning that they are abandoned to a senseless fate. And there are others who, encouraged by human success in extending control over nature, look forward like Nietzsche to the time when the Superman of the future will take over the supreme control. Such hybris is no doubt a pathetic illusion, but it may be no worse founded than Schleiermacher's belief that consciousness of absolute dependence implies consciousness of God. This may turn out to be the Achilles' heel of his system and specifically of his christology which, as we shall see, depends on this very point.

Throughout this book I have stressed the necessity of maintaining the full humanity of Christ, on the ground that if it is undermined in any way, Christ is made into an alien being and can no longer have any major significance for the human race. I believe that Schleiermacher had the same point of view, and so I called this chapter 'Humanistic Christology'. We must now consider just what this 'humanistic christology' is. We may begin with an important statement of Schleiermacher which seems to assert Christ's solidarity with the human race in terms that to some may seem to be extravagant:

It must be asserted that even the most rigorous view of the difference between [Christ] and all other men does not hinder us from saying that his appearing, even regarded as the incarnation of the Son of God, is a natural fact . . . As certainly as Christ was a man, there must reside in human nature the possibility of taking up the divine into itself, just as did happen in Christ. So that the idea that the divine revelation in Christ must be something in this respect absolutely supernatural will simply not stand the test.[25]

In the passage just quoted, we strike again that familiar but far from clear distinction between the natural and the supernatural. Schleiermacher is claiming first of all that the appearance of Jesus Christ in human history is a natural fact, and I think we must agree, if we are determined to maintain the full humanity of Christ. Perhaps Schleiermacher expressed himself badly when he spoke of human nature having 'the possibility of taking up the divine into itself', but I think he was right in claiming that what we may call a union with the divine was possible for Jesus of Nazareth only because this is a potency that is present in all human nature. Christ did not, so to speak, begin with a supernatural endowment that put him in a different category from all other human beings – then he would not be one of us and would have no significance for human life. Yet this is not to say that he was just a natural product of evolution. In a world created by God, the natural is not merely natural. If we remember what Schleiermacher said about the idea of miracle, we can acknowledge that the natural, perceived from the point of view of religion, is infused with the supernatural, while the supernatural always communicates itself in and through the natural. To speak of the incarnation as a 'natural fact' is not to

deny God's agency, his predestination of Jesus and his vocation of Jesus –
in short, his election of Jesus to his messianic office. Schleiermacher has
no wish to deny this other aspect of the matter. He is trying hard to hold
together both the solidarity of Christ with all humanity, and his
difference.

What then is the structure of this humanity which we know in
ourselves and which is the same in us as it was in Jesus Christ? We have
already seen what Schleiermacher considers the basic character of the
human constitution, that is to say, its radically finite and contingent
nature. His anthropology begins from the datum that a human being both
is finite and is conscious of his or her finitude – and perhaps we should
add, *immediately* conscious of this condition, which means that the
consciousness does not come about as the result of reflection but is there
from the beginning as a 'pre-reflective awareness', if we may borrow a
term which came into use only among some later students of human
nature.[26] The more clearly a human being is conscious of his absolute
dependence, then the clearer becomes its correlative, namely, his God-
consciousness. At least, so Schleiermacher claims, and he takes a further
step in maintaining that 'the feeling of absolute dependence [is] in itself a
co-existence of God in the self-consciousness'.[27] As I have indicated
already, I think it is a pity that Schleiermacher no longer used his earlier
language about the 'sense and taste of the Infinite' as at least a
supplement to his 'absolute dependence' language. But in any case, the
clarity of the feeling of absolute dependence is obscured in human beings
by sin, and this in turn means that the God-consciousness is correspondingly obscured. It is on the basis of this anthropology that the person of
Christ is defined in the following words: 'The Redeemer is like all men in
virtue of the identity of his human nature, and distinguished from all by
the constant potency of his God-consciousness, which was a veritable
existence of God in him.'[28] This implies in turn that the Redeemer is free
from sin, but Schleiermacher rightly claims that this does not detract from
his complete humanity. 'That the Redeemer should be entirely free from
all sinfulness is no objection at all to the complete identity of human
nature in him and others, for we have already laid down that sin is so little
an essential part of the being of man that we can never regard it as
anything else than a disturbance of nature.'[29]

The description which seems to me to catch the essential point in
Schleiermacher's doctrine of the person of Christ runs as follows: he is
'the one in whom the creation of human nature, which up to this point
had existed only in a provisional state, was perfected'.[30] We at once
recognize in this a type of christology which continues the ideas of Paul
and Irenaeus. In fact, Schleiermacher too uses the language of the 'second
Adam': 'As everything which has been brought into human life through

Christ is a new creation, so Christ himself is the second Adam, the beginner and originator of this more perfect human life, or the completion of the creation of man.'[31] This way of looking at the matter brings before us again a hypothetical or speculative question on which we touched briefly at an earlier point, and which has some interest. Was Christ sent only because of sin and to bring redemption from sin, or was the sending of Christ part of the creation-process, an event that was required to bring the creation of the human race to fulfilment? As I have said, the question is hypothetical, and Schleiermacher rightly points out that we cannot consider redemption (and that might be the wrong word) in abstraction from the sinfulness of humanity. But it is no doubt important that we should have an affirmative understanding of redemption (better, perhaps, salvation) as bringing the human person not only to the state of being freed from sin but also to the state of having fulfilled his or her potentiality for being. Perhaps these are merely two ways of describing one condition, but if so, Christian theologians have probably stressed too much the negative process of deliverance from sin and too little the unfolding of the person into that fulness or wholeness which is salvation. On the other hand, when we use an expression such as 'free from sin', although it sounds negative, it is really highly affirmative. But even so, there is a point here. The second Adam is not only successful in overcoming the sin of the first Adam, but also in advancing from the immaturity of that first Adam to the perfecting of hitherto undeveloped human potentialities. Yet equally one has to say that human beings have been not only immature in the sense of failing to realize the human potential, but that they have sinned in the sense of diverting their potential into wrong channels.

We must take note too of another interesting remark which Schleiermacher makes – 'that Christ even as a human person was ever coming to be simultaneously with the world itself'.[32] In saying 'even as a human being', I suppose Schleiermacher means that he is thinking of Christ here not just as the eternal Logos but as the incarnate Logos, and that incarnation did not take place on a particular date but was a process that had been going on during a very long period of preparation. The suggestion seems to be that incarnation is an aspect of world-history or an element in the cosmic process, so that even as the world was developing and assuming its form through the ages in which it has been in existence, Jesus Christ too as a physical existence was in process of formation in these events. This may remind us of that psalm-verse which was early given a messianic meaning, and which we found already quoted in the epistle to the Hebrews:[33] 'Sacrifices and offerings thou hast not desired, but a body thou hast prepared for me; in burnt offerings and sin offerings thou hast taken no pleasure. Then I said, "Lo, I have come to do thy will,

O God", as it is written of me in the roll of the book.' Schleiermacher's way of talking about Jesus' 'coming to be simultaneously with the world itself' would fit very well into an evolutionary context, and although Schleiermacher was writing between thirty and forty years before Darwin published *The Origin of Species*, evolutionary ideas had been circulating since the early part of the eighteenth century, and not only as biological theories but as applied to the wider history of the human race and even the cosmos. It may well be that some of the speculations of Johann Gottfried Herder (died 1803) lie behind Schleiermacher's words, and it was possibly from Herder too that he had learned the importance of *Gefühl* or feeling. Nowhere in *The Christian Faith* does Schleiermacher mention Herder's name, but Barth is correct in claiming that 'without Herder the work of Schleiermacher would have been impossible'.[34]

It will be remembered that Schleiermacher stated his intention of expounding the incarnation as 'a natural fact'.[35] We may think that to a remarkable extent he is succeeding – by concentrating on the humanity of Christ and by setting this in an evolutionary or developmental context, he does seem to be drawing the person of Jesus Christ into the stream of world-history without invoking a special supernatural intervention. I need hardly say that there is a strong appeal in this way of proceeding, and that all of us who live on this side of the Enlightenment are bound to feel this appeal. At the same time, it is decidedly odd to speak of the incarnation as a 'natural fact'. We try to think of it as something that has come about through the agency of events that can be assigned a place within the texture of world-happening, yet we also want to say that something new and decisive has appeared at this point. Perhaps it depends on how rich or how impoverished our conception of 'nature' and the 'natural' is. If our conception of nature is mechanistic or quasi-mechanistic, then incarnation is not merely natural, indeed, no human life is merely natural. But it does not follow that we have to choose as the alternative the 'supernatural', in the way in which that term was traditionally understood. Schleiermacher was very conscious of these difficulties, and we shall have to judge, whether his response to them was adequate.

He does make it clear that he does not think very highly of the doctrine of a virgin birth or virginal conception of Jesus, such as is taught by Matthew and Luke. Schleiermacher's point is that even if one accepts that a virginal conception took place, the exclusion of the male parent would not shield Jesus from the human heritage of sin, for he would still receive it through the female parent.[36] I shall not follow Schleiermacher into the complexities that arise if one posits an immaculate conception of the Blessed Virgin in order to meet the difficulties, but will simply reduce the problem to a stark dilemma: If one so completely identifies Christ with the human race so that one can say that the incarnation is a natural fact, then must not the Christ stand as much in need of salvation as all other men? Whilst if we think of him as Redeemer (to use Schleiermacher's favourite term), must we not put him in a category by himself and make him a supernatural figure?

As I have mentioned, Schleiermacher was very much aware of the problem. At quite an early stage in *The Christian Faith*, he discusses the question of heresy.[37] Quite in line with his definition of dogmatic theology, he sees heresy as teaching which, when we fully consider it, is seen to be at variance with some central doctrine of the Christian faith, or even to make Christian faith impossible. He claims that there are two basic christological heresies – the docetic and the Nazarean (or Ebionite). The first, regarding Christ as Redeemer, attributes to him such an exclusive superiority over all other human beings that it effectually separates him from the race and makes of him a purely supernatural figure, so that Christianity collapses through his irrelevance. The second so thoroughly assimilates Christ to the human creation that he too stands in need of redemption, and again Christianity collapses. How then does Schleiermacher himself handle the problem?

We have seen that he dismisses the doctrine of a virgin birth as an inadequate response to the problem, apart from the fact that it introduces a suspect kind of supernaturalism. Yet it seems to me that Schleiermacher's own answer is not altogether different. On the one hand, the person of Christ is explained in terms of Schleiermacher's anthropology – Christ is the completion of the creation of man, he is the one in whom sin has completely yielded place to an absolutely potent God-consciousness which is equated with the veritable presence of God in him. But Schleiermacher thinks that Christ's freedom from sin demands a break from earlier generations, and so he claims that the 'beginning of his life was also a new implanting of the God-consciousness'.[38] This is not the same as a virgin birth, and the mode of conception is left out of the picture, but is not this *theologically* the equivalent of a virgin birth – a new beginning, a new implanting of the God-consciousness? What is this 'implanting'? The expression is obviously a metaphor, but I think it is not a good metaphor. It pictures the God-consciousness as some distinct 'thing' that gets inserted into the person or soul. If this happened 'in the beginning' of Jesus' life, does this mean that we go back to the mythological idea that even in the womb Jesus was conscious of being the Son of God? Schleiermacher did not believe that, for he holds that '[Jesus] needs to have the whole human development in common with us, so that even this existence of God [in him] must have had a development in time'.[39] In that case, therefore, it must have been in the beginning of Jesus' life only a potentiality which was actualized later as he grew up. But if it were no more than a potentiality, then we have already been told that this potentiality belongs to all human beings. So there was no need for a 'new implanting' of the God-consciousness, the potentiality for which was already present in the humanity which Jesus shared with all other men.

At this point therefore there is a logical defect in Schleiermacher's christology. He has promised to expound the incarnation as a natural fact, but has introduced a 'new implanting' of the God-consciousness which appears to be no less supernatural than a virgin birth. Of course, someone might reply to this criticism that even if there is a logical defect in Schleiermacher's exposition, that is not so serious as would have been the theological defect if he had tried to exclude all supernatural influence from the incarnation. Perhaps the question at issue is just how far sin has so disabled the human race that it makes the emergence of a natural but unimpaired God-consciousness impossible. If one thinks that sin has reached such a pitch, then a supernatural intervention would seem to be needed to correct the situation. But if not, then other solutions might be possible. It might be the case that what we consider the 'natural' resources of human nature – and these resources are, after all, given by God – are greater than we think, and, in certain circumstances, might rise above the constraints of mankind's sinful history, to achieve an unclouded God-consciousness. Schleiermacher's stress on growth and development in Jesus might seem to favour such a view. One need not claim that he was already perfect in the beginning of his existence in the womb (an idea which makes no sense, if we are attaching to it any moral significance) but that, in the deeds and decisions of life, he was, in the language of Hebrews, 'perfected', so that what is called 'sinlessness' is not a static condition but the end of a process of growing into union with God. This will call for further discussion.[40]

Schleiermacher wavers on these matters. He wants to affirm the highest degree of solidarity between Christ and the human race, but he also wishes to ascribe to Christ an 'ideal' status, including an 'essential' sinlessness, and this gives rise to the inconsistency in his position. In the spirit of nineteenth-century theology, he starts off bravely along the road of a christology 'from below', that is to say, from the human Jesus, but when he comes to consider the divine input (that 'all this is from God'), he introduces it in a clumsy manner and fails to give an integrated account.

At the beginning of this chapter, I expressed the view that Schleiermacher had no wish to be reductionist in his christology, and tried to say in his own terms all that the traditional creeds and dogmatic definitions had affirmed about Christ – or *almost* all, for he was impatient, as we too have seen reason to be, with such subtleties as *anhypostasia* and the like. But while I believe he aimed at conserving the essential meaning of the traditional formulations, he was critical of some of these formulations in their way of putting things. I would say that his critique of classical christology was one of the most acute that has been made. It shows beyond doubt (if we still need to be shown it) that Schleiermacher was not a vague romantic who substituted moods for thoughts, but was capable when he turned his mind to it of the most penetrating conceptual analyses.

Let us glance briefly at his treatment of the two-natures doctrine, as it was embodied in the definition of Chalcedon and in formulations derived from it. Schleiermacher has three criticisms here, all of them telling. The first criticism questions the propriety of applying the term 'nature' to God on the one hand and to man on the other, when we talk of a 'divine nature' and a 'human nature'. Schleiermacher's question is simply. 'How can divine and human be thus brought together under any single conception, as if they could both be more exact determinations, co-ordinated to each other, of one and the same universal?' He points out that in modern usage the word 'nature' is commonly used for a summary of the essential characteristics of some finite substance or entity, and is not applicable to God, at least, not in the same sense.[41] The second criticism is even more damaging. 'In utter contradiction to the use elsewhere, according to which the same nature belongs to many individuals or persons, here one person is to share in two quite different natures. A nature is a universal, so that one nature can characterize an indefinite number of individuals. But one individual cannot simultaneously manifest two natures, especially two natures that are poles apart, such as the human and the divine.'[42] A third objection is not quite so clear as the two already stated. Schleiermacher rightly observes that it will make for clarity if terms are used in the same sense in different doctrines. Here the point affects christological doctrine in relation to trinitarian doctrine. In christology, it is asserted that the second person of the Trinity has two natures which concur in a unitary person. In the doctrine of the triune God, it is taught that three persons share a single essence, and the word 'essence' here appears to mean much the same as 'nature' as generally understood. Must not this introduce new confusions? Does the second person of the Trinity have one person comprising two natures, while at the same time he is one of three persons sharing one nature.[43] At a much later stage of the book, I shall try to sort out some of these problems, but for the present I simply mention that Schleiermacher raised them very acutely. In half a dozen pages of his book, he makes a very strong case for a radical rethinking and reformulation of the doctrine of the person of Christ. Of course, it is another question whether his own restatement of christology is adequate. Perhaps few would think that it is satisfactory as it stands, but it may nevertheless contain important clues that might lead to newer and better solutions of the problem.

It is useful at this point to consider also how Schleiermacher understood the work of Christ. It may be thought that so far Christ has been exhibited as the exemplary human being, the completion of the creation of humanity and the paradigm for a future humanity. But in what sense is he not just an exemplar but, as Schleiermacher often designates him, the Redeemer?

It is hardly necessary to say at this stage that Schleiermacher rejects all those views which stress the death or suffering or blood of Christ as a satisfaction of God's honour or the price of redemption or a punishment accepted on our behalf. He considers all such views 'magical', and looks rather to the inward transformation which Christ brings about in the believer, within the community of faith. 'The Redeemer assumes believers into the power of his God-consciousness, and this is his redemptive activity.'[44] That paradigmatic humanity realized in Jesus Christ is imparted to the believers in the corporate experience of redemption in the community. If we ask more closely about the nature of this redeeming relation to Christ, Schleiermacher is prepared to describe it as 'mystical', though, as pointed out earlier,[45] he is not very happy about the term. 'Such a presentation of the redeeming activity of Christ as has been given here, which exhibits as the establishment of a new life common to him and us (original in him, in us new and derived), is usually called by those who have *not* had the experience, "mystical". This expression is so extremely vague that it seems better to avoid it.'[46]

Nevertheless, whatever we may call the experience, it is for Schleiermacher the foundation of faith and theology. It takes precedence over scripture and tradition. If, for example, we believe in the resurrection of Jesus Christ, we do so primarily on the ground of our experience of redemption in him, not on the basis of the reports that have been handed down from a distant past.

I suppose, however, that when one ties theology so closely to the experience of a community, one is also limiting its claims. It testifies only to what the members of this community have known in their experience. If one wanted to claim objective or universal truth for theology, one would have to supplement the testimony to experience by bringing in some rational or 'natural' theology. But we have seen that Schleiermacher believed that religious experience carries enough conviction to make proofs of God's existence and the like superfluous. He sums up his claim in the following sentences:

> This exposition is based entirely on the inner experience of the believer; its only purpose is to describe and elucidate that experience. Naturally,

therefore, it can make no claim to be a proof that things must have been so; in the sphere of experience, such proof is only possible where mathematics can be used, which is certainly not the case here. Our purpose is simply to show that the perfect satisfaction to which we aspire can only be truly contained in the Christian's consciousness of his relation to Christ in so far as that consciousness expresses the kind of relation that has been described here.[47]

10

Idealist Christology

In this chapter we come to the contribution of Georg Wilhelm Friedrich Hegel and some of his more important disciples. I have entitled the chapter 'Idealist Christology' because it presents a view of Jesus Christ within the context of the vast system of philosophical idealism which Hegel constructed. The accusation has often been made from Kierkegaard onward that for Hegel Christianity was simply an appendage of the philosophical system. But this is not the whole truth of the matter. Certainly, Hegel believed that philosophy ranks above theology, for philosophy attains to the level of conceptual thinking, whereas theology still operates at least to a considerable extent with the pictorial or representational thinking that is characteristic of religion. Yet, on the other hand, Hegel firmly believed himself to be a Christian, and his Christianity affected his philosophy, so that the relation between them is to be understood as reciprocal. It is not just a case of absorbing Christ into the system, but (so Hegel believed) of letting the system articulate the significance that extends far beyond the historical individual, Jesus of Nazareth. In *The Philosophy of History*, Hegel sees Jesus Christ 'as a *particular person*, in abstract subjectivity, but in such a way that conversely, finiteness is only the *form* of his appearance, while infinity and absolutely independent existence constitute the essence and substantial being which it embodies'.[1] Already this sentence gives a hint of the difficulty and complexity of Hegel's way of thinking. We might equally well have called this chapter 'Speculative Christology' because it discusses what Hegel himself would call 'speculative' thinking, applied to Jesus Christ. But unfortunately in popular usage the word 'speculative' suggests a way of thinking that is unrealistic and even undisciplined, perhaps only a flight of fancy. For Hegel, on the other hand, speculation is thinking that is dialectical, that is to say, reaching beyond the simple appearance, gathering up loose ends, resolving contradictions, relating wider wholes. In one passage, Hegel relates speculative thinking to mysticism. 'Speculative truth, it may also be noted, means very much the same as what, in special connection with religious experience and doctrines, used to be called mysticism.'[2] But Hegel's usage at this point is peculiar. Mysticism may have access to truth that is beyond the reach of 'the abstract thinking of understanding', but it is not beyond the speculative reason, in Hegel's view.

During Hegel's career, it seems that sometimes the religious interest predominated, and at other times the philosophical. As a young man he attended the famous theological institute at Tübingen, where he had at least two other geniuses of the first rank among his fellow students, namely, Hölderlin and Schelling. But according to the account of these years given by Hans Küng, Hegel's heart was not really in his theological studies.[3] He much preferred the freedom and openness of philosophy. But after leaving the theological school, Christianity began to absorb his attention. He even produced in the last years of the eighteenth century some quite substantial theological writings. These never saw the light during his lifetime, but they have been published in the twentieth century.

One of these pieces, long enough to constitute a small book, is *The Positivity of the Christian Religion*, and this makes it clear that the starting-point for Hegel's thinking about Christianity and Jesus Christ was very close to the position expounded by Kant in *Religion within the Limits of Reason Alone*, published two years before he began writing his own piece. According to Richard Kroner, 'Hegel became a Kantian the moment he understood the revolution brought about by Kant's critical philosophy; and he remained a Kantian throughout his life, no matter how much he disputed many of Kant's doctrines and even his fundamental position.'[4] I think we shall see that Kroner exaggerates somewhat, but the rationalistic stamp remained on Hegel, even if he admitted 'speculation' to have a place as well as the more positivistic 'understanding'.

The word 'positivity' in the title *The Positivity of Christianity* is used in its customary sense in German, when it is applied to religion, though I should say that the titles of these early pieces were given not by Hegel but by the editor. This German use of the word 'positivity' (*Positivität*) is intended to refer to what in English we might more naturally call the particularity of a religion, that is to say, the particular doctrines and ways of thinking about the deity which are customary in that religion, the rites, ceremonies and liturgies used in its public observances, its forms of spirituality, its moral code, its scriptures, its offices and institutions. Contrasted with such a positive religion is 'natural' religion or 'rational' religion, consisting of a few general truths (like those held by Lord Herbert) and perhaps practised only in a private capacity, without any public liturgy or buildings or organized structure. According to Hegel, 'Jesus was the teacher of a purely moral religion, not a positive one.'[5] In fact, Jesus' teaching turns out to be remarkably close to Kant's! It was, in the main, the disciples who turned Christianity into a positive ecclesiastical system. At this point in his development, Hegel seems to have been completely unaware of how unhistorical his account of Christian origins was, or how he imposed on the founder of Christianity the fashionable rationalism of the eighteenth century.

Another unhistorical detail which Hegel took over from Kant was the belief that Christianity owes nothing to Judaism. Hegel went even further than Kant in this matter, for he claimed that the German people had been deprived of their own rich heritage of Teutonic mythology and forced to adopt the Old Testament. 'Christianity has emptied Valhalla, felled the sacred groves, extirpated the national imagery as a shameful superstition, as a devilish poison, and given us instead the imagery of a nation whose climate, laws, culture and interests are strange to us and whose history has no connection whatever with our own. A David or a Solomon lives in our popular imagination but our country's own heroes slumber in learned history books.'[6] In writing these words, Hegel was unwittingly providing material for the extreme nationalism of a later time, and its attempt to revive the old pagan gods of northern Europe.

If the writing just considered is saturated in the philosophy of Kant, we see the beginnings of a change in *The Spirit of Christianity and its Fate*, written probably in 1798–1799, that is to say, just about the time when Schleiermacher was working on his *Speeches*. Here we do see pointers toward the mature thought of Hegel. Thus, while he is again sharply critical of Judaism, what he deplores is its isolation and individualism, its feeling of separateness. Hegel, on the contrary, sees Christianity as seeking to transcend all constricting boundaries in the search for an all-embracing unity. I have elsewhere contrasted Hegel's criticism of Abraham as the individualist with Kierkegaard's admiration for Abraham as the man who even set aside morality for the sake of what he believed to be his individual integrity.[7] A related change can be seen in the way Hegel thinks of God. In his Kantian phase, it was still the God of deism, God the exalted giver of the law, not altogether dissimilar to the God of the Old Testament, who was in Hegel's mind. But now God's immanence and closeness to creation is being admitted. There must be a 'living connection' between God and his creation. This in turn means that a narrowly rational or conceptual knowledge of God is not enough. 'Nowhere more than in the communication of the divine is it necessary for the recipient to grasp the communication with the depths of his own spirit.'[8] And this leads to a further change, the one which touches most closely on our own christological interest. Jesus is no longer to be considered as simply the moral exemplar, the man whose life was well pleasing to God. Jesus is 'Son of God'. But what does this mean? 'The relation of a son to his father is not a conceptual unity (as, for instance, unity or harmony of disposition, similarity of principles, etc.,) a unity which is only a unity in thought and is abstracted from life. On the contrary, it is a living relation of living beings, a likeness of life. Father and son are simply modifications of the same life, not opposite essences, not a plurality of absolute substantialities.'[9] Is this a Hegelian translation of *homoousios*? One further change may be mentioned, since it sums up the others. We now meet with great frequency the word 'love'. I think Richard Kroner is once again exaggerating, though in the opposite direction, when he claims that 'Hegel's first original philosophy might be called a "pantheism of love",'[10] but we can say that in the short period between *The Positivity of Christianity* and *The Spirit of Christianity* there had been a development in the direction Kroner indicates. One must also be cautious about the claim made by some writers that we are seeing in Hegel a dialectical synthesis of the positions of Kant and Schleiermacher. Certainly, Hegel is abandoning the abstract rationalism of Kant, and his own central concept of spirit (*Geist*) is broader, more human, more existential, than Kant's reason, but one has only to read Hegel's many critical remarks on Schleiermacher to realize that for him intellect always retained its priority over feeling.

These early theological writings show that after an initial period of aloofness, Hegel took a keen interest in matters religious and theological, and although from about 1800 onward it was philosophy and not theology that occupied his mind, one cannot read far in any of his major works without coming to discussions of theological problems. For Hegel, philosophy and theology could not be closed off from one another in separate compartments. Philosophy for him was all-embracing, so its most profound problems led inevitably into the regions of theology, while on the other hand any theology that is securely founded must pass beyond the immediacy of feeling to strive for a conceptual grasp of religious truth.

Though Hegel's collected works occupy between twenty and thirty large volumes, only four of these works were prepared by him for publication and made available to scholars during his lifetime. We have seen that the early theological writings did not appear until long after his death. His late courses of lectures at the University of Berlin were likewise posthumously published, having been prepared from lecture notes. These include lectures on the philosophy of religion. So the 'essential Hegel', as he himself had given it public expression, is contained in four works: and perhaps one should immediately add, 'But what works!' They are, *Phänomenologie des Geistes* (1807), known in English as *Phenomenology of Mind* or *Phenomenology of Spirit*, possibly the most difficult book in all

Western philosophy – and I say this after having spent a great deal of time studying and translating Heidegger. Hegel's *Phenomenology* explores the nature and development of spirit, both finite spirit as we know it in our own human experience, and Absolute Spirit which Hegel takes to be the ultimate creative reality. Then in 1812–1813 appeared the two volumes of *Wissenschaft der Logik (Science of Logic)* which may be considered Hegel's system of philosophy in its pure ideality. In 1817 came *Enzyklopädie der philosophischen Wissenschaften*, comprising three parts, an abbreviated logic, a philosophy of nature, and a philosophy of spirit. This was intended to be a compendium of his philosophy for the use of students, and there were two revised editions before Hegel's relatively early death in 1831. Throughout his life, Hegel had been interested in politics and government, and in 1821 he published *Grundlinien der Philosophie des Rechts (Outlines of the Philosophy of Right)*. The influence of these books on philosophers, theologians, politicians (especially Marxists) and others is incalculable.[11]

The difficulties of the *Phenomenology* are occasioned by the fact that one is invited to look at the incredibly complex and multiple manifestations of spirit from one angle after another, to know the differences between the various points of view and yet at the same time to integrate them into one comprehensive concept of spirit. What then is 'spirit'? Hegel needs more than eight hundred pages to give us what he would consider no more than a sketch. Any simple answer to the question, 'What is spirit?' would be merely misleading. Indeed, we might say that one of Hegel's great achievements is to show the superficiality of over-simplified and one-sided answers. At this point we may contrast him with Schleiermacher. The latter stressed immediacy, especially the immediacy of feeling. Admittedly, what is immediately present to feeling or sensations seems to have a certainty that we cannot find elsewhere. But Hegel declares that 'this bare fact of *certainty*, however, is really and admittedly the abstractest and the poorest kind of *truth*. It merely says regarding what it knows: it *is*; and its truth contains merely the *being* of the fact it knows.'[12] But this apparently certain immediacy is deceptive.

> When we look closely, there is a good deal more implied in that bare pure being, which constitutes the kernel of the form of certainty, and is given out by it as its truth. A concrete actual certainty of sense is not merely this pure immediacy, but an example, an instance, of that immediacy. Amongst the innumerable distinctions that come to light, we find in all cases the fundamental difference – namely, that in sense-experience, pure being at once breaks up into the two 'thises' (this I and this fact before me). When *we* reflect on this distinction, it is seen that neither the one nor the other is immediate, merely *is* in sense-

certainty, but is at the same time *mediated*: I have the certainty through the other, namely, through the actual fact; and this, again, exists in that certainty through an other, namely, through the I.[13]

So begins the long trek that leads from immediate experience to absolute knowledge.

One would have to accompany Hegel on that long trek to arrive at his concept of spirit. It is typical of his way of thinking always to reach out toward the whole, to follow up the connections and relations that bind each existing entity to innumerable others. 'When we want to see an oak, with all its vigour of trunk, its spreading branches and mass of foliage, we are not satisfied to be shown an acorn instead.'[14] This means that 'the truth is only to be realized in the form of a system'. Nevertheless, since one cannot grasp the system in one go, so to speak – some would confess it cannot even be grasped *seriatim* – it is permissible for us to seek a preliminary answer to the question 'What is spirit?' from some brief statement which may point us in the right direction. Hegel himself provides such a statement in the lengthy preface to the *Phenomenology*, even before he has begun to comment on the limitations of immediate experience. 'Spirit is alone Reality. It is the inner being of the world, that which essentially is, and is *per se*; it assumes objective, determinate form, and enters into relations with itself – it is externality (otherness), and exists for itself; yet, in this determination, and in its otherness, it is still one with itself – it is self-contained and self-complete, in itself and for itself at once.'[15]

This is a very dense statement, and will bear some brief comment. To say that spirit is alone reality is a metaphysical assertion of the kind that earns for its author the designation 'idealist', but we should not misunderstand it as if it meant that matter is somehow unreal. Hegel is claiming that the active, structuring principle of the world, its 'life' or 'inner being' as he calls it, is spirit. Matter is real, but it serves the purposes of spirit. In Marx, as is well-known, Hegel's view is reversed. Matter becomes the ultimate reality and spirit is only an epiphenomenon of the material world. But Marx achieves this reversal only by endowing matter with that dialectical activity which Hegel had seen as characteristic of spirit, so that Marx's matter is a spiritualized matter, even a deified matter, a matter deprived of its pure materiality. Returning to Hegel's statement about spirit, we next learn what is the distinctive activity of spirit – 'it assumes objective determinate form, and enters into relations with itself'. It is this notion of self-relatedness that is central to the being of spirit. Spirit goes out from itself, objectifies itself, then relates itself to itself as objectified, and in turn relates itself as object to itself as subject. This is, in Hegelian language, very much the point which Heidegger,

Sartre and other twentieth-century philosophers, have made about the human existent. Such an existent differs from, let us say, a stone or a cloud by this capacity to go out from itself and relate to itself. We may notice too that this is reminiscent of the New Testament understanding of the Holy Spirit, who goes out or proceeds from the Father (John 15.26) and who in turn directs the prayers of the church to the Father. Finally, we take note also that spirit which goes out from itself to become other nevertheless remains one with itself. In the *Phenomenology*, the unfolding of spirit is traced at many levels and in many contexts – in the self-consciousness of the individual as he or she rises to greater heights of understanding and knowledge, in the collective experience of nations and historical events, including the Enlightenment and the French revolution that had been so decisive for Hegel's own time, in different types of spiritual experience, such as morality and religion, to which Hegel accords a very high place, and then to crown the system there is the unfolding of the Absolute Spirit as it goes out into the finite, knows itself in and through the finite spirits, and finally returns to itself in a vast circular sweep of *exitus* and *reditus*.

This movement of spirit as it courses through the universe is described more closely in the concept of dialectic. This, of course, is not a new idea in Hegel, for it has been circulating in one form or another since ancient times. Dialectic draws attention to the conflict of opposites in the world. Everything seems to posit an opposite – male and female, hot and cold, light and dark, good and evil, spirit and matter, and so on indefinitely. The world-process can be seen as the constant collision of these opposites, and their constant regrouping in new configurations. What fascinated Hegel was the unending resolution of these conflicts, leading in turn to new conflicts and further resolutions. Probably the best known word in the Hegelian philosophy is *aufgehoben*, which can be translated into English in half a dozen ways according to context – 'taken up', 'sublated', 'absorbed', 'reconciled', 'resolved'. The popular view of the dialectic sees it as a threefold movement: thesis, antithesis, synthesis. The initial thrust is met by its opposite, and the two are resolved in a coming together which provides the first moment in a new dialectical movement. But when one speaks of dialectic in this way, the impression given is too smooth and mechanical. While the threefold pattern is very pervasive of Hegel's thought, he has also to make compromises and admit untidiness-es, especially, for instance, when he is dealing with such a complicated subject as history. There is nothing merely mechanical in the dialectic which he describes in the following words:

The ultimate nature of life, the soul of the world, the universal life-blood, which courses everywhere, and whose flow is neither disturbed

nor checked by any obstructing distinction, but is itself every distinction that arises, as well as that into which all distinctions are dissolved;
pulsating within itself, but ever motionless; shaken to its depths, but
still at rest.[16]

Of course, the danger in believing that there is some universal pattern
of this kind in the happenings of the world is that we begin to impose it on
everything that comes to our notice and may end up by distorting the
facts so that they fit the *a priori* pattern. That first Hegelians and then
Marxists have done this with their dialectic is something that cannot be
denied.

But the fact that there have been abuses and exaggerations, especially
in the application of dialectic to specific and highly complex episodes of
history, does not deprive the general idea of dialectic of all validity. Our
own interest here lies in seeing how Hegel uses the idea in his concept of
God and of Jesus Christ. Here we are turning away from particular
manifestations of dialectic to its ultimate metaphysical or ontological
significance. The following paragraph sums up Hegel's teaching, in his
own words:

> The first and foremost moment is Absolute Being, Spirit absolutely
> self-contained, so far as it is simple eternal substance. But in the process
> of realizing its constitutive notion, which consists in being spirit, that
> substance passes over into a form where it exists for another; its self-
> identity becomes actual Absolute Being, actualized in self-sacrifice; it
> becomes a self, but a self that is transitory and passes away. Hence the
> third stage is the return of self thus alienated, the substance thus
> abased, into its first primal simplicity. Only when this is done is spirit
> presented and manifested as spirit. These distinct ultimate Realities,
> when brought back by thought into themselves out of the flux of the
> actual world, are changeless, eternal Spirits, whose being lies in
> thinking the unity which they constitute.[17]

Even a superficial reading of this passage suggests the Christian teaching
about the triune God. Whether Hegel derived his philosophical conception of Absolute Spirit from reflection on the theological doctrine, or
whether his philosophical idea of spirit as that which goes out from itself
to know itself in an other directed him back to what he had already
learned of the Christian understanding of God, is of little moment. We
can see that in his scheme, the first and foremost moment, the Absolute
Spirit, corresponds to the Father of the Christian Trinity. The Other, who
is actualized in self-sacrifice, is the Son. And the third stage, in which the
unity is restored, is the Holy Spirit, very much as conceived in traditional
Christian theology.

It is important to notice that it is the Trinity that constitutes God in Christianity, and likewise the 'three eternal spirits' in Hegel. God is not simply 'subject', as in Judaism or Kantian deism, but 'spirit' which has gone out of itself into the object. Thus in Hegel the immanence of God is more strongly stressed than in much traditional theism. This certainly does not mean that Hegel is a pantheist, as he has sometimes been called, but it would be correct to call him a 'panentheist', or, as I prefer to say, a 'dialectical theist'.[18] Only a complete failure to understand him could lead anyone to think of Hegel as an atheist, but one can see how the misunderstanding has arisen. If one identifies God with the first moment in Absolute Spirit – 'Spirit absolutely self-contained', in Hegel's language, the 'Father' in traditional theological language – then one might think that Hegel was an atheist, because 'Spirit absolutely self-contained' is only a hypothesis, that is to say, a hypothetical beginning or ground. But from the beginning, that is to say, from all eternity, spirit, in accordance with its nature, has been going forth into the other, has been manifesting itself in the realm of the finite. So if we conceive of God as the absolute Monarch containing in himself all power and being, then such a God has never existed. In Hegel's words, 'The Absolute Being must from the start have implicitly sacrificed itself.'[19] It has gone into the far country of the finite. This requires a doctrine not simply of creation, but of creation qualified by emanation. The Son is the historical Other in whom the Absolute Spirit has imaged itself, in whom the implicit sacrifice which that Absolute has been making since the beginning receives its actual historical realization. Hegel can sometimes talk about a 'speculative Good Friday' as distinct from the historical Good Friday, and by this speculative Good Friday he means, of course, the sacrifice that has always been there in the Absolute Spirit – an idea which is reflected in the New Testament language about the Lamb 'slain before the foundation of the world' (Rev. 13.8). This also requires a doctrine of incarnation, and Hegel does not hesitate to say that 'the thought of incarnation pervades every religion'.[20] The effect of such generalizing language is twofold. On the one hand, it reduces what is sometimes called the 'scandal of particularity'. If we think of one unique incarnation at a particular moment of world-history, then Christianity appears to be separated from all other religions, and the claims of these other religions are put in question. Furthermore, we seem to be faced again by Lessing's 'ugly ditch' which yawns between the particular historical event and its supposed universal significance. Hegel eases such problems, for by seeing the particular incarnation in Jesus as the historical counterpart of Spirit's universal incarnation and eternal sacrifice, he opens up for it an unlimited field of meaning. But there is another side to this generalizing process. The importance of the historical seems to have been reduced to a very low level, even to vanishing point. One cannot say that for Hegel, history was unimportant. On the contrary, history is necessary for the unlocking and manifestation of the riches of Spirit. In his own writings, Hegel spent a great deal of time and energy in the accurate portrayal and elucidation of historical developments. But even so, one is forced to ask whether the historical incarnation in Jesus of Nazareth has anything like the weight of the ontological self-externalization of the Absolute Spirit in the world of the finite, or whether the shattering event of Calvary is any more than a passing reflection of the speculative Good Friday of Spirit's eternal self-immolation. Sometimes Hegel speaks of Jesus as the individual man who is also God, almost in a naive way, as if God were walking the earth in Jesus. But doubtless he would explain this as the picture language of religion, and so he can also 'explain' what it really means by writing long stretches without any mention of Jesus and by transposing his argument into the concepts and universal truths of ontology.

The foregoing remarks on some of the ambiguities of Hegel's philosophical theology direct us to another problem which he raises. What does he mean when he speaks of the 'death of God'? As was true also of Schleiermacher, Hegel was deeply conscious of a tragic element in Christianity. Religion can easily become optimistic and triumphalist, and no doubt there are passages in Hegel's work where he could be accused of seeing things in that way. But the cross is too central and too obstinate a datum for it to be smothered in roses. Hegel speaks of 'the bitter pain which finds expression in the cruel words, "God is dead"'.[21]

These words are not to be understood in the atheistic sense which Nietzsche was to attach to them later in the nineteenth century. They are quoted by Hegel from a Lutheran hymn of the seventeenth century, and they refer to the death of Jesus on the cross.[22] If one accepts that in Jesus Christ there was a union of the divine and human natures, then this may be held to sanction paradoxical ways of speaking, in which divine attributes are applied to the human Jesus, or conversely, human attributes to God. We have seen that such ways of talking were to be found as early as Ignatius of Antioch.[23] The technical expression *communicatio idiomatum* was used for this transfer of attributes from divine to human or *vice versa*, and Luther and his followers seized eagerly on the practice in order to emphasize the unity of the divine and human in Christ. The hymn quoted by Hegel was meant for Good Friday, but the expression 'God is dead' may well suggest for one conversant with Hegel's ideas the speculative Good Friday rather than the historical Good Friday. The language 'God is dead' is so blunt that it must have been uncomfortable for worshippers using this hymn, for the words were changed in later editions to 'The Lord himself lies dead'. But if there is a sense in which we can say that Jesus Christ is God, then it is not meaningless to say that if Christ died, God died, though clearly explanation is needed. In the words of Eberhard Jüngel, 'The decisive event of Good Friday belongs to the divine *curriculum vitae*.'[24] He explains this to mean that God has entered the finite order and refuses to abandon it. The death of God, in this sense, means the death of the God who dwelt apart in untroubled bliss, but this is neither the God of Christian faith nor the God of Hegel's philosophy, for which Absolute Spirit, totally self-contained, is, as we have seen, a hypothetical idea posited 'in the beginning'. The death of God as the all-powerful, irresistible, triumphant God on account of his having gone into the finite and shared the experiences of suffering and death may at first strike us as unrelieved tragedy. 'God has died, God is dead – this is the most frightful of all thoughts, that all that is eternal, all that is true, is not, that negation itself is found in God; the deepest sorrow, the feeling of something completely irretrievable, the renunciation of everything of a higher kind, are connected with this.'[25] Yet this is also the moment when God has drawn near, when we can discover the rose in the cross, when we learn the meaning of resurrection. 'Spirit is spirit only in so far as it is this negative of the negative, which thus contains the negative in itself. When, accordingly, the Son of Man sits on the right hand of the Father, we see that in this exaltation of human nature its glory consists, and its identity with the divine nature appears to the spiritual eye in the highest possible way.'[26]

Profound though some of these insights of Hegel are, they are nevertheless leading away from the historically existing Jesus into the realm of universal ideas – notably, for instance, in the view of resurrection given here. It is significant too that Hegel's successors who turned their minds to theology almost all minimized the historical element – and this was true not only of radicals such as Strauss but equally of 'right-wing' Hegelians such as his Anglo-Saxon disciples. But we must be careful not to jump to one-sided conclusions about a thinker who was so consciously and consistently dialectical as Hegel. Alongside the tendency to dissolve the concreteness of the historical into the universal ideas of logic and metaphysics, he teaches also that the history of this world is programmed down to the last detail. This is a doctrine of providence, which Hegel calls the 'cunning' of reason. It does not abolish freedom or contingency, but it outwits them, runs ahead of them and causes them to serve unknowingly the ends of the universal Spirit. Jesus Christ has his important place in this providential history, yet, as Hans Küng has remarked, 'The last word is spoken not by Christ, but by the Spirit *qua* Spirit which knows itself as absolute Spirit.'[27] There is a sense in which incarnation is eternal, for the self-emptying of the Absolute into the world is coterminous with history. But the historical incarnation in Jesus Christ, though for Hegel it is real and has its designated place in that necessary stream of happening which is decreed by the cunning of reason, is not the last word. It points beyond itself to the eternal self-giving of Spirit. The historical Jesus is but a passing moment, and he is himself sublated into Spirit through his death and resurrection.

The very last paragraph in the *Phenomenology* contains an allusion to Calvary. This is not surprising in view of Hegel's belief that religion teaches the same truths as philosophy, and it is not surprising either that this mention of Calvary is not to the historical but to the speculative Calvary, to the eternal divine self-sacrifice. If one were to ask whether there is any biblical counterpart to these thoughts of Hegel, perhaps it would be found in Hebrews, though Hegel himself does not suggest any such parallel. But it will be remembered that in Hebrews the self-offering of Jesus appears to be understood as not simply the visible sacrifice of Calvary but, in a more mystical sense, as something that takes place beyond space and time, in 'the inner shrine behind the curtain, where Jesus has gone as a forerunner on our behalf, having become a high priest for ever after the order of Melchizedek' (Heb. 6.19–20). So Hegel speaks of 'the Golgotha of Absolute Spirit, the reality, the truth, the certainty of its throne, without which it were lifeless, solitary and alone'. And presumably if it were 'lifeless, solitary and alone' it might be the ultimate reality, but it would not be God. He adds a quotation from Schiller to drive home the point. 'Only

> The chalice of this realm of spirits
> Foams forth to God his own infinitude'.[28]

No matter how deeply or widely we read in Hegel, we find that on questions of religion and Christianity, there always remains a measure of ambiguity. There is no doubt that he believed in the truth of Christianity and believed further that his own philosophy taught essentially the same truth. I doubt if any philosopher has paid a nobler tribute to religion than we find in Hegel's *Lectures on the Philosophy of Religion*:

> Religion is for our consciousness that region in which all the enigmas of the world are solved, all the contradictions of deeper-reaching thought have their meaning unveiled, and where the voice of the heart's pain is silenced – the region of eternal truth, of eternal rest, of eternal peace. Speaking generally, it is through thought, concrete thought, or, to put it more definitely, it is by reason of his being spirit that man is man; and from man as spirit proceed all the many developments of the sciences and arts, the interests of political life, and all those conditions which have reference to man's freedom and will. But all these manifold forms

of human relations, activities and pleasures, and all the ways in which these are intertwined; all that has worth and dignity for man, all wherein he seeks his happiness, his glory and his pride, finds its ultimate centre in religion, in the thought, the consciousness and the feeling of God. Thus God is the beginning of all things and the end of all things.[29]

Yet when all this has been said, religion remains in Hegel's view subordinate to philosophy. The thinking of religion takes place on the level of images and pictures, whereas philosophy advances to concepts. Christianity is, for Hegel, the absolute religion, but beyond it one can still ascend to the absolute philosophy. I did say in our discussion of Kant that there is a knowledge derived from reason and conscience without which we could not recognize the truths of revealed religion. But this is carried to extreme lengths by Hegel, who erects a whole comprehensive system of rational philosophy as the criterion by which religious truth is to be judged. Is human reason quite so powerful as Hegel believed? We cannot withhold our admiration from this man's own vast knowledge, his powers of understanding and his incredible competence in both critical and constructive reasoning. But surely reason has here over-reached itself.

Hegel was carried off quite suddenly by a cholera epidemic in late 1831. At that time he was working on *Lectures on the Proofs of the Existence of God*, which shows that his lifelong interest in religion continued unabated. In these lectures, however, we find him saying that the ontological proof is 'alone the true one', and since this is the argument which rests on reason alone, without any appeal to experience, it is clear that his strongly intellectual bias also remained. The reconciliation of opposites had obviously not been carried through.

The unresolved conflicts in Hegel's own thought show themselves in the sharp differences among his disciples of the next generation, often classified as either 'right-wing' or 'left-wing' Hegelians, though that is only a rough and uninformative division. The new generation was in fact very diverse, and Hegel's philosophy or some aspects of it were combined sometimes with Lutheran theology (Marheineke), sceptical New Testament scholarship (Strauss) or even atheism (Feuerbach and Marx). Confining ourselves to the consequences of Hegel's thought for christology, we shall concentrate attention on two scholars who took very different directions.

Although David Friedrich Strauss had not himself been a student of Hegel's, he was captivated by his philosophy and lectured on it at Tübingen in the years immediately following Hegel's death. Strauss was only twenty-eight when he completed his famous *Life of Jesus* in 1836, a book so controversial that it led to his dismissal from Tübingen and his failure to obtain a position at Zürich. Why then was there such a violent reaction against a book which certainly paid attention to the historical side of Christianity in a way that Hegel had never done, and had examined the gospel material about Jesus with a thoroughness that has seldom or never been equalled by any single scholar? The answer to the question is that Strauss's findings were so negative that it seemed to many of his readers that he had utterly destroyed the foundations of Christian faith. I have already touched on the work of Strauss,[30] and we have seen how he had suggested that a study of what were thought to be messianic predictions may have had considerable influence in shaping the gospel narrative so that it would coincide with these alleged predictions, and also how he accounted for the rapid rise of Christian theology by the hypothesis that much of it had been prefabricated, so to speak, in the Jewish heritage, and then only needed to be applied to the historical figure of Jesus. This, we should notice, was a somewhat different and considerably more plausible idea than Wrede's supposition that Paul believed in a heavenly supernatural Christ whom he identified with Jesus after his conversion experience.[31]

Strauss, of course, was far from being the first critic of the life of Jesus as narrated in the gospels, and at many points he was simply restating doubts and questions that had already been aired during the hundred years or so before he wrote his *Life*. What was new was his introduction of the word 'myth' into New Testament studies. It had already been used in relation to the Old Testament, but it was a departure to apply it to the stories about Jesus. With Strauss, 'myth' is not to be taken as a bad or deprecatory word. Myth is a production of spirit, though it is on the level of picture thinking, what Hegel called *Vorstellung*, and contrasted with the conceptual thinking (*Begriff*) of philosophy. Strauss defined 'myth' as follows: 'a narrative relating directly or indirectly to Jesus, which may be considered not as the expression of a fact, but as the product of an idea of his earliest followers; such a narrative being mythical in proportion as it exhibits this character'.[32] The second part of this sentence indicates that a narrative may be more or less purely mythical. Strauss believed that the myths about Jesus had two sources. As we have already noted, they reflect what were taken to be messianic predictions in the Old Testament, for instance, the prediction that the messiah would come from Bethlehem, which would help to create the birth stories. But the myths also draw on the impression left by 'the personal character, actions and fate of Jesus', and the predictions may have to be modified to accommodate these; for instance, the crucifixion of Jesus was a well-known fact, and in the face of it the traditional predictions had to be reinterpreted to allow for a crucified messiah. Actually, what Strauss calls 'myth' or, more specifically, 'evangelical myth', would perhaps hardly qualify as 'myth' in the sense in which that term is used by modern historians of religion, and that includes the sense in which Bultmann has discussed 'myth' in the New Testament. But so long as we are clear about what Strauss meant by 'myth', we need not concern ourselves in the present context with the question of how Strauss's usage differs from that of later writers. Strauss offers two criteria by which the presence of myth can be recognized. One is that the event reported is inconsistent with known and universal laws of nature, for example, walking on water. The other is the use of poetic language and of ideas well-known in mythology throughout the world, for instance, the darkening of the sun or the earthquake at the time of the crucifixion.

Strauss reminds us that there has been a very long tradition of allegorical interpretation of the scriptures, going back to Philo the Jew of Alexandria, and such great Christian scholars as Origen. The language of religion is a pictorial language, and we miss what it is saying if we fasten exclusively on the literal sense. Much of his *Life of Jesus* is taken up with a minute discussion of the gospel narratives, in the course of which Strauss operates a dialectical hermeneutic based on Hegel. The three stages in this hermeneutic are the supernatural, the natural, and their synthesis in the mythical. Let us take as an example the story of Jesus walking on the lake. If the story is taken literally, then we have to understand it as a supernatural act. No one could walk on water except through magical or supernatural powers. Perhaps the story was originally meant that way, or perhaps not. Some orthodox believers may still understand it in this literal way, but they are people who do not share the modern mentality. Some modern commentators have tried to solve the problem by moving on to a different type of interpretation. They offer a natural explanation, for instance (as I have myself read), that Jesus was walking on a ledge of rock that stretched out into the lake just under the surface of the water. This would make the story credible, but it would at the same time deprive it of any point. For then it would mean only that the disciples in their ignorance and stupidity thought they were seeing a miracle worked by the *theios aner* when in fact he was doing what anyone could do, if he knew the topography of the lake. So, since both natural and supernatural explanations fail, we are driven to sublate them in the third term of the interpretation, which means that the story is taken as a myth, an imaginative narrative intended to express the disciples conviction that Jesus was no less than the agent of God in their midst.

The example I have given here is a rather trivial one, but there are many more in the pages of Strauss. An interesting illustration of his method is found in his treatment of the stories of Jesus' predictions of his passion and death. When we considered this question earlier,[33] we saw that these predictions are, in all likelihood, insertions into the narrative by the evangelist, looking back on the events long after they had happened. For the most part, we followed Bultmann's treatment of the text, but now we shall see that Strauss had arrived at much the same results by a different method.[34] The gospels attribute to Jesus a foreknowledge of his sufferings, even in matters of precise detail. 'There are,' says Strauss, 'two modes of explaining why Christ could so precisely foreknow the particular circumstances of his passion and death; the one resting on a supernatural, the other on a natural basis.' For the former type of explanation, we have to suppose that Jesus was possessed of a spirit which enables him to draw all this information about himself and his fate from various passages in the Old Testament; and Strauss, with his customary attention to detail, illustrates how Jesus might have put together a fairly precise expectation of what would happen on the basis of scripture. But all this goes on the assumption that these ancient Hebrew writers were intending to refer to the career of the coming messiah. Not so, says Strauss. 'To confine ourselves to the principal passages only, a profound grammatical and historical exposition has convincingly shown, for all who are in a condition to liberate themselves from dogmatic presuppositions, that in none of these is there any allusion to the sufferings of Christ.' Here too in his careful way Strauss considers each of the passages concerned, showing that in their original reference they had nothing to do with Jesus or a messianic figure. If then the supernatural explanation fails, may we try the natural explanation? On this view, common sense would be enough to inform Jesus of his coming fate, and he could even, as Strauss shows, anticipate some of the details of what would happen. But Strauss then points out that there were quite a few uncertain factors which appear in the predictions but could not have been confidently anticipated on the basis of common sense alone. 'If then Jesus cannot have had so precise a foreknowledge of the circumstances of his passion and death, either in a supernatural or in a natural way: *he cannot have had such a foreknowledge at all*: and the minute predictions which the evangelists put in his mouth must be regarded as a *vaticinium post eventum*.' It is interesting to note that the Latin expression used here by Strauss is repeated exactly and in the same connection by Bultmann roughly a century later. So Strauss in his own way had already reached the conclusion that the predictions of the passion in the mouth of Jesus need neither a supernatural nor a natural explanation, for in fact they were never made at all. They are 'mythical', in his very broad sense of the word.

Strauss has a field day when he comes to the stories of the crucifixion and resurrection. The remarkable embellishments in these stories – the darkening of the sun, the rending of the veil of the temple, the earthquake, the opening of the tombs – these things can be explained in neither supernatural nor natural terms. If we accept them as miracles or supernatural events, then we must say that they were miracles that failed and had no point. If we try to offer natural explanations (which would be rather futile in any case), we land in gross improbabilities. All the signs of myth are present – parallels to pagan mythologies, inconsistencies in the accounts of the several gospels, and so on. So even those narratives which recount the most significant events in the career of Jesus are infected with myth, and we cannot rely upon them for any factual information. It is important to notice, however, that Strauss never went so far as those later exponents of the 'Christ-myth' theory, such as Arthur Drews, who believed that Jesus was wholly a product of the religious imagination.

We can readily understand the devastating effect which Strauss's work had on the Christendom of his day. Theologians had for centuries quarrelled among themselves over the interpretation of the scriptures, but most of them were at least in agreement in the belief that these scriptures provided a faithful account of the life and teaching of Jesus Christ. Now everything seemed to be wide open to question. We must not forget that Strauss himself was shaken by the results of his work. Thrown out of Tübingen and denied entrance to Zürich, he was paying the price of his honesty, unlike some other scholars of the eighteenth and nineteenth centuries who kept their opinions to themselves. I think Karl Barth is unduly harsh in his essay on Strauss, especially in denying that there was anything tragic about him. Barth does admit that 'Strauss offered to his time the sight of the theologian who has become an unbeliever, for all to behold and without denying it.'[35] Is this not tragedy – the tragedy not just of Strauss but of the modern church, which since the time of the Enlightenment has been penetrated by the most chilling self-questioning?

Academic critics of Strauss have concentrated attention rather on his neglect of source criticism. As was noted when we discussed the witness of the synoptic gospels,[36] the priority of Mark was first seriously argued by Lachmann, though other scholars had considered it for quite a long time. Lachmann's article appeared in 1835, the same year as the first volume of Strauss's *Life of Jesus*. But Strauss still believed in the priority of Matthew, and even that Luke antedated Mark.[37] Of course, much of Strauss's argument is independent of the question of the dating of the synoptic gospels, but his neglect of the question does not help him. On the other hand, Strauss did raise questions about John's gospel and its claim to apostolic authorship. Already in 1835 he was placing it well into the second century (considerably later than scholars would date it today), but in his second biography of Jesus, published in 1864 as *Leben Jesu für das deutsche Volk*,[38] he expressed a clear preference for the synoptics over

John, and of course this was very important for christology, since it is John's gospel which represents Jesus himself as making large claims to a special relation to the Father. John had been the favourite evangelist among writers on christology, and the denial that his gospel was early or was the work of an apostolic eye-witness was felt to be quite devastating. But what was sensational and deeply disturbing in the middle of last century would scarcely raise a ripple of emotion today. Thus, in our discussion of John's gospel in Chapter 5, I said of the 'I am' sayings that 'we may well suppose that these expressions are placed on Jesus' lips by John or the community of believers to which he belonged' and that 'John ascribes to Jesus and sometimes to the disciples a consciousness, which they almost certainly did not have at the time, of what was going on, a consciousness which could only emerge as time passed and events could be seen in perspective.'[39] It is not only scholarship that has changed in the intervening years between Strauss and ourselves; we have also moved away from the excessive individualism that sharply separated Jesus from his community.

Strauss is today remembered chiefly for his radical and thoroughgoing criticism of what were taken to be the historical foundations of the Christian faith. In a 'Concluding Dissertation' to the *Life of Jesus*, he claims that faith can survive unscathed the collapse of the historical record. No doubt he is to some extent speaking tongue in cheek at this point. Nevertheless, he is drawing a distinction which has remained in Christian theology ever since, and the problem it presents has certainly not been solved. I mean, the distinction between the historical Jesus and the Christ of faith. This could be called the modern Nestorianism, though possibly the expression would be unjust to Nestorius.

What then does Strauss have in mind when he talks about 're-establishing dogmatically that which has been destroyed critically'? Whatever may have been Hegel's own thoughts on the matter, his followers interpreted him in such a way that the history is treated as merely picture-language, a pointer to eternal truth that can be expressed conceptually. For Strauss, at the time when he completed the *Life of Jesus*, the eternal truth is the union of God and man. In his own words

This is the key to the whole of christology, that, as subject of the predicate which the Church assigns to Christ, we place, instead of an individual, an idea; but an idea which has an existence in reality, not in the mind only, like that of Kant. In an individual, a God-man, the properties and functions which the Church ascribes to Christ contradict themselves; in the idea of the race, they perfectly agree. Humanity is the union of the two natures – God become man, the infinite manifesting itself in the finite, and the finite spirit remembering its infinitude . . . This alone is the absolute sense of christology; that it has been annexed to the person and history of one individual is a necessary result of the historical form which christology has taken.[40]

But it seems that Strauss himself was not satisfied with his own prescription for the reconstruction of faith. Perhaps he had excised so much from traditional Christianity that it was bound to bleed to death. At any rate, in his last phase he drifted away from Christianity altogether. In *Der alte und der neue Glaube* of 1872 (known in English as *The Old Faith and the New*) Strauss asks and answers four questions. Are we still Christians? The answer is negative – Jesus as a distant figure of the past can no longer be decisive for us. Do we believe in God? The answer is vague, and seems to hover between pantheism and atheism. How do we understand the world? Here the answer reflects the state of science in the nineteenth century. The fourth question is the ethical one – how should we behave? Strauss recommends a humanistic ethic which is not indeed opposed to Christianity but is not connected with it in any essential way.

Strauss had been a student of the famous Tübingen scholar, Ferdinand Christian Baur, who, in turn, had been deeply influenced by both Schleiermacher and Hegel. However, he believed that both of these thinkers had neglected the historical aspects of Christianity and, in particular, the historical career of Jesus, allowing it to be absorbed into the idealized Christ figure. We have seen that Strauss took up the problem of the historical Jesus, but his results were so negative that they constituted not so much a solution as a dissolution. So we turn now to another student of Baur's, an almost exact contemporary of Strauss.

This was Isaak August Dorner who held important academic and ecclesiastical positions in Germany in the middle decades of the nineteenth century. He too owed much to both Schleiermacher and Hegel, and like Strauss he used a method of inquiry based on Hegelian dialectic. Christology was a major interest throughout his career, and with that admirable thoroughness and industry for which German scholarship is renowned, he produced a monumental history of christological doctrine from the New Testament down to his own time – *Entwicklungsgeschichte der Lehre von der Person Christi*, published from 1839 onward. The English translation is in five large volumes and is entitled *History of the Development of the Doctrine of the Person of Christ*.[41] Very few theologians have ever attained to such a mastery of the history of christology as did Dorner, and the fruits of his long preoccupation with the subject finally appeared in his posthumous *System of Christian Doctrine*.[42]

In the introductory part of this work, he explains the dialectical method which he proposes to employ. The first stage on the way to a well-founded Christian knowledge is experience, a view which may remind us of Schleiermacher. But with Dorner, it is not religious experience in general that is the foundation, but the experience of the historical events that gave birth to Christianity, as these events are attested in scripture. But this experiential or historical knowledge is inadequate, and we move on to the intellectual or conceptual investigation of religious realities, as exemplified in the major philosophical systems. This reminds us now of Hegel's criticism of Schleiermacher. But clearly it is also a criticism of Hegel, at least, as Hegel was being interpreted by Strauss and many others. Dorner was trying to bring about a synthesis between the experiential/historical strand in christology and the intellectual/ideal strand. Though I have included him in this chapter on 'Idealist Christology', we should note that he explicitly dissociated himself from the extreme position of Kant, who had made the ideal Christ (the archetype) independent of the historical Jesus. But Dorner can rightly be numbered with the idealists because of his Hegelian methodology and because Hegel himself attached importance to history, even if he did not quite succeed in integrating it into his christology.

Dorner's great history of christology takes the development of the doctrine right down to his own time and includes criticism of some of his contemporaries, notably Thomasius and the kenoticists.[43] Part of this criticism was that the kenoticists were introducing change into God, and so going against the doctrine of his immutability. But in the course of making the criticism, Dorner himself was forced to think more deeply about the meaning of immutability.[44] He rejected the idea that God is an absolutely simple or monadic being, not least on the ground that such an idea makes anything like an incarnation virtually impossible. But if we acknowledge that there are distinctions in God and that these are eternal, then we can safeguard whatever was important in the doctrine of divine immutability and at the same time acknowledge the 'special mode of being of God in Christ'.[45]

He also thinks of God as having prepared the world for incarnation throughout its history by increasing its receptivity to the divine. Here we have echoes of both Schleiermacher and Hegel, but Dorner's treatment is more explicit. We see incarnation not so much as an irruption into world history but rather as itself an aspect of that history as God brings the creation into a reciprocal relationship with himself. To express this, Dorner quite naturally revives the first and second Adam language of Paul and other Christian writers, though he also insists that there is a clear distinction between the first Adam and the second. We must take care, he urges us, not to diminish the novelty of Christ, or to suppose that the human race represented by the first Adam would 'naturally' have evolved into the new humanity of Christ without Christ. He is likewise opposed to any view (such as that of Strauss) which would think of incarnation as simply the union of God with the whole human race. For Dorner, the individuality of Christ remains important. He calls him the 'central individual' of creation.

But perhaps the most original feature in Dorner's christology, and one which, I believe, still has importance, is his belief that incarnation was not only progressive in world-history but was progressive in Jesus Christ himself. Incarnation did not take place instantaneously in the womb of Mary when the archangel made his annunciation. It took place progressively throughout the lifetime of Jesus. It was a process of becoming (*werden*). In paradoxical language, Dorner talks about Christ's 'increasing external humiliation, together with increasing internal trans-figuration'.[46] The paradox comes to the height of paradoxicality in the death of Jesus, for it is in that moment of final self-surrender that the consummation of incarnation takes place, the full union of the human and the divine. 'Growth having been ordained for humanity, and Christ presenting true humanity in an actual human life, a truly human growth pertains to him.'[47] This growth is understood both as an increasing *assumption* by the Logos of the humanity of Jesus, and an increasing *receptivity* on the part of Jesus toward the Logos.

Since Christ's death was, as we have seen, the completion of the process of incarnation, then it was also the beginning of his risen life in God. It was the 'spiritual consummation of his person', and so 'the lowest stage of his outward humiliation is in itself the beginning of his exaltation'.[48]

Dorner's contribution to christology was certainly not a negligible one, and especially valuable was his attempt to conceive of the person of Christ and his relation to the Father in more dynamic categories than had been customary in much of the theology of the past. Historians of doctrine sometimes speak of Dorner as a mediating theologian, and this seems fair. His developmental or dynamic understanding of incarnation might have been understood in more radical ways, but his own sense of dialectic and of the need to give due weight to conflicting points of view kept him from one-sided positions, and his attempted synthesis of history and idea may have been close to what Hegel himself had intended.

But in general the consequences for theology of Hegel's idealism were a devaluation of history. Even moderate Hegelians who would have shrunk from the extreme historical scepticism of Strauss were neverthe-less inclined to lay so much stress on the *idea* of Christianity that its historical origins and the person of Jesus Christ himself were regarded as of little importance. This point will be confirmed if we glance briefly at Hegelianism in England, where it had very considerable influence in the later part of the nineteenth century, by which time it had pretty well faded out in its native Germany.

This British Hegelianism was considered an ally of Christian theology, though it introduced some ideas which did not quite fit the traditional dogmatic pattern. One of its most respected advocates was Edward Caird (died 1908), who taught first in Glasgow and then in Oxford. His Gifford Lectures, published in 1893, express a view of religion and Christianity which is, I think, very close to that of Hegel and also representative of the view held at that time by many philosophers and theologians in the English-speaking world.

Like Hegel, Caird believed that 'the world is a rational or intelligible system'[49] and that, in principle, everything is capable of rational explanation. But the mode of explanation must be adequate to the level of what is being explained. The higher may not be explained in terms of the lower, and this implies that in a universe which has brought forth spiritual life, the ultimate principle of explanation cannot be less than spiritual. But, Caird believes, it is in religion that the spiritual life reaches its most concentrated and essential character. So the quest for a rational understanding of the world coalesces with the religious quest. 'Every rational being as such is a religious being.'[50] 'God' is religion's name for that spiritual unity which holds together all things in the world-system.

All religions have a kinship within an evolutionary framework. Caird's dialectic begins from *objective* religion (illustrated from ancient Greece) in which the divine is seen as immanent in the objective world. In *subjective* religion (the type is Israel) God is manifested in the inner life of man, especially in the moral consciousness. The opposition of these forms of religion is overcome in Christianity, which Caird calls *universal* religion, much as Hegel had called it *absolute* religion. In this Christian synthesis, we reach a form of panentheism, not to be confused with pantheism. 'God is now conceived not, as in all objective religions, as a merely natural power or as the unity of all natural powers; nor again is he conceived, as in subjective religion, as a spiritual being outside of nature and dominating over it. He is conceived as manifesting himself alike in the whole process of nature and in the process of spirit as it rises above nature.'[51] These spiritual truths find their expression in the incarnation of God in Christ, but we are to think of Christ not so much as a person as an idea – the idea of a divine humanity, the incarnation of the divine in all human life. So long as the idea is grasped, the historical reality is dispensable, as is shown by the following passage: 'The general idea needs, so to speak, to be embodied or incarnated, "to be made flesh and to dwell among men", in all the fulness of realization in a finite individuality, before it can be known and appreciated in its universal meaning.' But then, it becomes possible 'to detach the idea from accidents of time and place and circumstances, and present it as a general principle'.[52] This seems scarcely distinguishable from Strauss, though he is never actually mentioned.

We shall see that the historical question cannot be quite so easily set aside as some of the idealist christologists would have liked.

] 11 [

Mid-century Misgivings

In the last three chapters, we have seen something of the radical changes in christology that were taking place in the Enlightenment and post-Enlightenment periods. The classical christology that had stood so long (and still stands as the official teaching of the churches) was increasingly subject to criticism. Both its historical content and its doctrinal formulations were now in doubt. Admittedly, new christological affirmations were also being made, but could they take the place of the old dogmas? Could they, in short, provide an adequate intellectual support for Christian faith? Jesus Christ was being humanized, supranaturalism was yielding to immanentism, revelation was being replaced by speculation, theology was being absorbed into philosophy. Whenever a powerful movement like the one described occurs, it calls forth a counter-movement, and this was apparent by the middle of the nineteenth century. Theologians and religious thinkers appeared who resisted or partially resisted the new trends and who sought to re-establish continuity between Christian faith and its origins in the Bible and the tradition.

I may here return briefly to a point which I made earlier[1] concerning the somewhat irregular pattern of christological development. I was apologizing for devoting only one chapter to the christology of the patristic period, the middle ages and the Reformation, as compared with the considerably fuller treatment accorded to both earlier and later periods. I invoked in support of my procedure Martin Hengel's remark that in christology more happened in the first two decades than in the next seven centuries. But now we are seeing that there were also major developments in the modern period. I mentioned in the last chapter the monumental work of Dorner on the development of christology, and it may be of some interest to note how he divides the subject chronologically. He too recognizes three periods. The first stretches from the origin to 381 (the condemnation of Nestorius) though sometimes he seems to extend it to 451 (Chalcedon). The middle period in his reckoning is once again of inordinate length, running from 381 to 1800. That is the time of the classical christology, not seriously interrupted either by the Reformation or by the wearisome debates between Lutherans and Calvinists in the time that followed. The modern period for Dorner began only in 1800, but was already densely packed by the time he was writing his history in the sixties. In his perceptive study of modern German christology, Alister McGrath remarks: 'In view of the fact that the Enlightenment is now widely recognized as constituting the most significant development in the intellectual history of the Christian faith – far surpassing even the Reformation in this respect – it is proper to argue that it defines the *terminus a quo* from which any account of modern theology in general, and modern christology in particular, must begin.'[2] But in this chapter, we have to take account of the fact that the new era had scarcely gathered momentum when it became clear that some people – and not just the 'old guard' – were beginning to worry about the direction in which things were going.

A Lone Protester

The best-known of all these mid-century religious thinkers who were swimming against the stream was Søren Kierkegaard. When he died worn out in his early forties in 1855, he had in a long series of brilliant writings opposed just about everything we have met in the last three chapters. Admittedly, he made little impact in his own time. A lonely eccentric, he was in the eyes of many a figure of ridicule on the streets of Copenhagen. Not until the twentieth century did he come into his own as an acute critic of Hegel, as the father of existentialist philosophy, and as an inspirer of Barth, Niebuhr and other leaders of the renascence of Protestant theology.

Yet one could hardly say that Kierkegaard himself was a theologian or even a philosopher. Such designations seem to imply the author of some coherent or systematic body of thought. Kierkegaard had no use for systems, but nevertheless he had many brilliant insights. The trouble for any would-be interpreter is that he will almost inevitably make Kierkegaard's thought seem more systematic and more unified that Kierkegaard intended it to be. The very titles of his books make it clear that he wishes to have nothing to do with system-building: *Philosophical Fragments; Concluding Unscientific Postscript; Training in Christianity; Fear and Trembling; Either/Or* – these titles show that we are not being presented with a rival intellectual system, but have turned away toward the problems of life with all its discontinuities and its refusal to fit neat logical patterns. This does not mean that we are to dismiss Kierkegaard as some philosophers have done, treating him as a mere irrationalist or perhaps as a fideist. Systematic interpreters, such as Louis Pojman, have shown that Kierkegaard did set up and defend theses by argument when he thought that was the appropriate procedure.[3]

Nevertheless, I would find it difficult to talk about a 'christology' in Kierkegaard. There are many christological pronouncements and many good criticisms of the christologies of other thinkers, but hardly a coherent body of teaching that one would call a 'christology' in the conventional sense. Kierkegaard certainly strikes a jarring note in nineteenth-century christology, yet it is hard to compare him with other writers on the subject, or to treat his writing as another 'christology'. I shall illustrate the difficulty by setting him alongside each of the three major figures considered in the preceding chapters – Kant, Schleiermacher and Hegel – and show that in each case there is a sharp conflict, yet at the same time Kierkegaard seems to carry even further some aspects of the thought of the philosopher concerned.

In the case of Kant, we have seen that the actual concrete figure of Jesus is made strictly unnecessary. At most he serves to awaken our awareness of the archetypal humanity already discoverable in our reason. But with Kierkegaard, the concrete Jesus cannot be dissolved into an abstraction. He distinguishes between the kind of teacher – Socrates is the example – who acts like a midwife in helping to bring to birth the ideas already in one's mind, and the kind of teacher – Jesus – to whom the learner owes everything, for he brings a divine revelation. Confronted with Jesus Christ, reason 'makes a collision', it encounters that which lies beyond its grasp, so that one has either to leap out beyond reason into faith, or else take offence and turn away.[4] Yet Kierkegaard seems to have been even more dismissive of the historical than Kant was. It is not that he himself thought of denying or doubting the historical reports about Jesus (he could be quite naive in this matter) but that for him the event of Jesus Christ was more than history. It was the appearance of the eternal in time, and debates over historical questions trivialized the issue. In words that have often been quoted, Kierkegaard wrote:

> If the fact spoken of were a simple historical fact, the accuracy of the historical sources would be of great importance. Here this is not the case, for faith cannot be distilled from even the nicest accuracy of detail . . . If the contemporary generation had left nothing behind them but these words: 'We have believed that in such and such a year God has appeared among us in the humble figure of a servant, that he lived and taught in our community and finally died', it would be more than enough.[5]

Whether it would have been enough is a question we shall not discuss at this point, for I have been drawing attention only to the complexity of Kierkegaard's relation to Kant.

If we now ask how Kierkegaard stands in relation to Schleiermacher, we find new contradictions. On the one hand, Schleiermacher's idea that Christ is the completion of the creation of humanity is simply not acceptable to Kierkegaard. For Kierkegaard, there is 'an infinite difference of quality' between God and the human race. So even if we say that Christ is a good man, a truly remarkable man, the greatest and best man that has ever lived and prolong the series by as many superlatives as we like, we can never say he is God. That would be a *metabasis eis allo genos*. 'Neither can I nor anyone else by beginning with the assumption that Christ was a man arrive in all eternity at the conclusion, Therefore it was God.'[6] So here Kierkegaard decisively rejects the so-called 'christology from below', though it is precisely in this context that he reveals the naivete mentioned above, for he says that Christ told us he was God. I shall not pause to ask whether, if there is an infinite qualitative difference between God and man, that would make anything like incarnation impossible, but go straight on to another side of the relation between Kierkegaard and Schleiermacher. The latter has often been accused of subjectivizing Christianity, even if that was not his intention. But does not Kierkegaard outdo Schleiermacher in this very matter of subjectivizing? For Kierkegaard tells us that truth is subjectivity.[7] However, it is not easy to know just what he means by this. He does not deny that there are objective truths – truths of historical fact, for instance, though we have seen that he does not rate them very highly. His own interest is concentrated on the task of becoming a person (and for him, this is the same as becoming a Christian), and the task is not accomplished by understanding Christianity in an abstract way, but in a passionate involvement in which one has to attain an inward certainty even in the face of objective uncertainties. All this of course has to be placed in the context of Kierkegaard's Denmark, where, in his judgment, becoming a Christian was simply a formality. 'To be a Christian is a thing of naught, something which everybody is as a matter of course.'[8] The talk of truth as subjectivity, then, is not to be taken as meaning that the criterion for truth is personal preference, but that the most important truths cannot be learned by the understanding alone but have to be experienced as events in one's inward being.

We have also to consider Kierkegaard in relation to Hegel. Here there is indeed a violent clash, yet we have also to recognize that the two thinkers share some deep convictions. But Kierkegaard believed that Hegel had 'changed' Christianity, he had incorporated it into the smooth rational texture of a reality that corresponds to the structure of thought. Thus the paradoxical, concrete, individual character of Christianity had been abolished. It had been dissolved, sublated, *aufgehoben* into the system. Kierkegaard had two arguments against the possibility of an all-embracing philosophical system (and here, incidentally, we see him deploying rational argument even against the mighty Hegel). One argument is that every thinker or philosopher is at the same time an existing individual, located at a definite point in space and time. He is within the system of reality and therefore cannot see it as a system in its wholeness. To do that, he would need somehow to transport himself to a point outside the system. Kierkegaard argues therefore that if indeed reality constitutes a rational system, it can be seen as such only by God, and not by any finite thinker. One might suggest, of course, that even God may not be able to view reality from the outside, unless he is a God external to and detached from the universe. Kierkegaard's second argument claimed that a system can be identified and understood only when it has become complete. But reality is always in process, on its way from one state of affairs to another. So there are always loose ends that do not or do not yet fit into a system.[9]

On the other hand, Hegel and Kierkegaard were at one in holding that the world is a scene of conflicts, where every tendency seems to call forth its opposite. In Hegel's dialectic – and it will be remembered that this dialectic operates in both thought and reality – the opposites are reconciled in a new synthesis. But Kierkegaard does not accept that reality can be conformed to thought or that its conflicts can be as easily resolved as Hegel's philosophy might suggest. So he aims not at the resolution of these conflicts but at giving each side its due. So in what he calls 'paradox' the conflicting elements stand side by side. But the paradox is not nonsense. Each side of the paradox asserts a truth which, taken in isolation, would become an untruth. They are not combined but they correct one another. The 'absolute paradox', for Kierkegaard, is the paradox of the God-man. There is no way, he thinks, in which this could be rationally justified. It is above and beyond reason, and invites either faith or offence. Kierkegaard will not even allow that considerations of probability can be admitted. His view of paradox may be compared with paradox in John's gospel, discussed at an earlier stage.[10] I took as an example the two sentences from the beginning of the prologue: 'The Word was with God' and 'The Word was God'. On the face of it, they seem to contradict one another, since the first tells us that God and the Word are two entities, while the second seems to identify them. Yet, as we saw, we are being directed to a way of thinking about the relation as one that hovers between identity and difference and which John expressed by putting down his two sentences side by side.

The relation between Hegel and Kierkegaard is a very complex one, and considering how much these two men wrote and how difficult they sometimes are to understand, it is obvious that to trace it in detail would be an enormous task. This task has in fact been undertaken by Professor Niels Thulstrup.[11] He sees the fundamental difference between the two thinkers in their conflicting views of the human being. For Hegel, the human individual is subordinate to the world-process and is determined by it. For Kierkegaard, the category of the individual takes precedence. If for Hegel the real is the rational, for Kierkegaard the real is the concrete individual, whose development is not rationally determined and who has freedom to make the leap of faith out beyond reason. From this difference over anthropology follow the wider theological and philosophical differences. For Hegel, Christian faith is a stage – admittedly, the highest stage – on the way to the absolute philosophy. But for Kierkegaard, faith stands higher than reason, and the awkward paradoxes of Christianity cannot be resolved into a rational system.

Without attempting to impose a system on Kierkegaard's christological thinking, let me set down seven points which seem to me to be at the heart of it and which we shall find being revived when Kierkegaard was rediscovered (or even discovered for the first time) in the earlier part of the twentieth century.

1. The foundation is Jesus Christ, the God-man, the Absolute Paradox. It is not wrong, I think, to say that Kierkegaard presents us with a 'take it or leave it' situation. The paradox is not explicable by any rational means – in fact, Kierkegaard thinks it is folly to attempt any explanation. Reason comes up against something with which it cannot deal. One has either to make the leap of faith or else take offence at the sheer absurdity that a man is God and declares himself to be God. But although the intellect can make nothing of this paradox, there must be some way of entering into it if faith is to be possible. It is here that Kierkegaard's 'existentialism' becomes important, in particular, his recognition that the human being has a passional and volitional nature, as well as being an intelligent being, and that the human situation may be lit up for us through our affective nature as well as through our understanding. So we are enabled to have faith in the paradox, but not through grasping it intellectually. Kierkegaard himself asks: 'How in the world can a person get the idea of accepting it? Quite simply, only the consciousness of sin can force one into this anxiety-laden situation – the power on the other side being grace.'[12]

2. The second point is implied in the first. Any thinking about Jesus Christ will get nowhere if it begins from his humanity. I use the expression 'thinking about Jesus' but it is hard to find suitable language to express Kierkegaard's view. He seems to hold that the human historical Jesus is not the 'real' Christ. The real Christ is God, God appearing in history but not historical, for this is the eternal in history. Whether one can make any sense of this or whether it would be wrong even to try, is a question. Again, if God is qualitatively different from man, and Christ is really God, not really man, are we not reduced to complete incomprehension? Consider the following sentences:

Can one learn from history anything about Christ? No. Why not? Because one can 'know' nothing at all about Christ; he is the paradox, the object of faith, existing only for faith. But all historical communication is communication of 'knowledge', hence from history one can learn nothing about Christ. For if one learns little or much about him, or anything at all, he [who is thus known] is not he who in truth he is, i.e., one learns to know nothing about him, or one learns to know something incorrect about him, one is deceived. History makes Christ out to be another than he truly is, and so one learns to know a lot about . . . Christ? No, not about Christ, for about him nothing can be known, he can only be believed.[13]

A passage like this raises the standard question addressed to docetic christologies: of what relevance to the human race is a Christ who is 'really' not human, or possibly at best half-human? And there is the further question: how can one believe in someone or something if one *knows nothing* about the object of belief?

3. Kierkegaard's claim that Christ is the eternal in time is not elucidated by him and he even seems to be saying that it cannot be elucidated, but it is important to notice that at this point he does admit metaphysics into his work. I say the point is important, because it shows the inadequacy of a purely existentialist christology. The appeal in such a christology is to immediate experience – in Kierkegaard's case, we have the mention of anxiety and sin as prerequisites for the emergence of faith – but christology, as a part of theology, needs reflection as well as experience. Here Hegel's critique of Schleiermacher would hold also against Kierkegaard. It is not illegitimate to ask, 'Why have faith in Christ?' Kierkegaard does give an answer, 'In Christ the eternal has become present in history'. But he does not or rather he will not explain the answer.

4. The next point to notice about Kierkegaard's view of Christ is his teaching about the incognito – a view which re-emerges in Barth, and which perhaps had its roots in the teaching of some early Lutheran theologians that there was a *krypsis* or hiddenness of the divine attributes of Christ. This in turn may go back to Paul's teaching that even the demonic powers failed to recognize the true being of Christ, 'for if they had, they would not have crucified the Lord of glory' (I Cor. 2.8). Kierkegaard certainly draws attention to an important problem here, though it is doubtful if he helps toward any solution. The problem is, basically, how is revelation possible. For if God can communicate with us only through things, persons, events in the world, there is bound to be an ambiguity. We may regard these as just naturally occurring in the world, and not understand them as divine communications. The great majority of people in the time of Jesus saw him only as a man, and probably as a

misguided man, and for only a very few was he 'revelation'. How then is revelation possible? Kierkegaard seems to have boxed himself in at this point, for he has denied that we can learn anything about the 'real' Christ from historical information about the career of Jesus. He does in fact make one assertion about Jesus, and makes it repeatedly, which does break the incognito. That is the assertion that Jesus himself declared that he was God.[14] But few scholars today would be able to go along with Kierkegaard in that assertion.

But there are other elements in Kierkegaard's teaching which may be inconsistent with his more robust affirmations of the divine incognito, but which, I think, save him from thoroughgoing docetism and also point to a very profound view of God on his part. I refer to his famous parable of the king and the maiden in *Philosophical Fragments*. The king seeks to win the love of the humble maiden, but the only worthwhile way to do this is to appear to her without his kingly majesty, for that might elicit her love for the wrong reasons. So what is he to do? Dress up as a beggar, as happens in fairy tales (myths)? That would be a form of *krypsis*, but also a form of deception, and no true relation could be founded on that. So, reverting from the parable to the Christian doctrine of the incarnation of the Word in Christ, we hear Kierkegaard saying 'God's servant form is not a mere disguise, but is actual from the hour that in the omnipotent purpose of his omnipotent love, *God became a servant*, he has, so to speak, imprisoned himself in his resolve and is now bound to go on (to speak foolishly) whether it pleases him or not. God's presence in human form, yes, in the humble form of a servant, is itself the teaching.'[15] At this point, we seem to have advanced beyond *krypsis*, 'hiding' or 'disguise', to *kenosis*, 'emptying', and we shall have more to say about this later. But the question remains: 'Even if the incognito is not a disguise, how does the eye of faith penetrate to the hidden revelation?'

5. I think we may find some answer to the question just raised in another of Kierkegaard's ideas, that of 'indirect communication'. The view that some of the most important things in life cannot be said directly is not new. The synoptic gospels make much use of parables, while John's gospel has its paradoxes, its ironies and its symbols. Kierkegaard too had a flair for indirect communication. His earliest work was a study of irony, and we have seen examples of his use of paradox and parable. Indirect communication is associated too with his habit of publishing many of his works (including those quoted above) under fictitious pseudonyms. Critics are not agreed about the precise significance of his use of pseudonyms, but the most likely explanation is that by using a variety of such pseudonyms, he gave the impression of offering different points of view so as to encourage the reader to make a choice.

And for Kierkegaard it was the freedom and intensity of choice that gave an action its worth and dignity, rather than the content.

But how indirect is it possible for a communication to be, without its ceasing to be a communication? If the Christ appears incognito, what is the point or where is the revelation?

Kierkegaard raises the question himself when he writes, 'God did not assume the form of a servant to make a mockery of men; hence it cannot be his intention to pass through the world in such manner that no single human being becomes aware of his presence. He will therefore doubtless give some sort of sign . . .'[16] But I do not find that Kierkegaard tells us what he thinks the sign is, though he does indicate that it may as easily occasion offence as awaken faith. Let us look then at another passage. Kierkegaard reminds us that John the Baptist sent messengers to Jesus with the question whether he was the one to come, or whether they should wait for another. Jesus replies, 'Go and tell John the things which you hear and see', and he mentions miracles of healing apparently as messianic signs. Kierkegaard comments: 'So Jesus does not answer *directly*. He does not say, "Tell John that I am the Expected One." That is, he requires faith, and therefore to an *absent* person cannot make a direct communication. To a person who was *present* he might well say it directly.'[17] This is puzzling, but we may note that the Kierkegaard scholar Walter Lowrie, in an explanatory note to this passage, expresses the view that Kierkegaard was at this time giving up his attachment to 'indirect communication'.

However, we have to push this question further, especially as it will arise again in a slightly different form when we come to Barth and the twentieth century. In our discussion of Kant, I suggested that he was right to the extent that we could only recognize Jesus Christ as the person well-pleasing to God if we already had in our minds some idea of what such a person would be like – if we already had some 'archetype', to use Kant's word. Now, at the time when he wrote the *Philosophical Fragments*, Kierkegaard's view was that Jesus is the teacher to whom we owe everything, in contrast to Socrates who awakens what is already hidden in our minds. In that case, we could only become aware of Jesus' significance if there were indeed some 'sign' or some 'indirect communication'. But a different possibility was already to be seen in the writing *Fear and Trembling*. The voice of God comes to Abraham, 'Go and sacrifice your only son'. But how did Abraham know that this was the voice of God, this outrageous idea that had come into his mind and would seem to call for offence rather than acceptance? Kierkegaard does face the question. 'Why does Abraham do it? For God's sake, and, what is exactly the same, for his own.'[18] In other words, there was something deep down in Abraham (we may call it his authentic conscience) which led him to accept this outrageous command as the command of God; and the command of God, which is 'exactly the same' as his own deepest conscience (How completely Kantian!) takes precedence over conventional morality.

6. This leads naturally into the next point, which is the notion of offence. Kierkegaard takes this idea directly from the New Testament. The word translates the Greek *skandalon*, 'scandal' or 'stumbling-block'. Christian apologists have laboured since the beginning to remove the stumbling-blocks and make it easier for people to believe. But Kierkegaard has no use for apologetics. The paradox of the God-man is bound to be an offence to reasonable people. And not just the God-man in the abstract, but the fact that it was this particular man, a nobody. 'Is not this the carpenter's son? And they took offence at him' (Matt. 13.55 and 57). The Christian believer has to struggle against the established order, both intellectual and social, for a Christianity that gives no offence has been reduced to a shadow. In the last tragic months of his life, Kierkegaard engaged in open warfare against the church which, he believed, had robbed Christianity of its offence and therefore of its meaning. 'The whole difficulty of being a Christian vanishes, being a Christian and being a man amounts to the same thing, and we find ourselves where paganism ended'.[19]

7. The last point I want to discuss is 'faith' in Kierkegaard. Faith is not for him an inferior form of knowledge or a stage on the way to knowledge. Hence his objections to any attempt to 'prove' the existence of God and even more to 'prove' that Jesus Christ is somehow God. Faith is not the result of argument or a calculation of probability, but is, in Kierkegaard's language, a leap, and that word 'leap' seems to designate the achievement of a new stance such that we cannot explain or analyse how we have come to that point. The word 'stance' is appropriate here, for it is not just an intellectual conviction but an attitude of the complete person, in which not only thought but the will and even the passions are involved. The attitude of faith may even be accompanied by intellectual uncertainties, for, as we have seen, it is primarily inward and subjective. Yet for Kierkegaard, in sharp opposition to Hegel, faith ranks above knowledge. It has a participatory character which gives its own certitude, even in the face of objective uncertainties.

The seven points I have mentioned (and the number could have been either reduced or increased) are more like a shopping list than the summary of a coherent theological position. I suppose that is the way Kierkegaard would have liked it. If we understand him as he probably understood himself, that is to say, as a gadfly, then I think we can recognize that he made an important contribution by asking so many awkward questions of nineteenth-century thinkers. But if christology is not simply faith in Christ but reflection on faith, then we find there are many questions where Kierkegaard does not help us. There may well be mysteries where reason makes its collision, but surely we have to pursue the path of reason as far as it can take us. It may well be true that the multiplication of historical details about Jesus would not advance the theological questions about him, but we cannot be indifferent to history, especially its negative findings. Kierkegaard teaches us to have misgivings about the humanistic and immanentist thrust of early nineteenth-century christology, and we do well to ponder some of his warnings. But he does not himself offer us a christology in which we can rest.

Kenotic Christology

By 'kenotic' christology' we mean a doctrine of the person of Christ which sought to understand him in terms of a *kenosis* or self-emptying of the Logos, whereby it was able to manifest itself in the finite life of a human being. Like Kierkegaard, the advocates of a kenotic christology were uneasy about the theological developments of their time, but they were prepared to see some merits in them, especially in the new stress on the humanity of Christ, and tried to make room for it. Thus kenoticism was a kind of mediating theology, incorporating the traditional incarnational understanding of Christ, but modifying it in such a way as to safeguard against those docetic tendencies which seem to have dogged the classical christology through the centuries.

The most persuasive statement of the kenotic view came from Gottfried Thomasius (1802–73) whose writings were almost contemporaneous with those of Kierkegaard. His views were tentatively presented in *Beiträge zur kirchlichen Christologie* (1845) and then in a more fully developed form in *Christi Person und Werk* (1853–61). The latter is a complete systematic theology with its centre in the person and career of Jesus Christ. The sub-title of the whole work is 'Exposition of Evangelical–Lutheran Dogmatics from the Centre-point of Christology'. There are three parts. The first, dealing with the doctrine of God, anthropology, and the general framework of Christian theology, is called 'Presuppositions of Christology'. The heart of the argument, and the ideas which chiefly concern us, is in the second part, called 'The Person of the Mediator'. The third, concluding part, draws the consequences in 'The Work of Christ'.

We met the word *kenosis* when we were discussing Kierkegaard, and I pointed out that when he offers his parable of the incarnation, he has in mind not merely a hiding (*krypsis*) but a genuine renunciation or emptying (*kenosis*). The word is an allusion to that famous hymn in praise of Christ, whether it is by Paul or, as many scholars believe, is pre-Pauline: 'Christ Jesus, though he was in the form of God, did not count equality with God a thing to be grasped, but emptied himself (*heauton ekenose*), taking the form of a servant, being born in the likeness of men. And being found in human form, he humbled himself and became obedient unto death, even death on a cross. Therefore God has highly exalted him and bestowed on him the name which is above every name, that at the name of Jesus every knee should bow, in heaven and on earth and under the earth, and every tongue confess that Jesus Christ is Lord, to the glory of God the Father' (Phil. 2.4–8). Exponents of kenoticism rely heavily on this passage, and, to a less extent, on another Pauline passage: 'For you know the grace of our Lord Jesus Christ, that though he was rich, yet for your sake he became poor, so that by his poverty you might become rich' (II Cor. 8.9).

Though Thomasius was not the first to explore the kenotic point of view, his statement is probably the best that has been offered. At a later time several British theologians took up kenoticism, but I would have to agree with Thomasius' American editor and translator, Claude Welch, when he writes, 'It is all very well to praise the imprecision or vagueness of the British kenoticism as theological modesty and restraint before a mystery, but the presuppositions on which the kenotic theory can really emerge are precisely those that demand pursuit to the limit of the metaphysical and even the psychological questions.'[20]

Thomasius explicitly dissociates himself from Schleiermacher's view that the person of Christ is to be understood as the completion of the creation of humanity, and even more strongly does he dissociate himself from Strauss's view that it expresses the general truth of the unity between the human and the divine. Both of these views fail to make an adequate distinction between creaturely being and the being of God. But Thomasius does not go as far as Kierkegaard in thinking that there is an infinite qualitative difference between the divine and the human. He holds that man has a capacity for receiving God and of being penetrated by God, and he claims that some such affinity is a necessary presupposition for a doctrine of incarnation. Furthermore, Thomasius stood by the teaching of Lutheran christology, the dominant tradition of which maintained that although the Logos infinitely surpasses in knowledge, life and action the bounds of a merely human existence, yet in the mystery of the incarnation, the Logos was wholly present in Christ and nothing of the Logos remained outside him. This was in opposition to the Calvinist view that during the incarnation the Logos also existed outside Christ – the view called *illud extra Calvinisticum*.[21] Thomasius believed that if one admitted such an existence of the Logos outside of Christ, then one would again get into the difficulties of a dual personality. For only if one holds (as orthodoxy is supposed to require) that though there are two natures in the incarnate Christ, there is a unitary person, and this is the divine person of the Logos, is dualism avoided. If one can perform the mental gymnastics needed to undersand what the argument was about, then

Thomasius certainly seems to have had a point. For if the person of the Logos *is* the person of Christ, yet the Logos is also at the same time outside of Christ, must we not postulate a double personality? But how can the infinite Logos be reduced or compressed (we can speak only metaphorically) into the compass of the human Jesus? Of course, Thomasius' problem here is the problem of all christology, and the language is always bound to be metaphorical. How can the infinite be revealed in the finite? This is not something that can happen literally. If we are to think of the infinite making itself known in and through the finite, whether in an incarnation or in some other way, there must be some dimming down, some filtering, some reduction of scale, some *kenosis*, to use the word popularized by Thomasius and others.

But then, one may ask, if such a dimming down, reduction or emptying takes place, must this not result in a failure to reveal, if the divinity of the Logos has been so diminished? Perhaps Schleiermacher had a possible answer to this question when he claimed that the human being has 'a sense and taste of the infinite', which seems to be the claim that in the mystery of the human person there is some strange coming together of finite and infinite. This is an idea we can put aside for the present, but we may want to come back to it at a later stage of our inquiry.[22] It is not an idea that was available to Thomasius, for we have seen that he explicitly rejected Schleiermacher's humanistic christology. But Thomasius had two answers of his own to the question. One of them anticipates, even in the language it uses, the point so eloquently made by Karl Barth that 'for God it is just as natural to be lowly as to be high'.[23] In Thomasius' language, it is of the very essence of love 'to accept every limitation . . . What seems to be the alienation or finitization of deity is the deepest internalization of deity itself, the concentration of its energies on one point which, in its significance, far outweighs the most inclusive manifestation of omnipotence'.[24] The second of Thomasius' answers turns on his well-known distinction between the immanent and the relative attributes of God. The immanent attributes are absolute power, truth, holiness and love. The relative attributes are omnipotence, omniscience and omnipresence, and they belong, as the name implies, to God's relations with the world. In the incarnation, it is claimed, the Logos divested himself of these relative attributes and now related to the world as a human being. But he retained and in his incarnate existence fully manifested those immanent attributes that belong to the very essence of deity. This, Thomasius claimed, is true even of power. The incarnate Lord was no omnipotent man, no miracle-worker or *theios aner*. 'He exercised no other lordship at all than the ethical one of truth and love . . . his whole exercise of power was absorbed in his world-redeeming activity.'[25]

Another point worth noting emerges in Thomasius' teaching. He makes a distinction between the 'emptying' by which the divine, pre-existent Logos sets aside his relative attributes to assume the finite human condition, and the 'humbling' which the incarnate Christ undergoes in his acceptance of the way of the cross. In Thomasius's language, there is an emptying of the *Logos asarkos* (the Word before incarnation) and a humbling of the *Logos ensarkos* (the Word in the incarnate state). But these two moments are closely connected, indeed, the humiliation of Jesus in his death is the earthly-historical counterpart or image of the divine self-limitation or self-emptying of the Logos. The humiliation of the human Jesus is no disguise but is continuous with the self-abnegation of God himself. All this presupposes a two-stage *kenosis*, a self-emptying by the pre-existent Logos and then a further humbling even to the death of the cross in the human life in which that Logos is believed to have become incarnate. At this point, some lines of connection are obviously established between kenoticism and the religious philosophy of Hegel, for in his philosophy the Absolute Spirit may be said to empty itself of its absoluteness and to enter the finite. But are any such ideas to be derived from the biblical passage or passages on which the kenoticists tried to found their theory of incarnation? The reader will remember that we discussed these passages in the context of Pauline christology, and we were persuaded to follow the interpretation placed on them by James Dunn. He showed that the Christ-hymn of Philippians fits very well into the two-Adams christology of Paul, and that it is not necessary to invoke a doctrine of the pre-existence of Christ to provide an interpretation. Although I gave reasons for preferring Professor Dunn's interpretation over rival views,[26] I did acknowledge that he might be mistaken, for in questions about what a New Testament writer may or may not have meant in a particular passage, it is impossible to reach complete certainty. But I think the weight of evidence certainly favours Professor Dunn, and the effect of this is to take away the main biblical basis on which the kenoticists rested their case. One could still argue that they had produced an interesting and even attractive christological theory, but they themselves thought they were building on scripture, and would have been very unhappy to have had their exegesis rejected.

But the kenotic christology was open to more criticisms than simply misinterpreting certain passages of the New Testament. The Oxford scholar William P. Sanday, while recognizing that kenoticism had several merits and offered a mediating position among the conflicts of nineteenth-century theology, objected that it had made too much of a relatively small section of biblical material and ignored the main thrusts of New Testament teaching about the person of Christ.[27] In fairness to Thomasius, however, it must be noted that he devoted a good deal of space to setting forth what he believed to be scriptural evidences for his view, and he went so far as to claim that 'the whole of scripture' was on his side.[28] But unfortunately, once one has adopted a theory, it is hard to resist the temptation to read all the evidence as supporting one's own view.

But there were other serious criticisms of Thomasius and those who thought like him. One of the most damaging came from Ritschl. He pointed to the difficulty of seeking to maintain that the essential or immanent attributes of the divine Logos are retained in the incarnate Christ, while the relative attributes are divested. 'For', he argued, 'even if omnipotence and the like are only relative attributes of God and of the divine Logos – relative, that is, in relation to the world – is not this very relation the limit within which alone any knowledge of God is possible, outside of which God is wholly inconceivable? Moreover, the conception of the divine Logos has its origin exclusively in the relation of God to the world, so that we cease to conceive the Logos of God in the way which the conception itself requires, if in any particular case we think away his relation to the world.'[29] Other critics complained that Thomasius seemed to be laying claim to a detailed inside knowledge of the pre-existent Word, even to the point of being able to classify its attributes. If one could know so much of the Logos prior to the incarnation, what was the point of the incarnation or what fresh revelation could it bring?

As had happened in the case of idealism, so with kenoticism – when it had run its course in Germany, it had a second flowering in England. Of several British theologians who developed kenotic christologies, the most prominent was Charles Gore (1853–1932), a former bishop of Oxford. The first mention of the kenotic point of view in his writings occurred in 1889 in his contribution to the famous symposium, *Lux Mundi*, of which Gore himself was the editor. The matter might seem trivial to us, but at that time biblical criticism was still a very controversial matter, and one way of arguing among conservatives was to search the sayings of Jesus for information about the biblical writings in the belief that this would settle disputes, Jesus being supposed to be infallible. Gore – to the dismay of some of his more conservative colleagues – could not go along with such views. For instance, Jesus argues with the Pharisees on the assumption of the Davidic authorship of Psalm 110, and this fact had been used to rebut the claims of Old Testament scholars that David was not the author. But Gore (perhaps he was remembering Aquinas)[30] does not appear to think that Jesus had any extraordinary 'natural' knowledge. 'It is contrary to his whole method to reveal his Godhead by any anticipations of natural knowledge. The incarnation was a self-emptying of God to reveal himself under conditions of human nature and from the human point of view.'[31]

Six years later, Gore gives his kenotic view of christology a more explicit statement in his *Dissertations on Subjects Connected with the Incarnation*. 'The real incarnation', he declares, 'involves a real self-impoverishment, a real self-emptying, a real self-limitation on the part of the eternal Word of God.' The church has systematically obscured this true humanity of Christ. 'There is no doubt, I think, that the general teaching of the Catholic Church for many centuries about our Lord has removed him very far from human sympathies, very much further than the Christ of the New Testament.'[32] One of Gore's most striking examples of the limitation of Jesus' knowledge touches on a subject which we have discussed earlier – how far did Jesus know in advance that he would be put to death? Gore believes that even in the very last hours, Jesus still did not see clearly the shape of coming events: 'It was only because the future was not clear that he could pray, "O my Father, if it be possible, let this cup pass away from me".'[33]

In his last major writing on the person of Christ, from the year 1922, Gore comes back to the notion of self-emptying as the clue to an understanding. He claims it is not just a self-limitation of knowledge but a general self-limitation within the bounds of human life. But this is no 'failure of power', rather the great manifestation of love and sympathy. Though he does not name Thomasius, Gore may well have been thinking of him when he distances himself from attempts to be too detailed in describing the mode of the self-emptying.[34]

The idea of *kenosis* is an important one in Christian thought, but the kenotic christologies, whether German or English, turned out to be no more than an episode in modern thinking about the person of Jesus Christ. Their authors were attempting to do justice to the humanistic demands of nineteenth-century thought, but alarmed by such extreme developments as had appeared in radicals like Strauss and Feuerbach, they wanted to cling also to the classical framework, the starting point of which is the pre-existent Logos. They were still too cautious in asserting the full humanity of Jesus Christ, and failed to appreciate that christology, if it was to escape from the docetic drift of centuries, had to be stood on its head, so to speak, and begin once more from the humanity of Christ, as indeed it had done in the beginning. There was needed more than a hundred years of further thinking before there emerged a balanced statement like that of Pannenberg:

> Methodological reasons do not permit us to work with the incarnation as a theological presupposition. To do so would be to make the humanity of Jesus' life problematic from the very beginning. To be sure, all christological considerations tend towards the idea of the incarnation; it can, however, only constitute the end of christology. If it is put instead at the beginning, all christological concepts are given a mythological tone.[35]

12

Positivist Christology

It was only after careful consideration that I decided to entitle this chapter 'Positivist Christology', and I shall briefly explain the reason for the decision. We have already met the expression 'positive religion', but the usage there is different. Both Kant and the young Hegel believed that in its pure form Christianity would be identical with the religion of reason, and would need no dogmas, rituals, priests or even Christ himself. These trappings belonged to what they called 'positive religion', that is to say, an institutionalized historical form of religion, and they believed that it was the disciples, not Jesus himself, who had given to Christianity its positive features. But now we are thinking of positivism in a different sense. It stands for a type of philosophy which deliberately restricts its field of inquiry to the realm of the positive, understood as constituted by observable and testable matters of fact, concerning which we can arrive at fairly reliable conclusions. On the other hand, a positivist philosophy excludes from consideration metaphysical or speculative questions, on the ground that they are in principle unanswerable, and perhaps also useless for practical purposes. So the positivist in christology would be an investigator who eschewed all metaphysical questions about Jesus Christ – questions such as whether he had two natures, or two wills, whether he was 'one in being' with the Father, whether the one person of Christ is a human person or a divine person, and so on. We have ourselves seen reason to be impatient with some of the refinements in the history of christological discussion. The positivist in christology would turn away from all such questions and concentrate on historical questions about the life and teaching of Jesus, and perhaps also on ethical questions about what we can learn from him about the ordering of human life in this world. So the tendency would be to restrict theology in general and christology in particular to questions of history and ethics. One advantage of this – strongly felt in the nineteenth century and even to some extent today – is that within the universities theology would begin to look much more like one of the sciences.

If it is asked whether God himself would not eventually have to disappear in this reduction of theology to history and ethics, the answer is that those theologians whom we are considering in this chapter did not go quite so far as that. Perhaps they were inconsistent, but they did believe in God. It is true that they rejected any natural theology and any metaphysical arguments for the reality of God, but they made up for this by asserting that there is a revelation of God in Jesus Christ, and that this is a positive datum. One cannot help wondering, however, whether such a combination of faith and scepticism must not remain uneasy. Some-times one hears the expression 'revelatory positivism' used to describe this state of mind in which one accepts the claim of a revelation while at the same time denying that there are any evidences in the cosmos that would support a belief in God. It reminds us of the utterance of a prominent Ritschlian theologian: 'If it were not for Jesus Christ, I would be an atheist.'

Already by the middle of the nineteenth century positivism was emerging as the dominant form of philosophy. This was not surprising and to some extent it merely reflected the growing importance of the sciences and their rising prestige as they gave proof of their ability to produce reliable knowledge. But a related development was the revival of the Kantian philosophy. The impressive fabric of Hegelian metaphysics had scarcely been erected when it was already coming under attack. In philosophical circles, neo-Kantianism became the new fashion. Kant had, of course, combined in his philosophy the conflicting tendencies we have been noting. On the one hand, his critique of metaphysics seemed to strengthen enormously the movement toward positivism. But possibly even more important for Kant himself had been his exaltation of the ethical and his acknowledgment that in moral experience we break through the limits of the phenomenal to spiritual reality. These two sides of Kantianism were both evident in the neo-Kantian revival, though they might be combined in different proportions and the combination was often weighted toward the one side or the other, that is to say, toward an agnostic positivism, or toward a spiritual realm of values which also constitutes part of the 'given' and to which we have access through the moral sense.

The major theologian in this new period of thought was Albrecht Ritschl (1822–89). His positivist tendency is clearly expressed in a footnote which appears near the end of his systematic theology and is typical of the work as a whole: 'I, too, recognize mysteries in the religious life, but that when anything is and remains a mystery, I say nothing about it.'[1] Ritschl, like many others of his generation, had begun as a Hegelian, but he came to reject metaphysics and also the traditional dogmas of the church, which seemed to him an illicit mixture of metaphysics and religion. Likewise, he had no time for mysticism, or for any kind of religion that stresses inwardness rather than life in human society in the world. Thus, although Ritschl's name is often linked with that of Schleiermacher, he took a very different line and was openly critical of the theologian of feeling. Schleiermacher, he believed, had made the mistake of thinking of religion as a relation between God and the human being, and so missing out a third point which determines the relation – the world; and he was scornful of Schleiermacher's claims for feeling – 'that discovery of post-Reformation times, that standard of an enervated generation, pretending to a scientific character which faith simply contradicts when it fills us with its proper power'.[2] To say that Schleiermacher and Ritschl are the great protagonists of 'liberal theology' is to overlook the differences between them and is in any case a statement so vague as to be virtually empty. For what is meant by 'liberal' theology? If it means only that the theologian to whom the adjective is applied has an openness to other points of view, then liberal theologians are found in all schools of thought. But if 'liberal' becomes itself a party label, then it usually turns out to be extremely illiberal.

Ritschl then turns away from mystery, feeling, speculation, and stresses the ethical significance of Christianity. In this respect, he shows his debt to Kant, but it is important once again to notice the differences as well as the similarities. Quite unlike Kant, Ritschl believed in the importance of history, and particularly in the revelation given in the historical Jesus. Whereas Kant stressed the archetype already present in the human reason, for Ritschl Christ brings something new: 'Beyond all doubt, Jesus was conscious of a new and thitherto unknown relation to God . . . Whoever has a part in the religion of Christ in the way Christ himself intended cannot do other than regard Christ as the final revelation of God.'[3] There follows from this a further difference. Kant hoped that a time would come when a rational ethical religion would have established itself without appeal to any historical or positive accompaniments. Ritschl believed that such an abstract religion is a chimera, and that the concrete historical features of Christianity are essential to it. 'There is no religion that is not positive, and there never has been; natural religion, so called, is an imagination.'[4]

As a good Lutheran, Ritschl assigned a central place to the doctrine of justification, and his principal writing, composed in the years 1870–74, is *The Christian Doctrine of Justification and Reconciliation*. The first two volumes of this massive work are mainly historical, while the third (and last) is a complete systematic theology. It is arguable, however, whether 'justification' or the 'kingdom of God' or the idea of 'value-judgments' is the real centre of his thinking. Of course, justification, the kingdom of God and value-judgments are all closely related. Justification is the fundamental Christian experience that sets the believer in a new relation to God and confers on that believer a new sense of worth in the eyes of God. But, according to Ritschl, 'justification is related in the first instance to the whole of the religious community founded by Christ, and to individuals only as they attach themselves to the community'.[5] So justification points beyond the individual to the community, the final realization of which is the kingdom of God. This expression 'denotes the association of mankind – an association both extensively and intensively the most comprehensive possible – through the reciprocal moral action of its members'.[6] There cannot be isolated individual Christians, for their very faith relates them within the community. The community, in turn, owes its foundation to Jesus Christ. He is not just the paradigm of the good life, set up for our imitation, but stands over against us as the author of forgiveness and the new relation to God. It is this significance of Christ for our lives, as we have experienced it in justification and the Christian life, that we are confessing when we acknowledge Christ's divinity. To say Christ is God is not to make any metaphysical statement about him. 'If Christ, by what he has done and suffered for my salvation, is my Lord, and if, by trusting to the power of what he has done for me, I honour him as my God, then that is a value-judgment of a direct kind. It is not a judgment which belongs to the sphere of disinterested scientific know-ledge, like the formula of Chalcedon. Every cognition of a religious sort is a direct judgment of value.'[7] I suppose we could express this in another way by saying that for Ritschl, as a positivist who rejects metaphysics, the word 'God' represents an unknown quantity, an x. But Christian experience solves the problem, that is to say, it is revelation, for in that experience, especially justification, Christ has for us the value of God and supplies the meaning for the word 'God'. There may be metaphysical mysteries here, but, in Ritschl's view, we need say nothing about them. 'We know the nature of God and Christ only in their worth for us.'[8]

In the course of his wide-ranging and carefully detailed argument, Ritschl makes many lesser points which should not be overlooked. I therefore mention a few of them. He asks what is meant by saying that Christ's kingdom is not of this world. This does not mean that we are to give to the idea an entirely otherworldly sense – this would in any case conflict with Ritschl's conception of the kingdom as an ethical common-wealth. It means, on Ritschl's interpretation, that the kingdom is a community resting not on legal rights but on loving conduct, a com-munity 'exempt from the standard of legal rights', that is, of claims and counter-claims.[8] He also visualizes a 'kingdom of sin' over against the kingdom of God, but this is no demonic realm, but rather a recognition of the corporate nature of sin, even in dulling the common conceptions of right and wrong, so that 'we become accustomed to standing forms of sin and acquiesce in them'.[9] The importance which Ritschl attached to the historical Jesus and to historical knowledge about Jesus is not as clear as one might have expected, in view of the fact that he leans away from metaphysics to the realm of inner-worldly fact. He does indeed say, 'If the Godhead of Christ or his Lordship over the world in his present state of exaltation is to be a postulate of Christian faith . . . then it must be demonstrated to us in Christ's influence upon ourselves. But every form of influence exerted by Christ must find its criterion in the historical figure presented by his life.'[10] Here we seem to have two sources which support each other – the Christian experience of salvation in the community and the historical witness to Jesus mediated through the tradition.

The account of Ritschl's christology given here makes it clear that what I called the 'mid-century misgivings' discussed in the last chapter were only an episode, and that with Ritschl the humanist, immanentist trends were again asserting themselves. In the words of historian Claude Welch, 'Though opposed to mid-nineteenth-century mediation theology, as well as to the apologetics of orthodoxy, Ritschl was representative of a new kind of mediation, cutting loose from the speculative and metaphysical and turning to the practical and historical as a new foundation and form for theology. His thought articulated the theological mood of a rising generation.'[11] We may say indeed that his christology made a good deal of sense for people of modern times, and that it might claim legitimacy in those stirrings which we noted in Luther and Melanchthon, but which were speedily aborted as the Reformation proceeded (or failed to proceed).[12] But although Ritschl can be defended from some charges, and although he has been treated with less than fairness by Karl Barth[13] and some other critics, there are without doubt serious questions that have to be raised about his christology, and we may now turn to these.

They centre chiefly on his idea of value-judgments and the use which he makes of it. Can he really make up for his rejection of metaphysics by his introduction of values and value-judgments, or is he simply reintroducing metaphysics in a new and concealed form? The answer to that question will depend finally on what we think is necessary for a responsible judgment of value, especially where we have to do with what might fairly be called the ultimate value. A judgment about ultimate value can hardly be a purely arbitrary matter. If such a judgment is responsible, then I ought to be able to say why I judge A to be of ultimate value and not B, or, to speak in more specific terms, I ought to be able to say why I believe that Christ has the value of God or supplies a content for the word 'God' rather than, let us say, Mohammed or Hitler or Marx or some other rival figure who is proclaimed by a community to be, if not actually God, then at least the ultimate criterion of value. And certainly, to be the ultimate criterion of value is one of the characteristics of God. With Luther, it was in fact the defining characteristic, and let us not forget that Ritschl was a good Lutheran, even if he irritated his more conservative co-religionists. Now, Luther's linkage of God to value is very definite:

> A god is that to which we look for all good and in which we find refuge in every time of need. To have a god is nothing else than to trust and believe him with our whole heart. As I have often said, the trust and faith of the heart alone make both a god and an idol. If your faith and trust are right, then your God is the true God. On the other hand, if your trust is false and wrong, then you have not the true God. For these two belong together, faith and God. That to which your heart clings and entrusts itself is, I say, really your God.[14]

Luther seems here to be saying that it is a value-judgment that constitutes God: 'That to which your heart clings and entrusts itself is, I say, really your God.' But he is wise enough not to leave the matter there. For he makes a distinction between God and an idol, and between a trust that is 'right' and a trust that is 'false and wrong'. So there is more than a value-judgment here. To be 'right' and to refer to God rather than an idol, the value-judgment cannot be separated from an objective judgment as to what really is the case. A judgment about what 'really is the case' in such a matter could, I suppose, be called a metaphysical judgment; but if that word is too controversial when discussing Ritschl, let us be content to call it an ontological judgment. Whatever we call it, the point is that the ascription of divinity to Jesus Christ is not *merely* a value-judgment but entails also the assertion of a relation between Jesus and God.

Indeed, we saw that Ritschl does claim very confidently that 'beyond all doubt, Jesus was conscious of a new and thitherto unknown relation to God'. He puts forward a complex argument to show that there is a coincidence of purpose between Christ and God. The life-work of Christ is the same as the work of God, the end to which Christ devoted himself is the same as the end which God has in view for the creation, namely, the bringing into being of a universal ethical kingdom.[15] If Christ's life-work is indeed the same as the work of God, if Christ is the founder of a universal ethical kingdom and such a kingdom is the end at which God himself is aiming, then of course we have very good reasons for making the value-judgment that Christ is God. But how does Ritschl know all this? It can hardly be read off from the history of Jesus' life as we find it in the gospels, or from his sayings. There is also what can only be called a metaphysical interpretation of the history, an interpretation which finds in it evidences of God's intentions for the creation and of the role of Jesus as God's agent. There are in fact plenty of mysteries here, and Ritschl has plenty to say about them, in spite of his declaration that when anything is a mystery, he will say nothing about it.

Ritschl's situation, whether he is willing to acknowledge it or not, is like that of any other theologian – he makes value-judgments but at the same time he cannot help making objective judgments about God, Christ, the world and the relations among these realities. If he tries to confine his theology to value-judgments alone (as he sometimes seems to do) then he cannot distinguish between God and an idol and his value-judgments are arbitrary and irresponsible. But as soon as he begins to give reasons for them, he is plunged willy-nilly into metaphysical or ontological problems which he has been trying to evade.

The difficulties that beset him can be seen at several points in his argument. We have noted, for instance, how he contrasts his own christology with the formula of Chalcedon, claiming that his view is a 'direct judgment of value' whereas the Chalcedonian formula is a 'judgment that belongs to the sphere of disinterested scientific (*wissenschaftlich*) knowledge'.[16] When one considers the passion with which theological matters were debated in the patristic age, it is hard to believe that the formulae being debated were 'disinterested'. Ritschl himself asks the question, 'How is religious knowledge related to theoretical or philosophical knowledge?' He realizes that to say that the former deals in value-judgments, the latter in objective judgments of fact (including metaphysical fact) is inadequate. Valuations enter into all our knowing. 'Value-judgments are determinative in the case of all connected knowledge of the world, even when carried out in the most objective fashion. *Attention* during scientific examination always denotes that such knowledge has a *value* for him who employs it.'[17] In other words, there is no knowledge that is completely value-free or interest-free. But at this point Ritschl appears to have proved too much, for he has undermined his own distinction between value-judgments and theoretical judgments, and so the distinction he makes between his own christology and that of Chalcedon falls to the ground. Or, if it does not altogether disappear, it becomes a matter of degree. He makes a distinction between concomitant judgments of value and independent judgments of value. The former accompany all investigations of facts, for 'without interest we do not trouble ourselves about anything'. But in the latter case, that of the independent judgments of value, the values have become the main concern. But even so, I would insist that the connection between fact and value has not been broken, and indeed cannot be broken if our value-judgments are to be responsible and intelligent. So what I have called the positivist christology of Ritschl turns out to be less positivist than he would have liked it to be. Obviously unhappy with a criterionless judgment of value, he searches desperately around for some objective support for the claim that 'Christ is God', but has little success. It would be difficult to dissent from the sarcastic remark of Bonhoeffer that Jesus has been 'declared divine by the community in a burst of enthusiasm'.[18]

The general direction mapped out by Ritschl was followed by Wilhelm Herrmann, professor for many years at Marburg and one of the most influential theologians of the late nineteenth century. He taught both Barth and Bultmann, and his writings reached more readers than those of Ritschl himself, not only in Germany but in the English-speaking countries as well. Herrmann well illustrates the neo-Kantian character of Ritschlianism – the repudiation of metaphysics and the practical emphasis on moral values. But along with this goes a reverential attachment to the person of Jesus, approaching sometimes almost to a Christ-mysticism. The attractiveness of Herrmann's writings is in part due to their existential tone – he writes as one who really cares for what he is writing about.

But the positivist tendency remains strong. Speculation and metaphysics can, in Herrmann's view, never be successful in solving the problems which they have set for themselves, and they can never attain to the kind of objective truth that is accessible to the natural sciences. Why then has so much energy gone into metaphysics when there had been so little return? The answer is that beyond the metaphysical quest there lies a practical motivation – the need of human beings to gain an orientation for their lives in this world. But this need cannot be satisfied by metaphysics or any theoretical system of belief. Only religion, expressed in a concrete faith, can respond to the need. Religion is perverted from its true nature when it is combined with metaphysics and turned into a system of dogmas, as has happened, in Herrmann's view, in the course of Christian history. I am not sure that it would be fair to say that Herrmann is a representative of what has been called 'revelatory positivism' but he does come very close to it. When he writes, 'We do not merely come to God through Christ. It is truer to say that in God himself we find nothing but Christ',[19] then he is virtually teaching not only that 'Christ is God' (as the great majority of Christian theologians have believed, understanding the 'is' in the sense of predication rather than identity), but also that 'God is Jesus' (a proposition which most theologians would reject as far too restrictive of what we mean by 'God').[20] I think what Herrmann wished to say would have been adequately safeguarded by some such formula that there is nothing in God which contradicts Jesus Christ. This is, of course, an affirmation of faith, but it is one that most Christians would presumably be willing to make, for if Christ is in some important sense the 'revelation' of God, then, though we admit that there are regions of deity beyond our comprehension, we could hardly claim Christ as revelation if we thought that these regions cancelled out what we think we have learned of God in Christ. But when Herrmann says 'we find in God nothing but Christ', he is going beyond the relatively modest affirmation of faith which I mentioned, and is bluntly asserting an identity – 'Jesus is God'. This, I think, does deserve to be called 'revelatory positivism'. That this is the case is borne out by some other things that Herrmann says. If we were to point out to him, as some of his contemporary critics did, that 'God' is not a specifically Christian word and that people have had some knowledge of God outside of Christianity, in paganism and in Jewish religion, for instance, that is to say, that there are and have been people who believe in God and, we must suppose, have some knowledge of God, but who do not think that God is Jesus, then what does Herrmann have to say? In his own words, 'we may reply that we by no means wish to assert, even for a moment, that the savages of New Holland have no knowledge of God, no pulsations of true religion, and therefore no communion with God'. He argues similarly about Judaism. But we cannot enter into the minds of such groups of people. 'We stand in such historical relationships that Jesus Christ alone can be grasped by us as the fact in which God so reveals himself to us that everything that hides him from us vanishes away.'[21] Though later in his argument Herrmann will introduce objective considerations of an ethical kind into his valuation of Jesus Christ, at this point it seems to be just a brute fact, part of the given historical situation in which the Western world finds itself. This is surely religious positivism carried to extreme lengths. The content of the word 'God' is determined for us purely by our cultural situation. Not only are we forbidden to reflect upon it metaphysically, we may not even compare it with the ideas of God current in other religions.

So far it may seem that Herrmann is driving us in the direction of a subjective faith, not held up by any supports outside itself. The basis of this self-authenticating faith is the power of Jesus' personality. The traditional two-natures christology is rejected by Herrmann as 'metaphysical' and as missing the inward religious relation to Jesus which is the primary foundation of faith. In his *Systematic Theology* (which is in fact only a brief summary of his lectures) he declares that 'Christian doctrine is only to be understood as the expression of new personal life'.[22] This may remind us of the similar limited claim made by Schleiermacher, who was as much admired by Herrmann as was Ritschl. Yet, as I indicated earlier, Herrmann did try to find some objective grounds for Christian belief, though he sought them not in the speculative realm but in the positive down-to-earth facts of history and ethics. 'The Christian's consciousness that God communes with him rests on two objective facts, the first of which is the historical fact of the person of Jesus. We have grasped this fact as an element in our own sphere of reality, and we have felt its power . . . The second objective ground of the Christian's consciousness that God communes with him is that we hear within ourselves the demand of the moral law. Here we grasp an objective fact which must be held to be valid in any historical study of life.'[23]

These two points, of course, repeat the teaching of Ritschl. When Herrmann describes the first of them as 'the historical fact of the person of Jesus', he does not mean historical research or the reconstruction of the career of Jesus built up by such research. It is the 'inner life' of Jesus that is the significant historical datum, and in Herrmann's view, we still know the power of that inner life through the New Testament. To use one of his favourite expressions, it makes an 'impression' on us today as it did on the original disciples. The word 'impression' (*Eindruck*) is not meant to be understood as the conveying of some rather vague atmosphere, as it often is in common speech, but a forcible imprinting, like the impression of a design on metal when a coin is struck in a mint. The precise nature or condition for the conveying of this impression of the inner life of Jesus is left vague by Herrmann, and perhaps it could not be otherwise. 'The inner life of religion is a secret in the soul.'[24] This language about a 'secret in the soul' as likewise Herrmann's stress on 'communion with God' could be taken to suggest something mystical. But like most German Protestant theologians, Herrmann has a deep suspicion of mysticism. His attitude is rather like that of Schleiermacher – an acknowledgment of the deep inner experiences of religion coupled with a rejection of the metaphysics implied in traditional mysticism. Herrmann is particularly anxious to avoid any suggestion of a direct mystical relation to God. Our relation to God takes place in and with our relation to Jesus Christ, for are not God and Jesus virtually identical in his way of thinking?

The other objective ground to which Herrmann appealed was that 'we hear within ourselves the demand of the moral law'. Here we have an easily recognized echo of Kant. This emphasizes that Herrmann's view of Christianity is not so much mystical as ethical. Like Ritschl, he emphasized Jesus' teaching about the kingdom of God. 'It is clear in these sayings of Jesus that in all history he was the first to express the real meaning of moral good, that it is the will to fellowship, issuing in inner freedom won in and through fellowship.'[25]

There were many other scholars at the end of the nineteenth century and the beginning of the twentieth who might be called Ritschlians, though like all such designations, this one easily becomes vague and uninformative. Whether it should be applied to Adolf Harnack (1850–1931) is doubtful. He must be acknowledged as probably the most erudite of all nineteenth-century students of Christianity, but it was also with him that the liberal-positivist tendencies which we have been considering in this chapter reached their logical conclusion, which turned out to be also their moment of dissolution. But at the turn of the century, in the winter of 1899–1900, he was exercising as great an influence as any theologian of modern times, as he gave his famous lectures in the University of Berlin on 'The Essence of Christianity' (*das Wesen des Christentums*). The book containing these lectures bears in English the title *What Is Christianity?*, but it is a pity that the word 'essence' has been lost in this translation, since it was important in Harnack's thinking. He believed that in spite of all the changes, doctrinal, liturgical, institutional and so on that the church has undergone in the course of its history, there is a central core – it might even be called an authentic Christianity – that has persisted through all the changes and that sometimes revives and shows its power, as it did (in Harnack's view) at the time of the Reformation. He believed that in spite of all our modern sophistication and our disillusionment with traditional Christian teaching, this essence, if it can be liberated, has still power to appeal to the deepest human aspirations. It could even be argued that the astonishing impact made by his lecture course proved his point.

But what is this essence, and how are we to determine what is the essence, and what are merely the outward, dispensable trappings? It is at this point that Harnack, as theologian and writer on christology, is in the closest relation to Harnack as historian. It is to critical history that we must look for the purification of the essence of Christianity. That essence has been covered over and hidden by the centuries-long development of dogma and ecclesiasticism, and this has happened not only in Catholicism but equally in the Protestant orthodoxy that arose in the centuries following the Reformation. The essential Christianity is not a doctrine but primarily a way of life. It is true that certain beliefs are implicit in this way of life, but its transformation into a doctrine and eventually the elaboration of a system of dogmas was, in Harnack's view, a deterioration. It was brought about by the fact that Christianity had to establish itself in the Hellenistic world, and this meant that it had to come to terms with it intellectually. 'Theology', he wrote, 'is dependent on innumerable factors, above all, on the spirit of the time; for it lies in the nature of theology that it desires to make its object intelligible'.[26] Unfortunately, the end result in the history of Christian dogma is that the essence of Christianity has been made unintelligible, indeed, invisible as it has become more and more covered up. The business of critical study is to penetrate back through all this accumulation of material until the essence is exposed. I do not think, however, that it is fair to Harnack to represent him as seeking simply to get back to the most primitive Christianity. That was the kind of criticism which Alfred Loisy made when he complained that Harnack had ignored the fully developed form of Christianity and occupied himself with only the original seed.[27] But Harnack was not trying to get back to some supposedly pure beginning. He says quite plainly that '"primitive Christianity" had to disappear in order that "Christianity" might remain'.[27] And what remains is something living, capable of new development.

One sometimes hears the criticism that Harnack was like a child peeling an onion in the hope that he will eventually come to the core, but in fact he ends up with nothing. This criticism, as I have said, has often been applied to Harnack, but the truth is that he himself used it to describe what he was *not* trying to do! 'We must not be like the child who, wanting to get at the kernel of a bulb, went on picking off the leaves until there was nothing left, and then could not help seeing that it was just the leaves that made the bulb.'[28] The purely historical labour of critically examining the rise and proliferation of Christian dogmas is not really analogous to peeling an onion. Harnack readily admits that it is not easy to know in every case what belongs to the enduring essence of Christianity and what to the accidents of a particular situation. Again, while he deplores the dominant role that doctrine has played in Christian history, he does not deny the need for some dogmas, for, as we have seen, some basic beliefs are already implicit in the Christian way of life. However, he does hope to arrive at 'the kernel of the matter' and certainly he expects that when that point is reached, the doctrinal baggage (if we may so speak) will have been very much reduced. Sometimes indeed Harnack seems to want to remove from Christianity all particularity and to commend the rational or natural religion of Kant and the deists. So we find Harnack actually writing 'that the gospel is in nowise a positive religion like the rest; that it contains no statutory or particularistic elements; *that it is, therefore, religion itself.*'[29] But Harnack took history too seriously to believe that some timeless abstract creed could serve the religious needs of the human race. The 'essence' is certainly not to be confused with its outward vesture, but it never appears without some such vesture. We get the impression that Harnack really agonized over the task of distinguishing kernel and husk:

> Truly the historian's task of distinguishing between what is traditional and what is peculiar, between kernel and husk, in Jesus' message of the kingdom of God is a difficult and responsible one. How far may we go? We do not want to rob this message of its innate character and colour; we do not want to change it into a pale scheme of ethics. On the other hand, we do not want to lose sight of its peculiar character and strength, as we should do were we to side with those who resolve it into the general ideas prevailing at the time.[30]

Obviously the historical figure of Jesus had for Harnack a power of attraction very much like that he had for Herrmann, and which could not be exercised by some bare 'archetype' of the life well pleasing to God. So we must not push to extremes the view that Christianity is not a positive religion, or is 'religion itself' if this was to be understood as an abstract essence. But how does Harnack interpret the figure of Jesus? What is his christology, if indeed it is permissible to use the word 'christology' in relation to Harnack?

The original gospel, in historical terms, was the preaching given by Jesus himself, not a preaching about Jesus. That original preaching of Jesus is summed up by Harnack under three major headings: 'The kingdom of God and its coming', interpreted very much along the same lines as we found in Ritschl and Herrmann, that is to say, as a universal moral commonwealth: 'God the Father and the infinite value of the human soul' – this is the element in his teaching that gives confidence and a sense of worth; 'The higher righteousness and the commandment of love' – this is the distinctively Christian element, proceeding from Jesus and lifting morality on to a new level.[31] Now, it is true that Harnack says about this original form of the gospel, 'The gospel, as Jesus proclaimed it, has to do with Father only and not with the Son'.[32] But he is not going back to being a 'Jewish Christian' or an 'Ebionite' of the primitive Christian community – indeed, quite in the tradition of Kant and Hegel, he minimizes the connection with Judaism, saying that Christianity's connection with it was very loose.[33] On the other hand, he insists on the closest connection between the gospel that Jesus preached and Jesus' own person and history. Jesus 'was himself what he taught; to steep ourselves in him is still the chief matter'.[34] But to say this is for Harnack quite compatible with rejecting the two-natures christology as a speculative metaphysical intrusion into Christianity. The Jesus in whom we must steep ourselves is the Jesus revealed by history, and Harnack remained confident that in spite of Strauss and other sceptical historians, the New Testament picture of Jesus remains reliable. So when he says, 'How great a departure from what [Jesus] thought and enjoined is involved in putting a "christological" creed in the forefront of the gospel',[35] this is not intended to remove Christ from the central place which he occupies in the Christian faith, but to purify by means of history. But to someone reading Harnack's works roughly a century after they were written, the question is bound to arise whether even this great and learned historian has the right to make the assertions he does about the historical Jesus. It is certainly an impressive figure that he sets before us, one whom Harnack himself does not hesitate to call 'Son of God'. But how far that figure is drawn 'solely from history' and how far it has its roots elsewhere are questions that would be raised by Harnack's critics in the new theological generation. And what about God, for belief in God is the main doctrinal element in the original gospel, even in its simplest form? Ought not Harnack – or any responsible theologian – to have offered some vindication of this belief in a secular age, and any such vindication could not proceed from history alone.

Though Ritschl, Herrmann and Harnack differ quite considerably among themselves, there is a definite 'family resemblance' and I think we have seen that there is justification for grouping them together under the heading of 'Positivist Christology'. This indeed might be seen in retrospect as the end product of those tendencies which were working themselves out in christology from the Enlightenment onward. Yet it was not quite the end, for there had not yet been faced in its full force the relativism which arises from putting history in the place once occupied by metaphysics. As we move from Kant to Ritschl and Harnack, we see the tide of the historical more and more submerging what had once been regarded as the eternal, timeless truths of metaphysics and epistemology. Strauss had indeed pointed out the great gulf that separates the modern conception of history from the ancient one and had consigned much of the New Testament record to the realm of myth. But even as late as Harnack there persists the belief in a permanent unchanging essence of Christianity that has been there from the beginning and can still address us as 'gospel'. Harnack believed that history could purify the gospel by pruning away extraneous developments, but would the reliance on history lead eventually to dissolution?

That question prompts us to consider the work of Ernst Troeltsch (1865–1923). In modern terms, we would probably call him a professor of religious studies rather than a professor of theology, for he combined theological with historical and sociological studies in what could fairly be called a scientific or even positivistic approach to religion, seen primarily as a human phenomenon. But this statement has to be qualifed at once by adding that Troeltsch had personal religious convictions which made him uneasy about the positivist and relativist directions in which his studies were moving.

Troeltsch's name is associated with 'historicism', the view that all sociocultural phenomena are historically determined, that truths and values are not absolute but relative to the cultural conditions out of which they have arisen. His views are expounded in *Der Historismus und seine Probleme* (*Historicism and Its Problems*).[36] The business of the historian, we are told, is to explain historical happenings by showing their position in the whole causal nexus of historical events. In doing this, he must observe three principles. The first is the principle of criticism – whatever the historian says can never be the last word – it is always liable to revision if new evidences are found; the second is the principle of analogy – a report will be credible only if the event it records is analogous to events in our present experience; the third is the principle of correlation – there is continuity in history, each event being correlated with others in a single series. One might say there was nothing new in these principles – something very like them underlies Strauss's work, and even Schleiermacher's intention to treat incarnation as a 'natural fact'. But Troeltsch gave them systematic expression, and their consequences for christology were obvious and they are still important today. In the present century, for instance, they have been accepted by Bultmann and contested by Pannenberg. One would say, however, that these principles are nowadays very widely accepted among secular historians, and if they are taken into christology and history is allowed to have the dominant role in christology, then very severe restrictions are laid on what may be claimed for Jesus Christ, and the task of constructing a christology which will both remain loyal to the traditional faith in Christ and will be respectful toward the canons of modern thought becomes very questionable.

At this point we may pause for a moment to note how Troeltsch's historicism not only carries further the concern with history in Ritschl and his successors, but radicalizes it in such a way as to react critically against that older generation. Ritschl and, even more, Herrmann believed in something like a 'revelatory positivism', so that the lack of any metaphysical knowledge of God was compensated by his self-revelation in Jesus Christ, so that Christ had the value of God. Harnack did not use the same language, but he did believe in a permanent essence of Christianity, so that a person in 1900 could go back to the original gospel and hear it as something that spoke directly to him in his own situation. But if historical relativism is accepted, Ritschl, Herrmann and Harnack are all alike in serious trouble. They had greatly oversimplified the problem of how a twentieth-century person can hear what was being said in a document of the first century. To put it in another way, they had modernized Jesus and understood him in their own frame of reference rather than in his. This kind of criticism of 'the quest of the historical Jesus' was going to increase in intensity in later years. But we begin to understand Troeltsch's personal anxiety as it became clearer that he had dealt a 'body blow'[37] to traditional Christian theology. Had he initiated an unstoppable slide into complete relativism, into a self-destroying scepticism in which finally the distinction between true and false disappears? Or is a rational person bound to say, 'This must not happen!' And there is a moral side to the matter as well as a logical one. Though we may agree that communication with a person of a very different culture is very difficult, as the history of human conflict shows, can we ever say that it is impossible or be content to accept that it is? And are there not great human geniuses, Jesus among them, who have had an incredible power to reach across barriers of time and space and race?

The problem of the absolute and the relative occupied Troeltsch's mind through much of his life. For centuries, Christian thinkers had simply assumed that the Christian faith has the fulness of truth, and that other faiths are in various degrees erroneous. Even Hegel had called Christianity the 'absolute' religion. Troeltsch's view of history and the correlation of all events within it meant that Christianity could not be considered in isolation from other faiths. We have already had occasion to notice the 'history of religions' school[38] and have seen how some of its adherents believed that early Christianity had taken over some of its teachings from Gnostics and other non-Christian groups. Troeltsch was a leading representative of this school, and he did not evade the question of how Christianity relates to other faiths in modern times. Do Christianity and its founder, Jesus Christ, occupy a uniquely authoritative place? Or must they not be compared and evaluated in relation to other faiths and other saviour-figures? And if one does so compare them, can one ever pronounce that such and such a faith is absolute or final or beyond comparison with others? Troeltsch took the view, rightly, I think, that in order to make such a pronouncement one would require 'a knowledge of God that exhausts its essence and idea, that is withdrawn from all change and enrichment, that overleaps the bounds of history.'[39] No one has this. Incidentally, it is worth noting the similarity between what Troeltsch says here, and what Kierkegaard said about Hegel's system of philosophy.[40] But Troeltsch did not think that his denial of the absoluteness of Christianity meant that he had to adopt an 'aimless relativism'. Sometimes he argues that Christianity is the point of convergence and culmination of all religions. In a late writing, he claims that Christianity is 'final and unconditional *for us*', but that this does not rule out the possibility that God communicates himself to others in different situations in different ways.

In the course of these chapters in which I have discussed the various types of post-Enlightenment christology, I have given attention mainly to German and other European theologians and philosophers, because one must frankly say that it is from them that the original ideas and formative influences have come. But since I assume that my readers will be mainly English-speaking, I have from time to time included a British or American representative, and I shall do the same in this chapter, for not only were the four Germans already considered widely read in English translations, there was in addition a special appeal in their positivist leanings to the non-speculative, pragmatic type of mentality that seems to go with the Anglo-Saxon temperament.

The United States was particularly receptive to Ritschlianism, which deeply affected the undogmatic ethical type of Christianity known as the 'social gospel'. The American exemplar I have chosen is Walter Rauschenbusch (1861–1918), for many years a pastor in a run down area of New York, then professor in the seminary at Rochester. Though born in the United States, his family had come from Germany and he received some of his education there and was well acquainted with the work of German philosophers and theologians. His first book, *Christianity and the Social Crisis*, was an indictment of the industrial urban society he had known in New York, a reminder to the church of the concern for justice among the Hebrew prophets and the concern of Jesus for the neighbour, together with a call to the churches to become involved in what he called the 'social movement'.[41] But it is to Rauschenbusch's credit that, unlike some church activists, he saw the necessity for providing a theological basis for the policies which he advocated.

He therefore constructed a complete theology, which began with these words: 'We have a social gospel. We need a systematic theology large enough to match it and vital enough to back it.'[42] The theology which Rauschenbusch proposes has obvious resemblances to the German theologies considered earlier in the chapter. It is a theology which 'must not only make room for the doctrine of the kingdom of God, but give it a central place and revise all other doctrines so that they will articulate organically with it'.[43] The United States was, of course, fertile soil for such a theology, for from the time of the Pilgrim Fathers, the symbol of the kingdom of God had been a powerful one. The kingdom had been central in the teaching of Jesus himself, but for various reasons it has never become the focus of the church's interest as it should. In the earliest days of eschatological expectation, this world was considered transitory and unimportant; in the time of the Roman Empire, the church was too weak to have any great influence on society; in the Middle Ages, otherworldliness again supervened in the form of monasticism. But now, in the modern industrialized world, the time has come for the church to turn to the long neglected social problem and to engage with what Rauschenbusch called 'the fundamental purpose of its existence'.

What kind of christology emerges in the context of this social gospel? As we might expect, Rauschenbusch sees Jesus primarily as the initiator of the kingdom of God, and this means that he set in motion the historical forces of redemption which aim at the transformation of human society into the kingdom. Like Ritschl, he also stressed the negative side of the task as a struggle against the kingdom of evil, understood as sin on a corporate or collective level. With this conception of the mission of Jesus, he is even more sweeping than his German counterparts in his dismissal of the classical christology. Like Harnack, he claims to have returned to the original gospel. His view of Christ is 'a return to the earliest messianic theology; whereas some of the other christological interests and ideas are alien importations, part of that wave of "Hellenization" which nearly swamped the original gospel'.[44]

One might wonder whether Rauschenbusch is heading for an entirely humanized, positivized christology, with Jesus no more than a social reformer. This is certainly how some critics understood the social gospel. But Rauschenbusch still maintained a belief in God and saw Jesus as the agent of God. Though he favoured socialism, Rauschenbusch was not a Marxist. But he did use some Marxist analysis in his treatment of the history of theology, seeing in particular the monarchical idea of God as a product of ideology. Jesus was the corrective to this. The cross of Christ teaches us to think of a suffering God who shares the striving of his creation toward the ideal kingdom. So it is not mere rhetoric when Rauschenbusch asserts: 'The kingdom of God is divine in its origin, progress and consummation; it is miraculous all the way, and is the continuous revelation of the power, the righteousness and the love of God.'[45]

13

Critical Responses and Theological Renascence

In chapter 11 which I called 'Mid-century Misgivings', I discussed some christological developments arising in the eighteen-forties in reaction against the rationalist and humanist tendencies that had dominated the most influential types of christology produced in the first half of the century. But these protest movements did not bring any lasting changes in the directions which were being followed in christology. They soon faded out as a new surge of liberal thinking came along – the surge I have described in chapter 12 called 'Positivist Christology', and I think that the use of the word 'positivist' has been justified from what we have seen of the teaching of Ritschl and others. For any transcendent or (to use a word that had become very unpopular) 'supernatural' element in Christianity had been either excluded or at least minimized, except that, somewhat incongruously, God lived on in the background, and there might even be an appeal to 'revelation' to fill in the gaps left by philosophical scepticism.

But inevitably the renewal of the reductionist and immanentist trend of nineteenth-century theology called forth a further reaction from those who believed that theologians were moving too far from their bases in the Bible and the tradition. This new reaction manifested itself strongly in the last decade of the century, and in retrospect we can see that it was something much more powerful and significant than what had occurred in mid-century. It turned out in fact to be the beginning of an important and distinctive new theological movement that was to dominate the first half of the twentieth century and even beyond, a movement that has often been called by its admirers the 'theological renascence'. Its greatest achievements were, of course, associated with the name of Karl Barth, but the ground had already been prepared for him. However, the theologians who initiated the change and made possible the renascence were not themselves thinking in terms of a new-style theology and still less of a neo-orthodoxy, but were expressing their dissatisfaction with the theological (and especially christological) productions of the nineteenth century, and exercising their critical faculties at the expense of the so-called 'liberals', especially the Ritschlians.

A pioneer of these new theological tendencies was Martin Kähler (1835–1912), professor at Halle for many years. His major work, *Die Wissenschaft der christlichen Lehre*,[1] was first published in 1883 and in its christological teaching has resemblances to the work of Dorner, described above.[2] In Dorner's teaching, it will be remembered, there was a progressive incarnation in Jesus, and this was constituted by a twofold activity: the *assumption* of the humanity of Jesus by the Logos, and the corresponding *receptivity* of the divine on the side of Jesus. Though the language is slightly different, it seems to be essentially the same understanding of the matter that we find in Kähler: 'The union of the Godhood and the manhood becomes intelligible, if it is regarded as a reciprocity of two personal movements; on the one hand, a generative activity from the standpoint of the eternal Godhood, and, on the other hand, a receptive activity from the standpoint of the developing humanity.'[3] It does not follow, however, that Kähler derived these ideas from Dorner. Though Dorner had been expounding such ideas for quite some time in his lectures, his *System of Christian Doctrine* was not published until after his death, to be precise, in 1885, two years after Kähler's book on dogmatics. But it matters little who was the first to write in these terms. I have already indicated in the discussion of Dorner that this idea of a progressive incarnation arising from a twofold activity appears to be a valuable one and is still worthy to be considered in a contemporary christology.

Although Kähler's book on dogmatics was highly regarded in its time, he is today chiefly remembered for a book which came out quite late in his career and which has been seen as one of the most damaging blows to liberal or positivist theology. This book, published in 1896, bore the somewhat longwinded and obscure title, *Der sogenannte historische Jesus und der geschichtliche biblische Christus*.[4] The title was originally that of an essay which Kähler had published in 1892, and the book of 1896 consisted of that essay with three others. I do not know whether Kähler was the first to make a distinction between the two German words *historisch* and *geschichtlich*, which are contrasted in the title of the book. Both would normally be translated into English by the same word, 'historical'. But in Kähler, and more recently in Bultmann, *historisch* has been used to refer to the 'facts' of history, what is discoverable by historical research, whereas *geschichtlich* has been used rather to designate the significance of historical happenings for human existence. In an earlier writing,[5] I made the distinction by translating *historisch* as 'objective-historical' and *geschichtlich* as 'existential-historical', and I still think this is a useful way of handling the problem. I should point out, however, that in the standard English translation of Kähler's book, the convention adopted is to translate *historisch* as 'historical' and *geschichtlich* as 'historic'. Thus the title of the book in English is *The So-called Historical Jesus and the Historic Biblical Christ*.[6]

This particular book is mainly critical and anti-Ritschlian in its thrust. A major section of the key-essay bears the title, 'Against the Life-of-Jesus Movement'. In opposition to attempts to derive a 'life of Jesus' from the biblical writings, Kähler commends the study of the entire biblical picture of Jesus. The critical power of Kähler's teaching was not lost on one of his young students, Paul Tillich, who preserved this recollection:

> The power of the Protestant principle first became apparent to me in the classes of my theological teacher, Martin Kähler, a man who in his personality and theology combined traditions of Renaissance human-ism with a profound understanding of the Reformation and with strong elements of the religious awakening of the middle of the nineteenth century . . . He was able not only to unite these ideas with his own classical education but also to interpret them with great religious power for generations of humanistically educated students. Under his influence a group of advanced students and younger professors developed the new understanding of the Protestant princi-ple in different ways.[7]

The 'Protestant principle' was understood by Tillich as a principle of criticism which needs to be constantly applied to what he called the 'Catholic substance' of Christianity. In a way, this makes Protestantism dependent on the Catholicism which provides the material for the essentially critical function of Protestantism. At the same time, the Protestant principle has an independent source, for it arises from the notion of justification by faith alone, on which Luther and his followers laid such stress. The Protestant principle therefore prunes away all that is extraneous in Christian theology, so that theology becomes a pure expression of faith. In the particular case which concerns us at the moment, what is to be pruned away is reliance on the findings of historical research. The objection is not just that because such findings are never more than plausible and because they are infected by the relativism of a historical point of view, they can never supply that 'objective' basis for faith such as Herrmann and others desiderated. From the strictly Protestant point of view, there is the further decisive objection that the objective props which research is expected to supply would contradict the nature of faith itself. Thus Kähler (and, to a large extent, Tillich after him) tried to make theology independent of the historian.

We find Kähler saying about the quest for the historical Jesus and the attempt to make this historical figure the objective basis for christology that 'the Jesus of the "Life-of Jesus" movement is merely a modern example of human creativity, and not one iota better than the notorious dogmatic Christ of Byzantine christology'.[8] The first part of the sentence declares that the historical Jesus unveiled by research is not objective reality but an artificial modernization of Jesus, reflecting the values of the investigator. It is as much an amalgam of historical data and superimposed ideas as were the dogmatic constructions of theology. The second part of the sentence makes it clear that Kähler's criticism of the liberals was not motivated by any desire to reinstate the classical christology, brusquely dismissed as 'the notorious dogmatic Christ of Byzantine christology'.

So where does one go from here? The Bible, we are being told, is not history, such that we could construct from it a reliable picture of the historical Jesus. Equally, the Bible is not dogma, standing ready to be translated into the language of Chalcedon. Kähler's alternative to history and dogma is kerygma, a word which means 'proclamation' and which has been very popular among New Testament critics since Kähler's time. 'It is as kerygma, as a deliverance of the divine commission to his heralds, that the ancient word of scripture acquires its significance in the Church.'[9] He can also say (and how provocative this must have been to those engaged in the historical quest!) 'The real Christ is the preached Christ.'[10]

Let us consider for a moment what could be meant by the sentence just quoted. I think we find an answer if we cast our minds back to the first chapter of this book, when I mentioned the remark of Gadamer on the function of a work of art.[11] That function is to set forth the essence of what is represented, so that, to quote his example, the Achilles of Homer is more than the original Achilles. It was in that connection that I first mentioned Kähler's claim that the real Christ is the preached Christ. There is an analogy here between the sermon and an artwork. The sermon and the Bible itself are not simply setting forth the objective facts of Jesus' career or his place in a conceptual dogmatic scheme. They are concerned with his meaning, his 'essence', if you prefer Gadamer's word, in so far as this touches the concerns of the hearers. Or, to put it in another way which also recalls the beginning of our inquiry,[12] they are less concerned to tell us who Jesus *was* than to say who he *is*. It is in this sense that Kähler wants us to see the Christ of the whole biblical witness, rather than any abstraction from that whole picture, such as a historical Jesus or a dogmatic Christ. But what would it mean to see Jesus in terms of the whole biblical witness? I think it would mean to see him in the context in which the Bible presents him, the context in which he is proclaimed, the context in which he has salvific significance. This context obviously includes a theistic worldview, a spiritual history, certain aspirations and expectations on the part of human beings, and so on. Some such context of relationships is presupposed if Christ is to have the kind of significance that the church has claimed for him. And even if the original aspirations and expectations (we discussed them in chapter 2) have in some cases disappeared, in other been radically transformed, we can, I believe, find analogues in the minds of people today. Potentially, they are 'hearers of the word',[13] if the church can find the kerygmatic word that can communicate today.

Deeper questions underlie some of these matters. Can we, for instance, be content with what Pannenberg and others have called the 'positivist' view of history, the view which confines itself to empirically verifiable happening?[14] Admittedly, such a view has largely established itself from the time of the Enlightenment, and finds perhaps its fullest expression in the Marxist view of history. I do not think Christian faith or theology can find a place within such a reduced conception of history. But the alternative is not necessarily a return to mythology, which would in any case be impossible for anyone who has learned the lessons of the Enlightenment. But we do have to be discriminating about the Enlightenment, for like other historical phenomena its truths were mixed with error and many of its promises have proved illusory. Although Troeltsch enunciated principles that would purge history of mythology, he recognized the special character of 'historical causation'.[15] Such historical causation includes the action of spirit, and perhaps it was to recognize this that Kähler did not hesitate to apply the term 'suprahistorical' to Christ.[16] This particular term may be unfortunate and I would not wish to use it myself without very careful definition, but it does act as a warning that if we want to do justice to the complexities of history as the activity of personal and spiritual beings, we must break out of positivist conceptions. So in a time when many people do think of history in positivist terms, the use of a word like 'suprahistorical' could claim justification among those who are dissatisfied with the positivist point of view.

Tillich believed that Kähler's aim was to make systematic theology completely free of the changing opinions of historical researchers, and clearly Tillich himself would have dearly liked that to happen. But I doubt very much that theology can escape from the constraints of historical research. Even so, Kähler remains important in showing that a positivist conception of history will not do, and that we need a more comprehensive idea of the historical if we are to come to grips with those things in history that are of chief importance for theology. In that sense, we have to heed his contention that 'the real Christ is the preached Christ'.

The year 1892 was a bad one for liberal Protestant theology. Not only did it bring forth, as we have seen, Kähler's essay on the so-called historical Jesus, it was also the year which saw the publication of a quite short but revolutionary book by the New Testament scholar Johannes Weiss (1863–1914). The book was entitled *Die Predigt Jesu vom Reiche Gottes*, or, in its English translation, *Jesus' Proclamation of the Kingdom of God*.[17] Ironically, Weiss was a son-in-law of Ritschl, and whether through tact or simply by accident the publication of the book did not take place until three years after the death of the older man. Its argument was indeed devastating to the Ritschlian position, but this was a different kind of attack from the one we found in Kähler. Whereas Kähler had found fault with the project of trying to extract from the New Testament writings a reliable historical portrait of Jesus, Weiss's complaint was rather that the job had been done very badly. He was in collision with Ritschl, Herrmann and even Harnack because, as he believed, he had done much more thorough research than they had, and had produced a much more authentic account of Jesus and his teaching. In particular, the idea of the kingdom of God which had been a central conception with the older writers was given a quite different interpretation by Weiss. He saw it not as an ethical or political conception that might give relevance to the message of Jesus, but as a product of eschatological and apocalyptic fantasies that are totally alien to the modern outlook.

Ritschl and his followers had uncritically interpreted the kingdom of God as an ethically ordered commonwealth embracing ideally all human beings, a commonwealth that had been founded by Jesus and given its moral ideals by him. Weiss had concluded that this lofty moral vision had little or nothing to do with what Jesus had in mind when he proclaimed the imminence of the kingdom. The kingdom of Ritschl and the others is a modern conception, based not on the teaching of Jesus but on that of Kant. According to Weiss, Jesus was not the founder of the kingdom but simply proclaimed its coming. God alone would bring in the kingdom by his supernatural power, and it would not depend on human efforts, least of all on any political revolution or evolution. 'To hope for the kingdom of God in the transcendent sense of Jesus and to undertake revolution are as different as fire and water.'[18] Nevertheless, this kingdom would be an objective reality, not an inward moral ideal, and the historical details of the kingdom of God as preached by Jesus can be ascertained by a more careful application of historical scholarship than the theologians of the previous generation had achieved. Such scholarship showed that 'Jesus' idea of the kingdom was inextricably involved with eschatological-apocalyptic views – its interpretation as an innerworldly ethical ideal is a vestige of the Kantian idea and does not hold up before a more precise historical investigation'.[19]

The shock which Weiss's teaching caused to the liberal establishment was remembered many years later by Bultmann, who had been a student in those days: 'I still recall how Julius Kaftan in his lectures on dogmatics said, "If the kingdom of God is an eschatological matter, then it is a useless concept so far as dogmatics is concerned".'[20] Presumably, it was useless because the idea of an end to the age is just unacceptable to the post-Enlightenment mentality. No doubt Weiss and Schweitzer after him exaggerated the significance of their discovery or rediscovery of eschatology. It could be argued too that Ritschl and the others were right to modernize the teaching of the gospels if it had become unacceptable and unusable in its original form. In fact, both Weiss and Schweitzer evaded the full implications of their own researches and introduced their own modernizations. But certainly a crushing blow had been dealt to the credibility of the old liberalism. It was clear that its teaching was not, as it had claimed to be, the pure message of Jesus stripped of ecclesiastical accretions. One might still find Harnack's lectures of 1899–1900 quite inspiring, but they should not have been entitled 'The Essence of Christianity' or have claimed to represent the authentic gospel of Jesus.

Weiss's later writings include a large work on primitive Christianity, entitled *Das Urchristentum*. (The English translation is called *Earliest Christianity*.) In this, he traces the development from Jesus as the proclaimer of the kingdom to Jesus as the centre of the new Christian cult. Paul is seen as the originator of this cult and, like Strauss and Wrede, Weiss accounts for the rapid rise of a 'high' christology in Paul in terms of the application of already available messianic ideas. He also makes the point (which we have already met in Jeremias' view of eucharistic origins)[21] that Jesus went to his death in the belief or hope that it would hasten the coming of the kingdom, and this is a point which we should bear in mind when we come to the systematic part of this book and have to ask about Jesus' death.[22]

But here we must note another train of thought which emerges in *Earliest Christianity*. Whereas in the book of 1892 Weiss had attacked the Ritschlian theologians on the ground that their historical investigations had been inadequate, in his later work he drives a new wedge between the modern interpreter and the figure of Jesus by anticipating some of the ideas of the form-critics. When this approach is applied, the gospels are seen as products meant to serve the apologetic, didactic and devotional needs of the early church, rather than as records of the historical Jesus.[23] As Weiss expressed it:

Every narrative that has been preserved, every saying that has survived, is evidence of some particular interest on the part of the primitive church. To this extent, the selection of what was handed down serves to characterize the interest of the group whose need it satisfied. In far greater measure must we learn to read the gospels not only for what they tell us about Jesus, but also for what we can learn from them about the life and faith of the earliest Christians.[24]

The attack which Weiss had opened on liberal theology on the basis of his eschatological studies was intensified by the work of Albert Schweitzer (1875–1965), better known to the world at large as a philanthropist than as a biblical scholar. From his early work, *The Mystery of the Kingdom of God*, published in 1901, to his latest, *The Kingdom of God and Primitive Christianity*, published only after his death, Schweitzer developed an interpretation of the New Testament based on 'thoroughgoing eschatology'. It is an interpretation which he summed up in the opening sentences of what has been called his 'theological testament', the posthumous work mentioned above: 'Christianity is essentially a religion of belief in the coming of the kingdom of God. It begins with the message preached by John the Baptist on the banks of Jordan, "Repent, for the kingdom of heaven is at hand" (Matt. 3.2). It was with the same preaching that Jesus came forward in Galilee after the imprisonment of the Baptist.'[25] Like Weiss, Schweitzer believed that Jesus went to his death to hasten the coming of the kingdom.

Of course, the most widely read of Schweitzer's theological books is *Von Reimarus zu Wrede*, known in English as *The Quest of the Historical Jesus*, with the subtitle 'A Critical Study of its Progress from Reimarus to Wrede'.[26] It appeared in 1906 and is a detailed survey of the attempts by biblical scholars and theologians to penetrate behind the pages of the New Testament to the historical human figure of Jesus of Nazareth, as he supposedly was before faith began to deck him out with religious embellishments and even with divine attributes. These attempts had already begun in the eighteenth century at the zenith of the Enlightenment, and they continued unabated through the nineteenth century. They were not entirely stopped in their tracks by the criticisms of such scholars as Kähler, Weiss and Schweitzer, but the enterprise of bringing to view the plain unvarnished historical Jesus was shown to be so highly problematical that any so-called 'new quests' for the historical Jesus have been much chastened compared with the earlier ones.

Many of the post-Enlightenment writers whom we have considered in the past few chapters appear in Schweitzer's survey, and his criticisms of them must still be considered well worth reading nearly a century after they were written. The main criticism is that these nineteenth-century scholars had not taken account of the fact that Jesus' teaching was given in the context of his own time, and that was a time when, if Schweitzer is correct, Jewish religious thought was completely dominated by apocalyptic conceptions. The main theme of Jesus' preaching was the imminent end of the world. But post-Enlightenment scholars cannot come to terms with such a mythological idea, so those of them who still want to be Christians and to commend the Christian faith can only 'modernize' Jesus, and this really means that they make Jesus the vehicle for their own nineteenth-century bourgeois values. It also means that in spite of their concern with history, they are in fact quite unhistorical in their approach to Jesus. Even the great Harnack is accused by Schweitzer of 'anti-historical violence'! Harnack, in his *What is Christianity?* almost entirely ignores the contemporary limitations of Jesus' teaching, and starts out with 'a gospel which carries him down without difficulty to the year 1899.'[27]

In Schweitzer's view, the scholars who 'have sought to pass over from the life of Jesus to Christianity have acted like men who find themselves on an ice-floe which is slowly dividing into two pieces, and who leap from one to the other before the cleft grows too wide'.[28] Even Jesus' ethical teaching was thought by Schweitzer to be strictly conditioned by the eschatological expectations of the first century. Weiss had been willing to allow that some of Jesus' ethical teaching was not affected by eschatology, but Schweitzer saw it as an 'interim ethic' applying to the supposedly short time remaining before the end of the age and not having universal application. At this point, however, we can scarcely help asking whether Schweitzer's critique has eroded not only the positions of Harnack and other nineteenth-century liberals but has cut away the grounds of his own Christian discipleship. Here we face again a question which confronted us in the discussion of Troeltsch.[29] Are cultural differences sometimes so great that communication has become impossible? If so, can anyone still be a 'Christian' or, at any rate, a Christian who claims a relation to Jesus Christ? Does Schweitzer give any answer to such questions? In one sense, he gave a decisive answer by his own outstanding life of Christian service to the sick and destitute. But his theoretical answer, his rationale for his actions, is much less clear. On the one hand, he tells us that 'we are obliged to admit the evident fact that religious truth varies from age to age'.[30] This is in line with his criticism of Harnack, but then, surprisingly, he finds with Harnack that there is an 'essence of Christianity', which he describes as follows: 'The essence of Christianity is world-affirmation which has gone through an experience of world-negation. In the eschatological world-view of world-negation, Jesus proclaims the ethic of active love.'[31] Another important idea with Schweitzer is perhaps even more difficult to relate clearly to the New Testament – 'reverence for life'.

But it is not our business here to try to sort out Schweitzer's religious convictions. Our own interest lies in his contribution to thinking about the person of Christ and the critical impact of that thinking on the liberal theology that prevailed at the end of the nineteenth century. And we are bound to say that his impact was, on the whole, negative. Indeed, he said it himself: 'There is nothing more negative than the result of the critical study of the life of Jesus.'[32] There is a sadness in the closing pages of Schweitzer's *Quest* when he drives home the point that the Jesus whom we meet in the pages of Renan or Harnack must fade from our minds, because

> . . . he never had any existence. He is a figure designed by rationalism, endowed with life by liberalism, and clothed by modern theology in a historical garb. The study of the life of Jesus has had a curious history. It set out in quest of the historical Jesus, believing that when it had found him it could bring him straight into our time as a Teacher and Saviour. It loosed the bands by which he had been riveted for centuries to the stony rocks of ecclesiastical doctrine, and rejoiced to see life and movement coming into the figure once more . . . But he does not stay; he passes by our time, and returns to his own.[33]

The title of this chapter is 'Critical Responses and Theological Renascence', and up till now we have been dwelling mainly on the first half of the proposed topic, the critical responses that were made at the end of the nineteenth century to the liberal tendencies that had characterized christology throughout the century, and had reached their fullest flowering in the teaching of Harnack. The three writers whom we have just been considering, Kähler, Weiss and Schweitzer, perceived and exposed the faults of their Ritschlian predecessors, but they had little in the way of constructive theology to put in the place of what they were discarding, and certainly, as we have seen, they were not contemplating a return to the orthodox christology that had held the field from the days of the early church until long after the Reformation. After the ground had been cleared, two more decades had to pass before the theological renascence and its work of reconstruction could make a beginning.

The leading figure in the renewal was Karl Barth (1886–1968), often hailed as the greatest Protestant theologian since Calvin. He was a native of Switzerland and spent most of his teaching years in the university of Basle, but in the earlier part of his career he held chairs in Germany and won distinction for his courage in standing up to Hitler's attempts to manipulate the German Church. Barth accepted the critique of nineteenth-century theology discussed in the earlier part of this chapter: like Kähler, he believed that theology's concern is with the kerygma, so his own theology was sometimes called 'kerygmatic theology' or 'theology of the word'; and like Weiss and Schweitzer, he accepted the eschatological character of the New Testament message, understood as a 'theology of crisis'. But he went much further in his criticisms of the development of Christian thought from Schleiermacher to Harnack and blamed it in large measure for the spiritual plight of Europe and for the dreadful events of

World War I and what followed it. As Barth saw it, the theologies of the nineteenth-century had been so anxious to adjust Christianity to the culture of the age that its genuine content had been submerged. Instead of God's revelation being set over against human culture as that by which all human achievements must be judged, the Christian faith had been made a part of culture. The villain of the piece, in Barth's eyes, was Schleiermacher, though Barth never denied the greatness of Schleiermacher or the permanent consequences of his teaching for Christian theology.

When we discussed Schleiermacher's teaching about the person of Christ, I entitled the chapter 'Humanist Christology'. It began from human experience, the religious experience of the human being who becomes aware of finitude and thereby becomes aware also of the infinite being of God, and Schleiermacher's christology was humanist in the further sense that it presented Jesus Christ as the completion of the creation of man. Barth objected to both aspects of this humanist approach. It was mistaken in basing itself on human experience, because this was to overlook the fact that human nature is flawed by sin and cannot find the way to God; and it was further mistaken in its attempts to represent Jesus Christ as virtually a natural development in the history of humanity. In Barth's view, religion never gets us out of human subjectivity; it is a search for God which leads only to idols fabricated by our own minds. Also, in Barth's view, Jesus Christ is so far from being the culmination of human development that he stands over against humanity in judgment as one who has been sent by God.

This reversal of the trends of nineteenth-century Protestantism found expression in his famous *Römerbrief*, a commentary on Paul's letter to the Romans. The first edition of the commentary appeared in 1918, when Barth was still pastor of a parish in Switzerland; its basic message was continued and strengthened in a second (completely rewritten) and several subsequent editions. Alister McGrath says about Barth's *Romans* that it is 'a work of prophecy rather than theology',[34] and certainly it is written with a passion and a consuming concern for the spiritual content of Paul's epistle that makes Barth's commentary a different *genre* from the books we usually think of as commentaries, with their linguistic and historical information, their speculations about the circumstances of writing, and so on. The name of Kierkegaard comes up quite often in the commentary. At this stage of his thinking, Barth shared Kierkegaard's belief that between God and man there is an 'infinite qualitative difference'. If we ask, 'How then is any relation between the two possible?' the answer is that from the human side it is impossible but that in Jesus Christ there is (again in Kierkegaard's language) the 'absolute paradox' whereby the relation is established: 'The positive relation between God and man, which is the absolute paradox, now exists'.[35] In a phrase that was much quoted, Barth spoke of God's action in Christ as 'vertically from above'.[36] The language we have been quoting seems to indicate an exclusive emphasis on the divine transcendence, and of course Barth did want to combat the pantheistic tendencies of the nineteenth century, visible from Schleiermacher on. But one has to remember that in Barth, the otherness of God is always counterpoised by his dialectical insistence on incarnation. The full meaning of this will become apparent to us when we come to the later developments in Barth's thought, but even at the time of *Romans* the dialectic is operative, and if God acts 'vertically from above', Barth also assures us that 'God must not be sought as though he sat on the throne of religious attainment. He is to be found in the plain where men suffer and sin.'[37]

The new stress on eschatology is also apparent in the early Barth. With exaggerated enthusiasm, he writes: 'If Christianity be not altogether thoroughgoing eschatology, there remains in it no relationship with Christ.'[38] But what did he mean by 'eschatology'? He says elsewhere in the commentary: 'The end of which the New Testament speaks is no temporal event, no legendary destruction of the world. Who shall persuade us to depress into a temporal reality what can be spoken of only in a parable?'[39] Like Weiss and Schweitzer before him, Barth, even at his most radical, felt unable to take eschatology in quite the literal way that we suppose Jesus and Paul took it. When Barth claimed that Christianity must be eschatology, I think he meant that it is always a message of 'crisis', another frequently recurring word in the commentary. Crisis is judgment, and the message of Paul's letter, both when it was written and when Barth launched his commentary is a message of judgment. God has confronted the human race with his living Word, Jesus Christ, and that Word brings both judgment and grace.

Obviously Barth's theology was taking a direction almost totally opposite to that of Harnack. In Harnack, Jesus Christ did represent the highest human aspirations – 'the forces and the standards which on the summits of our inner life shine out as our highest good', to quote his own language. In Barth, Christ is the judge of this 'highest good', and in that judgment, it is found wanting. An exchange of letters between the two men took place in 1923,[40] and it shows how wide was the gap between them. According to Harnack, 'the task of theology is one with the task of science in general'. But according to Barth, the task of theology 'is one with the task of preaching; it consists of taking up and passing on the word of Christ.'

From 1932 onward, Barth was engaged in carrying out the task just described, and the result was his *Church Dogmatics*, a statement of Christian theology even longer and more detailed than St Thomas'

Summa Theologiae, though like it in respect of being unfinished. It is to the *Church Dogmatics* that we must turn for Barth's mature view of christology.

Because God is other than man, some starting-points for theology are ruled out right away. We cannot begin from the human side, or we shall never get beyond the human. So we cannot begin with philosophical speculations, or even, as we have seen already, with religion. These are human attempts to reach out to God, but they are doomed to failure. This means in turn that for Barth there can be no 'natural theology'. Theology is possible only if God has spoken, so one could say that the fundamental proposition in Barth's enterprise is 'God speaks'.[41] There is therefore a 'word of God'. Although Barth insists that the proposition 'God speaks' is not a symbolic use of language, it might have been better if he had said, 'God communicates' or 'God communicates himself', for the fundamental form of the word which he utters is Jesus Christ, the Word or Logos. There are two subordinate or derived forms of the word – the scriptures which give their testimony to Christ, either as one who is to come (Old Testament) or one who now has come (New Testament); and the preaching of the word, the exposition of scripture, and, as we have already noted, Barth considered theology and preaching are very closely related.

Barth's christology reverts to the classical starting-point, that is to say, it begins with Christ as the divine Word. Already in the first half-volume of his great work, the doctrine of the triune God is laid down as the foundation of the whole edifice. Jesus Christ is the revelation of God, but only God can reveal God, so Jesus Christ belongs within the Godhead. The trinitarian structure of deity is itself derived from the fundamental activity of revelation, from the proposition, 'God speaks'. 'The ground, the root, of the doctrine of the Trinity . . . lies in revelation.'[42] This is because the event of revealing has a threefold form, described by Barth in the terms 'revealer', 'revelation' and 'revealedness'. The precise significance of these terms and their relations to one another are not entirely clear. I have suggested myself that Barth's doctrine of the Trinity, though said to be derived from revelation, is in fact derived from an analysis of the *concept* of revelation, so that any event of revelation would, through its form alone and without regard to its content, imply the idea of a threefold God.[43] But Barth's argument is not clear enough for me to be certain about this, and in any case he would probably have replied that there is only one revelation, and that other pretended revelations are merely products of 'religion' in his own tendentious definition of that word. So here we have a christology which begins from the divine Christ as a person of the Trinity. Actually Barth does not like the traditional language of 'persons' and prefers to speak of three 'modes' of the divine

Being. So not only is there no attempt to take a purely human Jesus as the starting-point for christology or to follow a path of exposition which would lead from the familiar and everyday into deeper and more mysterious regions, it is claimed that we have to begin with a divine being. 'The very definite order of being which Holy Scripture makes manifest . . . enforces an order of knowing corresponding to it.'[44] We may agree with him that there is in the New Testament no idea of a merely human Jesus who is not already the Christ of God, for the documents of the New Testament are products of faith. Yet in our own earlier studies of the New Testament material, we have seen that faith went through various stages of development. It was only after years of reflection and meditation that Christians arrived at their belief that Jesus is the very living Word of God and many years after that before they clearly formulated a belief in the triune God.

Of course, theology and therefore christology have to begin somewhere, and no science is without some presuppositions and assumptions. We may think, however, that Barth has begun with too many assumptions and skipped over too many hard questions. He admits himself that when God speaks, there is always an ambiguity about it – perhaps it was not really God. 'When God speaks to man, this happening is never so marked off from the rest of what happens that it might not promptly also be interpreted as part of this other happening.'[45] No doubt there are many people who in the end of the day would agree with Barth that God speaks – and has indeed spoken in Jesus Christ. But this would be at the end of the day. Before they got to that point, they would insist on asking what it would mean for God to speak in such a way, and why we should think that this had happened in the case of Jesus. Could anyone living in the twentieth century *not* ask such questions? So while Barth certainly carried further the destructive criticism of nineteenth-century christology, begun by Kähler and company, we do not read very far in the *Church Dogmatics* without beginning to doubt whether he is going to produce any credible affirmative statement that will speak to people two hundred years after the Enlightenment. Because of Barth's deliberate avoidance of what for many people today are the most troublesome questions about Jesus Christ, Dr McGrath goes so far as to write that 'Barth's christology belongs to the pre-modern period'. He adds (and this is certainly a fair comment on volume IV of the *Dogmatics*), 'It is perhaps significant that Barth appears to be most at home in his dialogue with the christology of the sixteenth and seventeenth centuries, rather than with that of the modern period.'[46]

The next important step in the construction of Barth's christology does in fact bring us into dialogue with the sixteenth century, in particular, with Calvin's doctrine of election. Any revelation of God must be a veiled revelation, for God cannot be revealed directly in a finite earthly medium. Therefore, as we have seen, a measure of ambiguity attends even the revelation in Christ. Yet Barth believes that the revelation is adequate, and that there are no hidden areas of God that are not in some manner illuminated by the revelation. Though Barth is usually in agreement with Calvin, he takes issue with the latter's teaching on election and predestination, on the ground that Calvin is entertaining an idea of God which is not derived from and is actually in conflict with the revelation in Christ. 'The electing God of Calvin is a *Deus nudus absconditus* (a merely hidden God) . . . all the dubious features of his doctrine result from the basic failing that in the last analysis he separates God and Jesus Christ.'[47] In Calvin's teaching, God had from all eternity predestined some human beings to salvation and others to condemnation. It must be counted very much to Barth's credit that he completely reconceived the meaning of election, which had been for so long a grim feature of Reformed Christianity. In this reconceived version of the doctrine, it is centred entirely on Jesus Christ. 'Jesus Christ is the electing God; Jesus Christ is the elected man.'[48] Admittedly, it is not easy to disentangle all the relationships involved, or to judge whether Barth's teaching here is quite coherent. But it certainly goes far to 'Christianizing' Calvinist teaching. Instead of an arbitrary sovereign decree by which some are elected to bliss and others damned to hell, Barth sees in predestination 'an overflowing of the inner perfection and joy of God'.[49] In Jesus Christ, God elects all of humanity to be his covenant partner. There are, as I have said, confusions and loose ends here. Jesus Christ both elects and is elected, Jesus Christ is both elected and reprobated. Barth does not succeed in welding it all together, but perhaps we should not expect that images of this kind can be more than suggestive. The point is that God's purpose in election is understood purely in salvific terms, and that the agent of this saving work is Jesus Christ who also embraces within himself the whole human race. In a phrase that recurs many times, Barth speaks of the election of Jesus Christ as 'the beginning of all the works and ways of God'.[50]

Many profound and far-reaching consequences follow from this rethinking of the doctrine of election. It looks like a turning-point in Barth's thought, and calls for a reassessment of his earlier teaching. I mention the following points.

1. In his early writings, Barth showed himself so strongly opposed to the humanistic trends of the nineteenth century that he was in danger of appearing as Luther did to Feuerbach, that is to say, for God but against man. In those days Barth had revived Kierkegaard's language about the 'infinite qualitative difference' between God and man. But now humanity is being accorded a hitherto unsuspected dignity. For if it was in the beginning of all God's works and ways that Jesus Christ elected and was

elected, and in him the entire human race was chosen to be God's partner, then there must be a sense in which humanity has been there from the beginning. There must be a sense in which God himself has never existed without man, at least, without the idea of man as a major concern and purpose, so there cannot really be an infinite qualitative difference. Barth does in fact say, 'The Christian doctrine of God cannot have only God for its content, but since its object is *this* God, it must also have man, to the extent that in Jesus Christ man is made a partner in the covenant decreed and founded by God.'[51] Barth himself explicitly drew some of the consequences of the teaching outlined above when some years later he produced a small book, entitled *The Humanity of God*. He went so far as to say, 'Theology would be better called theanthropology' and 'It is precisely God's deity which, rightly understood, includes his humanity.'[52] It is important to note, however, that he talks of the humanity of God, never of the divinity of man. Though talk of the 'absolute qualitative difference' between God and man was muted, there was still, in Barth's view, no way from man to God, no natural theology.

2. Another consequence of Barth's doctrine of election is universalism, the doctrine that in the end all shall be saved. The whole human race is elected in Christ. I have no quarrel myself with universalism, and find Barth's teaching about election very much more acceptable than the grim doctrine of Calvin. But the question is how Barth squares his universalism with all his solemn words about the magnitude of human sinfulness and the helplessness of the human condition. Was that just rhetoric? For it does not really matter. Whether they repent or not, whether they even know it or not, all human beings are *already* saved by the predestinating decree. This is *sola gratia* carried to extremes. The sinner does not need to raise a finger or even nod his head – he is completely passive in this matter of salvation. God's salvation through Christ is a purely objective event – it takes place 'outside of us, without us, even against us'. These words are quoted from a polemic of Barth directed against Bultmann, because the latter had stressed the decision of faith on the part of the person saved. Barth will not allow that the human being does anything, it is all done for him. There is no synergism or co-operation. He says, 'If the good shepherd gives his life for the sheep, he does so to save the life of the sheep, but without any co-operation on their part.'[53] But human beings are not sheep – indeed, one is tempted to say that there is an infinite qualitative difference between a man or a woman and a sheep, except that I would think the word 'infinite' is an exaggeration, as I think it also is when the corresponding contrast is posited between God and the human family. So in spite of Barth's doctrine of universal election and his talk about the humanity of God, I think he still takes a pretty poor view of the human race. God's saving act cannot be purely objective or external, for if

he is acting on a person, there must be some appropriation and response on the part of that person within an I-Thou relationship. Or, to express the matter differently, in Christianity there can be no purely forensic justification that is not at the same time the beginning, however minimal, of sanctification.

3. Still another serious question arises for Barth's position. What has become of history in the light of that predestinating decree that stands at the beginning of all God's works and ways? Barth stresses not only the *sola gratia* but equally the *eph' hapax* ('once-for-all') which engaged our attention in our study of Hebrews. In his view, everything is already finished and complete. It has all been settled in that moment before time and history began (if one may so speak), that moment of election. If one puts so much into the eternal decree, then where was the point of incarnation, of God's condescension and humility of which Barth so beautifully writes, or the death of Christ on the cross or his resurrection from the dead? Or what meaning is there in an individual's putting his or her faith in Christ if it has all been settled already? Perhaps at that time the individual does become a co-worker, but how important is this for Barth? It is difficult not to conclude that for Barth history is unimportant. Even when he wrote the *Römerbrief*, he declared that 'the resurrection is not an event in history at all',[54] but is it any different with the other 'key events' in the gospel narrative? In spite of all Barth's protests about philosophical intrusions into theology, is his position any different from that of Hegel, for whom the historical happening of Good Friday on 14 Nisan in the year 30 is only a reflection of the speculative Good Friday in eternity? I doubt whether Barth has any satisfactory way of sorting out these problems, and suspect that Van Harvey was correct when he wrote that 'Barth claims all the advantages of history but will assume none of its risks'.[55]

The heart of Barth's christology is to be found in Volume IV (containing four part-volumes) of the *Dogmatics*. I have already indicated that Barth's christology is (to use the common jargon) a 'christology from above', that is to say, it follows the classical pattern of speaking first of Christ's descent from the Father, and then of his return. So Barth begins with 'the way of the Son of God into the far country' but this is in due course balanced dialectically by his teaching on 'the exaltation of the Son'. About these two parts of his exposition, he says: 'The New Testament obviously speaks of Jesus Christ in both these ways: the one looking and moving, as it were, from above downward, the other from below upward. It would be idle to try to conclude which of the two is the more original, authentic and important. Both are necessary. Neither can stand or be understood without the other'.[56] The first of the two ways, as has been mentioned, is the way of the Son of God into the far country. Of great importance for Barth's exposition is the Christ-hymn of Philippians, which, in contrast to the interpretation which we followed in Chapter 3,[57] he understands in the more traditional sense as referring to the pre-existent Christ or Word who empties himself of his divinity or at least of some of his divine attributes to take the form of a servant. Indeed, as one reads this part of the *Dogmatics*, one at first gets the impression that Barth is going to follow the path of the nineteenth-century kenoticists. But he does not, and he is well aware of the severe problems that attend kenotic christology.[58] God cannot reveal himself if in the very act of revelation he ceases to be God. That remains true, even if we also have to insist that any revelation through a finite medium must be at the same time a veiling. Barth's decisive rejection of the nineteenth-century kenotic theories is expressed in the words: 'God is always God, even in his humiliation. The divine being does not suffer any change, any diminution, any transformation into something else, any admixture of something else, let alone any cessation.'[59] God cannot cease to be God, the ultimate reality and source. If we see God in Jesus Christ, it is not because God has changed his nature. Then we would not really be seeing God. Barth here has a much clearer grasp of the dialectical nature of God than had the kenoticists. The incarnation of God in Jesus Christ is 'a mystery which offends', that is to say, which offends our usual ways of thinking. We think of God in terms of power and transcendence, so then we think he must get rid of these attributes in order to appear in humility and weakness. But Barth's point is that humility and weakness are as fundamental to the being of God as are power and transcendence, and it is not necessary (indeed, it is absurd) to think that we have to deny one set of characteristics to make way for the other. So he claims: 'The mystery reveals to us that it is just as natural for God to be lowly as it is to be high, to be near as it is to be far, to be little as it is to be great, to be abroad as it is to be at home.'[60] This is what Nicholas of Cusa called the *coincidentia oppositorum*,[61] the coincidence of opposites, and it seems to me to be an essential element in our attempts to arrive at some understanding of what we mean when we use the word 'God'. God did not lose himself or dissipate himself in the journey into the far country, and did not cease to be God. Rather, there is a revealing of the depth of deity so contrary to our expectation that all our preconceived ideas of God are upset. That is why it is called a 'mystery which offends'. Barth at this point reminds us of the *extra calvinisticum*,[62] the teaching of Calvin that the union of the Logos with Jesus did not mean, in some absurdly literal fashion, that it was 'enclosed in the narrow tenement of an earthly body'. We may think that here we are being drawn into oversubtle speculation, but the point is simply that God, if there be a God, can never become that which is not God.

According to Barth – and also to Paul in Philippians – it is Christ's obedience even to the length of death on the cross that is characteristic of his relation to the Father. But what does this mean? In Barth's view, Christ is a divine person, the second person of the Trinity. We have to ask, then, as Barth himself very honestly does, can Christ obey God? Can God obey God? Are there, within God, relations of above and below, superordination and subordination? It is true that in early Christianity, Christ might be considered subordinate to the Father. We noted a passage in John's gospel which seemed to imply this, and in both Justin the Martyr and Origen we found statements which place Christ second to God.[63] This was in fact a common belief in the ante-Nicene period. It was, however, rejected by orthodoxy, and Barth too rejects it, on the grounds that it dissolves the divinity of Christ and inevitably brings us to think of him as an exalted creature. But I really wonder whether Barth is not wavering on the very edge of monophysitism. Much earlier in this book, we took note that in one of his more speculative flights of controversy with Lutheranism, he seems to be moving in a monophysite direction.[64] We have seen in the discussion of Paul's christology[65] that the Christ-hymn can be so interpreted that Jesus' obedience appears as a purely human obedience, and the question whether God can obey God is an artificial question that has plausibility only for someone who shares Barth's monophysite tendencies. We shall return to these matters later,[66] and I shall argue that it is far more impressive and worthy of our awed admiration if we take it as human obedience.

But in saying that, I am moving over to the second of the two ways which Barth recognized as equally necessary to an understanding of Christ's person, 'the exaltation of the Son', 'the royal man', the man who returns home from the far country to the Father. As Barth himself very succinctly puts it, 'It was God who went into the far country, and it was man who came home'.[67] In Jesus Christ there is both the self-manifestation of God in the world, and simultaneously the perfecting of the human being in a new relation to God. Already in the several parts of Volume III of the *Dogmatics*, the volume which deals with the doctrine of creation, Barth had claimed that the human creature is to be studied and understood in the light of Jesus Christ, as the true man. In spite of what I have claimed is a tendency to monophysitism, Barth's dialectic insists that he speaks unequivocally of Christ's humanity, as in the following: 'Jesus is man as we all are, and he is therefore accessible and knowable to us as a man, with no special capacities or potentialities, with no admixture of a quality alien to us, with no supernatural endowment such as must make him a totally different being from us. He is man in such a way that he can be the natural brother of any other man.'[68] No statement could be more forthright, and it was in the same understanding that we tried to interpret the New Testament material in the early chapters of this book. Now in Volume IV/2 Barth sets out the career of Jesus, his ministry of healing, teaching and reconciliation, his suffering and his atoning death, his resurrection and exaltation, as the bringing to light of true humanity. 'In the existence of the man Jesus, we have to do with the true and normal form of human nature, and therefore with authentically human life.'[69]

Barth's christology is complicated – more complicated than this summary can begin to suggest. After all, his entire theology is in the main a christology, and it takes six million words for its (uncompleted) expression. Sometimes he makes assertions that are bound to strike us as extreme and unbalanced, but usually one finds that within the vast dialectical framework can be found other assertions of an opposite tendency which correct the excesses. But this does not make for clarity and increases the difficulty of arriving at a fair assessment of Barth's teaching. Many critical questions are bound to arise in our minds. By beginning from the understanding of Christ as the eternal Word and the second person (mode) of the triune God, has he obscured the true humanity of Jesus Christ? By removing the centre of action from history to eternity (to God's decree of election before history begins) has he deprived of significance the claim that the Word was made flesh (was brought into history)? Has he really faced up to the results of biblical criticism? Though he stops short of a doctrine of the total depravity of man, one has to ask whether his emphasis on human passivity, sin, ignorance and general incapacity does not leave man incapable of being 'saved' in any worthwhile sense. These are only a few of the questions that may be and indeed have been raised against Barth. However justified his attack on nineteenth-century liberalism and however powerful his attempts to rebuild the classical christology, one can at most say that he forced theologians to think again about where they were going but did not himself provide a clear or adequate answer to the question about Jesus Christ in the twentieth century. By the time he died in 1968, Barth's influence had waned considerably, and the vaunted theological renascence had come to an end. Looking back on that whole movement, we can say about Barth and his associates what he had once said about Ritschl and the Ritschlians, namely, that it was an episode. In the meantime, many of the trends of the nineteenth century have reappeared in theology. But they have reappeared in a chastened and altered form because of Barth and the movement which he led.

Next to Barth, the major theologian of the theological renascence was another Swiss scholar, Emil Brunner (1889–1966). Though closely associated with Barth, there was a rivalry between the two and it sometimes erupted in sharp controversy. Brunner is important to our study because he devoted an extensive monograph to christology – Der Mittler, published in 1927. The English translation is entitled The Mediator, with the subtitle 'A Study of the Central Doctrine of the Christian Faith'.

Brunner made no secret of the polemical thrust of his study. He wrote:

'the present exposition of this theme is deliberately and uncompromisingly opposed to the modern conception of this [christological] dogma, introduced by Ritschl and Harnack.'[70] Even harsher is his comment: 'Paul of Samosata might be described as the first Ritschlian, or in a more general way as the first modern theologian.'[71]

At the same time Brunner, whether deliberately or not, expressed himself on some important theological issues less rigidly than Barth. Whereas the latter would have nothing to do with natural theology, Brunner was prepared to allow it a very minimal role. So we find him saying near the beginning of *The Mediator*, 'It is impossible to believe in a Christian way in the unique revelation, in the Mediator, without believing also in a universal revelation of God in creation, in history and especially in human conscience.'[72] However, one should not exaggerate this point, for it is the unique once-for-all revelation in Christ that really matters, not the timeless general revelation.

Like Barth, Brunner acknowledged the ambiguity of the revelation in Christ – it was at the same time a veiling, so we might fail to see it. 'The revelation in Christ is a manifestation of God of such a kind that it is possible to pass it by without seeing it; it is a form of the presence of God which it is possible to mistake for the exact opposite, as his complete absence.'[73] Brunner himself thought that his greatest contribution to theology lay in his exposition of the idea of revelation, and especially in the illumination of this idea by the personalist or 'I-Thou' philosophy of Ebner and Buber. This is not so obvious in *The Mediator*, though he does in fact mention Ebner and the need for 'a real relation to a real thou'.[74] In fact, the difference between Christianity and the religion that arises out of general revelation is that in Christianity there is a personal relation to a personal God, whereas in other forms of religion the relation is to an impersonal Idea – so Brunner believed. But the full application of the 'I-Thou' philosophy comes in later works. Its christological implications are to be seen especially in the second volume of Brunner's *Dogmatics*, written more than twenty years after *The Mediator*. It is in the encounter of person with person that revelation takes place, hence revelation is more than verbal. He writes: 'Jesus Christ himself is more than all words about him. The Word of God, the decisive self-communication of God, is a person, a human being, the man in whom God himself meets us';[75] and 'the truth which faith perceives and grasps is a personal self-disclosure, the truth of revelation, not the truth which can be discovered by research and the use of the intellect.'[76] It is probably true to say that Brunner's broadening of the idea of revelation so as to see it in terms of personal encounter rather than in the form of words has become very widely accepted among theologians both Protestant and Catholic. But its reception should not be uncritical. At least two points have to be borne in mind. The first is, that personal encounter, though certainly more than words, usually includes words, and what people say to each other is a very important constitutive element in their meeting. The second point is that Brunner's disparagement of 'the truth that can be discovered by research and the use of the intellect' could be interpreted as an encouragement to anti-intellectualism, and there has been more than enough of that in the history of theology.

In *The Mediator* Brunner's christology was so firmly rooted on the Godward side that some critics accused him of being docetic, but in the *Dogmatics* he seeks to correct this tendency and to begin from the human Jesus. He quotes Luther, 'We must begin at the bottom, and afterwards rise to the heights.'[77] He believes that following this path one comes to a doctrine of incarnation in which the mystery of Christ as *vere homo* and *vere Deus* is established. 'The truth that the eternal Son of God meets us in the man Jesus necessarily leads to the doctrine of the incarnation of the Son of God.'[78]

'What is bothering me incessantly is the question . . . who Christ really is, for us today.'[79] The words were written by Dietrich Bonhoeffer (1906–1945) in 1944 when he was in prison in Berlin, just about a year before he was hanged by the Nazis in the closing days of World War II. It is the question that is occupying us all through this book. No doubt it had for Bonhoeffer in prison a poignancy which we can only try to imagine. Yet for him too as a theologian it was an intellectual question.

Bonhoeffer was himself a product of the theological renascence and owed much to Barth. Yet the circumstances of his life had exposed him more harshly to twentieth-century society. He was in the tradition of Barth in the sense that he was christocentric and biblically oriented. But he belonged to the modern world in a way that Barth never did, the modern world which in Hitler's Germany he experienced as post-Christian, secular or perhaps one should say pagan.

If Bonhoeffer's life had not been prematurely terminated, he might possibly have attained as a theologian to the same kind of eminence that belonged to Barth and Brunner, or he might not. There is not enough evidence to decide this question. To most people, he is known for his Christian witness in the political sphere and is revered as a martyr. But he was also a thinker, and though his theology is no more than fragmentary, some of his ideas have been very influential.

The idea that Christ is at the centre stayed with him throughout his theological career. *Christ the Center* is the title of the American edition of a course of lectures in christology which he gave as early as 1933, though they were published only after his death. Toward the end of his life, when he was struggling with the task of trying to visualize the Christianity of the future, it is clear that Christ was still at the centre – indeed, his critique of religion is to be understood affirmatively as his attempt not to let Christ be deposed from the centre by the trappings of Christianity. When he declared in his lectures of 1933 that 'Christology is Logology – it is *the science* because it is concerned with the Logos',[80] he was making a claim for Christ that may have gone even beyond Barth. Must we not go to Pascal for an equivalent statement? 'Jesus Christ is the goal of everything and the centre to which everything tends. He who knows him knows the reason for all things'.[81] Heinrich Ott claims that Bonhoeffer did not avoid the ontological question – Ott says, indeed, that 'the question, "What is reality?" could be called the peculiar theme of all his theological thinking'.[82] The true ontological reality for Bonhoeffer is Jesus Christ. And, as the reader will remember from Bonhoeffer's somewhat sarcastic remark about the Ritschlians,[83] Christ's special status is not due to the value-judgment of the community, but is given its reality because of his relation to God the Father. Unfortunately, however, Bonhoeffer never himself explained what this relation of Christ to the Father is. But he did make it clear that he wanted nothing to do with the 'higher positivism' of Ritschl and company. It was Bonhoeffer's intention to give another lecture in the 1933 series, and this was to be entitled 'The Eternal Christ'. Perhaps this would have cast some light on the question of Christ's ontological relation to the Father. But apparently this lecture was never written. Thus Bonhoeffer's immense claim for Jesus Christ seems to stand as something quite arbitrary, a subjective preference. He was even supposed by some of the 'death of God' theologians of the nineteen-sixties to be an atheist. But this is a wildly inaccurate reading of his position. Both in his theological writings and in his letters from prison, it is clear that a deep religious faith was characteristic of him.

Yet at the same time he saw clearly that if faith in God or Christ is to mean anything in the modern secular world, it has to be related to secular concerns. His largest book, the *Ethics*, commends conformity to Christ, and acknowledges that this means that we look to a reality which is ultimate, transcendent and eschatological. 'But before the ultimate comes the penultimate, before the last things the next to last things, and these are the everyday social and ethical concerns of mankind.'[84]

Obviously we would like to know how he would have filled in some of the gaps in his account of Christianity. Would he have been more successful than others in the theological renascence, in reworking the themes of traditional christology in such a way that they could speak to men and women in a secular age? We shall never know, and those who have sought to assume the mantle of Bonhoeffer in the years since his death have not been convincing. Towards the end, he himself seems to have become increasingly disillusioned with the leading theologians of the day, most of them products of the new spirit that had breathed life into theology from the nineteen-twenties on. He finds fault for one reason or another with Heim, Althaus, Tillich, Bultmann. Karl Barth is praised for his critique of 'religion', because it let the revelation of the reality of Christ come through as revelation. But even he failed, for he gave no guidance in the 'non-religious' interpretation of dogmatics and ethics. There lies his limitation, and because of it his theology of revelation has become a 'positivism of revelation'.[85] So here again, near the end of his life, he makes it clear once more that his own solution, whatever it might have turned out to be, would not have been positivism.

But in spite of this criticism of Barth, Bonhoeffer remains in the same tradition. Like Barth, he believed that the human being is fulfilled in being open to others, and so he characterized Jesus as the 'man-for-others'. And like Barth, he believed that it is natural to God that he should appear in weakness rather than power.

14

Christologies of the Late Twentieth Century

Already by the middle of the twentieth century the so-called theological renascence had lost its momentum. An obvious sign of this was the extent to which the original leaders of the movement had drifted apart and were pursuing very different objectives. Such scholars as Bultmann, Tillich and Gogarten, who had once been associates of Barth in the revolt against the old liberalism, did not share his attachment to Reformation orthodoxy. At the same time, younger theologians were appearing and introducing new problems and new methods. One of the most important factors in changing the theological climate was the stirring in the Roman Catholic Church, expressing itself in the Second Vatican Council and in the outpouring of new theology both before and after the Council. Before the Council, the course of theology had been in the main decided by German Protestant scholars, as we have seen in the preceding chapters. But from about 1960 onward, the leadership has passed to Roman Catholic writers, though even among them German or German-speaking theologians have been pre-eminent.

Existentialist Christology

We begin with those former allies of Barth who came to follow different paths from the one which he had chosen. We did note that Barth in his early anti-liberal writings often quoted Kierkegaard, but that as time went on, he tried to free himself from any existentialist or anthropological influences that might come from a philosophical source. But some of the other theologians of the renascence were quite willing to embrace existentialism as a philosophical ally, and it is their work that we shall consider in this section.

Chief among them was Rudolf Bultmann (1884–1976), probably the greatest New Testament scholar of the century and one who both directly and indirectly exerted a great influence on systematic theology. Bultmann did not share Barth's scruples about consciously employing philosophical concepts or methods in theology, but he was concerned that it should be the 'right' philosophy, and for him that meant existentialism, and especially the analysis of human existence worked out by Martin Heidegger in his famous book of 1927, *Sein und Zeit* (*Being and Time*).[1] Bultmann's reason for making this choice was that the New Testament is primarily a message of salvation or new life, so that the question which we must address to it in order to elucidate its meaning is, 'What does this say to us, as existing human beings?' So he declares, 'The "right" philosophy [for the work of theology] is quite simply that philosophical work which endeavours to develop in suitable concepts the understanding of existence that is given with human existence.'[2] This method of existential interpretation is at the same time a 'demythologizing', that is to say, it translates the New Testament out of the objectifying mythological language in which much of it is expressed into a language which expresses a new possibility of human existence. Here we are concerned only with the question of how Bultmann handles the christological issue.

Bultmann's clearest and quite controversial statement of an existentialist christology is to be found in an essay, 'The Christological Confession of the World Council of Churches'.[3] This essay was published in 1951, three years after the formation of the World Council. Bultmann had been asked to give an address at a conference of liberal Swiss theologians on the statement adopted at its foundation that 'the World Council of Churches is composed of churches which acknowledge Jesus Christ as God and Saviour'.

Bultmann saw no special problem about the use of the word 'Saviour'. It has nowadays a somewhat archaic ring about it, but it is a functional term and expresses Christ's relation to the believer – it is, if you will, existential. The difficulty attaches to the other term, 'God'. What does it mean to call Christ God? Bultmann notes that the World Council used the strong formulation, 'acknowledge Jesus Christ as God', not anything less direct, such as 'Son of God' or 'Word of God'. What then does the assertion, 'Christ is God', mean? Are we speaking of Christ's nature or of his significance? Is the assertion metaphysical or soteriological, or could it be both? These are the questions Bultmann wishes to investigate.

Bultmann's first step is to look at the New Testament and find whether there is any scriptural precedent for calling Christ God. As the reader may remember from our earlier discussion of the titles of Jesus[4] Bultmann returns an almost completely negative answer to the question. In his view, the only clear case in which Jesus is called God is the confession of Thomas (John 20.28), and that is very plainly an existential, even an emotional or an exclamatory utterance, not a metaphysical or ontological one. Though other New Testament scholars are more affirmative than Bultmann in their views of the application of God-language to Jesus in the New Testament, it may strike us as rather odd that such an apparently central Christian affirmation as 'Jesus Christ is God' is so minimally attested in the scriptures that we have to hunt around for instances, and when we have found them, argue about what they really mean.

If then we accept that Jesus Christ is very rarely called God explicitly in the New Testament, and that when and if this does happen, the context is confessional or liturgical rather than dogmatic, we are prepared for Bultmann's statement of his existentialist christology. The question is whether this way of speaking of Christ as God is a description of him in the sense of an objectifying statement about his being, or whether it expresses his significance for the believer. Bultmann comes down strongly for the second of these interpretations. A christological pronouncement is not only about Jesus Christ, it is also a pronouncement about the person who makes it. It is not about Christ's nature or *physis*, but about the *Christus pro me*. He poses the question thus: 'Does [Christ] help me because he is God's Son, or is he the Son of God because he helps me?'[5] In sum: 'The formula "Christ is God" is false in every sense in which God can be understood as an entity which can be objectivized, whether it is understood in an Arian or a Nicene, an orthodox or a liberal sense. It is correct if "God" is understood here as the event of God's acting.'[6] Bultmann's use of the word 'event' is important. He can say, 'Christ's Lordship, his deity, is always only an event at any given time'.[7] That is to say, Christ's deity is not an eternal property of his person, nor is the confession of his deity an eternal dogmatic truth. Christ's deity is the event that takes place when the word of Christ is heard as word of God. In Bultmann, God too is understood as event. God is not a metaphysical entity to be conceptualized, but a power that in certain moments impinges upon us.[8] I think one could say that in Bultmann we meet an almost purely existentialist form of theology. For him, the great error is to 'objectify', to turn something or someone that can be known only in a living experience into an object to be examined, taken apart and put together again. That, in his view, is what we do with God in the philosophy of religion, or what we do with Christ when we argue about the two natures or the hypostatic union.

This does not mean that Bultmann was a reductionist in christology. There is indeed in Christ that which is human and that which is divine, but these are not 'natures'. The miracle of Christ is that a human word is heard as a divine word. Bultmann thinks that both the nineteenth-century liberals and the 'Amsterdam people' (his contemptuous term for those who constructed the World Council formula) are 'objectifiers'. The liberals objectified Christ by humanizing him, reducing him to the 'historical Jesus'. The orthodox likewise objectify him, but as the 'God-man', the one divine person in whom concur two natures. In each case (so Bultmann claims) one has dissolved the paradox of the 'eschatological event' – the critical moment when the human word of Christ is experienced as the event of God's action. One can see many parallels here to the teaching of Karl Barth, and understand how he and Bultmann, though following different paths, had come from a single origin and still had much in common.

I think however that one must judge that Bultmann's fear of 'objectifying' was exaggerated. Christology is not just confession of faith, like the confession of Thomas when he exclaimed 'My Lord and my God!' Christology also demands reflection on the utterances of faith, it searches for the grounds on which such utterances are made. So we cannot be content with Bultmann's view that Christ's deity is simply a confession of his significance in the moment of faithful encounter – the eschatological moment. To decide that the word that addresses us in and through Christ is the word of God (that is to say, is the ultimate word, the last or eschatological word) is not an arbitrary decision. At least, it should not be such in a rational being. It is a decision to be made in the light of all the knowledge and understanding we can muster. But such understanding need not be objectifying – on the contrary, it would have to be participatory. Bultmann's own studies of existentialism and particularly of the philosophy of Heidegger surely made it clear to him that there are ways of describing human experience that are non-objectifying.

We must take this a little further, for Bultmann's motivations are perhaps as much Lutheran as existentialist. We meet again the Reformation principle of *sola fide*. Bultmann, as is well-known, often reached very negative results in his historical researches into the New Testament. But he tells us that he never felt uncomfortable about this.[9] Faith has to stand on its own, it must not be supported by the work of historical research. Bultmann would presumably have said the same about metaphysical research, or even about any kind of ontological reflection. In this he stands by a tradition that goes back to Luther himself, though incidentally it reappeared in Ritschl. The classic statement came from Melanchthon: 'To know Christ is to know his benefits, not to contemplate his natures and the modes of his incarnation.'[10] But christology does have to carry the discussion beyond that. Bultmann appears to be content with Melanchthon, but I prefer Barth's judgment: 'It was an act of rashness when Melanchthon thought he should suppress the special doctrine of God in order to turn at once to the statement of the *beneficia Christi*. The *beneficia Christi* cannot be properly investigated if some consideration of the *mysteria divinitatis* as such has not been undertaken in its proper place.'[11]

There is no denying that Bultmann's existentialist christology has many merits. It is no mere doctrine *about* Christ but sets forth Christ as truly eschatological, that is to say, as one who calls for a fundamental decision about life, or, in Bultmann's language, invites us to make his cross our own.[12] But can such a radical decision be demanded unless one has grounds for believing that the word that comes to us through Jesus is indeed a word from God? This belief cannot rest just on a momentary feeling or on the majority vote of the Christian community. It can rest only on an ontological bond between God and Jesus, and that calls for ontological reflection and probably for historical investigation as well.

There are other difficulties in Bultmann's view. He is not interested in the personality of Jesus – not in the 'what' but only in the 'that', to use his own terminology. But can the 'what' and the 'that' be separated? The mere fact *that* Jesus existed seems to have little meaning unless we know and have been deeply impressed by the content of this existence. For Bultmann, Jesus is the bearer of the word, or rather, he is first the bearer when he proclaims the imminence of the kingdom of God, and then he is himself the content of the word in the apostolic preaching. But in traditional Christian language, Jesus was not called the 'bearer' of the word – it was the Blessed Virgin Mary who was the bearer (*theotokos*) and Jesus who in his own person *was* the word and, of course, still is. We can agree that Bultmann has reasons for being silent about Jesus as a person. As an honest historian, he has to say that only very scanty information is to be had. He is also aware that a devotion to the person of Jesus can become merely sentimental and falls far short of 'making Christ's cross one's own'. But perhaps Bultmann's insistence on identifying Christ with the *function* of being the bearer of the word arises from his excessive attachment to the strictly *verbal* understanding of the word. Preaching, verbal communication, is for Bultmann all-important. There is justice in the comment of the Jesuit L. Malevez: 'We are no longer confronted either by the ontological reality or the spiritual presence of the ever-living Christ. All that concerns us is the message of which he is the instrument.'[13]

One further problem in Bultmann's teaching is common to many of the existentialists, both theological and philosophical. This is their individualism. Earlier we alluded to Bultmann's contrast between Christ's nature (*physis*) as something objectified and the *Christus pro me* as his living encounter with the believer in the word of preaching. It is significant that Bultmann uses the expression, *pro me*, 'for me', not *pro nobis*, 'for us'. As we shall see, some theologians of the generation after Bultmann have made individualism a major reproach against him.[14]

Bultmann was primarily a New Testament scholar, whereas his near contemporary Friedrich Gogarten (1887–1967) was primarily a systematic theologian. Gogarten was very much in sympathy with Bultmann's existentialist methodology, but there are some differences between the two men, and it will be interesting to take note of Gogarten's contribution.

Like Bultmann, Gogarten thinks of himself as addressing the 'modern' man or woman, the post-Enlightenment person for whom Christianity needs to be demythologized and related to human existence as it understands itself today. But Gogarten takes more trouble than Bultmann in analysing the changes which the Enlightenment has brought about. In his view, what characterizes the modern age is the fact that metaphysics has been superseded by history:

> This historical approach is the expression of a profound change which has taken place since the beginning of the modern age in the relation of man to the world and to himself. This change means nothing more and nothing less than that by it the world has for man become his own world. It is his world now no longer in the sense that it is set before him with its form as a world, to which it is his task to adapt himself in accordance with its pre-established order. It now becomes his world in the totally different sense that it is for him to watch over it and provide it with a form and order.[15]

The phenomenon which Gogarten is describing is actually secularization. The term 'secularization' is understood in many ways and in many aspects, but fundamentally it is *historicization*, the bringing of everything into the age or *saeculum*. In the ancient and mediaeval worlds, there was an unchanging metaphysical framework, forming, so to speak, the stage on which the events of history took place. Everything was already determined and there was no place for human responsibility and creativity. But now the situation is reversed. Human beings themselves make history. Metaphysical systems are products of history, born out of the currents of history and eventually perishing in these same currents. So the problem for the modern theologian is to disengage theology and therefore christology from its traditional metaphysical setting and express it anew in historical terms.

But this cannot be done in the way attempted by the nineteenth-century theologians. Like Bultmann, Gogarten dissociates himself from the liberals and has no interest in reconstructing the historical Jesus. Rather, it is a question of reading the existential significance of Jesus' history in such a way that it illuminates our own history and presents us with a possibility of existence. In that sense, he can declare that 'the word of Jesus is the word of God'. It will be noted how close Gogarten's thought is to Bultmann's at this point. Gogarten even uses Bultmann's term 'demythologizing' to designate the kind of interpretation he has in mind.

But in a later book, *Jesus Christus, Wende der Welt* (English title: *Christ the Crisis*) Gogarten acknowledges more clearly than Bultmann did that to say that the word of Jesus is the word of God is to speak of an intimate relation between God and Jesus, a relation which is anterior to the existential relation between Jesus and the Christian. Of course, in acknowledging this, Gogarten may seem to be also acknowledging that he has not after all got rid of metaphysics, at least, not as long as he wants to bring God into the situation. Furthermore, he claims that Jesus' relation to the Father had about it a finality that makes him different from the line of Hebrew prophets who had also spoken the word of God. This special relation of Jesus to the Father is no longer expressible for us in the outmoded metaphysical terminology of the ancient creeds and conciliar pronouncements, but of course to say this is to say much less than that metaphysics *in all possible terminologies* is now impossible.

Can we say something more specific about this intimate relation between God and Jesus? According to Gogarten, Jesus was the first human being to accept full responsibility before God, and therefore the first to break with the confusion between God and the world, with its consequent idolizing of the world or of innerworldly being.[16] Gogarten's teaching at this point is based on his interpretation of Paul's teaching in the letter to the Galatians, where he claims that the Christian has come of age and has been delivered by Christ from the tutelage of the law and subordination to worldly powers. Jesus brought the old world to an end and inaugurated the kingdom of God, in which human beings can be free responsible co-workers with God (Gal. 4.1–9). This is also associated by Gogarten with secularization. Paul's talk of 'coming of age' is like a foreshadowing of Kant's essay on Enlightenment which challenged people to stand on their own feet and think for themselves.[17] For Gogarten, secularization (historicization) is not anti-Christian but rather an implicate of Christianity.

It is clear then that Gogarten does provide, at least in outline, an ontology of history, so that his existentialist christology does take up some of the questions that were left undiscussed by Bultmann. But we have seen that Gogarten has new problems of his own, and there are others that are still to be mentioned. Is liberation for historical responsibility really the central message of Jesus? Is this not another example of modernizing Jesus, and is Gogarten not reconstructing the historical Jesus in the image of the 'modern man', in spite of his criticisms of the nineteenth-century liberals for doing exactly this? We are in fact coming up against the ambiguities of any so-called 'secular Christianity', an idea which was popular in the nineteen-sixties. It may be a self-contradictory idea, for 'secularity' in most of its forms gets along without God and without Christianity. This seems to have been apparent to Gogarten when he wrote: 'The difference between modern historical thought and Jesus' understanding of history is that virtually nothing remains of responsibility *before God*.'[18] Again, when everything has been historicized and seen as the product of a historical situation, are we not plunged into a thoroughgoing relativism which threatens Gogarten's own position? What about his claim for Jesus' finality and the difference between him and the prophets who came before him? Must not Jesus too be deprived of any absolute status, any finality that would mark him off sharply from the earlier prophets and teachers of Israel? On Gogarten's own terms, would it not be correct to see Jesus as an inaugurator who was important for his own time and culture, but whose significance has increasingly diminished as human beings have 'come of age' and taken over their own responsibility, no longer understood as a responsibility before God?

I shall add a third example of an existentialist christology, this time taken from the teaching of Paul Tillich (1886–1965). In Tillich, however, we do not have what I characterized as the 'pure' existentialism of Bultmann. Tillich has an existentialist starting-point and its influence remains strong throughout his theological writings, but many other influences are combined with it, taken from the wide range of German philosophical and religious thought. So we find in him remnants of German idealism (Schelling), of the mystical tradition (Boehme and even Dyonisius the Areopagite), depth psychology (Jung) and more besides. Nevertheless, he did write that 'theology has received tremendous gifts from existentialism, gifts not dreamed of fifty years ago or even thirty years ago'.[19] The gifts he had in mind are mainly gifts of language, new terms which help to link the traditional Christian vocabulary to the living concerns of human beings at the present time. This is given more detailed expression in his exposition of a 'method of correlation'. What he seeks to exploit in this method is a correlation between the questions that are raised in contemporary culture in its own critical self-examination, and the answers that may be derived from the theological tradition. The task of the theologian is to listen to the questions arising out of the cultural situation and to rethink the tradition in response to these questions. In any culture, ancient or modern, the human being is motivated by what Tillich calls an 'ultimate concern'. That concern may take different forms in different historical epochs, but in the twentieth century Tillich sees it as a quest for meaning. Is there any sense, purpose or goal to life, or is it at most a series of episodes that finally do not add up to anything? It is clear that on this view theology is a strongly existential enterprise, even though Tillich did not embrace a purely existentialist methodology. Does this mean then that he was able to make good some of the deficiencies that we found in Bultmann's christology?

Before we try to answer that question, I think we may agree that Tillich did have a more adequate doctrine of God than Bultmann. He had two ways of talking of God – one was existential, and defined God in terms of the attitude of the believer, as 'ultimate concern'; the other was ontological and defined God as 'Being itself'. This latter expression is to be understood in something like Heidegger's sense of 'Being', that is to say, the reality which is not itself a being or anything that is, but which is present in and beyond all beings as the source of their existence. For Bultmann, the word 'God' had existential significance as the power which in moments of crisis compels a person to decision, but this power cannot be conceptualized. Tillich does not want to speak of God *only* as 'ultimate concern', which might make him no more than a subjective experience of the moment. So Tillich has his alternative way of talking, in which God is 'Being itself', a reality prior to human experience. But Tillich does not thereby objectify God, as Bultmann so much feared to do. I have mentioned that Tillich's language of Being is very close to Heidegger's, and one could say also that it is near to the mystic tradition. To call God 'Being' is not to turn him into an object, for 'Being' is not one of the beings, indeed, for those who are concerned with beings, God or Being might equally well be called 'nothing', in the strict sense of not being a thing or an entity or a being. The mystical tradition is evidenced further in Tillich's theory of symbols. In this we can discern a tradition that goes back to Dionysius' treatise, *The Divine Names*. Our language cannot be used literally of God, but we are not reduced to complete silence, for the language can be used symbolically. At one stage[20] Tillich took the view that the only non-symbolic statement we can make about God is that he is Being-itself, though later he seems to have had doubts even about that fairly modest claim. The function of a symbol is to point beyond itself to a reality which cannot be known in a direct literal way. On the other hand, if a symbol comes to be valued in and for itself, it has been transformed into an idol. This can happen even to the person of Jesus. Tillich warns against a Jesus-theology or a Jesusology in which the human Jesus has become the ultimate concern, instead of pointing beyond himself to the mystery of God or Being.

Does this mean then that Christ too is a symbol? I do not think that anywhere Christ is actually called a 'symbol' by Tillich. This is worth noting, because Tillich seems to lay so much stress on the significance of Jesus Christ that one could be excused for wondering whether Tillich is prepared to dispense with a historical reality for Jesus altogether. We have noted that as a student he was deeply impressed by his teacher Kähler, who was among the first to criticize the quest for the historical Jesus,[21] and later Tillich was further impressed by Schweitzer's negative estimate of historical research into Jesus.[22] But in theory at least, Tillich believed it necessary to claim that 'Jesus Christ is both a historical fact and a subject of believing reception'.[23] He took this view because otherwise one would miss out something that is essential to basic Christian faith: 'If theology ignores the fact to which the name of Jesus of Nazareth points, it ignores the basic Christian assertion that essential Godmanhood has appeared within existence and subjected itself to the conditions of existence without being conquered by them.'[24] But the other side is equally important, the universalization of Christ as a saviour figure significant to all human beings. In this second way, we are seeing Christ in his symbolic rather than his historical reality, and we have to see him in both ways if we are to understand his place in Christianity.

What more can be said about this symbolic or universal significance of the Christ? We have already met Tillich's expression, the 'new being', as an interpretation of Jesus as the Christ. What does he mean here by 'new being'? The expression is somewhat obscure. Tillich does insist that it is intended to make an *ontological* as distinct from a merely *anthropological* assertion about Jesus Christ. He contrasts it with the term *Urbild* (archetype) which would be appropriate to the christologies of Kant and Schleiermacher, where Jesus is primarily considered as the fulfilled pattern of humanity. I do not think Tillich is doing justice to his predecessors when he regards them as setting forth only an anthropological view of Christ.[25] But he believes that he himself overcomes their deficiencies with his idea of 'new being' which makes clearer the participation of Jesus as the Christ in God and the mediation through him of the power of new being. It seems to me that the difference between Tillich and Schleiermacher or Kant is less than he wants to claim. Surely too there is an ambiguity lurking in this expression, 'new being'. Is the word 'being' in the expression 'new being' the same in meaning as the word 'being' in 'being-itself'? If not, there is a grievous confusion here. But how can the word 'being' have the same meaning in these two cases? Tillich is very insistent that when we talk of 'being-itself' we have to do not with some particular being or entity but with being in general or, as he can also call it, the 'power of being' which is prior to every particular being. But Jesus is a particular being, so it is misleading to call him the 'new being', for this suggests that 'new being' is of the same ontological order as 'being-itself'.

Unlike Barth, Tillich was willing to acknowledge that there is revelation outside of the specifically Christian tradition. The human awareness of finitude sets up a quest for God which issues in natural theology, and though this in itself does not take people very far, it makes them open to the possibility of revelation. In Tillich's language, Jesus Christ is the 'final revelation' but it was not an isolated event but stands in a revelatory history which includes many 'preparatory revelations'.[26] I do not want to raise the question here as to whether Tillich's division of revelation into 'preparatory' and 'final' is satisfactory and does justice to non-Christian revelations (he seems to have been having second thoughts about this at the end of his life), but I do want to examine more closely what he says about 'final revelation', for I think there is some further serious confusion here.

Tillich often speaks of the biblical 'picture' of Jesus as the Christ. A 'picture', in his usage, would seem to be not much different from what he means by 'symbol'. It has also been called by one of his commentators a 'verbal icon'.[27] This expression is helpful in illuminating the problem, because it can hardly fail to make us think of the iconoclastic controversy in the Byzantine church. Those who defended icons claimed, like Tillich, that they point beyond themselves to the mystery of God and, indeed, participate in that mystery. Those who opposed the veneration of icons held that they were idols. Tillich, as we have seen, makes a similar objection to preoccupation with the historical Jesus, as in nineteenth-century liberal Protestantism. He holds that in order for the biblical picture of Jesus to be final revelation, the picture itself has to be negated or 'crucified'. But there seems to be a double confusion here. As D. H. Kelsey has pointed out, if the picture itself is done away, how can it point beyond itself?[28] And there is a further confusion in Tillich here, for it is not the picture that is negated or crucified, but the historical Jesus. Because he is crucified (and, one may add, risen) he is transformed from an individual of history into a universal icon. But the icon, picture, symbol or whatever one prefers to call it is not negated – it has power as a pointer to God precisely by preserving its image of the crucified Lord.

Georges Tavard makes a devastating comment about Tillich's christology; 'It is not biblical enough, not historical enough, not theological enough.'[29] I am tempted to add, 'It is not clear enough.' Although Tillich tries to supply the ontological element that is lacking in Bultmann, it is nevertheless Bultmann's christology that stands out as the clearest and most powerful christological contribution that has come from the existentialist camp.

Roman Catholic Christologies after Vatican II

There have been many Roman Catholic writings on christology since the Enlightenment, but we have passed them over since, in the main, they were variations on the Chalcedonian theme. Even as late as 1954, Karl Adam's excellent book, *The Christ of Faith* still reflected the traditional christology, though one must add that it showed the continuing strength of that christology.[30] However, as Karl Rahner was to point out a few years later, textbooks of Catholic dogma published in 1950 were hardly distinguishable from textbooks of 1750, in spite of all the shattering events that had taken place in the two centuries between them. But certainly such a complaint could not be made after Vatican II. Roman Catholic theologians have produced a great body of new theology that is lively and interesting. Some of it, admittedly, has proved to be superficial and ephemeral, but, as I remarked at the beginning of this chapter, the leadership in theology today belongs to Roman Catholic writers. To some extent they have incorporated into their own tradition insights derived from Protestant thought and from secular philosophies, but they have been more concerned than were Protestant theologians to reconcile the new theological thinking with the traditional teaching of the church.

The most illustrious of this new breed of Roman Catholic theologians is the German Jesuit Karl Rahner (1904–84). His written output has been enormous, comparable in sheer volume, I should think, to that of Karl Barth. Christology receives its due share of attention in this widely ranging engagement with theological topics, but before turning directly to the christological writings, we should take note of two books on the philosophy of religion in which Rahner sets out some of the basic ideas which then inform his treatment of specific areas of theology.

The philosophical foundation of Rahner's thought is Thomism, but it is Thomism in the new form which it has assumed in the twentieth century, often called 'transcendental Thomism'.[31] This philosophy began as an attempt to reconcile Thomism with the 'Copernican revolution' that Kant claimed to have brought about in philosophy when he turned it away from speculative metaphysics to the critical examination of our human powers of knowing, to a 'transcendental' inquiry into the conditions of knowing. This in turn led to a view of the human knower as 'transcendent', in the sense that such a knower is driven on relentlessly from one question to another, from one horizon of knowledge to another, without ever coming to a final stopping-place. To some extent, therefore, transcendental Thomism is primarily a philosophical anthropology, an understanding of the human being as a finite creature who is nevertheless conscious of moving toward an infinite horizon.

In his early book *Hörer des Wortes* (1963), in English, *Hearers of the Word*, the anthropology hinted at in the last paragraph is worked out by Rahner. What he is trying to establish is something like a capacity for hearing God or receiving revelation, a capacity which, he believes, belongs to the normal human constitution. In Rahner's view, 'man is spirit, that is, he lives his life in a perpetual reaching out to the Absolute, in openness to God'.[32] We can hardly help being reminded of some of the ideas of nineteenth-century Protestantism – the 'sense and taste of the Infinite' (Schleiermacher), the 'religious *a priori*' (Troeltsch), and so on, though Rahner is far from either Schleiermacher's glorification of feeling or Troeltsch's social analysis. He speaks rather in Thomistic terms of a *potentia oboedientalis*, a possibility for hearkening to a revelatory word that *may* come from that unknown horizon toward which the human spirit reaches out. 'Our task', says Rahner, 'is to demonstrate that the positive openness for a revelation which God may possibly give is part of the essential constitution of man . . . Man must possess an openness for the self-utterance of the One who possesses being absolutely, through the luminous word. This openness is the *a priori* presupposition for the possibility of hearing such a word.'[33] It is not easy to assess Rahner's argument at this point. Can he *demonstrate* an openness for revelation as part of the *essential* human constitution? It might not be difficult to show that as an empirical fact of history there has been an almost universal readiness among human beings to accept what purport to be divine revelations. But that is less than and different from what Rahner is claiming. He does however say that 'the absolute transcendence of man as spirit reveals the Infinite'.[34] Here the argument seems to be that we are aware of ourselves as beings in a limitless process of transcendence toward a spiritual Infinite, and that to be in this situation is to have the expectation that some revealing word will come from that Infinite. A difference between what Rahner is saying and what most Protestant theologians who acknowledge some kind of religious *a priori* have said is this, that Rahner is basing his case on an affirmative sense of the infinite possibilities of transcendence, whereas Protestant writers, such as Tillich and the existentialists generally, took as their basis the human sense of finitude. (This would be true also of the mature Schleiermacher, but not of the early Schleiermacher of the *Speeches*.)[35]

The teaching contained in *Hearers of the Word* has to be understood in the light of a still earlier work, *Geist in Welt* or *Spirit in the World*, first published in 1957. Here the traditional word 'spirit' is applied to the human being, and it is the analysis of spirit that serves as the clue to understanding what it is to be human, including the mysterious but undeniable sense of the infinite that belongs to the essence of humanity. Indeed, it would seem to be precisely this outreach toward the infinite that is taken by Rahner to be the defining characteristic of 'spirit': 'Man is spirit because he finds himself situated before being in its totality, which is infinite.'[36] We also find spirit described in the following terms, which stress in particular the dynamic character of spirit: 'Spirit is desire (dynamic openness) for absolute being . . . The human spirit as such is desire, striving, action . . . Every operation of the spirit can therefore be understood only as a moment in the movement toward absolute being as toward the one end and goal of the desire of the spirit.'[37]

With this anthropology in mind, we can now go on to consider Rahner's christology, for anthropology and christology are closely related in his thinking. The relation is succinctly expressed by Rahner in the twofold formula: christology is transcendent anthropology, anthropology is deficient christology.[38] Or we could say, christology shows us in Christ what humanity can be when brought to the fulness of its possibilities, and at the same time shows us how our everyday humanity falls short of its archetype in Jesus Christ.

As a good Catholic, Rahner takes his departure from the church's *magisterium*, from the Chalcedonian definition formulated by an ecumenical council in 451, and still officially the norm for christological belief in most of the mainline Christian churches and denominations.[39] At Chalcedon, the council of bishops solemnly pronounced its mind on the question of the person of Jesus Christ, and it was hoped (mistakenly, as it turned out) that its proffered solution might bring controversy to an end. But theological controversy never comes to an end, just as no scientific enterprise ever comes to an end. There are always questions that need to be rethought, issues that need to be reopened, conflicting theories that need to be reconciled. When the Chalcedonian formula was discussed at an earlier point, I quoted Karl Rahner's own remark that such formulae 'derive their life from the fact that they are not the end but the beginning, not the goal but the means, truths which open the way to the – ever greater – Truth'.[40] They are certainly not meant to save future generations of Christians the trouble of further reflection on the topics with which they deal. In fact, the danger of such formulae is that they tend to be merely *repeated*, without any true appropriation of what they are saying, and, still less, any participation in the intellectual struggles which produced them. Creeds and other formulations of belief are historical utterances, arising out of a definite historical situation. Thus each new generation has to find in its own situation the truth enshrined in the formula. If this is not done, the formula may come to obscure the truth, rather than express it, for, as Rahner points out, the history of theology has been as much a history of 'forgetting' as a history of learning. Such forgetting occurs when traditional doctrines are taken over externally with no genuine 'making present' of their truth. The 'primordial' truth of the doctrine is lost in a vague 'average' understanding. The reader who is familiar with Heidegger will recognize his teaching about philosophy in what Rahner (at one time a student of Heidegger) is here saying about theology.

How then can one avoid the danger noted? Both Heidegger and Rahner would seem to advocate a return to the sources, a retracing of the steps by which the teaching under discussion came to be formulated. In the case of christology, this means going back to the New Testament. The creeds and formulae of the early church claim to be founded on the New Testament, but, as Rahner points out, it is not claimed that they are an *adequate* condensation of the biblical teaching. Inevitably – and we saw this ourselves in our earlier studies of the development of christology both in the New Testament and in the patristic period – there is selection, and the consequent emphasis on some themes at the expense of others. So Rahner poses the awkward question: 'Is it true that the Chalcedonian dogma . . . is a condensation and summary of *everything*, without remainder, of which we hear in scripture about Jesus the Christ and about the Son, or, again, of what we might hear if only we were to speak once more of what has still not entered into scholastic theology?'[42]

In particular, we may ask whether in the development from the New Testament to Nicaea and then to Chalcedon, the humanity of Christ was progressively obscured in an increasingly metaphysical terminology. Here Rahner seems to lean toward those Protestant theologians who urge the claims of a christology that begins from Christ's humanity. Rahner thinks that the doctrine of the 'two natures' has been so reduced in our understanding of it, that the human nature is taken to be a mere instrument required for the incarnation, and the fully human life of Jesus is not taken seriously. Again, he points to the preaching ascribed to Peter in the early chapters of Acts, which certainly begins from a fully human Jesus, a suffering and dying Jesus. 'This Jesus, whom you crucified, God has made Lord and Christ.' Of course, this primitive preaching did not last, and in the New Testament itself it is eventually superseded by the more sophisticated teaching of John about the Logos who has been from the beginning and who became flesh. But Rahner asks: 'Is the christology of the Acts of the Apostles, which begins from below, with the human experience of Jesus, merely primitive? Or has it something special to say to us which classical christology does not say with the same clarity?'[43]

Of course, I hardly need to say that Rahner is not advocating some form of adoptionism or any purely existentialist type of christology. He explicitly rejects the idea that there could be an evolution towards Christ understood as a striving upward of what is below by its own powers. Likewise, although Christ is seen as the archetype of all humanity, Rahner does not share Bultmann's aversion to asking about the ontological relation between Jesus Christ and the Father.

This other side of the christological question, namely, the incarnational idea of the coming of God into the creation, is discussed by Rahner in connection with the idea of evolution.[44] He mentions the similarity of some of his views to those of Teilhard de Chardin, though it seems that both of them had worked quite independently. In the evolutionary process, Rahner believes, God has been progressively communicating himself both in and to the creation. Jesus Christ is the climax of this process of communication, so that he has for Rahner a cosmic significance, an idea which we have seen recurring in Christian theology from Ephesians onward. The ultimate goal will be achieved when God is communicated in the entire cosmos. Hence 'incarnation [in Jesus Christ] appears as the beginning of the divinization of the world as a whole'.[45]

It would seem then that Rahner must reject the teaching of Kierkegaard and the early Barth that between God and the world there is an infinite qualitative difference, for how could this be the case if God is ever to enter the created order in the intimate manner suggested by the idea of incarnation? It is at this point that we see the important part played by Rahner's anthropology. The God-creature relation is to be understood (so far as we can understand it) in terms of the God-man relation. The classical christology asserts the union, without either mixture or separation, of the divine and human natures in the one person of Christ. This becomes conceivable when we recall Rahner's way of describing the spiritual nature of the human being. Spirit is not a 'substance', however subtle, but the activity of 'transcendence', of reaching out. If we acknowledge that in Christ the spiritual dynamism of the human creature has reached out toward the infinite God who has himself prepared this point of entry into the creation, then we perceive the outlines of what Rahner has ventured to call the 'divinization' of the world.

The freedom and creativity of post-Vatican II christology can be seen in a very different account of the matter, in the work of the Belgian theologian, Edward Schillebeeckx (1914–   ). In three massive volumes[46] this Dominican scholar has provided perhaps the most detailed study of the person of Jesus Christ to have appeared in the twentieth century. Like Rahner, he goes back to the sources, and like most theologians today, he begins his reflections from the human Jesus. But he differs from Rahner in this respect, that whereas Rahner develops his christology from the basic datum that Jesus was a human being and therefore had the spiritual potentialities of a human being as described in Rahner's anthropology, Schillebeeckx tries to be much more specific in speaking of Jesus as an individual with ascertainable characteristics – the concrete historical Jesus. Thus for Rahner the link between Jesus and God is provided by the ontological constitution of the human being as such: 'Only someone who forgets that the essence of man is to be unbounded . . . can suppose that it is impossible for there to be a man, who, precisely by being man in the fullest sense (which we never attain), is God's existence into the world.'[47] For Schillebeeckx, on the other hand, a much more tortuous way has to be pursued from the historical Jesus to the dogmatic Christ of faith. And there is the further complication that Schillebeeckx is not content to go back to the Christ of the gospels but attempts to go even further into the layers of tradition that lay behind the gospels, so that he does not feel himself inhibited by Martin Kähler's warning that the real Christ is the biblical Christ, not the historical Jesus which research claims to discover.[48] Schillebeeckx acknowledges that his approach is 'unconventional' but thinks that the Christ of ecclesiastical dogma and even of ordinary preaching is so far removed from contemporary ways of thinking that drastic steps are needed if people today are to be persuaded that Christ is still a significant figure. He calls the first volume of his trilogy an 'experiment' in christology, and in the present situation I have no hesitation in saying that it was a worthwhile experiment. But only when we have critically examined it can we judge how successful it has been.

Schillebeeckx, as has been mentioned, seeks to uncover the original Jesus as he was in his lifetime. Admittedly, this is a very risky procedure. Our gospels tell us about Jesus already crucified, risen and exalted to christhood, but the material has all passed through the crucible of faith, so that the original Jesus has virtually faded from view. At most we get glimpses, or hear his voice in the teaching. Of course, we can say that there *must* have been a human figure back there before faith arose, and we can even begin to conjecture some of the things that *must* have been true about him. To quote my revered teacher, Ian Henderson, 'there must have been something about the actual Jesus at the time at which he was on earth, to make the New Testament witnesses summon men to decide for or against him'.[49] But can we, through source-criticism and other kinds of criticism, through a kind of biblical archaeology, as it were, dig back to the beginnings? Is this not what Schweitzer and company showed to be impossible?

Schillebeeckx did have the courage to embark on this task, though he acknowledges that during the three years that he spent on exegesis before beginning to write his book, he was assailed by doubts. 'The fundamental stimulus behind this whole project seemed at times to amount to an impossible enterprise; there is, more or less, no biblical pericope on the interpretation of which the experts on exegesis do not disagree among themselves.'[50] Of course, Schillebeeckx was not the first systematic theologian to be discouraged by the notorious lack of agreement among the biblical scholars! We can only say that Schillebeeckx has gone about his task with the greatest care and patience and has consulted a wide range of scholars. He reconstructs a picture of the ministry of Jesus, and I think one could say that it is this picture of the ministry that is decisive for Schillebeeckx' interpretation. Jesus is the proclaimer of the kingdom, liberating his hearers from constricting ideas of God and of human community; accompanying the teaching is the acted parable of Jesus' own life, his healings and exorcisms, and (of special significance for Schillebeeckx) his table-fellowship both with his own disciples and with sinners and social outcasts of various kinds. Those who attached themselves to Jesus in this pre-Easter ministry were already experiencing a new relation to God in and through him.

Can we be more specific about this? Schillebeeckx finds a clue in the Hebrew–Jewish understanding of the 'prophet'. In the gospels, Jesus is frequently called a prophet, and sometimes identified with the prophet like Moses who had been promised to the people of Israel (Deut. 18.15). It may be that Jesus did not quite fit the traditional image of the prophet (perhaps John the Baptist fitted it better) but nevertheless one could argue that Jesus was indeed a prophet, though one who in some respects burst out of the traditional image.[51] But in Schillebeeckx' view, the title of prophet is the oldest of all christologies (if indeed we can speak of a 'christology' which is pre-Easter and pre-messianic!). He writes: 'Because of what they had experienced in their intercourse with Jesus during his time on earth, the choice of the very first followers of Jesus (later to become Christians) fell upon the Jewish model of the eschatological prophet, with which they were familiar.'[52] He deplores the fact that exegetes have made so little of the image of the prophet, for he believes that it is an extremely rich one and already in the earliest period had the seeds of a christological development that might reach all the way to Chalcedon.[53] Incidentally, it seems that Schillebeeckx is not acquainted with the work of Heschel on the Hebrew prophets.[54] Heschel's views would help to strengthen Schillebeeckx' argument.

It is Schillebeeckx' appeal to the earliest Jesus traditions that is most characteristic of his position, so we can pass over his discussions of the later New Testament literature, though he has much of interest to say.[55] But readers may wonder how he can possibly see a way from the hypothetical salvific experiences of the earliest followers who called Jesus a prophet to, let us say, the Johannine christology and then in course of time to Nicaea and Chalcedon. The continuity is provided by the subsequent career of Jesus, his death and resurrection, then by the growth of incarnational christology which, in Schillebeeckx' view, gradually displaced alternative ways of expressing the significance of Jesus as the Christ. But there is, I think, a weak point in the chain of Schillebeeckx' argument, and that is his treatment of the resurrection of Jesus. A full discussion of this difficult topic is being deferred until we come to the systematic part of the book, but Schillebeeckx' somewhat unusual views may be noted and criticized here. He does not think of the resurrection of Jesus as having the pivotal significance that is usually assigned to it. Of course, when he maintains this, he seems to be going against the testimony both of the evangelists and of Paul and of the New Testament generally. But Schillebeeckx believes that the basic belief of the earliest Christians was not specifically in resurrection but in the exaltation of the Jesus who had suffered and died to the presence of God, so that he is now 'living with God'. Obviously the two ideas, resurrection and living with God, are closely related, and even in the gospels the relation among the events clustered around the end of Jesus' earthly career is a variable one – for instance, in Luke crucifixion, resurrection, ascension, the coming of the Holy Spirit are distinct moments spread over a period of fifty days or thereby, while in John they all seem to be collapsed into a single complex happening. Schillebeeckx' intention is to reconstruct the perception of these events as they might have appeared to one of the early Jewish believers in terms of his own Jewish background of belief and expectation. His basic position is expressed in the following sentences:

> What one can say is that with both the Jews and with the Jewish Christians the general belief in life after death (for the righteous) began more and more to assume the form of belief in physical resurrection (a trend quite evident in late Jewish literature); and this gradual ascendancy of the resurrection idea over other ways of conceiving of the actual form of an 'assumption into heaven' took place also in Christian circles during the first few generations. But with or without resurrection, *in no way does the affirmation of belief in Jesus' being taken up into heaven depend on a possible empty tomb or on appearances*; both these last presuppose belief in Jesus' assumption into heaven after his death, whether after a sojourn in the realm of the dead or 'from off the cross'.[56]

So in Schillebeeckx' view, it was not the discovery of an empty tomb or the vivid appearances of the risen Lord to the disciples that led them to believe that he was alive with God. It was the other way round. They believed that the God who had sent his servant Jesus had after his death exalted him to the heavenly places, and because of this prior belief, the disciples came to believe that Christ had risen from the dead and began to tell stories about an empty tomb and of appearances.

Frankly, this does not sound very probable. Schillebeeckx does add more detail. He accepts the tradition that Peter played a leading part in those events. After the crucifixion, the disciples had scattered and remained scattered until Peter brought them together again. Peter had had time to reflect on what had happened, in the light of the traditional teaching. As a result of his reflection, he underwent according to Schillebeeckx some kind of 'conversion' experience in the strength of which he rallied his fellow apostles. For he had found in the scriptures the assurance that when the righteous are persecuted and even put to death, though they seem to have been destroyed, God has a secret purpose for them and they live on in him. Schillebeeckx is referring especially to a well-known passage in The Wisdom of Solomon:

> [The wicked say]: 'Let us see if his words are true, and let us test what will happen at the end of his life; for if the righteous man is God's son, he will help him, and will deliver him from the hand of his adversaries.

Let us test him with insult and torture, that we may find out how gentle he is, and make trial of his forbearance. Let us condemn him to a shameful death, for, according to what he says, he will be protected.' Thus they reasoned, but they were led astray, for their wickedness blinded them, and they did not know the secret purposes of God, nor hope for the wages of holiness, nor discern the prize for blameless souls; for God created man for incorruption, and made him in the image of his own eternity, but through the devil's envy death entered the world, and those who belong to his party experience it. But the souls of the righteous are in the hand of God, and no torment will ever touch them. In the eyes of the foolish they seem to have died, and their departure was thought to be an affliction, and their going from us to be their destruction, but they are at peace. For though in the sight of men they were punished, their hope is full of immortality (Wisd. 2.17–3, 4).

No one could deny that these words might very readily be applied to Jesus by one of his followers, reading them or remembering them in the days following the crucifixion. But that they would have been potent enough to 'convert' such a person, in the sense of lifting him out of disappointment and despair and giving him a new unbounded enthusiasm for the cause which he had deemed to be lost, and potent enough not only to produce conversion in Peter but through him to produce a like effect in those who had been his companions in discipleship – this seems to me to impose an impossible strain on our credulity. In discussions of the resurrection of Jesus, one usually comes down to the question, 'What would be a sufficient reason for the rise of the belief that Jesus had been raised from the dead?' The discovery of an empty tomb might have caused the belief. Or the experience of seeing and hearing Jesus alive. But these experiences would be convincing because they were so dramatic (even if they were mistaken in one way or another). I do not think that reading or remembering a passage of scripture which speaks in a general way of a hope for the righteous beyond death would have been nearly percussive enough to produce in Peter and the others the radical turn-around or conversion they had at that time.

So in spite of all Schillebeeckx' ingenuity and learning, I do not find his christological speculations persuasive. He was right in his determination to go back to the human Jesus, but wrong in trying to build so much of his case on fragmentary and doubtful traditions, arbitrarily selected. We can go along with him when he declares: 'That the man Jesus, in the sense of "a human person", is for me the starting-point of all my reflection I would call a sort of palisade that needs no further proof or justification. It is a truism. There are no ghosts or gods in disguise wandering around in our human history.'[57] But who or what are the 'ghosts or gods in disguise'? I think Schillebeeckx had in mind docetic figures of Christ. But the expression could also be applied to the inventions of not-so-critical historians.

The Jesuit Pierre Teilhard de Chardin (1881–1955) belonged to an older generation than Rahner and Schillebeeckx, but theologically he must be grouped with them because it was only in the more liberated atmosphere of Vatican II and its aftermath that his works became known. During his lifetime, his religious and theological works were not permitted to be published, and his major book, *The Phenomenon of Man*, appeared only in the year of his death. Soon, however, he had become the most widely read of Roman Catholic theologians, with an influence extending far beyond the boundaries of his church. Already by 1962 Teilhard's writings were having such success that the Holy Office thought it prudent to issue a *monitum* or warning that the faithful should not be too uncritical in accepting his teaching.

What then was the reason for the sudden fame that came posthumously to a priest who had lived much of his life in China and was virtually unknown and undiscussed among professional theologians and philosophers? The answer to that question is quite simple. It was believed by his admirers that he had made significant progress toward bridging the gap that in the modern world yawns between the natural sciences on the one hand and Christian faith on the other. The strength of the response made to Teilhard is an indication of how deeply many people are concerned with the science-religion divide, itself part of that wider divide between secular and sacred which stems from the Enlightenment and which is the concern motivating this book. In his youth Teilhard had become interested in the biological sciences, and had been attracted by the philosophy of Henri Bergson. This philosopher's *Creative Evolution* (1907) and other writings, drawing on a wide range of biological data, had attacked the popular nineteenth-century materialism, and argued for a creative principle at work in the evolutionary process, though perhaps this was conceived more in pantheistic than theistic terms. Teilhard's own teaching was to follow somewhat similar lines, though it had a much more definitely Christian character than had Bergson's.

Teilhard sees evolution as a vast ordered process, moving, as he believes, toward a goal. He has been criticized by some scientists for taking too simple a view of evolution, as if it were a linear advance toward the fufilment of an inherent purpose. On the other side, he has been criticized by theologians who ask whether the immanent principle at work in evolution (if there is such a principle) can rightly be called 'God' or whether God appears only at the end in Teilhard's scheme and not at the beginning. There can be no doubt that Teilhard's views need much criticism and rethinking, partly because he got no criticism in his lifetime, because he was inhibited from publication. However, our concern in this book is to consider Teilhard's views on christology, not to make a general assessment of his theological method. It is enough to say that his merits and demerits as a theologian or philosopher of religion are still being debated.

In Teilhard's scheme, the history of evolution is exhibited as a history of increasing complexity. Elementary particles are built up into atoms, atoms into molecules, molecules form living cells, these in turn build up multicellular organisms. The law of this process is that as complexity increases, so there is movement toward life and eventually consciousness. There are crucial points or 'thresholds' in the process, when something new emerges – for instance, at some distant moment in the past, the first living things emerged, and at a much more recent point, the human race emerged as the bearers of consciousness, reason, personal being, and with humanity the possibility of the evolutionary process taking over its own direction. The end of the process, the eschatology, as it were, of this view of the world, is called by Teilhard the omega-point, the gathering up and fulfilment of all things in a spiritual culmination. Whether this is God or all things gathered up in God is not quite clear. Some critics claim that God will only exist at the end in Teilhard's scheme, but probably his own view is that God has always been guiding the process. For while there will be novelty in the future, he tells us that 'nothing could ever burst forth as final across the different thresholds successively traversed by evolution (however critical they may be) which has not already existed in an obscure and primordial way'.[58]

We are now able to see the place of Christ in this scheme. He is, so to speak, the reflection back into the very heart of the evolutionary process of that spiritual fulfilment which lies at the end as its goal. In Christ the end is already present. Teilhard's vision of the future is a hopeful one – the building up of the body of Christ on a cosmic scale, a vision that we first met when considering the letter to the Ephesians.[59] 'The exclusive task of the world is the physical incorporation of the faithful in the Christ who is of God.'[60] This may strike us as extravagant language, but the church's claim for Christ has always seemed extravagant, and those who speak of the cosmic Christ are only drawing out the implications.

For Teilhard, Christ is not only the end and the anticipation of the end, he has like every other novelty been hidden in the past, coming to be with the world, as Schleiermacher expressed it. In Teilhard's language, 'the prodigious expanses of time which preceded the first Christmas were not empty of Christ, for they were imbued with the influx of his power'.[61] Inherent in this teaching is a veneration for matter and the potentialities of matter, unequalled, I think, since the days of John of Damascus and the controversies over icons.[62] It is true that Teilhard seems to believe that at the omega-point the material will be transformed into the spiritual, yet he always thought of the material as having a capacity for transcendence, just as Rahner saw transcendence as the characteristic of spirit. So for Teilhard it is not only the human race but the whole material cosmos that is destined to be incorporated into the body of Christ. In a writing which is admittedly poetic and mystical rather than strictly theological, 'The Mass on the World', Teilhard gives expression to ideas which came to him in China, when, on the feast of the Transfiguration, he found himself in a desert unable to celebrate the eucharist, and imagined the whole universe being consecrated to become the body of Christ. 'When Christ says, "This is my body", these words extend beyond the morsel of bread over which they are said. They give birth to the whole mystical body of Christ. The effect extends beyond the consecrated host to the cosmos itself – the entire realm of matter is slowly but irresistibly affected by this great consecration.'[63]

This vision of a cosmic consecration or universal christogenesis is certainly a new development, though it is in the tradition of that cosmic christology which has been cultivated by some Christian theologians from New Testament times onward.[64] But in earlier ages Christ's cosmic Lordship was conceived in the context of a static universe. 'Now,' as Christopher Mooney has remarked, 'there is an opportunity to rethink the data of revelation concerning the person of Christ within a totally different physical framework. What is even more important, such rethinking will put theologians in a position to give a truly theological significance to the whole evolutionary process.'[65] Almost from the beginning of our inquiry in this book, we have been aware that the expression 'Jesus Christ' does not refer only to the individual human being who was called by that name, but to the 'Christ-event', the social reality of which Jesus was the centre and inspirer. In the language of Augustine, the whole Christ is both the head and the body, both Jesus and the community gathered about him. With Teilhard, this idea of the body of Christ is expanded to embrace the entire physical world. Obviously this implies a high conception of matter, comparable to that entertained by the Byzantine theologians. This universe of ours has over the ages brought forth life and mind and human persons and even (if we are considering the picture from below) the Christ. When one has in mind the astounding potentialities of matter-energy, it is not unreasonable to think of the whole universe as the 'body' of the Logos which is the principle of its order and unity. And one must immediately add that it is not unreasonable either to acknowledge that the creative Logos must be presupposed in the whole process.

I do not think, however, that we need go so far as Teilhard in thinking that the relation of Christ to the cosmos calls for the recognition of a third nature, the cosmic, along side the traditional divine and human natures in Christ's person.[66] Here his enthusiasm has carried him away. But this extravagant speculation does not detract from the value of his vision of a cosmic consecration, which lends a new dignity to the natural world.

Liberation Christology

Roman Catholic thinking about the person of Christ since Vatican II has taken other forms besides those discussed in the preceding section. Much attention has been paid to the 'liberation' theology that has developed in Latin America. Its philosophical affiliations have been more with Marxism than with transcendental Thomism, and its practical concern has been more for human society than for scientific interpretations of the natural world. But though it is not in the mainstream of Catholic thought, one should not exaggerate the differences. The kind of christology that has emerged among the liberation theologians is, on the whole, quite orthodox and traditional, though it has radical implications for ethics and politics. Again, although this liberation theology has arisen out of the peculiar situation of Christianity in Latin America and might therefore seem to be a regional theology and therefore at the opposite extreme from the cosmic thinking of Teilhard, Latin America itself is very much a cultural offshoot of Catholic Europe, and a glance through the index of names in any book of liberation theology would reveal a list of theologians and philosophers not much different from what would be found in theological books written in Europe or North America.

The most substantial work on christology to come from the liberationists is the book of Jon Sobrino (1938–), a Jesuit from El Salvador. The Spanish original edition appeared in 1976 and bore the very sober and descriptive title *Cristología desde america latina*, but the English version has the more dramatic title, *Christology at the Crossroads* (1978). From the strictly theological point of view, it is quite traditional. At a time when the classical christology had been severely criticized by a group of English theologians in the symposium *The Myth of God Incarnate* (1977), I myself at a symposium in New York heard Sobrino distancing himself from their views and declaring, 'No liberation theologian known to me has ever denied the divinity of Christ.' But what does happen in a 'liberation' christology is that some things about Jesus Christ that were passed over in traditional formulations are now brought into the foreground and given an emphasis which results in quite a different total impression of Christ.

Sobrino quite correctly tells us 'that there is no reason why christological titles should be the exclusive prerogative of one particular culture, even that of the New Testament writers'.[67] We have seen that in early Christianity titles drawn from the Jewish background such as 'messiah' began to be supplemented or even replaced by titles from the wider Hellenistic world.[68] There seems to be no good reason for refusing to let the process continue. Sobrino's suggestion is that today Jesus could very suitably be called the 'Liberator'. That particular title is one that has been used in Latin America for men like Simon Bolivar, one of the leaders in the revolt of the Spanish colonies in South America against the mother country in the early decades of the nineteenth century. Some of the republics still issue coins with Bolivar's portrait and the inscription 'Liberador'. Inevitably, such a title carries definite political overtones, but of course exactly the same was true of the term 'messiah' when first applied to Christ. In fact, 'liberator' and 'messiah' had somewhat similar meanings in the two very diverse cultures in which they were used. But just as 'messiah' or 'Christ', when it passed into Christian usage, took on a distinctively Christian meaning, so one might hope that 'liberador' would in a Christian and theological context acquire a somewhat different semantic range from the one that it had in Spanish-American history. It is very important to notice that when Sobrino advocates the title of liberator for Jesus, he adds a proviso: 'so long as we remember that it is through Jesus that we learn what liberation really is and how it is to be achieved'.[69]

In common with other liberation theologians, Sobrino holds that Christianity is more of a doing than a thinking, and that consequently orthopraxis or 'right doing' takes precedence over orthodoxy or 'right belief'. It is probably a fair criticism of the church to say that in the past she has often been too much concerned for orthodoxy, and too little concerned for a Christian 'praxis' that would translate faith into action. In extreme cases, the separation between belief and action was so great that it amounted to hypocrisy. But it is doubtful if one can simply claim that orthopraxis takes precedence over orthodoxy. The relation between belief and action is very complex, and certainly has some elements of reciprocity.

Belief and action are related by Sobrino to what he thinks were two stages in the Enlightenment. The first stage, associated with Kant, was concerned with the liberation of human reason from theological domination. It is this intellectual problem that has continued to be the main interest of European theology. The second phase (which Sobrino associates with Marx) 'championed the liberation of the whole person from a religious outlook that supported, or at least permitted, economic and political alienation'.[70] 'Christological reflection in Latin America', we are told, 'seeks to respond to the second phase of the Enlightenment. It seeks to show how the truth of Christ is capable of transforming a sinful world into the kingdom of God.'[71]

The starting-point for such a christology must be the historical Jesus. Sobrino is aware of the criticisms made against such an approach from Kähler onward, and he has no use for Harnack, whose Jesus was the 'model of bourgeois morality and citizenship in the nineteenth century'.[72] Sobrino himself thinks that the interpretation of the historical Jesus must

begin from his proclamation of the kingdom of God. But Jesus' understanding of the kingdom and the way to realize it developed as he went
along. Even his conception of God developed. He came to think of God
less in terms of power, more in terms of love. But it was no sentimental
love that we meet in Jesus.

> Jesus does not advocate a love that is depoliticized, dehistoricized and
> destructuralized. He advocates a political love, a love that is situated in
> history and that has visible repercussions for human beings. Rather
> than simply advocating the complete abolition of the zealot spirit, he
> proposes an alternative to Zealotism. Historically, Jesus acted out of
> love and was *for* all human beings. But he was for them in different
> ways. Out of love for the poor, he took his stand *with* them; out of love
> for the rich, he took his stand *against* them. In both cases, however, he
> was interested in something more than retributive justice. He wanted
> renewal and re-creation.[73]

Sobrino's emphasis on action rather than thinking occasionally leads to
something close to anti-intellectualism. For instance, he criticizes
Pannenberg as a theologian whose work is 'explicative' rather than 'transformational'. 'He works out a novel historical hermeneutics, but it is
designed to explain history rather than to transform it.'[74] No doubt the
aim of Christianity is ultimately to transform history, but theology is not
the whole of Christianity, but is that specifically intellectual work which
aims at explanation and understanding. It could be argued that only
when one has 'made sense' of Christian faith has one the right to apply it
in practical situations. Otherwise 'transformational' theology may be no
more than propaganda and the manipulation of people. Sobrino himself
cannot escape the explicative work. If his claims that christology should
begin from the historical Jesus and that his own reading of the historical
Jesus is preferable to Harnack's, then a great deal of careful and
academically demanding theological work has to be done.

Born in the same year as Sobrino is another Latin American theologian
who is author of a full-scale work on christology – Leonardo Boff
(1938–). He is a Brazilian and therefore writes in Portuguese, in
which the word for 'liberator' is '*libertador*'. His book on christology, first
published in 1972, is called *Jesus Cristo Libertador*, or in English *Jesus
Christ Liberator*, and is subtitled 'A Critical Christology of Our Time'.

Quite early in the book, he gives a list of five priorities which, he
believes, must characterize a christology constructed in the context of
Latin America. But these priorities are presented in a moderate way that
does not simply embrace one aspect and reject the other. Boff's first point
is that the anthropological element should have priority over the
ecclesiastical. This could also be expressed by saying that the church must

have a human face, to borrow an expression used by Schillebeeckx. According to Boff, the Roman Catholic Church in South America has traditionally been authoritarian, and if it is to present Christ to the people in a way to which they will respond, then that presentation will need to be in human rather than legal and dogmatic terms. The second priority is that of the utopian over the factual. The use of the word 'utopian' may be unfortunate, but all that Boff is asking is that the preaching of Christ should be hopeful and forward-looking, not judgmental and condemnatory. But this spirit of hope is characteristic of virtually all Catholic theology since Vatican II. The third point is the priority of the critical element over the dogmatic. This is not a call for radical doctrinal innovation, but for a principle of criticism in theology, so that Christian teaching does not stagnate in ancient formulae that are no longer generally understood, but is able to engage in dialogue with the world today. A fourth point is the priority of the social over the personal. We understand today much more than was the case in earlier times how much human life is moulded by the social and political structures in which people live. Human salvation needs not just individual conversions but a renewal of the sociopolitical framework. But here again Boff avoids a one-sided judgment. 'Jesus demands personal conversion and restructuring of the human world.'[75] Boff's last point is already familiar to us from Sobrino, and is a commonplace among the liberation theologians – the priority of orthopraxis over orthodoxy. I have already indicated the dangers of anti-intellectualism if this point is pushed too far. I think that not only in Europe but all over the world the difficulties that many people have in relating in any affirmative way to Jesus Christ are intellectual difficulties, and these will not be overcome by calls to action or 'praxis'. But Boff is once again moderate in his understanding of this priority. Whereas Sobrino in his mentions of traditional christology, particularly Chalcedon, is consistently critical of the abstract conceptual character of that christology, Boff might even be judged too uncritical. He speaks of Chalcedon as the time 'when orthodoxy formulated with full lucidity the fundamental truth that Jesus is wholly and simultaneously true man and true God'.[76] Not everyone will agree that Chalcedon spoke with 'full lucidity'!

I have drawn attention to a few points at which Boff and Sobrino take somewhat different views. But these are points of detail, and essentially these two liberation christologies are similar. Like Sobrino, Boff founds his christology on the historical Jesus. As he understands the matter, 'the historical Jesus puts us in direct contact with his liberative programme and the practices with which he implements it'.[77] But what is this liberative programme? There is an ambiguity in 'liberation' until we know *from* what and *for* what people are being liberated. Boff has already commended Marxist social analysis as the way to discern the factors that produce injustice and stand in the way of human fulfilment. But the liberation which this demands has to do with economic, social, political and ideological structures.[78] This is something less that the liberation which Jesus desired, yet it must not be overlooked. In a typically balanced statement, Boff says: 'The salvation proclaimed by Christianity is an all-embracing one. It is not restricted to economic, political, social and ideological emancipation, but neither can it be realized without them.'[79] There is probably little in the actual teaching of Jesus that would put us 'in direct contact' (to quote Boff's phrase) with a liberative programme that would deal with sociopolitical structures. Yet one could say that the conflict with 'principalities and powers' is present in the clash of Jesus with the authorities and in his condemnation and death. Let us remember that the first post-Enlightenment reconstruction of the picture of Christ (one could hardly call it a christology) was in political terms – I mean, of course, the reconstruction by Reimarus.[80] It could be said that the liberation christologies of Latin America are trying to state more adequately whatever truth there may have been in Reimarus's ideas, for if Christ is significant for all human life, that must include social and political life.

Eschatological Christology

At the end of the nineteenth century, the belief that the mind of Jesus had been dominated by eschatological and even apocalyptic ideas gave a major shock to the theological world. The liberals did not know what to do with an idea so primitive and so foreign to modern minds as that the world might have an end. Weiss and Schweitzer, the champions of the new eschatological interpretation of the New Testament, were embarrassed by their own discovery, and made no constructive use of it. When Barth wrote his commentary on Romans, he made enthusiastic remarks about all theology being eschatology, but eschatology was not to be understood in anything like its original sense but rather as a way of speaking of the crisis that had befallen Europe. Bultmann too paid lip service to the eschatological character of the kerygma, but he demythologized it by bringing it from a mythological future into the present, where 'eschatological' signifies the ultimacy and urgency of the decision that is demanded in face of the word. So if Weiss and Schweitzer were correct in claiming that primitive Christianity was through and through eschatological, there was a very long wait before their findings began to be taken seriously by systematic theologians. But eventually that did happen, and it has been a feature of some of the most interesting German Protestant theology in the post-Barthian, post-Bultmannian period.

A leader in this new phase of German theology is Jürgen Moltmann (1926–   ). He has been a very prolific writer, and much of his output has a direct bearing on christology. His reputation as a major theologian was established by his *Theology of Hope* (1964), subtitled 'On the Ground and the Implications of a Christian Eschatology'. This was the first volume of a trilogy, and the second volume, *The Crucified God* (1973), would have a good claim to be regarded as possibly the most important theological book to be published in the second half of the twentieth century. The third volume of the trilogy dealt with the church and makes little contribution to christology. But Moltmann then embarked on a new series of books designed to cover the whole field of Christian theology. Two of them are specially important from the christological point of view: *The Trinity and the Kingdom of God* (1980) and a volume devoted specifically to christology, *The Way of Jesus Christ* (1990).

In his *Theology of Hope* Moltmann took with full seriousness the eschatological and even apocalyptic beliefs of the New Testament and of Jesus himself. As I have noted above, eschatology had been on the theological agenda since the beginning of the century, but the heady ideas of primitive Christianity had been defused and rendered inoffensive to modern minds by a succession of theologians. Moltmann on the contrary, in conscious opposition to Bultmann in particular, accepted that eschatology is no mere accidental trapping of Christianity, a dispensable relic of the first century, but of the very essence. This bold recognition means that Moltmann has to face a number of intellectual difficulties and perhaps the accusation that he has embarked on a process of remythologizing, but it cannot be denied that it gives to his theology a certain vitality. As Kierkegaard pointed out long ago, a Christianity from which all offence has been removed is a pretty dull affair.

Another obvious feature of Moltmann's theology is his deep concern with the contemporary world, especially with situations of oppression, injustice and deprivation. He began his theological reflections when he was a prisoner of war at the end of World War II, and perhaps his own early experiences of hardship in a disordered world kindles his interest in the political and social implications of Christianity. At any rate, Moltmann could not be counted among those whom Marx accused of seeking only to understand the world without seeking to change it, nor could he be subjected to the kind of complaint which, as we have seen, Sobrino makes against Pannenberg.[81] Actually Moltmann has exerted quite a considerable influence on the liberation theologians, for his future-oriented theology combined with his interest in socio-political problems establishes an obvious link with the liberationists.

Moltmann's theological ideas were beginning to become known in the years when there was much talk of the 'death of God'. Moltmann does sometimes speak of the world as 'godless' in its present condition, but whereas 'death of God' was usually understood as meaning that God is no longer, because modern man has outgrown religion, Moltmann spoke of the world as 'godless' in the sense that God is 'not yet', the reign of God is a promise for the future. This suggests a comparison with Teilhard de Chardin, but the influence behind Moltmann here is more probably the neo-Marxist philosopher, Ernst Bloch, author of a lengthy work entitled *Principle of Hope*. Bloch visualized the whole universe, human and non-human, as imbued with a kind of *nisus* toward a future fulfilment. One of his major categories is the 'not yet' and 'not yet' suggests hope. This idea is central to Moltmann's theology of hope. Whereas the previous generation of theologians had laid great stress on revelation, Moltmann argues that the category of promise is more typical of the Bible. He sees the promise-fulfilment schema running through the whole of the Bible. This is not a denial of revelation, but the assertion that revelation is given in the form of promise.

Moltmann's stress on promise makes him unsympathetic to the so-called 'realized' eschatology that was so much in favour among twentieth-century biblical scholars. He wants to go back to the futuristic expectations of the very earliest Christians. In some ways, this may seem like a retreat from the modern world back to pre-critical ways of thinking. I shall come back to this problem in a moment, but first let us notice that Moltmann believes that his futuristic concern is a point of contact with the modern mentality. He points, for instance, to the importance of planning in modern societies and claims a kinship between hope and planning. He even wrote a book called *Hope and Planning*[82] but I think he fails completely to make a case, for secular plans for the future are entirely dependent on human resources, and such ideas as the promises of God or the resurrection of the dead are quite irrelevant to them. At best, it might be said that these Christian ideas or hopes were gropings toward modern ideas of progress, but Moltmann would get little comfort from such a concession, for his own position is that these ideas were *not* myths or symbols but central realities of Christianity. So here we have to come back to that question which we postponed – whether in his *Theology of Hope* Moltmann is putting back the theological clock, in the sense that he is trying to bring back into history ideas which in modern times have been judged mythological. Here Bultmann and Moltmann appear to be in head-on collision. Bultmann accepts the critical historical method, including Troeltsch's criteria for distinguishing history from myth or legend. Moltmann rejects these criteria, especially the principle of analogy. Jesus' resurrection, he holds, has no analogy. It is unique, a *novum*, so one must reject views of history that cannot find room for resurrection, and look for a new conception of history that will not be positivistic.[83] Unfortunately he does not supply the required conception of history, so there is a gaping hole in the fabric of this theology here. Even one of his more sympathetic critics, Christopher Morse, complains that Moltmann's 'conceptual vagueness' on these matters cannot be excused.[84]

When we pass to the second volume of Moltmann's trilogy, *The Crucified God*, attention shifts from resurrection to cross, though these two central items in Christian faith are kept closely related in Moltmann's thought. The great achievement of this second book is to present a fully (or almost fully) Christianized understanding of God. If Christ is believed to be the clue to the mystery of God, then our thinking about God must be derived from Christ. For too long, Western theology has been dominated by a monarchical conception of God, derived from natural theology, the Old Testament and various philosophical sources, but not radically rethought in the light of the crucified Christ as 'the visible revelation of God's being for man in the reality of his world'.[85] Moltmann is determined to know God through the suffering Christ, a God of love who participates in the suffering of his creatures. The history of Jesus is represented as the conflict between God and the gods, that is to say, between the God of suffering love and all the gods of power created by human ideologies.

But we may note a problematic area in *The Crucified God*. In spite of the tradition of the divine impassibility, Moltmann thinks of God *in* Christ or *with* Christ, even in the passion. But as a concession to the Reformed theological tradition to which he belongs, Moltmann also wants to speak of Jesus as abandoned by God. Jesus, it would appear from his cry of dereliction, did subjectively *feel* himself abandoned. But Moltmann wants to say he really was abandoned, and this is in plain contradiction to his claim that the Father was suffering in and with Jesus.[86]

But it is more typical of Moltmann to stress the closeness of God and Jesus than their separation. This is evident in the strongly trinitarian nature of his theology, already clear in *The Crucified God*. 'The history of Christ with God and of God with Christ becomes the history of God with us and hence our history with God.'[87] Moltmann can even say that 'the human God who encounters man in the crucified Christ involves man in a realistic divinization (*theiosis*)'.[88] He does not hesitate to use the word 'panentheism' for his doctrine of God.[89]

In his later book, *The Trinity and the Kingdom of God*, Moltmann continues to explore the significance of a trinitarian doctrine of God, and how it encourages freedom and openness in human affairs. He declares that 'the intention and consequence of the doctrine of the Trinity is not only the deification of Christ; it is even more the christianization of the concept of God'.[90] There is a hint of cosmic christology and perhaps also of eastern orthodox influence when he writes: 'To throw open the circulatory movement of the divine light and the divine relationships, and to take men and women with the whole of creation into the lifestream of the triune God: that is the meaning of creation, reconciliation and glorification.'[91]

The many strands in Moltmann's thinking about Jesus Christ have been brought together in *The Way of Jesus Christ*.[92] The subtitle of this book is 'Christology in Messianic Dimensions' which makes it clear that the futuristic and eschatological interests are still important with Moltmann. He takes his departure from the messianic hopes and promises of Israel, and then moves on to the depiction of Jesus in the New Testament. Again he insists on the need to see cross and resurrection in the closest association with one another and, indeed, to see the whole series of historical events as linked together. It is on this basis that he defends the resurrection of Jesus as a reality and not just mythology. Moltmann considers the criteria of Troeltsch, mentioned above, and agrees that if they are accepted, it becomes very difficult to conceive history in such a way that it could include resurrection. But is not the resurrection of Jesus the end of the kind of history which Troeltsch envisaged, the beginning of a new creation? This may seem such a sweeping idea that we might reject it out of hand. But Moltmann, with a reference to Pannenberg's concept of 'universal history', reminds us that the historian is not just concerned with analysing and investigating what has happened. Inevitably, any historian, has to weave these facts into a historical narrative, and in order to do that he needs some philosophy of history. While this is true of all historians, even those who would think of themselves as positivists, it is perhaps most evident in the case of the Christian historian for whom 'resurrection' will be an important *motiv* in the construction of his narrative. This is at least some advance toward repairing what I earlier described as a 'gaping hole' in Moltmann's christology.

Another important development in *The Way of Jesus Christ* is that what in the earlier writings were only hints and allusions to a 'cosmic' christology are here developed in a long chapter on this topic. In dialogue with Teilhard and Rahner, Moltmann considers Christ as the Logos through whom the worlds were created, and, with his usual concern for drawing the practical conclusions of his ideas, applies his cosmic christology to current anxieties concerning the environment.

Wolfhart Pannenberg (1928–) is another leading figure in the post-Bultmannian phase of German Protestant theology. He has several things in common with Moltmann – he rejects existentialism and demythologizing, he holds that resurrection and eschatology are realities essential to Christian faith, he searches for a new and more adequate philosophy of history. On the other hand, he does not share Moltmann's political aspirations, as indeed we noted in Sobrino's criticism of him. He is more philosophical and rationalistic than Moltmann in his theological method, but equally prolific in the volume of his writings.

In earlier parts of this book, we have already encountered some of Pannenberg's ideas, and it may be useful to recall them before we go into a more detailed discussion. First of all, we noted his insistence on not separating fact from interpretation in history. He criticizes the 'futile aim of the positivist historians to ascertain bare facts without meaning in history' and urges that 'we must reinstate today the original unity of facts and their meaning'.[93] Against whom is Pannenberg inveighing? The 'positivist historians' are presumably those whom Arnold Toynbee characterizes as 'one school of western historians in a post-Christian age of western history' and who (in his view) see only 'a chaotic, disorderly, fortuitous flux, in which there is no rhythm or pattern of any kind to be discerned'.[94] Pannenberg makes it clear that he is also dissatisfied with Bultmann and the existentialists who separate fact from interpretation, and though Pannenberg might have some sympathy with Kähler who likewise criticized the 'positivists', he does not like Kähler's category of the 'suprahistorical'. Where then does Pannenberg want us to look? The answer to this question we have also met in earlier discussion, when we found Moltmann alluding to Pannenberg's interest in 'universal history'.[95] Such 'universal history' is certainly not a popular idea at the present time. It seeks the unity of history and to gain a glimpse of the course of history as a whole. It is the opposite of that disjointed analytic approach which Toynbee claims to be typical of contemporary historians, and might be more like Toynbee's own vast canvases on which he depicts the rise and fall of complete civilizations. There is, of course, a long tradition of the writing of universal history, going back to Augustine's monumental *City of God* and represented nearer our own time by Spengler's *Decline of the West*.

The Christian theologian, in Pannenberg's view, needs a universal theory of history, with God himself as the principle of unity – indeed, Pannenberg seems to hold that any unitary concept of history entails a concept of God. But he insists that this does not mean that one must embrace supernaturalism. 'Proper theological research into history must absorb the truth of the humanistic tendency toward an "immanent" understanding of events. It may not supplant detailed historical investigation by supernaturalistic hypotheses.'[96]

Although God is posited as the source of the unity of history, we cannot know him *a priori* but only through his self-revelation in history. This is possible only if history moves toward an end, so that for Pannenberg the eschatological-apocalyptic framework of expectation is just as important as it is for Moltmann. He is at one with Moltmann when he declares:

'when one is dealing with the truth of the apocalyptic expectation of a future judgment or a resurrection of the dead, one is dealing directly with the basis of Christian faith.'[97]

It is in this framework that the person of Jesus Christ is to be interpreted. Jesus is the anticipation of the end of history. Thus, in Pannenberg as in Moltmann, a special stress is laid on the resurrection of Jesus. In accordance with his view that a theistic understanding of universal history does not excuse us from detailed consideration of particular events, Pannenberg appeals to the evidence for a resurrection of Jesus, understood as a historical event within the framework mentioned above. Pannenberg believes that there are two independent strands of tradition to be considered – the tradition of the empty tomb, and the tradition of the appearances. He disagrees with Bultmann, who sets aside the empty tomb stories as later legends. Pannenberg's view is that when one has considered the traditions, the critical objections, the alternative explanations and so on, resurrection stands as the most probable 'explanation' of what happened at this juncture in the rise of Christianity.[98] He supports his historical argument with further considerations drawn from anthropology, in particular, that 'it is inherent in man to hope beyond death, even as it is inherent in man to know about his own death'.[99]

I have put resurrection in the forefront of Pannenberg's christology because it does have an important role in his thought and connects closely with his philosophy of history. But this should not obscure the fact that he is not making an appeal to the supernatural but trying to consider even resurrection from the point of view of a rational (not 'positivist') historian. In fact, Pannenberg is very insistent that christology in the modern period must begin from the humanity of Christ. This principle is not breached through the importance he assigns to the resurrection for, as we have seen, the phenomenology of the human being in general reveals that he or she projects existence beyond death. So we find him going so far as to say, 'Where the statement that Jesus is God would contradict his real humanity, one would probably rather surrender the confession of his divinity than doubt that he really was a man.'[100] Of course, this insistence on Christ's humanity is not meant to exclude his divinity, only to rule out any premature assertion of the divinity that might place the humanity in doubt. Is it the resurrection of Jesus that marks the transition from the mere man to the God man? That may be implicit in the following sentences: 'All christological considerations tend toward the idea of the incarnation; it can, however, only constitute the conclusion of christology. If it is put instead at the beginning, all christological concepts . . . are given a mythological tone.'[101]

Pannenberg's work is impressive, but some aspects of it remain problematic. One of these is the concept of resurrection – or perhaps I should say, the image of resurrection. It is not to be understood literally, yet we are also told that it is not, as Bultmann would have it, mythological. Perhaps, of course, it just cannot be clarified any further so long as we live within the bounds of sense, or perhaps the only clarification is the one that Pannenberg offers, namely, to locate resurrection, whether of Christ or of human beings generally, within the horizon of an eschatological view of history. But that brings us to a second problem. Has Pannenberg succeeded in providing a philosophy of history that can really sustain his theology? Allan Galloway concludes an illuminating study of Pannenberg with what I think is a just verdict: 'Pannenberg has put forward suggestions which are theologically exciting and apologetically effective. But to work them out with the care and precision appropriate to their importance would require a much more carefully elaborated metaphysic than is at present available to Pannenberg.'[102]

Some British and American Christologies

Eighty years ago the Scottish theologian Hugh Ross Mackintosh wrote in his book, *The Doctrine of the Person of Jesus Christ*: 'We do not find in the theology of the English-speaking races much that needs to be chronicled.'[103] The remark seems harsh, but even today it would still be broadly true. Creative theological ideas have come from the European continent – mostly indeed from Germany – and English-speaking writers have been content to discuss and criticize these ideas. In this study of christologies since the Enlightenment, our attention has been mainly directed to the continentals, with only a few British or American representatives who were in any case expounding views that had originated elsewhere, Caird on idealist christology, Gore on kenotic christology, Rauschenbusch on the social gospel. But as the readership of this book is mainly British and American, this section will be devoted to English-speaking theologians who have made contributions to christology in the past fifty years or so.

We begin with Donald Baillie (1887–1954) whose book *God Was in Christ* has become almost a classic. It is taken up largely with expounding and criticizing the ideas of such continentals as Barth, Brunner and Bultmann but, as we shall see, it develops some independent ideas about the person of Christ. Baillie begins with a survey of the scene as it was about the middle of the century. He noted two apparently contradictory tendencies. One he called 'the end of docetism', for he believed that virtually all theologians were eager to uphold the full humanity of Jesus Christ. But over against that, he noted a new historical scepticism which had come about as an extreme reaction following the discrediting of the quest of the historical Jesus. Baillie was particularly critical of Bultmann's dismissal of the importance of having historical information about Jesus, and declared: 'I cannot believe that the rediscovery [of the historical Jesus] was from the Christian point of view a delusion, or was anything less than a recovery of something which is vital to Christian faith.'[104] But Barth, Brunner and Kierkegaard also incur judicious criticism for their alleged indifference to the historical Jesus, and Baillie makes the point that we must have some knowledge of Jesus if he is to mean anything to us.

Of course, he is not advocating a return to the historical Jesus in the nineteenth-century sense. There must also be christology, the theological study of the person of Christ. Baillie acknowledges that the idea of a God-man is the 'supreme paradox', but he is not taking refuge in paradox. He points out that paradoxes occur widely in human experience. One of his illustrations is map-making.[105] The spherical surface of the earth cannot be projected without distortion on to a flat sheet of paper. We therefore use several projections, any one of which creates a distortion, but if we take them together, one corrects another. The vital illustration for christology is the human experience of divine grace operative in our lives. We do things, yet we say that it is not really we who do them but God working in and through us. Paul expressed it by saying 'It is no longer I who live, but Christ who lives in me' (Gal. 2.20). Yet, according to Baillie, it is exactly in these moments we are most truly ourselves. This then is the substance of his christology. Christ is the man fully surrendered to God, the man in whom grace reigns supreme. Baillie attributes his teaching to Augustine, but among modern theologians, it seems to be quite unique and original. Questions have been raised about this christology. Is it adoptionist? Does it make the difference between Christ and other human beings one of degree only? I think myself the same questions could be raised about any christology which sets off from the humanity of Jesus, for instance, the christology of Rahner, but I think also that they can be satisfactorily answered, as I hope to show at a later stage.[106]

Baillie goes on to a full discussion of the atoning work of Christ. He makes at least two important points here. The first brings us back to the historical Jesus. The point is that the meaning of the cross cannot be understood apart from what we know about the one who dies on the cross. This is obviously directed against Bultmann, for whom it is the resurrection that brings the meaning of the cross while the preceding life of Jesus is left out of consideration. The second point, which would hold against Barth,[107] is that atonement cannot be purely objective, because it is 'a spiritual process in the realm of personal relationships' and cannot therefore be 'a transaction completed as it were behind our backs'.[108]

In connection with the second of these points, we may note that Baillie also comes out strongly for the view which I defended when we were discussing the teaching of the epistle to the Hebrews, namely, that the event of atonement was not a once-for-all happening in the past but an event which we are bound to call 'continuing' or perhaps 'eternal'. 'To reduce the importance of the historical event,' writes Baillie, 'would be contrary to every instinct of Christian faith: and yet it seems impossible to say that the divine sin-bearing was confined to that moment of time or is anything less than eternal.'[109] He reminds us of the phrase in the book of Revelation, 'the Lamb slain before the foundation of the world' (13.8), though he was, as I need hardly say, well aware that there is more than one way of reading the verse in which that phrase occurs.[110]

It is not surprising that this book of Baillie's has, as was mentioned, attained to the status of a modern classic, for it combines the post-Enlightenment approach to christology 'from below' with a deep spiritual sensitivity.

Eleven years after *God Was in Christ* there appeared an important American contribution to christological studies – *The Word Incarnate*, by Norman Pittenger (1905–). This book was later updated by a sequel, *Christology Reconsidered* (1970). Pittenger is a leading representative of the school of 'process theology' which has been very influential in the United States. The members of this school stress process and becoming as against any static world-view, and draw heavily on the philosophical categories of Arthur North Whitehead, Charles Hartshorne and other philosophers in the same tradition.

The process theologian tends to see events in terms of continuous development, rather than in terms of sudden jumps or irruptions from outside. Thus Pittenger sees the New Testament understanding of Jesus rising to its culmination in the Johannine application of the term Logos ('the expressive principle in Godhead'). The increasingly high estimates of Jesus finding their climax in the assertion of his divinity are seen by Pittenger no doubt correctly, as reflecting an experience of salvation in and through Christ, rather than an intellectual exercise. So he sees the patristic development toward the classical christology as continuing the New Testament development. Though he criticizes some details of the classical christology, he treats it with great respect and believes that his own statement preserves the *intention* of the ancient formulations, though not tied to their words. We find him writing: 'Thus we can see that to all eternity the whole issue of Christianity is found in the problems which the early Church faced, and if the intention which determined the classical formulations adopted at that time (although not necessarily the words) be denied, Christianity is certainly destroyed.'[111]

That is certainly a strong statement, and we may ask how it is reconciled with the somewhat naturalistic stress on process which is typical of Pittenger. More than once Pittenger insists that Jesus has his origin 'not by intrusion from outside but by emergence from within'.[112] But his understanding of emergence is taken from the philosophers of 'emergent evolution' who believed that in the evolutionary process there are points when something *novel* emerges, though it can also be seen to have been prepared by what has gone before. Jesus Christ is such an emergence, understood as 'a fresh intensification of the divine *nisus* in action in the creation'.[113] Jesus is not a visitor from another sphere, but neither is he just a product of evolution, originating entirely 'from below'. He is the expression of the Logos – 'the unique focus for a universal presence and operation',[114] the point at which 'the diffused activity of deity in and for the human race is concentrated . . . as a burning-glass concentrates the sun's rays'.[115] This language makes it clear that Pittenger, like his mentor Whitehead, has a strong doctrine of divine immanence, but Pittenger relates his 'panentheism' as Whitehead does not, to the Christian doctrine of the triune God: the Father is God above us, God transcendent; the Son or Logos is God with us, God concomitant; the Spirit is God in us, God immanent.

In his later and shorter book on christology, *Christology Reconsidered*, Pittenger relates his theology more directly to Whitehead and employs some of Whitehead's formidable battery of technical terms. We read: 'God sets before the historical existent Jesus his *initial aim*, through providing him with his vocational *lure*, and through the mutual *prehension* which is found when God and man are in openness and interpenetrate one with the other in love.'[116] I have italicized the technical terms in the sentence quoted and of course each of these terms is given quite a precise significance in the Whiteheadian philosophy. Whether they should be pressed into the service of theology is debatable, but one can say that Pittenger's broad appeal to process philosophy has been a clarifying exercise in christology and has shown that a fairly traditional understanding of Jesus Christ can still make sense in the context of modern thought.

Another important American contribution to christology has been made by Schubert Ogden (1928–   ). At the beginning of his theological career, Ogden was greatly attracted by the work of Bultmann, though not in an uncritical way. The result of his work on Bultmann was a book entitled *Christ without Myth* (1961) which Ogden himself summed up in two main theses. The first was: 'Christian faith is to be interpreted exhaustively and without remainder as man's original possibility of authentic existence, as this is clarified and conceptualized by an appropriate philosophical analysis.'[117] At this stage, Ogden did not hesitate to speak of his 'complete acceptance of Bultmann's demand for demythologizing and existential interpretation'.[118] But he realized that the position expressed in his first thesis could easily be misunderstood as a reduction of theology to anthropology, so we find him suggesting that theology needs some kind of metaphysical dimension as well as an existential one, and the metaphysics he suggests is process philosophy. Theology needs a philosophy which will adequately analyse and conceptualize divine existence as well as human existence. This resource, he claims, is supplied by process philosophy. 'We would suggest,' he says, 'that an adequate solution to our theological problem waits on an attempt to think through in an integral way the respective contributions of these two movements in contemporary philosophy'[119] – namely, existentialism and process philosophy. But whether these two very different ways of thinking can be 'integrated' must be very doubtful and, as we shall see, Ogden does not accomplish it.

The second main thesis in his christological reflection in *Christ without Myth* is this: 'Christian faith is always a possibility in fact because of the unconditioned gift and demand of God's love, which is the ever-present ground and end of all created things; the decisive manifestation of this divine love, however, is the event of Jesus of Nazareth, which fulfils and corrects all other manifestations and is the originative event of the Church and its distinctive word and sacraments.'[120] Here Ogden is recognizing that the Logos which was manifested in and through Jesus of Nazareth has spoken to human beings in other ways as well.

The next phase of Ogden's theological activity was rather different. He emerged in the 1960s as one of the most powerful critics of the so-called 'death of God' theology. In a collection of essays, *The Reality of God* (1966), Ogden offered a strong defence of theism, but it was not the traditional theism but what he called 'a neo-classical alternative' which has been developed in the work of Whitehead, Hartshorne and others. Ogden made large claims for this process philosophy: 'The ancient problems of philosophy have received a new, thoroughly modern treatment, which in its scope and depth easily rivals the so-called *philosophia perennis*.'[121] It was on the basis of process philosophy then that Ogden built his response to the 'death of God' writers. But it is significant that one of the essays in this volume, 'What Does It Mean to Affirm, "Jesus Christ Is Lord"?' reverts to a primarily existentialist way of thinking. Ogden organizes his essay around the assertion of Paul in I Cor. 8.4–6 that 'for us there is one God, the Father, from whom are all things and for whom we exist, and one Lord, Jesus Christ, through whom are all things and through whom we exist'. Ogden acknowledges that God is or exists, whether we think he does or not, but, in another sense, God exists *for me*, and he reminds us of Luther's existentialist or even subjectivist statement that 'the trust and the faith of the heart alone make both God and an idol . . . that to which your heart clings and entrusts itself is, I say, really your God'.[122]

For Ogden, God the Father and Jesus Christ the Lord are alike 'that to which the heart clings and entrusts itself'. The two descriptions have the same existential significance, the Son is not even subordinate to the Father but is the re-presentation in a human life of the God of the covenant, the God whom Ogden often describes by the expression 'boundless love'. So he can say very much in the manner of Bultmann, 'The human word that speaks to men in the event of Jesus, and thence in the kerygma and sacraments of the Church, is the same word always addressed to them in God's original revelation.'[123]

So while process philosophy has been important for Ogden's doctrine of God, his christology has drawn almost entirely on the existentialist approach. This continues to be true in a later book which he devoted specifically to the christological question – *The Point of Christology* (1982). Here he states: 'The point of christology is an existential point. Its assertion about who Jesus is, is even more fundamentally an assertion about who we are.'[124] He reminds us of Bultmann's view[125] of the 'I am' sayings in John's gospel, namely, that the true subject of these sentences is not the 'I' but the descriptive phrase. For instance, 'I am the light of the world' should be read, 'The light of the world – it is I'. The sayings do not answer the question 'Who is Jesus?' but a series of highly existential or soteriological questions – 'What is the light of the world?' and so on. Similarly he points out that according to the form critics, the gospel tradition tells us not who Jesus *was* in a historical sense, but who he *is* in his existential significance for us in the present. I hardly need to say that Ogden is happy with Melanchthon's statement, '*Hoc est Christum cognoscere, beneficia eius cognoscere*',[126] though we saw reason to think that the matter cannot just be left there. This could have been the point at which Ogden might have introduced some of the concepts of process philosophy, perhaps on lines similar to what we met in Pittenger, but he may be right not to 'mix' his conceptualities, or it may be that, like Bultmann in his unwillingness to shore up faith with historical research, Ogden fears to infringe the principle of *sola gratia* – something which he has accused the present writer of doing.[127]

Ogden does in fact agree with Bultmann that it is probably impossible and in any case unnecessary to accumulate historical information about Jesus. The history has been swallowed up in the existential significance. Ogden's masterstroke at this point is to supply the information that the great champion of the historical study of Jesus, Harnack, wrote his dissertation for habilitation in 1874 on the topic *Vita Jesu scribi nequit*.

Returning to the British scene, we attend now to the work of John Robinson (1919–83). Robinson acquired fame through his popular paperback *Honest to God* (1963) which was a critique of the image of God commonly held among churchpeople – an image in which God's transcendence of the world is exaggerated to the virtual exclusion of any sense of his immanence, so that he is a God 'up there' or 'out there', not a God 'in the midst'. Four years later, Robinson published his *Exploration into God*, a constructive sequel to the earlier book in which he now advocated a form of 'panentheism'. But if one tries to rethink a doctrine so central as the doctrine of God in Christian faith, there are bound to be repercussions on other doctrines, and not least on christology. So already in *Honest to God*, Robinson found himself also criticizing the popular incarnational christology of the Church of England. It had led, he believed, into a widespread docetism. (Readers will remember that Bishop Gore had said much the same thing in the 1890s.) Jesus was also a figure from 'out there', he had come from a heaven in which he pre-existed, sojourned for a brief time on earth, and then returned to the realm from which he had come. No doubt Robinson tended to caricature the popular view of Jesus as 'God dressed up' to look like a human being, but equally there is no doubt that there was a good deal of validity in his criticism, and the genuine humanity of Jesus had been obscured in spite of the quest of the historical Jesus and in spite of the Reformation and in spite of the carefully balanced orthodox teaching that Jesus Christ is consubstantial with us in his humanity, just as much as he is consubstantial with the Father in his divinity. If the idea of the God-man seems incredible in the twentieth century, this is in considerable measure due to distorted teaching on the part of the church.

It was ten years after *Honest to God* that Robinson published a full-length work on christology, entitled very significantly, *The Human Face of God*. I think one could also say that this was the most important book on christology to appear in Britain since Baillie's *God Was in Christ*, a quarter of a century earlier.

A major purpose of Robinson was to reawaken as far as he could the long lost sense of the humanity of Jesus Christ, his full sharing of our human condition. So not only does the word 'human' appear in the title of Robinson's book, the word 'man' appears in the titles of six out of the seven chapters – 'Our Man', 'A Man', 'The Man', 'Man of God', 'God's Man', 'Man for All'. It is as if the humanity of Jesus Christ is to be studied from every possible angle. Only so, Robinson believed, can some *rapport* be established between Christ and the people of the Western countries in our time. It is not only God who has been removed to the perimeters of life or beyond, the same fate has been suffered by Christ. It cannot be assumed that Christ encounters us with the 'existential question', for to a great many people, he is not a real person, certainly not an important one. Thus Robinson, rightly, I think, and in agreement with many theologians writing on christology in recent times, stresses the full humanity of Christ, even overstresses it (if that is possible) as a corrective against its long neglect and the false supernaturalism which is still so common within the churches. But it is important to notice that there is one chapter of the book in the title of which the word 'man' does not appear – the chapter entitled 'God for Us'. Robinson had a complex mind in which the new and the traditional were both represented and both had a secure place. Sometimes the new, even the sensational and ephemeral, seemed to captivate him; at other times a more conservative attitude, especially in regard to the Bible, made itself obvious. It certainly was his intention to affirm no less concerning Jesus Christ than he believed that the New Testament affirms. 'I am wishing to affirm Jesus as the Son of God as the New Testament speaks of him, as the one who was called at his baptism and vindicated at his resurrection to *be* God's decisive word to men, the embodiment of his nature and the enactment of his will.'[128] The determination of Robinson to affirm what he believed to be essential in the biblical and patristic tradition came out clearly some years after *The Human Face of God* in his sharply hostile criticism of the English symposium *The Myth of God Incarnate* (1977), in which some of the contributors were frankly reductionist or were even ready to dispense with 'incarnation'. Robinson had already anticipated their position in his own christology. Incarnation does not necessarily mean the pre-existence of a supernatural being who, at a certain moment of time, takes flesh. 'I believe,' wrote Robinson, 'that the word can just as truly and just as biblically (in fact, more truly and more biblically) be applied to another way of understanding it. This is: that one who was totally and utterly a man – and had never been anything other than a man or more than a man – so completely embodied what was from the beginning the meaning and purpose of God's self-expression (whether conceived in terms of his Spirit, his Wisdom, his Word, or the intimately personal relation of Sonship) that it could be said and had to be said of that man, 'He was God's man' or 'God was in Christ' or even that he *was* 'God for us'.[129] It is also the case that Robinson anticipated the interpretation which James Dunn gave to the Christ-hymn of Philippians 2, an interpretation which does not entail pre-existence. 'Jesus was not, I believe, for Paul . . . a divine being veiled in flesh or one who stripped himself of supernatural attributes to become human; he was a man who by total surrender of his own gain or glory was able to reveal or "unveil" the glory of God as utterly gracious, self-giving love.'[130] These last words, of course, remind us of another phrase, already used in *Honest to God*, and central to Robinson's understanding of Jesus, a phrase that had been impressed upon him by his reading of Bonhoeffer: the man for others.

Robinson's christology is not readily classified, and there is no single set of philosophical concepts which articulates it. Alistair Kee shows through a careful study of Robinson's doctoral thesis that the personalist philosophy of Martin Buber made a profound impression on him and in some respects remained an important influence.[131] At the time of *Honest to God*, the thought of Paul Tillich was in the ascendant. In his christology, Robinson seems to have felt the attraction of process philosophy, though he does not entirely accept it. This attraction is shown not only by his frequent quoting of and high praise for Norman Pittenger (he describes Pittenger's *The Word Incarnate* as 'one of the great books in this field') but equally by his stress on the growth and emergence of Jesus as the Christ within the temporal process. There was nothing 'ready-made' about Jesus, as there might be if he had 'dropped in' from another sphere. But Robinson bases himself on the biblical testimony, rather than on any philosophy. 'It is noteworthy that the epistle to the Hebrews, which is the only New Testament document to refer to Jesus' perfection, always uses of him the verb "perfected", never the adjective "perfect".'[132]

In concluding this chapter, we may note that as the twentieth century draws to its close, the debate about the person of Jesus, reopened by the Enlightenment, shows no sign of flagging. Though some lament that he has become irrelevant in the world of today, there are still plenty of theologians bringing fresh knowledge and fresh exertions of thought to bear on the question, 'Who really is Jesus Christ for us today?' Having, we hope, learned something from both the strengths and weaknesses of christological reflection from the Enlightenment down to our own time, let us now address the question for ourselves.

PART THREE

'Who Really Is Jesus Christ for Us Today?'

15

What Would Be Required in a Christology Today

In the preceding chapters, we have followed a long path on which we have had to take note of a quite bewildering variety of responses provoked through the centuries by the figure of Jesus Christ. Yet it has all been preparation for the decisive question that now faces us – what do we make of Jesus Christ in our time? We have gone back to the original Christ-event, to the earliest testimonies concerning a somewhat obscure figure who taught in the context of the beliefs and expectations of Judaism and aroused so much opposition that he was put to death; and we saw how in the succeeding centuries there arose the 'classical christology' that held sway in the Christian church for many centuries and is still the official teaching of most of the churches today. Then we saw how this carefully wrought structure was hit by the tidal wave of the Enlightenment. Quite suddenly, everything was placed in doubt. If we take the work of Reimarus, the so-called 'Wolfenbüttel fragments', as, shall we say, a kind of religious manifesto of the Enlightenment, then we see the extent to which the traditional christology was being challenged. The witness of the New Testament was read in terms of a naturalistic interpretation, the figure of Jesus was depicted not as a moral and religious leader but as a failed political revolutionary, the origins of the church were seen not in a saving mission but in fraud and deception.[1] Of course, Reimarus represents only the angry initial outburst against the long story of intellectual oppression. The more considered responses followed – not less radical than Reimarus, but more carefully thought out and not merely negative. I mean the story that we traced in the middle chapters of this book, the criticisms of Kant, Schleiermacher, Hegel, Strauss, Ritschl, Harnack, Troeltsch and all the others. Christology was into a new era, and we ourselves are still in that era. As Hans Küng has remarked, 'The christological debate that has persisted since the dawn of the modern age has not yet been resolved.'[2]

To return to my metaphor, the tidal wave struck and seemed to be sweeping everything away, but just as happens with tidal waves in real life, so with this metaphorical one, attempts at reconstruction began almost at once. People could not go back to the pre-Enlightenment mentality, apart from those discredited groups that we call 'fundamentalists'. Yet probably to most people it seemed that Christianity was something so precious that it could not be allowed to perish. And although Christianity has shown a steady decline in the two and a half centuries or so since the Enlightenment, there are still many people who think it is too precious to be abandoned and who look for ways of reconstructing belief. Those thinkers whom I mentioned – Kant and many of those who came later – were certainly stern critics of much that had come down from the past, but one can only be impressed at the astonishing wisdom and ingenuity of their efforts to present Jesus Christ and his message in ways that can still speak convincingly. We have surely had ample evidence of that in our studies. To quote Küng again: 'Whoever (as often still happens) sees in the development of the modern conception of Christ since the Enlightenment mere apostasy not only undervalues the fertile new impulses that emerged here, but also fails to appreciate the many flashbacks that are made to the representations of Christ from earlier ages.'[3]

So that Christ-event of almost two thousand years ago is still making its impact felt, and those who are aware of this are still compelled to ask the question about the person who was at the centre of the event. But they can ask the question and likewise formulate any answers to the question only in the language and conceptuality of today. That is why at the beginning of this third part of the book stands the question that Bonhoeffer was asking in prison in Berlin: 'Who really is Jesus Christ for us today?'

As a first step toward seeking an answer to the question, we have to ask ourselves: In what respects would a modern or post-Enlightenment christology differ from the classical christology that held sway during the seventeen centuries or thereabout of Christendom? I think there are at least five ways in which a modern statement would differ from the traditional ones.

1. First, there is the *historical* question. From the patristic age to the Reformation and even beyond, it was assumed that we have reliable, even perhaps infallible, historical knowledge about Jesus, especially in the four gospels. No attempt was made to distinguish in the records history from legend, or either of these from mythology – indeed, it would have been considered improper or heretical to suggest that parts of the

gospels are legendary or mythological. In the gospels, miracles are related in a matter-of-fact way, as if they were events of the same order as such everyday happenings as crossing the lake or entering a city. In the Apostles' Creed, as has often been pointed out, visible historical events in the career of Jesus are put in the same sequence as mythological or supernatural events: he 'was conceived by the Holy Ghost, born of the virgin Mary, suffered under Pontius Pilate, was crucified, dead and buried; he descended into hell; the third day he rose again from the dead, he ascended into heaven and sitteth on the right hand of God, the Father almighty'. Yes, we can *picture* it all (and mediaeval artists did picture it all in a wonderful way, even the descent into hell) but our picture is partly factual, partly imaginary. In the modern age, we cannot shut our eyes to distinctions which people of former times did not make or, at least, did not clearly make.

Again, no attempt was made to compare the historical trustworthiness of the various New Testament writers. Although, as we noted,[4] John's gospel was quite early considered a 'spiritual' gospel and different from the others, it was esteemed no less than the synoptics as a record of what Jesus had actually done, and likewise the sayings which John attributes to Jesus were regarded as *ipsissima verba* of the Lord.

That situation which lasted through all the time that produced the great patristic, mediaeval and Reformation treatments of christology no longer obtains. Reimarus' reinterpretation of the gospels was, historically, wide of the mark, but it signalled a new era of freedom and even scepticism in the critical study of the foundation documents of Christian faith. For more than two hundred years now, generations of critical scholars have given meticulous attention to this slim collection of documents that we call the New Testament. They have been trained not only in theology but, to varying degrees, in linguistic studies, in the history of cultures and religions, in psychology, sociology, anthropology, in literary forms, and no doubt in many other matters besides. Never, we may suppose, has such a small volume of material been subjected to such a close and long continued scrutiny, so that there can be scarcely a sentence or even a word that has not been weighed and pondered many times over. This fact alone is a tribute to the impression which the New Testament has made and the importance which is attached to it. Perhaps it is also the case that the sheer concentration of attention on these writings has led to the setting of impossibly high standards for their historical credibility. Even the most searching cross examinations in a court of law could not have been more thorough.

So where do we stand now? After these two or three centuries of close analysis, what if anything can we still believe with any confidence about the formative events at the beginning of Christianity? Has the record been completely eroded? I doubt if any responsible scholar today would go quite as far as that; the belief that the figure of Jesus is a mythical invention was indeed held by a few writers at the end of the nineteenth century, but is not taken seriously any longer. At an early stage in our inquiry, we noted that E. P. Sanders has claimed that there are a few basic historical facts about Jesus that can be regarded as certain (to the extent that anything can be 'certain') and we found an interesting confirmation of this in the earliest written evidence about Jesus, the letters of Paul, which mention a very similar series of facts about Jesus.[5] Sanders, moreover, is willing to concede 'probability' to many other stories which are told about Jesus in the New Testament. We are not entirely destitute of historical material, even if we have much less than was once believed. The question for us is whether we have enough that is still reliable.

But that question forces us to look at a prior question. Even if some historical information about Jesus is available, does the theologian really need it? Does he even need to know that Jesus in fact existed? Or can one get by with a purely ideal or mythological Christ? As we have seen, different answers have been given to this question. Kant claimed that we need no empirical example of the archetype of a life well pleasing to God, because we already have it *a priori* in the practical reason. Strauss, though he believed that Jesus had been a real figure of history, thought that he had pretty well destroyed the record of his life as we find it in the gospels, but that from the point of view of dogmatics, this made no difference. Among recent writers, Bultmann, Tillich and Ogden try to make themselves independent of questions of historical fact. But are they more deeply involved than they are willing to admit?

This whole nest of questions concerning the historical Jesus is still with us, and will call for some decisions before a contemporary christology can be worked out.

2. Where does christology begin? This is not just a matter of indifference, for in any inquiry the starting-point at once sets up a perspective, and even if one is considering the same phenomena, they may appear very differently according as one proceeds to examine them from one side or another. Not only is this so, certain value-judgments are also involved. What we put in the forefront of a theory or interpretation usually gets more attention than what only gets introduced subsequently.

We have noted several times that one way of classifying christologies is to divide them into those which begin 'from below' (as the current jargon expresses it), that is to say, from the humanity of Jesus Christ, and those which begin 'from above', that is to say, from his origin in God. The classical christology was a christology 'from above'. In the Nicene creed, we affirm of Jesus Christ that he is 'the only Son of God, eternally begotten of the Father, God from God, Light from Light, true God from true God, begotten, not made, of one Being with the Father'. Only after that exalted confession of his deity do we go on to say that 'he came down from heaven; by the power of the Holy Spirit he became incarnate of the virgin Mary, and was made man'. In the great musical settings of the Mass, the dramatic moment is the *'descendit'*, 'he came down', when there is a pause in the music and everyone bows or kneels. It takes a long time to get to the *'homo factus est'*, 'he was made man', and when we do get there, the humanity seems very much in second place after the glories of the pre-incarnate Logos. Hence the complaints of Bishop Gore and Bishop Robinson of an unconscious docetism in the churches. Hence also the determination of many contemporary theologians to break away from the traditional pattern and to begin their expositions of the person of Christ from an unequivocal affirmation of his complete humanity. We have seen this determination at an early stage of post-Enlightenment christology in the work of Schleiermacher, and today it is almost universal. One has only to mention Rahner, Pannenberg, Robinson as representative of a very broad agreement that christology must begin from the humanity that makes Christ consubstantial with ourselves, in the language of Chalcedon.

Apart from anything else, this is something that is demanded by the teaching situation in which the church currently finds itself. We live in a secular age, when the very word 'God' has become elusive for many people. How then can one hope to speak intelligibly of Jesus Christ if one begins by talking about his coming from God or identifying him with the divine Logos? But there is more to it than just the practical demands of the educational situation. If there is any truth in the idea of incarnation, then this must mean meeting people where they are, and in a secular age that means meeting them on the level of their everyday humanity. Perhaps they do not think very much about God or have much understanding of God-talk, but they have some understanding of humanity and even of the mystery of humanity, and if Jesus Christ is to be meaningful in such a situation, it will be as one who shares in humanity. Let us not be intimidated either by murmurings about adoptionism. In demanding that christology takes its departure from the human Jesus, one is simply going back to its original path in the earliest days of Christianity. Let us recall Peter's preaching: 'This Jesus whom you crucified, God has made both Lord and Christ' (Acts 2.36). This is an important and essential part of the kerygma but, as I have said more than once, it is not a complete christology. To say that a christology for the present day must *begin* from the humanity of Christ is not to decide in advance that it cannot go any further.

3. A third point to be borne in mind in the construction of a contemporary christology is the problem of metaphysics. The classical christology, both in the creeds and formulae of the church and in theological discussion, was strongly metaphysical in character. Its terminology, even in creeds

recited in the public liturgy, introduced technical philosophical terms such as *ousia*, 'being', *homoousios*, 'of the same being', *physis*, 'nature', *hypostasis*, 'subsistence'. I did in fact offer some justification for the use of such language at the time when Christianity was spreading through the Hellenistic world.[6] But that particular language, derived from Greek sources, has of course long ceased to be the universal language of learning that it once was. Nowadays, new philosophical terminologies have taken its place, and we have in fact seen how some of these new ways of speaking and thinking have been used in christology – idealism by the Hegelians, process philosophy by Pittenger, existentialism by Bultmann, and so on. I believe myself that some appropriate philosophical conceptuality and language does have its place in the theological discussion of christological problems. We cannot evade the hard questions by saying as Melanchthon did that to know Christ is to know his benefits. Metaphysics or ontology is indispensable if one is going to give an account of Jesus Christ that is intellectually well-founded. But we cannot forget that the New Testament managed to say all the important things about Jesus Christ without getting into the niceties of metaphysical discussion. We have to remember also that in our own age metaphysics has become unpopular and suspect even among philosophers, and that a heavy involvement in metaphysics could be more of a hindrance than a help in seeking to communicate the significance of Jesus Christ. In particular, one has got to recognize that there are limits to what can be discussed, and avoid becoming merely speculative or getting lost in scholastic distinctions, as has happened quite often in the past, and even the not so distant past. Metaphysics or ontology in some form or another is not finally dispensable in any adequate christology – we agreed on that for reasons discussed very near the beginning of this book.[7] But we have seen that even in the modern age there have been theologians who have allowed themselves to be drawn into abstruse speculative questions which really cannot be answered and, even if they could, would not yield knowledge of any importance. So we have to remain on guard against what might be called the temptations of an academic imperialism. I am opposed to every kind of anti-intellectualism and every attempt to short-circuit difficult problems, but I recognize that in the long run our interest in Christ must not be separated from his 'benefits' or turned into a game in which we guess at his inner constitution.

4. A fourth point concerns the relation of Jesus Christ to the human race as a whole – the question of his benefits seen from a different angle. What relation does he have to people living today, almost two thousand years after his birth? The classical christology did make some attempts to come to grips with this question, but not, I would say, successfully. Sometimes it was believed that just by assuming humanity in Jesus, the

eternal Word had more or less automatically reversed the effects of sin and restored to the whole race its integrity. This seems to me a quasi-magical way of understanding the matter, and I do not think it would be unfair to question whether such a view must not be attributed to the great Athanasius in his teaching that the coming of Christ was like the return of someone whose portrait had once been painted on a panel but has been obliterated, and is now restored.[8] Sometimes theories of atonement have been taught with such emphasis on the 'objective' character of what was done that it becomes, in Baillie's phrase,[9] a transaction carried out behind our backs. We have seen that Barth sometimes talks in this way, though he can speak in other ways as well. Such language may not be magical, but it is legal or forensic, and, above all, it is impersonal. These traditional ideas are not likely to commend themselves today, but they have been very influential in the past and have in some cases been taught by highly respected theologians.

Similarly, the concept of *anhypostasia* can be criticized not only as a confused product of over exuberant metaphysical speculation, but also as a most inadequate attempt to speak of the relation of Jesus Christ to the human race. According to this concept, Jesus Christ was 'man' in a generic sense without being 'a man', a human person or individual human being. But surely this is word-spinning, and I do not think that it is compatible with the belief that Jesus truly was a man, consubstantial with the human race.

So in this whole area the classical ideas need to be rethought, even in some cases discarded. The traditional teaching does not give any satisfactory answer to the question, 'How is it possible for this person, Jesus Christ, to have a vital significance or a saving significance for human beings living many centuries after his time in different parts of the planet? How is it possible for him to be a 'life-giving spirit' (as Paul expressed it) or the 'representative man'? We may hope that new understandings of interpersonal relations and new conceptions of representation may help us to work out a more satisfactory answer to such questions than has been offered in the traditional theologies.

5. As the fifth point, we have to ask what we can say nowadays about the supposedly unique place of Jesus Christ in the history of God's dealings with his creatures. What does it mean to say that he is 'the only Son of God'? Though indeed Jesus Christ occupies a unique and central place in the Christian religion, there are many other religions in the world and many other 'saviour figures', if I may use that expression. Christians, of course, have always been aware that there are other faiths – as Paul said, 'there are many gods and many lords' (I Cor. 8.5). From the beginning, Christians were aware of the alternatives, Judaism on the one hand and paganism on the other. But Judaism, it was supposed, had been

superseded, while pagan idolatry was supposed to be nothing but ignorance and sin. So there was no problem in claiming that in Jesus Christ alone is there a true self-communication of God.

Today that situation has completely changed. We realize that the range and variety of religions throughout the world is far greater than was imagined in the early centuries or even two hundred years ago. We even think it possible that in this vast universe there may be a multitude of alien cultures in which there is faith and therefore there have been mediators of faith. We recognize too that many of the non-Christian religions which we do know on earth have profound spiritual and ethical content, and hold out ways of life that are believed and experienced by millions to be ways of salvation. Many Christians today would be unwilling to dismiss these non-Christian ways as mere error, though some still hold to the old exclusive view. But increasingly, polemic or indifference has been replaced by dialogue, in which affinities and differences are discussed in a spirit of mutual respect.

But what are the consequences of this for the understanding among Christians of Jesus Christ? Can one still speak of him as the 'only Son of God' (Nicene creed) or claim that in him alone there is salvation? At least since the time of Troeltsch and his critique of the 'absoluteness' of Christianity,[10] there has been an urgent need to look again at such questions. Do Christians really need to use exclusive language about Christ? Norman Pittenger, whose views we discussed above,[11] did not hesitate to say that the difference between Jesus and all other human beings is a difference of degree, not of kind.[12] There is nothing terribly startling about this, or even unorthodox, for if the difference is one of kind rather than degree, then I think we have fallen into docetism, whatever we may say. But this opens the way to a more affirmative attitude to the non-Christian faiths. It does not, however, depend directly on Pittenger's general christology, and not specifically on his allegiance to Whitehead's philosophy. Virtually all modern theology has abandoned the idea of sudden irruptions from outside (the old supernaturalism or God's action 'vertically from above', in Barth's phrase) and sees things happening as gradual processes, though not without critical moments. If incarnation is a process and not an instantaneous happening to be dated to 25 March 4 BC or thenabouts, the notion of degrees of incarnation, even in the personal growth and development of Jesus, has some probability.

I have now listed the five points at which, I believe, we have to follow a different course from the classical christology if we are to answer the question, 'Who really is Christ for us today?' But how different is that course? How different is the answer? When we have completed the task that is still before us, I think we must face these questions too. They are of course part of a larger question which lies far beyond the scope of this book. That is the question, 'Is Christianity one thing?' Perhaps that is putting the question somewhat crudely. I mean, is there a unitary religion, faith or movement, called Christianity, having its origin in the life and teaching of Jesus and continuing with a recognizable identity to the present day? This is the kind of question with which Stephen Sykes dealt in his book *The Identity of Christianity*. At any rate, in fairness to my readers, I think the question has to be asked at the end of our inquiry whether the understanding of Christ at which we arrive is continuous with the catholic tradition.

16

The Historical Question

We have seen that anyone who would think or write about christology today must face the considerable disarray that has arisen over the historical question. What do we know with reasonable certainty about the historical figure Jesus of Nazareth? And how much do we need to know in order to evaluate the claims that have been made for him?

We begin with the basic question, 'Did Jesus ever exist?' The question was never asked until modern times, when a handful of writers have sought to show that the figure of Jesus is a product of the mythologizing imagination. Among them were Arthur Drews (1865–1935) who claimed that the figure of Jesus had developed out of the cult of a sun-god;[1] and the Marxists Albert Kalthoff (1850–1906) and Karl Kautsky (1854–1938) who believed that Jesus was a mythical figure embodying the longings of the oppressed underclass of the Roman Empire.[2] But these Christ-myth theories have virtually disappeared among serious scholars. Despite the comparative obscurity of his life, one can be as sure that Christ really existed as much as one can be sure that other remembered figures of the remote past have existed. The main evidence is the existence of the Christian church before our eyes, with a history going back to the first century. In words of John Knox, 'The principal argument the historians have for the existence of Jesus is the Church's prior knowledge of it – that is, a memory of Jesus which can be traced back continually through the centuries to the time when the Church first emerged into consciousness of itself.'[3] The church, of course, very early began to produce the writings which eventually were collected into the New Testament, so that we have written testimonies to the existence of Jesus, the oldest of them dating from within twenty years of his death. It is incredible that these testimonies could have been hoaxes, especially when we remember that they began as separate writings which were only gathered together long afterward. Historians usually add the evidence of a few non-Christian writers from the late first century or early second century – Josephus, Tacitus, Pliny, Suetonius, the Jewish Talmud.[4] These add nothing of substance to what we learn from the Christian sources, but some interest attaches to them because they do afford evidence that Jesus existed from writers who were either indifferent to Christianity or even hostile. So I think we can affirm with confidence that Jesus of Nazareth did live in the time of the Roman emperors Augustus and Tiberius, and I think we could add to the bare fact of existence that he was crucified, since this is mentioned in even the barest references, like that of Tacitus. It is no accident that in the creeds the words *sub Pontio Pilato*, 'under Pontius Pilate', are attached to the crucifixion, thus making the link between the Christ who is confessed and an identifiable moment in world-history.

But why is it important to insist on the real existence of Jesus? Would not the spiritual truth of Christianity remain intact even if Jesus were only an imagined figure, as indeed some of the idealist philosophers and theologians seemed to assert?[5] But the Christian claim is not simply that there is an ideal laid up in the heavens or an archetype imprinted in the structure of reason. Christianity differs from Platonism or from Kantianism not in upholding an ideal (which they also do) but in affirming that the ideal has been realized in history and embodied in an actual life. So we find Paul saying, 'Do not say in your heart, "Who will ascend into heaven?" (that is, to bring Christ down)' (Rom. 10.6). The Christian kerygma transfers the reality from heaven to earth. Christ is in the midst as the Man, the new Adam. This is surely an indispensable part of the Christian message. It requires as its minimal condition that Christ did exist as a human being, so the evidence that he did exist is not to be dismissed as merely trivial. I think Christianity needs more of a historical basis than just the assertion that Christ existed, but it certainly needs at least that much.

Why should we think that it needs more, and what grounds do we have for thinking that more is available? Bultmann is very sceptical about what can be known concerning the actual life (inward and outward), of Jesus and takes the view, as we have seen,[6] that it is enough to affirm the *dass*, the fact *that* Jesus lived (and was crucified), without asking about the *was*, *what* Jesus was in his own history. He thinks this was the view of Paul and John, who give adequate statements of the kerygma without becoming involved in the historical narration that we find in the synoptists. About Paul Bultmann says:

Paul proclaims the incarnate, crucified and risen Lord; that is, his kerygma requires only the 'that' of the life of Jesus and the fact of his crucifixion. He does not hold before his hearer's eyes a portrait of Jesus the human person, apart from the cross (Gal. 3.1), and the cross is not regarded from a biographical standpoint but as saving event. The obedience and self-emptying of Christ of which he speaks (Phil. 2.6–9; Rom. 15.3; II Cor. 8.9) are attitudes of the pre-existence and not of the historical Jesus . . . The decisive thing is simply the 'that'.[7]

Right away we see some things in this quotation with which we must disagree. In our study of Paul's christology in Chapter 3, we found persuasive the arguments of James Dunn (and John Robinson took a similar view) that the Christ-hymn in Philippians *does* refer to the obedience and self-emptying of the human, historical Jesus, and that so to read it produces a more economical and more persuasive interpretation than to bring in the conception of pre-existence. But, in a more general way, we have seen reason to suspect the emphasis on the *dass* in separation from the *was*, the 'that' torn away from the 'what', for what meaning can we give to the 'that' apart from the 'what'? Donald Baillie dealt with this point with plain common sense. It is not (as Bultmann held) the resurrection that primarily gives us the meaning of the cross; that meaning depends equally on the being of the one who was crucified.[8] After all, vast numbers of unfortunate people were done to death under Pontius Pilate and other tyrants of the Roman empire, but their crosses were not significant just from having happened. Their deaths would be significant only in relation to the antecedent lives.

If Bultmann's argument is unconvincing in the case of Paul, this is even more the case with John. For John does tell us something of the 'what'. 'John,' says Bultmann, 'gives all due emphasis to the humanity of Jesus, but presents none of the characteristics of Jesus' humanity which could be gleaned, for example, from the synoptic gospels.'[9] This is an opaque statement and would be difficult to square with what we have already seen of the teaching of John and the synoptics, when we were very attentive to Bultmann's own views on these writings.

But Bultmann has never been entirely negative on this matter of the 'what'. Though he has opposed any quest, new or old, for the historical Jesus, he has not denied that we can know something of the words and deeds of Jesus.[10] In fact, he gives his own summary of what we can know about the activities of Jesus, and Bultmann acknowledges that from these activities we can infer a few of his personal characteristics:

With a bit of caution, we can say the following concerning Jesus' activity. Characteristic for him are (1) exorcisms, (2) the breach of the sabbath commandment, (3) the abandonment of ritual purifications, (4) polemic against Jewish legalism, (5) fellowship with outcasts, such as publicans and harlots, (6) sympathy for women and children; it can also be seen (7) that Jesus was not an ascetic like John the Baptist, but gladly ate, and drank a glass of wine. Perhaps we may add (8) that he

called disciples and gathered about himself a small company of
followers – men and women.[11]

This brief list of eight historical characteristics of Jesus has some points
of resemblance to the two lists which we noted at a much earlier stage,
one based on Sanders' book *Jesus and Judaism* and the other extracted from
Paul's letters. There is more agreement between Sanders and Paul on the
content of such a list than there is between either of them and Bultmann,
but it is interesting that the quantity of material is about the same in each
case, suggesting that the amount of historical data about which we can
have reasonable certainty extends at the most to ten or twelve items. Does
a meagre list of the kind we are considering tell us enough about the
'what' of Jesus to make the 'that' identifiable, to give it some substance so
that it is not just the vague assertion that someone existed and was crucified, but we cannot say anything specific about that 'someone'?

As seems to be always the case in theology, and especially in
christology, we have to consider strong arguments on both sides of a
question, and then try to do justice to both. In the present case, we are
told by some scholars either that as a matter of fact we have only the
scantiest knowledge about Jesus or that as a matter of principle we do not
need to have such knowledge, but have only to affirm that he lived and
was crucified; while some other scholars tell us that this is inadequate and
we need to know something of the life and character of Jesus. To give a
concrete illustration of this clash, Kierkegaard made an often quoted
statement that if Jesus' contemporaries had left only the testimony, 'We
have believed that in such and such a year God appeared among us in the
humble figure of a servant, that he lived and taught in our community,
and finally died', it would have been more than enough. Against that, set
the view of Donald Baillie who denies that it would have been enough. He
denied it because we would need to know more about this person whose
life and death are mentioned to be able to judge on what grounds it was
claimed that he was God.

Kierkegaard, of course, was not influenced by the thought that we do
not in fact have much information about Jesus. He accepted the gospel
record as reliable, and even believed that Jesus himself had claimed to be
God. But on principle he held that all the historical information we could
possibly have about Jesus could not confirm such a claim, for it belongs to
a different realm of discourse. Kierkegaard went so far as to say that in
Jesus Christ God appeared 'in a strict incognito, an incognito impenetr-
able to the most intimate observation'.[12] This language of an 'incognito',
which was also taken up by Barth, was sharply criticized by Baillie. 'If no
revelation of the nature of God were to be found in the incarnate life, what
would be the gain of believing that God therein became man? If the

"divine incognito" remains in this extreme form, what saving virtue is there in the dogma of the incarnation? If there is no revelation, no "unveiling", of God in the human personality and career of Jesus, but only a "veiling"; if God in Christ is as much as ever a *deus absconditus*, not a *deus revelatus*; what are we the better of the coming of God in Christ?'[13]

Baillie, of course, would not deny that if God communicates himself through any finite entities, this must imply some 'veiling' of his infinite being. The root of the trouble may well be that Kierkegaard posited an 'infinite qualitative difference' between God and man, and I earlier expressed the suspicion, now perhaps being confirmed, that such a view of God makes impossible anything like an incarnation.[14] I wonder if Kierkegaard himself became aware of this, for in a late writing he modifies his position: 'The whole life of Christ would have been mere play if he had been incognito to such a degree that he was through life totally unnoticed – and yet in a true sense he was incognito.'[15] Barth too had modified his position from the one expressed in *The Epistle to the Romans* to the one he reached in *The Humanity of God*. The latter book allows for some affinity between God and man, and therefore for the possibility of something like incarnation. It does not, of course, do away with the ambiguity arising from the fact that any manifestation of the divine in the finite may remain unnoticed. As Barth pointed out, Jesus may be seen as simply the rabbi of Nazareth.[16] In the words of Matthew's gospel, 'flesh and blood' will not reveal anything more than flesh and blood, that is to say, the realm of the finite. But might it not be the case that a personal existence made to the image of God and having therefore some affinity to God might in the mysteries of love and obedience and faithfulness point us beyond the realm of flesh and blood?

About thirty years ago, when the demythologizing controversy was at its height, I was engaged in a detailed study of Bultmann's work, and not least this question about the need for some factual historical element in any adequate attempt to say who Jesus is or was. At that time I argued for what I called a 'minimal core of factuality'.[17] This would be not so much a short list of more or less indubitable facts as a more impressionistic picture of Jesus in which even legendary contributions might have a place in revealing something of what he was. I did claim that the existence before our eyes of the Christian community with its documents and traditions gives an 'overwhelming probability' to this picture prior to historical research. I found some support for this view in Althaus and Bornkamm, and though I did not know it at the time, I believe that just about then John Knox was thinking on similar lines, for he wrote very soon afterward his book, *The Church and the Reality of Christ* in which he spoke of the church's prior knowledge of Christ and its continuous memory of him. I would now, I think, avoid the expression 'core of factuality' since I believe that what concerns us is something more diffuse, something scattered through the various strands of the tradition. But from these strands a tolerably reliable picture can be constructed – as we have seen ourselves in considering Paul, the synoptists and the other New Testament witnesses. It falls far short of a 'biography' of Jesus but it is not negligible, and it has to be maintained alongside the 'that' if the latter is to be more than an empty assertion.

Let us now look more closely at a few specific historical assertions that seem to be of special importance for christology.

The first of these is the question of what is sometimes called the 'messianic consciousness' of Jesus. Older books of christology often had as their starting-point a chapter on Jesus' self-understanding. I suppose that very few contemporary writers on christology would follow that path. Investigators from Wrede to Bultmann have made out a strong case for believing that Jesus did not claim to be the messiah, and may even have actively discouraged any disciples or admirers who wanted to attach this title to him. But we have seen that the word 'messiah' was understood in more ways than one, and that it was in any case only one of several terms that came to be applied to Jesus. It may be, as Bornkamm suggests, that even in Jesus' lifetime people were speculating about who he was, and certainly after his death and resurrection he was called the messiah or Christ.[18] But it seems unlikely that Jesus himself laid claim to any honorific titles. If we follow the synoptic gospels, then what he proclaimed was not himself or his coming, but the imminent approach of the kingdom of God: 'Now after John was arrested, Jesus came into Galilee, preaching the gospel of God, and saying, "The time is fulfilled, and the kingdom of God is at hand; repent, and believe in the gospel' (Mark 1.14). Of course, one might say that if he felt himself called by God to proclaim the coming kingdom, then by implication he had a place in that kingdom as its proclaimer, even perhaps its founder. This is one possible way in which scholars have tried to bridge the gap between the historical Jesus who preached the kingdom, and the Christ of faith who was preached by the first Christian evangelists. It is the view that the kerygma concerning Christ was already implicit in the preaching of the kingdom of Jesus. But even if one could work out this complex relationship, it still would not throw light on Jesus' self-consciousness. We cannot say that he thought of himself as messiah or under any of the other titles that came to be applied to him. Perhaps none of them really fitted. Or perhaps, if we recall a speculation which came to our notice earlier, he believed that there was another figure, perhaps a supernatural figure, who was still to come and who would inaugurate the new age of the reign of God.[19]

This suggests another and more theological way of understanding the 'incognito'. Jesus obviously believed himself to have been called by God to announce the kingdom, he thought of himself as a son of God (though almost certainly not in the full sense which the expression came to have later), he spoke of God as a Father with whom he had an intimate relation. But he does not claim any grandiose title to express his relation to God or the kingdom, and may even have thought of himself as pointing forward to another than himself. I say that this gives a more theological meaning to the incognito. It reminds us that Israel looking back on its history understood itself as a non-people who had been called by God to become a people.[20] In the same way, Paul was to look back on Christ and his suffering, and see in him the wisdom of God, but a wisdom which chooses the weak and foolish things of the world for carrying out God's purposes. Historians may regret that Jesus had such a low profile and that we know so little about him. But is this not part of the revelation? This is how God works.

According to Aquinas, Jesus Christ had from the 'first instant of his conception' a full knowledge of God, including his own relation to God.[21] To believe this, I would say, would be utterly subversive of the true humanity of Christ. His knowledge of God and of himself in relation to God, if he was truly man, must have been what Thomas would call an 'acquired' knowledge, something learned through experience. It must have developed during his life, and not least in the formative years that are so important in the life of every human being. Luke's story about Jesus' getting lost in Jerusalem and then being found asking questions in the Temple is presumably a legend, but the point of it – 'Jesus increased in wisdom and in stature, and in favour with God and man' (Luke 2.52) – is an entirely accurate statement of what must have been going on in the so-called 'hidden years', and the growth in knowledge must have continued. While we cannot say that it ever reached the point when Jesus identified himself with a role designated by an expression such as 'messiah' or 'Son of Man', he must have reflected on what it meant for him to be a 'son' or agent of the Father in the proclaiming of the coming kingdom, though we cannot know exactly what he thought his relation to the Father was, and it does not seem to matter very much. What the disciples came to believe was that Jesus *is* the Christ, and also Lord, Son of God and so on, not that *he said he was* Christ, Lord etc. So we have to leave this question of Jesus' self-understanding as not clearly answerable, but this is not very important from a theological point of view.

However, if someone were to say that we just have no understanding at all of how Jesus thought of himself or of his message, I do not think that would be a probable judgment either. He was conscious of a vocation from God to proclaim the kingdom, and the record shows him as single-mindedly devoted to that vocation, even to the point at which it brought him to death.

This mention of the death of Jesus brings us to what is perhaps the most difficult of all the questions which need to be considered in relation to the historical problem. I have suggested that we need not bother ourselves too much whether Jesus ever claimed to be messiah or any other figure expected by the Jews at that time. But I do not think we can say that it does not matter how he understood his own death. Bultmann declares in one of his essays, 'The greatest embarrassment to the attempt to reconstruct a portrait of Jesus is that we cannot know how Jesus understood his end, his death.'[22] That embarrassment stands even for the very modest portrait or sketch which we have seen reason to believe is necessary for a theological account of Jesus. We have to know something about his death because that death on the cross came to be the centre of the church's proclamation of Jesus. From Paul right down to our own time, theologies of atonement have been built upon the cross. I have argued above that purely objective theories of atonement in which the men and women who are saved do not need to have any conscious awareness of the event – a transaction that goes on behind their backs, as Baillie put it – are quite inadequate, for atonement implies the reordering of personal relationships, and this is impossible without the conscious participation and consent of the persons involved. Now, if this is true of the Christians who experience salvation or the beginning of salvation through the cross of Christ, must it not be even more true of Christ himself? He is the central figure in what is going on, the mediator between God and the human race, and we can hardly suppose that he is unconscious of the meaning of the events in which he is involved. So we cannot avoid the question of how Jesus understood his own death. But is there any possibility of finding an answer?

The basic objective facts of the matter seem clear enough. As we have noted, the crucifixion of Jesus is just about as indubitable as the fact that he really did exist, and is often coupled with it.[23] At a certain point in his activity, Jesus appears to have decided to go up to Jerusalem. In the gospels, this is a dramatic moment which leads into the last act of the narrative, the passion, death and resurrection of Jesus. On the way to Jerusalem, Jesus tells the disciples that he will meet suffering and death in the city. When we considered these predictions, we saw that in all probability they are *vaticinia post eventum*, predictions put into the mouth of Jesus by the evangelists who knew what had been the outcome of his journey, and we rejected them mainly on the grounds that the detailed knowledge of the future attributed to Jesus is incompatible with an acknowledgment of his true humanity.[24] As we shall see in a moment, it is by no means certain that Jesus went up to Jerusalem knowing that he would die.

Was he then simply caught up in a chain of events outside his control?

Was his death something that came upon him simply through the machinations of his enemies? This is where we come up against the difficulty, for Christian theology and all the theories of atonement go on the assumption that his death was something that he freely accepted. Unless that death had a 'voluntary' character, it could not have the theological significance that has been claimed for it. The voluntary nature of his death is strongly asserted in the New Testament. He gives his life 'as a ransom for many' (Mark 10.45); he says, 'No one takes [my life] from me, but I lay it down of my own accord' (John 10.18); 'He offered up himself' (Heb. 7.27). But might not all of that language be the interpretation placed on his death by writers looking back from an interval of a good many years?

It is worth recalling at this point that Reimarus, who in the early days of Enlightenment criticism gave one of the most radical reinterpretations of the gospel story that have ever been made, claimed that Jesus went up to Jerusalem not to die but to raise a revolt against Roman rule. He was hailed by a crowd of supporters as a national hero when he made his entry into the city. His next step was to attempt to seize a public building, the Temple, following a pattern common among rebels. But he had overestimated his support among the populace. His followers faded away, he was arrested, tried, condemned and executed, and dies in disillusionment – 'My God, my God, why hast thou forsaken me?' (Mark 15.34). Like other attempts to turn Jesus into a political figure, that of Reimarus had to rely on a very selective treatment of the evidence, while his accusations of fraud against the apostles are mere speculations on his part. But his *Fragments* do have the effect of setting a question mark against the traditional gospel account of Jesus' last days or weeks. He reopened the questions of why Jesus went up to Jerusalem and how he understood the events that took place there.

It seems to me that we cannot be sure why Jesus was drawn to Jerusalem at the end of his career – and the main reason for this uncertainty is that probably Jesus himself was not entirely clear about the meaning of the step he was taking, or what the consequences would be. I do not think we can say, he went up to Jerusalem to die. Some scholars (Weiss, Schweitzer, perhaps also Jeremias) do seem to think that he did so, in the belief that his death would in some way hasten the coming of the kingdom of God.[25] Others (Bornkamm, Conzelmann) take the view that he went up to Jerusalem to confront the religious establishment with his message of the kingdom in the hope that even at that late hour they would hear the message and repent, or perhaps in the hope that the kingdom would break in at that time.[26] What seems to me decisive against the view that Jesus anticipated death on his journey to Jerusalem is the Gethsemane story. I have said already that by its very nature this story mustbe classified as legend. But I said it was 'true legend' in the sense that it embodies some memory that had survived in the tradition, the memory that Jesus had not, shall we say, thrown himself on death with the euphoria sometimes characteristic of a martyr, but had accepted it with reluctance. Human nature being what it is, and Jesus, as I have said again and again, being truly and fully human, I think he could only have gone to Jerusalem with some hope in his heart, very likely the hope that a last appeal to his opponents might awaken the desired response or, failing that, the hope that the apocalyptic kingdom would burst in in all its power.

Does this mean then that we abandon the traditional belief that Jesus' death had a voluntary character? No, for there is not a simple disjunction between 'throwing oneself on death' and suffering death at the will of others. There is another possibility, and it seems the most likely of all. Jesus may have set his face toward Jerusalem not meaning to die but hoping to convince the opposition, yet at the same time deeply aware of the danger of what he was doing and with the knowledge that death was a possible outcome. Am I indulging at this point in baseless psychologizing about Jesus? I do not think so. He knew as did every Jewish religious teacher that Jerusalem had a reputation for killing the prophets: 'O Jerusalem, Jerusalem, killing the prophets and stoning those who are sent to you!' (Luke 13.34). Just recently he had learned of the death of John the Baptist, and this must have suggested that he would suffer the same fate. So, although we must frankly say that we cannot know these things with certainty, the reconstruction offered here is far from improbable.

It is, however, enough to secure that voluntary element in the death of Jesus which seems to be important for the theological interpretation. There is an example from recent history which appears to me to provide an illuminating parallel. In the spring of 1968, Martin Luther King went to the city of Memphis to help resolve a bitter labour dispute with racial overtones. He did not go to Memphis to die, but in the hope that he could help to change people's minds there. As we all know, he was assassinated in the course of his visit, and many people looked on his death as a martyrdom. Though he had not gone there to die, and though his mind may well have been preoccupied with hopes for the future rather than with the prospect of death, he had known very well for a long time that death was a constant possibility so long as he continued to speak and work for his cause. In the case of Jesus, something similar must have been true. He was aware of the opposition and aware of the fate of the prophets, including John. He knew that if he crossed the Jordan into the remote areas to the east, he would be relatively safe.[27] But in fact he went up to Jerusalem.

Looking back on these events from an interval of several decades, the evangelists believed that they had taken place in accordance with God's plan for salvation, and so they believed also that Jesus was conscious of carrying out that plan, so they represent him as having predicted his death and as going knowingly to the cross. We have rejected this traditional account, on the grounds that it diminishes the humanity of Jesus by attributing to him a supernatural knowledge. But to reject the account of the synoptists at this point is certainly not to diminish the figure of Jesus himself – his stature is rather increased in a theological sense by recognizing the limits of his knowledge in virtue of his full humanity. This last point is well expressed by Raymond Brown:

> A Jesus who walked through the world knowing exactly what the morrow would bring, knowing with certainty that three days after his death his Father would raise him up, is a Jesus who can arouse our admiration, but still a Jesus far from us. He is Jesus far from a mankind that can only hope in the future and believe in God's goodness, far from a mankind that must face the supreme uncertainty of death with faith but without knowledge of what is beyond. On the other hand, a Jesus for whom the future was as much a mystery, a dread and a hope as it is for us, and yet at the same time a Jesus who would say, 'Not my will but yours' – this is a Jesus who could effectively teach us how to live, for this is a Jesus who would have gone through life's real trials. Then we would know the full truth of the saying, 'No man can have greater love than this – to lay down his life for those he loves' (John 15.13), for we would know that he laid down his life with all the agony with which we lay it down.[28]

We began this chapter by noting that critical scholarship has eroded much of the historical material of the New Testament. But we agreed that some minimum of factual history is needed in Christian theology, beyond the bare assertion that Jesus lived and was eventually crucified. In the limited areas which we have probed, we have found that historical criticism of the gospels is far from being merely negative. In fact, by pruning away the docetic tendencies that very early entered into the picture of Jesus, it has forced us to recognize that the one who confronts us in the gospels is no mythological demigod but a genuine human being in the fullest sense.

17

The Humanity of Jesus Christ

In the last chapter we have seen that although two hundred years of critical scholarship have led to a very different reading of the New Testament record from the one that was earlier accepted, it has certainly not destroyed that record or banished Jesus Christ to the realm of mythology, but has forced us to recognize that here we are confronted with a man, a human being of the same constitution as ourselves. It is obvious, of course, that there must have been something special about this man, to account for the fact that a person from such an obscure background rejected by his own society has risen to be the most influential person in a spiritual sense who has appeared in human history. But though he was obviously 'special', this does not separate him from the human race. As we have seen, he differs from other human beings in degree, not in kind. As far as his powers and limitations are concerned, they were of the same kind as belong to all of us. That very old christology of Paul which saw in Jesus the new Adam or new man and contrasted him with the first Adam of Hebrew mythology, the fallen man who failed to attain his stature as a man, already grasped the central point. We have seen that one of the demands on a contemporary christology is that it should begin in the same way as Paul, with an unambiguous recognition of the complete humanity of Christ. He is a man, indeed, we wonder if he is the Man. That is the way we are required to look on Jesus today, but it is also a return to the oldest way, not only to Paul's teaching about the first and last Adams but to that elusive phrase, the 'Son of Man', which appears in the very early tradition and then fades out.[1] Of course, it should be unnecessary to say that when the word 'man' is used here, it is the equivalent of the Hebrew *adam* and the Greek *anthropos*, and signifies a human being of either sex. Sexuality is an essential constitutive element in every human being, and Jesus was a man in the secondary sense that he was of the male sex. But I do not think that any theological importance attaches to this. Being human was essential to Jesus as the Christ, being male was, as far as I can see, contingent. But the question whether the Christ might have been a woman rather than a male human being is purely speculative and unanswerable, like Thomas' question whether the Father or the Holy Spirit might have become incarnate rather than the Son.

If we begin our christological reflection from the recognition that Jesus Christ was a man, a human being 'consubstantial' with ourselves, in the language of Chalcedon, then we have decided to follow a path which leads in the opposite direction from that of classical christology. The classical christology began from the divine Logos and asked the question in the form, 'How does God become man?' or 'How does the Word assume humanity?' Our question is rather, 'How does a man become God?' or 'How does a human life embody or manifest the divine life?' But finally I think one has to face both types of question. We have accepted that in the post-Enlightenment age we find good reasons for beginning with the humanity of Christ, but we certainly do not exclude the possibility or even the necessity of asking subsequently about the presence of God in this man. Likewise, in reverse order, Karl Barth discussed first the journey of the divine Son into the far country, but followed that up with the return of the Man (the 'royal man', he called him) from the far country to his home.

So we begin with the simple assertion that Jesus Christ was a man, a human being. But we would not have bothered to make this assertion or to speak of him at all unless we thought that there was something special about this man, that perhaps he is the Man, the archetype of humanity. These considerations point us to a prior question: 'Who or what is a man, a human being? Since we ourselves are human beings, I suppose we ought to know, but in fact the question who or what is a human being is one of the most difficult questions that there is, and it has been answered and still is being answered in a multitude of conflicting ways.

There is one conflict that stems from the Enlightenment itself, and has never been resolved. On the one hand, modern thought has downgraded the human race. It has stripped humanity of its claim to be a special creation of God and his special concern. It has exiled him from the centre of the universe to an obscure planet in an obscure corner. It has classed him with the animals and even with the plants and the bacteria. It has made him a part of nature and subjected him to the same kind of empirical studies that we employ for understanding other natural phenomena. That is one side of the picture.

But there is another side which looks contradictory. Kant, it will be remembered, singled out human autonomy as the central significance of the Enlightenment.[2] In course of time, Nietzsche drew the conclusion that the human race must now take over the functions once ascribed to God – the functions of governing this universe and shaping its future course. In two and a half centuries, the human race has vastly extended its powers until at last it seems that the dream of the builders of the Tower of Babel will be fulfilled: 'This is only the beginning of what they will do; and nothing that they propose to do will now be impossible for them' (Gen. 11.6). So if humanity has been in some respects downgraded, it has also been encouraged to think of itself as the highest being of which we have any knowledge and to be moving into an unlimited future in which the earth will be brought ever nearer to the heart's desire. So we find Iris Murdoch commenting thus: 'Our picture of ourselves has become too grand, we have isolated and identified ourselves with an unrealistic conception of will, we have lost the vision of a reality separate from ourselves, and we have no adequate conception of original sin.'[3] The criticism which she voices has not yet been generally accepted, but there is increasingly an anxiety for the future of the race and a corresponding disillusionment with secular 'progress'.

This anxiety is perhaps reflected in the fact that humanity itself has been increasingly the topic of philosophical reflection in recent decades. Is the human being simply a part of nature, to be understood exhaustively by the methods of empirical science, or are there some human characteristics that slip through this net, so to speak? Is there something new and distinctive in the human being that forbids us to regard him or her as no more than a highly complicated animal or has the appearance of the human race – 'hominization', as it is sometimes called – signalled the emergence of a new type of creature? Just as I shied away from the doctrine that there is an 'infinite qualitative difference' between God and man, so I would not want to urge some absolute difference between man and the lower animals. It is a difference of degree rather than of kind, just as we said in the case of the difference between Jesus Christ and other human beings, but a difference of degree can be quite decisive, and may be so great as to be virtually a difference in kind. The human race is linked to other living things and to the material cosmos in general in innumerable ways. It has arisen out of the cosmos in the process of evolution. All these living things share the same material basis and are subject to the same basic laws of nature. As investigators such as Skinner and Lorenz have shown, there are many parallels between human behaviour and animal behaviour. Yet when all this has been said, a yawning gap remains between man and even the highest of the animals. Kant was correct in seeing the distinctive characteristic of the human being in autonomy or freedom. The human being is shaped not just by the forces that act upon him in the natural environment, but by his own choice of goals. He is never set free from these environmental forces, but increasingly he has risen above them and achieved some control over them. Increasingly he has begun to make humanity according to his own ideas and values, or, to put it in another way, he has increasingly become a creature of history rather than of nature.

So we find that even as one powerful current of thought in the past two hundred years or so has been busily trying to incorporate humanity into the scheme of the natural sciences as one more natural phenomenon, this has called forth opposition in the form of another stream – or rather, several streams – which have emphasized what is distinctive in the human being. In some cases, these new philosophical anthropologies have been reacting so strongly that they have exaggerated the distinctiveness of the human to the point of cutting the links with the rest of the cosmos, and ending up with a dualism. Although these new doctrines about the nature of a human being have in some cases been reaching back to the past in the hope of recovering a religious view, others are quite secular or even atheistic. They are all agreed that with the emergence on this planet of *Homo sapiens*, a new type of entity has appeared, with limited freedom, intelligence, even conscience, and that for the proper understanding of this human reality, we need to use new personal categories and should not attempt a reductionist inclusion of the human within categories that have their validity only at lower levels of being.

The term that is commonly used for this distinctive characteristic of human beings to rise above the tyranny of natural laws and to form themselves is 'transcendence'. The term was for a long time used in relation to God, and referred to his 'superiority' (the metaphor of height is unavoidable in this way of talking of God's relation to the world) over the world. God, it was believed, possessed a different kind of being from the creaturely being of the world and the items within the world. Now, when the word 'transcendence' is used in relation to the human being, there is still something of this sense of being exalted above the natural world – and, of course, the rise of science in the past two or three centuries has, as we have seen, had the ambiguous effect of promoting the belief that humanity itself is part of nature and yet at the same time encouraging us to think that we are masters of the universe and eventually destined to control it. But the difference between that older meaning of 'transcendence', derived from theology, and its more recent anthropological connotations is that in the older usage it was understood in a static sense. God's transcendence and later man's transcendence were understood as a permanent relation of superiority over the world. In the more recent usage, 'transcendence' is taken in a much more dynamic sense – certainly when it is used of the human being, and, as we shall see in the next chapter, it can have an analogously dynamic sense when used of God. Etymologically, to 'transcend' means to climb over, to cross a boundary.

The language is still metaphorical or quasi-metaphorical, but the metaphor is slightly different. It is not the metaphor of being above or being in control, but the metaphor of advancing into new areas, perhaps overcoming obstacles in the way. We could also say that it is moving from one horizon to another. Wherever one stands, there is a horizon at the limit of vision, but as one advances toward that horizon, the horizon itself recedes. It is not a barrier, but discloses new horizons beyond. So the notion of transcendence seems to contain not just the idea that one can move out from where one happens to be, but that there is no limit. Here there may be at least the germ of a religious element, something like the 'sense and taste of the infinite' in Schleiermacher's language. Where could a finite human being get the idea of the infinite? I suppose one might say that one's sense of one's own finitude logically implies the idea of infinity. But this logical relation would present us only with a static infinite, a mere abstraction. Active transcendence is different. The infinite which it seeks exercises an attraction, perhaps on the basis of an already existing affinity. If there were an 'infinite qualitative difference' between God and man, God would be no more than a static infinite logically deduced. We shall return to these difficult questions when we look more closely at what we mean by 'spirit'.[4]

The flourishing in recent decades of these philosophical anthropologies which stress human transcendence is a fact of the highest significance for christology. If indeed christology should take its departure from the humanity of Christ, and if humanity contains within itself a principle of transcendence, then there may be a way here that, beginning from the total humanity of Jesus Christ, 'consubstantial' with all humanity, leads to the conception of a transcendent or transcending humanity which, in an older terminology, would have been called 'God-manhood'. We may remember Rahner's claim that christology is 'transcendent anthropology', and that expression would seem to imply not just a humanity that transcends itself but an anthropology which transcends itself to become theology (thus reversing Feuerbach). But it is time for us now to pass in review some of these anthropologies, and see whether we can glean from them something that may be helpful in our efforts to construct a christology based on the humanity of Christ. At the present time, I think there are at least four such anthropologies. The most obvious one is existentialism. Next, there are some forms of Marxism or neo-Marxism. Then, there are the process philosophies of Whitehead and others. Finally, there is the transcendental Thomism that has been characteristic of recent Roman Catholic thought. I propose to deal later with the bearing of the theory of evolution on christology, and, with the possible exception of the third, the four anthropologies mentioned are not directly concerned with evolution. Nevertheless, the evolutionary way of thinking that has been influencing modern thought for a long time provides a congenial background for theories of transcendence. We have moved away from a world of static unchanging essences into much more fluid conceptions.

Let us begin with existentialism which, as I said, is the most obvious example of an anthropology that stresses human transcendence. What distinguishes the human being from all the other beings to be found on earth is this: the human being not only *is* but knows that he or she is, and because of this knowledge has some say and some responsibility in determining what he or she will become. In the often quoted words of Jean-Paul Sartre: 'Man first of all exists, encounters himself, surges up in the world – and defines himself afterwards. If Man, as the existentialist sees him, is not definable, it is because to begin with, he is nothing. He will not be anything until later, and then he will be what he makes himself.'[5] This statement is no doubt exaggerated, and elsewhere I have criticized it.[6] It leads to that dualism against which I warned earlier in this chapter, a dualism which sets humanity (*pour soi*) on one side and nature (*en soi*) on the other with an unbridgable gulf between them. But, allowing for exaggeration, we can concede that Sartre is correct in seeing that the human being has to make or choose his essence, while natural and manufactured objects have their essence as something given. To the extent that this is correct, there is always something *more* to a human being, that which he or she may become and which is not yet determined. We can extend this thought to the human race as a whole. We do not know what potentialities of humanity are still to unfold. Human 'nature', to use the traditional expression, is still in process of formation.

Friedrich Nietzsche is usually considered one of the fathers of existentialism, though the label is not important. Perhaps as much as any philosopher of modern times, he has held strongly to the idea that the human being is in process of transition. There is indeed a streak of misanthropy in Nietzsche's philosophy. He could respect human beings only to the extent that he recognized they were on their way to becoming something other than the mean ignoble creatures that he considered so many of them to be. In his view, man is a thing to be surpassed. 'Man is a rope stretched between beast and superman.'[7] Nietzsche might have been writing a hundred years after the actual date, amid the fears and worries of the twentieth century when he remarked: 'The most anxious ask today, "How is man to be preserved?" But the question should be, "How is man to be surpassed?" The superman is my care; he, not man, is my first and only care.'[8] Nietzsche was not only atheistic but anti-Christian, yet this view of the human being as in need of radical conversion has some parallels with Christianity. Yet Nietzsche was looking in quite a different direction from Christianity. The human future, the true essence of humanity, is identified by him with the 'prodigious power' latent in the human life-form. But who is this superman that is coming – if indeed 'superman' is an adequate translation of *Übermensch*? The superman remains a human being and he belongs not just to the remote future. He is the human being who has attained full autonomy, who has discarded the conventional moral values to make room for new values that he has himself created, who has abolished God in order to take control of the world. Unlike the Christ of the Christ-hymn, the superman *does* think that equality with God is something to be seized, and that his own destiny is not to be a servant but a ruler. In Nietzsche we reach the apotheosis of the human autonomy which Kant had proclaimed as the essence of Enlightenment. Or if we want to trace the origin of the superman even further back, do we find it in that moment at the very beginning of the modern period when Descartes decided that the only reality we can really trust and make it the foundation for everything else is human self-consciousness? So Heidegger thought when he wrote, 'Modern metaphysics first comes to the full and final determination of its essence in the doctrine of the superman. In that doctrine, Descartes celebrates his supreme triumph.'[9]

Here we see both the similarity and the difference between the Christian and the Nietzschean ideals for humanity. Both see man-in-transcendence, reaching out to a 'more' in which humanity would have attained a higher level. We could even say that in both cases it is a reaching out to Godhood. Nietzsche's superman is a secularized and dechristianized version of the God-man. The superman, like Sartre's man, is the desire to become God and, above all to exercise divine power. The God-man, by contrast, immerses himself in God and manifests God's presence in him in terms of love and service.

The two existentialist philosophers whom I have brought into the discussion are both atheistic, Sartre and Nietzsche. That perhaps gives extra point to my claim that modern philosophical anthropologies are presenting us with a view of the human being which makes intelligible certain ideas which seem to be assumed in christology – that human 'nature' is something still taking shape and therefore capable of 'transcendence', and that it is through a transcendent anthropology that one might hope to come to some understanding of divinity, as the ultimate horizon of our transcendence. Of course, I remind the reader that for the present we are thinking of these matters only from the human side.

The idea of a transcendent or transcending humanity is to be found also in Marxism and its later developments. Marxism and existentialism are often contrasted, but they have in fact much in common. Both arose as reactions out of Hegelianism; both are primarily anthropological in character; both can combine in new syntheses, as one sees, for instance, in the philosophies of Sartre and Marcuse. The major difference is that existentialism has concerned itself primarily with the individual human being, whereas Marxism is a social philosophy.

As far as I can discover, Marx himself did not use the term 'transcendence' but the idea was clearly present in a sentence like the following: 'Since, for socialist man, the whole of so-called universal history is nothing but the formation of man by human labour, the shaping of nature for man's sake, man thus possesses a clear irrefutable proof that he is born of his own self, a proof of the process whereby he has come to be.'[10] This quotation is interesting for several reasons. It illustrates my point that Marxism and existentialism are both basically anthropological or even anthropocentric philosophies. But Marxism, unlike the existentialism of Sartre, does not set nature over against man, but incorporates it into the human task of shaping both humanity and the earth. Also, the place given to the concept of work is peculiar to Marxism. The second sentence of the quotation raises some problems and may even seem somewhat naive. Clearly, man is *not* born of his own self and the 'process whereby he has come to be' went on for a very long time before human labour had any part in it. But the general picture is highly compatible with modern theories of human transcendence.

This becomes clearer still when we move on from Marx to some of the later neo-Marxists. Herbert Marcuse, whose philosophy attempts to synthesize Marxism and existentialism, uses the term 'transcendence' quite freely. However, he gives it a social rather than an individual connotation. Attacking contemporary empiricism and its preoccupation with 'facts', he calls for the use of 'critical reason' to evaluate the facts, for he rightly holds that no philosophy is 'value-free'. His language is at times reminiscent of the evangelistic preacher, as he calls for 'a new type of human being'. Where this message gets across, transcendence takes place as an 'overshoot' within a society of the existing structures and institutions. If we think of Christianity as originating in a social happening, the 'Christ-event', then Marcuse's analysis helps us to understand the hostile reaction of both the Jewish and Roman establishments, which saw in the new movement a threat to their own security. For them, at least, it was the appearance of a new humanity.

The clearest and most interesting statement of the principle of human transcendence among neo-Marxists is found in the verbose writing of Ernst Bloch, especially his three-volume *magnum opus*, *The Principle of Hope*. Although professing himself an atheist, Bloch, as I have said elsewhere, would be better described as some kind of pantheist.[11] He rejected belief in God because 'God' is usually conceived as a power which oppresses man and stands in the way of human transcendence; but what was peculiar to Bloch was his extension of the idea of transcendence to the whole universe. There is a principle of 'hope' in everything, that is to say, a tendency to realize its possibilities for being. This brings Bloch close to those philosophers of process and emergence who talk about a *nisus* or drive in things. Such ideas of course go back at least as far as Aristotle who insisted that it is never enough to ask what something is (*ti esti*) without asking the further question, what it is capable of becoming (*ti en einai*). Obviously, this is true above all of the human being, the most plastic of all beings in nature and the only one that chooses what it will become. So in Bloch's view it is less correct to say, 'We are human' than to say 'We are becoming human'. 'We are still in a state of not-yet-being. I am. But I do not have myself. Thus we are only becoming.'[12] Here, as with Marcuse, we find ourselves on the borderline between Marxism and existentialism.

The human being is the bearer of the world's potentiality. 'Man is that which has still much before it. He is repeatedly transformed in his work and by it. He repeatedly stands ahead on frontiers which are no longer such because he perceives them, he ventures beyond them. The authentic in man and in the world is potential, waiting, living in fear of being frustrated, living in hope of succeeding.'[13] Man is therefore the microcosm, and his transcendence is, one may say, the spearhead of a universal transcendence. This is the element in Bloch's philosophy which, I think, places it in the category of 'pantheism' rather than 'atheism'. I have already drawn attention to the resemblance of Bloch to the process philosophers, and clearly there is a resemblance also to Teilhard de Chardin. I think the Marxist authorities of East Germany would have agreed with my diagnosis of pantheism, for they eventually deprived Bloch of his university post on the grounds of 'mysticism'. This may have been a fair intepretation, for, like Augustine, Bloch seemed to think that these distant areas of humanity toward which we may transcend, have a certain religious significance. He expressly disavows that his concern with the human means an abandonment of the religious. He says: 'The growing humanization of religion is not paralleled by any reduction in its sense of awe, but rather the contrary; the *humanum* now gains the *mysterium* of something divine, of something deifiable, gains it as the future creation of the kingdom, but of the right kingdom.'[14] This reference to a humanity that reaches out toward deification, and that connects this with the 'kingdom' can scarcely be anything but an allusion to Jesus Christ. His kingdom is the 'right' kingdom because it is not a kingdom of power or founded on an ideology of power. As we saw at an earlier stage, Bloch was impressed by Luke's Christmas story, as precisely the negation of an ideology of power.[15] Incidentally, Bloch's claim that preoccupation with the human being and the discovery of 'mystery' in that being do not abolish 'religion', has a bearing also on what we are doing in this chapter. In our quest for an understanding of the person of

Jesus Christ, we have committed ourselves to beginning from his humanity, and I am well aware that some theologians would be highly critical of such a procedure, believing that it could lead only to a much reduced conception of Jesus Christ as a 'mere' man. But if one accepts the principle of transcendence as a basic characteristic of the human being, then it is difficult to speak of a 'mere' man. Any human being who has entered on the path of transcendence is already showing that humanity is always 'more' than we think, and we have still to discover how far the mystery of the human may stretch toward the supreme mystery that we call 'God'.

Moving on from Marxism or neo-Marxism, it is not a long step to the philosophies of process. There we meet again the notion of the human being as an entity that is not fixed in its character but is in process of self-creation. Unlike the existentialists, Whitehead does not set humanity over against nature but includes it within nature. However, nature for Whitehead is much more than a physical process, and the human race shows us nature at its most creative point. 'Mankind is that factor in nature which exhibits in its most intense form the plasticity of nature.'[16] Sometimes he uses the word 'transcendence' in connection with the human capacity for self-creativity, as in the following passage, which will also help to throw light on the use of Whiteheadian terminology by Pittenger in the course of his christology:[17]

> The world is self-creative; and the actual entity as self-creative creature passes into its immortal function of part-creator of the transcendent world. In its self-creation the actual entity is guided by its ideal of itself as individual satisfaction and as transcendent creator. The enjoyment of this ideal is the 'subjective aim', by reason of which the actual entity is a determinate process.[18]

It may be useful to remind the reader at this point that a human being is one instance of an 'actual entity', in Whitehead's terminology. Other process philosophers and theologians have a similar view of the human being as self-creative, though they do not all use the word 'transcendence' in the sense which we have been employing in this chapter. Hartshorne, for instance, prefers to talk of 'surpassing' rather than 'transcending'. But since this entire group of process thinkers have a conception of God as possessing a 'consequent nature' or 'immanent pole' whereby he is closely related to the world and to nature, all of them could find room within their philosophical framework for the idea of a humanity that transcends toward God.

Just to complete the picture, I want finally to mention still another conception of human transcendence, that found among the transcendental Thomists. Most of them are Roman Catholics, and some of them have applied their anthropological theories to the problems of christology.

We took note briefly about this new type of Thomism when we considered some recent Roman Catholic contributions to christology.[19] I shall not repeat what was said there, but we are now in a position to see more clearly the significance of this philosophical development, for we can perceive it as part of a wider family of philosophies, including certain forms of existentialism, neo-Marxism, process thought and evolutionary philosophy. One could say that the traditional concepts of Thomism have been set in motion, as it were. They have been given a fluid, dynamic quality which they did not have in the older ways of thinking. Especially is this true of the concept of the human being. The best statement of transcendental Thomism in English is that of the Canadian Jesuit, Bernard Lonergan, in his book *Insight* (1949) and many other writings. Already, of course, there are several varieties of the new Thomism. Lonergan's version is close to the Thomist traditions in emphasizing the intellectual values. But it is a highly dynamic kind of intellectualism. Knowing is not the passive reception or entertaining of ideas, it is an active pursuit, a going out into the world. According to Lonergan, '"transcendence" means going beyond', and at each stage of knowledge, we go beyond what has hitherto been known to a deeper and more comprehensive level of knowledge. In some ways, *Insight* is comparable to Hegel's *Phenomenology of Spirit*, because it traces the successive stages by which the mind reaches out to grasp the various realms of phenomena, with absolute knowledge as the goal. The active character of the knowing mind is expressed by Lonergan when he writes, 'There is an intellectual desire, an eros of the mind. Without it, there would arise no questioning, no inquiry, no wonder.'[20] The mention of questioning here is important, for Lonergan can also say that 'transcendence' is the 'elementary matter of asking further questions'.[21] Every question leads to an answer which in turn raises a new question, and the mind follows the path through the various sciences and realms of knowledge until it comes to the ultimate questions. In his markedly intellectualist portrayal of transcendence. Lonergan is, among the transcendental Thomists, at a very considerable remove from the existentialists. The kinship with existentialism comes out more clearly in some of the other practitioners of the new Thomism.

I have in mind especially Karl Rahner. Though steeped in the writings of St Thomas, he was also at one time a student of Heidegger, and these influences combine in the anthropology which underlies most of his theological work. Just as Hegel sought to broaden the strict rationalism of Kant by substituting for reason the richer concept of spirit (*Geist*), Rahner too goes back to the traditional term 'spirit'. But he understands 'spirit' in such a way that it is primarily an activity, the activity of going out and also of returning. In the several anthropologies which we are presently considering, we could say that there is something like an equivalence among the terms existence, transcendence, spirit. These terms all refer to the capacity of the human being to go out from himself or herself to form relations with that which is other, yet it is precisely in this process that the self is created and grows. In Lonergan this reaching out was seen primarily in the 'eros of the mind', the reaching out for knowledge in the activity of questioning. But spirit reaches out in many other ways besides. These too are ways of transcendence. In Marcel, for instance, the individual transcends the narrow limits of individual being by relating to other persons, and this is how the individual's own personhood is developed. Art and esthetic experience is another obvious mode of transcendence. Art as the quest for the sublime is close to religion, the quest for the holy, that which in the highest degree is other to human finitude. It is on this aspect of transcendence that Rahner concentrates attention. Spirit is the desire for absolute being. On the other hand, he can say that God is the 'whither' of human transcendence. This, I suppose, is not meant to be a definition of God, for one would not define God by reference to the finite human creature, but it is a recognition of the reciprocity between God and man. It is that reciprocity which finds expression in the word 'spirit'. There is that in the human being which, so to speak, opens out toward God and finds its completion in God. So we may understand Augustine's famous words, 'Thou hast made us for thyself, and our hearts are restless until they find rest in thee.'[22] We come again to this mystery within the human being, that though finite, there is some vestige of the infinite in this being, even if only in the infinity of an outreach that surpasses everything finite. To come back to Rahner, he says 'by "spirit" I understand a power which reaches out beyond the world and knows the metaphysical'.[23] The presence in the human being, in virtue of his or her humanity itself, of spirit understood as the principle of transcendence, implies an affinity to God and a capacity for receiving God.

I have been trying to show that some of the most profound anthropologies of modern times, both religious and secular, have made the idea of transcendence central to their understanding of the human condition, and that there would be great difficulty in saying where the limits of human transcendence lie. This, I believe, is of the highest significance for an understanding of the claims that have been made for Jesus Christ. To call him the God-man (or whatever the preferred expression may be) is to claim that in him human transcendence has reached that point at which the human life has become so closely united with the divine life that, in the traditional language, it has been 'deified'. It has not, however, ceased to be human – rather, for the first time, we learn what true humanity is. In a typical sentence, Rahner says: 'Only someone who forgets that the essence of man is to be unbounded . . . can suppose that it is impossible for there to be a man who, precisely by being man in the fullest sense (which we never attain) is God's existence into the world.'[24]

Though the appeal in this chapter has been mainly to modern theories of the *humanum*, I want now to point out the interpretation of christology in terms of the raising of a human being to God has its roots as far back as we can go and has ample precedents in earlier theology, though it has been much overshadowed by the classical christology with its emphasis on a movement in the opposite direction, that is to say, the coming down or descent of God into man, or the assumption of humanity by the divine Logos. Eventually I shall try to reconcile these two points of view, but for the present I am urging the ascending christology.

I said that to find the roots of it, we have to go back as far as we can go, into what I called the 'prehistory' of christology, discussed in Chapter 2. We go back to the creation story, and to the creation of the human race in particular. The account is mythological, yet it is full of remarkable spiritual truth. 'Then God said, "Let us make man in our image, after our likeness; and let them have dominion over the fish of the sea, and over the birds of the air, and over the cattle, and over all the earth, and over every creeping thing that creeps upon the earth." So God created man in his own image, in the image of God he created him; male and female he created them' (Gen. 1.26–7). What was that image in which God created the first human couple? Various answers have been given. Some have seen the image as 'dominion', but that leads to the false gods of power and to the cult and ideology of power. Others have seen the image in 'reason', but that is too narrow, and we would do better to use what I called above the 'richer' concept of 'spirit'. God conferred on the human creature the gift of spirit, and therefore an affinity with himself, for God too in Christian teaching is spirit (John 4.24). So although the Hebrew scriptures are so strongly opposed to making any image of God, they teach that there is indeed a creature in the image and likeness of God, namely, the human creature. Even allowing for the defacement of that image by sin, something of it remains in every human being. If then there ever came into existence a human being in whom that image was not defaced but manifested in its fullness, would not that human being, precisely by being fully human, be God's existence into the world, so far as the divine can become manifest on the finite level? At the moment, of course, we are talking only of a possibility – the possibility of a being both human and divine. It seems to me that given the plasticity of the human being, the affinity of that being to God, and the capacity of that being for transcendence, then one can affirm that the possibility of a God-man is a real possibility within what we can know of the conditions of existence in this world.

We are presently considering only a possibility. But as we move on from the prehistory of christology into the actual story of its development, we are confronted with the assertion that the possibility has been actualized in history, that the God-man has appeared in the person of Jesus of Nazareth. As we have seen, the first written testimony came from Paul. The first Adam had been a failure. Though he was created in the 'image and likeness' of God, this became for him the sinful and insane ambition to seize equality with God, in the sense of usurping the divine rule. But the new Adam, Jesus Christ, eschews the temptation to become the superman who will challenge God, and becomes 'like God' or achieves a true transcendence by relating to others and creating a new humanity. 'He is the image of the invisible God, the first-born of all creation' (Col. 1.15). He is the Man who is exalted through service and obedience even to death, so that he receives the name above every name, the name that belongs to God (Phil. 2.6–11).

It is clear that there are two moments in the church's act of faith in Jesus as the God-man. The first, as I have said, concerns *possibility*, and depends on the belief that the human being is a being-in-transcendence with the capacity for growing toward God and manifesting the divine life. The second concerns *actuality*, and is the assertion that in Jesus Christ the possibility became a reality in history. Whether one can assent to the first of the two moments will depend on one's view of human nature and its significance in this universe. Whether one can assent to the second moment depends on the testimony of the New Testament writers, and that is why we thought it necessary in the early chapters of this book to go back to the sources and examine them in the light of modern criticism. One must also remember that the question of present experience in the church may have evidential value, but again I must ask to defer this question until we have inquired more closely into the meaning of Christ's resurrection and exaltation.

The relatively simple and – if I may so describe it – humanistic christology of Paul is, of course, supported by some of the other New Testament witnesses (we noted examples of this in Mark and in Acts),[25] even though it came to be subordinated to the christology 'from above'. But it was never quite forgotten, and we have seen that it came back from time to time in various Christian writers. We met it in Irenaeus, who not only stressed the notion of the image of God in man but also the progressive manner in which this image, given as potentiality, must be brought to realization as likeness.[26] We met this type of christology again (though not without some ambiguity) in the teaching of Maximus the Confessor.[27] But perhaps it is only with Schleiermacher at the beginning of the modern period that the humanistic christology comes into its own and receives expression in quite a thoroughgoing fashion.[28] Christ, according to Schleiermacher, is 'the completion of the creation of man' and, as such, the man in whom there is a 'veritable presence of God'.[29] Since Schleiermacher's time, many of the basic ideas have been re-expressed and given new applications, and we have met what I am calling the 'humanistic' christology in different forms in such near contemporaries with ourselves as Pittenger, Pannenberg, Rahner and others.

But I can readily believe that some readers will have serious doubts about this whole approach. Is not this way into christology that begins from the humanity of Jesus and from our own experience as human beings one that is riddled with adoptionism and Pelagianism? I can only reply to that by repeating a point that I already made in discussing Paul – that the christology from below is still only half of the story. It is, I have argued, the correct starting-point, but the way it opens up inevitably brings us to ask about God's place in it all. We do not forget Paul's words, 'All this is from God' (II Cor. 5.18).

The idea that there is an implacable conflict between adoptionist and incarnational christologies is quite mistaken. Each of these approaches needs the other. The former has chronological priority, the second ontological priority. 'The fact is,' as William Porcher DuBose once said, 'the whole truth of Jesus Christ is just as much man realizing and fulfilling himself in God as God realizing and revealing himself in man.'[30] In the next chapter, we shall look at the christological question from the other side, as God's coming down to the human race.

But just before we go on to that, there is one other aspect of the humanity of Jesus Christ that calls for at least a preliminary notice in this chapter. It is the question of his relationship to the human race in its totality. Why should this man be considered significant for all human beings? The question can be more fully answered only after we have thought further about the passion and death of Jesus. But the preliminary answer I want to give is that Jesus is the *representative* human being.

But on what grounds do we make such an assertion, and what precisely does it mean? As far as the grounds for the assertion are concerned, we have to rely on the testimony of the church, not just the New Testament writings produced by early members of the church but on the continual renewal of the tradition in the preaching and sacramental life of the church. Even today, something of the impact of Jesus Christ still reaches us, and some might even talk of a living presence of Christ in the church. Whatever channels or factors or mechanisms are involved, there can still be today an experience of Jesus Christ in which we recognize him as the fulfilment of our humanity, one with us in the whole spectrum of human experience, yet different from us in having brought the most central possibilities of humanity to a new level of realization. In some other words of that neglected American theologian, DuBose, whom I quoted a few lines back, 'We recognize by the instinct of a true humanity that Christ is the very truth of humanity.'[31] 'The instinct of a true humanity' – what is that? Let us call it conscience, but conscience at its deepest level, not the surface conscience which reflects simply the rules of the society in which we live. This deeper conscience is an awareness which we have in virtue of our status as rational and spiritual beings that if we follow some directions, we enhance our rationality and spirituality, if we follow others, we diminish them. This is where the rationalist christology of Kant has its due.[32] There is within us an archetype, an ideal, a lure which draws us on and which, we believe, we see fulfilled in a signal way in Jesus Christ, and not only fulfilled but transcending even what our consciences had set before us. We recognize him as the representative human being, the Word made flesh.

But just what does it mean to say 'representative'? He has attained this representative status not in any magical or instantaneous way, but through striving and the overcoming of temptation, though that striving was always in response to the gracious action of God. As the epistle to the Hebrews teaches, he was 'perfected' in a process of becoming perfect. But this does not mean that he brought every human potentiality to its perfect realization. Part of our human finitude is the demand that we set priorities and make some commitments more important than others. The perfection of a human being could not consist in being everything all at once, if that could even be imagined. If we trust the tradition – and I think we have seen reason to accept its general trustworthiness – then Jesus gave priority to love, love to God and love to fellow human beings, even love to the cosmos as God's creation. It was not a new *idea* – it had been in the conscience of Israel for centuries and was even enshrined in the scriptures, and no doubt in some form it was in the consciences of many men and women beyond the borders of Israel. But now the archetype took shape in an actual human being and a new humanity was formed.

18

The Divinity of Jesus Christ

Following what we have taken to be one of the requirements of a modern christology, we have begun our study of the person of Christ from the human side, and working with the idea of what modern anthropologies have termed the 'transcendence' of human nature, the idea that human nature is not a fixed essence but has an openness that seems to allow for indefinite development, we have seen that the Christian claims for Jesus Christ begin to make sense within the framework of such a dynamic anthropology. One can claim that in Jesus Christ a new level of humanity has been reached, and if this claim is linked to the traditional idea that the distinctiveness of the human being arises from the creation of humanity in the image of God, then what has taken place in Christ is the realization of that image. The ancient Christian writers did not hesitate to speak of the 'deification' (*theopoiesis*) of man, though this expression was applied primarily not to Christ but to the Christian believer who in Christ is restored or being restored to God's intention for humanity. In Christ himself, the movement was seen as following the opposite direction – it is an incarnation or 'inhumanization' (*enanthropesis*)[1] of the divine Logos. In the *Quicunque vult* or so-called 'Athanasian creed', it is explicitly stated concerning Christ that 'although he be God and man, yet he is not two, but one Christ; one, not by conversion of the Godhead into flesh, but by taking of the manhood into God'.[2] This looks like another attempt to spell out too exactly the meaning of incarnation and is an obscuring of the full humanity of Jesus Christ. The view taken consistently in this book is that deification and inhumanization are not to be regarded as opposing theories about the person of Christ but as complementary. They offer two different perspectives on the same event. In our exposition, we have given priority to deification, the raising of a man toward God for it has seemed necessary to maintain the full and utter humanity of Christ against all the tendencies that would turn him into an alien supernatural being. But we have never denied that finally we must come to terms with Paul's assertion that 'all this is from God' and that the raising of a human life to the level at which it manifests God is possible only through the descent of God into that life. In Jesus Christ we are confronted with both the deification of a man and the inhumanization (incarnation) of God. And though the first of these two ways of looking at the event has been put first in our exposition, for reasons that have been repeatedly stated, the second of the two ways is the more profound and is a necessary condition of the first. If there is a capacity for God in the human being, that can be the case only because there is already what Karl Barth called a humanity in God. But this is a very difficult idea, and is obviously more speculative than the idea of an indefinite capacity for 'transcendence' in the humanity which we all experience at first hand.

It is important, however, that we do not make the problem even more difficult than it actually is. It does seem to me that some theologians have in fact made it more difficult because they have assumed a concept of God which separates him so absolutely from the created order that the gulf between can never be bridged. If there is no affinity whatever between God and the human race, if God is *'wholly* other' and separated from us by an *'infinite qualitative* difference', then it seems to me that incarnation must be not only the 'absolute paradox' but a sheer impossibility. The language I have been quoting here is found in Kierkegaard and in the early Barth, and these two Christian thinkers were able to speak of incarnation only because in the course of their dialectical thinking they profoundly modified their stress on the otherness of God. They continued to believe that no human being could rise unaided to God, but in their several ways they found in God a humanity and even a humility which made contact across the gulf. So Kierkegaard in his famous parable describes the king who lays aside his majesty in order to meet the beloved on a footing of equality,[3] while Barth tells us that it is as natural for God to be lowly as to be high.[4] Even so, I think these two writers lacked an adequate doctrine of the divine immanence, and without such a doctrine, the difficulties in the way of thinking of an incarnation are enormously increased.

In much Christian theology there has been an almost exclusive stress on the transcendence of God, and when God is understood in this onesided way, it becomes very hard to see how he could enter human history in the manner that is implied by a doctrine of incarnation. Christianity, of course, inherited its understanding of God from the Hebrew and Jewish tradition, and in that tradition God is conceived in predominantly transcendent terms. This in turn meant that the first Christians moved only slowly toward a doctrine of incarnation, for it seemed to be an infringement of the belief in the otherness of God. We have seen that the use of God-language in relation to Jesus is minimal in the New Testament, and seems to have been admitted reluctantly.[5] Yet we have seen also that the Jewish scholar Abraham Heschel through his use of the concept of the *pathos* of God argued for an intimacy of God with his people, especially a bond between God and the prophets through whom he communicated his word.[6] Admittedly, this was not 'incarnation' as Christian theologians have understood the term, but the Hebrew prophets were much more than mere mouthpieces or transmitters who simply passed along the word without themselves being moulded or transformed by it. A figure such as Jeremiah in the final years of the kingdom of Judah was so enveloped in his prophetic vocation and so permeated by the word which he spoke that many writers and preachers have drawn a parallel between him and Christ. Christian theologians sympathetic to the Jewish tradition have given positive recognition to the affinity between the prophets and Christ, for instance, Schillebeeckx who uses the category of 'prophet' as a major constituent of his christology,[7] and Pittenger, who, while recognizing the 'novelty' of Jesus, places him in a history of revelation and sees his difference from other figures in that history as one of degree rather than of kind.[8] I hardly need to say that I am myself much more attracted by this view than by attempts to posit an absolute difference between Christ and the prophets. I have in mind, for instance, the view of Brunner, according to which the Old Testament prophet was 'a passive instrument for the message, an instrument without any value of its own', and so 'absolutely different' from Christ. If I understand him rightly, Brunner appears to hold that Jesus Christ is the *exclusive* revelation of God, while the prophets are merely pointers to revelation.[9]

But even if we allow that there are features of the Old Testament which qualify the transcendence of God over the creation and that it does not teach a stark monotheistic transcendence such as one finds in Islam and still less does it teach the doctrine of a distant God typical of the deists of the Enlightenment, the Old Testament doctrine of God is not, on the face of it, hospitable to a doctrine of incarnation. That explains why God-language about Jesus Christ (and such language seems to be inevitable once the idea of incarnation is accepted) was slow in commending itself to the first Jewish Christians, including most of the writers of the New Testament.

When we do see a development in that direction, it came not in the form of a directly stated doctrine of divine immanence, but in the specifically Christian doctrine of the Trinity or triune God. Through Jesus Christ, the members of the Christian community had had a new experience of God, nothing less than a 'revelation', to use the technical term. Their new experience of God was so closely bound up with Jesus Christ that they could not now think or speak of God apart from Christ, or of Christ apart from God. This development can be seen as early as Paul. 'For us', he tells us, 'there is one God, the Father, from whom are all things and for whom we exist, and one Lord, Jesus Christ, through whom are all things and through whom we exist' (I Cor. 8.6). In the famous Christ-hymn, which may be even older than the verse just quoted, Christ has received 'the name which is above every name' (Phil. 2.9). The doctrine of incarnation and the doctrine of the Trinity developed together, and clearly each implies the other.

I mentioned that it was through the doctrine of the Trinity rather than through a direct doctrine of divine immanence that incarnation was related to the general corpus of Christian teaching. There may have been several reasons for this. The associations of immanence were historically with paganism and with pantheism or even polytheism. Divine immanence suggests a religion of nature, and as such it must have been suspect in the eyes of those who came out of a Jewish background. Furthermore, when one speaks of divine immanence, this is more likely to convey the impression of a vague universal presence of God in everything, rather than a specific presence, as demanded by the notion of incarnation. Clearly, the emergence of Christianity and the special place that it gave to the person of Jesus Christ called for a major rethinking of the traditional understanding of God and the making of many new distinctions never made before. The work still goes on in the theology of our own time.

In earlier chapters, we have seen some of the moments in this historical development of christology, both in ancient and in modern times. The root of it all is the idea of God in the Old Testament, as inherited by the first Christians. As Barth tells us, this is a God who essentially speaks, or communicates himself, or utters his word.[10] This understanding of God is already assumed in the New Testament – indeed, *almost* every mention of God (*Theos*) in the New Testament refers to the traditional God of Israel, not to Jesus Christ or the Holy Spirit.[11] This word 'God' and what it stands for was a necessary presupposition for any Christian assertions such as that Christ had been sent by God or was the Son of God or was the Word of God or even was God. Yet if Christ was the Word of God (we have seen that this metaphor of the Word or Logos implies an 'utterance' or coming forth of God from his hiddenness)[12] then there is a reciprocity between the Hebrew inheritance and the revelation in Christ. Only the inherited understanding of God permitted the disciples to say Christ had come from God, yet as soon as this was said, it meant that God must be understood anew in the light of Christ, as his own self-communication. This reciprocal interpretation and interpenetration of the Hebrew God and the new revelation in Christ led, as we have seen, in the direction of the triune God of Christian theology. But now a further influence supervenes. As theologians grappled with the intellectual problems of Christian faith, they were inevitably drawn into the ambience of philosophical ideas. In particular, neo-Platonism was a powerful influence from the fourth century onward. This philosophy had originated with Plotinus (205–270) who, quite independently of Christianity had arrived at the idea of a Triad of divine hypostases. These were: The One, the nameless ultimate source of all that is, beyond all comprehension; the Mind, which has come forth from the One into the realm of order and intelligibility; and the Soul, a further emanation from the One extending through the universe and dwelling in all things. In spite of many differences, there is a broad similarity between this divine Triad and the Christian Trinity, and the neo-Platonist framework was taken up by some Christian theologians as a conceptual basis for their doctrine of God. They saw some correspondence between the One and the Father, between the Mind and the Logos, and between the Soul and the Holy Spirit.[13]

A good example of this merging of Christian and neo-Platonist ideas of deity is provided by the Christian mystic who wrote under the pseudonym of Dionysius or Denys (c. 500). Himself a mystic, he imagines a kind of divine ecstasy, in which God comes out of himself in an act of self-emptying or self-giving: 'We must dare to affirm (for it is the truth) that the Creator of the universe himself, in his beautiful and good yearning toward the universe, is through the excessive yearning of his goodness transported outside himself in his providential activities toward all things that have being . . . and so is drawn from his transcendent throne above all things to dwell within the heart of all things, through an ecstatic power that is above being and whereby he yet stays within himself.'[14] Though I have slightly abridged this passage, it is so densely packed with ideas that it calls for some comment. Dionysius is not speaking specifically of the incarnation, but of a more general descent of God into the world. Perhaps the incarnation is to be seen as the culminating moment in this descent, and perhaps it is in such a way that it ought to be understood – not as an isolated or anomalous happening, but as the focus of what God is always doing and has always been doing, that is to say, coming into his creation. The notion of God's being drawn by his love from his transcendent throne is reminiscent of Kierkegaard and Barth on the lowliness of God, and might even suggest a 'death of God', except that Dionysius, recognizing that God, if there is a God, must be immortal and inexhaustible, affirms that in spite of his self-outpouring, 'he yet stays within himself'. But we could say that he does envisage the 'death' of the solitary monarchical God, for Dionysius' God (he prefers to speak of the 'thearchy' rather than simply of 'God') is not only in some respects utterly transcendent ('above being' and 'beyond reason') but, as we have seen, 'dwells at the heart of all things'. It must be said that

Dionysius does not succeed in making clear the relation of his 'thearchy' to the Trinity of Christian theology, though one can see a broad correspondence. But he certainly does teach a conception of God that is highly compatible with such Christian ideas as Trinity and incarnation – the idea of a God who does not dwell in some kind of frozen immutable perfection, far from the material world, but a God who comes out of his transcendence in a generous overflow of love so as to identify with the world. Another important point to note here is that Dionysius, even if unintentionally, is offering us a new model of divine transcendence. The expression 'divine transcendence' has usually been taken to mean precisely that 'otherness' which distinguishes God from the world as the perfect from the imperfect, the infinite from the finite, the eternal from the temporal, the immutable from the mutable, the impassible from the passible, and so on. But this mode of being is what Dionysius' thearchy renounces in allowing itself to be drawn by love from its transcendent throne into the realm of earthly happening. This suggests an active type of transcendence, analogous to what we have called 'transcendence' in the case of the human being. Self-transcendence in a man or woman is the capacity to go beyond. Does God perhaps possess an analogous capacity? That would be a 'transcendence' not in the conventional static sense of the term as applied to God, but an active transcendence, a dynamic reaching out in creation and redemption, and this is surely an idea that is closer to Christian ways of thinking of God. The process philosopher, Hartshorne, talks of God as 'surpassing' himself.[15] If it is objected that to talk in this way is incompatible with a belief in the perfection of God, I think it may be replied that the objection would hold only if one's thinking is restricted to static ideas. If we accept that in some respects of his being God is involved in time and history – and it is hard to see how any Christian theologian could deny this – then as God fulfils his purposes, he is not just perfecting the world as exterior to himself, but is increasing his own satisfaction and therefore 'surpassing' himself, moving on to new levels of perfection.

As we ourselves move toward a more dynamic conception of God and think of him not as dwelling in a distant heaven in untroubled bliss but as transcending in the sense of constantly coming forth from himself, then the idea of incarnation will not seem to be some improbable speculation or some fragment of a fantastic mythology. Rather, we can see it as the meeting point at which the transcendence of humanity from below, as described in the last chapter, is met by the divine transcendence from above. We can see too that this way of conceiving incarnation arises out of the reciprocal type of interpretation mentioned early in this chapter. Ideas of God and his relation to the world, derived from various sources ancient and modern, are brought into contact with the Christian revelation of God in Christ. In particular, a non-monarchical idea of God, first conceived in ancient philosophy and further developed among the modern thinkers discussed in Chapters 8–14, both illuminates and is corrected by the Christian idea of the triune God.

But it may be objected that the approach to incarnation in this chapter and the preceding one is too general and abstract. It might suggest some universal presence of God in the world, but hardly the concrete, particular union between God and the man, Jesus of Nazareth. Let us agree that there is some force to this objection. But the approach has been deliberately adopted. Only if there is *in all human beings* a possibility for transcendence and a capacity for God, can there be such a possibility and capacity in the man Jesus; and only if God makes himself present and known in and through the creation generally can there be a particular point at which he is present and known in a signal way. Jesus Christ would not be a revelation if he was only an anomaly in the creation. He is revelation because he sums up and makes clear a presence that is obscurely communicated throughout the cosmos. Elsewhere I have called him the 'focus of Being'[16] and the same metaphor has been used by Norman Pittenger who writes, 'He is the unique focus for a universal presence and operation.'[17] Jesus Christ gets his significance from combining in himself a universality with his particular historicality. So far we have been thinking of incarnation in universal terms, but now we must heed the demand for a more particular discussion, oriented to the historical figure of Jesus.

When it was said, using the language of Dionysius, that God has been drawn from his transcendent throne 'to dwell within the heart of all things', this was not to be understood in a vague pantheistic sense, as if God were equally present or immanent in every part of creation. Even if we were willing to believe that God is in some measure present in everything, we would have to say that his presence would be more visible in some things than in others. It may be the case, for instance, that God is present in every atom of hydrogen, for even a hydrogen atom, though the simplest kind of atom that there is, is a pattern of energy so complex that it baffles understanding and excites in us the same kind of awe as Kant felt before the starry heavens. But if natural objects, from atoms to galaxies, can fill us with awe and can communicate something of God, is there not a much fuller communication when we turn our attention to a human being, who has been called a 'microcosmus', a being who sums up in himself or herself the whole range of reality comprised in the order of nature? More than that, the human being even transcends nature through the possession of spirit, so that he or she is not just a microcosmus but the image of God? So, if there is any entity on this planet in and through which God can be present and revealed, it would be in a human person. The Celtic philosopher Eriguena, who developed the neo-Platonist philosophy of Dionysius, spoke of human beings as both the recipients and the vehicles for 'theophanies' or revelations of God.[18] I think we could even say that if God is indeed a God who speaks, a God who communicates himself, then if he willed to communicate himself on this planet, it would need to be in and through a human being or a human community. I believe that to some extent God's image remains vestigially in every human being, but the Christian claim is that in Jesus Christ that image has clearly shone forth. But, as I have said more than once, the difference between Christ and other human beings is one of degree, rather than of kind. In the peculiar language of Schleiermacher, 'The Redeemer is like all men in the identity of his human nature, and distinguished from all by the constant potency of his God-consciousness, which was a veritable existence of God in him.'[19] Perhaps it is only when we think of Jesus Christ as the true Man within the framework of a humanity upon which God has universally breathed his life and bestowed his image that we can see incarnation not as the great anomaly of history but as a 'natural' step in the unfolding of creation. I may remind the reader of Athanasius' argument that if there is a sense in which the Logos has been embodied in the whole world, there is no difficulty in believing that the same Logos has been particularly communicated in a man.[20]

But why should we think that Jesus of Nazareth was that man? Surely it is improbable that God would have revealed himself in so obscure a person, a person about whom we can assemble, as we have seen, less than a dozen reasonably certain facts? I suppose one might answer that this is just the way history has turned out. Obscure though this man was, it is nevertheless in and through him that the Word has been heard and believed. But one might go further. The very obscurity of Jesus, the *incognito*, is paradoxically part of the revelation. It was all of a piece with the history of revelation in Israel. God 'chose' the gypsy tribes of the Hebrews rather than any of the great nations of the ancient world. In course of time, he called Jesus to his ministry – the Jesus concerning whom the townspeople said, 'Is not this the carpenter's son?' (Matt. 13.55).[21]

In the last chapter, I asked whether the approach to christology that begins from the human side and traces the path of a man transcending toward God must not be riddled with adoptionism and Pelagianism. I hope that the present chapter which speaks of the descent of God into the creation and the focussing of his presence and activity in the man Jesus of Nazareth redresses the balance, and while it must not in any way be allowed to detract from our recognition of the full humanity of Christ or even to obscure it by pushing it permanently into second place, nevertheless the new perspective which looks from the other side of the

God-man relation is necessary to make clear that in the last resort 'all this is from God'. I propose therefore to conclude this chapter by asking the question: How far does the christology so far expounded agree with the traditional teaching of the church as expressed in the formula of Chalcedon?

I think I have made it clear in earlier mentions of the subject that I am not saying that the actual words of Chalcedon must stand for ever – indeed, some of these words have become very poor vehicles of communication for our time, because they are time-conditioned like all words. Once they spoke the current idiom, but they no longer do so. We still retain them in our official books and documents, and they are not just museum pieces but are still invested with a certain normative status. The Chalcedonian formula is what the church in a solemn ecumenical council summoned at a critical juncture in its history confessed as the summary of its faith in Jesus Christ. We could hardly reject it without rejecting our identity as Christians. We would not be moving on to a new formulation of Christian doctrine, but moving on to a new religion. But what has to be retained does not lie in the words but in what is sometimes called the 'governing intention', something that can never be expressed apart from words, yet may be capable of expression in many verbal formulations. It is certainly my hope that the christology set forth in this book, though it does not use the traditional language and categories, stays within the parameters of the catholic tradition and is entirely compatible with the 'governing intention' of Chalcedon and other classic Christian pronouncements. But to establish this point, we have to look again at the language, and ask whether what has been said in the present exposition says, though in a different way and with different emphases, no less than the church has traditionally said in its confessional statements.

There are three more or less technical terms that are important in the Chalcedonian definition and that offer a stumbling-block to the modern mind: *ousia*, *hypostasis* and *physis*. The trouble with these three terms is not only that they have their home in an outmoded scheme of philosophy, but that even when they were current, they were ambiguous. Their meanings overlapped, and a glance at any good Greek lexicon will show that the three terms could in different contexts and usages have three distinct meanings, or sometimes they could all flow together in a gloomy semantic merging![22]

First of all, let us try to distinguish them. 1. *Ousia* is the most general of the three terms. It would be most naturally translated as 'being' since it is the noun related to the verb *einai*, 'to be'. But it is more commonly translated 'substance', which in ordinary usage might mean 'property' but in a philosophical or theological context would refer to the 'reality' of anything. But here a further ambiguity arises. When we hear the word 'substance', we think most commonly in the modern age of a material substance, and probably we think of it chiefly in terms of solidity. In earlier epochs, the conception of substance was not so narrowly circumscribed. This broader range of significance is seen when we use the word 'being' – there are many modes of being as well as that mode which is instantiated in the solid existing thing. There are, to mention only two obvious cases, the modes of being that we call 'human being' and 'divine being'. It must be counted a gain that translations of the Nicene creed in modern English liturgies speak of the Son as 'of one being with the Father', rather than 'of one substance with the Father'. Throughout this book I have been advocating dynamic rather than static categories in christology, and it seems to me that a dynamic understanding of 'being' as including 'becoming' is a legitimate interpretation of the traditional ways of speaking.

2. The term *'hypostasis'* is, from the etymological point of view, a much closer equivalent to the English 'substance' than is *ousia*. Literally understood, a *hypostasis* is the 'support' or 'foundation' underlying something, and in a philosophical context it might be contrasted with *phainomenon* as the outward 'appearance' of something. In this sense, *hypostasis* would be very close in meaning to *ousia*. But in traditional christology, *hypostasis* meant rather an individually existing thing, in particular, a 'person'. In the Chalcedonian formula, the word *hypostasis* is conjoined with the word *prosopon* to designate the person of Christ, when it is said that the two 'natures' concur in one personal entity (*eis hen prosopon kai mian hypostasin syntrechouses*). Here the model for understanding what is meant by *hypostasis* is a personal one, rather than the abstract impersonal idea of a substrate lying behind the phenomena.

3. Perhaps it is the term *physis* that is of primary importance for an interpretation of Chalcedon. The word is usually translated 'nature' and the word 'nature' in this usage is understood as the essential characteristics that make an entity one thing rather than something else. In the particular context with which we are dealing, we are asked to suppose that there is a 'human nature' and a 'divine nature' and that these 'concur' in the person of Jesus Christ. But the whole tenor of our argument has maintained that there is no human nature in the traditional sense, that is to say, no fixed stock of characteristics comprising the universal 'essence' of humanity, but rather that humanity is something unfinished, even now coming into being, so that its full shape is unknown; and if we have to profess that we do not yet know what is the essence of humanity, must we not be even more reticent in speaking of the nature of God? For God too, we have seen, is constantly surpassing himself in the outreach of his love and his 'nature' must lie beyond our understanding, except in so far as it has reached out and made contact with the creation. Indeed, the

question may be raised whether the word 'nature', understood in anything like its traditional sense, must not be applicable only to finite beings, and quite inapplicable to God. But if we move away from the static understanding of 'nature' (*physis*) as a fixed essence to the dynamic or processive understanding of *physis* as 'emergence' or 'coming into being', then the notion of the two natures 'concurring' in the person of Christ becomes intelligible. On the one hand, humanity is seeking its authentic being in its spiritual quest for communion with God, while on the other hand God is entering his creation and communicating himself through a human being who can both receive and express the presence of God.

The christology I have been expounding is so far from being a rejection of Chalcedon that I think one could claim that only in some such way can one make sense of Chalcedon in the modern age. Yet I do not believe this is an innovation. We have seen that a dynamic understanding of human nature was to be found among such early Fathers as Theophilus of Antioch and Irenaeus. Christopher Stead, in his scholarly treatment of the idea of substance or being, tells us that in Aristotle *physis* could mean 'an immanent formative principle that controls the development of living things'.[23] In Aristotle the nature (*physis*) of a thing (and he is thinking especially of the human being) is known only when its becoming has been completed. We have to ask not what it is (*ti esti*) but what it was to be (*ti en einai*). From where we are, we do not yet know what humanity is to be, but Christian faith points to Jesus Christ as the revelation of the fulfilment for which humanity is destined.

Before we leave the topics discussed in the present chapter, there is one item of unfinished business to which I must return here. In our survey of post-Enlightenment christology, we noted that several nineteenth-century theologians had offered severe criticisms of Chalcedon, among them Schleiermacher, Ritschl and Harnack. Schleiermacher's criticisms were by far the most acute,[24] and I promised that we would come back to them. I briefly remind the reader of the main points of his critique. How can one speak of a 'divine nature' and a 'human nature', as if there were a genus 'nature' of which the divine and the human, are specific determinations? And an even more serious point was raised by him. How can one 'in utter contradiction to the use elsewhere, according to which the same nature belongs to many individuals or persons', speak of one person's sharing in two quite different natures?

Schleiermacher's criticisms would, I think, be unanswerable if the word 'nature' were taken in the traditional sense as a fixed stock of characteristics. For then to say that one person possessed two different natures each in its entirety would be much like saying that the same animal was at one and the same time wholly a dog and wholly a cat. But if 'nature' is understood in the dynamic sense explained above, then

Schleiermacher's criticism falls to the ground. Nevertheless, although Schleiermacher rejects the traditional formulations of the 'two-natures' christology, I do not think that he rejects its 'governing intention' and would say that his own christology says in his language no less than the ancient formulation said in its language.

] 19 [

The Mysteries of Jesus Christ

This chapter will consider about a dozen 'happenings' in the career of Jesus Christ as it has been traditionally reported. I have put the word 'happenings' in inverted commas, because in the case of some of these occasions, it is hard to know what happened as an event in the actual history of Jesus, and what has been supplied by the imagination or theological creativity of his followers. In the title of the chapter, I have used the word 'mysteries'. This is not an ideal term, for it savours somewhat of the occult. But I have decided to use it for those reported moments in the career of Jesus in which we can discern both an element of historical happening and a penumbra of theological interpretation. In some cases, the historical element is clear and well attested, in other cases there is virtually nothing that could be claimed as historical. Correspondingly, the imaginative element in the report may be greater or less, but in each case it is this imaginative element that draws attention to the deeper significance of what is reported. The 'mystery' could, I suppose, be called a 'sign' – it points beyond the actual happening to the meaning of Jesus for our understanding of human life before God. Let me give examples. The death of Jesus on the cross is a well attested event of world history and can be dated with tolerable accuracy to the year 30 or thereabouts. But the New Testament, the creeds and Christian theology in general has seen this event as 'atonement', effecting a new relation between God and the human race. The ascension of Jesus into heaven is, on the other hand, a piece of mythology, inconceivable as a historical happening because our modern cosmography is so different from that which prevailed in the first century. The report is purely imaginative, and if there is any historical element here, it can be only the psychological experience of the disciples in their recognition of the Lordship of Christ. But let us turn to the mysteries themselves. Most of them have already come to our notice, either in our study of the New Testament witnesses or in the thought of later theologians.

Pre-existence

Since the 'mysteries' of Christ are not historical or temporal events in anything like the usual sense, we can hardly treat them in chronological order. But some belong more obviously to the beginning, others to the end, and most of them do have an order in the gospels. It would seem therefore right to begin with the mystery of the pre-existence of Jesus Christ.

Obviously, there are some parts of the New Testament that make more of pre-existence than others. In our study of Paul, we accepted the view of James Dunn that it is not necessary to invoke the idea of pre-existence to interpret his writings. What was decisive for me was not only Professor Dunn's careful and persuasive exegesis of the relevant passages in Paul, but the fact that his reading produces a simpler, more economical christology. I do not think that we need to introduce pre-existence in some of the other important New Testament witnesses, notably the synoptists. It is true that Peter's sermon on the feast of Pentecost mentions the 'plan and foreknowledge of God' (Acts 2.23), and we shall consider whether this implies some form of pre-existence, but there is nothing in the synoptic gospels that demands pre-existence, and some scholars have even argued that the stories of a virginal conception of Jesus in Matthew and Luke rule out pre-existence! Whether or not that is the case, it seems to be only in John among the evangelists that a clear doctrine of pre-existence is taught. Outside of the gospels, one could agree that some doctrine of pre-existence can probably be found in Hebrews, I Peter, Ephesians and Revelation. So there is hardly a strong case for claiming that pre-existence is essential to christology. Pre-existence is certainly taught by some of the writers, yet there are very important parts of the New Testament where the idea seems to be absent.

In the preceding paragraph, it is already suggested that there are several ways in which pre-existence may be understood. 1. Reflection on the being of God, even in philosophy or natural theology apart from any specific Christian revelation, leads, I believe, to the thought of a God within whom one must make certain distinctions. An example of such a non-Christian conception of God came to our notice in the last chapter, where we touched on Plotinus' understanding of God as a divine Triad. The explanation of why thinking about God moves in this direction is that perhaps necessarily, we think of God both as perfectly self-contained and yet at the same time as related as Creator to those beings which are not God. So, to begin with at any rate, we think of God's being in two modes – his being in himself and his being in relation to that which is other than himself. (Both Plotinus and the Christian Fathers went on to speak of a third mode, but for the present we need not follow them.) We already see this recognition of two modes in the divine Being in the Old Testament, especially in the Wisdom-hymn of Proverbs which I quoted in connection with John's doctrine of the Logos.[1] In the Old Testament, although Wisdom is spoken of as if she were a person in the hymn quoted, it is likely that the language is metaphorical and she has not yet been considered as a distinct hypostasis. But already by John's time that hypostatization has taken place. The Logos, as we have seen, is understood to hover between identity and distinctness in relation to God.[2] Now clearly this Wisdom or Logos is so close in being to God that it must share in the eternity of God. Thus John can say, 'In the beginning was the Word'. The Word pre-exists everything that has been created, for everything has been created through the Word. If then we are prepared to speak of God, there seems to be every reason for saying that God's Word is pre-existent.

But does this mean that Jesus Christ is pre-existent? Here we must remind ourselves that we had to raise the question, whether the word 'is' should be understood as the 'is' of identity when we say that Jesus is the Word. Strictly speaking, Jesus is the Word *incarnate*, so must we not say that prior to the incarnation, the Word pre-existed Jesus? Perhaps even during the life of Jesus, the Word was *more* than Jesus, for although the question is a highly speculative one, there are surely some reasons for assenting to the so-called *extra Calvinisticum*. So when Jesus says in John's gospel, 'Before Abraham was, I am' (8.52) or when he speaks of 'the glory I had with [the Father] before the world was made' (17.5), perhaps we are to understand that in John's intention it is the Word who is speaking in and through Jesus, and that although the Word pre-existed not only before Abraham but the whole creation, this is not the case with Jesus, as the Word incarnate. As I said when we were considering the teaching of John, I believe it can be read in such a way that while it undoubtedly affirms that the Logos has existed 'from the beginning', this does not imply a personal pre-existence of Jesus Christ.[3] Something similar could be said about some of the patristic passages, for instance, the claim of Justin that when God speaks to the patriarchs of the Old Testament, this is the Logos. It is, however, the Logos prior to the historical incarnation in Jesus, and so does not imply a pre-existence of Jesus. There is an apparent parallel to these passages from John and Justin in one of Paul's letters, where, recalling the exodus of the Israelites from Egypt and their survival in the desert, he writes that 'they drank from the supernatural Rock which followed them, and the Rock was Christ' (I Cor. 10.4). Is not Paul saying here that Christ was present at the migration from Egypt, and that therefore he must have been pre-existent? If we had to assent to this question, then clearly it would severely damage our earlier exposition of Paul's christology. In that exposition, we relied heavily on Professor

Dunn, and with regard to the passage now before us, again I think that he offers us a perfectly sound and persuasive interpretation that does not entail that Paul had any thought of pre-existence in his mind. In Dunn's view, Paul is using the incident from Israel's history as a type of what is now happening in the church:

> In this typological interpretation it is not actually implied nor does it follow that Paul intended to identify Christ with Wisdom . . . Nor does it follow that Christ was thought of as having existed at the time of the wilderness wanderings. All we can safely say is that the allegorical interpretation of Philo or of Alexandrian Judaism [in which the Rock was identified with Wisdom] may well have prompted the more typological interpretation of Paul: as Rock = Wisdom in Alexandrian allegory, so Rock = Christ in Christian typology. In short, it is not sufficiently probable that I Cor. 10.4 refers to Christ as pre-existent for us to make anything of it in our inquiry.[4]

I do not think it is necessary for us to go back and re-examine the other New Testament witnesses discussed in earlier chapters of the book. It would be a tedious exercise and would not materially alter the position we have already reached, namely, that while some of the New Testament writers do believe in a pre-existent Logos or Wisdom which could not be anything but pre-existent, since it is a mode of the divine Being, and while they also believed that this pre-existent hypostasis dwelt in the human Jesus, they did not teach that Jesus himself was pre-existent. If they had, that would have been a denial of his true humanity and a lapse into mythology.

But are we not now in danger of separating Jesus from the Logos or Wisdom? Are we suggesting that Jesus just came along by accident, as it were, and turned out to be a suitable candidate in whom the Logos could become incarnate? Here I think we must move on to a second way of understanding pre-existence.

2. If the early chapters of Acts do give us a genuine reminiscence of the primitive Christian preaching, then this second way of understanding pre-existence may be quite ancient. It is a way which includes the whole Christ, not only the Logos but the human Jesus, but not in any literal conception of pre-existence that would have to be judged mythological or a denial of Jesus' true humanity. According to Acts, the primitive preaching spoke of the 'definite plan and foreknowledge of God' (2.23) in the event of Jesus Christ. If one accepts this idea of a providential plan, of a purpose or intention of God, then one could say that from the beginning Jesus too has existed in the mind and purpose of God. This is not literal or personal pre-existence, but it may be the only pre-existence we can begin

to understand and the only kind that is compatible with Jesus' true humanity.

These ideas have been worked out most fully by Karl Barth.[5] The election of Jesus Christ is, according to Barth, 'the beginning of all God's works and ways'.[6] Some startling consequences follow from this. It means, for instance, that the human race has been in God's intention from the beginning, for in electing Jesus Christ, God elected in him all humanity. In Barth's view, there is and presumably always has been, a 'humanity' in God. In our earlier discussion of Barth, we have seen that there are some obscurities, possibly confusions, in his teaching on those matters, and that his apparent willingness to pack all the action into a prehistorical eternal decree of election places the whole historical aspect of Christianity in question, both as regards its significance and even its reality. Still, the notion of election does give an intelligible and non-mythological sense to belief in the pre-existence of Jesus Christ, understood not simply as the Logos but as the Logos united to the man Jesus of Nazareth. If someone objects that on such a view Jesus Christ pre-existed 'only' in the mind of God, I think one would have to reply that to be conceived and affirmed in the intention of God is to enjoy a very high degree of reality, even if it is different from the reality of existing in space and time.

3. There is a third way of understanding pre-existence, and once again it would include the human and material aspects of Jesus Christ. This way is made possible by the modern evolutionary understanding of the world. According to contemporary cosmologists (and, of course, we all know that scientific theories may change considerably in course of time) the universe had its origin in a great burst of energy some fifteen to twenty billion years ago. From that initial event the world as we know it has gradually taken shape – galaxies and stars have been formed, the chemical elements have been built up, planetary systems have been formed, on some planets, perhaps many, perhaps very few, life has appeared and on earth at least, there have come into being creatures possessing rationality and personality. Some writers tell us that all this was already determined within minutes of the beginning. There was, so to speak, a 'fine tuning' and if the values of the natural constants had varied just a little one way or the other, the present universe would not have come about, there would not be intelligent beings on earth, there would be no cosmological theories for these could arise only in an 'anthropic' or quasi-anthropic universe that had produced its own possibilities for self-understanding. I am not being so naive as to suppose that an argument from design could be easily based on modern cosmology, and in any case I have consistently argued that if there is some *nisus* or goal-seeking striving in the evolutionary process, it is better

understood in immanental terms than as imposed from outside by a transcendent 'watchmaker'. But I am saying that, (however one may interpret the matter), this earth, the human race, yes, Jesus Christ himself were already latent, already predestined, in the primaeval swirling cloud of particles. Schleiermacher understood this when he wrote that 'Christ, *even as a human person*, was ever coming to be simultaneously with the world itself'.[7] A century or more later, when evolution had become a well established theory, Teilhard de Chardin was saying much the same when he wrote, 'The prodigious expanses of time which preceded the first Christmas were not empty of Christ.'[8] I come back to the point that incarnation was not a sudden once-for-all event which happened on 25 March of the year in which the archangel Gabriel made his annuncia-tion to the Blessed Virgin, but is a process which began with the creation. If I were to offer a definition of 'incarnation', I would say that it is the progressive presencing and self-manifestation of the Logos in the physical and historical world. For the Christian, this process reaches its climax in Jesus Christ, but the Christ-event is not isolated from the whole series of events. That is why we can say that the difference between Christ and other agents of the Logos is one of degree, not of kind. In particular, the evolution of the cosmos resolves itself eventually into the history of the human race, and within that history a special significance belongs to Israel and the prophetic tradition, and out of that in the fulness of time is born Jesus Christ. It is in some such way, I believe, that the mystery of pre-existence is to be understood.

Nativity

We consider next the birth of Jesus. Though its celebration at Christmas has become perhaps the most popular festival in the world, and though its 'happenedness' cannot be doubted (Jesus must have been born!) our historical information is negligible. At the time when Jesus was born, no one outside of the family circle would be interested. By the time the gospels were written, the circumstances of the birth would be long forgotten, and those who had known anything about it would be dead. Paul, Mark and John make no mention of the birth of Jesus. Matthew and Luke provide us with short narratives of the event but these must have been written more than eighty years after it happened. Both writers place the nativity in the reign of Herod the Great, who died about 4 BC, so that the conventional date of Christ's birth, though it serves as the basis of our calendar, must be wrong. Likewise there is doubt about the place, for though both Matthew and Luke name Bethlehem, this may be simply to conform to the belief that the messiah would be of Davidic descent and would come from his city, for otherwise Nazareth has good claims, perpetuated in the designation 'Jesus of Nazareth'. But apart from these scraps of doubtful information, the birth narratives are manifestly legendary in character. The stories of apparitions of angels or of the star that led the wise men to Bethlehem, however much they have come to be loved in Christian tradition, have no historical value and, I suspect, very little theological value either. Indeed, the incidents which glorify the birth of Jesus – the angels and the star – belong to the same tradition as the *theios aner* christology which we criticized above – they try to enhance the significance of Christ by introducing supernatural prodigies. Though no doubt it is also legendary, the story that Mary and Joseph were turned away from the inn has far more theological significance – I ventured to call it 'true legend'.[9]

But the crucial issue raised by the birth narratives in Matthew and Luke is their contention that Jesus was virginally conceived, that he had no human father but was conceived in the womb of Mary by the action of the Holy Spirit of God. This belief, though it is not found in the earlier witnesses of Paul and Mark, has nevertheless been taken into the fabric of orthodox Christian faith and is affirmed in the catholic creeds. But in spite of the fact that the virginal conception of Jesus (commonly called the 'virgin birth') has the status of a dogma of the church, I think we have to look at this dogma very critically and ask whether it makes any worthwhile theological contribution to christology.

Would the belief that Jesus was born of one human parent alone in any way enhance his stature in our eyes or his authority as one sent by God or the claim that he is the paradigm of humanity? I do not believe so. On the contrary, it would encourage the wrong kind of christology, the *theios aner* christology which still lingers in some quarters today and which demeans Christ by turning him into a wonder-worker. And that leads to the further point, that if we suppose Christ to have been conceived and born in an altogether unique way, then it seems that we have separated him from the rest of the human race and thereby made him irrelevant to the human quest for salvation or for the true life. We would be saying not that he is the revelation of God shedding light in our darkness, but that he is an altogether unintelligible anomaly, thrust into the middle of history.

But while I think these things have to be said, there is more to the matter. In our study of John's gospel, we took note that while he does not say anything about a virginal conception of Jesus, he does say something which is reminiscent of the virgin birth stories, but which applies to the whole Christian community, to all who have part in the Christ-event. Those whom he calls the 'children of God' were born 'not of blood nor of the will of the flesh nor of the will of man, but of God' (John 1.12–13). This is equivalent to saying that in Christianity there has emerged a new humanity drawing its *life* (and this Johannine word with all its connotations has to be emphasized) from God rather than from the world. And if we apply the words specifically to Jesus rather than to the community generally, it is through him that the community has come into existence and received its life, and he in turn is not a chance mutation thrown up in the course of evolution but the one in whom is concentrated that progressive penetration of the universe by the Logos that has been going on from the beginning and was intensified in the history of Israel. Any truth in these remarks is not affected one way or another by the biological circumstances of Jesus' conception and birth.

Baptism

Mark's gospel, unlike those of Matthew and Luke, says nothing about Jesus' birth but begins with his public ministry when he was already, so Luke tells us, 'about thirty years of age' (Luke 3.23). Mark has therefore the advantage over the other evangelists of beginning his account of Jesus in the clear light of history rather than in legend. The event which marked the beginning of Jesus's ministry was his baptism at the hands of John the Baptist, and this is one of the best attested happenings in Jesus' career.[10] It is one of the best attested happenings because it became something of an embarrassment to the early Christians and there must have been a tendency to suppress the memory of it. The reasons for this are obvious. Mark tells us plainly that John preached a 'baptism of repentance for the forgiveness of sins' (1.4) and again he declares quite simply that 'in those days Jesus came from Nazareth of Galilee and was baptized by John in the Jordan' (1.9). This would naturally lead us to suppose that Jesus had accepted John's baptism in a spirit of repentance and seeking forgiveness. But at a very early point in Christian history there arose a belief in the sinlessness of Jesus – the earliest reference to this belief is probably Paul's remark that he knew no sin (II Cor. 5.21). Presumably it was believed that if Christ is to be the Saviour, then he must himself be free from sin. So the idea that he had received a baptism of repentance for the forgiveness of sins would seem to impugn his sinlessness and indeed disqualify him as the Saviour from sin. Anxiety about these questions presumably lies behind the way in which Matthew alters the story of the baptism as told by Mark. According to Matthew, when Jesus came for baptism, 'John would have prevented him, saying "I need to be baptized by you, and do you come to me?" But Jesus answered him, "Let it be so now; for thus it is fitting for us to fulfil all righteousness". Then he consented' (Matt. 3.14–15). If Matthew's version of the incident were correct, then we would have to say that the baptism was an empty ceremony performed for the edification of the people!

But although we must beware of psychologizing, the incident is remembered and told in the gospels because it must have been significant for Jesus. It is for this reason that we include it among the 'mysteries' – it is an observable historical event, yet it is told in such a way that it is meant to throw light on the person of Christ. All three of the synoptists embellish their account of the baptism by telling us that as Jesus came up from the water, he had a vision of the heaven opening and the Spirit of God descending like a dove (indeed, Luke turns this into a public spectacle, with the dove 'in bodily form') while a heavenly voice pronounces, 'Thou art my beloved Son; with thee I am well pleased' (Mark 1.11). In John's gospel, although there are strong suggestions that John has baptized Jesus, this is not explicitly stated – perhaps a baptism by the Baptist would have been too inappropriate in the case of the Johannine Christ, and this gospel insists on a number of occasions that John acknowledged his subordination to Jesus (John 1.30; 3.30). But John's gospel too records the spiritual significance of the baptism, the descent from heaven of the Spirit as a dove, and its resting on Jesus (John 1.32). In this case, however, it is John the Baptist who is the recipient of the vision.

The total effect of these gospel accounts of the baptism is to shift attention away from the historical happening of a baptism of Jesus by John to a decisive moment in the career of Jesus, the moment when he receives the Spirit of God as a kind of messianic anointing, the call to his messianic vocation as the proclaimer and inaugurator of the kingdom of God. Of course, we need not suppose that this is how Jesus or any of the others understood matters at the time. There is no need to suppose a dramatic moment of vocation at all. So far as we can reconstruct the events, we might plausibly suppose that the young man Jesus had been stirred by eschatological teachings such as were current at the time, and that quite naturally he had been drawn to John the Baptist as a famous herald of the coming new age, that he had accepted baptism from John and that he may even have joined himself to any community that had gathered around the Baptist. But there are conflicting opinions about whether John was the centre of any community, and also about his possible relations to the Qumran community, and such questions are not really relevant to our own inquiries. If Jesus at the outset of his public ministry had some relation to John, he soon became an independent figure, and it seems that he did not adopt the ascetic style of John who had apparently modelled himself on the prophet Elijah (Matt. 11.18–19; Luke 7.33–34).

If it was only in retrospect that Jesus' baptism was seen as a moment of vocation, this would agree with what we have hitherto seen of a messianic consciousness on the part of Jesus. If he had such a consciousness, it may well have had its origins in a sense of vocation intensified at the time of the baptism, then deepening toward the end of his life and perhaps only explicitly proclaimed by his followers after the resurrection. But although it is dangerous to psychologize, the testimony of all four evangelists does strongly suggest that for Jesus the baptism was a decisive time when he devoted himself to the coming kingdom even if such ideas as messiahship were not explicitly in his mind.

Temptations and the Question of Sinlessness

In the synoptic gospels the story of the baptism is swiftly followed by a story of temptations. In Mark, it is simply said that 'he was in the wilderness forty days, tempted by Satan' (Mark 1.13), while in Matthew and Luke this is expanded into a legendary account (slightly different in the two gospels) in which specific temptations are presented by Satan and rejected by Jesus (Matt. 4.1–11; Luke 4.1–13). Of course, the evangelists are not suggesting that Christ's temptations came only at the beginning of his career, and were once for all overcome. They indicate that the temptations recurred almost to the very end, but the actual temptation narratives in Matthew and Luke serve as a kind of summary of the temptations that must have come to Jesus once he embarked on his vocation. Though the accounts are legendary, they are not based on psychological reconstruction but simply on common sense. Given that Jesus followed the course that he did, he must have encountered temptations of the kind described.

One of the temptations we can recognize right away from earlier discussions – it is the temptation to be the *theios aner*, the wonder-worker who in the ancient world could impose his authority on the masses by his supposedly supernatural powers. 'Cast yourself down from the Temple, and the angels will ensure a soft landing!' Rejected too is the 'bread and circuses' style of leadership, which so many demagogues have found successful. 'Command this stone to become bread!' Perhaps the other rejected temptation, the vision of the kingdoms of earth made subject to him, represents the way of the zealots, the way that relies on force and political power, the way which Reimarus thought Jesus had actually taken. It could only be with the advantage of hindsight that one could say that Jesus chose the way of the cross in preference to these other ways. Probably the inevitability of the cross came to his mind only very late, as we saw when we asked why he went up to Jerusalem.[11] But I think one might venture to say that even at the beginning of his ministry he chose the way of non-violence, of service to his fellows, of teaching, discussion and communication, as we read about his methods in the gospels.

The claim of the evangelists and, indeed, of other New Testament writers is that Jesus resisted the temptations that pressed upon him and was sinless. How do we understand this claim, and how important is it?

First of all, I think we should be clear in our minds that the assertion of Jesus' sinlessness does not depend on any doctrine of virginal conception or virgin birth. It was, I believe, mainly through the influence of

Augustine that there arose the opinion that sin is transmitted from generation to generation though the sexual act involved in procreation, so that if Jesus was to be preserved from the inheritance of original sin, he would have to be conceived supernaturally, apart from sexual intercourse. But if one rejects this Augustinian idea of the transmission of original sin, then the need for any break in the heredity of Jesus is seen to be uncalled for. It would in any case compromise his genuine humanity, and again and again I have insisted that any belief that places in doubt the entire humanity of Jesus must be rejected, for at a stroke it would render him irrelevant to human beings. Equally, one must reject another Augustinian idea, that Christ *could not* sin (*non posse peccare*). This again would appear to infringe his true humanity. The New Testament teaches that Christ *did not* sin, not that he could not. If he could not, then the narratives of his temptations lose all meaning and come very close to being deceptions.

Karl Barth was surely correct when he said that if Christ took human flesh, then it must have been 'sinful flesh'. I would myself avoid the expression 'sinful flesh' which can be misleading in several ways, but the point is that Jesus Christ really participated in the life of the human race. Now, if the human race is fallen, can one really be a man or live in solidarity with one's fellow men, without in some way being affected by that fallen condition? We cannot have it both ways. If we affirm that Christ is truly and fully human, sharing our condition, then we cannot insulate him against the universal presence of sin in human life. Perhaps we can ease the situation somewhat by distinguishing between individual and corporate sins. We might believe, for instance, that Jesus in his individual dealings refrained from sinful acts, but how could he refrain from participating in the corporate sins of society? It seems, for instance, that he paid taxes to the Roman authorities and taught that it was right to do so; but does this not mean that at least in some slight degree, he participated in the sins of imperial Rome? When he went to John and received the baptism of repentance, even if he was not conscious of any individual sins for which he needed forgiveness, may he not have been repenting in and with and even on behalf of his fellow Jews? – a point to which we shall return later.

Are we then going to say that while Jesus Christ in those individual acts for which he bore full responsibility remained without sin, yet in virtue of his incarnation in solidarity with the human community he shared in the corporate sinfulness of humanity? I am not sure that one can even say that. If Jesus was *really* tempted, if he *really* won a victory over sin at the cross, must he not have grappled with sin on the individual level too? Some words of John Knox have to be pondered at this point. He has just quoted from the epistle to the Hebrews the passage which describes Jesus as 'one who in every respect has been tempted as we are, yet without sin' (Heb. 4.15). Knox comments:

> [The author] means, of course, that Jesus, when he was tempted, did not *consent* to sin, did not succumb to its enticements. But, we may ask, can temptation be real if sin itself is not in some sense or measure already present? Is not sin the precondition or presupposition of temptation, even when our resistance or God's grace keeps it from being, in overt act, its consequence? Am I really tempted if I do not, however briefly or tentatively or slightly, consent? Have I been really tempted if I have rejected only that which entirely repels me or that from which I stand entirely aloof? Can we then think of Jesus as tempted – and, moreover, tempted in all respects as we are – and yet as not knowing from within the existential meaning of human sinfulness? I am not now saying that we cannot; I am saying that there is no obvious way in which we can.[12]

We can understand Knox's hesitancy in the last sentence. The considerations which he has advanced create a dilemma for the Christian theologian. On the one hand, it is an absolute necessity for him to maintain the solidarity of Christ with the human race; on the other hand, if Christ is simply in the same boat with all the rest, then it would seem that he too needs to be saved and cannot be a Saviour.

There is, however, another way in which we can look at these problems. Throughout this book, I have tried to lay stress on the notions of growth, development, process. Sinlessness too must be understood in a dynamic fashion. It could be only the product of a history, not a static condition brought about by a virginal conception or anything of the kind. Here we may recall the paradoxes that we met in Hebrews, where Christ on the one hand is said to have been 'made perfect' in the course of his temporal life on earth.[13] To quote a significant verse: 'Although he was a Son, he *learned* obedience through what he *suffered*; and *being made perfect*, he *became* the source of eternal salvation to all who obey him' (Heb. 5.9).

Sin may be briefly described as alienation from God. Anyone born into human society is bound to know this alienation – that is what we call 'original sin'. Surely Jesus too must have known this distance from God as he grew up in ancient Palestine. His 'sinlessness', in spite of the negative formation of the word, consisted in his highly affirmative overcoming of the distance, his deepening union with the Father through the deeds and decisions of his life, in which he overcame sin. I would not hesitate to call this a progressive incarnation in the life of Jesus.

Transfiguration
The three synoptic gospels all tell the story of the transfiguration of Jesus

(Mark 9.2–8; Matt. 17.1–8; Luke 9.28–36). It is the story of a vision. Jesus, accompanied by the 'inner circle' of his followers, climbs a mountain (traditionally Mount Tabor) and there they see him transfigured, shining 'like the sun'. He is joined by two of the great men of the Old Testament, Moses and Elijah, and a heavenly voice is heard attesting, as at his baptism, 'This is my beloved Son.'

It would be hard to say what historical actuality, if any, lies behind this story. It may have been a post-resurrection experience of some of the disciples, and this has been projected back into the ministry of Jesus. In the gospels, the transfiguration follows soon after Peter's confession of Jesus as the Christ at Caesarea Philippi, and we did note that quite possibly that confession was itself post-resurrection.[14]

I think it would be fair to say that the story is more an account of the disciples' reaction to Jesus than of anything that happened in Jesus himself. In the rise of the earliest Christian faith, there must have been some moment when the disciples saw in Jesus a new depth of significance, a new 'glory', to use the traditional word, and this seems to be the experience attested in the transfiguration story. What was that new significance? It would certainly be going too far to say that it was already an understanding of Jesus as the incarnate Son or Word. But the incident may be taken as evidence of a gradual deepening in the disciples' estimate of Jesus, a deepening process which came eventually to the idea of incarnation. That point, however, was still a long way in the future.

If the story of the transfiguration was, as some scholars hold, originally the story of a post-resurrection appearance, why did Mark move it back into the ministry of Jesus? Perhaps it is meant to serve as a pointer forward to the resurrection, which, of course, was already long past when Mark was writing. But there is another possibility, and although it is little more than a guess, I would like to suggest it. We have seen that several very reputable scholars – Bornkamm, Baillie, Schillebeeckx and others – have been unhappy with the contemporary tendency to place all the emphasis on cross and resurrection and to ignore or discount the ministry of Jesus. As Baillie very pertinently demanded, would the cross and resurrection have significance apart from what Jesus was in the life and activity that brought him to the cross?[15] Would the disciples have attached themselves to Jesus and given him their allegiance in the course of his ministry if they had not already found some salvific significance in him? Perhaps this is not very different from saying that there were in the ministry of Jesus pointers forward to the climax which came only at the end, preliminary 'gleams of glory', so to speak. It is even possible, in spite of what the New Testament experts say, that Peter's confession and the transfiguration belong within the ministry of Jesus. At any rate, that is where the evangelists have placed them! And whether or not they were correct in doing this, it does seem to suggest a stronger continuity between the Jesus of the ministry and the Christ of post-resurrection faith than is allowed by some scholars – I suppose I have Bultmann specially in mind.

Passion, Death and Atonement

The closing events of Jesus' life show us most clearly what is meant by describing the major moments of his career as 'mysteries', for here we have observable historical events, events that we could have seen if we had been there, yet at the same time they are claimed to be events of profound theological significance. This theological significance is not something that could be empirically observed, but is, we could say, a 'seeing in depth' of the events, a seeing which discloses them in their relation to man's spiritual needs and aspirations. The significance is not something added on to bare factual happenings, but is part of the events themselves as they impinge on the human moral and spiritual consciousness. Perhaps there is an analogy between what I am trying to describe and an aesthetic experience in which we 'see' not just colours, shapes and so on, but that subtler quality which we call beauty.

What then is the significance that Christian faith has claimed to see in the passion and death of Jesus? Paradoxically, it has been seen as a saving event, something which in spite of its darkness and horror as a public execution offers the possibility of wholeness and authenticity. The killing of this man is a desperate crime perpetrated by civil and religious officers; but the evangelists have turned the story into 'gospel'[16] so that as this man goes to his death those who hear the preaching of the cross are impelled to follow him and find true life in this death. This is their baptism into the death and life of Christ. This is their obedience to his own challenge, 'If any one would come after me, let him deny himself and take up his cross and follow me' (Mark 8.34).[17]

But how can we begin to understand such an incredible transformation? How can a judicial murder be represented as a salvific event?

This is the kind of question that has driven the church to seek a theology of atonement. Many such theologies have been produced and there is no single one that is universally accepted. At the best, we can only hope to have a number of analogies and metaphors, correcting and supplementing each other but together conveying something of the mystery of the cross as it has been experienced in Christian faith.

It is not my intention here to present any detailed theology of atonement. That subject is so broad and has been so much discussed that it would need a book to itself. But one cannot write about the person of Jesus Christ without maintaining the closest contact with his work, understood as his saving activity. Who he is and what he does are questions that are closely intertwined, and neither can be answered in isolation from the other. So without becoming involved in too much detail, we must consider at least in outline the place of Christ's death and atoning work within this christological study.

We can first of all clear the ground by setting to one side some theologies of atonement which, though they have been very influential, appear to me to presuppose ideas of God which, from a Christian point of view, are very questionable. I mean, theologies which represent God as angry and offended, or as a punishing God intent on exacting the penalty for sin. To say this is to acknowledge at once that we cannot make use of two of the best-known theologies of atonement from the past, the theologies of Anselm and Calvin. At the centre of Anselm's view was the concept of 'satisfaction'. God's honour had been outraged by human sinfulness, and even a perfectly righteous life could not make up for the damage done. God required an additional satisfaction, and this was provided by the death of the righteous man, Jesus. I do not think one needs to be a sentimentalist to say that such a harsh, even tyrannical, picture of God is unacceptable. In the case of Calvin, the ideas are different, but again it is a sub-Christian conception of God that we meet. The human race deserves punishment for its sins, but Christ takes their place though he is righteous and not deserving of punishment. By a legal fiction, his righteousness is 'imputed' to us and our guilt is 'imputed' to him; he suffers vicariously for us. In these theologies of atonement, not only is the understanding of God a highly questionable one, but even the understanding of salvation is a poor one, for it is taken to be mainly negative, an escaping of punishment. How far this falls short of John's teaching that Christ came to bring life! Unsatisfactory too is the way in which the relation between Christ and other human beings is envisaged in these theologies. Christ is seen as a substitute, and already in a criticism of Barth[18] we have seen the problems raised by such a view.

The first step toward outlining a theology of the saving work accomplished by Christ in his passion and death is to clarify the relation between Christ and the Christian. In an earlier chapter,[19] I suggested that Christ's relation to other human beings may best be considered as that of 'representative'. As the true human being who has fulfilled in his humanity the image of God, he is representative of that authentic humanity which is striving for expression in every human person. Here we must note the valuable work of Dorothee Sölle, who, in her book *Christ the Representative*, made a careful distinction between a 'representative' and a mere 'substitute'.[20] A substitute stands in and does something for us, in our place; we remain passive while the substitute gets on with it – indeed, we would not even need to know that he had done anything at all. I protested strongly against any such view of human salvation, when we met it in Barth.[21] Rational, moral, responsible human beings cannot be saved like so many sheep. Some response, some co-operation or synergism is needed, otherwise there is only a quasi-magical manipulation on a subpersonal level. That is one reason, in addition to others, for rejecting the atonement theologies we found in Anselm and Calvin. A representative is quite different from a substitute. The representative also steps in for us, but he holds the place open for us so that we can step in ourselves. The Christian must consciously appropriate the work of Christ on his or her behalf, and take up the cross. To believe in or to have faith in the cross of Christ is well expressed by Bultmann when he says that it is 'to accept Christ's cross as one's own, to be crucified with Christ'.[22] But what does that mean? It is what Paul understood by baptism (Rom. 6.3ff.). It is a turning away with Christ from the temptations of the world, the temptations of power, wealth, sensual indulgence and so on, to the things of the kingdom of God. That is why in the earlier discussion in this chapter of the baptism of Jesus and his sinlessness, I suggested that we need not be embarrassed that this representative man accepted a baptism of repentance – we can think of him as repenting for the whole race as their representative, and as one who in true solidarity with the race knew something of the alienation that sin has brought about. This links up also with what I regard as probably the best theological treatment of atonement to be found in modern writing on the subject, the work of John McLeod Campbell.[23] He claimed that Christ's atoning work 'took the form of a perfect confession of our sins'. As such, 'it has all the elements of a perfect repentance in humanity for all the sin of man – a perfect sorrow, a perfect contrition, all the elements of such a repentance, and that in absolute perfection, all – excepting the personal consciousness of sin'.[24] Campbell is obviously thinking here not so much of the actual blood-shedding and physical death of Calvary as of the passion which preceded those moments, the acceptance of death by Jesus, the resistance of the temptation to avoid it, the agony of the garden of Gethsemane. Also in his book he stresses not so much the past event as the 'prospective' aspect of the atonement as a continuing work which is constantly going on as Christians join with Christ in his perfect repentance. This indicates that he understood Christ as a representative in the sense explained above, not as a substitute.

Campbell was aware that the traditional belief in Christ's sinlessness does make it difficult to see how he could offer a perfect repentance. He rejected the Calvinist fiction of an 'imputation' of sin. But without going quite so far as more recent scholars such as John Knox, Campbell does consider the view (which I accepted above) that Christ in his solidarity with humanity could not avoid some participation in corporate sin. Thus

Campbell was fascinated by the saying of Paul that Christ 'was made sin for us' (II Cor. 5.21) and by some words of Luther about Christ's 'joining the company of the accursed, taking unto him their flesh and blood'.

Lest our emphasis on repentance gives the impression that like Anselm and Calvin we may be taking too negative a view of salvation as simply deliverance from evil, it is desirable to supplement Campbell's theology of atonement with one of the other models that have been used, that of sacrifice. Again we have to distance ourselves from any interpretation that would suggest placating an angry deity. Sacrifice, as we learned from the epistle to the Hebrews, is self-sacrifice, the offering of the self to God. Perhaps, as some scholars have claimed, Jesus believed that by offering himself in an obedience even to death, he could hasten the coming of the kingdom. For the disciples, joining themselves to Jesus means joining in the self-offering of his sacrifice, and so living in God and for God rather than for any merely selfish or worldly ends. Hebrews (as we interpreted it) leads us to see this sacrifice once again in 'prospective' terms, to use Campbell's word – it is not just an event of the past (though it certainly is something that has once happened) but is an ongoing event renewed in every act of faith in Christ, and in every baptism and eucharist.

Ending A (The Happy Ending)

At this point I break off for a few moments our study of the 'mysteries' of Christ in order to look ahead at where we are going. I think we are faced with two possible endings to the story, and I believe that reasons can be found in support of each of them.

The first I shall call the conventional ending. It is conventional in the sense that it is the one commonly accepted. It is supported by the majority of New Testament writers, it is incorporated into the catholic creeds, and it is re-enacted year by year in the liturgical calendar of the church.

According to this conventional ending, the mystery of Christ's atoning death was followed by several other mysteries – the descent into hell, the resurrection from the dead, the ascension into heaven, the session at the right hand of the Father, the sending of the Holy Spirit and, to conclude the series, a mystery which has not yet taken place, Christ's coming again with glory. So it stands in the Apostles' creed. After saying that Jesus 'suffered under Pontius Pilate', we go on: 'he descended into hell; the third day he rose again from the dead, and ascended into heaven, and sits on the right hand of God the Father almighty. From thence he shall come to judge the living and the dead.' The chronology of these events is based on Luke's gospel and the Acts of the Apostles, and is followed faithfully in the liturgical calendar. On the third day after the crucifixion comes

Easter and the resurrection; then forty days elapse (the time of the appearances of the risen Christ) before we come to the ascension; then a further ten days bring us to Pentecost and the sending of the Holy Spirit; while beyond that there is an indefinite stretch of time that will be closed by Christ's coming again.

I have ventured to call this series of events the 'happy ending', and I think it is true to say that we all have the happy ending syndrome. We would not have been satisfied if the story had ended with the cross. The need for a happy ending is natural to us and arises out of our moral sense. Even that very austere moralist, Immanuel Kant, believed that the *summum bonum* or highest good must include not only moral goodness or virtue, but happiness conjoined with it. He declares that virtue is the *supreme* good. 'But it does not follow,' he continues, 'that it is the whole and perfect good as the object of the desires of rational finite beings; for this requires happiness also.'[25]

When even a man of such invincible rectitude as Kant, a man who insisted that our actions have no moral value unless they are done simply because we *ought* to do them, claims that virtue ought to be crowned with happiness, then perhaps it should not even cross our minds to struggle against the happy ending syndrome. Persons who are weaker than Kant and do not share his tough moral fibre (and the present writer would have to include himself among them) may well feel justified without more ado in accepting the conventional ending. After all, it is firmly based on some of the most basic New Testament writings, it is the universal teaching of the church and, as we shall see, very strong arguments can be brought in its support. If it is not the 'true' ending, surely it *deserves* to be – and here the moral demand for a happy ending makes itself heard. I shall do my best to present this ending to the reader in its strongest form.

But I cannot conceal from the reader that there may be another way of seeing these matters. If there are strong arguments *for* the conventional ending, there are also serious question marks to place against it. And the questions do not arise just out of the modern scepticism that was engendered by the Enlightenment. I think that some of the New Testament writers themselves hint at another ending. We have picked up hints of this in those earlier chapters where we were examining the New Testament witnesses to Jesus. We remember, for instance, the abrupt ending of Mark: 'And they (the women) went out and fled from the tomb; for trembling and astonishment had come upon them; and they said nothing to anyone, for they were afraid' (Mark 16.8).[26] If these were indeed the final words of the gospel, then no wonder they did not satisfy the happy ending syndrome of the readers, and almost at once some people began providing smoother endings, including appearances of the risen Christ and the affirmation that he had been taken up to heaven and seated at the right hand of God. But I think the most important question marks arise out of John's gospel, as was briefly indicated at the end of Chapter 5, and will be discussed more fully below.[27]

But now we turn to the post-crucifixion mysteries of Ending A.

Descent into Hell

The descent into hell is hardly typical of the mysteries being discussed in this chapter, because in introducing the term 'mystery', I said that it was meant to embrace both a historical element and a theological interpretation. As far as the descent into hell is concerned, there is no historical element at all, the story being purely mythological and based on conceptions of the universe that were current in the first century but have long ago been superseded. It cannot even claim to have a scriptural foundation, for the few scattered passages which are sometimes cited as such a foundation are ambiguous and scholars are not agreed about what they mean. In our discussion of the christology of I Peter, I was prepared to accept that something like the traditional belief may be found there,[28] though I think I made it clear that there are many conflicting views about what the writer is trying to convey. The absence of any universally accepted teaching on the subject is well represented by the fact that whereas the Apostles' creed affirms that Christ descended into hell or the place of the dead, the Niceno-Constantinopolitan creed makes no mention of the matter and does not propose it as an article of belief.

Leaving aside the exegetical arguments over what the relevant biblical passages were originally meant to say, it seems to me that the *theological* justification for the belief is that it can be read as supporting the universal nature of the salvation offered in Christ. There would be something incomplete about any conception of salvation for which there is a cut-off point in time, a salvation, for instance, which is available now and will be available in future, but is not available to the past. To make sense of such ideas, one would have to confront very difficult questions concerning the nature of time, and what we mean by 'eternity'. Has the past simply disappeared into unreality? Or is it still real to God and accessible to him? In the age of relativity, such questions will not seem quite so absurd as they might once have done.[29] Those who speculated about a descent into hell had no conception of relativity, but it may be that in the mythological terms available to them, they were trying to express a belief that God's salvific purpose in Christ is not limited to the present and the future.

Resurrection

'If Christ has not been raised', writes Paul, 'then our preaching is in vain, and your faith is in vain' (I Cor. 15.14). He seems to be selecting a particular Christian belief and saying, 'Everything stands or falls by this!'

I doubt very much whether in the case of such a complex system of beliefs as Christianity, such a simplistic mode of falsification is possible. But it is certainly true that the resurrection of Jesus Christ is a key element in what I have called the 'conventional' story. If it were taken away or even radically demythologized, it would certainly have left a major gap behind it; and the various items in Christian faith are so closely interrelated and interdependent that the knock-on effect, so to speak, would be pretty drastic. Yet for the post-Enlightenment mentality, resurrection is a very difficult idea to accept. Indeed, it always has been one of the stumbling-blocks in Christian faith. Just as surely, however, it was 'of first importance' in Paul's gospel or kerygma (I Cor. 15.1ff.).

Let us begin our consideration of this mystery in the same way as with most of the others – by asking about any discernible historical basis. By this I do not mean an actual rising from the dead, for contemporary historians would hardly regard such an event as historical within their sense of the word. Even theologians, including quite orthodox theologians, hesitate to say that the resurrection of Jesus was historical in any ordinary sense. Barth, for instance, says: 'The death of Jesus can certainly be thought of as history in the modern sense, but not the resurrection.'[30] But unquestionably there is here a historical event that calls for a sufficient explanation. That is simply the rise of the Christian church. This is, so to speak, the outward, visible, historically observable aspect of the resurrection, considered as part of the Christ-event and not only something in the career of Jesus. For the rise of the Christian church is not easily explained. The gospels give the impression that after the crucifixion the Twelve scattered in fear. In spite of the respect felt for them, they were obviously a group of rather mediocre people, not one of them, not even Peter, remotely approaching Jesus in moral stature or able to take over leadership. The enemies of Jesus had calculated well in getting rid of the leader of the new movement. It ought to have faded out in a very short time. But instead it burst forth with tremendous energy and spread through the Mediterranean and elsewhere. Writing about fifty years later, the Roman historian Tacitus mentions the execution of Christ by Pontius Pilate and says, 'a deadly superstition (Christianity), thus checked for the moment, again broke out not only in Judaea, the source of the evil, but also in the City (Rome)'.[31] Why did events take this unexpected turn? According to the testimony of these same Christians, it was because their leader, Jesus Christ, had risen from the dead and was still alive among them. There is a solid historical fact here, namely, that the birth of the church depended on the belief of the disciples that Jesus had been resurrected. Of course, their belief may have been mistaken. But we can begin from the datum that only a belief in the resurrection provides anything like a sufficient reason for the rise of Christianity after the death of Jesus.

We may notice first of all that belief in a resurrection of the dead was accepted by many Jews in the first century, though it was rejected by the conservative party, known as the Sadducees. The ancient tradition did not teach resurrection, though it acknowledged some kind of shadowy survival of the dead in an underworld – the belief we have already met in our discussions of Jesus' descent into hell.[32] But at the time of the Maccabean wars, when many young men were perishing in the cause of the Jewish faith, the belief took root that for them there would be more than the shadowy fate of Sheol or Hades, an existence that would be no less full and concrete than what they had known on earth, and that was represented as a bodily resurrection of the dead. There was therefore a background of belief in resurrection which might lend some plausibility to a claim that Jesus had risen.

But there was a further difficulty here. The Jewish expectation was of a general resurrection at the end of the age. The resurrection of Jesus fell outside of this expectation, as an isolated occurrence which had to be understood as an anticipation in an individual case of the general resurrection that would take place in the future. So there must have been some quite powerful experience in the Christian community that led its members to believe that God had acted specially in the case of Jesus by raising him from the dead.

Where then can we find the 'powerful experience' that produced belief in the resurrection? Several answers have been given. 1. Paul is our oldest written source for the resurrection, and he speaks of 'appearances' of the risen Christ to the disciples. Christ had appeared to him personally (I Cor. 15.8) and Paul reports that he had already appeared to other disciples, some of whom he names. Paul gives no details of these appearances (the descriptions of his own experience we owe not to his own laconic account but to the Acts of the Apostles), but the gospels describe with some detail quite a number of appearances to disciples in various circumstances. No doubt all these appearances were quite convincing to those who experienced them – they did believe that Christ had come back from the dead and was seen and heard by them. In our sceptical age, however, we would feel compelled to ask whether their experiences were subjective, and this is a question to which we shall turn shortly.

2. A different kind of experience is cited by some of the witnesses – the discovery of the empty tomb of Jesus. Bultmann thinks the story of the empty tomb is a later tradition, meant to give objectivity to the stories of appearances. Pannenberg, on the other hand, is prepared to accept the empty tomb story as an independent tradition. Paul, however, shows no knowledge of an empty tomb. But in any case, an empty tomb would not seem to provide much evidence. Today, if we discovered an empty tomb,

we would not dream of explaining it by a resurrection. Was the case much different in the time of Jesus, when the resurrection was not expected until the end of the world? There were all kinds of more plausible explanations of the empty tomb – the women might have gone to the wrong tomb, or the body had been removed. Certainly, in isolation, the empty tomb (assuming that it was indeed found empty) would not afford any decisive ground for belief in a resurrection.[33]

3. There is a third possibility, which has already come to our notice in a discussion of Schillebeeckx' christology.[34] On this view, it was a study of the Old Testament and some of the deutero-canonical literature that led Peter and then the others to believe that God would not desert his chosen servant, and it was this biblical promise that gave rise to the belief that Christ had risen and then to stories of an empty tomb and appearances, not the other way round. I have already sufficiently criticized this view on the ground that something much more dramatic than meditation on a few passages of scripture would be needed to bring about the belief that Jesus had risen from the dead. That there was indeed an intensive searching of the scriptures in the primitive church is attested by Luke (Luke 24.27) and was noted by Strauss in the early nineteenth century, but it is most improbable that it was a major factor in creating belief in the resurrection.

But can we reach a clearer idea of what we mean when we speak of the resurrection of Jesus Christ? Nothing could be more futile than to say that 'something happened' that gave rise to the belief. We have to be much more specific in saying what that 'something' was. Here I think we are greatly helped by Paul's extended discourse on resurrection in I Corinthians 15. He writes: 'But someone will ask, "How are the dead raised? With what kind of body do they come?"' (15.35). Perhaps these questions are unanswerable! But if we are going to talk about 'resurrection' then we have to give some indication of how we understand the idea. I think a little reflection, and also Paul's arguments, make it clear that what is resurrected is not the dead body that has been laid in the grave, not the body of flesh and blood and carbon chemistry by which human beings live on earth. (This point raises further problems about the story of an empty tomb.) That physical body is like an automobile – it has a built-in obsolescence, and though it may keep going for seventy or eighty or even a hundred years, it will eventually wear out and perish in death. So resurrection cannot be anything so simple as the resuscitation of a corpse, for that would be only a temporary postponement of death, which would come eventually. It would be quite different from the resurrection of Jesus Christ who, the New Testament claims, has conquered death and is alive for ever. To go back to Paul's argument, a natural body of flesh and blood could not be the bearer of a death- transcending existence.

So it is with the resurrection of the dead. What is sown is perishable, what is raised is imperishable. It is sown in dishonour, it is raised in glory. It is sown in weakness, it is raised in power. It is sown a physical body, it is raised a spiritual body. If there is a physical body, there is also a spiritual body (I Cor. 15.42–44).

The main point here is the assertion that there is a 'spiritual body'. We have to get beyond the thinking that 'body' means merely or even primarily the familiar structure of bones, flesh, blood and so on. Rather, 'body' is that aspect of one's being whereby one is inserted into a world, and so empowered to perceive, communicate and act in that world. The bodies that we have insert us into this earthly world of space and time, and empower us to perceive, communicate and act in this world. But may there be other 'worlds', other systems of relationships into which we are differently inserted? Are there, for instance, personal or interpersonal worlds, in which persons would be related in a manner different from that which depends on the bodily senses? Do we already have some hint of the possibility in our present experience, when people claim to be in communion with one another, though not using words or touching or looking at each other? I am not talking here about so-called 'paranormal' experiences, such as telepathy and I do not myself intend to get into that kind of area. But there are highly respected scholars, such as Hans Urs von Balthasar[35] and the Canadian philosopher of religion, Donald Evans,[36] who have looked sympathetically at the claims by mystics and others to have 'spiritual perceptions' of various kinds. The mystery of how mind and body are related in the human being is still far from being fully understood, and therefore the debate about the resurrection of Jesus Christ is still going on. Perhaps resurrection is transcendence to a new level in the being of the human person, a level which eludes our understanding so long as we are seeing it only from below. In any case, we are not confined to those visionary experiences recorded in the New Testament. Throughout the history of Christendom, men and women have claimed to have encounters with the living Christ, especially in a eucharistic context. Are these all to be dismissed as illusory, or must they not be added to the New Testament witness as further evidences that the crucified one lives on today?

Ascension

In the Luke–Acts chronology, the risen Christ continued to appear at intervals to the disciples for a period of forty days. Then there was a last encounter which they called the 'ascension'. Like the descent into hell, the ascension cannot be given any historical dimension, for it depends on a mythological conception of the universe. The mystery of the ascension is perhaps best understood like some of the others, as an event in the consciousness of the disciples rather than in the career of Christ himself. It is his final apotheosis when, in the traditional language, he takes his seat at the right hand of God.

The mystery of the ascension is drawing out a further meaning of the resurrection. Christ, who even in the appearance stories was still located at points in time and space, has now been raised to the side of God and has been universalized as a 'life-giving spirit', to use Paul's language (I Cor. 15.45). The meaning of the ascension for the disciples is the same as the message given to the women at the tomb: 'You seek Jesus of Nazareth who was crucified; he is risen, he is not here' (Mark 16.6). Henceforth he is with God and his life has been taken into the life of God, from whom it had drawn its power; and as ascended Lord, Christ now communicates that life to his followers everywhere. To express this in another way, we could say that the ascended Lord is not to be located in time and space, but lives at the centre of a different kind of world – a world of personal and interpersonal relation into which Christians are inserted, as I indicated briefly in the section on resurrection. The point is illustrated by an important insight of Karl Rahner: 'By his resurrection and ascension Jesus did not merely enter into a pre-existent heaven; rather, his resurrection created heaven for us.'[37]

Second Coming

The last mystery of Jesus Christ is different from all the others. It is something that has still to happen, whereas the other mysteries have all already taken place. Furthermore, when we talk of this final mystery of his coming again, the clouds of mythology thicken, and preoccupation with the expectation of Christ's return has been the source of many superstitions and has led to the growth of many deviant Christian or quasi-Christian sects.

As a future event, the second coming can as yet have no historical component. We may, however, investigate the historical origins of the belief. Did Jesus himself promise that he would return? Or was this expectation first formed by the disciples? When we turn to the New Testament in search of an answer to these questions, the suspicion arises that perhaps the belief originated in a mistake. Some of the disciples may have understood Jesus to be promising that he would return, but in fact he may not have intended his words in this way at all.

The reader may remember that in discussing the titles applied to Jesus, we considered among them the expression 'Son of Man'.[38] The phrase has different meanings in different contexts, but in some it has a definitely apocalyptic flavour. The Son of Man will come to hold judgment and to inaugurate the new age. When we read these passages of the New

Testament today, we assume that when Jesus speaks of the Son of Man, he is referring to himself, as undoubtedly he is in some other Son of Man passages. But when we look carefully, we find ambiguities. When, for instance, we read that Jesus said, 'When the Son of Man comes in his glory, and all the angels with him, then he will sit on his glorious throne' (Matt. 25.31), this verse and the verses following would most naturally be read as referring to some person other than Jesus. To quote another case, where we have two versions of the same saying: Luke records Jesus' words as, 'Every one who acknowledges me before men, the Son of Man also will acknowledge before the angels of God' (Luke 12.8) and here the Son of Man appears to be someone other than Jesus; but Matthew reports the words as, 'Every one who acknowledges me before men, I also will acknowledge before my Father who is in heaven' (Matt. 10.32), and here the saying applies to Jesus himself. It is quite possible or even probable that originally Jesus was thinking of someone other than himself. But after the crucifixion and resurrection, when Jesus was fully acknowledged as Lord and Christ, there was no room for some further apocalyptic Son of Man, and so any sayings of Jesus that spoke of the coming of such a person in the future had to be applied to himself. In any case, regardless of how the belief originated, the expectation that Jesus would come again from heaven became part of common Christian teaching and found a place in the catholic creeds. It would not be altogether unfair to say that in his early epistles Paul seems just as much preoccupied with the expected return of Christ as with what Christ has already done. But as time went on and the second advent did not take place, the expectation began to fade. It is much less evident in Paul's later letters. There may even have been something of a crisis in the church, as the initial hopes of a speedy return were disappointed. We get a hint of the complaints that were being made from a late writing of the New Testament: 'Where is the promise of his coming? For ever since the fathers fell asleep, all things have continued as they were from the beginning of creation' (II Peter 3.4). So the expectation of a return lost its urgency and was postponed to a distant future, where it still remains.

Can this doctrine of a second coming still find a place in a modern christology? We have seen that Moltmann has made an attempt to revive a futuristic eschatology. I suppose that one might say in a very general way that if Christ is the revelation of God and of the divine purpose for the creation, then in the end the spirit of Christ which is also the Spirit of God will bring all things to their destined fulfilment. But this would come about by the gradual processes of history, not by the dramatic return of a heavenly judge, which looks like the last kick of the *theios aner* christology.

Ending B (The Austere Ending)

I promised the reader that I would present the standard ending of the story of Christ in the strongest form I could find, and I think that has been done. That ending is enshrined in a series of mysteries, dominated by resurrection and ascension. This is the teaching of the church, and I think these ideas can make sense and be acceptable in the context of modern thought. I repeat too that the happy ending *deserves* to be true.

But the need to be absolutely honest compels us to look at an alternative scenario. Suppose in our account of the career of Jesus we had felt compelled to draw the bottom line under the cross? Suppose we omitted the 'joyful mysteries' that traditionally came after the cross? Would that destroy the whole fabric of faith in Christ? I do not think so, for the two great distinctive Christian affirmations would remain untouched – God is love, and God is revealed in Jesus Christ. These two affirmations would stand even if there were no mysteries beyond Calvary. This would be the austere ending to the story – so austere that we naturally shrink from it. But we have to give it a fair hearing.

It is obvious that we do not live in an ideal world. Any world of finite entities is bound to fall short of perfection, and even God is subject to constraints imposed by his own creation. In an ideal world, virtue and happiness would be joined together, as Kant visualized. But perhaps even God cannot arrange for this. If one had to make a choice between virtue and happiness, the choice would have to be virtue, for virtue can survive without happiness, but happiness cannot survive without virtue. We can imagine a virtuous person constantly racked by pain and ill-health, perpetually anxious over his or her children, deprived of every comfort and consolation. Though such a person might retain a certain peace of mind, it would be a misuse of language to say that he or she was happy.

If the highest virtue is the kind of love which the New Testament attributes to Jesus, then it seems to me that his victory over evil was already won in the agonizing hours before his death, and that it would remain decisive even if there were no subsequent events of resurrection and ascension – even if, as Pascal held, 'Jesus will be in agony until the end of the world'.[39] Pascal makes this comment in a passage where he depicts Jesus in Gethsemane, 'sorrowful even to death', seeking the solace of his friends, but not getting it, because they were asleep. Must not God be in agony over the sins and sufferings of his creatures, as long as the world continues?

Exaltation

Have I, in these last few paragraphs, been selling out completely to modern secular thought, to which ideas like resurrection and ascension are myths, not to be taken seriously? No, I think there are better reasons for saying what has been said. I want first to go back to the fact that John's gospel ends differently from the others. There is no series of mysteries spread over several weeks, as there is in Luke and in the conventional ending. Rather, everything is packed into one decisive happening. The clue to this occurs quite early in John, where we read: 'And as Moses lifted up the serpent in the wilderness, so must the Son of Man be lifted up, that whoever believes in him may have eternal life' (John 3.14–15). The allusion is to a story in the Old Testament of a plague which afflicted Israel, until Moses fashioned a serpent which he raised on a pole, and which healed the people when they looked toward it. Although the verse quoted does not make it explicit, the comparison is with Christ being raised up on the cross. The explicit connection is made later in the gospel: '"I when I am lifted up from the earth, will draw all men to myself". He said this to show by what death he was to die' (John 12.32–3). Of all the Johannine paradoxes, this one is surely the most striking. Jesus' exaltation *is* the cross! His exaltation *is* his humiliation! After this, a separate ascension into heaven would be an anticlimax. And the other post-crucifixion mysteries are also collapsed into one another. It is true that John, like the other evangelists, tells of the resurrection, the empty tomb and appearances to the disciples. But the significance of a distinct resurrection is reduced in a gospel in which the Saviour from the beginning has been the mediator of the eternal life of God, and in which the disciples have already received eternal life. 'Truly, truly, I say to you, he who hears my word and believes him who has sent me, has eternal life; he does not come into judgment, but has passed from death to life. The gift of the Holy Spirit is given on Easter day, not seven weeks later as in Luke–Acts. And it has been argued that for John the gift of the Spirit is the return or second coming of Jesus, for in this gospel the futuristic eschatology has become a realized eschatology. So it could be claimed that what I have called Ending B is not just a concession to modernity but has roots in John's gospel.

Among modern theologians, the one who comes nearest to setting forth something like Ending B is Rudolf Bultmann. According to him, 'faith in resurrection is really the same thing as faith in the saving efficacy of the cross'.[40]

We are compelled to ask whether all this mythological language [about resurrection and ascension] is not simply an attempt to express the meaning of the historical figure of Jesus and the events of his life; in other words, the significance of these as a figure and event of salvation. If that be so, we can dispense with the objective form in which they are cast.[41]

Does that mean then that resurrection is primarily an event in the disciples rather than in Jesus? One can answer this only with a 'yes and no'. Resurrection is an event in the believers, it is indeed the event of the church, which is Christ's living body, and which in its preaching and sacraments and community continues his life and work. But the meaning of resurrection is originally in Jesus himself – in the possession and mediation by him of true life, eternal life, which he brought to its highest pitch on the cross.

So I leave to the reader the choice between Ending A and Ending B.[42] Both, I think, can find roots in the scriptures, both conserve the essential truths of Christianity, both can find modern ways of being expressed, but I doubt if they can both be combined into an intelligible unity.

Christ and the Saviour Figures

There is one further important point to be discussed when we consider how we are to think of Jesus Christ today. We have become conscious as never before of both the unity and the diversity of the human race; of its unity, because in the technological age events which happen in one part of the world have their effects on what is happening virtually everywhere else; of its diversity because easy travel, instant communication, massive migrations and better education have made us aware of the many cultures, languages and religions that flourish in different parts of the earth. So Christianity is inevitably seen in the context of religious pluralism. How is it related to other faiths, especially to those half dozen or so great world religions which embrace among them the vast majority of human beings? Are there affinities among these faiths, or are they still – as they often have been in the past – rivals for the allegiance of mankind? In particular, a question arises about Jesus Christ. Does he have an absolutely unique and incomparable status? Does he provide the only way to a right relation to God, so that other ways and those who have taught them must be accounted mistaken? For many centuries, I think most Christians would have said that this is indeed the case, that the non-Christian religions including Judaism are erroneous and that salvation is to be found in Christ alone. However, I have urged several times in this book that the difference between Jesus Christ and other human beings (including the founders of world religions) is not one of kind but of degree, and this is to acknowledge that there must be some affinity. But this is far from saying that one must adopt a thoroughgoing relativism and say that one religion is as good as another or that the differences are merely cultural and do not raise questions of truth and falsehood. That kind of attitude is superficial and fails to treat the particular teachings of the religions with the respect due to them.

Although I have been saying that the question of religious pluralism is one that is peculiarly pressing in our own time, the church from the beginning has been aware of the claims of other faiths. In the earliest days, Christians knew both the Jewish religion from which they had sprung themselves, and also the many pagan cults that abounded in the world of the first century. The attitude of many of these early Christians was probably much like Paul's, when he wrote: 'There are many "gods" and many "lords", but for us, there is one God, the Father, from whom are all things and for whom we exist, and one Lord, Jesus Christ, through whom are all things and through whom we exist' (I Cor. 8.5–6). In saying this, Paul was speaking both as a Jewish monotheist for whom there is only one God, and as a Christian who believed that this one God had communicated himself in a new and decisive way in the person of the one Lord, Jesus Christ. Here we see, shall we say, the theological equivalent of the story of the ascension – the association of Jesus Christ with the one God in a relation which at a later time is defined in the doctrine of the Trinity, the new and distinctive Christian doctrine of God. But God the Father in the Christian scheme is still identified with the God of the Jewish and Old Testament tradition. On the other hand, the gods and goddesses of the pagan cults were kept at a distance, just as the Hebrew prophets had rejected any kind of syncretism between the God of Israel and the deities of Canaan. But there was this difference, that some of the early Christian theologians were sympathetic to Greek philosophical ideas of God. So one could say that from very early times there was a measure of ambivalence in the Christian attitude towards other faiths.

This is reflected in the New Testament itself, for it would be impossible to derive from it any one clear and consistent line of teaching on this question of the status of other faiths, even if one thought that an appeal to biblical texts could be decisive. We have ourselves taken note of a number of passages in the New Testament which seem to point in the direction of some kind of universalism, for instance, that great procession in Hebrews 11 of the men and women of faith, a procession which is led not, as we might have expected, by Abraham, the father of the people of God, but by what we may call 'universal' human beings, Abel, Enoch and Noah; or that introduction in the prologue to John's gospel of the Logos concept, 'the true light that lightens every man coming into the world' (John 1.9). But someone who was unhappy with this universalist interpretation could easily have found other passages with an apparently opposite intention, for instance, John's gospel also represents Jesus as saying, 'I am the way, the truth and the life; no one comes to the Father but by me' (John 14.6); while in Acts 4.12, we read of Peter saying: 'There is salvation in no one else [but Jesus], for there is no other name under heaven given among men by which we must be saved.' In the Nicene creed, we echo the Johannine language in confessing Jesus Christ as 'the *only* Son of

God'. It is, of course, understandable that in the early centuries, when Christianity was struggling to establish its identity over against both Judaism on the one side and paganism on the other, it had to express its faith in the strongest terms available. Those early Christian apostles and evangelists could not afford the luxury of academic debate, even if the thought had occurred to them. We cannot imagine them saying, 'Well, this is the message of Jesus Christ; but you have to consider whether it is saying anything that you cannot find in the Jewish tradition, or whether there is any wisdom in it preferable to what you can learn from Stoicism or some other school of thought.' That would not have been a kerygma or proclamation and it would not have gained any converts. If those early Christians really believed that something new and important had come about in Jesus Christ, if they had themselves undergone some deep salvific experience, and if they felt called to share the new spiritual truth, then inevitably they would put their energy into affirming their own beliefs. What is surprising is not that they did this, but that some of them, even in the midst of their desperate struggle for survival, were still able to voice those universal tendencies that were a part of their new faith.

But for us in the vastly altered circumstances of today, a different attitude is appropriate from that which prevailed in the early days of Christianity. I have already mentioned how to an extent that is unprecedented we have become aware of other cultures and other religions. But it is not just a case of having become aware of them. Many of us have met adherents of faiths other than our own, and been impressed by the deep spirituality that we have found among them. We find them manifesting qualities which Christian faith also encourages. Again, many of us have read the scriptures or writings of these faiths, now readily available in translation at almost any sizable bookstore, and we have found there teaching to which our consciences respond. And again, we cannot ignore the thinking and researches of the past two centuries. Troeltsch, without falling into what he called 'aimless relativism', showed the difficulty, if not the impossibility, of claiming 'absolute' truth. So today I think our attitude to other faiths would be much more affirmative than it has been in the past.

But at this point we must pause to clarify just what we mean when we speak of religions, and in particular what we mean when we speak of 'saviour figures', an expression which appeared in the title of this chapter. Religion is such a widely diversified phenomenon that I do not think anyone has ever produced a definition that has been universally accepted. Each religion has its own peculiar characteristics, and to bring them all within the scope of a single definition seems to be impossible. Karl Barth even went so far as to claim that Christianity is not a religion at all, but we felt unable to go along with his claim, because it rested on a very biased conception of religion.[1] Most theologians do not think that Christianity can avoid being counted as a religion, or that it should try to avoid being so counted.

Although it seems to be impossible to find a definition of religion that would cover all cases, there are certain characteristics that appear in almost every religion, certainly in what I have called 'world religions', that is to say, religions which have reached a relatively high level of moral and spiritual development and have gained for themselves a worldwide following or at least a worldwide recognition and respect. Some of them, such as Buddhism, Christianity and Islam, number many millions of adherents and have become international in character. Others, such as Hinduism, Shintoism, Confucianism and Taoism, also have millions of followers but are associated with particular nations or peoples. Still others are quite small numerically, but because of their lofty teachings have gained worldwide respect – I would mention Judaism, Parseeism and Sikhism.

What common characteristics can we find in the religions mentioned? It will be sufficient to name two, which are specially relevant to our concern in this book. The first is the recognition of what I shall call a 'holy reality'. In some cases this holy reality may be called God, but this particular word suggests a personal being, and in some religions the holy reality is conceived as an impersonal Absolute or in other ways for which God-language would not be appropriate. The second characteristic which we find in virtually all the world religions is a human figure who stands in a special relation to the holy reality. Perhaps this human figure has taught about the holy reality, or has brought some communication from the holy reality. Here I have in mind such figures as Buddha, Jesus, Moses, Krishna and so on.

Let me say just a little more about 'holy reality' and 'saviour figures'. Though I have said that 'holy reality' cannot be simply equated with 'God', nevertheless it appears that virtually every language has a word corresponding to the English word 'God'. Even where the 'holy reality is not a personal being, as in Theravada or Hinayana Buddhism, there may be recognition of 'gods', and it is inaccurate to describe this type of Buddhism as 'atheistic'.[2] In general, the religions of the West and also of the Middle East think of the holy reality as God (personal), while the religions of the further East think rather in terms of an impersonal (perhaps suprapersonal) Absolute. To include both types, I have in earlier writings used the expression 'holy Being', which is in some ways preferable to 'holy reality'.[3] But in using a common expression for both, I am recognizing a kinship between them. The two ways of conceiving holy Being (personal and nonpersonal) do not exclude one another and sometimes overlap. There are Christian mystics who have spoken of a

God who appears to transcend personal categories, while in both Hinduism and Buddhism there are personal manifestations of the ultimately nameless Being. Just as there are differences in the ways of conceiving holy Being, so there are very considerable differences among what I call the saviour figures. The expression 'saviour' is more applicable to some than to others. It is regularly used of Jesus, likewise of Krishna and of the Buddha in the Mahayana type of Buddhism. But one would hardly apply it to Confucius, except in a very broad way, or to Mohammed. Just as many titles were used of Jesus, so many have been used of the saviours in the various religions – 'prophet', 'teacher', 'founder', 'revealer'. I suppose the word 'mediator' might be widely acceptable, since all of these men did in fact mediate an understanding of holy Being to their followers. But here again we see the danger of sliding too easily into relativism with regard to these different faiths and their founders. In the name of tolerance or even a so-called 'liberalism', we tend to submerge the differences and to concentrate only on what we find is common ground. But this is to do much less than justice to those individual figures whom we try to force into some stereotyped pattern. Perhaps all we can say is that each one of them sought to bring about the enhancement of human life. We remember the words of Jesus, 'I have come that they may have life, and have it abundantly' (John 10.10). Though they would be differently understood in each case, I believe that these same words would express the intentions of the other saviour figures.

So I am saying that although our own study has been of Jesus Christ and although we have found in him, as I believe, a sufficient answer to human need and a sufficient revelation of God, we must respect those other teachers of the human race who have brought enhancement of life to people in other traditions. What they have in common with Jesus Christ is more important than their differences. What then is the common ground?

The first point is very simple – they are all human beings. They all, in spite of individual differences, share the human condition, the common human relationships and the common human problems. If there is one point that has been stressed repeatedly throughout this book, it is that theologians may not and must not in any way diminish or compromise the humanity of Jesus Christ. They may not, for example, make him so exalted and so different that he is turned into an alien type of being, not truly and fully human. If that ever happens, then he becomes irrelevant to us, for only one who has lived as a truly human person, has known the weaknesses and even the temptations of such a life, but has also known its possibilities for transcendence – only such a one can be a saviour and can push forward the frontiers of the human spirit. This is one of the great truths emphasized in Hebrews: 'In that he himself has suffered, being tempted, he is able to help them that are tempted' (Heb. 2.18). The difference between Jesus Christ and other human beings, including the saviour figures, is a difference *within* humanity – they have all shared that plastic raw material of the spirit that we call human nature, and each has fashioned it as he or she has been able.

The second point about Jesus and the other saviour figures is that all of them were seeking to realize the highest possibilities inherent in being a human person. In their several ways, they pursued justice, righteous-ness, love, compassion, peace and whatever else belongs to the well-being of the race. In them there is concentrated for us the greatest spiritual striving and aspirations that have been known on earth. They are figures of faith and hope who must not be forgotten or obscured in a world where opposing tendencies are also at work and there is the constant threat of a decline into aggression, greed, materialism, sensuality and whatever else makes finally for destruction and death.

The third point is that all of these saviour figures were mediators of grace. We have seen what this means in the case of Jesus Christ, yet these others too were emissaries of holy Being. They too had given themselves up to the service of a divine reality, who might work in them and through them for the lifting up of all creatures upon earth.

These saviour figures then were human beings, as Jesus Christ too assuredly was. But like him they gained such status in the eyes of their followers that in varying degrees their historicity and even their human-ity tended to be swallowed up in a mass of legendary accretion. Even Mohammed, one of the most recent founders of a great religion and one about whom a considerable amount of historical detail is known, has been made the subject of legendary exploits. On the other hand, figures such as Lao-tzu and Krishna are on the very margin between history and fiction. In the decades after the Enlightenment, historians tended to write off some of these ancient founders of religions as mere figments of the pious imagination. But probably scepticism went too far. We have seen that in the late nineteenth century Jesus too was declared by some to be a mythical figure, but that view never established itself among serious scholars. I think one can say that the others too have a good claim to have existed, even if information about some of them is very slight. Moses, for instance, is now a figure of the very distant past, and the early records about him have a minimal historical value, because even the earliest come from long after the time in which he is supposed to have lived. Yet the existence of Israel, with its distinctive religion of one God and its high moral teaching is evidence of some deep religious insight and therefore of the existence of one or more deep religious thinkers at some remote time several centuries before the appearance of the first writing prophets in the clear light of history. These deep insights from the past imprinted on Israel a distinctive character so profound that they preserved some memory of it all, and in their traditions told of a flight from Egypt under a prophetic leader, of the giving of a divine law (though this may well have taken place over a long period). They called that archetypal prophet Moses, and whether or not that was his name, there must have been some such figure, perhaps more than one, at the origin of these formative events. Similarly with even the most obscure among the saviour figures. Lao-tzu is very shadowy, and his name may not be a proper name at all. Yet we can hardly say that he is completely unknown, for we still have something of his teaching. Even Krishna is now claimed by some to have been a historical figure, and there does appear to be a two-thousand year old tradition that he was born in the city of Mathura, not very far from Agra.

But does it matter whether these saviour figures ever existed or not? Yes, it does matter, and for the same reasons that we took into account when we saw that it is important that Jesus Christ existed in history, and is not only a mythological figure. These saviour figures are figures of hope because their appearance from time to time on the face of this planet and their achievement in nudging the race forward toward a new and better humanity is a source of confidence in the worthwhileness of human life. And they have gathered around them followers who have continued to pursue their goals in communities of faith. Must we not say then of these founders that they had received in some measure the Word or Logos of God and had been to that extent vehicles of God's self-communication and agents of his in the salvation or making whole of mankind? In some cases, indeed, especially that of Krishna, there is something like a belief in incarnation, and this could be a helpful subject for dialogue among the religions.[4] At least, it could be so long as incarnation is not supposed to be an isolated event in Jesus Christ alone, but is seen to have been a continuous process of incarnation that began with creation, reached its climax in Christ and continues even today.

The non-Christian saviour figures too can be included in that long history of faith. I mentioned that in Hebrews the procession of the men and women of faith begins before Abraham, with some universal human figures. Should we not include some after Abraham as well? Suppose the procession has reached that point where Moses is passing, for obviously Christians too look back to him, as well as Jews.

By faith Moses, when he came of age, refused to be called the son of Pharaoh's daughter, choosing rather to suffer affliction with the children of God than to enjoy the pleasures of sin for a season.

By faith Mohammed, when he saw the people of Mecca degraded

by idolatries, brought them the message of the one invisible God who is righteous and merciful.

By faith Gautama Buddha, when he had perceived the damage done to human life by our undisciplined desires, taught the multitudes of Asia to restrain desire and to learn compassion for one another.

By faith Krishna brought the presence of the high God among the hosts so that they might know God cares for them.

By faith Confucius, living among the warring states of China, had a new vision of the blessings of rationality and sought to build up human relationships in accordance with the will of heaven . . .

And what more shall I say? For the time would not be sufficient to tell of Gideon and of Barak, of Zoroaster and of Lao-tzu and of Nanak and of others who through faith subdued kingdoms, worked righteousness, obtained promises, quelled aggressors.

'What more shall I say?' I think I must, as a Christian theologian, go on to say in the further words of the epistle to the Hebrews: 'All these, though well attested by their faith, did not receive what was promised, since God had foreseen something better for us' (Heb. 11.39–40). I would have to say as a Christian that the history of faith reaches its fulfilment in Jesus Christ. But I say that without the slightest disrespect for those who have found a relation to God in some other faith. When we hear the words ascribed to Jesus in John's gospel, 'I am the way, the truth and the life; no one comes to the Father but by me', we do not hear them in a narrowly exclusive way. In John's gospel, let us remember, the words of Jesus are the words of the Logos, not just of the individual human being, Jesus of Nazareth. That Word or Logos enlightens every one who comes into the world. Those of us who are Christians believe that we have heard it loud and clear in Jesus Christ and that we need not look beyond him. But we do not deny that the Word finds expression in other traditions and, indeed, in the whole creation. That does not lead us to become syncretists or relativists. It is only as we ourselves have accepted a commitment to the Word where that Word has encountered us that we can have an understanding of what it has meant to those following a different way. That will still be true if a day ever comes when theologians have to think not only of other terrestrial faiths such as those discussed in this chapter, but of what to us are unimaginable ideas of other intelligent races in remote parts of the universe. The mode of communication would be different, but it would be the same Logos speaking, and speaking the same words that we have heard through Jesus Christ: 'I am the way, the truth and the life; no one comes to the Father but by me.'

Notes

Part One: The Sources and the Rise of Classical Christology

1. Problems of Christology

1. Paul Tillich, *Systematic Theology*, vol. 2, University of Chicago Press 1957, p. 97.

2. Ibid.

3. Edward Schillebeeckx, *Jesus: An Experiment in Christology*, Crossroad Publishing and Collins 1979, p. 473.

4. A recent notable example is E. P. Sanders, *Jesus and Judaism*, SCM Press and Fortress Press 1985.

5. E. L. Mascall, *Jesus: Who He Is and How We Know Him*, Darton Longman & Todd 1985, pp. 38–9.

6. Friedrich Nietzsche, *Ecce Homo*, Vintage Books 1969, p. 300.

7. D. M. MacKinnon, '"Substance" in Christology – A Cross-bench View,' in S. W. Sykes and I. P. Clayton (eds), *Christ, Faith and History*, Cambridge University Press 1972, p. 288.

8. Maurice Wiles, *Explorations in Theology*[4], SCM Press 1979, p. 24.

9. J. D. G. Dunn, *Unity and Diversity in the New Testament*, 1977, revised second edition, SCM Press and Trinity Press International 1990, p. 56.

10. Ibid., p. 376.

11. Ibid., pp. 226–7.

12. Ibid., p. 56.

13. See above, p. 8.

14. Karl Barth, *Church Dogmatics* IV/2, T. & T. Clark 1958, p. 70.

15. Hans-Georg Gadamer, *Truth and Method*, Sheed & Ward 1975, p. 87.

16. Ibid., p. 13.

17. Ibid., p. 103.

18. Ibid.

19. Karl Barth, *Church Dogmatics* I/1, T. & T. Clark 1936, p. 188.

20. Martin Kähler, *The So-called Historical Jesus and the Historic Biblical Christ* Fortress Press 1964, p. 66.

21. Ibid., p. 43.

22. Rudolf Bultmann, *The Gospel of John*, Blackwell 1971, p. 648.

23. Wolfhart Pannenberg, 'The Revelation of God in Jesus of Nazareth' in J. M. Robinson and John B. Cobb, (eds), *Theology as History*, Harper & Row 1967, pp. 126–7.

24. See R. G. Collingwood, *The Idea of History*, Oxford University Press 1946.

25. Rudolf Bultmann, *Essays Philosophical and Theological*, SCM Press 1955, p. 286.

26. John Knox, *The Church and the Reality of Christ*, Harper & Row 1962, p. 23.

27. Ibid., pp. 22 and 122–3.

28. Wiles, op. cit., p. 22.

29. A curious story is told about Lord Herbert and his book, showing how the old superaturalism still mingled with rationalism – a phenomenon which we shall encounter again: Lord Herbert of Cherbury, having completed *De Veritate*, prayed: 'O Thou eternal God, Author of the light which now shines upon me and Giver of all inward Illuminations, I do beseech Thee of thine infinite goodness to pardon a greater request than a sinner ought to make. I am not satisfied enough whether I shall publish this Book, *De Veritate*; if it be for thy glory, I beseech Thee, give me some sign from Heaven; if not, I shall suppress it.' He had no sooner spoken these words than (as he affirms) a gentle noise came from Heaven such as he had never heard on earth, which he took for a sign and published his book in 1624 – J. Daniell, *George Herbert*, SPCK 1893, p. 294.

30. Immanuel Kant, *Critique of Practical Reason*, Longmans Green 1927, p. 260.

31. See H. S. Reimarus, *Fragments*, SCM Press and Fortress Press 1971.

32. Voltaire, Letters No. 96.

33. Kant, *Sämmtliche Werke*, Leipzig 1867, vol. 4, p. 159.

2. The Prehistory of Christology

1. D. F. Strauss, *Life of Jesus*, Swan Sonnenschien 1906⁵, p. 742.

2. A. J. Heschel, *The Prophets*, Harper & Row 1962, p. 224.

3. Ibid., p. 308.

4. Ibid., p. 25.

5. For a recent discussion of the place of covenants in Israel, see Ernest W. Nicholson, *God and His People*, Oxford University Press 1986.

6. G. von Rad, *Old Testament Theology*, vol. 2, Oliver & Boyd 1965, p. 319.

7. M. Eliade, *Cosmos and History*, Harper & Row 1959, p. 9.

8. R. Bultmann, *Theology of the New Testament*, vol. 1, SCM Press 1952, p. 4.

9. See above, p. 14.

10. Oscar Cullmann, *The Christology of the New Testament*, SCM Press 1959, p. 113.

11. Von Rad, op. cit., pp. 170–1.

12. W. Eichrodt, *Theology of the Old Testament*, vol. 2, SCM Press and Westminster Press 1967, p. 266.

13. See Cullmann, op. cit., pp. 86, 116.

14. See above, p. 3.

15. R. Bultmann, *The History of the Synoptic Tradition*, Harper & Row and Blackwell 1963, p. 257.

16. Ibid., pp. 258–9.

17. See Cullmann, op. cit., pp. 119–20.

18. Ibid., p. 56.

19. G. Bornkamm, *Jesus of Nazareth*, Hodder & Stoughton 1960, p. 172.

20. Morna Hooker, *The Son of Man in Mark*, SPCK and McGill University Press 1967, p. 71.

21. Bultmann, *Theology*, vol. 1, p. 9.

22. E. Stauffer, *New Testament Theology*, SCM Press 1955, p. 111.

23. Justin the Martyr, *Dialogue with Trypho a Jew*, 67.

24. Martin Hengel, *The Son of God*, SCM Press and Fortress Press, 1976, pp. 21–2.

25. R. H. Fuller, *The Foundations of New Testament Christology*, Scribner 1965, p. 115.

26. A. E. Harvey, *Jesus and the Constraints of History*, Duckworth 1982, p. 161.

27. See below, p. 109.

28. Bultmann, *Theology*, vol. 1, p. 124. Bultmann's views on this question were much influenced by the 'History of Religions' school, and especially by Wilhelm Bousset's book, *Kyrios Christos*, Göttingen 1913.

29. G. Stanton, 'Incarnational Christology in the New Testament', in M. Goulder, (ed.), *Incarnation and Myth*, SCM Press 1979, p. 155.

30. See below, pp. 293ff.

31. R. Bultmann, 'The Christological Confession of the World Council of Churches', in *Essays Philosophical and Theological*, SCM Press 1955, p. 275.

32. Raymond E. Brown, *Jesus, God and Man*, Bruce Publishing Co. 1967, pp. 28–9.

33. John C. Fenton, 'Matthew and the Divinity of Jesus' in E. A. Livingstone (ed), *Studia Biblica*, Sheffield 1980.

3. The Witness of Paul

1. See E. Schillebeeckx, *Jesus: an Experiment in Christology*, Crossroad Publishing and Collins 1979.

2. K. Barth, *Church Dogmatics*, vol. IV/2, T. & T. Clark 1958, p. 132.

3. John Knox, *Chapters in a Life of Paul*, A. & C. Black 1954, pp. 74ff.

4. J. A. T. Robinson, *Redating the New Testament*, SCM Press 1976, p. 84.

5. See above, p. 45.

6. S. Weinberg, *The First Three Minutes*, Collins 1978, p. 112.

7. Martin Hengel, *The Son of God*, SCM Press and Fortress Press 1976, p. 2.

8. See John Bowden, *Jesus: the Unanswered Questions*, SCM Press and Abingdon Press 1988, p. 204.

9. D. F. Strauss, *Life of Jesus*, Swan Sonenschien 1906[5], p. 86.

10. Ibid.

11. See above, p. 38.

12. William Wrede, *Paul*, Philip Green 1907, p. 151.

13. Of course, the fact that Paul apparently believed that Jesus was a descendant of David may simply be something he deduced from his belief that Jesus was the Christ, and may not rest on any specific information that he had. Indeed, what he says in I Cor. 1.18ff., about God's choosing 'what is low and despised in the world' might indicate that he would be little concerned about Davidic descent. According to Mark, Jesus himself discouraged the belief that the Christ is the son of David (Mark 12.35–37).

14. See below, pp. 405ff.

15. See E. P. Sanders, *Jesus and Judaism*, SCM Press and Fortress Press 1985. The list of events regarded by Sanders as having a high degree of certainty was made by John Bowden, op. cit., p. 43.

16. W. P. DuBose, *The Gospel according to St Paul*, Longmans Green 1907, p. 293. Reprinted in D. S. Armentrout, *A DuBose Reader*, University of the South 1984, p. 142.

17. John Hick (ed.), *The Myth of God Incarnate*, SCM Press 1977.

18. James D. G. Dunn, *Christology in the Making*, SCM Press and Westminster Press 1980, second edition SCM Press 1989, pp. 1, 13–14.

19. Ibid., p. 114.

20. Ibid., p. 117.

21. Ibid.,

22. See above, p. 14.

23. Barth, Church Dogmatics, IV/2, p. 33.

24. See below, pp. 245ff.

25. R. Bultmann, *Theology of the New Testament*, vol. 1, SCM Press 1952, p. 175.

26. See above, p. 56.

27. Dunn, op. cit., pp. 122–3.

28. See above, p. 57.

29. See below, pp. 348ff.

30. A. Deissman, *Paul*, Hodder & Stoughton 1926, p. 153.

31. John Knox, *The Church and the Reality of Christ*, Harper & Row 1962, p. 83.

32. See above, pp. 57–59.

33. Ibid.

34. Hans Urs von Balthasar, *A Theology of History*, Sheed & Ward 1963, p. 11.

35. Bultmann, *Theology*, vol. 1, pp. 191ff.

36. See below, pp. 405ff.

37. See G. Wainwright, *Eucharist and Eschatology*, Epworth Press 1971, p. 67.

38. Joachim Jeremias, *The Eucharistic Words of Jesus*, Scribner and SCM Press 1966, pp. 251–2.

39. Ibid., pp. 248–9.

4. The Witness of the Synoptics

1. See W. G. Kümmel, *The New Testament: The History of the Investigation of Its Problems*, SCM Press 1973, pp. 146–8.

2. See Humphrey Palmer, *The Logic of Gospel Criticism*, Macmillan 1968, p. 130ff.

3. Eusebius, *Ecclesiastical History*, III, 39.

4. See Rudolf Bultmann, *The History of the Synoptic Tradition*, Harper & Row and Blackwell 1963, pp. 1–7.

5. Ibid., p. 40, n. 1.

6. See above, p. 41.

7. Bultmann, op cit., p. 241.

8. See above, p. 72.

9. See above, p. 10.

10. William Wrede, *The Messianic Secret*, James Clarke 1971, p. 148.

11. See above, pp. 37–38.

12. Wrede, op. cit., p. 230.

13. Ibid., p. 18.

14. Alec McCowen.

15. Wrede, op. cit., p. 17.

16. See above, pp. 42–43.

17. Bultmann, op. cit., p. 241.

18. R. H. Fuller, *The Foundations of New Testament Christology*, Scribner 1965, pp. 227–8.

19. See below, pp. 335ff.
20. Strauss, *The Life of Jesus*, pp. 563ff.
21. See above, pp. 38–39.
22. Vincent Taylor, *The Atonement in New Testament Teaching*, Epworth Press 1940, p. 21.
23. Bultmann, op. cit., p. 161.
24. See above, pp. 38–39.
25. See above, pp. 82–83.
26. See below, p. 90.
27. John Knox, *The Death of Christ*, Abingdon Press 1958, p. 84.
28. E. P. Sanders, *Jesus and Judaism*, SCM Press and Fortress Press 1985, p. 305.
29. Joachim Jeremias, *The Eucharistic Words of Jesus*, Scribner and SCM Press 1966, p. 125.
30. Ibid., p. 115.
31. Ibid., p. 253.
32. Geoffrey Wainwright, *Eucharist and Eschatology*, Epworth Press 1971, p. 67.
33. R. Bultmann in H.-W. Bartsch, (ed.), *Kerygma and Myth*, vol. 1, SPCK 1957, p. 00.
34. G. Wainwright, *Doxology*, Epworth Press 1980, p. 426.
35. Richard Holloway, *Let God Arise*, Mowbray 1972, p. 147.
36. Bultmann, *History of the Synoptic Tradition*, p. 267.
37. A. E. Harvey, *Jesus and the Constraints of History*, Duckworth 1982, p. 170ff.
38. Sanders, op. cit., p. 319f.
39. Knox, op. cit., p. 21.
40. Jürgen Moltmann, *The Crucified God*, SCM Press and Harper & Row 1974, p. 000.
41. Bultmann, op. cit., p. 241.
42. Geza Vermes, *Jesus the Jew*, Collins and Fortress Press 1973, p. 41.
43. Wolfhart Pannenberg, *Jesus – God and Man*, SCM Press and Westminster Press 1968, p. 101.
44. See above, p. 82.
45. See above, p. 47.
46. C. F. D. Moule, *The Origin of Christology*, Cambridge University Press 1977, pp. 175f.
47. W. D. Davies, *The Sermon on the Mount*, Cambridge University Press 1966, p. 31.
48. Bultmann, op. cit., p. 367.
49. Ernst Bloch, *The Principle of Hope*, Blackwell 1986, vol. 3, p. 1256.
50. Charles Guignebert, *Jesus*, Kegan Paul 1935, pp. 96–104.
51. Barth, *Church Dogmatics*, vol. IV/2, pp. 150ff.

5. *The Witness of John*

1. See above, p. 89.
2. R. Bultmann, *Theology of the New Testament*, vol. 2, SCM Press 1955, p. 4.
3. This is the view of most scholars. For a different view, see J. A. T. Robinson, *The Priority of John*, SCM Press 1985, pp. 318–22.
4. See above, pp. 37–38.
5. See above, pp. 81–82.
6. See above, pp. 86–87.

7. Clement of Alexandria, quoted by Eusebius, *Ecclesiastical History*, vi, 14.

8. Clement of Alexandria, *Stromateis*, vi, 9.

9. Bultmann, op. cit., pp. 12–14.

10. J. A. T. Robinson, *Redating the New Testament*, SCM Press 1976 and *The Priority of John*, SCM Press 1985.

11. J. Louis Martyn, *History and Theology in the Fourth Gospel*, Harper & Row 1968.

12. Hans Jonas, *The Gnostic Religion*, Beacon Press 1963², p. 320.

13. E. Käsemann, *The Testament of Jesus*, SCM Press 1968, p. 9.

14. See above, pp. 80, 90.

15. Robinson, *Priority*, p. 366.

16. See above, p. 6.

17. J. Macquarrie, *Thinking about God*, SCM Press and Harper & Row 1975, p. 77.

18. See above, pp. 44–45.

19. K. Barth, *Church Dogmatics*, I/1, T. & T. Clark 1936, p. 150.

20. See above, p. 43.

21. See above, pp. 46–47.

22. See below, pp. 258–59.

23. Bowman L. Clarke, 'Reflections on God, Being and Reference' in *Being and Truth*, ed. A. A. Kee and E. T. Long, SCM Press 1986, pp. 54–5.

24. W. P. DuBose in *A DuBose Reader*, ed. D. S. Armentrout, University of the South 1984, p. 149.

25. Justin, *First Apology*, xlvi, 1–4.

26. C. H. Dodd, *The Interpretation of the Fourth Gospel*, Cambridge University Press 1953, p. 244.

27. See above, p. 103.

28. See above, pp. 66–67.

29. Bultmann, *Theology*, vol. 2, p. 66.

30. Ibid.

31. Bultmann, *Gospel of John*, p. 364. See also pp. 225–6, n. 3.

32. John C. Fenton, *Finding the Way through John*, Mowbray 1988, p. 17.

33. See below, p. 413.

6. Other New Testament Witness

1. John A. T. Robinson, *Redating the New Testament*, SCM Press 1976, p. 200.

2. A. H. McNeile, *An Introduction to the Study of the New Testament*, Oxford University Press 1927, p. 225.

3. See below, pp. 396ff.

4. See above, pp. 31–32.

5. John Henry Newman, *Tract One*, Rocket Press 1985, p. 16.

6. Myles Bourke in *The Jerome Biblical Commentary*, Chapman 1968, vol. 2, p. 395.

7. See below, pp. 212–24.

8. E. Jüngel, *God as the Mystery of the World*, T. & T. Clark 1983, p. 94.

9. See below, pp. 355ff.

10. See above, pp. 56ff. and 82ff.

11. The Shepherd of Hermas, *Commandment* 4, ch. 3.

12. See above, pp. 87 and 100.

13. E. Schillebeeckx, *Christ: The Christian Experience in the Modern World*, Crossroad Publishing and SCM Press 1980, p. 276.

14. Ibid.

15. *ARCIC Final Report*, SPCK and CTS 1981, p. 35.

16. John Baillie, *The Sense of the Presence of God*, Oxford University Press 1962, p. 133.

17. See above, p. 38.

18. Pannenberg, *Jesus – God and Man*; Schillebeeckx, *Christ*.

19. Schillebeeckx, op. cit., p. 230.

20. Pannenberg, op. cit., p. 271.

21. See below, p. 405.

22. Hans Jonas, *The Gnostic Religion*, Beacon Press 1963², p. 235.

23. John Knox, *The Humanity and Divinity of Christ*, Cambridge University Press 1967, p. 17.

24. Ibid., p. 38.

25. Ibid., p. 56.

26. See above, p. 59.

27. Knox, op. cit., p. 20.

28. Ibid., p. 37.

29. Ibid., p. 47.

7. The Rise of Classical Christology

1. See above, pp. 49–50.

2. Hengel, as we have seen, mentions seven centuries. Perhaps he had in mind the (sixth) ecumenical council, held at Constantinople in 680; or the theological activity of John of Damascus (died 749), often counted the last of the Fathers. Such dating can be only approximate, and some people might prefer to speak of four centuries, that is to say, up to the council of Chalcedon which dealt with far more significant issues than those which followed it.

3. See above, pp. 23–24.

4. Maurice Wiles, *The Christian Fathers*, Hodder & Stoughton 1966, pp. 9–10.

5. Bernard Lonergan, *The Way to Nicaea*, Darton, Longman & Todd 1976, p. 105.

6. Ibid., pp. 136–7.

7. Ignatius, *Rom.* 6. Quotations from Ignatius are from the Ante-Nicene Christian Library (ANCL), T. & T. Clark 1867ff.

8. Ignatius, *Eph.*, 7.

9. Ignatius, *Smyr.*, 2.

10. See above, p. 44.

11. Justin, *Dialogue with Trypho*, 127 (ANCL).

12. Justin, *1 Apology* 13 (ANCL).

13. Justin, ibid., 46.

14. See above, p. 117.

15. Irenaeus, *Against Heresies*, I, 26 and V, 1 (ANCL).

16. See J. Macquarrie, 'Some Thoughts on Heresy' in *Thinking about God*, SCM Press 1975, pp. 44–51.

17. Irenaeus, op. cit., IV, 38.

18. Ibid.

19. Ibid., IV, 20.

20. Ibid., V, 20.

21. Ibid., V, 1.

22. See above, p. 101.

23. R. D. Williams, *Arius: Heresy and Tradition*, Darton, Longman & Todd 1987, p. 158.

24. Origen, *De Principiis*, I, 2, 2 (ANCL).

25. Ibid., I, 2, 3.

26. Ibid., II, 8, 2.

27. See below, pp. 159–60.

28. Origen, op. cit., II, 6, 6.

29. Ibid., II, 6, 2.

30. Ibid., I, 2, 6.

31. Origen, *Contra Celsum*, VII, 17, ed. H. Chadwick, Cambridge University Press 1965.

32. Maurice Wiles, *Working Papers in Doctrine*, SCM Press 1976, p. 28.

33. Ibid., p. 37.

34. Ibid., p. 30, with reference.

35. For a brief account of these events, see J. N. D. Kelly, *Early Christian Doctrines*, A. & C. Black 1968[4], p. 231ff.

36. See below, p. 159.

37. See G. C. Stead, *Divine Substance*, Oxford University Press 1977.

38. See below, pp. 383ff.

39. Athanasius, *De Incarnatione*, 41, Oxford Early Christian Texts 1971.

40. See above, p. 154.

41. A. Grillmeier, *Christ in Christian Tradition*, Vol. 1, Mowbray 1975[2], p. 299f.

42. See Kelly, op. cit., p. 281ff.

43. Ibid., p. 292.

44. Ibid.

45. Gregory of Nazianzus, *Ep.* 101. Nicene and Post-Nicene Fathers, Parker 1894.

46. Augustine, *On the Trinity*, I, 12 and I, 2. Quotations from *Works*, ed. Marcus Dods, T. & T. Clark 1871ff.

47. Augustine, *On the Trinity*, IV, 9 and *The city of God*, XVII, 4.

48. Augustine, *Confessions*, VII, 9.

49. See F. Nau (ed.), *Le livre d'Heraclide de Damas*, Paris 1910 and F. Loofs, (ed.), *Nestoriana*, Halle 1905.

50. S. Cave, *The Doctrine of the Person of Christ*, Duckworth 1925, p. 110.

51. The texts of Cyril's letters, the Tome of Leo, the Chalcedonian definition and other related documents are collected and edited by C. A. Heurtley in *De Fide et Symbolo*, Parker 1889. Dr Heurtley furnished English translations in his companion volume, *On Faith and the Creeds*, Parker 1886.

52. See above, pp. 162–63.

53. Leo, *Tome*, 4.

54. S. Kierkegaard, *Philosophical Fragments*, Princeton University Press 1936, p. 29.

55. Karl Rahner, *Theological Investigations*, vol. 1, Darton, Longman & Todd 1961, p. 149.

56. John Meyendorff, *Christ in Eastern Christian Thought*, Corpus Books 1969, p. 99. See Maximus Confessor, *Selected Writings*, Paulist Press 1985.

57. See J. P. Migne, *Patrologia Graeca*, Vol. 91, c. 1080 ab.

58. See above, p. 156.

59. H. M. Relton, *A Study in Christology*, SPCK 1917.

60. See V. Lossky, *The Mystical Theology of the Eastern Church*, James Clarke 1957, p. 141.

61. T. Ware, *The Orthodox Church*, Penguin Books 1964, pp. 40–41.

62. Ibid.

63. John of Damascus, *On Icons*, I, 16. *Patrologia Graeca*, Vol. 94, c. 1245 a.

64. Anselm, *Our Deus homo*, John Grant Edinburgh 1909.

65. Thomas' christology is treated in *Summa Theologiae*, III, qq. 1–59 Blackfriars Edition, vols. 48–55, 1963ff.

66. Ibid., q. 3, a. 7.

67. See Gregory Palamas, *The Triads*, Paulist Press 1983.

68. P. Melanchthon, *Loci Communes*, ed. G. L. Plitt and T. Kolder, Erlangen 1890, p. 60.

69. John Calvin, *Institutes of the Christian Religion*, James Clarke 1953, vol. 1, p. 414.

70. K. Barth, *Church Dogmatics* IV/1, pp. 180–81.

Part Two: The Critique of the Classical Christology and Attempts at Reconstruction

8. Rationalist Christology

1. See above, p. 25.

2. Immanuel Kant, *Religion within the Limits of Reason Alone*, Harper & Row 1960, p. 9.

3. Immanuel Kant, *Critique of Pure Reason*, Macmillan 1956, p. 7.

4. See above, p. 24.

5. G. E. Lessing, *Theological Writings*, A. & C. Black 1956, p. 52.

6. Ibid., p. 53.

7. Ibid., p. 83.

8. Ibid., p. 97.

9. Kant, *Religion*, p. 15.

10. Ibid., p. 3.

11. Ibid., p. 56.

12. Ibid., p. 55.

13. Kant, *Pure Reason*, p. 93.

14. J. Macquarrie, *In Search of Deity*, SCM Press and Crossroad Publishing 1984, pp. 12–13.

15. Kant, *Religion*, p. 54.

16. Ibid., p. 59.

17. Ibid., p. 55.

18. Ibid., p. 179.

19. See above, p. 24.

20. Kant, *Critique of Judgment*, Oxford University Press 1928, Part 2, p. 131.

21. Kant, *Critique of Practical Reason*, Longmans Green 1927, pp. 200–201.

22. See E. Adickes, *Kants Opus postumum*, Berlin 1920, pp. 819, 824.

23. Some mystical writers might speak of God as 'suprapersonal'. But Kant was no mystic.

24. Kant, *Religion*, p. 105.

25. Professor at Marburg, 1876–1912.

26. Kant, *Religion*, p. 116.

27. Ibid.

9. Humanistic Christology

1. *On Religion: Speeches to its Cultured Despisers*, Harper & Row 1958.
2. Karl Barth, *Protestant Thought: From Rousseau to Ritschl*, SCM Press 1959, p. 306.
3. Schleiermacher, *Speeches*, p. 18.
4. Ibid., p. 61.
5. Ibid., p. 40.
6. See below, p. 202.
7. Karl Barth, *Church Dogmatics* I/2, T. & T. Clark 1956, p. 302.
8. Maurice Wiles, *What Is Theology?*, Oxford University Press 1976, p. 10.
9. Schleiermacher, op. cit., p. 89.
10. See above, p. 6.
11. Schleiermacher, op. cit., p. 89.
12. Ibid., p. 88.
13. Ibid.
14. Ibid., pp. 245–6.
15. Ibid., p. 248.
16. Ibid., p. 241.
17. Ibid., p. 238.
18. It is this second edition that is available in English translation: *The Christian Faith*, T. & T. Clark 1928.
19. Ibid., p. 5ff.
20. Ibid., p. 76.
21. See above, p. 197.
22. Schleiermacher, op. cit., p. 12.
23. Ibid.
24. Ibid., pp. 133–4.
25. Ibid., p. 64.
26. See J.-P. Sartre, *Being and Nothingness*, Methuen 1957, p. 74.
27. Schleiermacher, op. cit., p. 126.
28. Ibid., p. 385.
29. Ibid.
30. Ibid., p. 374.
31. Ibid., p. 367.
32. Ibid., p. 402.
33. See above, p. 133.
34. Barth, *Protestant Thought*, p. 200.
35. See above, p. 203.
36. Schleiermacher, op. cit., p. 405.
37. Ibid., p. 95.
38. Ibid., p. 389.
39. Ibid., p. 388.
40. See below, p. 398.
41. Schleiermacher, op. cit., p. 392.
42. Ibid., p. 393.
43. Ibid., p. 395.
44. Ibid., p. 425.

45. See above, p. 198.
46. Schleiermacher, op. cit., pp. 428–9.
47. Ibid., p. 428.

10. Idealist Christology

1. G. W. F. Hegel, *The Philosophy of History*, Dover Publications 1956, p. 318.
2. G. W. F. Hegel, *Logic* from The Encyclopedia of the Philosophical Sciences, Oxford University Press 1892, p. 154.
3. Hans Küng, *The Incarnation of God*, T. & T. Clark 1987, pp. 31ff.
4. In his introduction to Hegel's *On Christianity*, Harper & Row 1961, pp. 4–5.
5. G. W. F. Hegel, *On Christianity: Early Theological Writings*, Harper & Row 1961, p. 71.
6. Ibid., p. 145.
7. J. Macquarrie, *In Search of Deity*, SCM Press and Crossroad Publishing 1984, p. 129.
8. Hegel, *On Christianity*, pp. 256.
9. Ibid., p. 260.
10. Kroner, introduction to *On Christianity*, p. 11.
11. In the remainder of this chapter, references to Hegel's works will be by abbreviated titles, as follows: *Phen.* = *Phenomenology of Mind*, Allen & Unwin 1931; *History* = *Philosophy of History*, as in n. 1; *Logic* = *Logic*, as in n. 2; *Religion* = *Lectures on the Philosophy of Religion*, 3 vols., Routledge & Kegan Paul 1895.
12. Hegel, *Phen.* p. 149.
13. Ibid., p. 150.
14. Ibid., pp. 75–6.
15. Ibid., p. 86.
16. Ibid., p. 208.
17. Ibid., p. 555.
18. Macquarrie, op. cit., pp. 14–15.
19. Hegel, *Phen.* p. 722.
20. Hegel, *Religion*, vol. 1, p. 77.
21. Hegel, *Phen.* p. 753.
22. The hymn dates from 1641, and was written by a certain Johannes Rist. In the German, the line reads '*Gott selbst liegt tot*', 'God himself lies dead', rather than 'is dead'. For a comment, see Gerhard Ebeling, *Dogmatik des christlichen Glaubens*, Tübingen 1979, vol. 2 pp. 202–5.
23. See above, p. 000.
24. E. Jüngel, *God as the Mystery of the World*, T. & T. Clark 1983, p. 76.
25. Hegel, *Religion*, vol. 3, p. 91.
26. Ibid., p. 91, n. 1.
27. Küng, op. cit., p. 382.
28. Hegel, *Phen.*, p. 808.
29. Hegel, *Religion*, pp. 1–2.
30. See above, pp. 29, 50
31. See above, pp. 50–51.
32. D. F. Strauss, *The Life of Jesus Critically Examined* (from fourth German edition) Allen & Unwin 1906, p. 86.
33. See above, pp. 80–81.
34. Strauss, op. cit., pp. 563ff.

35. K. Barth, *Protestant Thought from Rousseau to Ritschl*, SCM Press 1959, p. 368.

36. See above, p. 71.

37. Strauss, op. cit., p. 71.

38. This second life by Strauss is known in English as *A New Life of Jesus*, 2 vols., Williams & Norgate 1879.

39. See above, p. 120.

40. Strauss, *Life of Jesus*, p. 780.

41. I. A. Dorner, *History of the Development of the Doctrine of the Person of Christ*, 5 vols., T. & T. Clark, 1871.

42. I. A. Dorner, *System of Christian Doctrine* 4 vols., T. & T. Clark 1891–7.

43. Dorner, *History*, vol. 2/3, pp. 239ff. and 249ff.

44. Dorner, *System*, vol. 3, p. 285ff.

45. Ibid., p. 288.

46. Ibid., p. 280.

47. Ibid., p. 328.

48. Dorner, *System*, vol. 4, p. 125.

49. E. Caird, *The Evolution of Religion*, Maclehose 1893, vol. 1, p. 4.

50. Ibid., p. 68.

51. Ibid., vol. 2, p. 117.

52. Ibid., p. 221.

11. Mid-century Misgivings

1. See above, p. 147.

2. A. E. McGrath, *The Making of Modern German Christology*, Blackwell 1986, p. 1.

3. L. P. Pojman, *The Logic of Subjectivity*, University of Alabama Press 1984, p. 144.

4. S. Kierkegaard, *Philosophical Fragments*, Princeton University Press 1936, p. 35.

5. Ibid., p. 87.

6. Kierkegaard, *Training in Christianity*, Princeton University Press 1941, pp. 28–31.

7. Kierkegaard, *Concluding Unscientific Postscript*, Oxford University Press 1945, p. 182.

8. Kierkegaard, *Training*, p. 71.

9. Kierkegaard, *Postscript*, pp. 79, 107.

10. See above, p. 108.

11. Niels Thulstrup, *Kierkegaard's Relation to Hegel*, Princeton University Press 1980.

12. Kierkegaard, *Training*, p. 71.

13. Ibid., p. 28.

14. Ibid., p. 33.

15. Kierkegaard, *Fragments*, p. 44.

16. Ibid.

17. Kierkegaard, *Training*, p. 96.

18. Kierkegaard, *Fear and Trembling*, Penguin Books 1985, p. 88.

19. Kierkegaard, *Attack on Christendom*, Princeton University Press 1968, p. 156.

20. Claude Welch, (ed.), *God and Incarnation in Mid-nineteenth-century German Thought*, Oxford University Press 1965, p. 9, n. 11.

21. See above, p. 171.

22. See below, pp. 363 and 369–70.

23. Karl Barth, *Church Dogmatics* IV/1, T. & T. Clark 1956, p. 192.

24. G. Thomasius, *Christ's Person and Work* (in *Mid-nineteenth-century German Thought*), p. 61.

25. Ibid., p. 70.

26. See above, pp. 58–59.

27. W. Sanday, *Christologies Ancient and Modern*, Oxford University Press 1910, p. 73.

28. Thomasius, op cit., p. 56.

29. A. Ritschl, *Justification and Reconciliation*, T. & T. Clark 1900, p. 410.

30. See above, p. 170.

31. C. Gore, *Lux Mundi*, John Murray 1890, p. 359.

32. Gore, *Dissertations on Subjects Connected with the Incarnation*, John Murray 1895, pp. 205–6.

33. Ibid., p. 83.

34. Gore, *The Reconstruction of Belief*, John Murray 1926, pp. 521–2.

35. W. Pannenberg, *Jesus – God and Man*, SCM Press and Westminster Press 1968, p. 279.

12. *Positivist Christology*

1. Albrecht Ritschl, *Justification and Reconciliation*, T. & T. Clark 1900, p. 607, n. 1. The best recent treatment of Ritschl is James Richmond, *Ritschl: A Reappraisal*, Collins 1978. This book has had the very unusual distinction of being translated into German for the benefit of Ritschl's compatriots: *Albrecht Ritschl, eine Neubewertung*, Vandenhoeck & Ruprecht, Göttingen, 1982.

2. Ritschl, *Justification*, p. 158.

3. Ibid., p. 386.

4. Ibid., p. 539.

5. Ibid., p. 139.

6. Ibid., p. 284.

7. Ibid., p. 398.

8. Ibid., p. 212.

9. Ibid., p. 338.

10. Ibid., p. 406.

11. C. Welch, *Protestant Thought in the Nineteenth Century*, vol. 2, Yale University Press 1985, p. 2.

12. See above, p. 171.

13. K. Barth, *Protestant Thought from Rousseau to Ritschl*, SCM Press 1959, pp. 390–97.

14. M. Luther, *The Book of Concord*, Fortress Press 1959, p. 365.

15. Ritschl, op. cit., p. 451.

16. See above, p. 254.

17. Ritschl, op. cit., p. 204.

18. D. Bonhoeffer, *Christ the Centre*, Harper & Row 1966, p. 71.

19. W. Herrmann, *The Communion of the Christian with God*, Williams & Norgate 1909, p. 32.

20. See above, p. 110.
21. Herrmann, op. cit., p. 63.
22. W. Herrmann, *Systematic Theology*, Allen & Unwin 1927, p. 64.
23. Herrmann, *Communion*, pp. 102–3.
24. Ibid., p. 19.
25. Herrmann, *Systematic Theology*, p. 46.
26. Adolf Harnack, *History of Dogma*, Williams & Norgate 1894, Vol. 1, p. 9.
27. A. Loisy, *The Gospel and the Church*, 1903, p. 16.
28. Harnack, *What Is Christianity?*, Williams & Norgate 1901, pp. 14–15.
29. Ibid., p. 63.
30. Ibid., pp. 55–6.
31. Ibid., p. 51.
32. Ibid., p. 144.
33. Ibid., p. 16.
34. Ibid., p. 11.
35. Ibid., p. 147.
36. E. Troeltsch, *Der Historismus und seine Probleme* is in Vol. 3 of the *Gesammelte Schriften*, Tübingen 1912–25.
37. The expression 'body-blow' is used by James Luther Adams in his Introduction to the English edition of Troeltsch's *The Absoluteness of Christianity*, SCM Press 1972, p. 8.
38. See above, pp. 45 and 102.
39. Troeltsch, *Absoluteness*, p. 119.
40. See above, pp. 238–39.
41. W. Rauschenbusch, *Christianity and the Social Crisis*, Macmillan 1907.
42. W. Rauschenbusch, *A Theology for the Social Gospel*, Macmillan 1918, p. 1.
43. Ibid., p. 131.
44. Ibid., p. 147.
45. Ibid., p. 139.

13. Critical Responses and Theological Renascence

1. M. Kähler, *Die Wissenschaft der christlichen Lehre*, Leipzig 1905[3].
2. See above, pp. 230–32.
3. Kähler, op. cit., p. 339.
4. M. Kähler, *Der sogenannte historische Jesus und der geschichtliche biblische Christus*, Leipzig 1896.
5. J. Macquarrie, *An Existentialist Theology*, SCM Press 1955.
6. M. Kähler, *The So-Called Historical Jesus and the Historic Biblical Christ*, Fortress Press 1964.
7. P. Tillich in Introduction to Kähler, *The So-Called Historical Jesus*, pp. 8–9.
8. Ibid., p. 43.
9. Ibid., p. 131.
10. Ibid., p. 66.
11. See above, pp. 15–16.
12. See above, pp. 4–5.
13. See Karl Rahner, *Hearers of the Word*, Herder & Herder 1969.
14See above, pp. 18–19.
15. See Troeltsch's article, 'Historiography', in *Hastings Encyclopedia of Religion and Ethics*, vol. 6, pp. 716ff.

16. Kähler, op. cit., p. 47.

17. Johannes Weiss, *Die Predigt Jesu vom Reiche Gottes*, Göttingen 1892: E.T. *Jesus Proclamation of the Kingdom of God*, SCM Press and Fortress Press 1971.

18. Ibid., p. 103.

19. Ibid., p. 133.

20. R. Bultmann in Foreword to *Jesus' Proclamation*.

21. Weiss, *Earliest Christianity*, Harper 1959, vol. 2, p. 495.

22. See below, pp. 400ff.

23. See above, p. 72.

24. Weiss, *Earliest Christianity*, vol. 1, pp. 12–13.

25. A. Schweitzer, *The Kingdom of God and Primitive Christianity*, A. & C. Black 1968, p. 3.

26. Albert Schweitzer, *The Quest of the Historical Jesus*, A. & C. Black 1954[3].

27. Schweitzer, *Quest*, p. 252.

28. Ibid.

29. See above, p. 265.

30. Schweitzer, *My Life and Thought*, Unwin Books 1966, p. 49.

31. Ibid., p. 51.

32. Schweitzer, *Quest*, p. 396.

33. Ibid.

34. McGrath, *German Christology*, p. 95.

35. K. Barth, *The Epistle to the Romans*, Oxford University Press 1933[6], p. 94.

36. Ibid., p. 102.

37. Ibid., p. 132.

38. Ibid., p. 314.

39. Ibid., p. 500.

40. See K. Barth, *Theologische Fragen und Antworten*, Zürich 1957, p. 10ff.

41. Barth, *Church Dogmatics* I/1, p. 150.

42. Ibid., p. 357.

43. J. Macquarrie, *In Search of Deity*, SCM Press and Crossroad Publishing 1984, p. 232.

44. Barth, *Church Dogmatics* I/2, p. 5.

45. Ibid., I/1, p. 188.

46. McGrath, *German Christology*, p. 115.

47. Barth, *Church Dogmatics* II/2, p. 111.

48. Ibid., pp. 115–16.

49. Ibid., p. 412.

50. Ibid., p. 350, etc.

51. Ibid., p. 509.

52. K. Barth, *The Humanity of God*, Collins 1967, pp. 9, 42.

53. Barth, *Church Dogmatics* IV/1, p. 231.

54. Barth, *Romans*, p. 30.

55. Van Harvey, *The Historian and the Believer*, SCM Press and Westminster Press 1967, p. 158.

56. Barth, *Church Dogmatics*, IV/1, p. 135.

57. See above, pp. 56ff.

58. See above, pp. 247ff.

59. Barth, *Church Dogmatics* IV/1, p. 179.

60. Ibid., p. 192.

61. J. Macquarrie, *In Search of Deity*, p. 99.
62. See above, p. 171.
63. See above, pp. 152, 156.
64. See above, pp. 13–14.
65. See above, pp. 56–57.
66. See below, p. 358.
67. Barth, *Church Dogmatics*, IV/2, p. 21.
68. Ibid., III/3, p. 53.
69. Ibid., IV/2, p. 452.
70. E. Brunner, *The Mediator*, Lutterworth Press 1934, p. 249.
71. Ibid., p. 276.
72. Ibid., p. 32.
73. Ibid., p. 441.
74. Ibid., p. 209.
75. Brunner, *Dogmatics* vol. 2, Westminster Press 1949, p. 15.
76. Ibid., p. 61.
77. Ibid., p. 322.
78. Ibid., p. 350.
79. D. Bonhoeffer, Letter to E. Bethge, 30 April 1944, *Letters and Papers from Prison*, revised and enlarged edition, SCM Press 1971, p. 279.
80. D. Bonhoeffer, *Christ the Center*, Harper & Row 1966, p. 28.
81. Blaise Pascal, *Pensées*, No. 17 (my translation).
82. H. Ott, *Reality and Faith*, Lutterworth Press 1971, p. 46.
83. See above, p. 258.
84. Bonhoeffer, *Ethics*, SCM Press 1955, p. 79ff.
85. Bonhoeffer, *Letters and Papers*, p. 280.

14. *Christologies of the Late Twentieth Century*

1. Martin Heidegger, *Being and Time*, Harper & Row 1962. German original, *Sein und Zeit*, Tübingen, 1927.
2. Bultmann in *Kerygma and Myth*, ed. H.-W. Bartsch, vol. 1, SPCK 1957, p. 193.
3. In Bultmann, *Essays: Philosophical and Theological*, SCM Press 1955, pp. 273–90.
4. See above, pp. 46–47.
5. Bultmann, op. cit., p. 280.
6. Ibid., p. 287.
7. Ibid., p. 286.
8. See J. Macquarrie, 'Bultmann's Understanding of God' in *Thinking about God*, SCM Press 1975, pp. 179–90.
9. *Glauben und Verstehen*, Band 1, Tübingen 1933, p. 101.
10. See above, p. 171.
11. Barth, *Church Dogmatics* II/1, p. 259.
12. *Kerygma and Myth*, vol. 1, p. 36.
13. L. Malevez, *The Christian Message and Myth*, SCM Press 1958, p. 124.
14. See below, pp. 319–20.
15. F. Gogarten, *Demythologizing and History*, SCM Press 1955, pp. 25–26.
16. Gogarten, *Christ the Crisis*, SCM Press 1970, p. 196.
17. See above, p. 25.

18. Gogarten, op. cit., p. 157.

19. Paul Tillich, *Theology of Culture*, Oxford University Press 1959, p. 126.

20. Tillich, *Systematic Theology*, vol. 1, Nisbet 1953, p. 264; but see also vol. 2, 1957, p. 10.

21. See above, p. 271.

22. *Systematic Theology*, vol. 2, p. 102.

23. Ibid., p. 98.

24. Ibid.

25. Ibid., p. 150.

26. Ibid., p. 143.

27. D. H. Kelsey, *The Fabric of Paul Tillich's Theology*, Yale University Press 1967, p. 107ff.

28. Ibid., p. 152.

29. G. H. Tavard, *Paul Tillich and the Christian Message*, Burns & Oates 1962, p. 167.

30. Karl Adam, *The Christ of Faith*, Burns & Oates 1957. German original, *Der Christus des Glaubens*, Düsseldorf 1954.

31. A useful introduction to transcendental Thomism is provided by E. L. Mascall in the first two chapters of his Gifford Lectures, *The Openness of Being*, Darton, Longman & Todd 1971. For a full statement of this philosophy, see Bernard Lonergan, *Insight*, Philosophical Library, Darton, Longman & Todd 1970.

32. K. Rahner, *Hearers of the Word*, Herder & Herder 1969, p. 66.

33. Ibid., pp. 27, 33.

34. Ibid., p. 76.

35. See above, p. 202.

36. K. Rahner, *Spirit in the World*, Sheed & Ward 1968, p. 186.

37. Ibid., pp. 28off.

38. K. Rahner, *Theological Investigations*, vol. 1 Darton, Longman & Todd 1961, p. 164, n. 1.

39. See above, pp. 164–65.

40. Rahner, *Investigations*, vol. 1, p. 149.

41. Ibid., pp. 151ff.

42. Ibid., pp. 154f.

43. Ibid., p. 155.

44. Rahner, *Theological Investigations*, vol. 5 Darton, Longman & Todd 1966, pp. 197–92. The same subject is treated in similar terms in Rahner's *Foundations of Christian Faith*, Darton, Longman & Todd 1978, pp. 178–203.

45. Rahner, *Investigations*, vol. 5, p. 161; *Foundations*, p. 181.

46. The three volumes have been translated from the original Dutch into English with the following titles: *Jesus: An Experiment in Christology*, Crossroad Publishing and Collins 1979; *Christ: The Christian Experience in the Modern World*, Crossroad Publishing and SCM Press 1980; *Church: The Human Story of God*, Crossroad Publishing and SCM Press, forthcoming 1990.

47. Rahner, *Investigations*, vol. 1, p. 184.

48. See above, p. 272.

49. I. Henderson, *Myth in the New Testament*, SCM Press 1952, p. 49.

50. Schillebeeckx, *Jesus*, p. 36.

51. See G. Vermes, *Jesus the Jew*, Collins and Fortress Press 1973, pp. 86–102; A. E. Harvey, *Jesus and the Constraints of History*, Duckworth 1982, p. 57ff.

52. Schillebeeckx, *Jesus*, 473.

53. Ibid., p. 479.

54. See above, p. 31.

55. Most of this discussion is in *Christ*, the second volume of the trilogy, and we took note of some of it in Chapter 6 above, especially pp. 134–35.

56. *Jesus*, p. 538.

57. Ibid., p. 33.

58. P. Teilhard de Chardin, *The Phenomenon of Man*, Collins 1959, p. 71.

59. See above, p. 140.

60. P. Teilhard de Chardin, *The Future of Man*, Harper & Row 1964, p. 318.

61. P. Teilhard de Chardin, *Hymn of the Universe*, Collins 1970, p. 70.

62. See above, p. 168.

63. Teilhard, *Hymn*, p. 13.

64. See A. D. Galloway, *The Cosmic Christ*, Harper & Row 1951.

65. Christopher Mooney, *Teilhard de Chardin and the Mystery of Christ*, Collins 1966, pp. 197–98.

66. See J. A. Lyons, *The Cosmic Christ in Origen and Teilhard de Chardin*, Oxford University Press 1982, pp. 183–84.

67. Jon Sobrino, *Christology at the Crossroads*, Orbis Books and SCM Press 1978, p. 379.

68. See above, pp. 36ff.

69. Sobrino, op. cit., p. 379.

70. Ibid., p. 348.

71. Ibid., p. 349.

72. Ibid., p. 8.

73. Ibid., pp. 369–70.

74. Ibid., p. 27.

75. Leonardo Boff, *Jesus Christ Liberator*, SPCK 1980, p. 64.

76. Ibid., p. 183.

77. Ibid., p. 279.

78. Ibid., pp. 274–5.

79. Ibid., p. 275.

80. H. S. Reimarus, *Fragments*, SCM Press and Fortress Press 1971. See above, p. 25.

81. See above, p. 318.

82. J. Moltmann, *Hope and Planning*, SCM Press 1971. This book was originally intended to be a sketch for a sequel to *Theology of Hope*, but the actual sequel was a very different book – *The Crucified God*.

83. Moltmann, *Theology of Hope*, SCM Press and Harper & Row 1967, p. 180.

84. Christopher Morse, *The Logic of Promise in Moltmann's Theology*, Fortress Press 1979, p. 95.

85. Moltmann, *The Crucified God*, SCM Press and Harper & Row 1974, p. 208.

86. Ibid., p. 243. The language is ambiguous or even unintelligible: 'In the forsakenness of the Son, the Father forsakes himself'.

87. Ibid., p. 277.

88. Ibid.

89. Ibid.

90. Moltmann, *The Trinity and the Kingdom of God*, SCM Press 1980 (= *Trinity and the Kingdom*, Harper & Row) pp. 131–2.

91. Ibid., p. 178.

92. *Der Wag Jesu Christi*, Munich 1989; *The Way of Jesus Christ*, SCM Press and Harper & Row 1990.

93. See above, pp. 18–19.

94. Arnold Toynbee, *An Historian's Approach to Religion*, Oxford University Press 1956, p. 76.

95. See above, p. 324.

96. W. Pannenberg, *Basic Questions in Theology*, vol. 1, SCM Press 1970, p. 79.

97. W. Pannenberg, *Jesus – God and Man*, SCM Press and Westminster Press 1968, p. 83.

98. Ibid., p. 98ff.

99. W. Pannenberg, *What Is Man?*, Fortress Press 1970, p. 44.

100. Pannenberg, *Jesus*, p. 189.

101. Ibid., p. 279.

102. A. D. Galloway, *Wolfhart Pannenberg*, Allen & Unwin 1973, p. 131.

103. H. R. Mackintosh, *The Doctrine of the Person of Jesus Christ*, T. & T. Clark 1913², p. 275.

104. Donald Baillie, *God Was in Christ*, Faber & Faber 1955², p. 52.

105. Ibid., p. 107.

106. See below, pp. 373ff.

107. See above, p. 284.

108. Baillie, op. cit., p. 200.

109. Ibid., p. 190.

110. Ibid., p. 192, n. 2.

111. Norman Pittenger, *The Word Incarnate*, Harper & Row 1959, p. 85.

112. Ibid., p. 192.

113. Ibid., p. 242.

114. Ibid., p. 192.

115. Ibid., p. 167.

116. Pittenger, *Christology Reconsidered*, SCM Press 1970, p. 143.

117. S. M. Ogden, *Christ without Myth*, Collins 1962, pp. 170–1.

118. Ibid., p. 171.

119. Ibid., p. 177.

120. Ibid., p. 179.

121. Ogden, *The Reality of God*, Harper & Row 1966, p. 56.

122. Luther's *Larger Catechism*. See above, p. 000.

123. Ogden, *Reality*, p. 203.

124. Ogden, *The Point of Christology*, Harper & Row and SCM Press 1982, p. 42.

125. See above, p. 120.

126. See above, p. 171.

127. Ogden, *Christ without Myth*, p. 214.

128. J. A. T. Robinson, *The Human Face of God*, SCM Press and Westminster Press 1973, p. 197.

129. Ibid., p. 179.

130. Ibid., p. 166.

131. A. A. Kee, *The Roots of Christian Freedom: The Theology of John A. T. Robinson*, SPCK 1988, pp. 57ff.

132. Robinson, op. cit., p. 77.

Part Three: Who Really Is Jesus Christ for Us Today?

15. What Would Be Required in a Christology Today

1. See above, p. 25.
2. Küng, *The Incarnation of God*, T. & T. Clark 1989, p. 19.
3. Ibid., p. 97.
4. See above, p. 101.
5. See above, pp. 52–53.
6. See above, pp. 148ff.
7. See above, pp. 6ff.
8. See above, p. 159.
9. See above, p. 328.
10. See above, pp. 265–66.
11. See above, pp. 329–30.
12. Pittenger, *The Word Incarnate*, Harper & Row 1959, p. 189.
13. Stephen Sykes, *The Identity of Christianity: Theologians and the Essence of Christianity from Schleiermacher to Barth*, SPCK 1984.

16. The Historical Question

1. A Drews, *The Christ-Myth*, Fisher Unwin 1911.
2. A. Kalthoff, *The Rise of Christianity*, Walts 1907; Karl Kautsky, *The Foundations of Christianity*, Allen & Unwin 1925.
3. Knox, *The Church and the Reality of Christ*, Harper & Row 1962, p. 60.
4. See J. Stevenson and W. Frend, (eds), *A New Eusebius*, SPCK 1960, pp. 1–3.
5. See above, pp. 229, 233.
6. See above, p. 119.
7. R. Bultmann, 'The Primitive Christian Kerygma and the Historical Jesus' in C. Braaten and R. Harrisville (eds), *The Historical Jesus and the Kerygmatic Christ*, Abingdon Press 1964, p. 20.
8. See above, p. 328.
9. Bultmann, 'The Primitive Kerygma', p. 20.
10. Bultmann, *The History of the Synoptic Tradition*, Harper & Row and Blackwell 1963, pp. 40, 50.
11. Bultmann, 'The Primitive Kerygma', pp. 22–3.
12. S. Kierkegaard, *Training in Christianity*, Princeton University Press 1946, p. 27.
13. Donald Baillie, *God Was in Christ*, Faber & Faber 1955[2], p. 49.
14. See above, pp. 240–41.
15. S. Kierkegaard, *The Point of View for My Work as an Author*, Harper & Row 1962, p. 16.
16. See above, p. 16.
17. J. Macquarrie, *The Scope of Demythologizing*, SCM Press 1960, pp. 90–5.
18. See above, pp. 38–39.
19. See above, pp. 39ff.
20. See above, p. 29.
21. Thomas Aquinas, *Summa Theologiae*, 3a, 34, 4.
22. Bultmann, 'The Primitive Kerygma', p. 23.
23. See above, pp. 348–49.

24. See above, pp. 80–81.
25. Jeremias associates this idea with eucharistic sacrifice, see above p. 87.
26. Bornkamm, *Jesus of Nazareth*, p. 154; H. Conzelmann, encyclopedia article, 'Jesus Christus' in *Religion in Geschichte und Gegenwart*, 1959³.
27. Cf. John 10, 40. This incident is regarded as historical by J. A. T. Robinson, *The Priority of John*, SCM Press 1985, p. 171.
28. Raymond E. Brown, *Jesus, God and Man*, Bruce Publishing, Milwaukee 1967, pp. 104–5.

17. The Humanity of Jesus Christ

1. See above, pp. 39–42.
2. See above, p. 25.
3. Iris Murdoch, *The Sovereignty of Good*, Routledge & Kegan Paul 1970, p. 47.
4. See below, pp. 369–70.
5. Jean-Paul Sartre, 'Existentialism is a Humanism' in *Existentialism from Dostoyevsky to Sartre*, ed. W. Kaufman, Harper & Row 1956, p. 290.
6. J. Macquarrie, *In Search of Humanity*, SCM Press and Crossroad Publishing 1982, p. 12.
7. F. W. Nietzsche, *Thus Spake Zarathustra*, Dent 1933, p. 7.
8. Ibid., p. 5.
9. M. Heidegger, *Nietzsche*, Harper & Row 1982, vol. 4, p. 28.
10. Karl Marx, *Economic and Philosophical Manuscripts of 1844*, quoted by L. Kolakowski, *Main Currents of Marxism*, Oxford University Press 1978, vol. 1, p. 137.
11. Macquarrie, *Twentieth-Century Religious Thought*, revised edition, SCM Press 1988, and Trinity Press International 1989, p. 403.
12. E. Bloch, *Man on his Own*, Herder & Herder 1970, p. 59.
13. E. Bloch, *Principle of Hope*, Blackwell 1986, vol. 1, p. 246.
14. Bloch, *Principle of Hope*, vol. 3, pp. 1196–7.
15. See above, p. 95.
16. A. N. Whitehead, *Adventures of Ideas*, Penguin Books 1942, p. 222.
17. See above, p. 330.
18. A. N. Whitehead, *Process and Reality*, Cambridge University Press 1929, p. 118.
19. See above, pp. 304ff.
20. Bernard Lonergan, *Insight*, Philosophical Library, Darton, Longman & Todd 1970, p. 74.
21. Ibid., p. 636.
22. Augustine, *Confessions*.
23. K. Rahner, *Spirit in the World*, Sheed & Ward 1968, author's introduction, p. liii.
24. K. Rahner, *Theological Investigations*, vol. 1, p. 184.
25. See above, pp. 92, 96.
26. See above, pp. 153–54.
27. See above, p. 167.
28. See above, p. 204.
29. Ibid.
30. W. P. DuBose, *The Soteriology of the New Testament*, Macmillan 1899, p. 147.
31. Ibid., p. 80.

32. See above, pp. 182–83.

18. The Divinity of Jesus Christ

1. See above, pp. 116–17.
2. *Quicunque vult*, as translated in *The Book of Common Prayer*.
3. See above, p. 242.
4. See above, p. 286.
5. See above, p. 46.
6. See above, p. 31.
7. See above, p. 310.
8. Pittenger, *The Incarnate Word*, Harper & Row 1952, p. 189.
9. Brunner, *The Mediator*, Lutterworth Press 1934, pp. 352–3.
10. See above, p. 281.
11. See K. Rahner, '"Theos" in the New Testament' in *Theological Investigations*, vol. 1, pp. 79–148.
12. See above, p. 44.
13. J. Macquarrie, *In Search of Deity*, SCM Press and Crossroad Publishing 1984, p. 69.
14. Dionysius, *The Divine Names*, 1v, 13.
15. See above, p. 368.
16. J. Macquarrie, *Principles of Christian Theology*, SCM Press and Macmillan 1977, p. 300.
17. Pittenger, *The Incarnate Word*, p. 192.
18. Eriguena, *Periphyseon*, 449D.
19. Schleiermacher, *The Christian Faith*, T. & T. Clark 1928, p. 385.
20. See above, p. 159.
21. See above, pp. 30, 244.
22. I have discussed these questions more fully in an article 'The Chalcedonian Definition' in *The Expository Times*, vol. 91, pp. 68ff., reprinted in C. S. Rodd (ed.), *Foundation Documents of the Faith*, T. & T. Clark 1987, pp. 23–36.
23. Christopher Stead, *Divine Substance*, Oxford University Press 1977, p. 71.
24. See above, p. 209.

19. The Mysteries of Jesus Christ

1. See above, pp. 107–8.
2. See above, p. 109.
3. See above, pp. 120–21.
4. J. D. G. Dunn, *Christology in the Making*, revised edition, SCM Press 1989, p. 184.
5. In *Church Dogmatics*, II/2.
6. Ibid., p. 350.
7. Schleiermacher, *The Christian Faith*, T. & T. Clark 1928, p. 402.
8. Teilhard de Chardin, *Hymn of the Universe*, Collins 1970, p. 70.
9. See above, p. 95.
10. See above, pp. 52–53.
11. See above, pp. 356–57.
12. John Knox, *The Humanity and the Divinity of Christ*, Cambridge University Press 1967, p. 47.
13. See above, pp. 126–27.

14. See above, pp. 37–38.

15. See above, p. 328.

16. See above, p. 10.

17. As was pointed out on p. 84, mention of the word 'cross' here does not imply that the saying comes from post-resurrection times.

18. See above, p. 288.

19. See above, pp. 373–4.

20. Dorothee Sölle, *Christ the Representative*, SCM Press 1967, especially pp. 89 and 123.

21. See above, p. 284.

22. In H.-W. Bartsch (ed), *Kerygma and Myth*, SPCK 1957, p. 36.

23. John McLeod Campbell, *The Nature of the Atonement*, James Clarke 1959.

24. Ibid., pp. 135–6, 137.

25. Kant, *Critique of Practical Reason*, p. 206.

26. See above, p. 91.

27. See above, p. 122, and below, p. 413.

28. See above, pp. 137ff.

29. See J. Macquarrie, *Christian Hope*, Seabury Press and Mowbray 1978, pp. 106ff.

30. Barth, *Church Dogmatics* IV/1, p. 336.

31. Tacitus, *Annals*, XV, 44, 2–8. Translation from J. Stevenson and W. H. C. Frend (eds), *A New Eusebius*, SPCK 1987[2], p. 2.

32. See above, p. 405.

33. See above, p. 91.

34. See above, pp. 310ff.

35. H. U. von Balthasar, *The Glory of the Lord*, Vol. 1, T. & T. Clark 1982, p. 365ff.

36. Donald Evans, 'Can We Know Spiritual Reality?' in *Commonweal* 13 July 1984, and other writings.

37. See P. C. Phan, *Eternity in Time – A Study of Karl Rahner's Eschatology*, Susquehanna University Press 1988, p. 167.

38. See above pp. 39ff.

39. Pascal, *Pensees*, No. 739.

40. Bultmann, *Kerygma and Myth*, p. 41.

41. Ibid., p. 35.

42. Though I have called Ending A 'The Happy Ending', I have called Ending B 'The Austere Ending', not 'The Unhappy Ending'. It would have been the unhappy ending only if Jesus had turned away from his commitment to the reign or kingdom of God.

20. *Christ and the Saviour Figures*

1. See above, pp. 198–99.

2. See John Bowker, *The Religious Imagination and the Sense of God*, Oxford University Press 1978, p. 260.

3. Macquarrie, *Principles of Christian Theology*, SCM Press and Macmillan 1977, p. 103ff.

4. For a fuller discussion, see John Macquarrie, *Theology, Church and Ministry*, SCM Press 1986, pp. 151–3.

Index of Scripture References

Index of Names and Subjects